Lifting The Veil

A Plain Language Guide
to the Bible

PETER HERMON

The Lutterworth Press

Published by
The Lutterworth Press
P.O. Box 60
Cambridge
CB1 2NT

www.lutterworth.com
publishing@lutterworth.com

First published 2007

Cataloguing in Publication Data

A Catalogue Record is available from the British Library

ISBN: 978 7188 3063 2

Unless otherwise indicated, biblical quotations are
from the New Jerusalem Bible © Darton, Longman and Todd, 1986

Book design and production for the publisher by
Bookprint Creative Services <www.bookprint.co.uk>

Printed in Great Britain by
Athenaeum Press, Gateshead

To Norma

This guide is not intended to stand alone and should be read together with the Bible itself, with the Appendices and Notes being studied at the same time

Contents

The New Testament

Moses veiled his face in daily life
and only removed the veil when he spoke with God or instructed
the people on what God had told him.

Ex 34:29–35

Preface

This book is intended for serious but non-specialist readers who would like to become more familiar with the Bible but who are deterred by its size and obscurities, or who simply do not know how to go about it. What messages do the various books convey? How do they interrelate? The extracts read in church may be familiar but what about the rest? Can one get a balanced overview, one that avoids the morass of detail, without losing the essence? My aim is to meet those needs in plain language.

We begin with a survey of the entire Bible setting it against the backcloth of secular history, drawing out its main characters and demonstrating its unity in the golden thread of Promise that links Genesis to Revelation. As God's plan unfolds it shows how the Old Testament insistently points to the New and Christ, prefiguring in Israel of old the spiritual realities of the age to come, while the New Testament shows how the Old is fulfilled, either already in Christ's new Israel of the Church or in the consummation yet to come.

Within this framework each of the Bible's books is taken in turn. First a brief overview to enable the reader to grasp its milieu and see how it relates to the rest. Then a more detailed synopsis which parallels the Bible (usually chapter by chapter) so that wherever he delves the reader should quickly be able to find his bearings and see a familiar landscape of woods where before there was only a straggle of trees.

I have attempted to steer a course that eschews the detail found in commentaries without on the one hand falling prey to concentrating on the better known texts and leaving whole tracts as *terra incognita*, and on the other of resorting to insipid generalities that, lacking the leavening of detail, rob the text of zest and cutting edge. Readers keen to delve deeper, including alternative interpretations where relevant, are recommended to consult one of the many modern commentaries now available.

I cover not only the sixty-six books found in Protestant Bibles but also the 'Deutero-Canonical' additions recognised by the Roman Catholic church. These are made up of seven complete books: Tobit, Judith, 1 and 2 Maccabees, Wisdom, Ecclesiasticus, Baruch, together with additions to Esther and Daniel. These constitute most, but not all, of what Protestants call the Apocrypha. (Catholics reserve the name Apocrypha for a separate collection of non-canonical books which broadly corresponds to books Protestants call the Pseudepigrapha.)

With the light it has shed on authorship, literary genre and historicity, scholarship has made an enormous contribution to Bible study. However it has often assumed that the text can be interpreted only after an exhaustive study of its formative process and it is hard to escape the impression that this has become almost an end in itself with the Divine Word sometimes treated as an afterthought. There is a tendency to fragment the text and to discount what the Bible says in favour of critical reconstructions that themselves rest on controversial foundations and add little to religious knowledge.

Old Testament prophecy is discredited and the Gospels themselves severely questioned. Peter's confession of Jesus as the Christ and Jesus' agony in Gethsemane are both widely characterised as legend. Many theologians and critics see Jesus' literal resurrection and promised Second Coming, events outside normal experience and understanding, as stumbling blocks. Yet what more monstrous example of the sin of human pride could there be than to insist that anything that savours of mystery and which stretches understanding beyond existing bounds must be discounted?

The fact is that countless millions have found nurture in the Bible without paying the slightest regard to such concerns. My aim therefore is to let the Bible speak for itself, to present it 'as it is', rather than through the prism of research. Like Everest, 'it is there'. Whatever the process by which it evolved, whoever the inspired authors were, vastly more important is the final edifice itself. It was after all Scripture 'as it is', vibrant and alive, that was the inspiration of the early church and which Jesus read, obeyed, endorsed and fulfilled. Cannot what was inspirational and authoritative to Him also feed us today?

None of this is to deny the value of scholarship when kept within bounds. I am not advocating fundamentalism and do touch upon questions of authorship, literary genre etc. where they assist understanding. It is essential to recognise symbolism and imagery (especially in Genesis and Revelation) and helpful to know that the stories of Samson may be folk tales, that Jonah may be a work of fiction written to convey religious truth and to know a little of modern views regarding the authorship of the Pentateuch, Isaiah and Daniel. But where such issues are aired it is in the shadow of the Bible, not the other way round.

The acid test is whether the Bible, presented in this way, blends into a convincing harmonious whole that satisfies minds, inspires hearts, feeds faith and leads to Christ. Every reader must judge for himself. My response is a resounding yes!

The Bible harbours no doubts about its own authority. Well over 3,500 times the Old Testament intones some rubric like 'Thus says the Lord'. The prophets all claim that their messages come direct from God. Jesus quite clearly upholds the Old Testament's authority, Mt 5:17; Jn 10:35. He speaks of the prophets pointing to Him, Lk 24:25–27,44; Jn 5:39. He came to fulfil the Scriptures, Lk 4:21,18:31; Mk 14:21,27 and constantly appealed to them to settle arguments, Mt 12:3–7;22:32, even to confound Satan, Mt 4:4–10.

Jesus promised a similar authority in the case of the apostolic testimony yet to be made, Jn 14:26; 15:26; 16:12–15. Paul certainly saw his authority as coming from Jesus, Ga 1:12, while the authors of 1 John and Revelation both affirm that their messages are from Christ Himself, 1Jn 1:5; Rv 1:1. Significantly Jesus ascribes to God what is Scripture, Mt 19:4, while Paul describes God's words as Scripture, Rm 9:17. Peter puts Paul's writings on a par with the rest of Scripture, 2P 3:15–16.

I believe that the Bible is 'inspired' in the sense that though written by fallible humans it is the divinely guided story of God's activity in the world: why He created it, what went wrong, His plan to put things right. It shows that history is not the chance collision of blind forces without meaning or purpose but the execution of an intelligent design fulfilment of which will no more depend upon human achievement than sin can block it. It is timeless.

It is timeless because we live in an increasingly secular world where spirituality is on the wane. A world where morality is tailored to need; where perversion rides in harness with virtue and affluence cohabits with deprivation and want. A world intoxicated by materialism and pleasure; one that harbours genocide, its leaders in thrall to vanity and pride. A world that deposes God and proclaims 'Glory to Man in the highest'. As a result the prophets' tirades against idolatry, self-interest, social injustice, immorality, greed, oppression and corruption ring as true today as ever they did.

This book is intended to encourage people to read the Bible for themselves. This is not the tall order it may seem. For though it is profound enough to engage the sharpest intellects the Bible is open to the simplest soul for the qualifications needed to harvest it are spiritual rather than intellectual. And the harvest is rich indeed:

> the holy scriptures – from these you can learn the wisdom that leads to salvation through faith in Jesus Christ. All scripture is inspired by God and useful for refuting error, for guiding people's lives and teaching them to be upright, 2T 3:15–16

Amos said:

> Lord Yahweh has spoken: who will not prophesy?, Am 3:8

Given that it is God revealing Himself can our stance be any less robust than:

> Lord Yahweh has spoken: who will not listen?

Reading the Bible

Although we start from the premise that the Bible is God's Word to man, written under the inspiration of the Holy Spirit, it soon becomes apparent that divine revelation does not make it easy reading. Like Jacob we have to wrestle to become Israel. There are occasional loose ends, inconsistencies, misplaced text that distorts the chronology, repetitions and abrupt changes of subject. Sometimes we have to read things into the narrative or deduce them from related texts. Small wonder that the Bible's meaning is not always immediately clear.

Ancient traditions, handed down for generations by word of mouth before being committed to writing, would inevitably have gathered embellishments and anomalies along the way. There are occasional variations (nothing fundamental) in the earliest manuscripts that have come down to us. Scribes were sometimes guilty of omissions and duplications. Early texts only had consonants and so errors may have crept in when vowels were later inserted or as 'glosses' where readers' margin notes were included as part of the text.

The redactors who produced the final version would have been as aware of these shortcomings as we are but they were simply not interested, as a modern editor would be, in smoothing out anomalies to make everything neat and tidy. Their aim was not to lose the smallest scintilla that bore upon divine revelation. For the same reason where they had multiple sources to draw upon, rather than editing them into one smoothed account, everything was kept. But they were not concerned with peripheral detail. Their sole aim was the propagation of religious truth. Where Cain's wife came from did not matter. What did matter was to show the tentacles of sin starting their insidious growth.

Add to these the facts that some passages contain material that was added retrospectively to benefit from hindsight, and that some writings are presented as from the pen of a seer of a bygone age, and it is small wonder that reading the Bible is not as easy as it might be.

It goes without saying that the Bible should be read in context, chapters rather than verses, books rather than chapters, best of all the whole Bible. By taking texts out of context it is possible to prove almost anything. As Christians we should read the Old Testament as forerunner to the New.

In order to communicate more easily with people of different cultures and ages the Bible uses many literary forms: narrative, parables, allegories, fable-like stories, poetry, apocalyptic. A poem or story, and the use of symbols, is often a better way to convey truth of an infinite God than simply stating facts. Sometimes truth is blended with fable. Where we would use logical argument to make a point the Bible may use discourse.

Each of these genres should read appropriately. No one today would read a newspaper and interpret news, political commentary and the fashion and sports pages in the same way. Familiar with our own conventions we adjust accordingly. We should treat the Bible similarly. In particular we should acknowledge the Old Testament's use of stories in the same way that we accept Jesus' use of parables. It is a mistake to worry about whether the creation narratives, or stories like Noah's ark, are literally true. The better question is 'Why is this passage in the Bible and what is it meant to teach me?'

Sometimes we need to distil the essence to arrive at deeper truth. Leviticus' ruling not to gather the gleanings of the harvest is telling us to care for the poor. St Paul's teaching about eating food that had previously been dedicated to pagan gods is urging us to avoid offending the consciences of people who might see things differently from ourselves.

Some texts are hard for us to follow because they involve Jewish customs or a style of argument based on Biblical quotations with which we are not familiar. The obscurity of some of St Paul's writings is in part due to the fact that he dictated his letters with scant opportunity to edit. Our problems are compounded because sometimes we are like eavesdroppers, hearing preaching or reading letters intended for others without always knowing the problems being addressed.

God has revealed Himself gradually over centuries. He has chosen to work in history through the words and deeds, the thoughts and feelings, of imperfect men and nations, letting history run its course with few interventions to assist the unfolding of His design. It would have been beyond our comprehension if we had been given God's revelation all at once, rather like giving a degree course to an infant. Instead God takes people as he finds them, building on perhaps meagre foundations to lead them step by step to ever purer ideals. So the Bible progresses from the rather stern and irritable tribal God of judgement of the Exodus to the monotheistic universal God of love revealed by Christ.

Because God's Word unfolds gradually we occasionally come across ideas that are later modified. The Mosaic law allowed divorce. Jesus forbade it. Similarly the absence of judgement on acts that today we would regard as of dubious morality should not be taken as indicating approval. A distinction must be drawn between what is positively approved and what is merely tolerated for a time. Equally events that seem to portray God as cruel or capricious are often no more than the Ancients' predilection to ascribe everything to God as the ultimate cause rather than seeing them as the results of man's own folly. We should always treat with caution any passage that seems to be at variance with the general trend.

Although the Bible is rich in history and biography its main aim is the dissemination of religious truth. It is out to promote God. Its overriding concern is man's salvation. History and biography are therefore included only in so far as they are needed in support. So a politically important king of Israel like Omri receives less mention than a widow of Shunem whose life carries a clear religious message. Similarly the Gospels tell us little of Jesus' early life while Acts concentrates almost exclusively on Peter and Paul whose deeds and writings – more than those of their fellow apostles – underpin the Christian faith.

Just as God took human form in Jesus who was both divine and a man of His time, so He recorded His Word in a book inspired by the Holy Spirit yet written by men of their time. And just as Jesus in His human nature was limited in knowledge except where religious truth was concerned, so too the Bible's inerrancy is limited except in matters to do with the meaning of life, morals and salvation.

In reading the Bible we need the help of the Holy Spirit as much as those who wrote it. We need the eye of faith and to seek out the simple straightforward meaning rather than trying to be too clever. The Bible should never be seen as the province of experts. The humble are open to spiritual truth more than the sophisticated.

> I bless you, Father, Lord of heaven and of earth, for hiding these things from the learned and the clever and revealing them to little children, Mt 11:25.

The Bible has fathomless depths. It does not yield its treasure easily and we can never fully plumb its deeps. Yet anyone who reads it, having invoked the Holy Spirit, will find that despite occasional obscurities the overall sweep of its message breaks through as gloriously as early sunlight piercing the morning mist.

THE BIBLE: A SURVEY

Readers new to the Bible are advised to begin by familiarising themselves with the following Survey which is intended to bring out the main themes of the Bible and to show how its various books fit harmoniously together. As even that is long, we begin with a brief overview.

Overview

The Bible begins in the distant past with God's creation of life and a perfect world where man would live with Him for ever. Then, with the (symbolic) story of Adam and Eve it describes the world as it actually is, a world where man's folly in rejecting God's sovereignty generates disorder, injustice and strife, putting man himself in need of redemption. The rest of the Bible is the story of what God is doing to bring that about.

It begins with God's promise to Abraham that he would indeed retrieve the situation and follows up with His election of Israel to be His tool to achieve this end. Having used Moses to rescue her from slavery in Egypt, God formally adopted Israel at Mount Sinai, where, in the Old Covenant, He gives her the Law to guide her and (animal) sacrifice to atone for sins when things go wrong.

Unfortunately, Israel was querulous from the start, and only after a long refining in the wilderness did God allow Joshua to lead her into the Land He had promised her (Canaan). Yet, despite this inestimable gift, Israel's subsequent history under Samuel, Saul and a line of kings beginning with David and Solomon was a litany of apostasy and sin. Warnings from the prophets – men like Isaiah, Jeremiah and Ezekiel called to speak in God's name – fell on deaf ears. Punishment was inevitable; loss of Canaan and exile to Babylon the result.

When eventually the captives were allowed to return home, life was hard. But hope remained. For along with their warnings against moral degeneracy the prophets had foreseen a New Covenant whereby God would remould and purify men's hearts and forgive sins. There would be a King of David's line, whose reign would have no end, and God would regather His people in a new Jerusalem ringing with joy. Gradually, with Daniel, the idea gained ground that these hopes belonged to a world after death.

Then, with Israel unfit to fulfil her divine mission, God stepped into history Himself, becoming man in Christ, treading a path of humility and suffering, and preaching a Gospel of love. With His sinless life, He broke the power of evil, and with His sacrificial death made reparation for sins as animal sacrifice never could, establishing the New Covenant whereby those who repented and turned to Him in faith would be forgiven their sins and, quickened by the Holy Spirit, reborn to eternal life.

We can now see that the Old Testament dealt only in shadows, showing how man is unable to save himself, and pointing to Christ, who really does offer salvation to all. He is the reality. He is the King who will reign forever over His people, not in Caanan in this world, but in a Kingdom infinitely more wonderful, the new Jerusalem of eternity, where, after a dire tribulation as evil makes one final fling at the end of time, He will gather the faithful for blessings beyond Abraham's wildest dreams: that life with Himself that God planned for His children before ever the world began.

The Old Testament

The Primeval Prologue

With the soaring refrain of a hymn, its chords evoking awe and wonder, the greatest story in the world begins with God's creation of the world. In poetic vein the author intones a paradise world conceived in love. Then in the (symbolic) stories of Adam and Eve, Cain and Abel, Noah and Babel, he shows how man, tempted by a snake representing some malevolent power outside of himself (evil, Satan or the Devil) uses his free will to defy his Maker, preferring self-love rooted in pride to the selfless love of God and neighbour. Sin is born. The results are calamitous: discord and dissonance and the seeds of the blighted world of injustice and suffering we know today where, in battle with the wiles of evil, man is pitted against man and nature herself cries out in pain. Worst of all it brings death and estrangement from a God who cannot abide sin. With sin there can be no paradise.

If we see the Bible as the story of Man's redemption, God reaching out to break the power of evil and save him from the sin that imperils the life in heaven He created him for, then these opening chapters of GENESIS, the PRIMEVAL PROLOGUE, explain why salvation is needed in the first place. They speak timelessly to all races and ages and stand in relation to the rest of the Bible as problem to solution, a problem that Christ answers on the Cross.

But first the way has to be prepared. And so the focus narrows to one man, Abraham (initially called Abram), as God embarks upon a plan that, beginning with Israel and climaxing in Christ, will save the world and make all things new.

The Patriarchal Age

The second part of GENESIS, the PATRIARCHAL AGE, begins with words that reverberate throughout the Canon. God's clarion call to Abraham, c1850 B.C., to uproot himself and migrate to an unknown land, Canaan (modern Palestine), which He will give his progeny, opens the way to the resolution of the dilemma with which the Prologue ended. Abraham's descendants will become a great nation 'as numerous as the stars of heaven' *and through them all families on earth will be blessed*. These promises, pointing to reconciliation, are ratified in a solemn covenant to which God, in an act of grace, binds Himself irrevocably. And so it is with a simple nomadic tent-dweller that God embarks upon the long campaign that will ultimately crush the cohorts of evil and redeem the human race.

But for the moment Genesis focuses on the remote origins, the founding fathers, of the nation God will employ to enact His redemptive will: Abraham himself, the archetypical man of faith who believed even when God asked him to sacrifice the son Isaac on whom His promises hinged; Jacob, the man of guile who cheated his brother Esau out of his birthright for a plate of stew yet later wrestled with God to win His blessing; Joseph, whose God-given ability to interpret dreams saved Egypt from famine and raised him to high office where he was able to save the brothers who had earlier given him up to suffering and death.

In tempo and essence these stories show that God's mills grind slowly. They suggest that the road to salvation will be strewn with obstacles, entail suffering, demand faith, move in mysterious ways, and attain its goal only in God's good time. In Joseph we see not only God harnessing the tide of history and working quietly in the ups and downs of daily life to overcome evil designs and save His people, but also a pointer to that greater Son whose suffering and death would one day win the final victory. To his repentant brothers it was as if he had come back from the dead to forgive them and bring new life.

Genesis ends, c1700 B.C., with Jacob and his twelve sons, the progenitors of the twelve tribes of Israel, domiciled in Egypt, safe from the famine they had gone there to escape, but far from the land of promise. This was providential. Thanks to Joseph they were a favoured community and able to grow in numbers and mature in nationhood in Egypt in a way that would have been impossible in the more turbulent Palestine. The stage was being set for the epic events of Exodus.

Deliverance from Egypt

When the curtain rises in EXODUS it is some four centuries later. The memory of Joseph has faded and the Israelites (as henceforth we shall refer to Jacob's descendents) are now languishing as slaves. It was at this juncture that God raised up Moses to deliver them out of Egypt and lead them to the Promised Land of Canaan, a 'land flowing with milk and honey'. The cardinal facts of Moses' early life are well known: how he was reared at Pharaoh's court after his mother hid him in a papyrus basket among the reeds of the Nile to escape infanticide; how God appeared to him in a burning bush, revealed His name, Yahweh, and gave him his great commission; how Pharaoh let the Israelites go after suffering ten calamitous plagues; and how, when Pharaoh had a change of heart and gave chase, his army was destroyed as the sea, which had earlier been parted by the wind to allow the Israelites to escape, suddenly returned to engulf it.

God's mighty act in rescuing Israel from bondage through the waters of the sea, c1250 B.C., is the greatest act of salvation in her history, the defining event of her nationhood. Together with its immediate antecedent, God's protection or 'passing over' of the Israelites (each identified by the blood of a lamb) as He slew the Egyptian first-born in the climactic tenth plague, it is commemorated forever in the Jewish Passover. It is equally significant to Christians who see it as prefiguring their own salvation as God acts through the death of His own first-born and the waters of baptism to rescue those who identify with the blood of a Lamb from the tyranny of sin.

The Sinai Covenant

Israel begins her long trek to the Promised Land and three months later is encamped at the foot of Mount Sinai. There God calls her to His service. He has carried her 'on eagle's wings' out of Egypt and now, if she is obedient, she will be of all peoples His personal possession, a kingdom of priests, a holy nation, the channel He will use to bring light to a sin-darkened world in pursuance of His promise to Abraham to confer blessings on all mankind.

This agreement, the Old Covenant, is conditional on Israel being obedient. But obedient to what? The answer comes in an awesome theophany accompanied by peals of thunder, lightning, dense cloud and trumpet blasts as God delivers the Ten Commandments and the Book of the Covenant, the first of the Old Testament's great law codes that together with the Commandments define the Law as the basis of Man's relationships both with his Creator and with his fellows. This is followed by a detailed specification for the Dwelling, a portable shrine where God will dwell among His people and where Israel can come to worship and seek forgiveness for her sins. Moses' brother Aaron and his sons are consecrated into the priesthood which Israel's calling now demands.

But already Israel's faith is wilting. Despite their miraculous deliverance from Egypt the people had begun to mutter and complain even before Sinai. Now, in Moses' absence on the mountain communing with God, they succumb to outright apostasy, venerating a golden calf. Only Moses' intercession averts God's wrath.

LEVITICUS brings more legislation in the laws of Purity and Holiness. However, appropriately for a book which exults in the holiness of a God who dwells among His sinful creatures, pride of place goes to the sacrificial rituals that are to be followed for hallowing her worship, giving thanks, expressing devotion and seeking forgiveness for sins.

Israel in the wilderness

NUMBERS is the melancholy tale of Israel's journey to the Promised Land through the Sinai wilderness, a saga of grumbles and ingratitude, faithlessness and sin, matched only by God's forbearance and providence as He guides her in a cloud by day, a pillar of fire by night, and miraculously succours her with water from the rocks, manna and quails. God gave Israel the chance to enter Canaan early on but when a reconnaissance party revealed the strength of the native tribes her courage failed. God responded to this lack of trust by decreeing that an entire generation must now pass away before she could enter the Promised Land. So as Numbers ends it is a new Israel, an Israel reborn, forged and refined in the harsh cauldron of the desert, that stands poised on the Jordan opposite Jericho ready to claim her inheritance.

DEUTERONOMY records three farewell addresses given by Moses just prior to his death on Mount Nebo overlooking the Promised Land which God had forbidden him to enter. In impassioned tones he recalls the wonders and blessings God had lavished on Israel and warns her, once she is enjoying the more affluent lifestyle of the land of milk and honey and living alongside a pagan community, never to forget that she owes everything she has to Yahweh. Faith and obedience to the Law, an inward spirituality, must be paramount. There must be no truck with idolatry.

It was now that Moses also delivered the last of the Old Testament's law codes. Like its predecessors the Deuteronomic code is a blend of civil and criminal law, of moral precepts and religious ceremonial, at once general and specific, but now tuned to the more settled and urban lifestyle Israel will lead in Canaan. Ominously God warns that while compliance will be rewarded with blessings, disobedience will bring down curses and exile. One day He will raise up another prophet like Moses.

Conquest of the Promised Land

JOSHUA takes its name from Moses' successor. It describes the miraculous crossing of the Jordan, c1210 B.C., the wondrous capture of Jericho 'when the trumpet brought the walls tumbling down' and three brilliant campaigns in which Joshua conquered Canaan and apportioned the land among the tribes. It ends with the people repledging their loyalty to Yahweh at a great assembly at Shechem.

The age of the judges

JUDGES paints a less rosy picture. Far from forming a cohesive nation the tribes were little more than a loose federation at this time, united only by their common faith. Many pockets of Canaanite resistance remained, especially in the plains, while neighbouring tribes like the Ammonites and Edomites took advantage of the unsettled conditions to launch their own incursions. To meet these threats God raised up, c1200–1050 B.C., a number of so called judges, not judges in the legal sense but rather local or regional chieftains, charismatic leaders, to act as deliverers. It was a violent degenerate age and the same theme recurs again and again. Israel sins. God hands her over to an oppressor. Israel repents. God sends a 'judge' – one like Ehud, Deborah, Gideon or Jephthah – to rescue her. Then, as soon as the judge dies, the dismal cycle of sin, punishment, repentance, and salvation is repeated all over again.

RUTH may belong to this era. It is the tale of a Moabite widow who risked everything by opting to accompany her widowed Israeli mother-in-law when she decided to return to Israel from Moab whence she had earlier emigrated with her husband to avoid a famine. It shows God working quietly behind the scenes to bring happiness out of seemingly hopeless situations and reveals that His providence knows no bounds where sex and race are concerned. The book's universalist slant is underlined by the revelation that Ruth was an antecedent of David, Israel's greatest king.

Samuel and Saul

1 and 2 SAMUEL open with the lackadaisical priesthood of Eli and Israel chafing under the Philistine yoke. To counter this, c1040 B.C., God again sent a deliverer. Samuel combined the roles of priest, judge and prophet. He led a religious revival and routed the Philistines. But as he grew old the people clamoured for a king 'to be like the other

nations'. Samuel was sure this was wrong. Israel already had a King in Yahweh. But he obeyed God's command to let the people have their way and anointed a personable young man named Saul. This was a pivotal point in Israel's history. Samuel's concerns about a monarchical system were well founded. Hitherto Israel's leaders had been chosen by God for their strength and charisma. In future many of the kings who became (at least nominally) guardians of the covenant faith would be swayed more by intrigue and force of arms and, as hostages to the stormy seas of political adventure, prove to be obstacles to the very faith they were supposed to defend.

Saul was a valiant warrior but lacked spiritual depth. He was eventually rejected by God who sent Samuel secretly to anoint a young shepherd boy named David as the king who would in due time succeed him. Following his victory over the Philistine giant Goliath David became a folk hero. This aroused Saul's jealousy and David was forced to seek refuge first as an outlaw in the Judaean wilderness and then, playing a double game, posing as a Philistine mercenary. Saul, a tragic figure at the end, was killed in battle with the Philistines on Mt Gilboa c1010 B.C.

David

David seized his chance and made himself king of all Israel. He captured Jerusalem from the Jebusites, c1000 B.C., and made it both his political capital and the focal point of the nation's worship by installing there the Ark, a gilded wooden chest from the Dwelling that was the seat of God's very presence. A string of victories against the Philistines and Israel's other neighbours extended his empire from Egypt to the northern Euphrates and with it came peace and prosperity. But transcending temporal glory was God's promise, delivered by the prophet Nathan, that David's dynasty would rule in perpetuity, a prophecy the significance of which would not even remotely have been dreamt of at the time.

David's life ended in tragedy. Adultery with Bathsheba was followed by filial strife and revolt, and by the time 1 and 2 KINGS opens with his death he is a lonely forlorn figure. Yet his stature endures. What other crowned head, and where else but in Israel, would a king accept the rebuke of a prophet for his sins and humbly and publicly accept his punishment?

David's name has always been associated with the PSALMS, the hymnal of ancient Israel. With their mood of piety and devotion reflecting an intense personal relationship with God the Psalms strike a responsive chord even today. To what extent David was the author of individual psalms may never be known. That he was the impulse behind the psalm as a medium for Israel's worship and praise is much less open to doubt.

Solomon

Under David's son Solomon Israel enjoyed a golden age. The Temple was built. She was protected by a powerful army equipped with cavalry and chariots while explosive growth in commerce and trade, coupled with a bevy of marriage-alliances, fuelled unprecedented prosperity (at least for the nobility) and exposure to foreign cultures. Solomon himself was hailed as a patron of wisdom and the arts and the SONG OF

SONGS, a poem of soft-hued beauty celebrating the wonder and joy of human love, is attributed to him although this may be no more than a literary fiction.

But storm clouds were gathering. David's empire was starting to crumble abroad while unrest was simmering at home. Solomon's extravagant wealth, a bloated hedonistic court and his grandiose building projects – lavish in their use of gold, silver and ivory – leaned heavily on forced labour and penal taxation. Swayed by his polyglot harem Solomon began worshipping the pagan gods of his wives in blatant contempt of the Law. On his death in 931 B.C. latent rumbles of resentment erupted into open revolt with the ten northern tribes breaking away to form their own kingdom of Israel. Henceforth Judah, the kingdom of the two southern tribes that remained loyal to Solomon's son Rehoboam, and Israel in the north would go their separate ways, mere pawns in a landscape in which their dabbling in power politics would drain them politically as much as the leaning of nearly all their kings to 'do what was displeasing to Yahweh' would maim them spiritually.

(Despite this, the reader will find that 'Israel' is still widely used to denote the totality of God's people, irrespective of kingdom, both during the time of the two kingdoms and later.)

This is a convenient place to note that 1 and 2 CHRONICLES provide a second set of annals largely paralleling Samuel and Kings. However the chronicler focuses almost entirely on Judah, and his history is even more theologically based with the Temple, the priesthood and the liturgy his prime interests. David and Solomon are presented as paragons of virtue.

From Solomon to the fall of Samaria

Israel made a disastrous start. Idolatrous shrines at Dan and Bethel, hostilities with Judah, dynastic upheavals and civil war, all sapped her vitality. Later on Omri imposed the stamp of firm government and built Samaria as a permanent capital but under his son Ahab Israel's spiritual mettle experienced its sternest test yet. Ahab's rabid wife Jezebel was fanatical in her promotion of the Canaanite cult and, had it not been for the prophet Elijah's dramatic victory over the massed prophets of Baal on Mount Carmel, Yahweh worship might well have succumbed altogether in the northern kingdom.

Elijah's mantle was taken up by his disciple Elisha. Between them they embodied the covenant faith. Ministering to the lowly, defying kings, and buttressed by a spate of signs and wonders, they sustained Israel during testing years that involved not only religious challenge but a succession of debilitating wars with her northern neighbour Aram.

Nor was Judah spared these convulsions. Rehoboam was powerless to prevent the Temple being ransacked by Egypt. And when Athaliah, a princess of Israel who had married into Judah's royal House, seized the throne and all but exterminated David's line, only a priestly coup prevented the baneful influence of Israel permeating the southern kingdom too.

The first half of the eighth century brought a remarkable change of fortune. With the attention of Assyria, the regional superpower, focused beyond the Euphrates, both kingdoms, under Jeroboam II and Uzziah, were able to extend their frontiers to limits not known since the heady days of David and Solomon. Peace and a revival of trade brought renewed prosperity. But the cost was high: rupture of the social order as the gap between merchant and peasant, the wealthy land-owning class and the poor, grew ever wide.

With the accession of Tiglath-Pileser III to the Assyrian throne in 745 B.C. this Indian summer came to an abrupt end. Pursuing a policy of westward expansion he crushed Aram, annexed Israel's northern provinces and reduced Judah to a vassal state. With six kings in her last twenty years – four murdered, one deposed – Israel was in a state of near anarchy and terminal decline. The end came in 721 B.C. when, after a desperate three-year siege, Samaria fell and the people of Israel were deported to Assyria, never to return. The northern kingdom ceased to exist. The Bible insists that this was due to her unbridled depravity. Venerating pagan gods, she fired Yahweh's fury by ignoring the Law and treating His warnings with contempt.

The early prophets

It was at this juncture that God raised up the first of a line of prophets whose oracles have come down in written form. Like their earlier counterparts – Moses, Samuel, Elijah – they were called to be bearers of God's Word in times of crisis, to quicken His people's conscience, to warn and encourage. AMOS and HOSEA both declared that Israel was on the road to ruin. Their censure was drawn by the rottenness, the social and moral corruption, eating away at the heart of her society. Outwardly thriving, Israel was riddled with injustice and greed. She did not understand that what God wanted was not more and more ritual and endless sacrifices, all divorced from inner spirituality, but a complete change of heart and renunciation of evil in favour of love and justice. Yahweh alone could save her. But He was ignored. So judgement was only a matter of time.

Amos was the first of the prophets to give voice to the 'Day of Yahweh', a time when God would intervene decisively in history. The concept gradually evolved to a Day of Judgement that would come after God had finally quelled the forces of evil: but to Amos it was a day of retribution against an Israel wedded to sin. Here he differed from the more tender-hearted Hosea who tempered equally barbed imprecations with his vision of God first as a husband who will one day take back His faithless wife (Israel) and then as an anguished parent; a parent who recoils in distress at the thought of separation from the infant Israel He had led out of Egypt; a parent who will one day, in a way he cannot divine, cure her disloyalty.

For all their harsh reproaches Amos and Hosea lived in hope. It was Amos who first articulated the idea of the 'remnant'. Whatever befell God's people a remnant would always survive as the seed of a purified and more faithful community to continue carrying the torch. With Hosea he foresaw a future age of reconciliation when a repentant Israel would be restored to live forever in a land of unparalleled prosperity and astonishing fertility.

MICAH, who ministered both before and after the fall of Samaria, also included

Judah in his strictures. Fond hopes that the Temple would save Jerusalem from the fate that had overtaken Samaria would soon be dashed. But God had not forsaken His people. All He asked was for justice, brotherly love and humility and a time would come when He would rescue them and humble their enemies. And from Bethlehem would come a ruler 'whose origins go back to the distant past' who would shepherd them and bring lasting peace.

In a long ministry extending from c740 B.C. until at least the turn of the century ISAIAH directed his barbs at Judah. She had hatched her own downfall: brimming with sham piety as she smugly took pride in her status as God's own people; seduced by wealth and pleasure; brandishing the rod of extortion on the weak and lowly. Consumed by politics and idolatry she was no better than a harlot, relegating God to a role of bystander and oblivious of the love and tender parental care He lavished on her. Even so she had only to repent and 'though her sins were like scarlet, they would be white as snow'. Otherwise it would not be long before she too groaned beneath the Assyrian lash.

But doom was not Isaiah's final word either. In the last days, after He had purged their guilt, God would regather His people from the ends of the earth in a glorious homecoming. The (gentile) nations too would hasten to Jerusalem to walk in His ways in a world of justice and idyllic peace. Dominion would be vested in a Son, Immanuel, of the House of David. He would be endowed with the Spirit of Yahweh and his reign would have no end.

(As will be explained in the main text we divide Isaiah into three parts ascribing chs 1–39 to Isaiah, chs 40–55 to another prophet known as Deutero Isaiah, and chs 56–66 to a third prophet referred to as Trito Isaiah. Zechariah is likewise divided into two parts, chs 1–8 being attributed to a certain Zechariah son of Iddo, chs 9–14 to a later Deutero Zechariah.)

Judah to the fall of Jerusalem

Israel's fate gave Judah a much needed wake-up call. King Hezekiah heeded Isaiah's strictures and bore down on idolatry. Politically he was less astute. Revolt against Assyria led in 701 B.C. to a devastating invasion from which Jerusalem only escaped when divine intervention annihilated the besieging Sennacherib's army.

Manasseh, the next king, reversed his father's reforms and it was left to Josiah in 622 B.C. to revive and extend them, fostered by a Book of the Law, probably an embryonic Deuteronomy, discovered in the Temple during repair work. But despite ZEPHANIAH breaking a prophetic silence of two generations with a fiery denunciation of Jerusalem's dissolute society it was all too late. Judah's defections and her appetite for idolatry were by now so insatiable that, with Jeremiah's and Ezekiel's calls to repentance and threats of judgement also being ignored, God invoked the curse of the covenant.

Assyria was now on the wane. Babylon was the emergent power and in 612 B.C. Assyria's fate was sealed when Babylon, supported by the Medes, sacked her capital Nineveh, an event that NAHUM applauds with vehement fire and passion. A bid by Egypt to challenge Babylon's hegemony ended in defeat at Carchemish in 605 B.C. Judah was now a Babylonian vassal and an attempt in 597 B.C. to throw off the yoke led to Nebuchadnezzar seizing Jerusalem and despatching the young king Jehoiachin to exile in Babylon along with the leading citizens. The sacking of the city ten years later after a second revolt, together with the razing of the Temple and further deportations, brought Judah's history to its ignominious end, an event commemorated with moving pathos in the poems of LAMENTATIONS.

It was his anticipation of this catastrophe that prompted HABAKKUK to question how God could use the bloodthirsty Babylonians to punish (for all her faults) the less wicked Judah. It is likely that OBADIAH also relates to this period and that his invective against Edom was sparked by Edom taking advantage of Judah's plight to annex parts of her territory. (Oracles like Obadiah's, revelling in the annihilation of Edom, Israel's archetypical enemy, are best seen as symbols of God's eventual destruction of evil and all His enemies.)

The years of Assyrian and Babylonian dominance provide the backdrop to two works of religious fiction that find a place in the Deutero-Canonical Scriptures. TOBIT is a fanciful tale of Jewish piety and family life showing God, though hidden, tirelessly at work in everyday life to reward the just. JUDITH relates how a devout Jewess used her feminine charms to lure the commander of an invading army to his death in order to save her people.

Jeremiah and Ezekiel

Judah's last days set the stage for two of her greatest prophets, JEREMIAH and EZEKIEL. Jeremiah's call antedated Josiah's reforms yet he was still active some forty years later to witness Judah's dying gasps and the sacking of the Temple. Ezekiel prophesied from Babylon, having presumably been a victim of the deportation of 597 B.C. Both condemned the abominations that were leading Judah to destruction. Her hands were stained with the blood of the poor and innocent. She rushed headlong into sin like a horse charging into battle and chased false gods like a whore her lovers; spurning the love Yahweh showered on her. Yet forgiveness was there for the asking if only she would repent.

Both insisted that God rewarded everyone according to his deserts and that the future belonged to the exiles in Babylon. They would become the nucleus of a new Israel. Jeremiah spoke of a day when God would snap His people's bonds and restore them to their ancestral land, a land ringing with laughter and joy, raising up a 'Branch' of David (fresh growth from the stump of a felled tree) to rule beside the priests.

Ezekiel, who continued his ministry after the fall of Jerusalem, envisioned a future no less splendid. God would regather His scattered flock, segregate the good from the bad, and lead them to rich pastures under a shepherd prince of David's House. With a vision of God breathing new life into a valley of dry bones he saw a national resuscitation. With the defeat of Gog he signalled the great tribulation that would precede God's final annihilation of evil in the latter days. Then there would be a new Jerusalem, a new Temple and a Promised Land even more fertile than the old.

In one of the peaks of Old Testament theology Jeremiah and Ezekiel both prophesied a New Covenant (which Jesus would inaugurate at the Last Supper) whereby God would infuse His Spirit into men's hearts, enabling both willing obedience to His will and forgiveness of sins, and leading to the fulfilment of the great covenant promise of old:

I shall be their God and they will be my people.

BARUCH, a composite work, purports to be from the hand of Jeremiah's secretary. It begins with the exiles confessing that their downfall was due to their disobeying the Law. Then a personified Jerusalem holds out hope of eternal joy. Finally it warns the exiles to be on their guard against the idolatry they will encounter once they are living in Babylon.

The Exile

Little is known of life during the exile but it was probably not too arduous. Extra-biblical sources speak of flourishing Jewish communities integrated into local society and able to earn their living. (From now on we shall usually refer to the exiles and their descendents as Jews.) Certainly when the exiles were given the opportunity to return home there was no rush to do so, while those who did go back were not short of money and treasure to help pay for the restoration of the Temple.

The exile would have shattered most faiths but for the Jews it was the springboard of new life. With the demise of the monarchy and the death of political aspirations they were able to devote themselves single-mindedly to their faith. Indeed they were impelled to. They saw the exile as the penalty for sin and so their whole future as dependent on fulfilling the Law's most stringent demands. Deprived of the Temple and so unable to offer their traditional worship, these now centred around prayer, the dietary laws, the Sabbath and circumcision.

All the hallmarks of later Judaism find their origins here: the supremacy of the Law, the authority of the priesthood, the synagogue. The exile was the start of the process that converted the body politic into the body ecclesiastic with the high priest as sole ruler. Buttressed by the Word of God as unveiled by the prophets, the Jews bonded together in exile in the conviction that they were the inheritors of a divine legacy.

Deutero Isaiah

Babylon's ascendancy was brief. A new star was rising in the east. In 550 B.C. Cyrus, the enlightened vassal king of Anshan in southern Persia, seized control of the Median empire. Victory three years later over Lydia, which comprised most of Asia Minor, consolidated his power and founded the Persian empire. It was probably at this time, when Cyrus' remorseless advance seemed increasingly likely to engulf a weak and divided Babylon, that DEUTERO ISAIAH composed his poems.

In stanzas of lyric beauty he acclaims the majesty of Yahweh, the one true God: omnipotent, omniscient, eternal, Saviour. Israel's punishment was over. God still loved her and would use Cyrus to lead her home in a new Exodus even more glorious than the first to a new Jerusalem even more beautiful than the first, a city singing with joy and gladness. There she would live in justice and peace with God as King. Pilgrims from every nation would hasten to join her. Salvation knew no bounds.

Alongside this effusion of joy Isaiah introduced the mysterious figure of the Servant. As Yahweh's disciple, and quickened by His Spirit, He would assume Israel's missionary role, bringing light and salvation to the ends of the earth. A despised man of sorrows, he would suffer grievously. But by giving his life as a sin offering and taking upon himself the guilt of many he would pave the way to reconciliation with God.

Return from exile

In 539 B.C., having defeated her armies in the field, Cyrus entered Babylon unopposed. He had long adopted a policy of freeing captive peoples in the lands he subdued in the hope of placating their gods and soon authorised the Jews to return home. But just as the exile was not the end for Israel, so the return to Palestine was not the dawn of a sunlit new age. Life for the little community that availed itself of Cyrus' dispensation was far from easy. Living under foreign tutelage, shorn of power and wealth, the Jews now inhabited but a small pocket of their former territory. The devastation of the Babylonian invasion would have left few homes standing and much of the land, where it was not claimed by migrants, would have reverted to wilderness.

EZRA describes how the first pilgrims to return to Jerusalem built an altar and then set to work to restore the Temple. However opposition from the local populace led to delays and it was some twenty years before the Temple was finally rededicated in 515 B.C..

Post-exilic prophets

Three prophets ministered in the early post-exilic years. The denunciations with which TRITO ISAIAH begins have a familiar ring. Despite the trauma of exile sin still cast its deadly stamp. Yet the embers of hope were aglow. Jerusalem and the ruined cities of Judah would be rebuilt bringing peace and lasting joy. Indeed the prophet goes further. Although he is never quite able to raise his sights beyond life in this world he nonetheless envisions new heavens and a new earth with a new Jerusalem of incredible splendour that will endure for ever and to which all nations will throng. This will happen suddenly, like a woman giving birth without ever going into labour.

HAGGAI strove to overcome the apathy that was delaying work on restoring the Temple. Following Deutero and Trito Isaiah he believed that this would be followed by God's long awaited intervention in history with Zerubbabel, the heir to David's throne, leading the Jews into the new age. In a series of elaborate and difficult visions ZECHARIAH saw a purified and restored Israel led jointly by Joshua the high priest and 'God's servant the Branch' who, for a time at least, he also (mistakenly) identified with Zerubbabel.

The Persian era

We are ill informed of the years 515 to 458 B.C. One source of information is MALACHI who reveals that morale was poor. Cynicism over evil-doers who prospered, ingrained immorality and injustice, mixed marriages – all inflamed by a priesthood that had lost its sense of vocation – indicate that spirituality had sunk to a low ebb. To all this the prophet responds with a much needed wake-up call. God will intervene, first through a messenger, an 'Elijah', then in person, 'like a refiner's fire', to punish the wicked and reward the virtuous.

EZRA and NEHEMIAH then pick up the story. In 458 B.C. Ezra was authorised by his Persian overlords to go to Jerusalem to teach the Law and fortify the ancient faith. He was followed in 445 B.C. by Nehemiah who restored the walls and repopulated the city. Both hammered home strict observance of the Law, including the dissolution of mixed marriages, as the duty of every Jew. It was disregard of this that accounted for their present plight – that of 'slaves in the country which God gave to their ancestors'.

We depend upon ESTHER for the only other intelligence we possess about the Persian era although few would champion its historicity. It is the tale of how God, without showing His hand (and without even being mentioned), saved the Jews from extermination at the hands of extremists at the Persian court and then turned the tables on their enemies.

The legacy of Ezra and Nehemiah

Nothing short of a miracle was quietly being enacted. The Jews' resistance to assimilation while in Babylon, their return to their ancestral land against every worldly expectation, the latitude given by the Persians in allowing them to observe their faith without molestation, and the way the Jews sustained it as an island of monotheism and holiness in a sea of polytheism and superstition so that the ashes of exile blossomed into the buds of a new beginning – all this is so far beyond parallel that only God can account for it.

But there was another side. While Ezra was right to recognise that lines had to be drawn if the Jews were not to be absorbed into the heathen world around them, his reforms eventually went too far, leading to such meticulous observance of ceremonial and legalistic hair-splitting that the Law became a fetish and Judaism gradually degenerated into the rigid exclusivism and intolerance we find in the Gospels. (Yet without the spiritual walls provided by Ezra and Nehemiah it may not have survived at all).

The later prophets

The bigoted community that JONAH addresses could well have been living in the aftermath of Ezra's reforms. His aim was to remind his readers of their missionary calling and that God's desire for repentance and salvation extended to the entire world, even to nations like Assyria whose barbarity and cruelty had made them bywords for wickedness.

JOEL extrapolates the penance and prayer that saved Israel from the devastation of a locust plague to the last days when repentance will similarly transform the Day of Yahweh, a day of judgement, into a day of deliverance. In a foreshadowing of Pentecost he prophecies a day when God will pour His spirit out on all humanity.

Much of DEUTERO ZECHARIAH is obscure but the Church has long seen its prophecy of a king who, while riding a donkey, will bring peace to the whole world, together with the allegory of the rejected shepherd and references to 'one who was pierced', as pointers to Christ. With echoes of the New Covenant it speaks of God pouring a spirit of grace and prayer on the people so that they turn to Him, and a fountain for washing away sins and impurity. Israel has a glorious future under a restored House of David. It ends with a portrayal of the great tribulation that must precede God's final victory in the end days.

The Seleucid and Maccabean eras

The Persian Empire held sway for two centuries before falling to Alexander the Great. Alexander's empire was the most extensive the world had yet seen but it barely survived his early death in 323 B.C. Within a few years it split into Thrace, Macedonia, Ptolemaia (Egypt) and Seleucia (centred on modern Syria). Initially Palestine lay under Ptolemaic tutelage but in 200 B.C. Ptolemy V was defeated by the Seleucid Antiochus III whose fiefdom it then became.

1 and 2 MACCABEES pick up the story in 175 B.C. when the Seleucid king Antiochus IV Epiphanes, intent on a rigorous program of Hellenisation to unify his empire, began a regime of oppression aimed at suppressing the Jewish faith. He profaned the Temple and forbade observance of the Law. He was opposed by a priest named Mattathias who raised the flag of rebellion that was later taken up by his sons Judas Maccabeus, Jonathan and Simon. Thanks to incredible valour and dedication, but aided also by internal squabbles among the Seleucids, the revolt prospered. In December 164 B.C. Judas was able to enter Jerusalem and rededicate the Temple. By the time MACCABEES ends, with Simon's murder in 134 B.C., the Jews had consolidated their right to religious freedom and gained a measure of political autonomy as well. Simon's line, the Hasmonaeans, maintained their grip on power until 63 B.C. when Pompey incorporated Palestine as a province of the Roman Empire.

DANIEL begins with heroic tales set in the days of the Babylonian exile – Daniel himself in the lions' den, his companions in the fiery furnace – showing how God is always in control, rewarding loyalty and humbling the mighty. These are followed by a sequence of visions claiming to give a preview of history that foretells Antiochus' tyranny and climaxes in the end days when, after a period of dire tribulation, the principalities of this world will give way to the universal and everlasting kingdom of God, resurrection, and the final felicity of the just.

The book purports to have been written in, and to be looking forward from, the sixth century of Nebuchadnezzar. However it may well have been composed shortly before the death of Antiochus Epiphanes – that is, after most of the events it claims to foresee – and put into the words of a seer of a bygone age. In this way appearing as prophecy that had already been fulfilled up to and including the tribulation of Antiochus' day, it would inspire its audience, smarting under Antiochus' persecution, to hold fast to their faith in the expectation that the rest, namely God ushering in His own everlasting rule, would also come to pass soon to bring an end to their suffering. It is in one of these visions that Daniel sees a figure that Jesus would later make His own: 'One most venerable conferring kingship on One like a son of man coming on the clouds of heaven'.

The Wisdom literature

The Old Testament books fall into four groups. The Pentateuch runs from Genesis to Deuteronomy, from the Creation narratives and God's election of Israel down to the death of Moses. The historical books, Joshua to Esther/Maccabees, carry us from Israel's conquest of the Promised Land to the exile and beyond. The third group, Isaiah to Malachi, comprises the prophets. Finally, placed somewhat awkwardly between the historical books and the prophets are the Psalms and the Song of Songs, together with five books that make up what is known as the Bible's Wisdom literature, a literary genre that uses the voice of reflection and experience to suggest guides to everyday living and explore life's enigmas.

JOB, one of the world's poetic masterpieces, wrestles with suffering, a problem to which it maintains there is no answer in this world save faith and unquestioning surrender to a God who has ordered everything for man's ultimate good but whose ways meanwhile are past understanding. Noteworthy is the prescient passage where Job (the subject of the poem), the faithful servant of God who is afflicted with such terrible suffering, comes close to transcending the bounds of the only world then known as he appeals to a 'Defender in heaven' who will vouch for his integrity.

ECCLESIASTES is a monologue on the apparent futility and injustice of existence in which the author encourages his readers to enjoy life's pleasures while they can. Yet beneath a sceptical veneer he cannot avoid clinging to a God who, in a way he cannot articulate, will one day settle accounts and make sense of it all.

PROVERBS enjoins its readers to let their lives be directed by fear of Yahweh and knowledge of God. Those who do so enjoy God's favour. The only alternative is the road of folly that leads to death. This general thesis is supplemented by anthologies of short pithy sayings, proverbs, to help the reader in his daily life. ECCLESIASTICUS is in similar vein but breaks new ground by equating wisdom with the Law, the Word of God. It concludes with a eulogy to Israel's stalwart ancestors: 'let us now praise famous men'.

The book of WISDOM offers its readers a stark choice: immortality for the virtuous who espouse wisdom, oblivion for the wicked. It dwells on the nature of wisdom and ends with an excursus celebrating its role in Israel's history, especially the Exodus.

All the Wisdom books are remarkable for their personification of Wisdom as a feminine celestial being; created by Yahweh; with Him for all eternity; at His side during Creation; deputed to carry His revelation to Israel.

REFLECTION

The Saviour God

The Old Testament reveals a Creator God who is omnipotent, omniscient, eternal; God of the cosmos and of every nation; a hidden God shrouded in mystery, demanding faith; utterly holy, transcendent, the only God; a personal God of love, justice and righteousness who judges the inner heart; who abhors evil and acts to save

His people from their sins; a God whose love never wavers no matter how often He is rebuffed; One who, though He punishes wrongdoing as a father would a child, never lets His anger deflect His resolve to save and invariably returns with a new initiative, inviting repentance and a fresh start; a God whose wrath is the well of His mercy and at whose command the ashes of judgement call forth the green shoots of salvation; a Saviour God.

Israel's inadequacy

Yet as the Old Testament ends God's promise to Abraham to bless all nations remains just that, a promise. How can this be? For God to go back on His Word is unthinkable. The answer lies in one word, Israel. At Sinai God chose Israel to be a holy nation, the tool for His salvic will. But this high calling was conditional on obedience and, unfortunately, despite enjoying a treasure house of God's saving acts and new beginnings – the miracle of the Sea, the passage of the Jordan, the conquest of Canaan, victories under the Judges, deliverance from the Philistines, the inspiration of the prophets, the return from Babylon, the zeal of Ezra and Nehemiah – obedience was something to which Israel could never consistently aspire.

There was a time under David when Israel might have grasped her missionary role. Despite the sins that stained his character David wanted nothing more than to be God's loyal servant. But it was not to be and Israel never again achieved the delicate balance of theocracy through monarchy her calling required. Instead a monarchical regime rooted in the secular steadily undermined the theocratic ideal. Time and again the prophets inveighed against the immorality and injustice, the insatiable appetite for pagan cult, that was alienating her from God. But it all fell on deaf ears. Israel had to learn at first hand the force for self destruction that temporal power and affluence possessed and that they could not provide the sort of society God wanted. The result was deportation and exile and a restoration that left her under foreign tutelage, as emasculated politically as she was still unfitted spiritually for her divine mission.

The new age

Yet, despite her chequered history there was never a time, even while declaiming the inevitability of God's judgement and with oblivion apparently staring her in the face, that the prophets left Israel devoid of hope. God would never renege on His promises. However grim the outlook a 'remnant' would survive to carry the torch. God would honour His promises. Beginning with Amos, Hosea and Isaiah, they foresaw an age – albeit postponed to a distant future, the means hidden from their sight – when God's people would be regathered to a new Eden, a land of astonishing fertility where they would live for ever in justice and peace, free of sickness and sadness, enemies vanquished, old enmities forgotten, sins forgiven. Inspired by Israel, pilgrims from all over the world would flock to Jerusalem to walk in God's ways and acknowledge His rule.

Yet for all its ideals – universal peace, the rule of righteousness, an Israel purified of her vices and restored to communion with a Yahweh dwelling among His people – this vision was, to begin with, firmly rooted in the material and a nationalistic colouring was rarely absent. To Micah it meant each man sitting contentedly under his vine. For Trito Isaiah it was an Israel restored to a Jerusalem with her walls rebuilt and free from marauders. In Ezekiel's eyes it meant a new Temple and a repurified cult. Zechariah delighted in the thought of old men sitting in the city squares with children playing merrily around them.

Deutero Isaiah was convinced that this new age would dawn with God leading His people in triumphant procession out of Babylon back to the new Jerusalem. But the reality of the homecoming was very different. Life in the restored community was hard, the land impoverished, and when it eventually became clear that the new order had not arrived the expectation of a visible breaking-in of God's power in history began to fade.

Gradually, spasmodically, beginning with Ezekiel and continuing with Deutero Zechariah and Daniel (and Trito Isaiah to a degree), the expectation gradually transmuted to belief in a transcendental event when, at some indefinite time in the future, God would put an end to history. After a tribulation in which evil would plumb incredible depths and plunge His people to the very brink of defeat, God would destroy the powers of darkness once and for all. He would create new heavens and a new earth, eclipsing the old order and issuing in His own universal and never-ending reign. In revealing the hope of resurrection and everlasting life Daniel goes further, bringing us to the threshold of the Gospels.

Thus the seeds were being sown that it is not in this world, as Abraham and the early prophets would have supposed, that God's promises will be realised but in a new creation, a new dispensation beyond the grave, outside history and time in God's own Kingdom.

The New Covenant

Absolutely crucial to any idea of a new age was the New Covenant prophesied by Jeremiah and Ezekiel whereby sins would be forgiven and men given new hearts that, quickened by the Spirit which Joel saw would one day be poured out on all humanity, would be freely responsive to God's will. Without this, given the frailty of human nature, the new age would be no better than the old. Deutero Zechariah's vision of God pouring a spirit of grace and prayer over His people and washing away sins spoke in similar vein.

The Messianic hope

Concurrent with the idea of a new age and stemming from Nathan's prophecy, hopes gradually centred on a king, of David's House, who later came to be known as the Messiah. Isaiah was the first to give this clear expression prophesying a Son, Immanuel, who would be inspired by the spirit of Yahweh and be endowed with the noblest titles imaginable: Wonder-Counsellor, Prince-of-Peace. Micah saw this future ruler hailing from Bethlehem.

Jeremiah and Zechariah echoed this hope in a Branch, a scion of David whose dynasty would rule beside the priests. Ezekiel cited a future David ruling as shepherd and prince as God's viceroy. Deutero Zechariah also linked deliverance with the House of David, prophesying a king who would be victorious yet humbly riding a donkey. Some of the psalms have Messianic overtones.

There is no evidence that the Jews linked this expected king with other figures of expectation: the future prophet like himself that Moses foretold, Deutero Isaiah's mysterious Servant, or Daniel's son of man. Much less, even though ideas began to evolve from a human and national figure towards a universal and transcendental being, did they expect a divine Messiah. Indeed, although the Jewish world of the first century was certainly looking for the advent of the Messianic age, what form it would take was the source of much confusion. Most expected a warrior king leader who would throw off the Roman yoke and restore David's empire. None expected a King who would be rejected and who would die on a Cross.

Expectation

As the Old Testament draws to a close it is thus with a sense of unfinished business. Diverse strands of prophecy, albeit some of them only delivered in scattered half-poetic glimpses, still await fulfilment. Life after death is but briefly touched upon in Daniel and Wisdom. The new age of blessing, the New Covenant, the Messianic hope, the conversion of the nations: all remain bedded in the future. The repeated failures of God's people and the consequent frustration of His promises hint that the story is not yet over but pointing beyond itself for its consummation. So as the Old Testament ends it is with the door of hope ajar and an air of expectancy of God's further action in the world.

The New Testament

The man of prophecy

With the coming of Jesus Christ all the hopes and prophecies of the Old Testament, all its uncertainties and enigmas, are brought to perfection and gloriously resolved either already or in the consummation yet to come. Christ is the pivot on which history turns. Centuries of expectation, diverse titles and roles, converge in Him. Strands that are scattered in the Old Testament Christ braids together as He climaxes its mighty deeds. He is the apotheosis of all it stood for, the synthesis of prophecy down the ages, the culmination of God's self-revelation and His saving acts, God's love expressed in history in a human life.

Son of God, He is the Messiah who fulfils God's promise that the House of David would reign forever, although unlike David His will not be a kingdom of this world. (Christ is the Greek equivalent of the Hebrew Messiah.) He is Isaiah's Immanuel, the ruler from Bethlehem heralded by Micah, the promised Branch, prince and shepherd who unites in Himself the spiritual and temporal powers that Jeremiah, Ezekiel and Zechariah saw as near yet apart. He is Daniel's son of man who, following the great tribulation He prophesied while seated on the Mount of Olives, will 'come on the clouds of heaven' to bring the Day of Yahweh to a close and judge the living and the dead. His Kingdom will have no end. It is Christ, whose coming was postponed until His Way became the only way, whom John the Baptist, Malachi's messenger, announced. He is at once the remnant of Old Israel and the nucleus of the New, the Church of God's missionary call, His channel for bringing blessings to all mankind.

He is woven into the very fabric of Scripture. Just as God granted new life on account of one good man, Noah, so it is with Christ. Where the first Moses saved his followers from physical slavery He, the second Moses, offers deliverance from the spiritual bondage of sin. Christian tradition has long seen Christ as Job's Defender in heaven and as the full flowering of the Old Testament's personification of Wisdom as 'pure emanation of the glory of the Almighty'.

Following Isaiah He gives hearing to the deaf and sight to the blind. He makes the lame walk. He is the light of the world, the living water. He frees prisoners and soothes the broken-hearted. He personifies the lowly who will be exalted. He is manna, the bread of life. Like Moses' bronze serpent He was 'lifted up' to save. Jonah's entombment in the belly of the sea-monster prefigured His own burial.
Appendices 1, 2 refer

The Saviour

Above all He opens the road to salvation. 'Not counting equality with God something to be grasped, and emptying Himself of His divinity' He became man, the supreme example of 'the first shall be last and the last shall be first'. Where man as (exemplified in) Adam aspires to be God, God became man in Jesus. Where man as Adam falls prey to the narrow demands of self-love and pride, Jesus lived a life of selfless love and humility.

With His sinless life of love and obedience, a life that was patterned on Isaiah's Servant and culminated with His death on the Cross, Jesus overcame evil and atoned for our sins as animal sacrifices in the Temple never could. Lamb of God, He bore the sins of the whole world; past, present and future. In St Paul's words 'He became sin'. In so doing He 'reversed the Fall'. He wrested back from evil the fruits of its victories, the ground already lost to sin, from creation to the end of time. He healed the breach between creature and Creator, dying that we might acquire His holiness to live anew after death, and revealing the depths of divine love as nothing else could. Where the first Adam begat death He, the second Adam, annihilates death. He came to give life and to give it abundantly. He is the perfect priest, bringing to fruition all that the Old Testament sacrificial system merely anticipated.
Appendix 3 refers

Jesus' resurrection brought visible evidence of His invisible victory. It bears witness that He was indeed who He claimed to be, Son of God, and that God approved of what He did, turning what looked like being evil's greatest triumph into total defeat. Indeed in rising from the dead Jesus was the first beneficiary of His own redeeming act and in the fullness of time His resurrection will be seen not as an extraordinary event but rather as extraordinary evidence, due to its timing, of an ordinary event.

After He ascended into heaven Jesus sent the Holy Spirit to continue His work by transforming men's hearts, thus fulfilling Joel's prophecy and completing the New Covenant which He inaugurated at the Last Supper for the forgiveness of sins.

The New Testament

Virtually all we know of Jesus Christ comes from the New Testament. The Old Testament was compiled over many centuries during which it followed the fortunes of God's chosen people. It includes biography, history, law, prophecy, a hymnal and Wisdom literature. The New Testament, by contrast, focuses squarely on the person of Christ. It was all written in the space of a few score years and in their different ways all its books interpret His life, death and teaching. The Gospels tell us what we know of His earthly life. The Acts of the Apostles show how the good news He brought spread from the mother Church in Palestine across the Roman empire. The epistles, twenty-one of them, deal with particular problems and questions Christians were wrestling with in the early years but still feed faith today two millennia later and are key to acquiring a deeper understanding of who Christ was and the implications of His teaching. Revelation, the Bible's finale, probes the future and is still being played out even today. It shows that despite every vicissitude God is firmly in control and looks forward to the time when history itself will be wound up, evil destroyed and, in a glorious renewal, God's original intentions will at last be fully realised.

The Gospels

The Gospels, MATTHEW, MARK, LUKE, JOHN, concentrate on Jesus' works and teaching and the events of the last week of His life. Biographical detail is sparse and secondary. They bring the good news ('Gospel' means 'good news') that God had at last made His decisive move by stepping into history Himself, not as a warrior king like David, as many had expected, but as Isaiah's Suffering Servant. As a result the Kingdom of heaven – deliverance from Satan and sin, healing and the age of righteousness, restoration and blessedness – is a present reality; present in Christ's person, attested in His victory over evil and death, and open now to all who repent and accept Him as their Saviour. For with His death Christ made reparation for sins, restored fellowship with God, overcame death and reopened the gates of heaven to all who join with Him in faith and allow themselves to be born anew and led by the Spirit to a life of love, their wills in union with God's, a perfection that will only be complete when the Kingdom comes in all its fullness after death.

The Gospels show a Jesus at One with His Father, sent to save the world, to be Way, Truth and Life. With His miracles and exorcisms He gave a glimpse of the wonderful world to come and His defeat of evil. With the example of His life, His teaching and His command to love He showed what God demands of those who are to share eternity with Him. With His atoning death on the Cross He made it all possible.

The Acts of the Apostles

ACTS opens with Jesus' ascension and the outpouring of the promised Holy Spirit at Pentecost. It then describes the travails of the early Christian community and how Jesus' followers, fired by the resurrection and empowered by the Spirit, carried the good news from Jerusalem, establishing churches across the Mediterranean, even to Rome itself. In a climactic event the conversion of Cornelius showed that the new faith was open to everyone. Moreover despite its Jewish roots Christians did not need to become practising Jews. In the event Jews generally rejected the Gospel and it was overwhelmingly gentiles who became its mainstay. God's promise to Abraham of blessings for all mankind was beginning to be fulfilled.

Following a dramatic conversion on the road to Damascus, Paul is the key figure in the second half of Acts, the narrative focusing almost exclusively on his three missionary journeys and taking us right up to his imprisonment in Rome. The letters making up the next thirteen books all bear his name.

The Pauline letters

The theme of ROMANS, the most closely argued of all Paul's letters, is that although everyone, whether Jew or gentile, is a sinner and thus properly stands condemned in God's eyes, acquittal and salvation are offered to all through faith in Christ who gave His life to that very end, that everyone might be reconciled with God. This is an act of pure grace on God's part, a free gift. We cannot earn salvation by ourselves, either by keeping the Law or in any other way. Paul then argues that just as Christ died for the forgiveness of sins, so as the risen Lord He works with the Holy Spirit to help us grow in holiness in our earthly lives, a process that only reaches completion after death with glorification as God's children.

He then wrestles with the tragedy of Israel's rejection of the Gospel concluding that Israel will be saved in the end, once the gentile conversion is complete. The letter ends, like several others, with counsel for Christians in their daily lives. They form one Body in Christ and must put to good use whatever gifts they have been endowed with. They must be good citizens and be guided by love and concern for others taking Christ as their role model.

GALATIANS covers some of the same ground though in less detail. It is the most outspoken of Paul's epistles and was written to rebuke critics who, following his mission to Galatia, were questioning His credentials and arguing that gentile converts to Christianity must first be circumcised (the distinguishing mark of the Old Covenant) and observe the Mosaic Law, in short become Jews in all but name. All of which ran directly counter to his teaching that salvation came as a gift from faith in Christ and in no other way.

1 CORINTHIANS is the apostle's reply to various problems that were taxing the newly founded church at Corinth: arguments between rival cliques, fellow Christians going to law to settle disputes between themselves, questions about marriage and celibacy, whether it was right to eat meat that had previously been offered to idols, decorum for public worship and so on. As part of his response Paul denounces sexual sin in the strongest possible terms. The book is also noteworthy for Paul's great

panegyrics on the spiritual gifts, the Body of Christ, the supremacy of love and the resurrection of the body.

2 CORINTHIANS followed a little later when relations with Corinth had become strained. In it Paul is forced to defend himself against detractors who were distorting the Gospel and questioning his character and motives. Here, more than anywhere else, he reveals the weight of the burden on his shoulders, the perils and frustrations that were his daily lot, and the unshakeable love and resilience that sustained him. The letter also contains an appeal for a generous offering to help the poor of the mother church in Jerusalem.

Despite its attribution to the church at Ephesus EPHESIANS was probably a circular letter to all the churches in Asia Minor. It is a hymn of praise to God for His grace and love in enabling everyone, gentiles as well as Jews, to become adopted sons, showered with blessings and forming one Body in Christ whose blood it was that redeemed them. But for the moment there is a constant battle against the powers of evil and only by donning the armour of God can Christians prevail.

PHILIPPIANS finds Paul at his most genial. He urges the congregation at Philippi to stay united and work as a team, remembering Christ's example and eschewing jealousy and selfishness. Let them never forget that what matters is not circumcision or the Law but faith in Christ. God is never far away.

COLOSSIANS was prompted by news that the church at Colossae was being infiltrated by deviant ideas linked to secular philosophy, pagan festivals, angel worship and asceticism. Paul's response is to underline the deity, supremacy and sufficiency of Christ, God incarnate. Everything else is a snare and delusion.

Despite again having to defend his motives 1 THESSALONIANS is full of warmth as Paul rejoices in the Thessalonians' staunch faith and reassures them that those who have already died will be at no disadvantage when Christ returns. 2 THESSALONIANS is a follow-up letter in which he refers to speculation over Christ's return and describes the terrible tribulation that will both precede and herald it.

1 TIMOTHY, 2 TIMOTHY and TITUS stand together. They urge that the best counter to false doctrine is to concentrate on the positive teaching of the Gospel and not to get sidetracked into idle speculation and semantics. They consider some of the problems faced by a young church, such as choice of leaders and the care of widows, and stress the need for sound doctrine to be matched by dedication and moral excellence.

PHILEMON is a personal letter asking Philemon, a Christian convert, to take back as a brother an ex-slave who had absconded with some of his master's valuables and subsequently taken refuge with Paul in Rome.

Hebrews

HEBREWS is one of the most difficult but important books in the New Testament. Here, more explicitly than elsewhere, it reveals how the Old Testament foreshadows the New and how the New fulfils the Old and brings it to perfection. It tells how the former dispensation based on the Old Covenant and the Law, a priesthood of fallible mortal men, man-made sanctuaries and animal sacrifice, was quite incapable of remitting sins and opening the way to fellowship with God. It was only ever intended as something temporary, a pointer and foretaste of something more efficacious that would come in God's good time.

The heavenly reality came with Christ. Blameless and divinely appointed, seated at God's right hand, yet in His humanity able to understand our weaknesses, He is the ideal priest. With His once-only perfect sacrifice of Himself He inaugurated a New Covenant that really does bring forgiveness of sins and peace with God, something the Old Covenant sacrificial rites, despite being repeated again and again, could never do. In place of the Promised Land of Canaan Christ offers rest in God's own heavenly abode. These are the realities of which the former designs were mere shadows now superseded. The gulf between sinful man and his holy God can only be bridged by one who is Himself both God and man.

Letters to all Christians

The remaining seven letters are known as the general or catholic (i.e. universal) epistles. Where Paul's epistles were written for a particular church and situation, these (except for 2 and 3 John) appear to have been intended for wider audiences.

JAMES is intensely practical, full of tips for grappling with the challenges of daily life. However it is dominated by one great theme. Christianity is not only about believing but also about doing. Faith without works (good deeds) is dead. At first sight this seems to be at variance with Paul's teaching that faith alone opens the door to salvation. Yet there is no contradiction. To James works are an obligation arising out of faith. True faith will inevitably produce good works while the absence of works would imply a defective faith.

1 PETER is a message of encouragement to Christians facing persecution. Let them model themselves on Christ and become models of virtue and reverence, accepting whatever suffering comes their way, being above reproach, full of love, and standing firm in the faith. Those who share Christ's suffering will also share His glory. 2 PETER warns against false teachers and people who scoff at God's apparent inactivity. When Christ returns to usher in the new creation that God has promised there will be no warning. So let them live pure and holy lives and be prepared.

1 JOHN was written in response to a sect that maintained a sharp distinction between the spiritual, which they believed to be pure, and the material, which was evil. As such they denied Christ's human nature: how could the holy God adopt a material body? They held that they were free of sin and in no need of redemption since conduct at the material level could never tarnish their spiritual standing.

God is light, moral perfection, John begins. Therefore we deceive ourselves if we think we can share in His life while walking in the darkness of sin. No one is free from sin. So let us confess our sins and be cleansed to walk in Christ's footsteps, letting light and love guide us in our lives. For God is love and it is only by following the example of that unfathomable love that we can become His children in eternal life. Christians must guard against the Antichrist who will come one day. Already his disciples are at work in the world denying Jesus as the divine Son of God come in human flesh.

2 JOHN also warns against teaching that deviates from the orthodox Gospel, particularly on Christ's humanity. 3 JOHN addresses a local problem, an unseemly squabble in a church of John's acquaintance where the pastor refused hospitality to itinerant preachers.

JUDE resembles 2 Peter. It is yet another warning against infiltrators who are perverting the Gospel and denying Christ. It urges the faithful to persevere, pray, and patiently await their Lord and the gift of eternal life.

Revelation

REVELATION balances the Genesis prologue as, in an elaborate series of visions and symbols, it shows history moving towards a towering climax when God's plan will at last achieve its goals. In the meantime this world will continue to be riven by strife, want, injustice, disasters and torment until the end of time. For, though Satan has been defeated on the Cross, he is still at large, although on the run, as long as this world remains. Yet the future is not in doubt. The Church will survive and finally, after a last frenzied assault by the powers of darkness (the great tribulation), Christ will return and the full fruits of God's plan, worked out through His redeeming blood, will at last be harvested. We shall become children of God. Satan, suffering and death will be destroyed for ever to be followed by the last judgement, a new heaven and a new earth, and a glorious new Jerusalem where the just will enjoy God's presence forever in eternal bliss.

REFLECTION

Paradise regained

We have seen how the Old Testament is incomplete, pointing to a time beyond itself for the realisation of God's promises: the destruction of evil, renewal and restoration, the age of blessing and bliss. With the New Testament, sculpted from the bedrock of Christ, what the Old imparts in enigma and diversity is, in Christ, woven together and given a new perspective; one that dispels its obscurities and, through the Cross, reconciles the tension between man's sin and God's holiness.

Hopes that were disappointed by the modest reality of the homecoming from Babylon after the expectation raised by Isaiah will be more than satisfied in the greater homecoming from the bondage of sin that Christ won for His people at Calvary. Abraham and his spiritual heirs are indeed a 'great nation'. As the Church, the new Israel of the redeemed, the new 'holy nation', it is now their job to spread the Gospel and they will be rewarded not with the paradisiacal restoration of the historic Israel, not with blessings in this world, not with the Promised Land of Canaan (all of them but tokens of spiritual blessings to come) but, thanks to God's love and Christ's blood, with the 'Promised Land' of life with God in a new creation beyond the grave, freed from the corruption that has held sway since the Fall and with Christ as their King. Their destiny is to become children of God in a Jerusalem of unimaginable splendour and boundless joy, illumined by the glory of a God who will wipe away every tear and dwell in their midst. Death will be no more.

And so the divine will triumphs over every adversity. Where in Genesis man was seduced by Satan, estranged from God and barred from the tree of life, as Revelation ends Satan is destroyed, man is reconciled with God and free to feed not from one tree of life but many, each bearing twelve crops a year. Life in abundance, as by God's grace the paradise of Eden, lost by man's folly, is finally regained in a new Jerusalem in Christ.
Appendix 4 refers

The Old Testament

THE PENTATEUCH

'Pentateuch' is the name of the first five books of the Old Testament: Genesis to Deuteronomy. They cover an immense period of time yet share a unity of theme that knits them closely together. Beginning in the distant past with Creation they trace the origins of life and man's Fall from perfection and continue with the start of God's plan to put things right, the call of Abraham and His choice of Israel to be a holy nation to proclaim His name throughout the world. They include the giving of the Law, prescriptions for sacrifice for giving thanks and seeking God's forgiveness, and they outline the trials and tribulations of Israel's journey from Egypt to the very threshold of the Promised Land.

*   *   *

Although authorship was traditionally attributed to Moses significant variations in style make a single-author thesis problematic. Ever since the seminal work of J Wellhausen in the late nineteenth century it has been widely accepted that it is a blend of four documents distinguished by the letters J, E, D and P.

J, so-called because it refers to God as Yahweh (the original spelling was Jahweh), is thought to have been compiled in the tenth or ninth century B.C. in the southern kingdom of Judah. It is largely narrative and characterised by clear vivid story telling and anthropomorphises.

E, referring to God as Elohim, probably stems from the eighth or seventh century B.C. and the northern kingdom of Israel. Again it is largely narrative but it also contains legal sections. It has a drier style than J and God is more remote communicating through dreams, visions and angels. It refers to Horeb where J uses Sinai, and Amorites where J talks of Canaanites.

D is virtually confined to Deuteronomy. It is marked by a distinctive exhortatory and moralising style: obedience leads to blessings, disobedience to curses. It was probably an early edition of Deuteronomy that was discovered in the Temple as the Book of the Law in 622 B.C., 2K 22, although its origins were certainly much earlier.

P, the 'priestly' source, concentrates on ritual, ceremonial, law, statistics and genealogies. It emphasises God's holiness and transcendence. The style is heavy and redundant. It probably dates from the Babylonian exile or shortly thereafter.

Modern research suggests that the situation is more complex and that each of

J,E,D,P is itself an amalgam of ancient traditions, oral as well as written, emanating from many sources over centuries ranging from the post-exilic era back to Moses or even earlier. Even relatively late passages sometimes have traditions of ancient origin embedded in them.

During and after the exile these various sources, which probably continued to evolve, would have been combined and edited by the priesthood into the Pentateuch as we know it today. In short, what is suggested is an elaborate mosaic, an interweaving of narrative and law, history and ceremonial, composed by many authors at different times with the four prime sources, each of them the result of editorial reworkings, crystallisations of their own mosaics at particular points in time.

Today sees growing scepticism about the classic documentary hypothesis so that in lieu of any consensus on new theories we have to confess that much is still shrouded in mystery. At the same time there is a growing acceptance that even if it is unlikely that Moses wrote the Pentateuch as it exists today he was certainly its inspiration and may well have been at least the originator of the stream of literary activity that gave it birth.

Genesis

Genesis is in two parts. It begins with a prologue telling how God created the cosmos and life and how, by sinning (choosing his own way over God's) man then brought discord and suffering into the world, putting himself at odds with his Creator and in need of salvation. As such it provides the *raison d'être* for the redemptive history that forms the rest of Scripture. The drama proper starts in part two with Abram as God unveils His plan to heal the breach that sin has hatched, the means whereby man will be reconciled with his Maker and Creation restored to the perfection and peace of its original design.

Genesis: The Primeval Prologue

Cast in poetic and symbolic mode the prologue is one of the richest veins in the Canon. The key to the riddle of life, it is cut on the grand scale taking the reader back to the dawn of time. With rich imagery it tells how God created a beautiful world where man would live for ever. Then, with the story of Adam and Eve, it shows how man allows evil to lead him astray. Refusing to accept God's sovereignty he brings turmoil into what was meant to be paradise rendering himself unsuited for the destiny God created him for and fit only for death. With Cain and Lamech it shows how, once it is launched, sin spreads like a plague while in the epic of Noah and the flood it reveals that were it not for the uprightness of one man (a foreshadowing of Christ) humanity would have been wiped out long ago by a God to whom sin is anathema. But even that warning is not enough to bring man to his senses as the story of the giddy pride of the men of Babel and their aspirations to god-like status makes all too clear.

By tempering censure with mercy at each provocation (clothing Adam, protecting Cain, renewing life in Noah) God indicates that judgement is not His final word, that redemption is in the air. But as the prologue draws to a close, apart from noting the arrival on the stage of a certain Abram (later renamed Abraham), it is without any hint of how this might come about.

That the prologue is meant to be read symbolically, applying to all men, is evident from the profusion of imagery: the tree of life, the snake that talks. The fact that 'Adam' carries the connotation 'mankind' in Hebrew while Eve derives from the Hebrew word for 'life' makes it abundantly clear how the sacred author viewed his composition. Few people would accept God walking in the garden of Eden or coming to earth to view the tower of Babel as historical.

To be preoccupied with science or history is equally misguided. The Bible's concern is with religious truth, with the 'why' of the world rather than the 'when', 'where' or 'how', and to respond to its delicate imagery with narrow literalism – to wonder if God really created in just seven days or to debate the size of Noah's ark – is to submerge the divine word in irrelevancy. Now in poetic vein, now with the thrust of an expert raconteur, but always enriched with imagery, its inspired epics are vehicles for truths that transcend simple narrative. So instead of 'did things really happen this way?' the better question is 'what does this story tell me?' It is only when we approach the prologue in that way, recognising Adam, Eve and the rest as part of the symbolism, that its message attains its full flowering and we can see, in our own propensity to sin, its stories re-enacted in our lives today.

None of this means that we should necessarily dismiss the prologue as entirely fiction. Presented as a narrative of earth's earliest generations it may well be underpinned by historical events. But the times are so remote and the details so sparse that we may never know. Nor does it matter. What does matter is that, whatever its historical basis, it tells us that Creation was not the result of mindless chance but the purposeful act of a loving God, and that by sinning man jeopardizes the eternal destiny God created him for.

Creation of the universe (1:1 – 2:3)

The 'book of origins' opens with a poem on the creation of the universe, life and man. In solemn hymn-like tones that have echoed down the ages, their simple austerity conveying awe and grandeur, we read of a transcendent, sovereign, eternal, all powerful God who, Himself apart from time and space, created everything from nothing by divine fiat: 'let there be . . . and so it was'. He ensured that all He created – light, sky, land and seas, vegetation, heavenly bodies, every kind of living creature – was good, the mark of a truly loving Creator.

As the peak of creation, the crowning glory, God made man, male and female, in His own image, to be master of all other creatures. The earth is to be man's home and he is to tend it as God's viceroy on earth. God blesses man and woman just as earlier he had blessed the animals. They are to be participants in the very act of creation itself by being fruitful and filling and subduing their earthly realm. This is a golden age, a peaceful paradise world. Man is to live in harmony with the animals, and they with one another, seeds, fruit and foliage providing food. On the seventh 'day' God rests thereby establishing the weekly cycle of our lives. He blesses it and makes it holy.

Creation of man and woman (2:4–25)

A second creation narrative focuses on life: man, animals, woman.[1] God shapes man from the soil of the earth and blows the breath of life into his nostrils thus fashioning him as a fusion of two worlds; physically like the animals, but uniquely with the spark of divinity too. God plants a garden in Eden watered by four great rivers, symbolic of idyllic beauty, peace and lush fertility. Every kind of tree grows there, enticing to look at and good to eat. God settles man in Eden. He is to tend the garden. Purposeful work is healthy and good.

Two trees are special. The tree of life symbolises immortality. The tree of the knowledge of good and evil represents morality and man may choose to eat from any tree in the garden save this. God reserves to Himself the right to decide the norms of behaviour, right and wrong, and the penalty for disobedience is death.[2]

Man is meant to be a social creature. So God creates the animals as companions and calls on him to name them thereby indicating his authority over them.[3] But no suitable companion is found. So God creates woman from the man's rib. Woman thus shares man's high calling at the peak of creation.

In telling us that a man becomes attached to his wife and that they become one flesh Genesis underlines the sanctity of marriage and sexuality. Both are God's gift and therefore good, giving man a role in creation and in his own parentage a faint glimmering of God's own Fatherhood. Although naked neither the man nor the woman feel shame. Their relationship is one of joyful innocence. Sin is as yet unknown. *Appendices 1, 2, 3 refer*

The Fall of man (3:1–6)

Having portrayed the paradise world of beauty and harmony that God intended, Genesis now relates why it has degenerated to the blighted world we know today. A snake, symbolising the devil or the force of evil in the world, tempts the woman to disobey God by eating the forbidden fruit of the tree of the knowledge of good and evil.[4] In other words she is encouraged to challenge God's moral prerogative.

How deftly the Fall, man in revolt before God, is described; how lifelike its portrayal of human perfidy. The snake sows doubt on exactly what God had prohibited, disingenuously denies that disobedience will incur death, and implies that God was motivated by meanness and jealousy, at the same time appealing to the woman's vanity by telling her that by eating the forbidden fruit she will become god-like. She rejects the temptation at first but desire and self-assertion are not to be denied. So she eats the fruit and her husband quickly follows suit. And so it is that sin, man rebelling against God, enters the world.

Shame and disharmony (3:7–13)

Straightaway the delinquent pair experience shame symbolised by nakedness and their feeble efforts to overcome their feelings of guilt by covering their loins with fig leaves are of no avail.[5] They are frightened to face God when He calls to them in the cool of the day. Nor are they any more at ease with one another. With acute psychological insight Genesis exposes the self-deception by which they rationalise what they have done. The man blames the woman and comes close to accusing God Himself. The woman blames the snake.

Consequences of the Fall (3:14–24)

The consequences are catastrophic; lasting enmity between the woman's offspring and the snake's, unrelenting war between man and evil willed by God who said to the snake:

> I shall put enmity
> between you and the woman,
> and between your offspring and hers;
> it will bruise your head
> and you will strike its heel.[6]

Pain, discord and drudgery – typified by child-bearing, marital strife, and backbreaking toil in husbandry – enter a world that previously yielded its fruits so plenteously. Earth is no longer subject to man's dominion.[7] Man must suffer alienation from God and death, marked by banishment from the garden and denial of access to the tree of life, now guarded by a fiery flashing sword. He has lost the everlasting life in paradise God created him for.

But even in this darkest hour God's providence pierces the gloom.[8] Eve, as the man named his wife, will have descendants. Despite its wanton behaviour humanity will go on and God shows that He still loves His creatures by clothing them. And out of bounds though they may be, the tree of life and the garden of Eden, symbols of immortality and paradisiacal life with God, remain.

Yet for now the spoils of sin could not be more stark. With paradise lost, all that remains is a tarnished wearisome world beset with disruption and social disharmony, where life has lost its zest and man is estranged from God and doomed to die.
Appendix 4 refers

Cain and the cancerous spread of sin (4:1 – 5:32)

Brotherly love gives way to rivalry and murder when the man's son, Cain, kills his brother Abel in a fit of pique because God preferred Abel's sacrifice to his own. Cain's subsequent, 'Am I my brother's guardian?', when God questions him has become the slogan of man denying his social responsibilities down the ages.[9] He is cast out of the community and condemned to the life of a wandering nomad. Yet in a signal example of unmerited mercy God agrees to protect him from avengers nonetheless.

Two genealogies, 4:17–24; 5:1–32, differently sequenced but broadly similar, carry Adam's line down to Noah.[10] The first, centred on Cain, shows how the world degenerates into strife and bloodshed as Lamech cries out for seventy-sevenfold vengeance.[11] The list condenses centuries for it refers to the rise of city life and the birth of husbandry, the arts and industry. The second stems from Seth, the son Adam was given in place of Abel. Despite everything man continues to be in God's image, 5:3; 9:6. Seth fathered Enosh, the first man to use the name Yahweh.[12] Enosh's progeny included Enoch, Lamech and Noah. Enoch 'walked with God' i.e. lived righteously and 'then was no more because God took him'.[13]
Appendix 5 refers

Sons of God and women (6:1–4)

In a mysterious interlude 'sons of God' marry earthly women. 'Sons of God' may be an allusion to fallen angels or simply to descendants of Adam's son Seth, while the beautiful earthly women are generally identified with Cain's progeny. Intermarrying would have corrupted the 'good' Sethites by the 'bad' Cainites and so called down God's judgement. Whatever the meaning it is hard to escape the cast of a heavenly dimension, a corruption of demonic proportions, in the mystery of sin and evil that these timeless verses convey. One result is that God limits man's earthly lifespan to one hundred and twenty years.

Noah and the flood (6:5 – 9:17)

God is grieved at man's rampant wickedness and is minded to purge the earth of all life. Even the animal world has been corrupted by the Fall. Total oblivion is only averted because one man, Noah, 'walked with God'. So when God sends a flood to destroy all other life Noah, his family and representative animal pairs, are saved in an ark which God had earlier commanded him to build.

After the waters subside Noah worships God and God blesses Noah. Man is again commanded to fill the earth and in an act of divine grace God unilaterally binds Himself in a covenant with all living things, human and animal. Never again, despite the sinful bent in His wayward creatures, will God devastate the earth and destroy its life. Moreover the delicately balanced seasons on which man depends will continue to provide life's necessities.[14] God nominates the rainbow, like a war bow laid aside, to commemorate this covenant.[15]

And so creation was reborn from the chaos of the flood. But now there is recognition of the ravages of sin. Fellowship with the animal world is lost for man may now eat flesh provided the sanctity of life is recognised by abstaining from blood. As further acknowledgement of man's violent nature God ordains capital punishment for murder. The world is no longer as God intended but as man has made it.

Noah's drunkenness (9:18–29)

This story has several loose ends but exactly what Ham's misdemeanour was or why it was his son Canaan who was cursed are unimportant. In covering their father's nakedness, symbolising shame as before, Shem and Japheth were acknowledging man's guilt. They are blessed. Ham, who did not avert his eyes, typifies those who have no sense of shame before God. They are cursed. Despite the flood sin is still rampant.

The re-peopling of the earth (10:1–32)

The aim is to show how Noah's sons people the whole earth.

Babel (11:1–9)

In his overweening pride man persists in futile attempts to master his destiny, challenging God by trying to build a tower reaching to heaven 'to make a name for himself'. However in accord with His promise to Noah God's response is muted. He

cuts man down to size and limits his ability to unite in rebellion by confusing his language and scattering him throughout the earth.[16]
Appendix 6 refers

From flood to Abram (11:10–32)

Another genealogy introduces Terah, a descendant of Noah's son Shem, who leaves his home in Ur in Lower Mesopotamia to go to Canaan, accompanied by his son Abram, Abram's barren wife Sarai and Abram's nephew Lot. However on arrival at Haran in north west Mesopotamia Terah settles there instead.

Reflection

Genesis reveals a God of power outside space and time. A God of love who created man to live with Him in eternity. Yet that does not satisfy man's pride. With immortality in his grasp he challenges God's moral authority. He wants to run the world his way. The result is disharmony and suffering.

And so Genesis is forced to reveal a God of judgement. God will not tolerate sin for ever. Punishment is inevitable. In his woeful state man cannot enjoy fellowship with a God to whom sin, because it is destructive of all that is good, is repugnant. Yet this is not a God red in tooth and claw. The divine solicitude is evident in the way God repeatedly reaches out to mitigate punishment with acts of grace. No sooner had sentence been passed in Eden than God clothed the errant pair. He protected the murderer Cain. Before unleashing the flood on a vagrant world it was God Himself who shut Noah in the ark for his safety. Much as man deserves oblivion God will not forgo him so long as a single spark of goodness remains.

Given this conjunction of judgement and grace, punishment and hope, God's resolve to fulfil man's destiny is never in doubt. That is why God created him and despite his failings he will not be denied. Man was created for life with God, hence the restlessness of spirit, the yearning for greater meaning to life, the urge for fulfilment, that will not be assuaged.

Yet as the prologue ends sin is pandemic. The lesson of the flood has done little to halt man's precipitous decline. Despite advances in commerce and culture he remains a moral dwarf and it is evident that sin is too deeply ingrained for him to be able to heal himself. Only divine intervention can save an egocentric world. And that is exactly what is now about to happen. The rebellion at Babel with which the prologue ends was not, as in earlier instances, immediately followed by some countervailing act of grace. Instead, in the midst of discord and dissonance, the worldview which Genesis has so far presented abruptly ends and the spotlight narrows to the family of Terah and his son Abram. The stage is being set for the beginning of God's plan to save the world and it is to the gradual unfolding of that plan, for turning pride-ridden man into sin-resistant man, that the Bible now turns.

Genesis: The Patriarchal Age

The call of Abram (12:1–9)

Few events in history have had such an unremarkable beginning as God's call of Abram. Yet this was a turning point in history, the start of God's plan to redeem the world. Out of the blue came the voice of God to Abram in Haran telling him to:

> Leave your country, your kindred and your father's house for a country which I shall show you; and I shall make you a great nation, I shall bless you and make your name famous; you are to be a blessing! I shall bless those who bless you, and shall curse those who curse you, and all clans on earth will bless themselves by you.

Abram journeyed from Haran to the land of Canaan eventually arriving in the Negeb. He was accompanied by Sarai and Lot. As he travelled he built altars acknowledging Yahweh as Lord of the land. When Abram reached Canaan God added further promises:

> I shall give this country to your progeny, 12:7

> Your issue will be kings, 17:6

> I will be their God, 17:8

God confirmed these promises on several occasions both to Abram and later to Isaac and Jacob.[17] In each case it is evident from the tenor of the language that the promises are unconditional, depending solely on the unchangeable nature of the One who made them. In an act of divine grace nothing is asked in return.[18] They stand as the missing words of grace for want of which the Prologue ended in enigma.

Reflection

We can distinguish four key elements in God's promises:

> God will bless Abram and his progeny and He will be their God
> Abram's progeny will inherit Canaan, the Promised Land
> They will be a great nation, including kings
> They will bring blessings to all nations.[19]

Like the covenant with Noah these promises have a universal dimension.

Abram enjoyed God's favour during his lifetime but his inheritance of land was limited to the tiny plot he bought to bury Sarai. The key to the promises' greater fulfilment comes later at Sinai when God elected Israel, the nation descended from Jacob's twelve sons, to a special role in the divine plan. Provided she was obedient she would be His chosen people, a holy nation to carry His name to the whole world.

For a time Israel was a great nation ruled by kings descended from Abram. She lived in Canaan and enjoyed God's favour. But it was only temporary. For she was unfaithful and never attained the spirituality demanded for her mission. The result was dispossession of both nationhood and land and the need for a new beginning.

That new beginning was Christ, the 'remnant' of Israel, the one perfect descendant of Abram. Christ took upon Himself the missionary role God had earlier entrusted to Israel and it is through Christ that the promises made to Abram will be fulfilled. Today Christ's Church, the spiritual heirs of Abram, the faithful who acknowledge Abram's God as their God, are indeed a great nation with Christ as their King. And as the new Israel it is they who, in Christ's name, will bring blessings to all mankind.

That work is still not complete. Only in God's good time will all His promises be fulfilled. When they are, Canaan in this world having been won and lost, God's promises will be honoured more splendidly than Abram or anyone could ever imagine for the faithful now have the assurance that at the end of time they will inherit as their Promised Land not the rocky ground of Palestine but a new heaven and a new earth, a realm where they will enjoy eternal life as children of God.

Abram in Egypt (12:10 – 13:1)

Famine forces Abram to migrate to Egypt. He passes Sarai off as his sister to protect himself and she is taken into Pharaoh's harem. However when God intervenes by inflicting plagues they are both allowed to return home.[20]

Abram separates from Lot (13:2–18)

Abram and Lot agree to part as the land can no longer support their joint flocks. Abram gives first choice of pastures to Lot who opts for the fertile surrounds of the Jordan valley. He settles near Sodom, a town noted for its ungodly ways. Abram is left with the harsher hill country and makes his home near Hebron. God renews His promises.

The meeting with Melchizedek (14:1–24)

In an obscure episode Abram pursues invaders as they withdraw with their loot. He recovers the booty and rescues Lot who had been taken prisoner. Back home he declines to keep any of the spoils of war for himself and is brought bread and wine and blessed by Melchizedek who is both king of Salem and a priest of 'God Most High'.[21]

The covenant (15:1–21)

God reaffirms His promises and assures Abram that the heir on whom they depend will be his own son, not a member of his household as he had proposed. His descendants would be as countless as the stars. Then Abram put his faith in Yahweh and this was reckoned to him as uprightness.

God binds Himself to His promises in a solemn covenant sealed by a flaming torch, representing Himself, passing between two lines made up of the severed parts of slaughtered animals. This was an ancient ritual whereby the contracting parties in an agreement became bound by the blood of the sacrificial victims and accepted that they would incur the same fate as the animals if they violated their accord. What is significant here is that God alone passes between the parts indicating unilateral commitment on His part. Abram learns that his descendants will have to suffer slavery and exile for 400 years before returning to their own land.

Appendix 7 refers

Hagar and Ishmael (16:1–16)

Still without an heir ten years later Abram agrees to Sarai's suggestion to father a child by her slave girl Hagar.[22] However he stands aside when Hagar and Sarai quarrel and Sarai forces the pregnant Hagar to run away. But after God intervenes not only is Hagar allowed to raise her son, Ishmael, under Abram's roof but she too is promised numerous descendants.

The covenant (17:1–27)

Years later God appears to Abram to renew His covenant promises yet again. Circumcision is to be the sign of the covenant relationship and Abram and Sarai are to be renamed Abraham and Sarah.[23] He tells the incredulous Abraham that the ninety year old Sarah will bear him a son who is to be named Isaac and that he, not Ishmael, will be the promised heir. But Ishmael too will father a great nation.

Retribution on Sodom and Gomorrah (18:1 – 19:38)

When three men visit Abraham it soon becomes clear that they are Yahweh with two angels. Yahweh promises Sarah a son within the year as 'to Him nothing is impossible'.[24] Later on as Yahweh muses over destroying Sodom and Gomorrah for their heinous sins Abraham bargains with Him to prevent the innocent perishing with the guilty.[25] As a result God promises to spare Sodom if as few as ten upright men can be found. However when the two angels reach Sodom that evening they find such debauchery that the next morning Yahweh destroys it in a hail of brimstone and fire sparing only Lot and his daughters.[26] Later on Lot's daughters ply him with wine and seduce him. Their sons become the ancestors of the Moabites and Ammonites.

Appendix 8 refers

Abraham's contretemps with Abimelech (20:1–18)

In a story with several loose ends Abraham settles in Gerar and again asks Sarah to pose as his sister, this time to protect him from Abimelech a pagan king. Although Abimelech acts honourably he is threatened with death by God and both he and his harem are stricken with sterility. Healing comes as a result of Abraham's intercession. Sarah is revealed as Abraham's half-sister.

Appendix 9 refers

Birth of Isaac (21:1–34)

Sarah at last gives birth to the promised son who is named Isaac. Hagar and Ishmael are expelled from the household but God ensures they are well provided for.[27] Following disagreement over a well Abraham concludes a treaty with Abimelech.

Abraham's sacrifice of Isaac (22:1–24)

Abraham faces his supreme test as God instructs him to go to the land of Moriah and sacrifice Isaac as a burnt offering.[28] Only at the eleventh hour is Abraham's hand stayed when, as he raises the knife to kill Isaac, an angel instructs him to sacrifice a ram instead. Abraham thus passes his supreme challenge of faith, in moral grandeur.[29] Because of this the covenant promises are repeated in their most expansive form. A family list introduces Rebekah, Isaac's future wife.

Death of Sarah (23:1–20)

Sarah dies and after a typical bout of oriental haggling Abraham buys a burial site for her in a cave near Hebron. The first small plot of the Promised Land is his.

The marriage of Isaac (24:1–67)

Abraham sends his senior servant to Haran to choose a wife for Isaac. The ensuing betrothal of Isaac and Rebekah is one of the Bible's most beautiful stories.

Death of Abraham (25:1–18)

Abraham's new wife Keturah bears him more sons including the forefather of the Midianites. When Abraham dies Isaac and Ishmael bury him beside Sarah. Some time later Ishmael also dies.

Esau and Jacob (25:19–34)

Isaac prays for a child because Rebekah is barren. When she at last conceives Yahweh tells her that she will bear twins and that thery will be rivals with the younger prevailing. This was borne out years later when Esau, the elder, returning from hunting one day pinched with hunger, sold his birthright to his brother Jacob for a plate of stew. Esau's shallowness was matched by Jacob's avarice in insisting on a formal oath before allowing Esau to indulge his appetite.[30]

Isaac (26:1–35)

The stories of Isaac at Gerar passing off Rebekah as his sister, and concluding a treaty with Abimelech to end a dispute over wells, have similarities with similar incidents involving Abraham. God bestows the covenant promises on Isaac both at Gerar and later at Beersheba. Esau, meanwhile, marries two pagan wives.

Jacob obtains Isaac's blessing (27:1 – 28:9)

Urged on by Rebekah Jacob tricks Isaac into giving him the blessing that was rightfully Esau's. Soon afterwards he leaves for Haran both to avoid Esau's vengeance and to choose a wife from among the daughters of Rebekah's brother Laban.[31] A somewhat chastened Esau marries one of Ishmael's daughters.

Jacob's dream (28:10–22)

At the very time he is a fugitive from the land of promise God appears to Jacob in a dream and confirms his inheritance of the covenant promises. The dream, in which Jacob sees a staircase reaching to heaven with angels ascending and descending, symbolises the meeting of heaven and earth, God and man. Jacob is being told that he has a role in the divine plan of salvation. Once again his duplicitous nature comes out. Though over-awed, he makes his obedience conditional upon God providing his creature comforts.

Jacob at Haran (29:1 – 30:43)

At Haran Jacob is tricked by Laban into marrying his daughter Leah before her younger sister Rachel, the true love of his life, whom he marries later.[32] Including children by his wives' slave-girls Jacob fathers eleven sons and one daughter at Haran. After fourteen years there, shortly after Rachel has given birth to Joseph, he is minded to return home but decides to stay on when he spots an opportunity to outwit Laban in a deal involving the sheep and goats he will receive for wages if he does so. The wily Laban agrees to the deal but then tries to cheat Jacob. However by a skilful breeding technique Jacob turns the tables and becomes very rich.

Jacob's flight (31:1 – 32:3)

Laban and his sons grow jealous of Jacob's prosperity so he seizes the opportunity presented by Laban's absence sheep-shearing to return home. Unbeknown to him Rachel removes the household idols. Laban pursues Jacob to challenge him over his precipitate departure and the whereabouts of the idols. Neither were aware that as Laban vainly searched Jacob's camp Rachel was sitting on the idols using her monthly period as an excuse not to stand. After much bluster Jacob and Laban part in peace.

Jacob wrestles with God (32:4 – 33:20)

Jacob sends conciliatory messages on ahead to Esau but divides his retinue in two as a precaution all the same. Then one night, alone by the ford of the Jabbok, came the hauntingly mysterious encounter that changed his life as he wrestled with a mysterious stranger whom he recognised as God. After battling until daybreak Jacob suffered a dislocated hip but still would not release his opponent until he had received His blessing and with it a new name signifying a new destiny.

We can best interpret this experience at the Jabbok as that of a tormented soul who could no longer rest without God's blessing. At Bethel, Genesis chapter 28:10–22, after his youthful excesses as an avaricious schemer and years of relegating God to the background, God became alive to Jacob, perhaps for the first time. He was not yet ready to commit entirely but the seed was sown and from then on he was left wrestling with himself, the old man versus the new yet to be born, until that fateful night twenty years later when he surrendered completely and Jacob, erstwhile trickster and seeker after God, became Israel, man of God, 35:10.

Jacob wrestled, as all who seek God's blessing must, not against God but for God and because of his persistence went away a changed man, marked by a new name, but carrying for ever in his hip the mark of that fateful night and a reminder that blessing cannot be won without suffering. His experience is everyman's. The quest for God is a struggle demanding perseverance but those who hold fast are changed. No one can encounter God and be the same again.

Jacob's fears about meeting his brother prove groundless. Esau is overjoyed to see him. However after giving Esau the impression that he would join him in Seir Jacob proceeds instead to Shechem where he buys a small plot of land.

The rape of Dinah (34:1–31)

Jacob's daughter Dinah is raped by Shechem. In revenge her brothers pillage Shechem's village and slaughter all the males while they are recovering from the circumcision they had agreed to in return for the incident being forgiven.

Jacob returns home (35:1 – 36:43)

Jacob outlaws foreign gods. He journeys on to Bethel where God reveals that his new name is to be Israel and endows him with the covenant promises. Rachel dies near Bethlehem giving birth to Benjamin. Jacob arrives back at Hebron shortly before Isaac dies. Esau joins in burying him. The chapter ends with listings of Esau's descendants, the Edomites.

Judah and Tamar (38:1–30)

Jacob's son Judah had a son Er who married a certain Tamar. When her husband died leaving her childless and neither of his brothers, Onan and Shelah, was prepared to father her child as was the custom, Tamar disguised herself as a harlot to entice Judah to sleep with her. She conceived twins of whom the elder was named Perez.[33]

Joseph in Egypt (37:1–36; 39:1 – 41:57)

Joseph is resented by his brothers because of his superior airs. So they sell him into slavery in Egypt where he eventually rises to a position of trust in the house of Potiphar, one of Pharaoh's officials. Before long Potiphar's wife falsely accuses him of trying to seduce her and he is imprisoned. There he makes a name for himself as an interpreter of dreams, so much so that when Pharaoh himself is troubled by dreams it is Joseph he sends for. Joseph's explanation, that Egypt faces seven years of fine harvests to be followed by seven years of famine, so impresses Pharaoh that he appoints Joseph governor of Egypt with responsibility for administering the nation's grain stocks. Joseph marries an Egyptian who bears him two sons, Manasseh and Ephraim.[34]

Joseph meets his brothers again (42:1 – 45:28)

Canaan is hit with famine and Jacob despatches all his sons except Benjamin to Egypt for supplies. When they appear before Joseph, whom they do not recognise, Joseph accuses them of being spies but allows them to return home on condition they leave Simeon behind and return with Benjamin. This kindles the brothers' guilty conscience over their treatment of Joseph and they suffer further disquiet when they discover the money they paid for the grain mysteriously returned to them in their sacks (unbeknown to them on Joseph's orders).

When the brothers are compelled to return to Egypt for further supplies, Benjamin accompanies them. This time Joseph not only arranges for their money to be returned in their sacks as before but also has his silver cup hidden in Benjamin's sack.[35] When, on Joseph's orders, his chamberlain pursues them and 'discovers' the cup Joseph decrees that Benjamin must become his slave. The rest may go. Judah sees this as God's punishment for their long ago betrayal of Joseph and insists they must all serve as slaves. When Joseph insists that Benjamin alone must pay the price Judah voices one of the noblest speeches in the Bible pleading, with an eloquence fuelled by the anguish Benjamin's loss would cause his father, to be allowed to take Benjamin's place as Joseph's slave. Joseph is now convinced that his brothers' change of heart is genuine and can contain himself no longer. He reveals his identity and invites Jacob and his family to domicile in Egypt.

Jacob settles in Egypt (46:1 – 47:31)

As he sets out God assures Jacob that He will make his progeny a great nation in Egypt and one day He will bring them back again.[36] Joseph suggests they tell Pharaoh that they are shepherds in the hope, subsequently realised, that he will allow them to live in Goshen where there is ample pasturage.[37] Joseph promises to bury Jacob with his ancestors.

Jacob's testament and death (48:1 – 50:26)

Jacob tells Joseph of the covenant promises. He blesses Ephraim and Manasseh and adopts them as his own sons. However he places his right hand, which would normally bless the elder son, on Ephraim, the younger, thereby indicating that he would be the greater.[38]

On his deathbed Jacob reviews the destinies of his twelve sons in a poetic blend of prophecy and judgement in which the prophecy for Judah bears strong Messianic overtones. Jacob dies and is buried alongside Abraham. Meanwhile in words that echo down the ages to Christ, Joseph reassures his brothers that he harbours no grudge. The evil they planned had by God's design been turned to good, the survival of His people.

Years later, after voicing his confidence in God's promises and asking to be buried in the Promised Land, Joseph himself dies. And so Genesis ends with Abram's progeny living quietly in Egypt, the age of blessings still seemingly far away.

Exodus

In Genesis God promised Abraham that he would be the father of a great nation whereby all nations on earth would be blessed. But as Genesis ends we find his descendants, forebears of the twelve tribes, living far from their homeland in Egypt. Their time had not yet come. Indeed four centuries were to elapse before the story is resumed in Exodus. Centuries during which the lot of the Israelites, now seemingly forgotten by God, slipped from honoured guest to servitude.

Exodus, where God starts to fulfil His promises, divides into two parts. The first tells how God raised up Moses to rescue His people from their bondage in Egypt. The second begins at Sinai with God's election of Israel to her role on the world stage as the nation He would use to offer blessings to all mankind. Straightaway He begins to forge her into the theocratic community, the kingdom of priests, that commission entails. He binds her with a solemn covenant, bequeaths her His Law and establishes a Dwelling to live in her midst. Exodus is thus a book of redemption and adoption whose twin foci are Egypt and Sinai.

* * *

If Exodus reveals a God of majesty and power, a God of ineffable holiness, the great I AM, it also reveals a God who acts in history and saves, even in apparently hopeless situations. A God who cares for the human condition and used His omnipotence to rescue Israel from captivity. Redemption came as a gift. There was no question of Israel earning it. The purpose of the Law when it came was not to enable communion with God but to preserve it.

We see a God whose detestation of sin is surpassed by mercy and love. No sooner had Israel promised obedience than she feebly succumbed to apostasy in the golden calf. In shattering the tablets of the Law, Moses signified God's judgement. In granting new tablets God demonstrated His love. Despite a repetitious saga of ingratitude, murmurings and rebellion, Israel had only to ask for succour for God to provide: water, manna, quails. Hosea likened Israel to a wilful child. We may extend the simile to an Israel too immature to respond to God's bountiful grace, too wayward to listen and to trust.

Exodus shows a God who demands faith, of Moses and Israel no less than of Noah and Abraham. What else but faith could have led Moses to accept God's prodigious commission to lead Israel into the harsh desert waste? What better example of faith is there than Moses' call for calm as the avenging Egyptians pinned his terror stricken band by the sea? What better proof of the power of prayer than Israel's victory over the Amalekites?

Unapproachable and transcendent though the grandeur of the theophany at Sinai proclaims Him to be, the God of paradox also reveals Himself as a God who wants to be near His people. Despite His awesome power we see a gentle God who protects the baby Moses in a cradle and derives good from evil as He uses Pharaoh's own daughter to thwart her father's evil designs by choosing Moses' own mother as his nurse.

Moses bestrides Exodus like a giant. He saved his people time and again, from themselves no less than from their enemies. But it is God, not Moses, who is the true hero. Only His love and power, not human will or piety, could deliver Israel as Moses was well aware. Israel never forgot the Exodus. It made an indelible impression and was the foundation of her faith. It pervades the Old Testament and the prophets saw it as a golden age. They never claimed to be founding a new faith, only recalling the old Exodus faith. At 6:7 God said: 'I shall take you as my people and I shall be your God.' At Sinai God took Israel to be His people. As Exodus ends He is dwelling among them as their God.

Moses' early life (1:1 – 2:25)

Genesis ends with the deaths of Jacob and Joseph. Exodus picks up the story some four hundred years later. The memory of Joseph had faded and the Pharaoh then in power had enslaved the Israelites because they had become so powerful as to be a potential source of sedition. When their numbers continued to grow he ordered all new-born boys to be put to death. This is the setting in which Exodus introduces us to Moses, God's choice to lead Israel to freedom.

Moses was born of Levite parents and when a baby his mother hid him in a papyrus basket among the reeds beside the river bank. He was discovered by Pharaoh's daughter who, taken with pity, adopted him. When she decided to recruit a nurse to rear him the woman she selected turned out to be none other than Moses' own mother.

Grown to manhood Moses fled to Midian after his killing of an Egyptian taskmaster who was striking a fellow Hebrew came to light.[1] He chivalrously helped seven sisters tending their father's flock by a well and eventually married one of them, Zipporah.[2] Meanwhile God heard the Israelites groaning in misery and remembered His covenant with Abraham.

God commissions Moses (3:1 – 4:17)

While Moses was pasturing his sheep near Horeb Yahweh appeared to him in a burning bush. He told Moses He would rescue His people from their slavery in Egypt and guide them to a land flowing with milk and honey, 'the Promised Land'. Moses was to be their leader. To Moses' nervous, 'Who am I to go to Pharaoh', He responded with the ever reassuring, 'I shall be with you' and promised Moses that the people he would lead out of Egypt would worship Him on the very mountain, Horeb, where he now stood.[3]

God tells Moses His name is 'I am He who is, Yahweh, the God of your ancestors'.

He must tell the elders of Israel all he has learned and ask Pharaoh to allow them to go into the desert for a three day retreat.[4] In telling Moses of the wonders He will have to perform Yahweh leaves Moses in no doubt as to the magnitude of the task that lies ahead and reveals that Israel will be given jewellery and clothing when she finally leaves Egypt.
Appendix 1 refers

Yahweh assuages Moses' doubts on his credibility by granting him miraculous powers: a staff that turns into a snake; the ability to make his hand leprous or clean at will; the means to change river water into blood. To offset his lack of eloquence his brother Aaron will act as his spokesman.

Moses returns to Egypt (4:18 – 6:1)

Moses returns to Egypt. On the way God tells him of the wonders He will perform and looks ahead to the deaths of the Egyptian first-born as the final means to force Pharaoh's hand. Success will not come easily. Pharaoh will be stubborn.
Appendix 2 refers

Verses 4:24–26 are difficult. One possibility is that God was angry with Moses for not being circumcised and that Zipporah circumcised him by proxy by circumcising their son and then touching Moses' genitals (for which 'feet' is a euphemism) with the child's foreskin. Another that God's anger was directed at Moses for not having circumcised his son in which case Zipporah associated Moses with her circumcision of their son as before.

Back in Egypt Moses and Aaron approach Pharaoh. However far from sanctioning the desert retreat he burdens the Israelites even more severely, insisting that they now gather the straw for their brick-making themselves rather than having it delivered to them as before. The people blame Moses for this unfortunate turn in events. Moses, for his part, appeals to Yahweh who again refers to the mighty deeds He will perform to force Pharaoh to release Israel.

An alternative account of Moses' call (6:2 – 7:7)

A second account of Moses' call includes genealogy showing Moses' and Aaron's descent from Levi. 'Yahweh' is said to replace 'El Shaddai' as God's name.

Confrontation with Pharaoh: the plagues (7:8 – 11:10)

After Moses and Aaron fail to impress Pharaoh by turning a staff into a serpent, Yahweh subjects Egypt to a succession of nine plagues: the Nile turning to blood and the fish dying, frogs, mosquitoes, horseflies, death of the Egyptians' livestock, boils, hail and lightning, locusts, and darkness. But despite all these travails Pharaoh remains obdurate and refuses to let Israel go.

Moses then announces the final blow, the death of the Egyptian first-born, human and livestock, which Yahweh says will cause Pharaoh not simply to let Israel go but to drive her out! Everyone must ask the Egyptians for silver and jewellery as they leave.

Israel leaves Egypt: death of the first-born: the Passover (12:1 – 13:16)

This complex section has three themes. The first is a blend of the story of Israel's escape from Egypt with God's institution of the Passover as a family feast to commemorate it in perpetuity. Celebrants must be dressed as if for a journey. An animal from the flock, a sheep or a goat, must be sacrificed and its blood daubed over the lintels and door-posts of their homes. The meal must be eaten hurriedly with unleavened bread (to recall the suddenness and haste of Israel's deliverance), with bitter herbs (to call to mind the bitterness of slavery), and using an unblemished animal none of whose bones has been broken (only a perfect offering is suitable for God). The whole animal must either be eaten or burned (signifying complete dedication to God).

On the actual night of the first Passover when Yahweh went through Egypt striking down the Egyptian first-born, the Israelites were identified by the blood marking their lintels and door-posts and 'passed over', i.e. spared. Overwhelmed, Pharaoh ordered them to leave. Such was the haste there was no time to bake bread so they made-off with their dough still unleavened. So glad were the Egyptians to see them depart that they plied them with gold, silver and clothing. The Israelites had been in Egypt for four hundred and thirty years (12:1–14, 21–51).
Appendix 3 refers

The second theme is the inauguration of a further feast commemorating the Exodus, Unleavened Bread, when for seven days, as a further reminder of that great event, only unleavened bread may be eaten (12:15–20, 13:3–10). Finally we have the law on first-born. All male first-born, human and animal, are to be consecrated to God in memory of His great act involving the deaths of the Egyptian first-born that led to Israel's rescue from slavery and her adoption as His first-born son (13:1–2, 11–16).
Appendix 4 refers

The miracle of the sea (13:17 – 15:21)

The Israelites avoid the direct coastal route to the Promised Land, through what was later Philistine territory, as that would have been patrolled by the Egyptians. Instead they take a more circuitous inland routing through the desert via the Sea of Reeds. Joseph's bones accompany them. Yahweh precedes them in a pillar of cloud by day and of fire by night.

Pharaoh changes his mind about letting Israel go and sets out in pursuit. The Israelites are pinned against the sea and begin to panic but Moses is a tower of faith. Yahweh will do the fighting for them, all they have to do is just to keep calm, 14:14. And so it was that the next morning after a dark cloudy night, as Moses raised his staff and stretched his hand over the sea, a strong easterly wind parted it and created a channel through which the Israelites were able to cross dryshod. But when the Egyptians gave chase the sea returned and they were drowned to a man. The triumphant song of victory that

follows – its refrain taken up by Moses' sister Miriam – is a paean of praise to the God who had so amply fulfilled His promise of salvation.
Appendix 5 refers

Israel journeys on to Mount Sinai (15:22 – 18:27)

Despite these epic events the story quickly becomes a saga of the people's groans and grumbles at their privations, matched only by God's unfailing providence. Bitter water at Marah is made sweet. When food is scarce God provides quails and manna, one day's ration at a time with a double portion every Sabbath eve. When water is again in short supply, and the near mutinous people hark back to Egypt, God shows Moses how to obtain water by striking a rock with his staff. Finally in a battle where Joshua is mentioned for the first time as Moses' lieutenant, a band of Amalekites is defeated thanks to Moses' sustained supplication.[5]

Zipporah and her two sons come to meet Moses in the desert. They are accompanied by their father Jethro, who worships Yahweh and advises Moses to delegate lest he wear himself out.

God adopts Israel (19:1 – 20:21)

After three months Israel pitches camp facing Mount Sinai where she remains until Nb 11. At once God makes known His purpose in rescuing her. Having borne her out of Egypt 'on eagles' wings' He intends to conclude a covenant with her. If she is obedient He will make her a kingdom of priests, a holy nation, His personal possession.

This is Israel's election to her unique role in world history. She is to be God's vehicle for bringing blessings to all nations in accord with His covenant with Abraham, reflecting His character and proclaiming His glory. However unlike the covenants with Noah and Abraham this is no unilateral act on God's part but one dependant upon obedience, an obedience that time was to show was not forthcoming.

Yahweh descends on the mountain in an awesome theophany, demonstrating His majesty and glory, His might, the gulf that separates Him from man. Lightning, dense cloud, smoke, fire, and earthquakes indicate the divine presence; thunder and trumpet blasts His imperious voice. He defines the terms of the covenant in the Decalogue, the Ten Commandments that form the bedrock of the Law. The first four deal with Man's duty to God, the remainder with his responsibilities to his neighbour.[6] The people are terror-stricken and ask Moses to mediate. At this point the narrative abruptly breaks off to be resumed at 24:1.

The Book of the Covenant (20:22 – 23:19)

The Book of the Covenant may be regarded as an expansion of the Decalogue with examples drawn from daily life. It is the first of the Pentateuch's law codes that together with the Decalogue constitute the Law.[7]

God will indicate where He may be worshipped.[8] Idols are forbidden. Altars should be of earth or unhewn stone and must not be approached by steps.[9] Detailed laws for slaves include provision for Hebrew male slaves to be given their freedom after six years. But any slave wishing to remain with his master may do so.[10] Wilful murderers, abductors, and anyone striking or cursing his parents must be put to death but cities of refuge will be established where people who kill accidentally can seek sanctuary from avengers. There follow a variety of laws concerned with quarrels and brawling, including the law of exact retribution, 'eye for eye, tooth for tooth'.[11] Special prescriptions applied to pregnant women and slaves (20:22 – 21:27).

Animals harming humans are to be put to death. Their owners are also to be punished, even to the extent of death themselves if they act irresponsibly. Penalties are laid down for instances where animals are hurt through carelessness, where one animal harms another, and for animal theft. Thieves may only be killed when caught at night. Any thief who is unable to make full restitution may be sold into slavery (21:28 – 22:3).

Further laws cover disagreements over illicit grazing, starting fires, assets entrusted to another's care and disputes over ownership. Anyone violating a virgin must compensate her father. Sorcery, bestiality and worshipping other gods are condemned. There must be no oppression of widows, orphans and aliens. The rich must not take advantage of the poor by charging interest on loans. If a cloak is retained as a pledge it must not be kept overnight when the owner needs it for warmth. God must not be reviled. Proper respect must be shown to secular authority. First-fruits should be offered willingly. First-born children and animals belong to God. Only correctly slaughtered meat may be eaten (22:4–30).

Evidence at law must be true and given without fear or favour. The example of returning a straying animal is used to illustrate that help should even be accorded to one's enemies. Judges must ensure that the poor get their due rights at law. There must be no fraud, bribery, or oppression. Every seventh year will be a sabbatical year when the land will lie fallow and all produce will be left for the poor. Israel must observe the Sabbath and shun other gods. Instructions for feasts and first-fruit offerings are followed by an edict to avoid pagan rites like boiling a kid in its mother's milk (23:1–19).
Appendix 6 refers

God calls for fidelity (23:20–33)

God reveals the boundaries of the Promised Land and promises to send an angel to lead His people there provided they remain faithful. The Canaanites will be driven out little by little and exterminated. Their cultic stones must be smashed, their religion destroyed, lest it become a snare and lead Israel astray.[12]

Ratification of the covenant (24:1–18, 31:18)

This passage, of which 31:18 is logically part, follows on from 20:21 and describes the ratification of the covenant. Many scholars consider it to be an amalgam of three of the Pentateuch's four sources, J,E and P. If so it provides an excellent example of how the editor, anxious not to lose a single word of the ancient traditions, wove his material together.

Verses 1,2,9–11 are J. Moses, together with Aaron, his two sons, and seventy elders, climbed the mountain where they sealed the covenant by sharing a meal with God.

Verses 3–8, 12–15a, 18b, 31:18 are E. Once the people had pledged obedience to the covenant, Moses wrote down Yahweh's edicts and the covenant was sealed by a ceremony at the foot of the mountain using an altar composed of twelve standing-stones.[13] Sacrificial blood was sprinkled both on the altar, representing God, and on the people, to signify the bonding of God with His people. After the ceremony Moses climbed the mountain where he remained for forty days at the end of which God gave him two stone tablets on which He had inscribed the Law in His own hand.

Verses 15b–18a are P. Moses climbed the mountain on which the glory of Yahweh rested for six days.

Instructions for the priesthood and the Dwelling (25:1 – 31:17)

Yahweh calls for contributions for a Dwelling where He can reside among His people. The greater part of this long section, with the details so lovingly dwelt on, then consists of instructions for its construction.

The Dwelling was basically a tent structure with a large surrounding courtyard. It became the focal point of Israel's religious life and at its heart was the Holy of Holies, a small room containing the Ark, a gilded wooden chest on top of which was the mercy-seat. This was the site of God's very presence, the focus of Israel's worship and the place where the tablets of the Law which God gave to Moses were kept. The whole edifice was mobile, in keeping with Israel's missionary role, and so acted as a portable house of worship. As we shall see later it was the Dwelling that led Israel throughout her desert wanderings.[14]
Appendix 7 refers

Instructions are also given for: providing oil for the lamps, 27:20–21; the priestly vestments, 28:1–43; the consecration of Aaron and his sons into the priesthood which Israel's relationship with Yahweh now demanded, 29:1–37; two daily burnt offerings, 29:38–42; a poll tax for the upkeep of the Dwelling, 30:11–16; the production of anointing oil and incense, 30:22–37; appointing craftsmen, 31:1–11; and the keeping of the Sabbath, 31:12–17.

Apostasy and renewal (32:1 – 34:35)

No sooner was the covenant sealed than, with Moses away on the mountain meeting God, the people persuaded Aaron to forge a golden calf, a pagan symbol of divinity, which they then proceeded to worship. God was minded to destroy them and only relented when Moses interceded (32:1–14). When he descended the mountain and saw the scene for himself Moses angrily shattered the tablets bearing the Law, destroyed the calf, and called on the Levites to slaughter the dissidents while Aaron feebly sought to excuse his complicity by talking as if the calf had somehow made itself[15] (32:15–29).

When Moses offered himself in expiation of Israel's sin God would not hear of it. Punishment would be borne by those who had sinned and an angel, not God Himself, would now lead them to the Promised Land. However after the people discarded their ornaments and repented, and Moses had again interceded, Yahweh relented and promised to lead them in person as before (32:30 – 33:6,12–17). An isolated passage introduces the Tent of Meeting where Moses used to speak with Yahweh face to face[16] (33:7–11).

When Moses asks God to show him His glory God replies that no one may see His face and live and reveals the gratuitous nature of His favours. Nevertheless He promises Moses a partial revelation (His 'back'). So Moses climbs the mountain again for God to pass before him (33:18 – 34:9). God renews the covenant and promises awesome wonders. He will drive the Canaanites out of the Promised Land. In return there must be no pact or fraternisation. Their religion – altars, cultic stones, sacred poles – must be utterly destroyed lest it lead them astray. The ensuing commands are a small selection of those pronounced earlier but convey the same ideal of total devotion to Yahweh.

Moses remained on the mountain with Yahweh for forty days and wrote the words of the covenant on new tablets. After he came down from the mountain his face shone with such radiance that he was compelled to wear a veil. It was the same whenever he returned from Yahweh's presence[17] (34:10–35).

The Dwelling is built (35:1 – 40:38)

These chapters tell, often word for word, and with only minor variations, how the instructions for the Dwelling were carried out and Yahweh took possession.[18] In addition we learn that the people responded to Yahweh's invitation for contributions so generously that Moses had to call a halt. A cloud, ablaze with fire at night, always covered the Dwelling and Israel marched only when it rose.

Leviticus

Exodus closed with the glory of God filling the Dwelling as He came to live among His people. He had rescued them from captivity in Egypt and given them the Decalogue and the Book of the Covenant, laws to help mould them in holiness in preparation for their mission to enlighten the world. Leviticus follows these germinal events with further legislation in the Laws of Purity and Holiness. Law is thus one of Leviticus' twin pillars. The other is sacrifice. Errant man needed to be shown how he could be forgiven and restored to fellowship with God once he lapsed into sin. God's answer, a temporary answer, lay in sacrifice for which Leviticus provides both a general manual and prescriptions for an annual Day of Atonement. The book is in seven parts:

- The ritual of sacrifice (1:1 – 7:38)
- Aaron's consecration into the priesthood (8:1 – 10:20)
- The Law of Purity (11:1 – 15:33)
- The Day of Atonement (16:1–34)
- The Law of Holiness (17:1–25:55)
- Blessings and curses (26:1–46)
- An appendix on vows and tithes (27:1–34)

The practice of sacrifice whereby man makes offerings, often slain animals, to the deity is a worldwide phenomenon central to many religions and going back to the most ancient times. What is common is a consciousness of guilt, man feeling at odds with God, and a desire to make amends by an offering that recognises God's sovereignty and seeks His mercy.

Israel was no exception. Sacrifice had been offered from the days of Cain and Noah. In Leviticus God formally appropriates it. Firstly as a means to thank Him and acknowledge His Lordship. Secondly as the way for men alienated from Him by sins to be forgiven. It is with good reason that Leviticus has been called a gospel for sinners enshrined in sacrifice and that the sacrificial rites in Leviticus follow the disclosure of Law in Exodus.

Leviticus makes it clear that the efficacy of sacrifice stems from God. Man cannot atone for sin by himself but only through God's grace expressed in His accepting the sacrifice of an unblemished victim in place of the sinner's own life which would otherwise be forfeit. Only a life can bridge the gap that separates God's ineffable holiness from man's delinquent waywardness.

However in revealing that He would accept a sacrifice of doves or pigeons, or even

0a bloodless portion of cereal, as a sin offering where an individual supplicant could not afford the prescribed bull, goat or ram, God indicated that in the last resort the efficacy of sacrifice depended not on the value of the victim, nor even on his offering a substitute life at all, but on his inner disposition for forgiveness.

We now know that there was nothing truly efficacious in animal sacrifice. It worked simply because God chose to regard it as effective for the time being. It was not His final answer and must be seen in its proper perspective as God taking over an existing human institution to provide a temporary solution, something that Israel at an early stage in her religious education could understand and which can be seen as a pointer to the future, the perfect sacrifice of God's Son which really does enable sins to be forgiven.

The sacrificial system was a constant reminder of the need for obedience. It drove home as nothing else could God's detestation of sin and its dreadful consequences: banishment from His presence and death, a theme that reached its apogee in the solemn, presentient Day of Atonement, a landmark on the long road to redemption that led to Calvary.

Despite its heavy emphasis on Law, sacrifice and sin, Leviticus ends with a message of hope. Despite His strident curses on the unfaithful, God promises that His punishment is remedial not vindictive, medicinal not terminal. He will remember His promises of old. Mercy and promise will have the last word. In calling for love of neighbour the Law of Holiness foreshadows the Gospel of Christ and amply refutes any suggestion that Leviticus is overly concerned with externals.

The prevailing motif in Leviticus is God's moral perfection, His abhorrence of sin and the demand that His people be like Him.

> Be holy, for I, Yahweh your God, am holy, 19:2

This, and the cry for Israel to be a race apart, a kingdom of priests,

> Be consecrated to me, for I, Yahweh, am holy, and I shall set you apart from all these peoples, for you to be mine, 20:26

reverberate as a heartbeat from every page.

THE RITUAL OF SACRIFICE (1:1 – 7:38)

Prescriptions are laid down for five types of sacrifice. These are detailed and repetitious and the text is not without its obscurities. To make matters worse the rituals are split between a main section in chapters 1–5 and a supplement in chapters 6–7. To highlight the main points without getting immersed in myriad detail we therefore restrict our synopsis to identifying the different types of sacrifice and giving an outline of the animal sacrifice for sin as a typical example.[1]
Appendix 1 refers

The burnt offering (1:1–17; 6:1–6)

Sometimes known as the holocaust this was used to give thanks to God and to express commitment and devotion, Gn 8:20; 22:2; Ex 18:12; 24:1–8; 1S 6:14, although on occasion it was also invoked when seeking God's help, 1S 7:9. Lv 1:4 indicates that it was also available to atone for sins. As the examples show it dates back to the earliest times. By consuming the whole animal on the altar fire the supplicant showed that he consecrated his whole being to God.[2] In cases of poverty a turtledove or pigeon could substitute for the more usual bull, lamb or goat.

The cereal offering (2:1–16; 6:7–16)

The cereal offering seems to have been used as a bloodless act of worship and to give thanks. It often accompanied a burnt offering or communion sacrifice, Ex 29:38–42; Nb 15:1–12. Only a token portion was burned as an offering to God, the remainder reverting to the priests.[3] It is suggested by 2:12–16 that this was the rite used when first-fruits were offered to God.[4]

The communion sacrifice (3:1–17; 7:11–38)

This was offered in praise, in fulfilment of a vow, to accompany a voluntary sacrifice or to express fellowship with God, Ex 24:1–8; Jos 8:30; 2S 6:17; 1K 8:63. Part of the victim was offered to God, the rest being shared between priest and supplicant, possibly including his family and friends. The partaking in a meal indicated renewed harmony with God just as sharing a meal is still regarded as a sign of friendship today. Of all the Old Testament forms of sacrifice this is the one closest to the Eucharist. The rules in 7:11–34 distinguish different types of communion offering, prescribe that participants must be ceremonially clean, forbid the eating of the victim's blood and fat, and stipulate how long the sacrificial meat may be kept before it is eaten.[5]

The sin offering (4:1–5:13; 6:17–22)

The sin offering was for the forgiveness of inadvertent sin, examples of which are given at 5:1–6, where the need for confession is also stressed.[6] There were separate rites for the high priest, the whole community, secular leaders, and private individuals. If an individual supplicant could not afford the prescribed lamb or goat, he could offer doves or pigeons or even a portion of cereal instead.

The reparation sacrifice (5:14–26; 7:1–10)

This was also offered for inadvertent sin and it is unclear how it differed from the sin sacrifice. Its main application seems to have been in cases where a person unlawfully withheld something that was due to God, such as first-fruits or tithes, or to another person in which case the guilty party was required to make good the shortfall together with a surcharge of one fifth. The ritual was similar to a sin sacrifice for a private individual.[7]

AARON'S CONSECRATION INTO THE PRIESTHOOD (8:1 – 10:20)

The ceremony for consecrating Aaron and his sons into the priesthood was given at Ex 29, embedded in the directions for constructing the Dwelling. We might therefore have expected to find the ceremony of investiture included in Ex 35–40 which records the building of the Dwelling and its acceptance by God. However its positioning here, after the manual of sacrifice, is eminently logical. Sacrificial rites were not only among the chief duties of the priests but also played a major role in their inauguration.

The ceremony culminates with a flame leaping from the Dwelling to indicate Yahweh's acceptance of Aaron and his sons into the priesthood. Then tragedy strikes as two of Aaron's sons are consumed by fire for some unspecified irreverence related to the altar fire. Aaron and his surviving sons are forbidden to exhibit any sign of mourning such as disordering their hair or tearing their clothes. There follows an injunction that priests must refrain from wine prior to undertaking their sacred duties. Finally Moses reprimands Aaron's surviving sons over their treatment of some of the meat from the recent sacrifices.

THE LAW OF PURITY (11:1 – 15:33)

These laws introduce the concept of (ritual) cleanliness; how a state of uncleanliness could arise; how long it lasted (sometimes only until the same evening); and the rites needed to regain cleanliness (sometimes quite elaborate, at other times no more than washing). The concern was not with physical cleanliness but with a state in which a person could be 'unclean' in the sense of being unable to approach God, join in worship, or mix with his fellows. Uncleanliness did not necessarily involve moral stigma. Childbirth incurred a state of uncleanliness for instance.

The origins of these laws are lost in antiquity. Some acts that other nations regarded as sacred may have been pronounced unclean as a way of setting Israel apart. Other things may have been ruled unclean because they were based on superstition, transgressed feelings of decency or aroused natural aversion. Many of the prohibitions are soundly rooted in hygiene.

Clean and unclean animals (11:1–47)

The purity laws start by distinguishing clean animals that could be eaten from the unclean that could not. Uncleanliness could be incurred by touching the carcase of an unclean animal or the body of a clean animal that had died a natural death.

Childbirth (12:1–8)

Childbirth incurred uncleanliness and two offerings were prescribed for subsequent purification: a burnt offering to thank God for the new life and a sin offering to restore cleanliness.[8] Offerings of turtledoves or pigeons were permitted in cases of poverty.[9]

Skin diseases (13:1 – 14:57)

Uncleanliness could also arise as a result of certain skin diseases and the purification rites incorporate what were essentially an early set of quarantine regulations. They also cover problems with clothing and buildings that were afflicted with mildew, fungi or dry rot. It was probably the association with decay that linked all these phenomena with uncleanliness.

Sexual impurities (15:1–33)

The purity laws end with a long list of sexual impurities.

THE DAY OF ATONEMENT (16:1–34)

Leviticus now returns to sacrifice. Earlier rites have addressed inadvertent sin. The annual Day of Atonement goes further and is for the expiation of all sin: wilful sin, 'sins committed with a high hand', acts of rebellion. It was a day of fasting and rest, the apogee of the sacrificial system. Enacted once a year it was an occasion of special solemnity when the high priest performed a ceremony to reconcile the entire nation with God.[10]

The rite began with a sin offering for the priest and his family. Lots were then drawn over two goats provided by the people, one to be their sin offering, the other reserved for Azazel, a mythological demon who dwelt in the wild remote from God. The priest, and he alone, then entered the Holy of Holies, burning incense as he did so to conceal the Mercy Seat, and thus the majesty of God, from his sight. The priest then sprinkled some of the blood of the bull of his own sin offering followed by some of the blood from the people's sacrificial goat, firstly in the Holy of Holies around the Mercy Seat, and then on the altar of burnt offering, thereby cleansing the Dwelling from the defilement it received from human sin.

The climax came as the priest confessed the nation's sins while laying his hands on the head of the remaining goat, thereby transferring the sins to the goat. The goat was then driven into the desert, bearing away 'all the guilt of the Israelites, all their acts of rebellion and all their sins' to Azazel's far away desolate haunts in the desert where they would no longer stand between the people and God.

Finally, having bathed and changed his vestments (infected by contact with the goat) the priest offered a ram as a burnt offering both on his own account and for the people while the bull and goat offered in the sin sacrifices were burned outside the camp.

Permeating this ritual was the realisation that wilful sin has a collective dimension and demands a communal cleansing. Everyone is contaminated by his neighbour's sin.

THE LAW OF HOLINESS (17:1 – 25:55)

On slaughter and the sacredness of blood (17:1–16)

Anyone slaughtering a bull, lamb, or goat (i.e. any animal acceptable for sacrifice to God) must do so at the Dwelling and then offer the animal as a communion sacrifice.

Slaughter must not be performed in the open countryside. No one must consume blood because 'blood is what expiates for a life'. Even the blood of animals that are not acceptable for sacrifice but which are lawful to eat, such as game, must be treated reverently by being covered with earth.[11]
Appendix 2 refers

Sexual prohibitions (18:1–30)

A list of sexual prohibitions, and an injunction against sacrificing children to Molech, is prefixed and suffixed by stern warnings that Israel must not follow the customs of Egypt and Canaan lest she too is punished like them.[12] Whoever obeys God will find life.

Miscellaneous laws (19:1–37)

This medley of laws begins with calls to respect parents, to observe the Sabbath, and to shun idols. A repetition of some of the rules for the communion sacrifice is followed by a plea for charity by leaving the gleanings of the harvest for the poor. Then come injunctions to refrain from stealing, deceit and fraud; against profaning the divine name by perjury; not to exploit one's fellow men – e.g. by being slow to pay wages; not to take advantage of the handicapped; to administer justice fairly, irrespective of status; to avoid slander and false witness; not to harbour hatred; to help others by correcting them; to eschew vengeance and grudges; in short to love one's neighbour as oneself (19:1–18).

Commands against mating different breeds of cattle, sowing two kinds of seed in a field and making garments from two fabrics probably had their origins either in a reaction against superstition or in an attempt to maintain Israel's distinctiveness by avoiding pagan customs. A detailed ruling on sexual relations with concubine slaves is followed by an edict that the fruit from a tree is not mature enough for offering to God before its fourth season. Further admonitions forbid eating blood, divination and magic, trimming one's beard at the edges, self mutilation in grief and tattooing[13] (19:19–28).

The next verses outlaw prostitution, call for respect for the Sabbath and the Dwelling, and forbid contact with dead spirits and magicians.[14] The chapter ends with calls to honour age, to fear God, to treat resident aliens as if they were native-born, and to desist from sharp commercial practice[15] (19:29–37).

Nowhere is God's concern for every aspect of human life more fully revealed than in the wide-ranging ambit of this remarkable chapter. No aspect of life, from secret sins of the heart to public action, is outside God's concern.

Penalties (20:1–27)

A penal code, closely related to the laws of chapter 18, includes both human impositions (the death penalty) and divine sanctions (dying childless). Israel must keep Yahweh's laws so that she may be a race apart and not 'vomited' out of the Promised Land as the present incumbents are about to be.

Regulations concerning priests and sacred food (21:1 – 22:33)

Regulations for priests and high priests, the latter being stricter, legislate on contact with corpses, marriage partners and mourning.[16] The function of priests is to offer sacrifice. They are consecrated to God and must not profane His name. They must be holy and be treated as such. Various physical infirmities are described which disbar from the priesthood but not from eating sacred food. Priests must not approach sacred objects nor eat sacred food while they are unclean. Only certain members of a priest's household may eat sacred food. Sacrificial animals must be unblemished, at least eight days old and never slaughtered on the same day as their young.[17]

A festal calendar (23:1–44)

We are now given a catalogue of Israel's feast days.[18]

Miscellaneous prescriptions (24:1–23)

The chapter opens with ordinances that logically form part of Exodus' excursus on the Dwelling. The golden lampstand must be replenished with oil so that it never stops burning. The loaves of permanent offering must be replenished each Sabbath, the stale bread being eaten by the priests. Then comes a case history illustrating the death penalty for blasphemy followed by laws governing murder, restitution for killing an animal, and assault.

Sabbatical and Jubilee years (25:1–55)

Every seventh year will be a sabbatical year of rest when the land must lie fallow. Spontaneous growth must not be stored but left to be gathered as food by anyone in need, landowner or servant, visitor or cattle. In addition every fiftieth year is to be a jubilee year when the same prohibitions (plus others) will apply. Yahweh promises sufficiency of food from earlier harvests during the fallow sabbatical and jubilee years. Anyone selling land has a right of redemption but in a jubilee year land reverts to its original owner automatically. Special rules for repossession apply to the Levites and to dwelling houses in walled towns.

A fellow Israelite may not be charged interest and if he falls upon hard times he must be given help. If he sells himself into service to redeem debts he must be treated as an employee, not as a slave, and freed in the jubilee year.[19] Foreigners may be engaged as permanent slaves however. If an Israelite is slave to a foreigner he must be freed in the jubilee year but may be redeemed earlier.

BLESSINGS AND CURSES (26:1–46)

Israel must eschew idols, keep the Sabbath and revere the Dwelling. Fidelity to God's commandments will bring peace, prosperity and plenty. God will live among His people and never reject them. Apostasy on the other hand will incur warfare, terror, penury, pestilence, famine, oppression, calamities without measure. Israel will be destroyed, scattered among the nations, there to pine away her guilt.

Yet mercy is not far away. There will be survivors and they will humbly admit their guilt and accept God's punishment. God will not reject Israel completely. He will remember His covenant.

VOWS AND TITHES (27:1–34)

An appendix introduces tithing and specifies the regulations and valuations to be used when anyone who had consecrated a person, animal, house or field to Yahweh, or who had an unclean first-born animal, sought to redeem it with a payment. Animals offered to God in sacrifice and to mark unconditional vows may not, however, be redeemed.[20]

Appendix 3 refers

Numbers

Numbers blends legislation with an outline of Israel's wilderness pilgrimage from Sinai, where Exodus left us, to the threshold of the Promised Land where Deuteronomy picks up the story with Israel encamped across the Jordan from Jericho. It is a litany of faithlessness, ingratitude and rebellion during which God's constancy and care never wavers: witness the unfailing manna, the miracles that produced quails and water, protection from the wiles of Balaam and victories over her many foes. Time and again God answered Moses' prayer: commissioning elders to help him, curing Miriam's leprosy, healing with the bronzed serpent, reprieving Israel when He was minded to destroy her after her early refusal to enter the Promised Land.

It was then that God swore that of all those who left Egypt only Joshua and Caleb who never lost faith would cross the Jordan. Otherwise it would be the children, Israel reborn, who would inherit. But even then only after forty years of trial and tribulation as desert nomads, receiving the chastisement of a loving parent seeking to open his children's eyes. Those who turned their backs on God also got their wish, ending their days in the desert.

Numbers highlights the immense gulf between God and man, His inapproachability and holiness. Ordinary people were barred from His presence on pain of death. Reverence was paramount. Yet at the same time God was near His people, His Dwelling in the centre of the camp making Him the centre of the nation's life.

Census and preparations for the journey (1:1 – 4:49)

Yahweh decrees a census of males aged twenty and over fit for military service and gives the order of march. The Levites are to be covered in a separate census because they are to be consecrated to Yahweh's service in place of human first-born. They are to assist Aaron and his sons, Eleazar and Ithamar, in their priestly duties and to help with the Dwelling: dismantling and carrying it when on the march and erecting it and pitching their tents around it as an inner ring when encamped (the secular tribes forming an outer ring). They are to act as a shield since no unauthorised person may approach the Dwelling on pain of death. The progeny of Joseph's sons, Ephraim and Manasseh, are recognised as tribes in their own right (instead of a Joseph tribe) thereby maintaining the number of secular tribes at twelve.

Appendices 1, 2 refer

Law (5:1 – 6:27)

Anyone unclean from a contagious skin disease, a discharge, or from touching a corpse must be expelled from the camp. Certain sins where restitution is possible must be confessed and the damage made good with a surcharge of one fifth. A ritual is given for testing a wife's fidelity (5:1–31).

The Nazirite vow which follows was for anyone, man or woman, who wished to be consecrated to God's service, either for a limited period or for life. It involved abstention from wine and strong drink, leaving the hair uncut and avoiding contact with the dead.[1] The passage ends with Yahweh's words of blessing for Israel: 'May Yahweh bless you and keep you . . .' (6:1–27).

Preparations for moving the Dwelling (7:1–89)

The tribal leaders donate wagons and oxen for transporting the Dwelling. We learn that when Yahweh spoke to Moses in the Dwelling it was from between the two cherubim above the Mercy Seat.[2]

Law (8:1 – 9:14)

Instructions are given for the purification of the Levites prior to their embarking upon their sacred duties in substitution for human first-born.

Anyone genuinely prevented from keeping the Passover at the appointed time due to uncleanliness from touching a corpse or from having been on a long journey may celebrate it one month later. This would allow time for purification.[3]

Departure from Sinai (9:15 – 10:36)

We are reminded that the Israelites broke camp when and only when the cloud (fiery red at night) marking God's presence rose from the Dwelling. Instructions are given for forging two silver trumpets for use when summoning the community, in battle, when breaking camp or at religious festivals.

At last, just over ten months after arriving at Sinai, the cloud lifts and the Israelites break camp. They march for three days led by the Ark.[4] Moses unsuccessfully tries to persuade Hobab, his father-in-law, to join them as he was familiar with the local terrain.

Troubles along the way (11:1 – 14:45)

Murmurings at Taberah are only quelled when fire destroys part of the camp. At Kibroth-ha-Taavah, bored with the manna, the people start complaining again. Yahweh is angry at their ingratitude and promises such a glut of meat they will become sick of it. When the meat duly arrives in the form of quails the people devour it greedily before a plague breaks out and many die.

When an overwrought Moses pleads for his burden to be eased, Yahweh endows seventy elders with some of his spirit so that they may help him. However when the spirit also comes down on two men who did not receive the spirit in the appointed manner Joshua becomes alarmed, probably thinking that Moses' authority might be jeopardized. But Moses is only thankful that an additional two men are fired up with Yahweh's spirit (11:1–35).

When Miriam and Aaron criticise Moses, ostensibly for his marriage to a foreigner but more likely, as Yahweh's response suggests, because they were jealous of his privileged role, Yahweh replies that Moses, 'the humblest man on earth', is no ordinary prophet as evidenced by the way He speaks to him face to face rather than through visions and dreams. Miriam is punished with a form of leprosy but is cured when Moses intercedes. Israel moves on to the desert of Paran (12:1–16).

Yahweh commands Moses to despatch a reconnaissance party to the Promised Land. It returns bearing fruit as evidence of a land 'flowing with milk and honey'. However only two of the party, Joshua and Caleb, favour occupying it at once. The rest counsel caution because the towns are heavily fortified and their inhabitants strong and powerful. The prospect of languishing in the desert any longer incites the people to talk of stoning Moses and appointing a new leader to take them back to Egypt.

Yahweh is angry at Israel's faithlessness and is minded to destroy her, only relenting when Moses intercedes. Even so, of those aged twenty and over who were counted in the census, only Joshua and Caleb will enter the Promised Land. Otherwise it will be their children, and even then only after they have spent forty years as desert nomads. Their forebears will die in the wilderness as punishment for their lack of trust.

So Israel is ordered back into the desert while all the members of the reconnaissance party except Joshua and Caleb are struck down. When they hear of Yahweh's anger the people set out to occupy Canaan. But it is too late. Neither Yahweh nor Moses is with them and they are heavily defeated[5] (13:1 – 14:45).

Law (15:1–41)

Every sacrifice must be accompanied by a cereal and wine offering. A first-fruits offering of bread must be set aside for Yahweh. Two rites for expiating inadvertent sin are followed by an edict that deliberate sinners must be outlawed.[6] After a story of a man stoned to death for gathering wood on the Sabbath, the Israelites are ordered to sew tassels on the hems of their clothes to remind them to obey God.

Rebellion (16:1 – 18:7)

We now have, interwoven, the stories of what were probably two separate rebellions. One under Korah, a Levite, is described in verses 1a, 2b–11, 16–24, 35; the other led by laymen Dathan and Abiram in 1b–2a, 12–15, 25–34. The references to Korah in verses 27, 32 were possibly attempts to fuse the two together.

The Korah party questions Moses' authority on the ostensible grounds that all the people are consecrated to Yahweh. However verses 8–11 suggest that the real reason for their ire was that as Levites they were not content merely assisting in the

Dwelling but had designs on the priesthood itself. The Dathan incident was sparked by disenchantment with Moses' leadership: where was the Promised Land of milk and honey they had heard so much about? Korah and his followers are consumed by fire from their censers while the families of Dathan and Abiram are taken down to Sheol in an earthquake (16:1–35).

Appendix 3 refers

To protect the censers from profanity (use by Yahweh had made them holy) they are hammered into sheets to cover the altar and serve as an object-lesson. Next day the people blame Moses for the rebels' deaths and the plague with which Yahweh then punishes them is only abated when Aaron performs the rite of expiation (17:1–15). To prevent any further aspirations to the priesthood gaining ground the authority of Aaron, and under him the Levites, is confirmed with the miracle of Aaron's branch (17:16–26).

Terrified by these events the people bewail their fate: how can they survive the Divine Presence in their midst? Yahweh replies that it is only the priests who are at risk. The Levites are in no danger provided they do not approach the sacred vessels or the altar while lay people are shielded by the priests and Levites (17:27 – 18:7).

Law (18:8 – 19:22)

Priests and Levites will not be assigned any land when Canaan is occupied. Instead priests will be entitled to the sacrificial offerings and to everything Yahweh receives as first-fruit and first-born offerings and from the curse of destruction for their support. The Levites will live off the people's tithes. However the Levites, for their part, must set aside a 'tithe of their tithes' for the priests[7] (18:8–32).

A ritual involving a red heifer is prescribed for purifying anyone rendered unclean by contact with the dead (19:1–22).

On to Transjordan (20:1 – 22:1)

The Israelites arrive at Kadesh where Miriam dies and the people become rebellious at their meagre diet and lack of water. The tension is relieved when Yahweh indicates a rock and tells Moses that he has only to order it to yield water for it to do so. However no sooner has Moses struck the rock than Yahweh decrees that neither he nor Aaron will enter the Promised Land.[8] Shortly after leaving Kadesh Aaron dies on Mt Hor. His son Eleazar succeeds him as priest (20:1–29).

Despite victory over the Canaanites at Hormah as they bypass Edom, the people yet again complain at lack of food and water. Yahweh punishes them with a plague of venomous serpents whose bite meant death. Interceding, Moses is told to make a bronze replica of a serpent and to raise it up like a standard. Anyone who was bitten had only to look at it to survive.[9] Victories over Sihon, king of the Amorites, and Og, king of Bashan bring Israel to the plains of Moab opposite Jericho where she encamps (21:1 – 22:1).

Balaam and Balak (22:2 – 24:25)

Balak, king of Moab, afraid of being overrun, recruits Balaam, a soothsayer, to curse Israel. Balaam initially declined Balak's entreaties in obedience to Yahweh, but after a second delegation arrived with offers of inducements, Yahweh instructed him to go to Balak but only to do as he was told. However Yahweh was angry with Balaam. We are not told why. Possibly Balaam was secretly hoping to be told to go so that he could claim Balak's proffered reward. What we do know from the sequel is that while disapproving of Balaam Yahweh decided to use him to derive good from evil (22:2–22).

On his journey to Balak, Balaam's way is three times barred by an angel. Balaam does not see the angel but his donkey does and he strikes the beast as it turns aside to protect him from the angel's drawn sword. The donkey responds in speech and Balaam's eyes are opened.[10] He recognises the angel who says he would have killed him but for his donkey. Acknowledging his sin Balaam offers to return home but the angel orders him to go on but to speak only as directed (22:23–35).

Three times Balaam rejects Balak's call to curse Israel, pronouncing blessings instead. In a final poem he foretells of a great king and the future overthrow of Israel's enemies[11] (22:36 – 24:25).

Apostasy at Peor (25:1–18)

Encamped at Shittim the Israelites sleep with Moabite women and worship the Baal of Peor.[12] Those involved are publicly put to death. An Israelite who is found brazenly consorting with a Midianite woman is slain by Phinehas, son of the high priest Eleazar. As a result of his zeal a plague that had been ravaging Israel on account of her apostasy is arrested and Phinehas and his descendants are promised the priesthood in perpetuity. Yahweh orders Moses to punish the Midianites for leading Israel astray.[13]

Preparations to share out the land (26:1–65)

A new census is taken as a prelude to sharing out the land the tribes will shortly possess. The siting of each tribe's allocation will be determined by lot while the area will be proportionate to its headcount. The Levites are enumerated separately as they will not be assigned any land. As Yahweh had warned, of those counted in the earlier census at Sinai, only Joshua and Caleb now remain.

Law (27:1–11)

Daughters can in future inherit property where a father dies without male issue.

Joshua appointed (27:12–23)

Yahweh invites Moses to view the Promised Land from a mountain top before he dies. Joshua is appointed as his successor although in future it would be the priests who would consult Yahweh through the urim.[14]

Law (28:1 – 30:17)

Liturgical prescriptions for the daily burnt offerings, the Sabbath, the Day of Atonement, and the various feast days are followed by a decree that a man's word under oath is his bond and by rules governing vows made by women.

War on Midian (31:1–54)

Israel puts Midian to the sword. However when he hears that the women have been spared Moses is enraged and orders all the male children and all except the virgins among the women to be put to death. It was the women who led Israel astray in the first place.[15]

The soldiers divide the booty between those who went to war and those who stayed at home. Portions are also set aside for Yahweh and the Levites, Yahweh's share being passed on to Eleazar for the priests. The army chiefs consecrate their spoils to Yahweh in thanksgiving that not one of their men had been killed.

Settlement east of the Jordan (32:1–42)

The tribes of Gad and Reuben ask to be given the territory east of the Jordan which Israel already occupies as their inheritance. Moses opposes this at first seeing it as a threat to unity and as discouraging the other tribes from continuing with the conquest of the rest of the Promised Land west of the Jordan. However when they reassure Moses that they will join in the rest of the campaign, provided they can first built sheepfolds and towns to protect their flocks and families while they are away, he agrees. Meanwhile the Manassehites conquer Gilead, also east of the Jordan, and settle there.[16]

The Canaanites to be driven out (33:1 – 34:29)

After a summary of the trek from Egypt to Moab Yahweh orders Israel to drive out the Canaanites and destroy their religious emblems in their entirety.[17] Any Canaanites who remained would be 'thorns in their eyes and thistles in their sides'. The boundaries of Canaan are defined and nominees from each tribe set to work with Eleazar and Joshua to share out the land.

Law (35:1 – 36:13)

Since the Levites will not be given a tribal homeland of their own, the other tribes are told to cede forty-eight towns for them to live in, each surrounded by pasture for their animals.[18] Six of these towns, three on either side of the Jordan, are also to be cities of refuge where anyone who has killed can take refuge from avengers while awaiting trial. Wilful killers must be put to death while an accidental killer is to be detained until the death of the high priest when he would be free to return home. An accidental killer may be killed by an avenger if he strays outside his city of refuge during his period of confinement.

A single witness is not enough to sustain a capital charge. The payment of a ransom to redeem a wilful murderer or to obtain early release for an accidental killer is forbidden (35:1–34). Women who own property must marry into their own tribe to avoid land transferring from one tribe to another (36:1–13).

Deuteronomy

Deuteronomy records a trio of speeches delivered by Moses as Israel was encamped by the Jordan ready to enter the Promised Land. Their aim was to prepare her for the temptations that lay in wait once she exchanged the harsh nomadic desert lifestyle to which she had become accustomed, and where her dependence on God had been total, for the more affluent urban conditions of the 'land flowing with milk and honey' where she would be subject to the malign influence of Canaanite religion. Deuteronomy is addressed to the people just as surely as Leviticus was written for the priestly caste.

Obedience will bring blessings, Moses proclaims. But it must be total, as disobedience will spell disaster. The Law must not be tampered with in any way and must be taught ceaselessly until it becomes embedded in life itself. The obedience God wants is more than mere external observance. It amounts to a 'circumcision of the heart', an inward spirituality that He Himself will engender. Loyalty is paramount. There must be no dallying with other gods.

What other nation has known such marvels, Moses continues, why is Israel so richly blessed? It is because God loves her and is faithful to the covenant He swore with her ancestors. All she has she owes to Him. Despite this a time will come when her infidelities will lead to exile. But even then, if she repents, God will remember His promises of old and restore her. And one day, Moses affirms, God will send another prophet like himself.

Embedded in the second discourse is a caucus of law, the Deuteronomic Code. To a degree this is an adaptation of Exodus's Book of the Covenant to meet changing social conditions. But there are pronounced differences. It has a more humane tone with particular concern for the weak and lowly and, to protect the purity of Israel's faith, legislates that worship must in future be confined to just one sanctuary.

Deuteronomy ends with Moses calling on Israel to reaffirm her commitment to the Sinai covenant. Then, shortly before his death, and having commissioned Joshua to lead her across the Jordan, he climbs Mount Nebo to view the Promised Land he himself may not enter.

MOSES FIRST DISCOURSE (1:1 – 4:43)

Historical review (1:1 – 3:29)

After recalling his appointment of leaders and judges Moses reviews some of the landmarks of the long trek from Sinai. He recalls the faint-heartedness of the people in refusing to put their trust in Yahweh and occupy Canaan after a reconnaissance party had reported the strength of the existing inhabitants. As a result Yahweh swore that only Caleb, Joshua and the children would enter Canaan and ordered Israel back into the desert. A subsequent foray, unsanctioned by Yahweh, ended in defeat (1:1–46).

He next reviews how Israel peacefully transited Edom, Moab, and Ammon by which time an entire generation had passed away just as Yahweh had said it would.[1] Yet all the time Yahweh had ceaselessly watched over His people. They were never in want. The kingdoms of Sihon and Og were conquered and their land partitioned out on the understanding that the recipients helped conquer the rest of the land west of the Jordan.

Moses records how even he was not to be allowed to enter the Promised Land. It would be his lieutenant Joshua who would lead Israel across the Jordan (2:1 – 3:29).

Obedience (4:1–43)

Moses reminds the people that Yahweh's laws must be kept in their entirety, nothing added, nothing taken away. All those who worshipped the Baal at Peor had perished whereas those who had kept faith were still alive. What other nation was as close to its gods as Israel to Yahweh or had such just laws and customs? So take the Law to heart, Moses goes on, and teach it to your children. Always remember that Yahweh revealed Himself at Horeb only as a voice, not as a shape. So make no images and shun false gods.

Moses predicts that the day will come when Israel will anger Yahweh and she will be banished from the Promised Land. She will be destroyed and only a remnant will remain, scattered among the nations. However in the final days she will repent and be reconciled for Yahweh is merciful and will not forget the covenant He made with her ancestors.

Moses then extols the glory of having been chosen by Yahweh, the God who created the human race. Has ever a people heard the voice of the living God speaking from the heart of the fire as they had? Has any god ever enacted a rescue to compare with theirs from Egypt? No. Yahweh is the true God, in heaven as on earth, He and no other. So keep His laws, Moses concludes, so that you may prosper and have long life in the country He is giving you for ever.

Moses nominates three cities of refuge in the newly conquered territory east of the Jordan.

MOSES SECOND DISCOURSE (4:44 – 11:32)

The Decalogue (4:44 – 5:33)

Moses restates the Ten Commandments and tells the people that although the covenant at Horeb was made with their ancestors it applies equally to them today.[2]

The great commandment and God's grace (6:1–25)

If you fear Yahweh, Moses continues, and keep His commandments you will enjoy long life and prosperity. Yahweh is the only God. You must love Him with all your heart, soul and strength and impress His laws on your children day and night, 'fastening them on your hand as a sign and on your forehead as a headband'. Recognising the danger of Israel turning to false gods once she was in the Promised Land, Moses reminds her that all her blessings – blessings she has done nothing to deserve – stem from Yahweh. So they must have no truck with Canaanite gods. Yahweh is a jealous God.

Israel: a race apart (7:1–26)

The Canaanites must be put under the curse of destruction, their religion wiped out.[3] There must be no treaty, no fraternising lest Israel be seduced by their gods. Israel is a race apart, chosen by God as His own. He will be with her as she conquers the Promised Land so success is assured, not all at once but little by little. He chose her because He loves her and is faithful to His promises. He confers blessings without measure on those who love and obey Him but punishes those who hate Him.

Training and temptation (8:1–20)

Israel's wilderness years were a probation. God was training her as a man trains his child, humbling and sustaining her to show that men live not on bread alone but need God as well. Now that He is leading her to a fine land where she will want nothing, Moses goes on, she must never become proud and forget that her blessings are all due to Yahweh and not on her own account. If she ever forgets that and serves other gods she will perish.

Yahweh faithful to His covenant (9:1 – 10:11)

Moses recites a long list of rebellions Israel had perpetrated since leaving Egypt to drive home that although Yahweh will deliver Canaan into her hands it is not because of any merit on her part but because the Canaanites are wicked; and to honour His promises.

Israel must love God (10:12 – 11:32)

Israel must fear Yahweh.[4] He is wholly just. She must keep His commandments and love Him with all her heart. Everything belongs to Yahweh in heavens and on earth yet He chose Israel and it was for her that He performed the mighty wonders she has seen. So let her 'circumcise' her heart, forego her obstinacy and honour the God who bestows His bounty without favour and succours the needy[5] (10:12–22).

Recalling Yahweh's great deeds in Egypt and the desert Moses again stresses that Israel must love and obey Him. Only then can she possess the Promised Land. She must keep his words forever in her heart and teach them to her children. She has a choice: blessings if she obeys Yahweh; otherwise His curse[6] (11:1–32).

THE DEUTERONOMIC CODE (12:1 – 26:15)

Concerning worship (12:1 – 16:22)

Canaanite places of worship, their altars and sacred emblems, on hill tops and under trees, must be destroyed. Israel must in future worship in just one sanctuary that God will nominate in place of the multiplicity previously allowed (by Ex 20:24). That is where offerings for sacrifice, first-born and tithes must be brought and that is where they must be eaten, joyfully and shared with one's household and the Levites. When animals are needed for food as opposed to cultic purposes they may be slaughtered at home just like gazelle or deer.[7] However their blood must still be treated reverently by being poured on the ground and must never be eaten (12:1–28).
Appendix 1 refers

Israel must beware the snares of Canaanite religion, a faith so depraved it even extends to child sacrifice. Anyone promoting other gods must be put to death even if it means wiping out a whole town. Loyalty to God is paramount. A prohibition against pagan mourning rites is followed by a resume of the Lv 11 rules on clean and unclean animals (12:29 – 14:21).

The people must eat the tithe and first-born offerings in God's chosen sanctuary along with the Levites. If this involves a long journey the tithe may be commuted and the money used to buy an equivalent offering on arrival at the sanctuary. However every third year the entire tithe must be given to the Levites and the poor[8] (14:22–29).

Every seventh year debts from brother Israelites (but not from foreigners) must be cancelled and any Israelite slaves freed and sent away laden with gifts. But any slave who so wishes can be kept on as long as he wishes.

Clean first-born male animals must be dedicated to Yahweh and eaten in the sanctuary but any animal with a defect must be eaten at home. Eating of blood is again forbidden (15:1–23). The feasts of Passover, Unleavened Bread, Weeks and Shelters will in future be pilgrimage feasts celebrated at Yahweh's chosen sanctuary rather than locally as hitherto. Judges must be appointed in each town and strict justice must prevail. Altars to Yahweh must not be sited near Canaanite sites (16:1–22).

Miscellaneous laws (17:1 – 18:22)

Animals intended for sacrifice must be unblemished. Anyone proven to have worshipped other gods must be put to death. Difficult legal cases must be referred to the priests and judges whose verdict will be binding on pain of death. If a king is needed he must be chosen by Yahweh and he must be an Israelite. He must not set about amassing military strength, wives or riches, nor set himself above his brothers but fear God (17:1–20).

Apart from (possibly) special portions (the text is ambiguous) the priests' entitlements to sacrificial and first-fruit offerings are extended to the Levites who now also have the right to leave their towns for the central sanctuary to minister with fellow

Levites already there. Pagan practices like child sacrifice, divination and spiritualism are prohibited. God will one day send another prophet like Moses.[9] False prophets must be put to death (18:1–22).
Appendix 2 refers

Concerning criminals (19:1–21)

Cities of refuge are to be established – three now, three later when the occupation of Canaan is complete – where anyone who kills accidentally may shelter from vengeance. However if a wilful murderer shelters there he must be handed over and put to death. Boundary marks must not be tampered with. More than one witness is needed for a conviction. False witnesses must suffer the penalty they sought for their victim.

Concerning the conduct of war (20:1–20)

Israel must not fear her enemies in times of war. Yahweh will be with her. Anyone with a new house, a new vineyard, engaged to be married, or simply frightened must be excused military service and allowed to go home.[10] While Canaanite cities are to be laid under the curse of destruction, other enemies must be offered peace terms. If these are accepted the people are to be conscripted into forced labour otherwise the men must be killed with the women, children and livestock spared and treated as booty. Unnecessary destruction, like cutting-down fruit trees, must be avoided.

Miscellaneous laws (21:1 – 25:19)

A procedure for making atonement in cases of unsolved murder is followed by rules for marrying women taken captive in war, establishing birthrights when a man has two wives, and dealing with rebellious sons. Anyone hanged must be buried the same day (21:1–23).

Cases involving straying animals bring home that everyone should offer neighbourly help. A man must not dress like a woman or vice versa. Birds and chicks are cited to teach that nature must be treated with compassion (though whether this was for its own sake or to preserve the food supply is unclear). Regard must be paid to the safety of others; roofs should have parapets, for example (22:1–8).

Commands that vines should not be mixed with other crops, that oxen and donkeys must not plough together and that wool and linen should not be mixed in clothes are possibly relics of ancient taboos.[11] Cloaks must be trimmed with tassels.[12] Rules then follow for dealing with disputes over a wife's virginity, cases of extra marital relations, participation in public worship and hygiene (22:9 – 23:15).

Slaves who escape from foreign masters must be given asylum. Sacred prostitution is outlawed. Interest may not be charged on loans to fellow Israelites but may be recovered from foreigners. Vows must be honoured promptly. Passers-by may satisfy their hunger by eating a few grapes or ears of corn from their neighbour's land but they must not abuse this privilege by taking grapes away or cutting the grain with a sickle (23:16–26).

Remarriage after divorce is prohibited. A newly married man must be excused public duties for one year. Restraint must be exercised when taking collateral for a loan. Kidnapping is outlawed. The priest's directions must be followed to the letter in cases of skin disease. Creditors must not be hounded but treated with dignity. If a cloak is taken in surety, for example, the owner must not be deprived of it at night. The poor must be paid their wages promptly and not exploited. Everyone is responsible for his own crime. The poor and defenceless must be treated with respect and compassion. Gleanings should be left for the poor (24:1–22).

Judges must be impartial and fair. Punishment must stop short of inflicting injury or humiliation. Domestic animals must be treated humanely. When a husband with brothers dies childless one of his brothers must marry the widow (the levirate law). Wives who seek to help their husbands when fighting must stop short of seizing his opponent's genitals. Dishonest business practices are prohibited. The chapter ends by reminding Israel that one of her traditional enemies, the Amalekites, must be destroyed (25:1–19).

Liturgical directions (26:1–15)

These consist of a ceremonial for offering first-fruits, recalling Israel's rescue from Egypt and the gift of the Promised Land, and a liturgy for the third year tithe (14:28 refers). First-fruits will in future only be offered in God's chosen sanctuary.
Appendix 3 refers

MOSES SECOND DISCOURSE RESUMED (26:16 – 28:68)

Blessings and curses: ceremonies at Shechem (26:16 – 28:68)

Moses tells the people yet again that Yahweh will be her God and she His people only if she keeps His commands (26:16–19). He then moves to impress it on their minds by ordering them, once they are across the Jordan, to inscribe the Law on standing stones and erect them on Mount Ebal beside an altar. Six tribes must then stand on Mount Gerizim to bless the people, while the other six stand on Mount Ebal to receive curses voiced by the Levites[13]. (27:1–26).

The speech concludes with a long catalogue of blessings for fidelity and curses for disobedience. Embedded in the curses are references to exile, to sieges imposed by a distant nation, and a forecast that only a small group will be left of those who were once 'as numerous as the stars of heaven'[14] (28:1–68).

MOSES THIRD DISCOURSE (28:69 – 30:20)

The Moab covenant (28:69 – 30:20)

Moses invites the people to recommit themselves to Yahweh by renewing the Sinai covenant, a covenant not just for those physically present there and then but for generations as yet unborn. He follows the oft repeated warning never to abandon

Yahweh for other gods with a further caution that God will not forgive anyone who hears His commands and yet convinces himself that all will be well if he still stubbornly ignores them. Looking ahead he describes how future generations will see the country devastated and the people uprooted and exiled for forsaking Yahweh (28:69 – 29:28).

Yet curse is not the last word. If, when she is in exile, Israel repents, God will take pity and restore her. He will 'circumcise' her heart so that she will love and obey Him. The curses will then recoil on her enemies. In a final appeal Moses stresses that observance of the Law is neither difficult nor beyond Israel's reach. God has not left His will in doubt and the choice is simple: blessings and prosperity or death and disaster (30:1–20)

MOSES' FINAL ACTS (31:1 – 34:12)

Joshua commissioned: the Law inscribed (31:1–30; 32:45–47)

Joshua is commissioned to lead Israel across the Jordan.[15] Yahweh will be with her so she has nothing to fear. Moses commits the Law to writing and the Levites are commissioned to keep it beside the Ark as a constant reminder. The elders must proclaim it to the people every seven years at the feast of Shelters. Yahweh then warns Moses of Israel's future apostasy and the disasters that will befall her. He is told to commit this message to song and teach it to the people as a grim reminder of their fate.

The Song of Moses (32:1–44)

The song summons heavens and earth as witnesses, laments Israel's ingratitude, proclaims God's loving care, describes how Israel spurned His love, and portrays God passing sentence on her. Yet despite all this God will not abandon His people. He will take pity on them and liberate them from their oppressors.

The death of Moses (32:48 – 34:12)

Moses blesses the tribes before climbing Mount Nebo to view the Promised Land he may not enter. There the prophet who 'knew Yahweh face to face' died and Joshua was filled with the spirit of wisdom he had previously enjoyed.[16]

THE HISTORICAL BOOKS

The Historical books begin their story with Israel on the Jordan, poised to enter the Promised Land, and carry it down some seven centuries to the Babylonian captivity. Joshua describes the conquest of Canaan, Judges the early struggles before the tribes welded into nationhood, 1 and 2 Samuel the early monarchy of Saul and David. 1 and 2 Kings, paralleled by 1 and 2 Chronicles, opens with Solomon and with few exceptions (such as the restorative balm of Elijah and Elisha) recites the long litany of obstinacy and infidelity that ended with God abandoning His people to punishment; the destruction of the Temple and exile. Ezra and Nehemiah open a window into the Persian age while 1 and 2 Maccabees jump to the second century and the revolt against the imposition of Hellenistic culture.

Although each of the remaining four books – Ruth, Tobit, Judith, Esther – is given a historical setting, they are probably novellas, works of religious fiction that owe their places in the Canon to their shedding light on God's providential activity in the lives of their participants.

Nor are the other books 'historical' in any conventional sense. Their prime concern is the relationship between Israel and her God. So martial arts and politics are of little concern and are disregarded unless at the same time they shed light on God and the promulgation of His salvic will.

Joshua

Joshua describes the conquest of the Promised Land and its partition among the tribes. It is prefaced by a reminder that God's help is conditional upon fidelity and ends with Israel renewing her allegiance to Yahweh in a covenant at Shechem.

The cardinal message of Joshua is that God keeps His promises. 'Of all the promises that Yahweh had made to the House of Israel, not one failed; all were fulfilled', 21:45. Overcoming all obstacles, and despite her infidelities, God had at last given Israel the land He had promised Abraham. The subjection of the native peoples in Joshua stands with the deliverance from Egypt as one of the pivotal events in Israel's emerging nationhood.

While it is true that Israel's path was eased by Canaan being a plurality of jealously autonomous city states, and that the narrative probably idealises what happened to extol God's power, it is no less true that the conquest was God's doing, a sustained miracle. It was He who engineered Israel's victory and He alone who made it possible. 'One man of you was able to rout a thousand of the enemy, since Yahweh your God was Himself fighting for you, as He had promised you', 23:10. It is impossible to explain the victory of a band of desert nomads over a settled and powerfully armed populace in any other way. The narrative positively revels in God's power. The division of the land is tantamount to a hymn of praise.

Preparations (1:1 – 2:24)

Yahweh orders Joshua to lead Israel across the Jordan to possess the Land He is giving her. Provided he keeps the Law he will succeed in everything he does. Joshua allows three days for mobilisation and reminds the three tribes who already have land east of the Jordan of their obligation to help in the forthcoming campaign (1:1–18). Meanwhile a prostitute named Rahab shelters two spies Joshua sends to reconnoitre Jericho, his first objective. She hides them on the roof of her house and later lowers them down by a rope from her window to escape. In return she is promised safe haven for her family during the coming invasion provided they all remain in her house and display a scarlet chord[1] (2:1–24).

Crossing the Jordan (3:1 – 5:15)

The Israelites strike camp and advance to the Jordan opposite Jericho following a respectful distance behind the priests and the Ark. Although in spate the river stops flowing the moment the priests carrying the Ark set foot in it, and they are able to stand on dry ground in mid-stream while Israel crosses the river dryshod. When everyone is safely across the river resumes flowing in full flood as before. The men are circumcised and the Passover is celebrated. Then the manna ceases[2] (3:1 – 5:12).

At this time of supreme trial, with the Jordan behind him and the way ahead barred by the fortified city of Jericho, and in a theophany reminiscent of Moses and the burning bush, Joshua learns that he is not alone.[3] A 'Man' (yet not a man) appears to him grasping a naked sword and describing Himself as 'captain of the army of Yahweh' (5:13–15).

Joshua's campaigns (6:1 – 12:24)

Jericho is captured. The Israelites march round the city walls for seven days led by seven priests walking ahead of the Ark blowing trumpets.[4] Then on the seventh day as they raise a mighty war cry the walls tumble down and the city is stormed. Everything is devoted to Yahweh under the curse of destruction. The people, men and women, young and old, are slaughtered along with their animals while anything of value is given to the treasury. Only Rahab's family is spared.[5] A curse is proclaimed on anyone who rebuilds Jericho (6:1–27).
Appendices 1,2 refer

Joshua's forces push on into the hill country but an attack on Ai fails because one of the assailants, a certain Achan, had kept for himself some of the spoils from Jericho that should have been devoted to Yahweh. He is identified by lot and stoned to death[6] (7:1–26). A second attack is successful as a frontal feint lures the enemy out of the town for an ambush party to take it from the rear. After the battle Joshua builds an altar on Mount Ebal and reads the Law to the Israelites as prescribed by Moses at Dt 27 (8:1–35).
Appendix 3 refers

The Canaanite kings form an alliance against Israel. However the Gibeonites take an independent line and trick Israel into a treaty guaranteeing their lives. When their emissaries arrive they are dressed in old clothes and have only stale bread to lend credence to their story that they hail from a distant country and are not Canaanites. By the time their ruse is discovered the pact is sworn and cannot be revoked. They are punished for their deceit by being confined to being wood-cutters and water-carriers (9:1–27).

Alarmed by the bridgehead that Israel now holds in central Canaan five kings join forces and attack Gibeon. Joshua hastens to their aid and after a forced overnight march wins a resounding victory in which the fleeing enemy forces, taken unawares, are thrown into even greater disarray by a violent hailstorm. This is the battle in which Joshua famously prays:

> Sun, stand still over Gibeon,
> and, moon, you too, over the vale of Aijalon![7] (10:12)

The five kings are entombed in a cave at Makkedah and later executed. Having subdued the central highlands Joshua next goes on to conquer Canaan's southern provinces. Everything is put under the curse of destruction (10:1–43).

In another lightning campaign Joshua defeats the northern kings by the Waters of Merom, burning their chariots and crippling their horses. At last 'the country has rest from warfare' (11:1 – 12:24).

Appendix 4 refers

Distribution of the land (13:1 – 19:51)

Although much of the land has still to be won, Yahweh instructs Joshua to divide it between the tribes. Moses had already promised Reuben, Gad and Manasseh heritages east of the Jordan and their boundaries are recorded first (13:1–33). With Eleazar the priest Joshua then begins to allocate by lot the land west of the Jordan. Caleb is given Hebron as reward for his trust in Yahweh at the time of the ill-fated reconnaissance (14:1–15).

Judah and Ephraim are allocated their portions. Caleb enlarges his land at the expense of the Canaanites. However Jerusalem remains inviolate in the hands of the Jebusites. The Manassehites are given a second allocation, west of the Jordan, and although they are unable to expel the Canaanites they are eventually able to enslave them. When Ephraim and Manasseh complain that their allocations are inadequate Joshua challenges them to clear the wooded areas and expel the remaining Canaanites, though he agrees this will be difficult due to the Canaanites possessing iron chariots[8] (15:1 – 17:18).

Israel assembles at Shiloh and the Tent of Meeting is erected there. Joshua allocates land to the remaining seven tribes. The Danites are unable to hold on to their territory and migrate north.[9] Joshua receives a personal settlement in the highlands of Ephraim (18:1 – 19:51).

Levitical cities and cities of refuge (20:1 – 21:45)

All six cities of refuge ordered by Moses are now designated as are forty eight towns for the Levites to live in.[10] The allocation is complete. Yahweh has honoured all His promises, overcoming all Israel's enemies and giving her land and tranquillity just as He had sworn to her ancestors.

Return of the eastern tribes (22:1–34)

Joshua releases the tribes with land east of the Jordan, commending their loyalty but warning them to remain faithful to Yahweh. A dispute arises over an altar they erect beside the Jordan on their way home. The other tribes misconstrue this as an attempt to establish their own sanctuary and a serious breach is only narrowly averted.

Joshua's farewell address (23:1–16)

In an address when he is getting on in years, Joshua warns Israel that she must never fraternise with the Canaanites but keep the Law and love Yahweh. He has given her all she has. He has fulfilled every promise and failed none and will drive out the remaining Canaanites if she stays loyal. Otherwise she will find them 'thorns in her sides and thistles in her eyes' and be driven out herself.

The Shechem covenant (24:1–33)

Joshua summons all Israel to an assembly at Shechem. He reviews her history from Abraham to the present day where they live in a land they have done nothing to deserve. He offers a stark choice: to banish the false gods of their ancestors and the Canaanites and serve Yahweh; or be destroyed. It is urgent. They must decide at once.[11] The people repledge their allegiance to Yahweh and Joshua seals it in a solemn covenant.

Joshua dies. Joseph's bones are interred at Shechem. The return from Egypt is complete.

Judges

Judges covers the period between Joshua and the inauguration of the monarchy in Saul, a span of perhaps one hundred and fifty years. In contrast with Joshua's picture of outright conquest by a united people, Judges shows the tribes holding only a precarious foothold in the Promised Land as, scattered and largely autonomous, they were bonded only by their common faith. They could not control the plains and were often forced to live alongside the Canaanites, even intermarrying, rather than displacing them.

Judges is a set of variations on a theme. Israel does evil in Yahweh's eyes and incurs His wrath. He hands her over to an oppressor. Israel cries out for help. God sends a liberator, one of the judges. Harmony and peace are restored. The saviour judge dies. Israel lapses and the cycle of impiety, punishment, repentance and salvation recurs all over again.

Despite their title the judges were not basically judicial men but charismatic leaders, men of action, liberators divinely empowered by God for a mission of rescue. Though they are portrayed as national figures their writ probably ran no further than the particular tribe or tribes they were deputed to rescue. Rarely, if ever, would their mandate have extended to all Israel. Deborah enjoyed the support of about half the tribes, Gideon only four. Equally although the judges are presented as following sequentially, there was probably some overlap. What the Book of Judges offers therefore is not so much a systematic history of these turbulent times as a picture gallery, snapshots of localised tribal groups.

Reading Judges we can only marvel at the sorts of people God enlisted to His cause and His forbearance at the debauchery and slaughter that accompanied the way they went about their business. They were desperate times. 'In those days there was no king in Israel and everyone did as he saw fit', 21:25. The dynamic that would eventually lead to exile was already rearing its head.

Judges concentrates on six main judges together with Gideon's son Abimelech. Six further judges are alluded to briefly. It concludes with appendices on the Danite migration and the Benjaminite civil war.

Tribal campaigns (1:1–36)

After Joshua's death Judah campaigns in southern Canaan accompanied by Simeon.[1] Hebron is captured and given to Caleb. Judah also captures Gaza and other Philistine towns but the main success is in the highlands. The plains cannot be held because Israel cannot compete with the Canaanites' iron war chariots.[2]

In central Canaan Bethel is taken by Ephraim and Manasseh but in the north the situation is less favourable. None of the tribes is able to expel the Canaanites although they are able to settle among them and even enslave them. The Danites fare even worse, the Amorites driving them out of the plains back into the hill country.[3]

The theological background to Judges (2:1 – 3:6)

After Joshua's death Yahweh's mighty acts were forgotten and Israel worshipped the local Baals. As a result Yahweh gave notice that He would not drive out the remaining Canaanites but leave them to torment her.[4] Even so He did send judges to rescue her when enemies oppressed her but no sooner did a judge die than she became as rebellious as ever.

Appendix 1 refers

Othniel (3:7–11)

The story of Othniel, Caleb's nephew, succinctly encapsulates the book's recurring theme. The Israelites deserted Yahweh to serve the local Canaanite gods. So He handed them over to Edom and slavery. Then when they cried out for a deliverer He sent Othniel to defeat Edom and free her. But as soon as Othniel died Israel stumbled again.

Ehud (3:12–31)

Moab invades Israel, capturing Jericho 'the city of palms' and enslaving the people. Yahweh sends Ehud, a Benjaminite, to rescue her. Ehud slays Eglon, the Moabite king, with a dagger while paying tribute and subsequently wipes out the Moabite invaders by seizing the fords across the Jordan that controlled their line of retreat. A single verse relates how the next judge, Shamgar, delivered Israel from the Philistines.

Deborah and Barak (4:1 – 5:31)

Soon after Ehud's death the Canaanites enslave Israel.[5] Deborah, a prophetess, enlists Barak to lead an army against them. Inspired by Deborah, Barak charges down from Mount Tabor and scatters the Canaanites under their commander Sisera. Sisera flees for sanctuary to Jael, the wife of Heber, a supposed friend, only to be treacherously killed when she drives a tent peg through his temple as he sleeps.[6]

Deborah's ancient victory song is a poetic rendering of the same event and clearly shows the dire straights Israel was in. Her villages were abandoned and her people restricted to stealthy movement along back roads as it was too dangerous to travel in caravans.[7]

Gideon (6:1 – 8:35)

When the Midianites reduce Israel to living in mountain clefts and plunder her crops, an angel appears to a sceptical Gideon to order him to the rescue. Gideon requests, and is given, a sign (his offering being consumed by heavenly fire). Despite this, when Yahweh then orders him to replace his father's altar to Baal with one to Himself, he is so frightened of his neighbours' and family's reaction that he can only bring himself to do it at night.

Then the spirit seizes Gideon and he musters Israel for battle as the Midianites mass near Jezreel. But before risking battle he insists on two further signs to bolster his confidence, both involving a woollen fleece[8] (6:1–40). To remove any grounds Israel might have had for boasting Yahweh then cut Gideon's army to three hundred, a mere hundredth of its original size: first by releasing the fearful, then depending on how they drank from a stream. At the same time He emboldened Gideon by allowing him to eavesdrop on one of the Midianites recalling a dream in which they were defeated.[9] The dream was soon borne out. That same night, when Gideon launched a three-pronged attack with blasting trumpets, fiery torches and fierce war cries, the Midianites assumed they were surrounded by a superior force and fled in panic without a fight (7:1–25).

When the Ephraimites complained at their minor role in the war Gideon smoothed their ruffled feathers by minimising his own role and praising Ephraim's part in the final pursuit. Meanwhile he hunted down two Midianite kings who had killed his brothers and took vengeance on two towns that had earlier withheld supplies from his famished troops until they were sure he really had won the war.

Gideon's life ended in paradox. Having declined an invitation to become king because Yahweh was their king he made an *ephod*, some form of cultic object, from the war booty and did nothing to stop it becoming a focus for idolatry. After his death Israel again relapsed into Baal worship (8:1–35).

Abimelech (9:1–57)

Abimelech, Gideon's son by a concubine, has himself proclaimed king at Shechem.[10] He hires mercenaries to murder Gideon's other seventy sons. Only one escapes, Jotham, who denounces Abimelech's base motives in a poetic fable.

In the event Abimelech's reign is brief. After three years the Shechemites plot to overthrow him. And although a coup led by Gaal is betrayed and fails, resulting in Abimelech razing Shechem and incinerating its inhabitants, he is fatally wounded soon afterwards when a millstone thrown by a woman cracks his skull.

Jephthah (10:1 – 12:15)

After briefly acknowledging two minor judges, Tola and Jair, the narrative moves to a time when, having once more deserted Yahweh, Israel is under the heel of the Philistines and Ammonites. After she repents Yahweh sends a deliverer in Jephthah, a prostitute's son and ex-brigand.[11] After peace negotiations fail the spirit of Yahweh seizes him and he vows to sacrifice as a burnt offering the first thing to come out of his house to meet him if he returns victorious from the now inevitable campaign (10:1 – 11:31).

Israel inflicts a stunning defeat on the Ammonites. But for Jephthah the flush of victory is tragically transformed into anguish when, on his return in triumph, it is his only daughter who greets him dancing to the tambourines. Her nobility of character as she gently encourages her father to keep his vow, asking only for two months grace to wander the hills and bewail her virginity, makes her one of the Bible's great heroines[12] (11:32–40).

Ephraim complains at not being invited to help in the war.[13] In the civil war that follows Ephraim is defeated with severe loss of life and Ephraimite fugitives trying to make their way home across the Jordan are identified by their inability to pronounce 'Shibboleth' properly and killed. Three minor judges, Ibzan, Elon and Abdon, are briefly mentioned (12:1–15).

Samson (13:1 – 16:31)

The Angel of Yahweh appears to the wife of a Danite named Manoah as Israel is groaning under the Philistines. She is barren but will bear a son, Samson, who will start to rescue Israel from the Philistines. He will be a nazirite[14] (13:1–25).

Samson marries a Philistine. Visiting her one day he sets the thirty Philistines who had been assigned to him as a bridegroom escort a riddle.[15] Unable to solve the riddle they threaten Samson's wife with death until she coaxes the answer out of him. Realising what has happened Samson flies into a rage and kills thirty other Philistines in order to acquire the festal robes he offered as prizes. Assuming the marriage is over Samson's father-in-law gives his daughter away to Samson's best man (14:1–20).

Samson devises a novel form of revenge. He catches three hundred foxes, ties them in pairs by their tails, fixes burning torches in the knots and sets them loose in the Philistines' cornfields and orchards. The Philistines retaliate by burning Samson's wife and family to death. However, pressurised by a deputation of Judahites who are disenchanted with the problems he is causing, Samson gives himself up. But no sooner has he done so than he uses his phenomenal strength to break loose and slaughter the Philistines with a donkey's jawbone. Yahweh miraculously relieves his thirst (15:1–20).

Samson narrowly escapes capture at Gaza while patronising a prostitute, barging through the city gates and carrying them away on his shoulders. Soon afterwards he falls in love with Delilah, a Philistine. The Philistine chiefs offer her a substantial reward if she can discover the secret of his strength. After much cajoling Samson confides that it stems from his nazirite vows and unshorn head. Betrayal follows. Delilah gets one of the Philistines to shave off Samson's hair while he is asleep in her lap. His legendary strength gone Samson is overpowered. His eyes are put out and he is imprisoned at Gaza turning the mill.

Later on the Philistines call on Samson to amuse them by performing feats of strength. But his hair has regrown and in a final gesture of defiance he pulls down the pillars supporting the building they are in, killing hundreds of Philistines at the cost of his own life[16] (16:1–31).

The Danite migration (17:1 – 18:31)

In the highlands of Ephraim a certain Micah establishes a shrine with idols paid for with money originally stolen from his mother. He installs an itinerant Levite as his priest. When a party of Danites passes by, following an earlier reconnaissance, they steal the *ephod* and other objects from Micah's sanctuary and persuade his priest to join them as they migrate to a new homeland at Laish. They put Laish to the sword, rename it Dan, and settle there, establishing a sanctuary with the stolen idols.[17]

The Benjaminite civil war (19:1 – 21:25)

A Levite returning home from Bethlehem with his concubine is forced to night stop in Gibeah in Benjaminite territory. During the evening some local perverts demand sexual relations with the Levite. His host offers his virgin daughter instead but the molesters will not hear of it and the Levite then proffers his concubine. She is gang-raped and dies. As soon as he arrives home the Levite dissects her body and sends a piece to each of the tribes with a call for vengeance. War follows in which Benjamin suffers a crushing defeat (19:1 – 20:48).

There was now a problem. As the Benjaminite women had all perished, and the other tribes had sworn not to inter-marry with Benjamin, how could the six hundred remaining Benjaminite men who had hidden in the desert preserve the tribe? It was noted that no one from Jabesh had participated in the attack on Benjamin despite a solemn oath to do so on pain of death. Troops were therefore sent to kill everyone in Jabesh except for four hundred virgins who were given to the Benjaminite male survivors. The remaining unpaired Benjaminite men were then told to hide in the vineyards near Shiloh and to choose a wife as the local girls came out to dance on an annual feast day (21:1–25).

Appendix 2 refers

Ruth

After the apostate barbarism of Judges, Ruth is an isle of tranquillity. It is the story of an ordinary godly family that despite life's misfortunes never lost hope and in the end found happiness. There are no villains, just the loyalty, generosity, kindness and devotion of simple honest people.

Like the stories of Joseph, Tobit and Esther, Ruth is an object lesson in how God, while remaining hidden, can bring about good by working through everyday events whose ripples rarely progress beyond the pools of the participants' own lives. It is impossible to read Ruth without the feeling that although He was hidden behind coincidence and human artifice, God was in control all the time. When we are told that 'chance' led Ruth to Boaz's plot we know that it was anything but 'chance'. Nor can we escape the conclusion that when religion nationally was in distress, it was through islands of faith in the families of people like Naomi that God preserved a nucleus of faith.

But whilst God was caring for ordinary families He was equally at work on the stage of history. For when Ruth remarried it was to become the great-grandmother of David and an ancestress of Christ Himself. In recounting this the sacred author is showing through Ruth, a woman with the Moabite blood of one of Israel's staunchest foes in her veins, that when it comes to race or sex God has no favourites.

In the time of the Judges a certain Elimelech, his wife Naomi and their two sons, leave their home in Bethlehem to seek refuge in Moab to escape a famine. Both sons subsequently marry Moabite women.[1] Some ten years later, after Elimelech and his sons have died, Naomi decides to return to Bethlehem. One of her daughters-in-law, Orpah, opts to remain in Moab but the other, Ruth, is reluctant to leave her mother-in-law to a lonely old age. In a poem that touches the sublime in a paradigm of devotion and piety she elects to accompany her back to Bethlehem and to adopt Naomi's God as her God (1:1–22).

Ruth decides to earn a living by gleaning and by chance starts working in the fields of a well-to-do man named Boaz who was a relative of Naomi through her late husband. Knowing of Ruth's kindness towards Naomi, Boaz ensures that she is well looked after. Naomi observes that Boaz has a right of redemption over them both[2] (2:1–23).

Prompted by Naomi, Ruth makes herself up and goes to the threshing floor where Boaz is sleeping after a day's winnowing and lies at his feet. But first she turns back the covering over his feet so that he will wake up during the night and give her the chance to speak to him privately. When he does awake she asks him to apply his right of redemption and 'spread his cloak over her'.[3] Boaz agrees to marry her subject to his first checking that a closer kinsman does not wish to exercise his prior right of redemption (3:1–18).

Boaz goes to the city gate the next morning where he meets the kinsman in question and acquaints him with his redemptive rights both over Ruth and also over some land of Elimelech's which Naomi wished to sell. The relative is agreeable to acquiring the land but when he realises that any redemption necessarily extends to marrying Ruth as well he waives his rights.[4]

Boaz marries Ruth. She has a son Obed, the father of Jesse father of David. An epilogue tells us that Boaz was descended from Perez son of Tamar and Judah, Gn 38[5] (4:1–22).

1 Samuel

The two books of Samuel cover a period of monumental change in Israel's fortunes, from a loose tribal confederacy to a nation united at the height of its power, from worshipping in a simple shrine at Shiloh to the splendour of the Temple at Jerusalem. This transformation was the legacy of three men: Samuel, prophet, priest and judge; Saul, Israel's first king; David, her greatest king.

As Samuel begins Israel is in a parlous state, subservient to the Philistines and spiritually bankrupt. But God raises up a champion to save her. Samuel led a religious revival and expelled the Philistines. However as he grew old the people clamoured for a king 'to be like the other nations'. Samuel was opposed but bowed to God's command to heed their wish. And so was fuelled that tension between the profane and the spiritual that sowed the seeds of Israel's long descent to Babylon.

Saul was a force to be reckoned with in battle but lacked spiritual depth. David, God's choice as his successor, famously slew the Philistine giant Goliath, and rose to be his army chief. However the more successful he was the more it fuelled Saul's jealousy and he was eventually forced to flee, becoming in turn a guerilla leader and then a Philistine mercenary.

Following Saul's death 2 Samuel tells how David was anointed king first of Judah and then of all Israel. He wrested Jerusalem from the Jebusites, made it his capital and extended Israel's frontiers to their widest bounds. The high point of his life came when God promised him that his dynasty would endure for ever. Thereafter, following adultery with Bathsheba, the tide flowed the other way. With his family racked by rape, murder and rebellion, his later years were a monument to sin's disruptive power and, though he retained his throne and Israel her empire, his life ended in pathos and tragedy.

Samuel's birth and dedication (1:1 – 2:11)

A woman from Ramah named Hannah, God-fearing but barren, prays for a son and swears that if her prayer is answered she will dedicate him to Yahweh Sabaoth for life.[1] It says much for the state of religion at the time that Eli the priest initially mistook her lips moving in silent prayer for drunkenness. Hannah's prayer is answered with a son, Samuel, and, true to her word, as soon as he is weaned she leaves him with Eli at the sanctuary at Shiloh where the Ark was now housed.[2] Her song of jubilation and praise echoes Mary's Magnificat, Lk: 1:46–55.

Eli and Samuel (2:12 – 4:1)

When Eli does not discipline his sons properly for treating the liturgy irreverently he is quickly taught that indulging family at the expense of God carries a heavy penalty. A man of God tells him that his family will be punished and lose its right of succession to the priesthood. Yahweh meanwhile continues to make Himself known to Samuel and by the time Eli grows old, with his sons persisting in their godless ways, it is Samuel to whom the people look as His spokesman.

Israel is defeated at Aphek (4:2 – 7:1)

Israel is routed by the Philistines at Aphek and the Ark, which had been brought to the battle in the hope of ensuring victory, is itself captured.[3] Eli's two sons are killed in the fighting and Eli himself has a fatal fall when he hears the news. The Philistines install the Ark in the temple of their god Dagon. But they get more than they bargain for. Dagon topples over in the presence of the Ark and the people are ravaged by tumours[4] (4:2 – 5:12).

After seven months the chastened Philistines have had enough and return the Ark to Israel in a cart drawn by two cows without any previous yoke experience and which had just had their calves taken from them. Despite this the cows steer a course straight back to Israel at Beth-Shemesh.[5] Seventy townsmen who do not rejoice at the Ark's return are struck dead whereupon the onlookers persuade Kiriath-Jearim to take it instead[6] (6:1 – 7:1).

A religious revival (7:2–17)

Twenty years go by during which Samuel leads a religious revival. As a result when hostilities with the Philistines resume the newly repentant Israel wins a great victory at Mizpah helped by a miraculous thunder storm. Land previously lost to the Philistines is regained and with it peace. Samuel remains a circuit judge for the rest of his life.

The people ask for a king (8:1–22)

When Samuel grows old the people ask for a king so as 'to be like the other nations'. Samuel thinks this is wrong as it amounts to rejecting the King they already have. He warns that a monarchy would bring conscription, taxes, corruption and extortion. But the people persist and Yahweh directs Samuel to do as they wish.

Saul becomes king (9:1 – 11:15)

A Benjaminite named Saul – tall, handsome and in the prime of life – approaches Samuel in the hope that as a man of God he will be able to help find his father's stray donkeys. Their meeting occurs the day after Yahweh had told Samuel that Saul was the man he was to anoint as king. Samuel secretly anoints Saul at dawn the next day and acquaints him with various signs he will experience on his way home as proof of his calling. One of these is that the spirit of Yahweh will make a new man of him.[7] He also charges Saul that in time of war he is to muster his forces at Gilgal and then wait seven days for Samuel to come to him to offer sacrifice and tell him what to do (9:1 – 10:16).

Although he is still personally opposed to a king, Samuel calls an assembly at Mizpah so that the people can make their choice. Saul is selected by lot and, after being found modestly hiding among the baggage, publicly acclaimed although there are a few dissenting voices. Saul quickly shows his mettle, routing a band of marauding Ammonites whereupon, on returning home, he is now acclaimed king without dissent (10:17 – 11:15).

Samuel hands over to Saul (12:1–24)

In a handover speech Samuel reminds the people of the wonders Yahweh has performed on their behalf since leaving Egypt. Despite this they have insisted on a king even though Yahweh was already their King. This is a very wicked thing.[8] Nevertheless if they and the king keep faith all will be well. If not, Yahweh's hand will turn against them.

Saul is rejected (13:1–15)

When Saul's son Jonathan assassinates the Philistine governor at Gibeah the Philistines retaliate by concentrating a huge force at Michmash prompting many Israelites to hide in caves or flee across the Jordan. Saul musters his troops at Gilgal and then waits the prescribed seven days for Samuel to arrive. When Samuel does not appear, and mindful of the facts that his force was being depleted by desertion and that a Philistine attack seems imminent, he decides to offer sacrifice himself. He had just finished when Samuel arrived and angrily prophesied that because of his disobedience his sovereignty would not endure. Yahweh's choice of king had fallen elsewhere[9] (13:1–15).

Victory at Michmash (13:16 – 14:52)

Helped by a diversionary feint by Jonathan, an earthquake and the return of deserters, Saul routs the Philistines. However his impetuosity nearly costs Jonathan his life. Saul thought that his inability to get a response from Yahweh when he sought guidance was because of some sin and swore that whoever was responsible would die. Divination pointed to Jonathan who had earlier refreshed himself from a honeycomb in contravention of Saul's order that no one was to take food until the battle was over. Despite Jonathan having been unaware of this order Saul was only restrained from having him put to death when the people shouted him down.[10]

Saul won many other victories over Israel's enemies displaying great personal valour. He consolidated his rule and raised a standing army.[11]

Saul is again rejected (15:1–35)

Samuel orders Saul to crush the Amalekites and impose the curse of destruction. However instead of applying it rigorously Saul takes the Amalekite king Agag alive and puts the best cattle and sheep to one side in deference to the people's wish to offer them in sacrifice.

When Samuel hears of this he is outraged and tells Saul that Yahweh has rejected him as king.[12] A penitent Saul pleads for forgiveness and tears Samuel's cloak as he tries to stop the uncompromising prophet walking away and summarily disowning him. But to no avail. Samuel himself kills Agag but Saul remains king for the time being.

The call of David (16:1 – 17:58)

Yahweh sends Samuel to Bethlehem to anoint one of Jesse's sons as Israel's future king. The mantle falls on the youngest, David a shepherd.[13] David is anointed and the spirit of Yahweh seizes him. At the same time it leaves Saul and he begins to suffer fits of depression. Saul's servants recommend music to calm him and David is engaged as his minstrel. Before long he becomes Saul's armour bearer too (16:1–23).

When war with the Philistines breaks out again Goliath, a giant of a man, challenges Israel to settle the issue by one-man combat. David volunteers to act as Israel's champion and slays him with a single shot from his sling. The Philistines flee in disarray and David is presented to Saul by Abner his army commander[14] (17:1–58).

Saul grows jealous of David (18:1 – 19:24)

Saul's son Jonathan and David become staunch friends. Saul puts David in charge of his fighting men and his reputation soars to such an extent that Saul grows jealous of him, especially when the people start singing 'Saul has killed his thousands and David his tens of thousands'. He can see that David enjoys the blessing that once was his and in one of his dark moods threatens David with a spear (18:1–16).

Hoping to get David killed Saul promises him one of his daughters if he will go on fighting the Philistines. But his plan backfires. David returns from the wars with double the agreed bride-price of one hundred Philistine foreskins and duly marries Saul's daughter Michal. Saul's paranoia continues to grow and after David routs the Philistines yet again he tries to impale him with his spear as he plays the harp. Later that same night Saul sends his henchmen to murder him but Michal helps him escape from his bedroom window. David flees to Ramah where he joins Samuel and a community of prophets. When Saul sends men to Ramah to arrest him, and later goes himself, they are all overcome by the spirit (18:17 – 19:24).

David on the run (20:1 – 23:28)

After Jonathan warns him that his father is still bent on killing him David flees to Nob where, requesting food from Ahimelech the priest, he is given the consecrated loaves from the sanctuary.[15] He carries on to Gath in Philistia where he feigns madness to conceal his identity from Achish the king (20:1 – 21:16).

After arranging custody for his parents in Moab, David takes refuge in Judah with some four hundred followers.[16] Meanwhile Saul, alerted by one of his officials who had spotted David at Nob, has Ahimelech and his fellow priests slaughtered for helping David. Only Abiathar, one of Ahimelech's sons, escapes to join David who was quick to acknowledge his responsibility for the massacre (22:1–23).

David relieves the Philistine siege of Keilah but has to flee to avoid entrapment by Saul. In the desert he meets Jonathan for the last time. He has a narrow escape when Saul spots him across a gorge. Luckily Saul has to break off the chase when messengers bring news of a new Philistine attack (23:1–28).

David spares Saul (24:1 – 26:25)

David takes refuge near En-Gedi. When Saul resumes the hunt he unknowingly puts himself at David's mercy when he enters a cave where David and his men are hiding in the recesses at the back. However David merely cuts off the hem of Saul's cloak. Even then he is conscience stricken 'at raising his hand against Yahweh's anointed'. After Saul leaves the cave David hails him from a distance and attests his goodwill. Saul weeps, contrasting his own malign behaviour with David's uprightness and makes David swear that he will not persecute his descendants when he becomes king (24:1–23).

Samuel dies at Ramah. When Nabal, a wealthy farmer, refuses David's demand for food in return for not molesting his herd, his wife Abigail, clearly fearing what David might do, supplies him instead. Nabal dies from a heart attack when he hears of it and David, who had earlier married Ahinoam, now takes Abigail as a wife as well (25:1–44). Before long David again has Saul at his mercy. This time he sneaks into his camp by night and removes the sleeping king's spear[17] (26:1–25).

David among the Philistines (27:1 – 30:31)

David decides that the best survival strategy is to become a Philistine mercenary domiciled in Ziklag. He plays a double game raiding Judah's foes while presenting the spoils to his Philistine overlords as if they came from Judah. Since he is careful never to take prisoners who might give the game away he is able to convince the Philistines of his loyalty while simultaneously ingratiating himself with the men of Judah (27:1–12).

When war with Israel resumes David becomes Achish's bodyguard while Saul consults a medium who conjures up Samuel from the grave to tell him that Yahweh has abandoned him for David. He will be slain the next day and Israel defeated (28:1–25).

When the Philistines refuse to allow David to fight with them against Israel, he returns to Ziklag to find it sacked by the Amalekites and its inhabitants taken prisoner. He hunts down the raiders and recovers everything: women and children, sheep and cattle. He then cleverly shares the booty amongst all his followers, baggage-minders as well as front line troops, together with an allotment for the elders of Judah (29:1 – 30:31).

The death of Saul (31:1–13)

Israel is defeated at Mount Gilboa. Jonathan and Saul's other two sons are killed. Saul himself falls on his sword to avoid capture. The Philistines hang their bodies on the walls of Beth-Shean where they are later recovered by the inhabitants of Jabesh and given a proper burial.[18]

2 Samuel

David becomes king of Judah (1:1 – 2:32)

When an Amalekite boasts that he finished-off Saul at his own request when he came upon him at Gilboa badly wounded and with the enemy bearing down upon him, David has him slaughtered. The beauty and nobility of the ensuing elegy make it one of the Bible's poetic masterpieces.

David proceeds to Hebron where he is consecrated king of Judah, a region where his earlier exploits would have won him many supporters. Meanwhile Abner, a cousin of Saul, 1S 14:50, and his former army commander, installs Saul's son Ishbaal as king of Israel although he himself is clearly the power behind the throne. War breaks out between David's supporters and Ishbaal's. After individual combat fails to settle the issue battle is joined at Gibeon. David's forces under Joab carry the day and in the ensuing pursuit Abner kills Joab's brother in self defence.

David becomes king of Israel (3:1 – 5:5)

Sons are born to David including Amnon, Absalom and Adonijah. As the war drags on David gradually gains the upper hand. Ishbaal and Abner clash when Ishbaal accuses Abner of intimacy with one of his father's concubines.[1] As a result Abner decides to throw his weight behind a move to make David king of Israel. However David insists on having Michal returned to him before he will negotiate.[2]

Abner continues drumming-up support for David, even lobbying Saul's own tribe of Benjamin. However his scheming comes to an end when, following a visit to David in Hebron, he is murdered by Joab in revenge for his brother's death. David is appalled but does not yet feel secure enough to antagonise Joab. When Ishbaal is also murdered the opposition of Saul's erstwhile supporters collapses and David is anointed king of Israel in his stead.

David takes Jerusalem (5:6 – 6:23)

David captures Jerusalem, hitherto an independent Jebusite enclave, probably by his men scaling a tunnel supplying water to the city, bored through the rock of the hill on which the city stood. He builds a palace and makes it his capital. This was an astute move. Jerusalem enjoyed a commanding position yet had no tribal affiliation. (By later housing the Ark there he also made it the centre of the nation's spiritual life.) David would rule in Jerusalem for thirty-three years following his seven and a half years as king of Judah in Hebron.

Envoys and presents from the king of Tyre show that David is now a force to be reckoned with and the Philistines realise that they can no longer treat him as a vassal. Twice they attack him and twice they are repulsed, David's advance in the second battle being guided by the sound of Yahweh's footsteps leading the way in the tops of the balsam trees (5:6–25).

David travels to Baalah to recover the Ark which had languished there since Samuel's day. He brings it to Jerusalem amidst scenes of great rejoicing and installs it in a tent. Uzzah, one of the Ark's attendants, is struck down as he steadies it with his hands (6:1–23).

The Davidic covenant (7:1–29)

David resolves to build a house for the Ark. Yahweh responds through the prophet Nathan that He does not want that. Instead He will create a 'house' for David, a dynasty that will endure for ever. David's fame will be as great as anyone's on earth. Israel will be settled in peace and never be oppressed again. Individual kings may stray but any punishment they receive will be the sort a father metes out to a son. Yahweh's love will never be withdrawn. David's own son will be his (immediate) heir and it is he who will build a Temple. David's prayer in response to these unsolicited promises is a model of faith, praise and piety. He recognises what Yahweh has already given him and is overcome at His generosity in promising even more.
Appendix 1 refers

David's campaigns (8:1–18)

In a series of campaigns David defeats the Philistines, Moab, Zobah, Aram, and Edom. Joab was David's army commander, Zadok and Abiathar his priests.

David befriends Jonathan's son (9:1–13)

Out of regard for his friendship with Jonathan, David returns Saul's estates to his crippled son Meribaal and gives him an honoured place at his court. Ziba, one of Saul's old servants, is deputed to look after him.[3]

David's affair with Bathsheba (10:1 – 12:31)

The Ammonites provoke war by humiliating David's representatives. Twice their Aramaean mercenaries are routed in battle. In a follow-up campaign David delegates the conduct of the war to Joab and stays behind in Jerusalem. There he seduces Bathsheba, wife of Uriah the Hittite, one of his officers with the army at the front. She becomes pregnant. David tries to cover his tracks by summoning Uriah back to Jerusalem and encouraging him to sleep with his wife so that he would think the child was his. But Uriah was a man of high principle and refused even to call upon his wife in accord with the custom that normal marital relations were inappropriate for those on active service, 1S 21:6. Thwarted, David despatches a message by Uriah's own hand to the compliant Joab ordering him to station Uriah in the thick of the fighting and then abandon him to his fate. As David had intended Uriah is killed and he duly marries Bathsheba (10:1 – 11:27).

In a forceful parable Nathan induces David to condemn himself. Then comes Yahweh's judgement. David's household will be stricken by the sword and his wives ravished for all to see.[4] He is forgiven but Bathsheba's child will die. David is truly contrite. He makes no attempt to deny his guilt and is grief stricken when the child duly dies. Later on Bathsheba conceives again and Solomon is born.

The Ammonites are finally defeated. Rabbah, their capital, is captured and its inhabitants consigned to forced labour (12:1–31).

Amnon's violation of Tamar (13:1 – 14:33)

David's son Amnon rapes Tamar the sister of his half-brother Absalom. Two years later Absalom has Amnon murdered at a sheep-shearing festival to which he had invited him.[5] Absalom flees to escape David's wrath and it is three years before Joab is able to engineer his return using 'a wise woman of Tekoa' as an intermediary. Even then it is two more years before David agrees to receive his son.

Absalom's revolt (15:1 – 17:23)

Absalom begins to undermine David's authority and stir discontent, ingratiating himself with litigants by implying that he would lend a more sympathetic ear to their complaints if he were king. After four years he throws caution to the winds and raises his standard in Hebron. When David hears that the northern tribes have defected he flees Jerusalem, a pitiful figure, barefoot and weeping, evicted by his own son and deserted by his trusted counsellor Ahithophel.[6] However before leaving David persuades his friend Hushai to stay behind in Jerusalem to gather intelligence and counter Ahithophel's influence (15:1–37).

Ziba brings David and his retinue food as they pass the Mount of Olives and breaks the news that Meribaal has remained in Jerusalem in the hope of recovering his kingdom. In disgust David gives Meribaal's estate to Ziba. Back in Jerusalem Hushai is worming his way into Absalom's confidence while Ahithophel advises Absalom to demonstrate his ascendancy by publicly taking David's concubines (16:1–23).

Ahithophel advocates a quick strike aimed at killing David and averting the risk of civil war. Hushai argues that as David is a seasoned campaigner it would be better for Absalom to wait and gather a larger force so that he could then overwhelm him by weight of numbers. Hushai's counsel prevails and when David hears of it he retires to safety beyond the Jordan. His advice spurned, Ahithophel commits suicide[7] (17:1–23).

David returns (17:24 – 19:44)

Absalom catches up with David near Mahanaim only to be overwhelmingly defeated. But for David everything is overshadowed by Absalom's death, entangled in the branches of an oak and finished-off by Joab and his henchmen. David is irreconcilable and only composes himself when Joab insists on a brave front for the sake of morale.

David makes Amasa his army chief in succession to Joab and makes his way back to Jerusalem.[8] He receives a mixed reception. Israel is of two minds, Judah cautious. At the Jordan David is met by Meribaal who claims that he did not join David because Ziba had deceived him. Not knowing whom to believe David orders Meribaal and Ziba to share Saul's former estate.

Sheba's revolt (20:1–26)

David had barely returned to Jerusalem before a Benjaminite named Sheba took advantage of David's lukewarm support to fan the flames of rebellion yet again. But Judah remained loyal and the revolt fizzled out after Sheba was beheaded in a town under siege from Joab who had regained command of the army after murdering Amasa.

Six appendices (21:1 – 24:25)

In the first of six appendices David hands over seven of Saul's sons to be dismembered by the Gibeonites in return for Saul's violation of a covenant guaranteeing their lives, (21:1–14). The next four consist of fragments of incidents in the Philistine wars, a victory hymn attributed to David, David's last words, and a memorandum recalling the exploits of David's most valiant warriors (21:15 – 23:39). The final appendix tells how Israel was punished with an epidemic after David conducted a census (24:1–25).

1 Kings

The books of Kings carry the history of God's people from the death of David down to the Babylonian exile some four centuries later. They glory in David's son Solomon whose reign was a golden age of peace and prosperity, splendour and empire. But the high hopes of his early years, flowing from his fountain of God-given wisdom and his building of the Temple, were not sustained. Affluence and pagan wives fuelled an impiety that brought judgement. After his death the kingdom split: Israel with a non-Davidic king, Jeroboam, in the north; Judah with Solomon's son Rehoboam as king in the south. Political division was soon matched by religious schism as Jeroboam, the paradigm of apostate Israel, established sanctuaries with Canaanite emblems at either end of his kingdom.

The narrative traces the fortunes of Israel and Judah in parallel shuttling from one to the other as it sketches the ebb and flow of their fortunes. But always, despite occasional mentions of insurrections and invasions, tribute and pillaging, with religious affairs to the fore.

It is a chastening story of pride, brutality, disloyalty and depravity driven by flawed leadership. The destinies of the little states lurch inexorably downhill. The last vestiges of Solomon's empire are soon lost while in the spiritual realm the verdict is equally grim. Every king of Israel, without exception, is condemned as 'doing what was displeasing to Yahweh in following the example of Jeroboam'.

The kings of Judah fare little better. Only Hezekiah and Josiah receive unstinted commendation while Asa, Jehoshaphat, Jehoash, Amaziah, Uzziah, and Jotham get approval that is qualified by their failure to sever Judah's addiction to the Canaanite cult. The rest are judged in the same trenchant terms as their peers in Israel. The depths to which religion sank are nowhere better attested than in the telling list of aberrations that Josiah is lauded for having outlawed.

Samuel's warning about a monarchical system is vindicated. Solomon may have ruled over a people economically in advance of the simple peasant community bequeathed by Saul but the price was shattering. Seduced by politics and affluence God's people drifted away from Yahweh and forgot their missionary call. Eventually the tide came in. The northern kingdom was deported to Assyria never to rise again. Judah fared little better. Reforms initiated by Josiah were too little too late to reverse an ever-tightening noose of apostasy. So Judah too found the sword of God drawn against her with the result that the melancholy tale that began with the glory of Solomon ends with Jerusalem sacked, her people exiled to Babylon, the Temple a smoking ruin.

Embedded in Kings are the stories of Elijah and Elisha, prophets God sent to fortify His people at a pivotal time in their history. Elijah was contemporaneous with Israel's king Ahab whose rabid wife Jezebel was bent on imposing Baal worship come what may. Only his humiliation of Baal on Mount Carmel saved the day. The spate of miracles that Elisha performed gave further assurance over the testing years ahead.

The death of David (1:1 – 2:46)

Alerted to a bid by Adonijah to get himself accepted as heir to the throne, David has Solomon anointed king shortly before he dies. Solomon's reign begins with bloodshed. First Adonijah is killed when he effectively makes one last desperate bid for the throne by seeking to marry Abishag, the nurse-concubine who had comforted David in his declining years.[1] Then Joab and Shimei are slaughtered in deference to David's deathbed advice.[2] Zadok is appointed priest in place of Abiathar.[3]

Solomon's early years (3:1 – 5:14)

Solomon marries Pharaoh's daughter. Although he loves Yahweh he also offers sacrifice on the high places and permits the people to do the same.[4] He chooses wisdom and moral discernment when Yahweh offers him gifts and is promised riches and glory too. His wisdom is exemplified in the story of the two harlots arguing over a smothered baby.
Appendix 1 refers

Twelve administrators are appointed to organise provisions for Solomon and his entourage, one for each month of the year. This is a time of peace and plenty, security and military might. In territorial terms the kingdom is at its height. Solomon becomes famous for his wisdom and composes many songs and proverbs.

Solomon builds the Temple (5:15 – 9:25)

Solomon obtains cedar wood and juniper from Hiram, king of Tyre, in return for wheat and oil. He levies a task force for carving the trees and quarrying stone and builds a Temple in fulfilment of God's word to David, 2S 7:12–13. The work takes seven years and Yahweh promises to make it His home provided Israel follows His precepts. Solomon then spends another thirteen years building himself a palace.

As soon as the Temple is complete the Ark is installed there and Yahweh takes possession. In a public address Solomon extols God's majesty and praises His love and faithfulness. Although Yahweh has a presence in the Temple, he continues, He cannot be contained there. Even the heavens cannot hold Him. May Yahweh honour His promise that one of David's descendants will always rule over Israel. May He dispense justice, forgive His people's sins and heed their prayers if they sincerely repent. May He hear the prayers of foreigners too. May Yahweh turn His people's hearts to obedience and be with Israel so that all peoples may come to know the one true God (5:15 – 8:66).

God assures Solomon that his dynasty is secure so long as His laws are kept. Otherwise

Israel will be banished.[5] We now learn that Solomon ceded twenty towns to Hiram in return for the timber and gold he received for the Temple and how he conscripted Canaanites still living in the land into labour gangs and employed them not only on the Temple and his palace but also to strengthen Jerusalem's defences, to create fortress towns, and to build granaries and stabling for his horses and war chariots[6] (9:1–25).

Solomon at his zenith (9:26 – 10:29)

Solomon commissions a Red Sea fleet and a flourishing trade results. When the Queen of Sheba pays a visit she is amazed at the splendour of his court. Solomon enjoys an international reputation for wisdom and enjoys a huge income from trade and taxes. He garrisons Israel with chariots and cavalry.

God's judgement on Solomon (11:1–43)

Solomon takes foreign wives and as he grows older worships their gods as well as Yahweh. As a result God tells him that he has forfeit the kingdom though this will not happen until his son's lifetime. Edom and Damascus, crushed by David, regain their independence. The empire is beginning to get whittled away.

Ahijah, a prophet, tears his cloak into twelve strips and gives ten of them to Jeroboam, an Ephraimite officer in charge of labour gangs, as a sign that he will be king over ten of the tribes on Solomon's death. He flees to Egypt when Solomon gets wind of the prophecy and tries to kill him. Solomon dies after a forty year reign.

The division of the kingdom (12:1 – 13:34)

At an assembly at Shechem called to proclaim Solomon's son Rehoboam king, all the tribes except Judah and Benjamin rebel against the harsh conditions they had suffered under Solomon and when Rehoboam, misjudging the mood, brusquely refuses to countenance reform, declare their independence with Jeroboam as the king of Israel in the north. Judah and Benjamin stay faithful to Rehoboam as king of Judah in the south.[7]

To discourage his people from going to Jerusalem to worship, Jeroboam establishes two shrines with golden calves at either end of his realm, at Bethel in the south and Dan in the far north. He also establishes shrines on the high places and appoints non levitical priests.[8] A man of God from Judah prophesies the future destruction of the altar at Bethel by a son of the House of David named Josiah.[9]

Early kings of Israel and Judah (14:1 – 16:34)

Jeroboam learns from Ahijah that because of his infidelity his dynasty faces a violent end. Pagan rites also proliferate in Judah. As a result Judah is invaded by Egypt and both the Temple and Rehoboam's palace are plundered. In an act which symbolises the end of Judah's golden age Rehoboam is forced to replace with bronze the golden shields which Solomon had made for the palace guards.

Rehoboam is succeeded by Abijam and then Asa. Asa is commended for introducing religious reforms although these stop short of abolishing the high places. He is at war with Israel throughout his reign and forced to strip the treasury to enlist Aram's help. His son Jehoshaphat becomes king on his death (14:1 – 15:24).

In Israel Nadab, who succeeded Jeroboam, is murdered after a two year reign while campaigning against the Philistines.[10] His assassin, Baasha, seizes the throne and fulfils Ahijah's prophecy by slaughtering Jeroboam's entire family. Baasha is succeeded by his son Elah but survives only two years before he too is murdered along with all his kinsmen.

Elah's assassin, Zimri, is ousted after only seven days by Omri the army chief and commits suicide. Omri wins the ensuing civil war and founds Samaria as Israel's capital. He is followed by his son Ahab who marries Jezebel, an unholy union that, with its unfettered support of Baalism, poses Yahwehism its severest challenge so far (15:25 – 16:34).

Elijah defeats Baal on Mount Carmel (17:1 – 18:46)

It was in these dark times that God raised up a great prophet. Elijah the Tishbite enters the arena without preamble of any kind, standing before Ahab and proclaiming a drought.[11] He goes into hiding where he is fed by ravens before moving on to Sidon where he miraculously succours a widow and restores her dead son back to life.

When, in the third year of the drought, Ahab sent his chamberlain Obadiah to find Elijah it was to usher in one of the Bible's most epic confrontations. Jezebel was set on wiping out Israel's faith even if it meant butchering Yahweh's prophets to a man.[12] The people were hedging their bets between Yahweh and Baal, 'hobbling first on one leg then on the other'. Faced by four hundred and fifty prophets of Baal on Mount Carmel Elijah threw down the gauntlet. He called for two bulls to be slaughtered, one for Baal, one for Yahweh so that each side could invoke heavenly fire to consume them and thus demonstrate who really was the true God. He sarcastically goaded the prophets of Baal as they vainly appealed to their god, 'perhaps he is busy or asleep', and when it came to his turn rubbed salt in the wound by soaking his offering in water. His trust was rewarded. When Elijah finally invoked Him, Yahweh showed that He was God and Baal no god at all by sending down fire so intense that it not only consumed Elijah's bull but burned up the remains of the water as well.

To Elijah this was a holy war between Yahweh and false prophets leading others astray and his subsequent ruthless slaughter of the Baalists must be seen in that light. Later the same day a downpour ended the drought.[13]

Elijah encounters God at Horeb (19:1–21)

Despite his triumph Elijah is forced to flee as Jezebel thirsts for revenge. Pausing in the desert near Beersheba, depressed and lonely, he feels a failure and wishes he was dead. He is fed by an angel and then makes the long trek to Horeb where, spending the night in a cave, he bewails his fate. Despite all his efforts Israel has abandoned the covenant.

God's prophets have been slaughtered. His own life is in danger and he is all alone.

God orders him out on to the mountain to witness a hurricane, an earthquake and a fire. Then He speaks to him in a still small voice. God assures him that he is not alone. There are seven thousand others who refuse to bend the knee to Baal. There is work for him to do. He is to anoint Hazael as king of Aram, Jehu as king of Israel and Elisha as his own successor. Between them they will punish Israel.[14] Leaving Horeb Elijah comes upon Elisha while ploughing. Elisha accepts his call, cooking his oxen for food to mark a new beginning.

Naboth's vineyard: start of the Aramaean wars (20:1 – 22:54)

Guided by a prophet Ahab defies overwhelming odds to defeat Ben-Hadad of Aram in two campaigns. However another prophet condemns him for his clemency in letting Ben-Hadad go free when he had him in his power. He will pay for this lapse with his life and Israel will also suffer for it.

Incited by Jezebel Ahab has a landowner named Naboth stoned to death on a trumped up charge of blasphemy because he covets his vineyard. Elijah declares that because of this sin his House will be wiped out and Jezebel will also come to a violent end. However after Ahab repents Yahweh defers these disasters to a later generation.

Three years later Ahab forges an alliance with Jehoshaphat of Judah to recover Ramoth-Gilead from Aram. His own prophets promise success but Jehoshaphat insists on consulting a prophet of his own who, after some sarcastic overtures, prophesies the disaster that in fact befalls. Ahab is wounded by a chance arrow and dies bravely on the battlefield as his demoralised troops run for home. His son Ahaziah reigns in his stead while in Judah Jehoshaphat is succeeded by his son Jehoram.

2 Kings

Elijah and Ahaziah (1:1–18)

Moab rebels against Israel. Ahaziah king of Israel injures himself falling from a balcony and sends messengers to enquire of a Philistine god if he will recover. Elijah intercepts them and prophesies that because he did not consult Yahweh Ahaziah will die. Two companies of men sent to bring Elijah to report to the king in person are engulfed by fire. However Elijah agrees to accompany a third contingent and delivers his prophecy to the king's own ears. Ahaziah duly dies and his brother Jehoram succeeds him.

Elijah is taken up to heaven (2:1–13)

Accompanied only by Elisha, Elijah parts the Jordan with his cloak and makes a miraculous crossing. Elisha asks to inherit a double share of Elijah's spirit (tantamount to being designated his heir). Shortly afterwards a chariot and horses of fire appear and Elijah is taken up to heaven in a whirlwind. As he sees this (the fact of seeing it confirming his double share of his master's spirit) Elisha cries out 'My father! My father! Chariot of Israel and its chargers', probably meaning that Elijah had been of more value to Israel than all its chariots and chargers.
Appendix 1 refers

Elisha's early miracles (2:14 – 6:7)

Empowered with Elijah's spirit Elisha performs his first miracles. Retracing his steps he parts the Jordan with Elijah's cloak, purifies foul water at Jericho, and allows bears to maul a gang of small boys for disrespectfully calling him 'baldy'.

Supported by Judah and Edom, Jehoram attacks Moab. During a long desert march his forces run out of water and are only saved from disaster when Elisha, stimulated by music, orders them to dig ditches. Next morning the ditches are full of water.[1] The Moabites are routed and fall back on their capital where the king of Moab engineers the allies' withdrawal by sacrificing his eldest son on the city walls[2] (2:14 – 3:27).

Elisha multiplies a widow's oil to save her from insolvency and her sons from slavery; promises a child to a well-to-do woman of Shunem married to an elderly husband; restores the boy to life after he dies a few years later; purifies poisoned stew at Gilgal; and satisfies the hunger of a hundred men with twenty barley loaves.[3]

Elisha heals Naaman, the Aramaean army chief, of a skin disease.[4] The same ailment is later contracted by Elisha's servant Gehazi as punishment for dishonestly soliciting payment from Naaman for the cure. Elisha miraculously retrieves an axe that had sunk in the Jordan (4:1 – 5:27).

Elisha and the Aramaean wars (6:1 – 8:29)

After war breaks out between Aram and Israel the king of Aram sends a task force to capture Elisha after he discovers that the prophet is able to anticipate his war strategy. Elisha is surrounded but is protected by fiery horses and chariots seen in a vision. As they start to move towards him the Aramaeans are temporarily sun-blinded, enabling Elisha to lead them into Samaria where they are later released unharmed.

On another occasion when the Aramaeans besieged Samaria the famine was so acute that the people resorted to cannibalism. The king blamed Elisha and only stayed his hand from having him beheaded when Elisha predicted that the siege would be lifted the next day.[5] That evening Yahweh caused the terrified Aramaeans to hear the sound of a great army advancing against them and fled in disarray (6:1 – 7:20).

Thanks to Elisha's prestige the Shunemmite woman's property is restored to her when she returns home after spending seven years in Philistia to escape a famine. In Damascus Elisha meets Hazael and foretells the terrible atrocities he will inflict on Israel as the future king of Aram. Next day Hazael smothers the king of Aram and seizes the throne.

Jehoram king of Judah marries Athaliah, one of Ahab's daughters. He is succeeded by his son Ahaziah who joins forces with Israel in a campaign against Aram in which Jehoram of Israel is severely wounded. Edom regains her independence from Judah (8:1–29).

Jehu's revolution (9:1 – 10:36)

Elisha has a prophet secretly anoint Jehu king of Israel and direct him to stamp out Jezebel and Ahab's entire family. Wasting no time Jehu hastens to Jezreel where he slays the convalescing Jehoram. Ahaziah king of Judah, who had been visiting Jehoram, is fatally wounded while trying to escape. Jezebel, taunting and haughty to the end, is thrown out of a window and run over by Jehu's chariot. Keen to eliminate all possible rivals Jehu then has Ahab's whole family butchered along with Ahaziah's kinsmen. Finally he massacres the followers of Baal and their priests and destroys their temple (but not the shrines at Dan and Bethel). Yahweh tells Jehu that his dynasty will survive until the fourth generation. Israel loses all her territory east of the Jordan to Hazael. Jehu is succeeded by his son Jehoahaz.

From Athaliah to the death of Elisha (11:1 – 13:25)

In Judah Athaliah, the queen mother, seizes power by massacring the entire royal family except Ahaziah's infant son Jehoash who is hidden in the Temple. David's line is all but extinct. Six years later she herself is murdered following a coup led by Jehoiada the high priest and supported by the army. Jehoash (or Joash) is crowned king. Jehoiada pledges fidelity to Yahweh and the temple of Baal is demolished.

Grown to manhood Jehoash assumes responsibility for refurbishing the Temple from the priests who had shown little enthusiasm for the task. He buys off Hazael from attacking Jerusalem with gold from the palace and Temple treasuries. He is eventually murdered by his servants and succeeded by his son Amaziah (11:1 – 12:22).

Israel is defeated by Aram during Jehoahaz's reign and her army reduced to a shadow of its former strength. His successor Jehoash (or Joash) is more successful, defeating Aram in three campaigns and recapturing the ground lost by his father. This series of victories is the subject of Elisha's last recorded act as he takes Jehoash to task for his lack of persistence in striking the ground with his arrows to symbolise victories over Aram. Elisha dies. But even in death one last miracle attends God's indefatigable prophet. The body of a Moabite thrown into his tomb comes to life when it touches Elisha's bones (13:1–25).

Amaziah and Jeroboam II to Ahaz (14:1 – 16:20)

Emboldened by a victory over Edom Amaziah recklessly challenges Israel to battle. He is heavily defeated and the Temple ransacked. A coup results in Amaziah being murdered and replaced by his son Uzziah while in Israel Jehoash is succeeded by his son Jeroboam II. (Both kings presided over periods of great prosperity and recovery of lost land.)

Uzziah is succeeded by his son Jotham and he in turn by his son Ahaz. Israel now enters a period of turbulence. Jeroboam II's son Zechariah is murdered after only six months. His killer Shallum assumes the throne only to be murdered himself after one month by Menahem who reigns for ten years during which time he is forced to pay tribute to Assyria. Menahem's son Pekahiah succeeds him but is assassinated after two years by Pekah. Pekah manages to cling to power for twenty years but then he too falls victim to a murder plot following a reign which sees large tracts of Galilee and Transjordan lost to Assyria. Pekah's killer, Hoshea, becomes Israel's last king (14:1 – 15:38).

In contrast to the good intentions of his two predecessors Ahaz in Judah reverts to worshipping on the high places and even performing child sacrifice. When Aram and Israel unite to attack Judah he plies Tiglath-Pileser, king of Assyria, with gold and silver to come to his aid. During a visit to Damascus after the war Ahaz is so impressed by an altar he sees there that he has a copy made for the Temple in Jerusalem to replace the original installed by Solomon. Ahaz is succeeded by his son Hezekiah (16:1–20).

Israel's deportation to Assyria (17:1–41)

Israel is invaded by Assyria and forced to pay tribute. When Hoshea makes overtures to Egypt and withholds tribute the Assyrians put him in chains and launch a full scale invasion. Samaria is captured after a three year siege and the people are deported to Assyria.[6] The Assyrians settle people from other parts of their dominions in Samaria resulting in a population with a hybrid religion, partly pagan, partly Yahwist.[7] In a long excursus Kings tells us that this all happened because despite many warnings Israel had treated the covenant with contempt and abandoned Yahweh for other gods.

Hezekiah's reforms: Jerusalem's deliverance from Assyria (18:1 – 20:21)

In Judah Hezekiah abolishes the high places and other emblems of Baal worship and even destroys Moses' bronze serpent because it had become an object of idolatrous worship. He rebels against Assyria and pushes back the Philistines.

Some years later Sennacherib of Assyria mounts an invasion. He appeals to the people to surrender but when Isaiah is consulted he prophesies that Sennacherib will abandon the attack and return home where he will fall by the sword. His prophecy is fulfilled the same night. As morning breaks the Assyrian camp is littered with corpses. Sennacherib strikes camp and returns home where he is later murdered by his two sons[8] (18:1 – 19:37).

Yahweh grants Hezekiah an extra fifteen years of life after he prays to be delivered from a grave illness. He sees his shadow shortening rather than lengthening in the setting sun as a sign of God's favour. When a delegation from Babylon arrives to congratulate him on his recovery, and the flattered Hezekiah shows them all his treasures and armaments, Isaiah rebukes him on the grounds that Babylon will one day be an enemy. Hezekiah digs a tunnel to safeguard Jerusalem's water supply. His son Manasseh succeeds him (20:1–21).

Apostasy under Manasseh and Amon (21:1–26)

Manasseh reverses Hezekiah's reforms, restores the high places, allows child sacrifice and sets up altars to Baal, even in the Temple. As a result Yahweh decrees that Jerusalem will suffer the same fate as Samaria. Manasseh's successor Amon is no better and after a two year reign is murdered by his palace officials in favour of his son Josiah.

The Book of the Law: Josiah's reforms (22:1 – 23:27)

During Temple repairs Hilkiah the high priest discovers the Book of the Law.[9] When it is read to him Josiah realises how far the nation has lapsed. Huldah, a prophetess, confirms his fears and foretells that Yahweh's wrath will result in disaster striking Judah. However because of his piety and penance this would not happen in Josiah's own lifetime.

Josiah embarks upon a program of reform. He orders that worship must be confined to one sanctuary. He burns the Baal cult objects, unsanctifies the high places, outlaws sacred prostitution and child sacrifice, and tears down the sacred pillars and poles. He slaughters illegitimate priests (those who had officiated at high places following Canaanite rites) and calls others (those who, despite worshipping at high places, had followed the orthodox Yahwist liturgy) in to Jerusalem where, although they would receive their keep, they would not be able to preside at the altar (because there were too many of them). He destroys the altar at Bethel and extends his reforms into Samaria.

The Passover is celebrated with more devotion than at any time since the days of the judges. Yet Yahweh's wrath is unassuaged.

Judah's last days (23:28 – 25:30)

Josiah is killed at Megiddo in battle with the Egyptians under Necho. His son Jehoahaz succeeds him but after only three months Necho deposes him in favour of his brother Jehoiakim and extorts a heavy tribute. Jehoahaz is carried off to Egypt where he dies.

A few years later Nebuchadnezzar king of Babylon invades Judah and reduces her to a vassal state. When Judah revolts three years later he encourages raiding parties from the neighbouring tribes to harass her. After a reign of eleven years Jehoiakim is succeeded by his son Jehoiachin and Nebuchadnezzar again invades Judah. Jerusalem surrenders and after a reign of just three months Jehoiachin is carried off to Babylon along with treasures from the palace and the Temple, the nobles, the artisan classes and all the men of military age. Nebuchadnezzar installs Jehoiachin's uncle Zedekiah on the throne.[10]

Nine years later Zedekiah launches a rebellion. Nebuchadnezzar returns to the attack and after an eighteen month siege captures Jerusalem for the second time. This time there is no mercy. The Temple is burned down and plundered, the city walls demolished. Zedekiah is blinded and deported to Babylon with all except the poorest people. Nebuchadnezzar appoints Gedaliah as governor of the rump of Judah. When, after a few months, he is assassinated the remaining people flee to Egypt in fear of retaliation.

After thirty-seven years in exile Jehoiachin is freed from prison and given an honourable position at the Babylonian court. Kings ends on a ray of hope.

1 Chronicles

1 and 2 Chronicles constitute a second set of historical books alongside Samuel and Kings. However almost half of Chronicles is paralleled in Samuel and Kings, often word for word. Elsewhere the Chronicler is highly selective in his choice of material with a viewpoint slanting to the Temple, the priesthood and the liturgy. He devotes seven whole chapters to David's plans for the Temple and its personnel. Even more than in Kings secular concerns have only minor walk-on roles.

The Chronicler is very much his own man. Where Kings blames Solomon for the schism that followed his death the Chronicler casts Jeroboam as the villain. Unlike Kings he sees Abijah as one of Judah's worthier sovereigns. He ascribes to Manasseh a conversion of which Kings knows nothing. After Solomon he concentrates exclusively on the southern kingdom of Judah. By cutting themselves off from the Ark in Jerusalem and rejecting the House of David, the Chronicler implies that the northern tribes had effectively rejected God Himself.

David and Solomon are painted as paragons of virtue. Virtually everything that could tarnish their reputations, such as David's affair with Bathsheba, is studiously ignored. According to Chronicles both gained the throne with unqualified support.

'God is with those who are with Him but deserts those who desert Him', 2Ch 15:2. This is the Chronicler's leitmotiv. Yahweh answered Asa's prayer for victory over the Cushites but withdrew His favour when he later sought Aram's help, 2Ch 14:8–12; 16:7–9. He rewarded Jehoshaphat's loyalty but punished him with the loss of his fleet when he formed a trading partnership with the idolatrous northern kingdom, 2Ch 17:3–11; 20:1–30, 35–37. Yet despite these examples of divine justice the Chronicler is very much alive to God's mercy to the humble and contrite, 2Ch 7:14; 30:9. Twice, under Rehoboam as under Hezekiah, He held His hand when Judah repented, 2Ch 12:5–8,12; 32:26. Even the evil Manasseh was restored to God's favour once he recanted, 2Ch 33:11–20.

The Chronicler's aim seems to have been to encourage the post-exilic community living in poverty and obscurity around Jerusalem. The glorious days of David and Solomon might have passed but God had not forsaken His people. With genealogies he called to mind their descent from Abraham and their election as God's people. He recalled God's promise to David of an everlasting dynasty. He glorified the Israel of David and Solomon as a golden age with life centred around the Temple. By ignoring the northern tribes, who had been deaf to Yahweh, he underlined that Judah was now the 'true Israel', the rightful heir to God's covenant promises.

It was true that Judah had also proved unfaithful and suffered but God's punishment of evil and blessing of righteousness in the past must surely foster hope for the future. David's line might have lapsed for the moment but God's promises endure and if Judah remained faithful all would be well. And so it is that Chronicles ends with the pale glow of dawn as Cyrus commands the rebuilding of the Temple.

Genealogies: Adam to David (1:1 – 9:44)

Chronicles opens with genealogies, beginning with Adam but quickly focusing on the twelve tribes and then Judah and Levi, David and Saul. David's line is extended to post-exilic times and Saul's descendants are also traced for several generations. The lists are selective – Cain and Abel are omitted – and there are occasional discrepancies and ambiguities. Chapter 9 jumps from ancient times to list the first exiles to return from Babylon with special reference to Temple personnel and their duties.

David (10:1 – 29:30)

The Chronicler leans on Samuel as he relates: Saul's death, 10:1–12; David's anointing as king of Israel at Hebron and his capture of Jerusalem, 11:1–9; David's champions, 11:10–47; how the Ark was moved to Jerusalem, 13:1–14; 15:1 – 16:3; victories over the Philistines, 14:1–17; Nathan's prophecy that David's dynasty would endure for ever, 17:1–27; David's campaigns against Ammon and Aram, 18:1 – 20:8; and how the Temple came to be built on the site of a former threshing-floor, 21:1 – 22:1.

He adds to Samuel and Kings: his judgement that Saul's death was the result of his infidelity to Yahweh, 10:13–14; lists of men who espoused David's cause in his early years, 12:1–41; a hymn of thanksgiving for the recovery of the Ark, 16:4–36; the appointment of priests to minister before the Ark in Jerusalem and at the Dwelling at Gibeon, 16:37–43; preparations for building the Temple,[1] 22:2–19; 28:1–21; David's prayer of thanksgiving for gifts to help pay for the Temple, 29:1–30; his redeployment of the Levites when they were no longer needed to carry the Dwelling,[2] 23:1 – 26:32; and various secular appointments, 27:1–34. He omits David's struggles with Saul and Ishbaal, his adultery with Bathsheba and Absalom's rebellion.

2 Chronicles

We highlight the main differences from Kings as each king of Judah is reviewed in turn.

Solomon (1:1 – 9:31)

Chronicles follows Kings in tracing Solomon's wisdom, his military might and wealth, and his building of the Temple.[1] However he makes no mention of the murders of Joab and Shimei nor of Adonijah's attempted coup. Equally he ignores the profligacy of Solomon's later years and makes only the most fleeting reference to his palace.

Rehoboam (10:1 – 12:16)

Two items are additional. First a reported migration of priests and Levites from Israel to Judah after Jeroboam appointed his own priests. Secondly a claim that Yahweh spared Jerusalem even worse ravaging than she in fact received from the Egyptians under Shishak once Rehoboam and his generals repented.

Abijah (13:1–23)

Chronicles has Abijah (Abijam in Kings) placing the blame for the break up of Solomon's kingdom squarely on Jeroboam's and Israel's shoulders rather than Solomon's as in 1K 11.

Asa (14:1 – 16:14)

Three items are additional to Kings. First the Chronicler describes how Yahweh routed invading Cushites after Asa invoked His help. Second he gives greater weight to Asa's religious reforms than Kings and attributes them to the inspiration of the prophet Azariah. Third he reports the seer Hanani condemning Asa for enlisting Aram's help to repel an attack from Israel rather than relying on Yahweh.

Jehoshaphat (17:1 – 21:1)

Chronicles gives a more rounded picture of one of Judah's worthier kings. After reporting how a prophet rebuked him for supporting the impious Ahab it describes the zeal with which he despatched a team of laymen and priests to teach the Law throughout Judah. It relates his creation of a strong army, his reformation of the judiciary, and how Yahweh rewarded his faith with a resounding victory over a massive invasion of Moabites, Ammonites and Edomites. It also tells how later on, when he parleyed with the northern kingdom, he came to grief.

Jehoram, Ahaziah, Athaliah and Joash (22:1 – 24:27)

Chronicles reveals that Jehoram suffered bowel disease and that Judah suffered invasion as punishment for his sins.[2] It adds little else to Kings apart from reporting Joash's abandonment of Yahweh in later life and his murder of the prophet Zechariah as a result of which the invasion by Aram is portrayed as divine punishment.[3]

Amaziah, Uzziah and Jotham (25:1 – 27:9)

The chronicler augments Kings' reference to Amaziah's victory over Edom by ascribing it to Amaziah trusting Yahweh rather than employing mercenaries. His subsequent humiliation at the hands of Israel is interpreted as punishment for worshipping the captured Edomite gods (25:1–28). Kings' brief treatment of Uzziah is amplified with details of a successful campaign against the Philistines and by attributing his skin disease to his contravening the Law by burning incense in the Temple[4] (26:1–23). Except for mention of a war with Ammon the Chronicler's record of Jotham accords with Kings (27:1–9).

Ahaz and Hezekiah (28:1 – 32:33)

The review of Ahaz's reign differs from Kings in two respects: in the story of Israel heeding the prophet Oded and releasing prisoners of war from Judah; and in blackening Ahaz's character even more than Kings (28:1–27). Whereas Kings concentrates its survey of Hezekiah's reign on Jerusalem's escape from Sennacherib, Chronicles gives pride of place to his religious reforms: the purification of the Temple, the restoration of the traditional liturgy, the celebration of the Passover and the re-establishment of the priestly and levitical orders, none of which is in Kings (29:1 – 32:33).

Manasseh and Amon (33:1–25)

Kings paints Manasseh as the worst of Judah's kings. Chronicles agrees but goes on to relate how, after reneging on his father's reforms, Manasseh was imprisoned in Babylon where he repented. Returning home he cleansed the Temple of its pagan emblems and accepted Yahweh as God. However it would appear from the retrograde conduct of his son Amon, about whom the Chronicler adds nothing, that these reforms had no lasting impact.

Josiah (34:1 – 35:27)

Chronicles places Josiah's reforms before the discovery of the Book of the Law and casts a shadow over him by reporting that when he engaged Necho in the battle that cost him his life he was acting against God's will.

Judah's last days (36:1–23)

The chronicler adds mention of a deportation to Babylon in Jehoiakim's reign (also reported at Dn 1:1–2) and Cyrus' call, many years later, to rebuild the Temple in words that are repeated as the opening lines of Ezra.

Ezra

Ezra and Nehemiah are closely related. They form a sequel to Kings and Chronicles and describe the Jews' return from exile, featuring the main events in their religious history over the next hundred years: the rebuilding of the Temple and the reinforcement of the Law.

Ezra's contribution was enormous. When he arrived on the scene the Jews were an island of wavering faith in a sea of paganism that could easily have engulfed them. He countered the threat by imposing the Law. He gave the little community, whose hopes were strained by the hardships of life back in Palestine and the non-realisation of Deutero-Isaiah's exultant prophecies, a new spiritual vitality. Having been divested of statehood all the Jews had left was their religious patrimony. So he used this to give them a new focus, converting their aspirations to be a nation state into becoming the covenant people they were always meant to be.

With hindsight his reforms were unbalanced. They were strong on banning mixed marriages, Sabbath observance and tithing but light on justice, mercy and humility. Ezra wanted the Jews to be a special people but forgot what for. He is silent on Israel's missionary role. And gradually the Jews' devotion to the Law degenerated into the self-righteous legalism that Jesus so roundly condemned.

However it would be wrong to lay the blame wholly at Ezra's door. The fault also lay with those who perpetuated measures like the embargo on mixed marriages long after they were necessary. One thing is certain. Without Ezra's reforming zeal it is by no means certain that the Jews could have resisted the encroachment of paganism or that the embers of Yahweh worship could have been fanned back to life as quickly as they were.

Ezra was a religious zealot. His contemporary Nehemiah, although also imbued in prayer and piety, was more a man of the world. Courageous, an inspiring leader, an achiever, he provided the physical security of city walls without which Ezra's reforms could not have taken root. When, on his second visit to Jerusalem he discovered the abuses that had re-emerged during his absence, he acted with a dynamism and fervour worthy of Ezra himself. But whereas Ezra broke up mixed marriages Nehemiah saw fit only to denounce them.

The exiles return from Babylon (1:1 – 2:70)

Cyrus issued an edict allowing the Jews to return to Jerusalem and rebuild the Temple. He also returned the Temple vessels (which Nebuchadnezzar had removed) to Sheshbazzar, the leader of the first contingent.[1] Those who did not wish to return contributed gold, silver and other offerings. A manifest of the group includes Zerubbabel and Joshua.[2] On arrival the people went to their own towns while the priests and Levites settled in Jerusalem.

The rebuilding of the Temple begun (3:1 – 4:5)

Seven months after their arrival Zerubbabel and Joshua rebuilt the altar of burnt offering despite fear of the 'people of the country', and the traditional liturgy was resumed. Some months later the foundations of the new Temple were laid amidst outpourings of great emotion from those old enough to remember the former Temple.[3] 'Enemies' offered to help but began to stir up trouble when they were rebuffed.[4]

Complaints (4:6–23)

From the names of the Persian kings that are quoted this passage clearly relates to events some decades after the rebuilding of the Temple. Nothing is known of what 4:6 and 4:7 refer to but 4:8–23 is an exchange of correspondence resulting in an attempt by the Jews to restore Jerusalem's walls being forcibly stopped.[5]

The rebuilding of the Temple completed (4:24 – 6:22)

When the narrative resumes we learn that work on the Temple was also held up for some 16 years. Then, inspired by the prophets Haggai and Zechariah, Zerubbabel and Joshua make a fresh start. Tattenai, the Persian governor, questioned their authority and petitioned the Persian king Darius to search the archives to confirm that they were complying with Cyrus' original decree. Darius not only did that but ruled that the Temple restoration be given every assistance and paid for out of the royal exchequer. The Temple was completed in Darius's sixth year.

Ezra journeys to Jerusalem (7:1 – 8:36)

We now jump nearly 60 years when, with the blessing of the then king Artaxerxes Ezra, a scribe and descendant of Aaron, journeyed from Babylon to Jerusalem with a caravan of returning exiles, a journey lasting four months.[6] Despite carrying a large consignment of gold and other valuables for the Temple, donated both by the Persian authorities and the Jews in Babylon, he declined the king's offer of a military escort, putting his trust in God. His commission was to apply the Law and restore the ancestral faith. Ezra accordingly made sure that his party included Levites for service in the Temple.

Ezra condemns mixed marriages (9:1 – 10:44)

On arrival Ezra was appalled at the prevalence of mixed marriages.[7] He made the community promise to dissolve them and send the alien wives and children away.

Nehemiah

See Ezra

Rebuilding Jerusalem's walls (1:1 – 4:17)

It was in the twentieth year of the reign of Artaxerxes king of Persia that Nehemiah, his cupbearer, learned of the lamentable state Jerusalem was in. The walls were in ruins, the people demoralised. So at great personal risk he persuaded Artaxerxes to let him go to Jerusalem to rebuild it.[1] Shortly after arrival he went out secretly at night to survey the walls and only then did he divulge his determination to rebuild them. There was an enthusiastic response and work began. However Sanballat and his friends made fun of it[2] (1:1 – 2:20).

After specifying who was responsible for each section of the wall the narrative relates how Sanballat became increasingly incensed as the work progressed, so much so that Nehemiah was forced to mount guards. He armed the workers and persuaded them to lodge in the city at night to help protect it rather than going home (3:1 – 4:17).

An economic crisis (5:1–19)

Some economic crisis led Nehemiah to ask the nobles to cancel their creditors' debts. He made the point that as governor he himself had never drawn the subsistence allowance he was entitled to.[3]

Rebuilding the walls continued (6:1 – 7:72a)

Sanballat and his confederates made repeated attempts to intimidate Nehemiah. It got to the stage where a prophet named Shemaiah attempted to entice him to take refuge in the inner sanctum of the Temple on the pretext that his life was in danger, a bait he contemptuously refused.[4] After 52 days, despite a rump of disaffected nobles stirring up trouble, the walls were complete (6:1–19).

Nehemiah now made arrangements for securing the city gates and ordered a census. A listing he discovered of the names of the first exiles to have returned is in substantial agreement with that quoted earlier at Ezr 2 (7:1–72a).

Ezra expounds the Law (7:72b – 8:18)

Everyone gathered to hear Ezra read the Book of the Law.[5] He stood on a wooden dais and read from dawn until noon while the people stood in rapt attention with the Levites on hand ready to explain. The people were moved to tears until he told them that it was a time for joy rather than sadness. Next day they began celebrating the feast of Shelters.

Public confession of sin (9:1–37)

Later that month, dressed in sackcloth and with dust on their heads, the people convened for a fast. Those who had severed mixed marriages confessed their sins. Then Ezra led them all in penitential prayer. Acknowledging God as creator, he reviewed the turning points in Israel's history from Abraham onwards. He recalled Israel's rebellious nature and God's compassion and admitted that Yahweh had been just in disciplining her. He had remained faithful while Israel had proven unfaithful. The prayer ended with a recognition of their present plight: slaves in the country He had given their ancestors.

The climax came in a solemn act of renewal when the people pledged to obey the Law. In particular they undertook to eschew mixed marriages; to refrain from trading on the Sabbath; to observe the sabbatical year; to pay the Temple tax; and to make tithe and other offerings as prescribed by the Law (10:1–40).

Jerusalem re-populated: various lists (11:1 – 12:26)

Lots were drawn to determine which families (one in every ten) would be required to move to Jerusalem.[6] Various lists follow: the names of Jews living in Jerusalem; other towns where Jews lived; priests and Levites who returned from Babylon with Zerubbabel and Joshua; the names of other priests and Levites.

The dedication of the walls (12:27–43)

The dedication ceremony involved two processions, each with a choir, making their ways along the walls in opposite directions, one led by Ezra, the other followed by Nehemiah. They entered the Temple to offer sacrifice amidst scenes of great rejoicing.

Supplementary notes (12:44 – 13:3)

Nehemiah notes how supervisors were appointed for the storerooms where first-fruit and other offerings were kept. He pays tribute to the priests and Levites, and also the Temple musicians and guards, for their devotion to the liturgy and recalls how everyone contributed to their upkeep. The passage ends with a reminder that foreigners must be excluded from the community.[7]

Nehemiah's second visit to Jerusalem (13:4–31)

During a second visit to Jerusalem Nehemiah took steps to eliminate various abuses that had crept in during his absence. He reprimanded the Temple officials when he found that the Levites and musicians were not receiving their proper subsistence and were being forced to return to their villages to earn a living. He reinstituted tithing and forbade trading on the Sabbath, posting guards at the city gates to prevent merchants importing their produce before the Sabbath was over. Tradesmen who tried to set up their stalls by the city walls were threatened with eviction. He flew into a rage when he discovered men with foreign wives. Some of their children could not even speak Hebrew! As the crowning ignominy he discovered that one of the high priest's grandsons had married a daughter of his old adversary Sanballat! Finally he drew up regulations for the priests and Levites defining their roles.

Appendix 1 refers

Tobit

Tobit, one of the deutero-canonical books, is a work of religious fiction set shortly after the northern kingdom's fall to Assyria. It is a story of domestic harmony and piety, about people who recognise God as responsible for their blessings and who are never slow to thank Him. Tobit himself is a man of wholesome integrity, zealous in his faith to the point of risking his life but without ever appearing sanctimonious.

The book is intended to show that despite the ups and downs of life, during which even the most virtuous of people may have to contend with misfortunes they have done nothing to deserve, goodness finds its reward in the end. God is continually at work in ways we can rarely discern at the time. Tobias' journey to Rhages was intended to recover Tobit's silver but God used it to heal Tobit and Sarah and bring happiness to their families. Every turning point in Tobit is marked by prayer.

The author is free with his use of history. Sennacherib was Sargon's son not Shalmaneser's, 1:15. Tobit could not have witnessed both the division of the kingdom after Solomon's death, 1:4, and banishment to Nineveh, 1:10, two hundred years later. But these are incidentals.

Tobit was a devout man who excelled in the Law and charitable deeds and persisted in pilgrimage to Jerusalem when the rest of his family worshipped the idolatrous calf at nearby Dan.[1] With his wife Anna and son Tobias he was exiled to Nineveh where, alone among his fellow exiles, he continued to observe the dietary laws. Shalmaneser was king of Assyria at the time and, thanks to God, Tobit became his purveyor. While on a business trip he took the opportunity to deposit some sacks of silver at Rhages in Media. Tobit fell foul of the next king, Sennacherib, and was forced to flee but his successor allowed him to return (1:1–22).

After Tobit had been blinded by bird droppings Anna took up spinning and weaving to make ends meet. One day she came home with a kid in addition to her normal wages. Tobit suspected it was stolen and ordered her to return it. Piqued, Anna questioned what good all his good deeds had done him. Downcast Tobit prayed for death (2:1 – 3:6).

Meanwhile at Ecbatana in Media a maiden named Sarah, daughter of a certain Raguel, also prayed for death. She had been married seven times but a demon had killed all her husbands on their wedding nights.[2] God heard both prayers and sent Raphael to help them (3:7–17).

Preparing for death Tobit counselled his son Tobias to live virtuously and to go to Rhages to recover the silver he had left there. Raphael, who now is revealed to the reader as an angel but who the characters in the story think is a kinsman named Azarias, is chosen as a travelling companion (4:1 – 6:1).

On the journey Tobias caught a fish. Azarias told him to keep the creature's gall, heart and liver because the gall was useful for curing blindness and the heart and liver for expelling demons. On arrival in Ecbatana, two days journey from Rhages, they straightaway went to the home of Raguel and his wife Edna. (We now learn that Raguel was Tobit's brother, 7:1). Tobias, who had discussed Sarah with Raphael on the journey, asked for her hand in marriage. Raguel gave his consent and they were duly married.

That night in the bedroom Tobias placed the fish's heart and liver on the incense. Distressed by the reek the demon who had killed Sarah's previous husbands fled to Egypt where it was strangled by Raphael. Sarah and Tobias prayed for God's blessing. When he found that all was well Raguel also thanked God and had his servants quickly fill in the grave he had had dug as a precaution. Tobias sent Raphael to Rhages to collect the silver while he remained behind with Raguel to continue the wedding festivities (6:2 – 9:9).

Just as Tobit and Anna were becoming concerned at their son's long absence Tobias and his bride set out for home. After a joyful reunion Tobit's sight was restored as the fish's gall was applied to his eyes and he blessed God (10:1 – 11:18). When Tobit and Tobias attempted to pay Raphael for his help he revealed that he was one of seven angels always on hand to do God's bidding so it was God they must thank for their blessings with prayer, fasting and almsgiving.[3] Tobit's blindness had been a test of his faith. Tobit's final hymn is an effusion of praise and thanks followed by a vision of a Jerusalem gloriously restored as a light for distant nations (12:1 – 14:1).

On his deathbed Tobit urged Tobias to leave Nineveh for Media for he was sure that Nahum's prophecy (that Nineveh would be destroyed) would be fulfilled. Jerusalem and the Temple would also be laid waste and the people exiled before being restored in glory once 'the time was fulfilled'. When that happened all races would be converted. Those who loved God would rejoice while sinners and wickedness would vanish from the earth.

After Tobit and Anna had died Tobias moved his family to live with Raguel in Media where he lived to see Nineveh meet the fate his father had foreseen (14:2-15).

Judith

Judith is another of the deutero-canonical books. It is a tale of the triumph of faith and virtue over the arrogant power of evil. Judith, the heroine, is the archetype of Jewish piety, steadfast in faith and prayer: Holofernes, the enemy she outwits and overcomes, the incarnation of evil, loud in threats and blasphemy. The moral is plain. Even when all seems lost God can protect His own and thwart their enemies. With God's help even an unarmed woman is more than a match for the most powerful of armies.

As history the story is implausible. It is so riddled with inaccuracies that it is as if the author never intended it to be read as anything other than an edifying story and that he deliberately infused it with allusions to different periods – Assyrian, Babylonian, Persian – in order to portray a timeless enemy.[1]

After routing the Medes Nebuchadnezzar sent Holofernes, his army chief, on a punitive campaign against Persia and other countries that had declined to support him against the Medes. As Holofernes approached the Israelites they took up defensive positions and prayed (1:1 – 4:15).

Meanwhile back at army headquarters the Ammonite leader Achior was briefing Holofernes on Israel's history, telling him that he would only defeat her if she lapsed into sin and thereby lost God's favour. Holofernes contemptuously rejected this advice. He broke with Achior and had his orderlies escort him to nearby Bethulia, an Israelite stronghold, to share its fate (5:1 – 6:21).

Holofernes then proceeded to blockade Bethulia. Food and water were soon in short supply and the people began to think that God had abandoned them because of their sins. They were all for surrendering but Uzziah, an elder, persuaded them to hold out for five more days to give God a chance to come to their rescue (7:1–32)

When Judith, a beautiful well-to-do widow and devout upholder of the Law, heard of this she upbraided the elders for putting God to the test by setting a time limit. Unlike their ancestors, she went on, they had not been unfaithful. So they should pray and wait patiently for God's providence. The fate of all Judaea was at stake and God was using this ordeal to test them. Judith then revealed that she herself would be the tool God would use to save Israel (8:1–36).

After praying Judith dressed as alluringly as possible, packed a supply of ritually pure provisions, and made her way to Holofernes' camp where she pretended to be an informer. On being ushered into his presence she told Holofernes that Achior's assessment would work to his advantage since the Israelites were planning to sin by eating the first-fruits and tithes, food set aside for the priests which ordinary people were forbidden to touch. She therefore proposed going outside his camp every night to pray to be told when this had happened so that she could then alert him when to attack (9:1 – 11:23).

For three days Judith followed the same routine, leaving camp early every morning while it was still dark to purify herself and pray for her plan to succeed. On the evening of the fourth day Holofernes invited her to a banquet intending to seduce her. However by the time they were alone he had collapsed in a drunken stupor on his bed.

With a murmured prayer Judith seized her opportunity. She beheaded Holofernes with his own sword and then left the camp as usual as if to pray. But now she had Holofernes' head in her food bag and instead of going to pray made for Bethulia where she told the people all that had occurred and giving all the credit to God (12:1 – 13:20).

When he heard the news Achior became a believer. The Israelites hung Holofernes' head on the ramparts and mustered on the mountain slopes as if preparing for battle. On seeing this the Assyrians roused their commanders but when they came upon the headless Holofernes they panicked and fled. All Israel joined in the chase, massacring the Assyrians and capturing vast amounts of booty. Once the fighting was over Judith led a triumphant procession to Jerusalem, everyone singing God's praises for the epic events that had saved them (14:1 – 16:20).

Judith returned to Bethulia where she was held in high esteem. She never remarried and eventually died at the ripe old age of 105 (16:21–25).

Esther

Esther tells how the tables were turned when one man hatched a plot to wipe out the entire Jewish race. The episode is set in Susa, the winter capital of the Persian Empire, but how much is historical is debatable. Details of life at the Persian court are accurate but there are other inconsistencies and so the book is best read without concern for historicity as a story showing how God prospers the righteous and humbles the wicked.

Esther is controversial. God is never mentioned. Nor is there any mention of religious observance apart from brief references to fasting, Est 4:3,16; 9:31, and Mordecai's allusion to 'deliverance coming from another quarter', Est 4:14. However the book has Deutero-canonical additions (shown in italics below) and these do introduce a religious element, especially Mordecai's dream which purports to show how everything that happened was within the planned providence of God.

Where the unbeliever would see Esther riddled with coincidences the believer sees God in control, working through events that could easily be attributed to chance but which never override individual freedom.[1] He sees God protecting His people wherever they may be: even the Jews of Susa who never returned to their homeland. And he learns that evil brings its own settlement. Haman plotted Mordecai's death only to die himself. The script he wrote for his own glorification was used to glorify Mordecai.

The scene is set in the reign of the Persian king Ahasuerus.[2] Mordecai is a Jew holding high office at the royal court at Susa. He has a dream depicting the ultimate triumph of the upright after a period of darkness and distress. On a separate occasion he warns the king of a plot against his life. A certain Haman, a favourite of the king, resolves to take revenge against Mordecai[3] (1:1a–1r).

Heady with wine Ahasuerus banishes Vashti his queen for refusing to appear at a state banquet. After a lengthy search Esther, a Jewish maiden, wins the king's favour to become his new consort. Esther was the cousin and adopted daughter of Mordecai, a Jew employed in the Chancellery, whose family had been deported to Babylon by Nebuchadnezzar. Mordecai forbids Esther to divulge her race (1:1 – 2:18).

Mordecai warns the king of a plot to assassinate him. The perpetrators are executed and the incident is recorded in the Annals. Unfortunately Mordecai falls foul of the king's newly appointed grand vizier, Haman, for not showing him proper respect. When he discovers Mordecai is a Jew Haman resolves to avenge the affront by liquidating every Jew in the realm (2:19 – 3:6). He casts lots to determine the best day to implement his plan (it turns out to be eleven months away) and prevails upon Ahasuerus to let him issue a decree under his seal calling for all Jews, young and old, women and children alike, to be slaughtered on that day citing their non conformity as justification (3:7–15). *The actual decree is quoted* (3:13a–13g).

Mordecai persuades Esther to petition the king. She is reluctant because under court protocol she would be risking death by approaching the king without being invited. However Mordecai observes with brutal clarity that if she remains silent deliverance will surely come from 'another quarter' but she will perish anyway. Perhaps, he observes, she has come to the throne for just such an emergency as this (4:1–17). *Mordecai implores Esther to invoke the Lord (4:8a–8b).*

Mordecai beseeches God to spare His people. He did not bow before Haman because he would not place the glory of a man above the glory of God. Esther prays for help when she approaches the king (4:17a–z).

Esther takes her courage in both hands and goes to see the king. She decides that a private banquet would provide the best setting to broach her request and invites the king and Haman there and then. Her intuition must have warned her that the opportune moment had not yet arrived because over the meal she does no more than invite them to another banquet the next day (5:1–8). *A deutero-canonical addition dramatises Esther's approach to the king emphasising her terror and piety (5:1a–2b).*

Prompted by his wife Haman decides to have Mordecai hung the next day. That night the king cannot sleep and calls for the Annals to be read to him. He is reminded how Mordecai revealed the plot to kill him and decides to reward him. He asks Haman, who was about to seek his permission to have Mordecai hanged, what he should do for someone he wishes to honour. The vain Haman thinks the king is referring to himself and is aghast when he is ordered to lead a parade in Mordecai's honour (5:9 – 6:13).

Later that day at her second banquet Esther confesses her Jewish ancestry, tells the king of Haman's plan to kill the Jews and begs him to save them. The king is outraged. Haman is hung on his own gallows while Mordecai is promoted to Haman's former office. His first act is to issue an edict in the king's name giving the Jews permission to defend themselves and to kill and plunder anyone who attacks them on the day designated for their own slaughter[4] (7:1 – 8:17). *The actual edict advises recipients that they would do well not to act on the earlier decree, gives the Jews permission to observe their own customs, and calls on the Persians to come to the help of any Jews who are attacked* (8:12a–12v).

When the day came it was in fact the Jews who took the initiative, putting their enemies to the sword. And because of Mordecai's influence the authorities supported them. Indeed Esther asked the king for the Jews in Susa to be allowed to continue the slaughter for a further day.[5] When it was all over Mordecai and Esther nominated the two days as annual feast days to commemorate the Jews' remarkable deliverance[6] (9:1 – 10:3). *Mordecai interprets his dream in terms of the drama that has just been enacted* (10:3a–3l).

1 Maccabees

The (deutero-canonical) books of Maccabees are set in the second century b.c. Persian rule of Palestine had been brought to an end by Alexander the Great and following his death Palestine fell between two dynasties; first the Ptolemies in Egypt and then the Seleucids who ruled from Antioch in Syria.

Maccabees is the story of the Jews heroic resistance to attempts by their Seleucid overlords to consolidate their dominions by getting them to renounce their traditional ways and adopt a Hellenistic lifestyle. The suppression was begun by the tyrannical Antiochus IV Epiphanes around 169 B.C. and carried on by his successors so that for many years the Jews suffered persecution and were forced to fight for their religious freedom.

Some Jews were content to bow to the Seleucid yoke. But Mattathias, a priest, was made of sterner stuff. He hunted down renegade Jews and started a resistance that under the leadership of his sons Judas (Maccabaeus), Jonathan and Simon erupted into open warfare. Aided by internal dissension within the Seleucid empire, but above all driven by a religious fervour based on fidelity to the Law and faith in God, the Jews overcame overwhelming odds and eventually emerged victorious. The Temple, which the Seleucids had profaned, was reconsecrated and Judaea regained a very large (at times total) measure of political and religious independence.

Maccabees is a story of God in action in mighty deeds that call to mind the Exodus and the return from Babylon. It is one more example of God intervening in history to preserve the seedbed of His revelation. For His and His alone was the power that gave victory.

1 Maccabees begins with a sketch of the events leading up to Antiochus' persecution. It shows how Mattathias lit the fire of rebellion, and then describes the progress of the revolt under the successive leaderships of Judas, Jonathan and Simon.
2 Maccabees is in five parts. Part 1 comprises two letters to the Jews in Egypt. Part 2 is a brief preface. Part 3 shows how the office of high priest gradually became embroiled in politics and tainted by corruption. Part 4 describes the onset of Antiochus' persecution along with stories of martyrs who refused to submit. Part 5 broadly parallels 1 Maccabees 3:1 – 7:50 as it sketches the fight for freedom under Judas.
The two books are very different in style. Whereas 1 Maccabees is content to let

the facts speak for themselves 2 Maccabees is infused with a spirit of piety and stresses supernatural intervention. It demonstrates a firm belief in resurrection and is noteworthy for its belief in the value of intercessory prayer for the dead and the efficacy of the prayers of the righteous dead for the living.

The text has been slightly reordered to conform with what is nowadays thought to be the correct sequence.[1]

Introduction (1:1–64)

After a brief reference to Alexander the Great the scene is set in the reign of Antiochus IV Epiphanes who ascended the Seleucid throne in 175 b.c. It was at this time that certain Jews began to adopt a Hellenistic life style, building a gymnasium, disguising their circumcision and abandoning their ancestral faith.

Returning from campaigning in Egypt in 169 B.C. Antiochus marched on Jerusalem and looted the Temple. Two years later his chief tribute collector pillaged Jerusalem again, demolishing its walls and building a citadel in which, along with a garrison, he quartered some of the renegade Jews. Antiochus then issued a proclamation in which he forbade observance of the Law. The sacrificial liturgy, Sabbath observance, circumcision, even possessing a copy of the Law; all were punishable by death. Altars and shrines for idols were built throughout the land. The crowning profanity was the building of the 'appalling abomination' on top of the altar of burnt offering in the Temple.[2] Some Jews acquiesced in Antiochus' attempt to eradicate their faith. Others held fast and were put to death.

Mattathias (2:1–70)

Incensed at seeing a fellow Jew about to offer sacrifice on one of the new altars, a priest named Mattathias struck him down, raised the flag of rebellion and took to the hills. He was soon joined by a strict sect known as the Hasideans. They organised themselves into an armed force demolishing the pagan altars, imposing circumcision and hunting down the renegades.[3] One especially devout community, however, allowed itself to be slaughtered by Antiochus' officials rather than defend itself on the Sabbath. Mattathias nominated his son Judas Maccabaeus to lead the resistance after his death.

Judas Maccabaeus (3:1 – 9:22)

Exhorting his men to trust in Heaven Judas gained quick victories.[4] Antiochus was enraged. But as he was short of funds he decided to devote his own energy to an expedition to extract tribute from his Persian provinces and to entrust the quelling of the Jews to a nobleman named Lysias. Lysias' efforts were doomed from the start. A force he despatched under Nicanor and Gorgias was routed at Emmaus and next year at Beth-Zur Lysias himself suffered a similar humiliation at Judas' hands (3:1 – 4:35). Antiochus died shortly after receiving news of these disasters while still on campaign in Persia convinced that his misfortunes were punishment for his crimes against the Jews.

Lysias proclaimed his young son king as Antiochus V Eupator. It was the year 164 B.C.
(6:1–17).

Judas now marched on Jerusalem. Stationing part of his force to contain the garrison
in the citadel, he reconsecrated the Temple and fortified the surrounding area with walls
and towers. Beth-Zur, which guarded the approaches from Idumaea, was also fortified.
A new feast was inaugurated to celebrate the dedication of the Temple[5] (4:36–61).

Further successes followed in Idumaea, Ammon and Philistia. With his brother
Simon Judas rescued pockets of Jews under siege in Galilee and Gilead (5:1–68). In
162 B.C. he laid siege to the citadel itself. On hearing this Antiochus marched to the
rescue. He defeated the Jews at Beth-Zechariah, regained Beth-Zur (which was in no
position to withstand a siege because it was the sabbatical year) and invested Jerusalem
and the Temple Mount.[6] However he was forced to lift the siege when news came
that Philip, whom Antiochus Epiphanes had deputed as regent for his young son,
had returned from Persia and was planning a coup. Under the terms of the ensuing
treaty the Jews were granted their religious freedom. However before hurrying back to
Antioch where he defeated Philip, Antiochus broke faith and treacherously razed the
walls guarding the Temple[7] (6:18–63).

In 161 B.C. Demetrius, the son of Antiochus Epiphanes' elder brother Seleucus,
landed in Syria to claim the throne. Antiochus and Lysias were put to death and
Alcimus, a man with pronounced Hellenistic sympathies and hostile to Judas, was
made high priest and put in charge of Judaea under Bacchides the regional governor.
Frustrated by Judas' continuing guerilla activities Alcimus appealed to Demetrius for
help. However the army Demetrius despatched under Nicanor was cut down by Judas
at Adasa, Nicanor himself falling early on. There was then a brief interval of peace
(7:1–50).

Judas used this lull to conclude an alliance with Rome (8:1–32). However in 160
B.C. Demetrius sent another army to Judaea, this time under Bacchides himself.
Battle was joined at Beer-Zaith. Heavily outnumbered, Judas was defeated and killed
(9:1–22)

Jonathan (9:23 – 12:53)

Jonathan, who succeeded his brother as leader of the uprising, was forced to take
refuge in the desert at first but by adroitly playing-off rival factions in the Seleucid
ranks he eventually came to be appointed high priest in 152 b.c. and governor-general
of Judaea in 150 b.c.. He continued to exploit Seleucid divisions and strengthen his
position until he was murdered by an erstwhile ally in 143 b.c.

Simon (13:1 – 16:24)

Simon, the last of Mattathias' sons, built on Jonathan's success and the Bible records
how in 142 b.c. 'the gentile yoke was lifted from Israel' with Simon becoming high
priest and effective governor of the Jews, 1M 13:41. 1 Maccabees ends with Simon's
murder by his son-in-law in 134 b.c., and henceforth we are dependant on extra-
Biblical sources to tell us how despite continuing warfare and intrigue Simon's line

continued to rule, with the country enjoying varying levels of autonomy, until with Pompey's invasion in 63 b.c. Judaea became part of the Roman province of Syria and the independence won for the Jews by the Maccabees finally came to an end.

2 Maccabees

Letters to the Jews of Egypt (1:1 – 2:18)

The first of two letters to the Jews of Egypt from the Jews of Judaea is a reminder urging them to keep the feast of Dedication in the year 124 b.c. (1:1–9).[1] The second has five parts: thanksgiving for the death of Antiochus Epiphanes; an account of how the perpetual fire on the altar of burnt offering was preserved from the time of the Babylonian exile to Nehemiah;[2] a report that Jeremiah concealed the Tent, the Ark and the altar of incense from the invading Babylonians on Mount Nebo; a reference to Nehemiah's library; and an invitation to celebrate the inaugural feast of Dedication (1:10 – 2:18).

Preface (2:19–32)

The author's aim is to condense an earlier five volume work by Jason of Cyrene.

The decline of the high-priesthood (3:1 – 4:50)

The first of two stories tells how the money in the Temple treasury was supernaturally protected when Seleucus IV, Antiochus' elder brother, sent his chancellor Heliodorus to appropriate it following a tip-off by a certain Simon, who was seeking to settle scores with Onias the high-priest, that the amount held was out of all proportion to liturgical needs (3:1–40).

The second is set soon after Antiochus Epiphanes came to power when Onias' brother Jason bribed the king to replace Onias by himself whereupon he embarked upon a rigorous program of Hellenisation. Three years later Jason was replaced by Simon's brother Menelaus who offered the king an even larger inducement. When Onias got wind that Menelaus was stealing some of the Temple vessels, Menelaus had him murdered. But everything soon came to light and when it did Menelaus' brother Lysimachus was lynched by the mob when it was learned that he too was implicated in the thefts. Menelaus himself was put on trial but managed to bribe his way to an acquittal (4:1–50).

Persecution and martyrdom (5:1 – 7:42)

Jason seized on a rumour that Antiochus had died on campaign in Egypt to attack Jerusalem in an attempt to supplant Menelaus. Interpreting this as a Jewish revolt

Antiochus hastened back from Egypt, put Jerusalem to the sword and pillaged the Temple. Following a second assault under Apollonius, carried out while the Jews were resting on the Sabbath, Judas Maccabaeus and some companions took to the hills (5:1–27).

Antiochus now moved to stamp out the Jewish faith and impose Hellenisation. The Temple was profaned and dedicated to the Greek god Zeus. Sabbath observance and circumcision were banned and Greek customs enforced on pain of death (6:1–17). Some Jews chose martyrdom rather than compromise their faith. Eleazar, a teacher of the Law, died on the torture wheel for refusing to eat a piece of pork (6:18–31). Another story, noteworthy for the unshakeable belief in resurrection conveyed in their dying words, tells how a mother and her seven sons all suffered agonising deaths – having their limbs severed and being scalped and fried alive – when they too refused to contravene the dietary laws[3] (7:1–42).

The fight for freedom (8:1 – 15:39)

Judas rallied support for the resistance movement and harassed the enemy with surprise attacks on isolated towns and villages. His first major victory came when he routed an army under Nicanor and Gorgias. A second force under Timotheus and Bacchides met a similar fate (8:1–36). After Lysias, the king's chief minister, had also been defeated in a battle at Beth-Zur in which the Jews saw 'a rider attired in white at their head, brandishing golden weapons', peace was agreed on terms favourable to the Jews[4] (11:1–21; 11:27 – 12:1).

Just as he was on the brink of returning from his Persian campaign Antiochus Epiphanes fell from his chariot and died, but not before repenting for his persecution of the Jews. His young son succeeded him as Antiochus V (9:1–29; 10:9–13).

Judas purified and reconsecrated the Temple (10:1–8). He reduced a number of enemy fortresses in Idumaea and again defeated Timotheus whom he pursued to the fortress of Gezer where he was slain and the town stormed (10:14–38). Further accounts tell of Judas avenging an atrocity at Joppa, launching a pre-emptive strike against Jamnia, campaigning in Gilead and again defeating first Timotheus and then Gorgias.[5] Once the fighting was over Judas, prompted by his belief in resurrection, and confident in the power of intercessory prayer for the dead, organised a collection for a sacrifice for sin to be offered in Jerusalem for those of his men who had fallen in battle and who were found to be wearing pagan amulets contrary to the Law (12:2–45).

In the year 163 B.C. Antiochus V and Lysias advanced into Judaea. Menelaus joined them but when it became apparent that he was only serving his own interests he was put to death. The advance was checked at Beth-Zur and when news came of a revolt back at Antioch Antiochus agreed to a settlement which acknowledged the Jews right to the Temple and guaranteed their religious freedom (13:1–26; 11:22–26).

Three years later Demetrius, son of Seleucus IV, seized the throne and had Antiochus and Lysias put to death. Spurred on by Alcimus, a former high-priest and keen Helleniser, Demetrius sent an army under Nicanor to defeat Judas and reinstate Alcimus. Nicanor was at first inclined to a peaceful accommodation with Judas but on orders from Demetrius instigated by Alcimus reverted somewhat reluctantly to threats and force. When Nicanor tried to make an example of a devout elder named Razis he committed suicide, falling on his sword and tearing out his entrails as he called on God to restore his life one day.

Shortly before the crucial battle in which Nicanor was defeated and killed Judas encouraged his troops by describing a dream in which he had seen Onias and Jeremiah interceding on their behalf, the righteous dead interceding for the righteous living (14:1 – 15:39).

THE WISDOM LITERATURE

After the Pentateuch and the Historical books come seven books of quite different character. Psalms and the Song of Songs, a poem on human love, stand apart. The other five – Job, Proverbs, Ecclesiastes and the two deutero-canonical books, Ecclesiasticus and Wisdom, make up what is known as the Wisdom Literature.

Job and Ecclesiastes address particular problems. Job probes the mystery of suffering. Qoheleth, the author of Ecclesiastes, is preoccupied with what he sees as the futility of life. Proverbs, Ecclesiasticus and the Book of Wisdom focus on the nature and acquisition of wisdom. Proverbs and Ecclesiasticus supplement this overall thesis with hints for daily living, typically expressed in short crisp sayings, proverbs, that make shrewd observations about life in a memorable way. The Book of Wisdom is notable for its doctrine of immortality.

The Bible does not define wisdom but its meaning is never in doubt. Put simply wisdom is knowing how to conduct one's life in accord with God's Will. It is the key to life and those who spurn it tread the path of darkness and death. Yahweh alone has true wisdom and it cannot be gained by human endeavour alone. It is a gift from God which may be summed up as fear of Yahweh in the sense of reverential submission to His Will reflected in obedience to His Law. Contrary to modern norms that often see wisdom as an obstacle to faith, the Bible teaches that trust in God is a prerequisite for true wisdom.

The welter of instruction in Proverbs and Ecclesiasticus shows that far from being philosophical in any technical sense, or reserved for an intellectual elite, wisdom is within everyone's grasp. It is intensely practical and pervades every aspect of life, religious and secular. It is concerned for example with how to get on with people; self-control; humility; maintaining a temperate tongue; resilience in adversity and so on. As the voice of reflection and experience it pertains to discernment and astuteness, behaviour and character, rather than knowledge and intellect.

The Wisdom books compare the wise man with the fool. A fool was not someone who lacked ability but the antithesis of the wise man. Someone who turned his back on Yahweh, spurned wisdom and espoused folly, the negation of wisdom, instead.

Wisdom and Israel's other traditions

The Wisdom literature is distinct from Israel's other sacred writings. Until Ecclesiasticus and Wisdom, the last of the genre to be written, it makes few references to the great themes that dominate the rest of the Bible – Election, Covenant, Law, Priesthood and Temple, the

Messianic hope. However this changes with Ecclesiasticus. Ben Sira, its author, calls for reverence towards the priesthood and purity in worship. Indeed Ecclesiasticus and the book of Wisdom both equate wisdom with obedience to the Law. From Jeremiah onwards the sages or scribes who recorded wisdom were regarded as one of the three pillars of Israel's religious heritage along with the priests as guardians of the Law and the prophets.[1]

The retribution principle

The main concern of the sages was the destiny of the individual so it is not surprising that the retribution principle finds a prominent place in their deliberations. This held that God rewards virtue and punishes evil: suffering is the wages of sin. Moreover since death was final justice must be dispensed in this life. By equating wisdom with the path to happiness and folly with doom, Proverbs upholds this dictum. Job challenges it. Not only does Job's own experience as a good man stricken with suffering give it the lie but the world is full of rogues who live to a ripe old age while the upright languish. However, apart from being shown that God's wisdom is beyond human understanding, and hence being left with no option but to trust in God's justice and goodness, Job receives no answer to his conundrum.

Qoheleth is equally alive to the dilemma. Life's manifold injustices are there for all to see and since the jaws of death claim everyone in the end what is the point of it all? The best anyone can hope for is to enjoy life while one can. Yet despite this fatalism, and his belief that death is the end, Qoheleth somehow manages to cling to a God who will one day call both the upright and sinners to account.

Ecclesiasticus stands on similar ground. Ben Sira, its author, knows that the retribution thesis is unsatisfactory and he has a shrewd idea that the answer is in some way linked to the moment of death. But although, like Qoheleth, he comes close to the idea of judgement he cannot articulate his intuition. The problem finds its solution in the Book of Wisdom with its teaching on immortality. It is beyond the grave that the scales of justice are balanced.

The nature of wisdom

Few things are more mysterious than those texts where Wisdom almost takes on a life of its own and is personified as a woman.[2] She is the first-fruits of God's fashioning, with Him from eternity, at His side during Creation, Pr 8. She comes forth from the mouth of the Most High and is deputed to carry God's revelation to Israel, Si 24. Ws 7 portrays her as a breath of the power of God, pure emanation of the glory of the Almighty. She renews the world. Evil cannot prevail against her. Jb 28 tells us that God alone knows where she is to be found.

As personified in this way Wisdom is at once distinct from God but immeasurably close operating almost as His 'agent'. Not strictly a person she assumes a personality that reflects the essence of divinity. These ideas, only partially and imperfectly expressed in the Old Testament, attain their full flowering in the Word of St John. Like Wisdom, the Word is at once in God and apart, existent from the beginning and active in creation. He is the source of life and evil cannot prevail against Him, Jn 1:1–5. The Wisdom of the Old Testament is thus assimilated into the Word of the New and so into Christ Himself.[3]

Job

Job is written against the then belief that God blessed the righteous and punished the wicked, the so-called retribution principle. Moreover as there was no belief at the time in a future life, justice must be meted out in this world. The converse was also held: if a man suffered it was because he was a sinner. He should therefore repent and throw himself on God's mercy. This philosophy presented few problems when Israel believed in corporate accountability as blessings or disaster could always be attributed to the behaviour of the majority. But once Jeremiah and Ezekiel had enunciated the principle that everyone was responsible for his own actions it led to obvious difficulties. What about the good man who suffers or the villain who prospers? This is the problem that Job grapples with.[1]

Job is a man of impeccable character and deeply religious spirit and in the story God allows Satan to afflict him with horrendous suffering to test his loyalty. Job's friends who come to comfort him know nothing of this, any more than Job does, and enter into a long debate in which they argue that his suffering must be due to past sins for which he must repent. Job will have none of it and stoutly defends his innocence. A tortured soul, he shouts defiance at God and questions His justice, coming close to blasphemy as he does so. How can it be right that virtue goes unrewarded while rogues thrive?

Job's own life belies any belief that suffering is the harvest of sin. Otherwise the debate sheds little light apart from observations that God may use suffering to chide, to cure pride or to test fortitude. The argument ends in stalemate: without the revelation of life beyond the grave it could scarcely do otherwise. Then right at the end, but significantly after a poem ascribing wisdom to God and God alone (and an intervention by a bystander named Elihu) Yahweh Himself intervenes.

But far from addressing Job's dilemma He totally ignores it. Instead He unleashes a barrage of thunderbolts demonstrating His power and wisdom as revealed in nature and the moral order. Was Job present at creation? Could he master the forces of evil? Job's self-assurance is shattered. He had been seeking a relationship based on justice and rights. Now he realises that he has been falsely arraigning a Creator of his own making. God is working on a different level and His wisdom so far transcends his own that it is presumptuous to question His ways. Ultimate wisdom, he learns, lies in trust in a God whose ways are past man's understanding.

To a suffering humanity, faced with a world where virtue and justice often seem to be out of step, the message of Job is thus a demand for humility and faith. Faith in a

God whose inscrutable ways it can never fathom but who has ordered all things for its ultimate good. Faith that must hold when understanding fails.

In the epilogue Satan, the ultimate source of suffering, is gone, thwarted by Job's loyalty just as he will finally be defeated by Christ's. And the manifold rewards Job receives reflect the blessings all the faithful will enjoy at the end of time.

Apart from its religious value Job is one of the peaks of Old Testament literature. Tennyson called it 'the greatest poem of ancient and modern times'.

Prologue (1:1 – 2:13)

Job is a godly prosperous man, a model of virtue. When Satan suggests that his piety is motivated by self-interest God allows him to attack Job to prove his faithfulness.[2] In a series of hammer blows that shatter his world Job loses everything: his animals, his family, and finally his health as he is afflicted with malignant sores from head to foot. Yet despite his wife's chiding he refuses to reproach God in any way. Three friends, Eliphaz, Bildad and Zophar come to offer sympathy and consolation.

Job's lament (3:1–26)

In stanzas of searing poignancy Job bemoans his fate and curses the day he was born as his friends sit silently beside him. Why does God let people go on living in misery?

First cycle of discourses (4:1 – 14:22)

Eliphaz opens the first of three speech cycles. Can Job recall anyone guiltless who perished? No, it is those who sow iniquity who reap disaster. He tells of a dream where a voice pointed out the impossibility of anyone being righteous in God's sight. He even finds fault with the angels (4:1–21). Resentment is foolish where God is concerned. People bring trouble on themselves. He urges Job to appeal to God's mercy. God is kind and just and Job should accept His correction. He who wounds is He who soothes and His chastisement is for our ultimate good (5:1–27).

Job's afflictions overwhelm him. He has lost his zest for life and eagerly awaits the release of death. Why won't God answer his prayer? He protests his innocence and challenges his friends to point out his faults.[3] He berates God for his suffering. Why must He take man's sins so seriously? What harm do they do Him? Why cannot He forgive? (6:1 – 7:21).

Bildad observes that God is just. Job's sons perished because they sinned. Job must plead with God. If he is as pure as he says his former blessings will be as nothing compared with what God has in store for him. God never abandons the good or condones evil (8:1–22).

Job questions the point of trying to establish his innocence before a God who is so wise and powerful. All he can do is beg for mercy. But will God listen? He destroys innocent and guilty alike wounding again and again for no apparent reason. He is sick of living. If God were human his case could be settled in court. But who would arbitrate (9:1–35)? Job asks why the God who so lovingly created him hunts him down so remorselessly for every little sin yet never gives him credit for the good he does. What is the charge against him? Cannot he be left alone for the little time he has left? (10:1–22)

Zophar rejects Job's claim that he is blameless. God, who fathoms depths that are inaccessible to man and sees all his misdeeds, is holding him to account for his sins. If only Job would repent all his troubles would fade away and his life would be brighter than the midday sun. But all the wicked can look forward to is death (11:1–20).

Job again questions God's justice. Everything is under His control yet virtue is laughed at while scoundrels prosper (12:1–25). Boldly maintaining his innocence he challenges God to tell him what he is charged with. Why does He treat him like an enemy? (13:1–28) Man is a feeble transient creature and once he dies that is the end of him. So why cannot God let him finish his days in peace? Then, for a wonderful moment, Job imagines God sheltering him in Sheol until His anger was spent (14:1–22).

Second cycle of discourses (15:1 – 21:34)

Eliphaz returns to the attack. Job's irreverence betrays him. No one is upright in the sight of God. Humanity soaks up wickedness like water and the wicked face unceasing torment. Their days are numbered (15:1–35). Job cries that his wretched condition is driving him to distraction. God is like an archer piercing him with arrows from all sides. Then suddenly, in a burst of inspiration, his thoughts leap from the profoundest depths to the greatest heights, to a Defender in heaven who will argue his case:

> my defender is there on high.
> Interpreter of my thoughts there with God (16:1–21)

But his elation fades as quickly as it came as he again contemplates his plight and the imminence of the grave (17:1–16).
Appendix 1 refers

Bildad reiterates that the wicked get their just deserts (18:1–21). In desolation Job claims that God has wronged him before his vision soars again to his living Defender:

> After my awakening, he will set me close to him,
> and from my flesh I shall look on God.
> He whom I shall see will take my part (19:1–29)

Zophar has nothing new to say. Any prosperity the wicked enjoy is short lived. Doom is inevitable (20:1–29). Job takes issue with this and questions whether there is any justice in the world at all. The wicked prosper and end their days happily despite flying in the face of God. How often does disaster overtake them? Sinners should bear their own punishment, not their children. Yet death strikes indiscriminately (21:1–34).

Third cycle of discourses (22:1 – 27:23)

Eliphaz repeats that Job is being punished for his sins. But now he lays specific charges against him: avarice, greed, cruelty, oppression, lack of charity. Job thought God was too remote to notice. However if He humbly repents joy will again be his (22:1–30).

Wrapped up in his own thoughts Job ignores Eliphaz's accusations. Confident that he has followed God's precepts he seeks the opportunity to put his case to God direct. But how can he find Him? In any case what is the use? Once God has made up his mind who can change it? Injustice and evil are everywhere[4] (23:1 – 24:17,25).

Bildad has run out of arguments and simply eulogises God's limitless power and purity before which man is a cipher who can never be judged virtuous in God's eyes (25:1–6; 26:5–14). Job too is exhausted and simply declaims his righteousness once again (26:1–4; 27:1–12). Zophar muses the dread fate awaiting the wicked (27:13–23; 24:18–24).

A poem in praise of Wisdom (28:1–28)

The debate is interrupted by the introduction of Wisdom. Man gropes tirelessly for precious minerals but Wisdom – personified as a woman – is more valuable even than gold. She lies beyond his reach and cannot be bought, her whereabouts known only to God. Wisdom is fear of the Lord, avoidance of evil.

Job's final speech (29:1 – 31:40)

Job recalls the days when he enjoyed God's blessings: family, prosperity, esteem, deference. He was scrupulous in caring for the needy and upholding justice (29:1–20). Now, with God turning him a deaf ear, he is a laughing stock, reviled and ravaged by disease. If only God would treat him as generously as he treated others (30:1–31). He vehemently rejects a catalogue of sins that might have been imputed to him: lust, falsehood, deceit, avarice. He has done nothing to warrant his suffering and ends with yet another plea for God to grant him a hearing (31:1–40).

Elihu (32:1 – 37:24)

A young bystander named Elihu now intervenes. After explaining why he feels compelled to speak (32:1–22) he asserts that Job is wrong in believing that he is sinless and that God keeps inventing excuses to punish him. God is too great to behave like that. He is forever trying to save people from sin and pride. Sometimes he speaks in dreams and visions. At other times he uses sickness to make His point[5] (33:1–33).

God treats everyone justly. It is inconceivable that He could be unjust. He knows our every step. If the wicked do not appear to be punished it is because God is tempering justice with mercy. Job is now adding rebellion to his sin (34:1–37). He is wrong in suggesting that because his sins do not harm God he should not be punished.[6] His sins may not touch God but they certainly affect his fellow beings. If God does not help sufferers it is because their prayer is empty (35:1–16).

God neither rejects the pure nor protects the rogue. If those who are suffering repent they will prosper once again. If not they will perish. God uses suffering to warn people in the hope of saving them. That is what He is doing with Job whose present travails stem from past sins (36:1–21). Elihu concludes with a hymn to God's greatness, invoking the glories of nature as witness to His splendour and might (36:22 – 37:24).

Yahweh's discourses and Job's responses (38:1 – 42:6)

Human wisdom has exhausted itself and God Himself now intervenes with all the force of the tempest from which He speaks. In spellbinding verse He arraigns Job with a battery of questions that bring him up against the unfathomable mysteries of His sovereignty. Could he have laid the earth's foundations? Could he herald the dawn, produce dewdrops or feed the baby ravens? Job's doubts and his suffering are not even mentioned (38:1 – 40:2).

In a second discourse God focuses on His control of the moral order – can Job humble the haughty or strike down the wicked? – before relentlessly reverting to the marvels of nature in the figures of two beasts, Behemoth (a hippopotamus) and Leviathan (a crocodile), that would have been a source of wonderment in the ancient world (40:6 – 41:26).

The effect is to convince Job that he is out of his depth. He acknowledges God's omnipotence and confesses his ignorance. He should not have questioned God in the way he did. God can be trusted. He does what He says. So he retracts what he has said and humbly repents (40:3–5; 42:1–6).

Epilogue (42:7–17)

Job's three friends are admonished for having spoken incorrectly about God.[7] Job intercedes on their behalf. His own fortunes are more than amply restored.

Psalms

The psalms were composed as anthems to the glory of God. With their diverse moods – praise, thanksgiving, elation, hope, confidence, sorrow, contrition, bewilderment – they reflect the aspirations, doubts, fears and certainties of the human heart. Yet, rooted in real life as they are, it is rarely possible to recover a psalm's historical background. This may be the despair of the exegete but it is also a strength. For it means that the psalms have a universal, timeless appeal which enables them to speak to later generations and in new situations. Historically non-specific, they are always relevant. Today we are puzzled by the same problems, stirred by the same emotions, experience the same needs, and worship the same God as the psalmists of old. As a result the psalms can act as the devotional handbook of the Christian church just as they were once the hymnal of ancient Israel.

Structure

The one hundred and fifty psalms that make up the Psalter are divided into five books, Pss 1–41; 42–72; 73–89; 90–106; 107–150, possibly reflecting the way they were collected, possibly in imitation of the fivefold division of the Pentateuch. Each of the first four books ends with a brief doxology as an interlude of praise, while Ps 150 rounds off the entire Psalter.[1] There are several smaller groupings. Pss 113–118, known as the Hallel, were sung on feast days. Pss 120–134, the songs of ascent, are so called because they are thought to have been sung by pilgrims en route to Jerusalem. The Alleluiah collection, Ps 146–150, concludes the Psalter in an exultant hymn of praise.

Titles

Many psalms have superscriptions or titles.[2] These may be musical or liturgical directions (many of which are obscure), historical associations or personal names with which the psalm is associated. Pss 3, 51 have all three. David's name appears at the head of some seventy-three psalms and the 'sons of Korah' and 'Asaph' in about a dozen instances each.[3] It is now widely accepted that these headers were not part of the original text but later additions. They are thus of limited use in determining a psalm's pedigree.

Authorship

It would be rash to assume that the psalms with attributions to David were all by his hand. Diversities in style and content underline this point as does the fact that Semitic prepositions have a wide semantic range with the result that 'by David' or 'of David' could equally well be translated 'for David', 'about David' or (named) 'after David'.[4] At the same time it would be wrong to deny any link between David and the Psalter. The Bible introduces David as a musician, 1S 16:14–23, portrays him as a poet, 2S 1:19–27; 3:33–34, as a devotee of the liturgy, 2S 6:5,14–15, and as a 'singer of songs', 2S 23:1. He invents musical instruments, Am 6:5, and organises the musical accompaniment for the Temple liturgy, 1Ch 6:16; 15:16; 25:1. We would therefore probably not be far wrong if we saw the David whom Jewish tradition regards as the author of the whole Psalter as the composer of at least a nucleus of psalms and as the inspiration behind the psalm as a vehicle for Israel's devotion, much as Moses is regarded as the founding father of the Law and Solomon of the wisdom tradition.

Formation of the Psalter

No more is known of other authors nor are we any the wiser about when the caucus was compiled.[5] The most we can safely conjecture is that the psalms contain elements spanning close on 1000 years from pre-monarchial times onwards. During that time various collections would have begun to form. These would have been edited, added to, re-edited and eventually combined, with the Psalter as we know it today most likely emerging somewhere in the second or third century B.C.

The Psalter and the liturgy

Some psalms were probably composed for private devotion, others to express national joy or sorrow, others still for recitation at a festival or for liturgical use. Whatever their origins, it seems clear from the element of praise in many of them, their communal character, and the musical and liturgical directions in their titles that, with the possible exception of a few historical and didactic psalms, they were eventually appropriated by the worshipping community, and became the hymnbook of Israel just as songs from various sources are incorporated into hymnals today.

TYPES OF PSALM

It is helpful to classify the psalms under eight headings: hymns of praise, thanksgiving, laments, songs of trust, didactic or Wisdom psalms, songs of Zion, songs of the Kingship of God and Royal psalms. However these categories are far from watertight. There is a large element of subjectivity and exegetes do not always agree. Some psalms combine the attributes of more than one type. Ps 19 for example, while undeniably a hymn of praise, modulates into the Wisdom style along with a plea for forgiveness. A small residue does not lend itself to any neat labelling. None of this matters. It is one of the glories of the Psalter that it defies rigorous categorisation. Classification is helpful but the important thing is to let each psalm speak for itself.

Hymns of praise

These psalms (Pss 8, 19, 24, 29, 33, 68, 100, 103–105, 111, 113, 114, 117, 135, 145–150) laud God as Creator and Lord of history and rejoice in His majesty and might.[6] The lyrical Ps 8 touches heights rarely scaled as it ranges from God in heaven to man at the peak of creation.

> I look up at your heavens, shaped by your fingers,
> at the moon and the stars you set firm
> what are human beings that you spare a thought for them?

Ps 29 sees God's awesome glory in the thunderstorm. Others dwell on the God of tenderness and love who cares for the oppressed, blesses the upright and frustrates the wicked; the God who providentially provides for His creatures' needs and has concluded an everlasting covenant with His servant Israel. The trilogy of Pss 103–105 is the supreme example of this genre. Ps 103 is a meditation on God's love. Ps 104 extols the glories of creation. Ps 105 recalls the epic of God's mighty deeds from Abraham onwards.[7]

Thanksgiving psalms

These (Pss 9, 30, 65–67, 92, 107, 116, 118, 124, 136, 138) are similar in many ways to the hymns of praise but are characterised by the psalmist offering thanks for deliverance from distress or for some other kindness. Ps 30 thanks God for recovery from illness, Pss 65, 67 for fertility and a good harvest, Ps 92 for the joy of the just and the ruin of evil-doers. Ps 107 is on the grand scale, thanking God for deliverance from Egypt, the return from exile, healing the sick and rescuing voyagers from the perils of the sea. Ps 136 thanks God for His love as revealed in the wonder of the cosmos, the Exodus and the gift of the Promised Land.

Laments

Laments, in which the psalmist appeals to God for deliverance from some woe or enemy, form the largest category. They may be either individual (Pss 3, 6, 7, 10, 13, 14, 17, 22, 25, 26, 28, 31, 35, 38, 39, 42, 43, 51, 53–59, 64, 69, 70, 71, 77, 86, 88, 102, 109, 120, 130, 140–143) or communal (Pss 12, 44, 60, 74, 79, 80, 83, 85, 90, 94, 106, 123, 137) in which case they may be voiced on behalf of a community or the whole nation.[8]

The object of supplication is often veiled in general or symbolic terms: unspecified enemies, evildoers, pursuers. At other times pleas may be for recovery from illness, Pss 6, 38, 102; following defeat in battle, Pss 44, 60, 74, 79, 80; against unjust judges, Ps 58; for God to judge the wicked, Ps 94. Or by someone subjected to false accusations, Pss 35, 109, 120; deserted by a friend, Ps 55; unjustly accused of theft, Ps 69; or simply looking for reconciliation with God following personal sin, Pss 51, 130. Sometimes the psalmist seems to be wrestling with doubt: has God forgotten them, Pss 13, 80? Is He asleep, Ps 44? On other occasions he bewails the fact that society seems to be falling apart, Ps 12. He depicts the fool who flouts his independence from God, Ps 14, and reflects on the transience of life, Pss 39, 90.[9] Some laments contain strong protestations of innocence, Pss 7, 17, 26. Ps 137 recalls the exiles in Babylon mourning at the memory of Zion.

One of the best known laments is Ps 22. It begins with Christ's cry of dereliction on the Cross and has other allusions to the suffering Messiah. Ps 44 is notable for a sense of self-justification that brings the psalmist close to rebuking God for His lack of support. Ps 51 is thought to be a prayer of the repentant David after his adulterous affair with Bathsheba. In its portrayal of a heart humbled by guilt yet raised from despair by the mercy of God it has no peer.

A remarkable feature of the laments is that they contain so little self-pity and often modulate into praise or thanksgiving, Pss 22, 31. This may be because the supplicant voiced his lament before a priest who assured him that God had heard his prayer, thereby enabling him to praise and thank God in certain knowledge of His grace. *Appendix 1 refers*

Songs of trust

Songs of trust (Pss 4, 5, 11, 16, 23, 27, 52, 62, 63, 91, 121, 125, 129, 131) resemble laments except that trust in a Yahweh who performs wonders for His faithful but detests the wicked is now the dominant theme. The sublime confidence and quiet beauty of Ps 23, expressing contentment and trust in God the good shepherd, have made it one of the most beloved of all the psalms. Elsewhere God provides shelter in the recesses of His tent, Ps 27, or under His wings, Ps 91. In Ps 16 the psalmist's relationship with God is so close that he cannot imagine even death breaking it. In the diminutive Ps 131 the psalmist trusts in God like a child in its mother's arms.

Didactic or Wisdom psalms

These (Pss 1, 15, 32, 34, 37, 49, 50, 73, 78, 112, 127, 128, 133) recall the Old Testament's Wisdom literature. In contrasting the opposing lifestyles of the upright and the wicked, the one resembling a tree planted near water, the other like chaff, the one destined for reward, the other for punishment, Ps 1 not only sets the tone for the entire Psalter but summarises the moral teaching of the Old Testament as a whole. Ps 15 defines the conduct that fits a man to live with his God, Pss 112, 128 the resultant blessings.

Several psalms grapple with the problem posed by the prosperity of the wicked and the suffering of the just. Pss 34, 37 counsel patience and trust. Justice will prevail in the end. After wrestling with doubts Ps 73 is equally convinced of the doom facing the wicked and finds solace in communion with God. Ps 49 exposes the futility of wealth while speaking of God ransoming the godly 'from the clutches of Sheol'.[10]

Ps 50 echoes the prophetic tradition in condemning formalism and hypocrisy in favour of worship that is sincere and comes from a heart that is morally pure.[11] Ps 32 voices the joy of confession and forgiveness. Ps 127 emphasises the futility of human effort when divorced from the God on whom everything depends. Ps 133 is a poem on brotherly love.

Songs of Zion

This little collection (Pss 46, 48, 76, 84, 87, 122) hymns the glory of God in His abode on Mount Zion. God is Israel's refuge and strength, the safe stronghold who defeats the nations gathered against her and puts an end to war, Pss 46, 48. Ps 84 is a pilgrim song lauding God in His Temple. Ps 87 is noteworthy for its universalism. Zion will become the mother of all peoples.

Songs of the Kingship of God

Pss 47, 93, 96–99 acclaim God's greatness and universal sovereignty. He is the victorious King of all the earth, Ps 47; the great creator, holy and just, Ps 96. He hates evil and protects His faithful, Ps 97. He is judge of all the world, Ps 98; a holy God of majesty and power who loves justice and uprightness, Ps 99; God for all eternity, Ps 93.

Royal psalms

These psalms (Pss 2, 18, 20, 21, 45, 61, 72, 101, 110, 132, 144) are so named because a king, presumably the reigning king at the time, is either the speaker or the focus of attention. They include a prayer for victory in battle, Ps 20; for long life and God's protection, Ps 61; thanksgiving for victory already achieved, Pss 18, 21; a royal wedding song, Ps 45; a plea for victory in war and prosperity for the people, Ps 144; a portrait of a future ideal king, Ps 72; an expose of the principles that should guide an ideal king, Ps 101; and a poem recalling David's transfer of the Ark to Jerusalem, celebrating both God's choice of Zion as His home and of David as the head of the dynasty that will reign for ever, Ps 132.[12]

Several have Messianic overtones. At face value Ps 2 exposes the absurdity of earth's puny rulers challenging the king whom God has already appointed. It probably originated at a time when vassals were rebelling against Israelite rule and originally had no further significance. But the grandeur of the language, in which the psalmist contrasts the futile agitation of the nations with the equanimity and immutable purpose of God, subsequently led the New Testament writers to give it a deeper Messianic interpretation with Jesus as the designated king: Lk 3:22; Ac 4:25–28; 13:32–33; Heb 1:5; 5:5.

Ps 110, in which the psalmist reveals to his Lord, the Davidic king, Yahweh's promise of worldwide dominion and everlasting priesthood, is especially portentous.

> Yahweh declared to my Lord, 'Take your seat at my right hand,
> till I have made your enemies your footstool.'
> Yahweh will stretch out the sceptre of your power;
> from Zion you will rule your foes all around you.
> Royal dignity has been yours from the day of your birth,
> sacred honour from the womb, from the dawn of your youth.

Composite and unclassified psalms

Pss 36, 40, 41, 89, 108, are hybrids. Ps 40 combines thanksgiving and praise with a lament. After beginning in didactic mode Ps 41 modulates into a lament from someone recovering from serious illness and abandoned by his friends. Ps 89 is in three parts: a hymn of praise; an oracle recalling God's covenant with David; and a lament after a defeat calling the future of the ruling dynasty into question.

Pss 75, 81, 82, 95, 115, 119, 126, 134, 139 fall outside the canonical types. Ps 75 is an oracle on God's justice, Ps 81 a festival song with the theme, 'If only My people would listen to Me'. Ps 82 depicts God in divine assembly condemning injustice. Ps 95 is an invitation to worship coupled with a warning to the community to avoid their ancestors' errors. Ps 115 contrasts the worthlessness of idols with the glory and might of Yahweh. The monumental Ps 119 (it has twenty-two stanzas of eight verses each) is best described as a hymn venerating the Law. The enigmatic Ps 126 is a song of the returning exiles, Ps 134 a call to prayer and benediction. Ps 139 is the meditation of a man who delights in God's all pervading presence in his life and even invites His scrutiny.

> God, examine me and know my heart,
> test me and know my concerns.
> Make sure that I am not on my way to ruin,
> and guide me on the road to eternity.

Theology of the Psalter

So embracing is the theology of the Psalter that it is sometimes described as the Old Testament in miniature. But there are two differences. Firstly, because it is a collection of one hundred and fifty individual compositions, the Psalter does not unfold God's word systematically so much as reveal it in a series of vignettes. Secondly edification comes not in the word of God declaimed to man but more indirectly through the medium of man addressing God.

No matter. If Israel had only known the psalms she would still have had a sound grounding in her faith. Celebrations of creation Pss 8, 19, 89, 104; acknowledgement of man's sinfulness Ps 51; summaries of history Pss 78, 105, 106, 135, 136; exposes on the fates of the godly and the wicked Pss 1, 11, 34, 37, 73, 91, 92; eulogies of the Law Pss 19, 119; sketches of the upright man Pss 15, 112, and of the ideal ruler Pss 72,101; poems on the lure of riches Ps 49; on God's love Pss 90, 103, 136; on forgiveness Pss 32, 51; on God the Shepherd Pss 23, 80; on God the rock who never lets His people down Pss 16, 18, 25, 31, 91; on the Davidic promise Pss 89, 132, and on God's concern for all nations Pss 2, 67, 87, 110, not to mention the joy and promise of the Zion and Kingship psalms, would still have yielded the bone and marrow of her belief.

Messianism

We have already noted the Messianic overtones of Pss 2, 110. These are underscored by St Luke who explicitly equates the son of Ps 2:7 with Jesus, Lk 3:22, while we have

Jesus' own authority to apply Ps 110:1 to Himself, Mt 22:44.[13] Heb 1:8–9 applies the wedding song of Ps 45 to Christ and Christian tradition has long seen it prefiguring the 'marriage' of Christ to His Church. The Royal psalms, Pss 72, 101, 132 are also undeniably Messianic.

Nor is this all. In anticipating a future victory when God will banish war and rule the whole world, the Zion and Kingship psalms also have an eschatological dimension, as does Ps 85 with its hope of a future grounded in peace, justice, love and loyalty.[14]

The Gospels recognise numerous allusions to Jesus in the Psalter, His cry of dereliction from the Cross, Ps 22:1 = Mt 27:46, and the casting of lots for His clothes, Ps 22:18 = Jn 19:24, being among the best known.[15]

Proverbs

Proverbs is in three parts: an extended prologue; seven collections of wise sayings or proverbs; an epilogue on the ideal wife. The prologue urges its readers to acquire wisdom and live according to its precepts. This is supplemented by warnings against loose living and interventions by Wisdom herself, now personified as a woman, in which she reveals her nature and origin as the first-fruits of creation and drives home the two paths in life. The way of wisdom, stemming from fear of Yahweh and knowledge of God, that results in blessings and life. And the way of folly, the rejection of wisdom, that leads to death.[1] The wise sayings that follow are intended to show how to apply wisdom in everyday life.

Prologue (1:1 – 9:18)

The sage states that his aim is to impart wisdom, especially to the inexperienced, though even the wise can benefit. Wisdom teaches uprightness and fair dealing and stems from fear of Yahweh, something that fools spurn. A warning against the blandishments of crooks who offer quick returns is followed by the arrival of Wisdom herself. Traipsing the city streets and squares she warns that those who mock her will live to regret it while those who heed her call have nothing to fear[2] (1:1–33).

When the sage resumes it is to teach that wisdom, which may be identified with fear of Yahweh and knowledge of God, comes from Yahweh Himself and He gives it to those who diligently seek it.[3] They enjoy His protection and a discernment that leads to uprightness, justice and happiness. It helps them resist the wiles of evil men and licentious women. They remain in God's favour while the wicked are rooted out (2:1–22).

Trust God rather than yourself, fear and revere Him, accept His correction and eschew evil (3:1–12). Wisdom is a pearl of great price, a tree of life. Never let her go (3:13–26). This advice is buttressed by proverbs commending good neighbourly relations and a warning against any inclination to envy the wicked (3:27–35). In another impassioned plea the sage counsels the light of virtue over the darkness of evil. The first step towards wisdom is to make its acquisition one's overriding priority (4:1–27).

The sage now warns against the lure of loose women. 'Delight instead, my son, in the fresh waters of the wife you married in your youth'. He warns against underwriting a stranger's debts; reproves laziness (praising the humble ant as an object lesson in industry) and castigates mischief makers and the ungodly (5:1 – 6:19). He concludes with further warnings against the seductive wiles of the adulteress[4] (6:20 – 7:27).

Wisdom herself now takes centre stage presenting herself as upright and truthful, the implacable opponent of evil, pride and arrogance. She is the champion of justice, more precious than jewels, mistress of thought, the source of power. Whoever seeks her finds her. Whoever loves her is loved by her. She endows her disciples with lasting riches. She was the first-fruits of God's creation and has been with Him from all eternity. She was at His side when He fashioned the universe. Whoever finds her finds life and Yahweh's favour. Those who reject her solicit death (8:1 – 36).

The choice facing humanity is thrown into stark relief as two women send out invitations to a meal.[5] But where Wisdom has prepared a sumptuous banquet with her own food and promises life, the silly woman offers only a snack of stolen food to be eaten clandestinely in death's very shadow (9:1–6; 13–18). The invitations are divided by aphorisms that contrast the willingness of the wise to accept correction with the intransigence of the mocker (9:7–12).

At this point, with Man torn between the calls of Wisdom and Folly, virtue and vice, life and death, the prologue ends. The scene is set for the guides to help him through life's vicissitudes.

The seven collections of proverbs (10:1 – 31:9)

These are distinguished by captions at various points in the text as follows:

- Proverbs attributed to Solomon (10:1 – 22:16)
- A selection from the sages (22:17 – 24:22)
- A further selection from the sages (24:23–34)
- Further proverbs attributed to Solomon (25:1 – 29:27)
- The sayings of Agur (30:1–14)
- Numerical proverbs (30:15–33)
- The sayings of Lemuel (31:1–9)

It is believed that Proverbs was edited into its final form during or after the exile. Much of the material is older, however, so there is no reason why Solomon could not have composed, or at least promoted, the two collections bearing his name. However the other attributions reveal that he was not the author of the whole book as 1:1 would suggest. Nothing is known of the other authors except that Agur or Lemuel were members of Massa, a north Arabian tribe descended from Ishmael, Gn 25:12–14.

The proverbs are not without ambiguities. One proverb may qualify or even deny another. But this is to be expected. Although stated as absolutes, as their literary form requires, they are generalisations to be applied in specific situations, not diktats to be used in every eventuality. Knowing when and where to use a proverb is all part of wisdom.

The sayings are not arranged in any recognisable order and defy summary, being as diverse as life itself. They commend hard work 10:4, humility 11:2, integrity 11:3, kindness to animals 12:10, a temperate tongue 12:18, truthfulness 12:19, encouragement 12:25, diligence 12:27, disciplining children 13:24, equability 15:18, honesty 16:11, self-control 17:27, temperance 20:3, generosity 21:26, resilience in adversity 24:10 and kindness to enemies[6] 25:21–22.

On the other hand, the sayings also condemn laziness 10:4, corrupt business practice 11:1, beauty without discretion 11:22, lying and slander 13:5, schemers 14:17, the quick tempered 14:29, idle gossip 20:19, gluttony and drunkenness 23:20–21, misbehaving with women 23:26–28, false-witness 24:28, vengefulness 24:29, people who are unreliable 25:19 or never satisfied 25:27, conceit 26:12, meddling in other people's affairs 26:17, quarrelsomeness 26:21, jealousy 27:4, self-deception 28:11, covetousness 28:25, people who can never accept correction 29:1, and the self-righteous 30:10–12.

A wise man should choose his wife, 12:4, and friends, 13:20, with care. He is circumspect in the face of authority, 16:13–14; 23:1–3, and does not wear out his welcome with neighbours, 25:17. He never responds without first listening, 18:13, and then speaks with restraint, 15:1, expressing himself persuasively, 16:23. The man who can control his choice of words will avoid trouble, 21:23, and be able to handle any situation,[7] 18:21.

Many of the proverbs have a religious character. Some echo the prologue by contrasting the wise man and the fool, the upright and the wicked, 10:1,3,7,23, 27; 14:26–27; 15:9,16,33; 16:6; 19:23; 22:4; 23:17–18; 28:5,18. Others teach that humility, not pride, is the hallmark of wisdom, 11:2); that nothing is hidden from a God who reads the heart, 15:3,11; 16:2; that God looks for sincerity of heart before ritual observance, 15:8; 21:3; that uprightness, not riches, is what will count on judgement day, 11:4); that anything is possible with God's help, 16:3,7; and that whoever trusts God has nothing to fear from men, 29:25.

The ideal wife (31:10–31)

This beautiful poem, acclaiming a wife who was a paragon of wisdom and virtue, forms a fitting finale to a book dedicated to promoting wisdom as the one true guide in life. The book ends as it began with fear of the Lord.[8]

Ecclesiastes

Qoheleth, the author of Ecclesiastes, plunges straight into his theme. Life is pointless, without rhyme or reason, futile, meaningless. Everything repeats itself. Learning merely increases one's sense of frustration. Nor is there lasting satisfaction in a life of pleasure. Money is another false trail. All it brings is worry and then, after a lifetime of work, it is left to someone else. The world is riddled with injustice. The good fall by the wayside while scoundrels prosper. And to cap it all is the finality of death where we all end up, humankind and animals alike. God's ways are unfathomable and there is nothing anyone can do about it. What is, is.

Qoheleth's conclusion is to enjoy life while we can. Stated so baldly this sounds humanistic and many have questioned Ecclesiastes' place in the Canon as a result. However Qoheleth is merely expressing the feelings and positing the questions on the meaning of life that tax even the most ardent believer from time to time while his insistence on enjoyment is a useful counterweight to people who regard pleasure as incompatible with religion.

Indeed far from being an obstacle Qoheleth's fatalism and pessimism actually enhance his message. He shows how it is possible, while sharing the difficulties that many find stumbling blocks, still to sustain a faith that upholds the way of wisdom over iniquity and folly; a stance which he sums up as 'fear God and keep His commandments'.

We must remember too that Qoheleth's melancholy refrains are directed against life bounded by the horizons of this world (there was no belief in an after-life in his day). So it is not the futility of life as such that he rails against but life where God, the source of all existence, has given so much but, it would seem, to such frustratingly little purpose. In short, life without Christ.

Paradoxically, despite being unable to articulate how it can be reconciled with the view that death was the end, Qoheleth also manages to cling to a God who will one day judge everyone and see that justice is done.

Ecclesiastes can be difficult. It tends to ramble with abrupt changes of subject, much repetition and no obvious progression. In his oscillations of mood we are in the presence of a man who, like Job, is confronting a vast mystery at the limits of his intellect; possessing some of the notes but unable to hear the melody.

Apart from the prologue and epilogue it is helpful to take Ecclesiastes in eight parts. Four develop Qoheleth's core themes. These are interlaced with 'words of advice', similar to the pithy sayings found in other parts of the Wisdom literature. They are often cryptic and only loosely connected to the sage's main thesis. There is also a poem on old age.

Prologue (1:1–3)

The author introduces himself as Qoheleth, a Hebrew word meaning something like 'Preacher' (Ecclesiastes is the Greek equivalent) and identifies himself, almost certainly as a device to gain authority for his work, with Solomon, Israel's traditional patron of Wisdom. Immediately he states his theme: the futility and wearisomeness of life.[1] What is the point of it all?

First development of the theme (1:4 – 2:26)

Life is an endless and meaningless grind. Nature operates in circles, history repeats itself. There is nothing new under the sun, no progress (1:4–11). Even the quest for wisdom is wearisome. What is, is. In fact the wiser one gets the greater one's sense of frustration. How futile it all is[2] (1:12–18).

Neither pleasure, wealth nor luxurious living – 'having a good time' – bring lasting satisfaction (2:1–11). However wisdom is preferable to folly even though the sage and the fool both meet in the oblivion of death. At least the wise man has his eyes open and sees where he is going whereas the fool walks in the dark (2:12–17). What is the point in working all one's life only to leave everything to someone who has done nothing to deserve it? The only happiness is in eating, drinking and enjoying whatever God gives us in return for our labours[3] (2:18–26).

Second development of the theme (3:1 – 4:16)

There is a time for everything: a time for tears, a time for laughter; a time for embracing, a time to refrain from embracing; a time for war, a time for peace; and so on (3:1–8). However, although God has determined these times and given us the ability to reflect on the passage of time, how everything fits together is beyond our comprehension. We cannot see the grand design. All we can do is enjoy whatever pleasures come our way never forgetting that they all come from God. (3:9–13). What God has decreed cannot be changed. There is nothing anyone can do about it. Miscarriages of justice abound but everyone will be judged by God.[4] However that is no great consolation because humans die just like animals and who knows what happens then? So enjoy your achievements while you can (3:14–22).

With all the oppression in the world there is a lot to be said for either being dead or never having been born. Rather than always striving to be one step ahead, or giving way to the sloth that leads to ruin, it is far better to steer a middle course that leaves room for inner peace (4:1–6). Better the joys of companionship than the miserly accumulation of wealth. Better, too, a wise youngster than an old fool who will no longer listen; not that his popularity will last for long either (4:7–16).

First words of advice (4:17 – 5:6)

Know what you are doing when you approach God. Be sparing of speech. Listen.[5] If you make a vow honour it without delay. Why risk angering God?

Third development of the theme (5:7 – 6:12)

Extortion is only to be expected in a society where officials at all levels are out to feather their nests. However money never brings happiness. The more you have the more you want and the more worries it brings. It can all get lost in some ill-fated venture but in any case you cannot take it with you when you die. So enjoy whatever God gives you (5:7–19).

Someone rich may die young with no one to bequeath his wealth to or live to a ripe old age but never have the time to enjoy it. A stillborn child is better off (6:1–6). Men's desires are insatiable. Better to enjoy what you already have than to keep on grasping for more (6:7–9). It is useless to try to change things. How can we tell what is best for us or what will happen after we are gone (6:10–12)?

Second words of advice (7:1 – 8:9)

An honourable name is better than luxury, the day of death better than the day of birth. Better the sobriety and mourning of the wise than the levity and feasting of the fool. The reprimand of a wise man is preferable to the compliments of a fool (7:1–7). Do not jump to conclusions or become exasperated. Avoid meaningless comparisons with the past. Wisdom has one great advantage over wealth; it bestows life. Accept things as they are since everything is determined by God (7:8–14).

Life is topsy-turvy. Good people die, scoundrels survive. So aim for moderation, being neither over righteous nor unduly wicked.[6] Wisdom makes the wise even stronger. No one can avoid sinning altogether. Do not listen when others gossip and criticise you; you have probably done the same yourself (7:15–22). True wisdom lies beyond one's grasp. At the same time folly is stupid and evil madness. Women are a snare. It is hard enough to find a good man but to find a good woman is almost impossible. Man was created upright. His deviousness is his own doing (7:23–29). Attend to what the wise man says. It is folly to oppose a king since he will please himself anyway. There is a time and place for everything (8:1–9).

Fourth development of the theme (8:10 – 9:12)

There is scant justice in life. Upright people get treated as if they were wicked and vice versa. Nevertheless everyone will eventually get his just deserts. Meanwhile we should be grateful for whatever enjoyment God gives us in this life in return for our labours. God's designs are hidden from human understanding. No wisdom can penetrate them (8:10–17). Qoheleth puzzles over the fact that although the upright and wise are in the hands of God they suffer the same fate as the wicked. But at least there is hope for the living – 'better to be a live dog than a dead lion' – for the dead are forgotten and unaware. So live life to the full and enjoy it while you can. Life is full of uncertainties and rewards do not always go to the deserving. We none of us know when our time will come (9:1–12).

Third words of advice (9:13 – 11:6)

Wisdom is superior to force but the wisdom of a poor man is not appreciated. It is not the shouting of fools that wins arguments but the calm voice of wisdom. A single sin can undo a great deal that wisdom has accomplished just as a dead fly can ruin a perfume (9:13 – 10:1). The wise man gravitates towards righteousness, the fool to perfidy. The sensible course when attacked by authority is restraint and composure. One of life's frustrations is seeing fools appointed to positions of authority and better men passed over (10:2–7). There is risk in every human endeavour. Plan ahead; one has to work twice as hard with a blade that needs sharpening. Just as a snake charmer will get bitten unless he uses his bent, so wisdom is of no avail unless it is used (10:8–11).

A fool talks endlessly but nobody knows what will happen next or after we die. Qoheleth bemoans inexperienced, hedonistic rulers who let things go to rack and ruin. Watch whom you criticise. A 'little bird' might give you away (10:12–20). Life is full of uncertainties. Therefore a man should widen his interests and take risks if he is to achieve anything. People who wait until they are certain wait for ever. No one can fathom God's ways. A man never knows which of his ventures will succeed and which will fail (11:1–6).

On old age (11:7 – 12:8)

Although some of the symbolism is obscure this is a poem of outstanding poignancy and power which the sage uses to reinforce his keynote themes: enjoy life while you are young; never forget that God will one day call you to account; only old age and death, the ultimate futility, lie ahead.

Epilogue (12:9–14)

A disciple commends Qoheleth's teaching and succinctly sums it up as to fear God and keep His commandments. God will call all our deeds to judgement, all that is hidden, be it good or bad.

Song of Songs

'Song of Songs' is a Hebrew idiom meaning 'greatest of all songs'. Yet despite this accolade nothing is known of when it was written or by whom.[1] Few works have provided such a fertile field for imaginative interpretation. It has been variously construed as a two-character drama involving Solomon; as a three-character drama; and as an anthology of nuptial poems. For centuries Jewish tradition took it as an allegory of Yahweh's love for Israel while Christians saw it as symbolising the marriage of Christ to His Church.

Today it is recognised that while the Song may recall these ideas, there is nothing that justifies relating the detail of its overtly erotic language to the spiritual realm, attempts to do so are both forced and unconvincing. As a result there is a growing consensus to take it at face value as a loosely related collection of poems extolling the passion and joy, the beauty and wonder, of human love. These are centred around a country girl (the beloved or bride), a shepherd (the lover or groom) and the daughters of Jerusalem, a chorus that the poet invokes from time to time.[2]

Employing metaphors that convey a chasteness and modesty that less poetic speech would preclude, the Song adopts a lofty tone and delights in physical attraction and the bond that binds the lovers. It knows the anguish of separation and the joy of reunion. It has nothing to say about procreation, extolling love for love's sake alone, and its warnings against stimulating love artificially are a valuable antidote to the modern world's commercialisation of sexuality. With its pastoral setting the Song recalls the Garden of Eden. It is as if we were witnessing the restoration of love to its pre-Fall bliss.

There is little progression. The lovers' passion is as intense at the beginning as at the end. A love longed for when apart, enjoyed when together, exclusively for one another. A love as strong as death, freely given yet beyond price. The Song's beauty of expression not only fits it to exalt the closest of all human relationships but recalls a love that is higher still.

First poem (1:1 – 2:7)

The beloved yearns for her lover's caresses and for 'the king' to take her away.[3] She longs to know where he grazes his flock so that she may join him (1:1–7). The daughters of Jerusalem tell her to follow the tracks.[4] The lover now makes his entrance. He compares his beloved's beauty to one of Pharaoh's mares and promises earrings and beads to enhance her loveliness even more (1:8–11).

The lovers express their mutual adoration in metaphors drawn from nature: exotic fragrances, flowers, doves, lawns, an orchard. She is the rose of Sharon, sick with love as she reclines in her lover's arms. He concludes by charging the daughters of Jerusalem 'not to rouse his beloved before she pleases'[5] (1:12 – 2:7).

Second poem (2:8 – 3:5)

The maiden describes her lover coming to visit her in the idyllic freshness of spring, bounding over the hills like a young gazelle. He invites her to the countryside to see the miracle of nature blossoming into new life with flowers, the first figs, the fragrance of the vines and the cooing of turtledoves. She urges him to catch the foxes that despoil the vineyards.[6] Their love is all consuming: 'my love is mine and I am his' (2:8–17).

The scene changes. Alone at night she cannot bear to be parted from her lover and goes about the city seeking him. When she finds him she brings him back to her mother's house, to the very room where she herself was conceived. Again the shepherd charges the daughters of Jerusalem not to rouse his beloved (3:1–5).

Third poem (3:6 – 5:1)

Possibly prompted by the lovers' own wedding the poet recalls Solomon's wedding procession[7] (3:6–11). The shepherd glories in his bride's charms. The tresses of her hair are like goats trailing in waves down Mount Gilead, her lips a scarlet thread. She is a 'garden enclosed, a sealed fountain'.[8] The bride picks up the metaphor and invites her groom to enter her garden and make it his own.[9] Guests are invited to the celebrations (4:1 – 5:1).

Fourth poem (5:2 – 6:3)

Ecstasy turns to anguish. When the shepherd comes by night and knocks on his beloved's door she is already in bed and slow to respond so that when she does eventually turn the bolt he has gone. Passion drives her to the darkened city to find him. The watchmen, taking her to be up to no good, beat her and take away her cloak. She charges the daughters of Jerusalem, if they should find her lover, to tell him that she is sick with love (5:2–9).

Now it is the maiden's turn to praise her lover. With his ruddy complexion, his head of purest gold and eyes like doves, he is one in a million (5:10–16). The daughters of Jerusalem enquire where he is. She replies that he has gone down to his garden to pasture his flock. They are together again (6:1–3).

Fifth poem (6:4 – 8:4)

The groom delights in his bride. She is the only one for him, an object of adoration, loveliness and desire, fair as the moon, resplendent as the sun[10] (6:4 – 7:10a). The bride calls her lover away to the serenity of the countryside – it is spring again with the vines budding and the blossoms opening – where she can give him the gift of her love (7:10b–14).

If only they were brother and sister so that she could display her love more openly.[11] As she nestles in his embrace the groom again appeals to the daughters of Jerusalem not to force their love (8:1–4).

Sixth poem (8:5–14)

The couple return from the desert, the bride leaning on her lover as she declaims the depths of her love: a love as strong as Death, passion as relentless as Sheol, love no flood can quench, no torrents drown (8:5–7).

Appendices

These concluding verses appear to be a collection of disparate fragments for which lack of context makes interpretation all but impossible (8:8–14).

Wisdom

Wisdom is one of the deutero-canonical books. The author is not named but assumes the mantle of Solomon. However it is widely agreed that this was merely a device to give the book a cachet and that it was composed by a Jew living in Alexandria during the first century B.C. Alexandria was a centre of the Jewish Diaspora and a great seat of Hellenistic learning. His audience would therefore have been fellow Jews whose faith was under challenge through exposure to the novelties of Greek philosophy and a pagan population with a vibrant cultural life. However his message of encouragement and hope transcends time, making it as relevant now as it was then. It is in three parts.

The book opens with a clear statement of man's immortal destiny although nowhere does it speak of bodily resurrection. Death brings a parting of the ways. The virtuous, those who embrace wisdom, will enjoy immortality, dwelling with God. The wicked face eternal loss. Death is the devil's doing. God created life. In part two the sage reveals Solomon's understanding of Wisdom and how he acquired her.

Part three, centred on the Exodus, shows Wisdom at work in history, contrasting the help God meted out to upright Israel with the punishment inflicted on reprobate Egypt. The author's intent was clearly to encourage the Alexandrian Jews by showing how their forebears had suffered in Egypt once before. God intervened on their behalf then and could confidently be expected to do so again.

Human destiny (1:1 – 6:21)

The author purports to be addressing his fellow kings. He enjoins them to live virtuously and to seek God in simplicity of heart. He will reveal Himself to those who trust Him. Perverse thoughts on the other hand separate people from God. Nor can Wisdom dwell in a body defiled by sin.[1] Nothing escapes God's gaze. His spirit fills the world and those who do wrong court death. Not that death was any part of God's design. On the contrary He created life and the upright are assured of immortality (1:1–15).

The godless invite death in everything they do. 'Life came about by chance', they say, 'it will pass away like wisps of cloud so let's enjoy it while we can'. So they go on throwing their weight about, ignoring the poor and weak, and reproachful and contemptuous of the upright whose way of life sticks in their throats. 'He claims to have God as his father' they say. 'Very well let's torment him and see if God comes to his rescue'. How misguided they are! God created man in His own image to be immortal and immortality is the reward the upright will receive. Death only came into the world because of the devil (1:16 – 2:24).

It may seem a disaster when the upright die but they are at peace with God and nothing can trouble them any more. Any ordeals God may have subjected them to in this life to test them are as nothing compared with the blessings to come. At the time of their visitation they will shine out and live forever with God as king.[2] But the wicked have nothing to look forward to (3:1–12).

No matter how many children the wicked have, or how long they live, they count for nothing. It is the virtuous God grants immortality to.[3] If an upright man dies young it is because God has taken him from this world to save him from contamination (3:13 – 4:19).

In a judgement scene after death the wicked, who were once so self-assured, see that the good people they used to mistreat are now with God and the horrible realisation dawns on them of the tragic waste of the godless lives they led. What good are their riches and arrogance now? They are left with nothing. The upright will live for ever with God while they will be annihilated (4:20 – 5:23).

The sage reminds his fellow kings that their power comes from God and He will hold them accountable if they do not rule justly. So they should heed his words about Wisdom. Wisdom is readily found by those who seek her. Those who love Wisdom keep her laws. And keeping her laws guarantees immortality[4] (6:1–21).

Solomon's quest for Wisdom (6:22 – 9:18)

Solomon began life like everyone else. He prayed and Wisdom came to him bringing all other good things with her. She is a priceless gem and those who acquire her win God's friendship. She is intelligent, holy, unique, all-powerful, pure; a mirror of God's power and goodness, an emanation of His glory. More splendid than the sun, unchanging, spanning the entire world, she can accomplish anything, drawing people nearer to God and renewing the world. God loves only those who embrace Wisdom. Evil cannot prevail against her. She governs the whole world for its good (6:22 – 8:1).

Solomon fell in love with Wisdom and sought her as his bride. She shares God's life and the secrets of His knowledge. She is the source of wealth, knowledge, experience and uprightness. She teaches the virtues of temperance, prudence, justice and fortitude. He decided to adopt her as his counsellor and comforter so that he would be a good ruler. After much thought he also concluded that Wisdom was the key to immortality. So he prayed to possess her for he realised she was a gift from God (8:2–21).

Solomon asked God for Wisdom so that he might rule justly and walk in God's ways. Without Wisdom, who was present when God made the world and who knows what pleases Him, he would count for nothing. It is difficult enough to fathom what is happening on earth. What hope would we have of understanding God's ways had He not given us Wisdom and His Spirit from above? (9:1–18)

WISDOM AT WORK IN HISTORY (10:1 – 19:22)

From Adam to Moses (10:1 – 11:3)

The sage now demonstrates how Wisdom has been at work in Israel's history from Adam right down to Moses and the Exodus.[5] The recollection of Moses paves the way for the five antitheses (summarised in italics) that occupy the remainder of the book.[6] In these the author contrasts the way God treated Israel and Egypt during the Exodus, and attempts to show that Israel benefited from the very things that afflicted the Egyptians.[7]

First antithesis (11:4–14)

Whereas the Egyptians had only the polluted Nile to drink from, God provided Israel with water from a rock. God had let Israel go thirsty up to that time both to teach her a lesson and to show her how severely the Egyptians were suffering.[8]

Second antithesis (11:15 – 16:15)

When the Egyptians sinned by worshipping reptiles and beetles God punished them with swarms of vermin.[9] The thought of these destroyed their appetites at a time when Israel was enjoying a diet of luscious quails. This antithesis is in three parts (11:15–16; 12:23–27; 15:18 – 16:4) divided by a reflection on God's mercy (11:17 – 12:22), a digression on idolatry (13:1 – 15:17), and an apologia for Israel's own privations (16:5–15).

The sage maintains that God could easily have destroyed the Egyptians but stayed His hand to give them a chance to repent.[10] Even the Canaanites were exterminated gradually. This leniency demonstrates that God is master of His strength and teaches His people to be kind when they judge and to hope for mercy when they are judged (11:17 – 12:22).

In an exhaustive digression on idolatry the sage warns that instead of worshipping the marvels of nature men should look beyond the created to their Creator. He ridicules the woodcutter who uses wood left over from making artefacts and cooking his meals to carve an idol he then worships. No less absurd is a traveller in a storm-tossed ship praying to a piece of wood that is even frailer than the ship. The potter is equally culpable, earning his living making idols he knows are worthless. Idols are a human creation, typically made by a father to venerate a dead child or by a ruler for his subjects to worship. They are at the heart of evil whereas the key to immortality is knowing God (13:1 – 15:17).

The author hastens to forestall any riposte based on the Israelites themselves once having been plagued by serpents, Nb 21:4–9. That was but a brief episode intended as a warning. Also it demonstrated God's power over life and death to her enemies (16:5–15).

Third antithesis (16:16–29)

Whereas the Egyptians' crops were ravaged by incessant rain, hail and unquenchable fire, God fed Israel with manna from heaven.

Fourth antithesis (17:1 – 18:4)

Whereas the Egyptians were terrorised by a plague of darkness Israel was guided on her journey by a pillar of fire.[11]

Fifth antithesis (18:5 – 19:21)

Whereas Egypt suffered disaster in the Sea Israel escaped across the Sea singing God's praises (19:1–21). This antithesis is preceded by a heart-rending description of the night the Egyptian first-born were slain (18:5–19) and an attempt to play down the time Israel was stricken by plague in the desert by explaining that it was quickly brought to an end by intercession[12] (18:20–25).

Conclusion (19:22)

God has made His people great and glorious. He has never failed to come to their aid.

Ecclesiasticus

Ecclesiasticus, also known as 'The Wisdom of Jesus ben (son of) Sira' or sometimes simply as 'Sirach', is one of the deutero-canonical books. The author identifies himself as Jesus son of Sira at 50:27 and in the subscript after 51:30. He is usually referred to as Ben Sira. The book is in six parts.

First comes a foreword in which Ben Sira's grandson tells how he made a translation of his grandfather's work while domiciled in Egypt in the thirty-eighth year of king Euergetes, with the aim of helping Jews domiciled abroad to live according to the Law.[1]

The core of the book is a long compendium of musings on the nature and origins of wisdom together with maxims and longer aphorisms on a wide range of topics, both religious and secular, after the style of Proverbs. This is discussed below (1:1 – 42:14).

The remaining four parts comprise a poem extolling the glory of God as revealed in nature (42:15 – 43:33); eulogies to Israel's great ancestors – 'let us praise famous men' – running from Enoch and Noah to a near contemporary high priest called Simon (44:1 – 50:29); a hymn of thanksgiving for deliverance from some life-threatening danger (51:1–12), and finally a poem describing the author's zeal in pursuit of wisdom (51:13–30).

WISDOM AND OTHER WORLDLY ADVICE (1:1 – 42:14)

Although Ben Sira made some attempt to organise his material according to subject matter, the book still lacks orderly arrangement and is no easier to summarise than Proverbs. We shall therefore attempt no more than to give a flavour by highlighting its main topics, starting with wisdom, the thread that binds it together.

Wisdom

Wisdom comes from God who alone possesses her fully. She was created before all else and is with Him for ever. The fount of wisdom is fear of God and keeping the Law, 15:1; 19:20; 21:11. Everything will turn out well for those who exercise fidelity, gentleness and patience. But those who yield to anger, duplicity and self-exaltation will be disgraced (1:1–30).

Fearing God demands constancy in the face of trials and ordeals. Those who hold fast will enjoy His support, mercy, forgiveness and blessings but woe to fainthearts and sinners (2:1–18). Although she tests them severely Wisdom rewards her followers and God loves those who love her (4:11-19). The pursuit of wisdom requires a rare single-mindedness. Only those who fear the Lord and obey the Law will find her (6:18–37; 14:20 – 15:10).

In the lyrical chapter 24, Wisdom sings her own praises.[2] She came forth from the mouth of the Most High, 'covering the earth like mist', and is enthroned with Him for all eternity. By God's command she made Israel her inheritance. Her fruits are available to everyone and once tasted prove irresistible. No one who obeys her will ever sin.

In equating wisdom and fear of God with the Law, Ben Sira breaks out of the narrower confines of Proverbs and ties wisdom into Israel's mainstream traditions. He travels further down this path when he enjoins reverence for the priesthood (7:29–31) and shows himself to be an ardent devotee of the liturgy[3] (35:1–10). However he rejects worship that is impious or tainted by sin (7:9; 34:18–26).

Other advice

Ben Sira accepted the orthodox view of his day that virtue is rewarded and evil punished in this life.[4] However he appears not to have been completely convinced and to have been struggling for some recognition of the injustices of the world. He seems to have had an inkling that death was the key: on their dying day the righteous will be blessed, 1:13; those who remember the inevitability of death will not sin, 7:36; in a man's last hour his deeds stand revealed and it is a trifle for God to repay him as he deserves, 11:26–28. It is almost as if Ben Sira had a presentiment of a personal judgement. But he does not articulate this nor make the jump to the idea of life beyond the grave, so how exactly he understood the final realisation of God's justice remains unclear.

Ben Sira commends charity to the poor, 3:30 – 4:11, while at the same time disapproving of undue self-deprivation, 14:3–19. He affirms man's freedom to choose between good and evil 15:11–17, acknowledges his propensity to sin, 8:5; 17:31; 37:3, the inevitability of retribution, 16:1–23 and calls for repentance, 17:24–32; 35:3. He proclaims God's justice, 35:11–24, His compassion for the cipher that is man, 18:1–14, and man's wretchedness, 40:1–11. He offers prayers to combat evil, 22:27 – 23:6, and for the restoration of Israel, 36:1–17. He hymns poems on creation and man's moral nature, 16:24 – 17:24, in praise of God, 39:12–35, and on death, 41:1–4.

That Ben Sira made some attempt to group his maxims by subject is evident from his homilies on parental respect, 3:1–16; pride and humility, 3:17–29; 10:6–18; friendship, 6:5–17; 22:19–26; 37:1–6; enemies, 12:8–18; women, 9:1–9; 25:13 – 26:18; 36:21–27; and control of the tongue, 19:4–12; 20:1–8, 18–26; 23:7–15; 27:4–7; 28:13–26. Even so there is sometimes more than one collection.

At other times it is difficult to detect any rationale in his arrangement. All the aphorisms of 8:1–19 and 9:10–18 have in common are relationships with different sorts of people; the rich and influential, repentant sinners, the elderly and so on. Chapter 7 ranges over shunning evil, seeking honours, presumption, seeking public office, prayer, kindness to the downcast, lying, respect for elders, shirking hard work, avoiding sin, humility, barter, slaves, care of cattle and more. Nothing seems to escape the sage's gaze whether it be advice on staying in other people's homes, 29:21–28, behaviour at dinner parties, 31:12–24, manners at a banquet, 32:1–13 or observations on wine, 31:25–31.

THE PROPHETS

The sequence of books from Isaiah to Malachi is known collectively as the Prophets. In everyday parlance a prophet is someone who foretells the future. Although this has its place in Biblical prophecy it is not the defining characteristic. In the Scriptures a prophet is someone who speaks in God's name. And although his vision may sometimes probe the future he is more often immersed in the urgency of the here and now, warning of reliance on the powers of this world rather than of God, and condemning idolatry and injustice. He is usually called at some crisis point and his message is usually aimed at the nation as a whole, rather than individuals, with the aim of quickening its conscience with warnings of judgement and visions of hope.

Samuel is sometimes called the last of the judges and the first of the prophets but there were prophets before his time e.g. Moses, Dt 34:10, Miriam, Ex 15:20, Deborah, Jg 4:4. Elijah and Elisha were prophets, 1K 18:36; 19:16, as were many others of lesser stature like Nathan, 2S 7:2, Ahijah, 1K 11:29, and Huldah, 2K 22:14. Nor was the office of prophecy unique to Israel. Elijah had to contend with 400 prophets of Baal, 1K 18:19.

We have reports about these earlier prophets but except in isolated instances we do not have their precise words or thoughts. The books from Isaiah to Malachi purport to give us the prophets' actual words. However even these later seers were basically preachers rather than writers so it is problematical how much they actually inscrolled themselves. With the possible exception of Ezekiel probably not very much and so the term 'writing prophets' that is often used to describe them is somewhat wide of the mark. Rather they are prophets whose oracles have been recorded in writing, often at the hands of disciples who would sometimes have added their own prophecies in the style of the master while they were about it. The original material would often have been delivered over the course of many years and it would also have been worked over by editors before being recorded in its final form.

Modern readers may well be sympathetic to Luther's observation that 'the prophets seem to observe no order but ramble along from one subject to another'. A typical chapter is a collection of fugitive pieces, some quite possibly only a verse or two long, shorn of connecting narrative, only rarely arranged in any discernible order, independent in form and content, uttered in varying circumstances and at different times. It is sometimes uncertain where the boundary lies between one effusion and the next. Much is in verse and so like all poetry allusive and cryptic. (All this results in a somewhat staccato effect when the prophets are presented in synopsis mode.)

The prophets were in no doubt that their message was from God. Their oracles are peppered with 'Thus says Yahweh', 'The word of Yahweh was addressed to me as follows', 'Yahweh declares' and so on.

A characteristic of prophecy is for time scales to be 'telescoped'. Future events are seen in a foreshortened perspective so that the distinction between the near term and the far distant becomes blurred with events that are historically separate getting merged and presented as if they were contiguous. One of the best examples is found at Mt 3:1–12 where John the Baptist (the last of the prophets), with his references to 'preparing a way for the Lord' and 'burning chaff in a fire that will never go out' telescopes events relating to Jesus' first and second Comings. However this peculiarity no more invalidates the prophets' utterances than it does those of Christ Himself who similarly telescoped events in His Olivet discourse, Mt 24.

Isaiah

Isaiah is one of the most inspiring books in the Bible. It sings prophecies of the Messiah which are the most exalted of any in the Canon. In its vision of the transcendent God who, after judgement and purging will regather the repentant faithful in a new Exodus, it is unsurpassed. Straddling two worlds, one portraying sinners before an angry God, the other a remnant receiving salvation from that same God, its thought ranges from the present to the end of time. Nor is it just in the religious order that Isaiah is pre-eminent. Its verse has a richness and grandeur that touches the sublime.

The book divides into three. Chapters 1–39 are set in the self-assured Judah of the eighth century, at a time when she was steadily falling under the shadow of Assyria's imperialist ambitions. They point to a future king, Immanuel, who will reign in glory but meanwhile stress Israel's infidelity and God's justice, conveying an air of menace and impending doom.

Chapters 40–55 address the exiles in Babylon in the sixth century. Punishment having been meted out, the prophet is looking to the Persians under Cyrus to restore them to their homeland. In addition they present a mysterious Servant who will reconcile the world with God through suffering. The backdrop to chapters 56–66 is the restored community living in Jerusalem soon after their return.

Because of these different settings it is likely that only chapters 1–39 belong to the Isaiah, son of Amoz, of the inscription at 1:1. Chapters 40–55 are generally attributed to another prophet, usually referred to as Deutero or Second Isaiah, who lived among the exiles in Babylon. Chapters 56–66 were long thought to be the work of yet another prophet, Trito or Third Isaiah. In fact they may well be a composite work.

Isaiah Son of Amoz

The Isaiah of the book's first thirty-nine chapters was called in 740 B.C., the year king Uzziah died, 6:1, and his ministry to Judah and Jerusalem spanned the reigns of the next three kings, 1:1. Since the latest of his oracles that can be reliably dated refers to Sennacherib's attack on Jerusalem in 701 he must have been active for at least forty years. He seems to have moved easily in court circles and to have had an extensive knowledge of world affairs. He wrote a history of Uzziah's reign, 2Ch 26:22, and so may have been a courtier. For at least part of his ministry he was a contemporary of Amos, Hosea and Micah.

Isaiah's call, when he saw God enthroned in majesty surrounded by seraphs, made an indelible impression and brought home to him with the force of a thunderbolt the gulf between God's ineffable holiness and the depravity of man.

It is against this background that his oracles denounce Judah's moral decadence so vehemently. She oozes at every pore with idolatry, hollow piety, pride, social injustice, oppression of the weak. She is preoccupied with wealth, pleasure and power, relegating God to the sidelines. From the citadels of their closed minds her leaders wilfully go their own ways preferring human wisdom to the divine.

Against conduct that so offends God's holiness there can be but one response. No one will escape God's just punishment. Neither Judah, for whom Assyria will act as His chastening whip, nor Assyria herself. The whole earth will reel under God's winnowing arm. For He is Lord of all.

But Isaiah is no prophet of despair. Even the most hardened sinners will be forgiven if they repent. Despite chastisement a remnant will survive. Purged of her guilt Jerusalem will once again become the 'Faithful City' and, in the latter days, the nations will gather in her squares to walk in God's ways.

These prophecies of judgement, doom and hope are scattered throughout the book but there are also four other collections. In chapters 24–27, 'Isaiah's apocalypse', the prophet looks beyond his own times to envision the end of the world: cosmic catastrophe, God's victory over tyranny and pride and the end of death culminating in God's reign over a vast concourse drawn from all nations. In chapters 34–35, the so-called 'little apocalypse', he sees the destruction of God's enemies and the bliss of salvation. In chapters 13–23, like several other prophets, he thunders prophecies against Israel's neighbours. Finally in chapters 7–11, in one of the Old Testament's great foreshadowings of Christ, he prophecies a Son, Immanuel, who will one day rule for ever as King with the spirit of Yahweh in justice and boundless peace.

Historical background

As many of Isaiah's oracles are written in the shadow of Assyrian aggrandizement (e.g. the Syro-Ephraimite war and Sennacherib's invasion) it may help the reader find his bearings to explain how these events interrelate. The first half of the eighth century B.C. had been a time of great prosperity for both Israel and Judah but with the accession of Tiglath-Pileser III to the Assyrian throne in 745 B.C. the writing was on the wall for both states. Over the coming decades Assyria would be ruled by a succession of predatory kings bent on empire. Conquered peoples would be ruthlessly transplanted and rebellion quashed with ferocious barbarity.

In 740 B.C. Israel was forced to pay tribute to Tiglath-Pileser. Shortly after she concluded an alliance with Aram (a state around Damascus) in the hope of averting further aggression and invited Judah to join them. When Judah's king Ahaz declined Aram and Israel invaded, intending to replace Ahaz with someone more sympathetic to their cause. This sparked the so-called Syro-Ephraimite war. When Ahaz appealed for help Tiglath Pileser needed no encouragement. He crushed Aram and stripped Israel of her northern provinces. But the price was high. Judah was reduced to little more than a vassal state.

Following Tiglath-Pileser's death in 727 Israel refused to pay tribute to his successor Shalmaneser V and flirted with Egypt. This was her death knell. In 721 Samaria fell to Shalmaneser's successor Sargon II and the northern kingdom ceased to exist. Her people were deported and her land resettled by immigrants from other parts of the Assyrian empire.

Sargon's death in 705 B.C. precipitated a spate of revolts in which Judah's king Hezekiah became embroiled, toying with the idea of a protective alliance with Egypt. Sargon's successor Sennacherib did not forget these presumptions. In 701 he overran Judah and Jerusalem itself barely escaped capture.

Oracles of promise and rebuke (1:1 – 5:30)

The devastation Judah has suffered from invasion is self-inflicted, the result of a stubborn ungrateful sinful nation rebelling against the parental care Yahweh has lavished on her. She has come within an ace of being wiped out like Sodom and Gomorrah. Even oxen and donkeys have more sense[1] (1:1–9).

Isaiah condemns worship that is hollow because it is accompanied by evil and wrong-doing rather than justice and kindness (1:10–17). Then in sharp contrast he announces that although those who persist in opposing God face His wrath, even those whose sins are like scarlet will be white as snow provided they repent (1:18–20).

Isaiah likens the once faithful Jerusalem to a harlot. But again judgement is tempered with hope, for after chastisement God will purge her of her guilt and she will become the 'City of Saving Justice, Faithful City.' (1:21–28). He next attacks pagan worship linked to sacred trees. Those who indulge will go up in flames like the parched leaves of the trees that were once their delight (1:29–31).

In a vision of the final days Isaiah sees every nation hastening to Jerusalem to walk in God's ways and live in a world that God will rule in justice and idyllic peace with swords hammered into ploughshares (2:1–5).
Appendix 1 refers

He attributes God's rejection of His people to their preoccupation with divination, wealth, armaments and idols. He prophesies a Day when God will intervene to abase human pride and arrogance; a time when men will hide in terror at the brilliance of His majesty and cast their idols aside as the rubbish they are (2:6–22).

A time of famine and anarchy is coming when inexperienced complacent rulers, parading their sin like Sodom, will lead the people astray. They hatch their own downfall (3:1–15).

Isaiah next berates the fashion-crazed society women of Jerusalem. Given over to flirtation and coquetry and besotted by self-adornment, what an awakening they face! A time of tribulation is coming when their tawdry baubles will count for nothing and seven women will plead with one man to bear his children[2] (3:16 – 4:1).

Another glimpse of the end days shows the fruits of Yahweh's 'seedling' living in Jerusalem under His protection after He has cleansed and judged them (4:2–6).

In an allegory of unrequited love Yahweh tells how He tended and nurtured His vineyard (Israel) with loving care on a fertile hillside (He bestowed blessings on her).

He naturally expected fine grapes (loyalty) in return. But all He got were the wild grapes of rebellion. So He will withhold rain and give the land over to brambles and thorns (5:1–7).

In a catalogue of 'woes' Isaiah again drags Israel's rebellious ways to the light of day as he castigates the greedy and extortionists; escapists, playboys and pleasure seekers who never give a thought to God; the proud; scoffers; perverted thinkers who have lost all sense of right and wrong; intellectual snobs; perpetrators of corruption and injustice. In an ominous coda he reveals that God has already summoned a distant nation (Assyria), its warriors 'growling like lions as they seize their prey', as His rod of anger (5:8–30).

The Divine call (6:1–13)

Only now does Isaiah relate how he received his prophetic call in a vision in the Temple in which he saw God enthroned in majesty and holiness. He was overcome by the realisation of his own uncleanliness but was purified when a seraph from God's presence touched his lips with a live coal taken from the altar. He was told that his words would fall on deaf ears and that before anything changed the land would be laid waste and abandoned with the people cutback to a 'stock', a holy seed[3] (6:1–13).

The book of Immanuel: Messianic portents (7:1–17; 8:23 – 9:6; 11:1–16)

Isaiah now gives voice to three prophecies that from the earliest times have been seen as portents of the Messiah. The first had its origins in a contemporary crisis. Aram and Israel had invaded Judah in an attempt to replace her king Ahaz with the son of a certain Tabeel who supported their plan to enlist Judah into their alliance against Assyria. Isaiah told Ahaz that if he trusted Yahweh the danger would pass. He was even offered a sign. Ahaz's rejection of this – 'I will not put Yahweh to the test' – sounds pious but Isaiah's rebuke shows that he saw Ahaz for the hypocrite he was.[4] Addressing the House of David he went on to prophecy that God would offer a sign in any case:

> The young woman is with child
> and will give birth to a son
> whom she will call Immanuel.

Furthermore before the child knew the difference between right and wrong (i.e. within a few years) Aram and Israel would be devastated[5] (7:1–17).

This is precisely what happened. Aram fell to Assyria within two years while the inhabitants of the northern kingdom of Israel were deported a few years later. Who the son was who figured in the prophecy at the time we do not know.

If this prophecy stood alone the belief that it also pointed to a wider realisation in Christ, way beyond the immediate circumstances that occasioned it, would rest on three foundations. First the name Immanuel, meaning 'God with us', obviously implies some quite extraordinary divine favour. Second, God giving a sign despite Ahaz's rejection also indicates that something of unusual importance was in the offing.

Addressing the prophecy to the whole House of David rather than simply to Ahaz also enhances its significance.

However the issue is put beyond doubt when the Immanuel prophecy is read together with two others. The exalted titles these give the Son, the promise that He will reign for ever, the virtues He will be endowed with emanating from the Spirit of Yahweh, the boundless idyllic peace He will inaugurate, not to mention the solemnity with which they are made and their exultant tone, make a reading limited to Ahaz's time untenable.

The second prophecy starts by revealing the glory that will come to the land of Zebulun and Naphtali (the area around Galilee).[6]

> The people that walked in darkness have seen a great light;
> on the inhabitants of a country in shadow dark as death
> light has blazed forth.

before continuing

> For a son has been born for us,
> a son has been given to us,
> and dominion has been laid on his shoulders;
> and this is the name he has been given,
> Wonder-Counsellor, Mighty-God,
> Eternal-Father, Prince-of-Peace (8:23 – 9:6)

When the Messianic theme resumes it is to reinforce that this mighty King will be of the House of David.[7]

> A shoot will spring from the stock of Jesse,
> a new shoot will grow from his roots.

before describing the wonderful gifts He will be empowered with: the spirit of Yahweh, of wisdom and insight, of counsel and power, of knowledge and fear of Yahweh, uprightness and constancy. He will bring perfect peace: the wolf will live with the lamb. Everyone will walk in God's ways (11:1–9).

There follows a vision of the last days when Gentiles too will seek out the Lord and God will gather the remnant of His scattered people from the ends of the earth in a glorious homecoming. Israel and Judah will live in harmony both with one another and with their traditional enemies, Edom, Moab, Ammon (11:10–16).
Appendix 2 refers

The book of Immanuel: diverse oracles (7:18 – 8:22; 9:7 – 10:34; 12:1–6)

Isaiah warns of an invasion when the land will be so devastated it will revert from vines to brambles and thorns and be fit only for cattle and sheep (7:18–25). He gives his second son a symbolic name ('quick pickings, easy prey') to draw attention to his earlier prophecy of the downfall of Aram and Israel at Assyria's hands and prophesies that Judah will be ravaged 'up to the neck' by the raging 'flood of Assyria' for not trusting in God's smooth flowing waters of Shiloah[8] (8:1–10).

Isaiah relates how God instructed him not to follow a populist line but to preach without fear or favour. He enjoins his disciples to preserve the words God has given him and to warn people not to dabble in mediums and fortune-tellers. A poetic fragment harrowingly portrays the anguish and despair of someone wandering in a land ravaged in the night of God's judgement (8:11–23).

Isaiah launches a fierce diatribe against arrogance, pride, apostasy, injustice and moral decay in the northern kingdom of Israel.[9] She is impenitent. God has chastened her already but His anger is still not spent (9:7 – 10:4).

Assyria will be destroyed for her pride and abusing her power. For although she has been acting as God's 'rod of anger' on His wayward people, she herself is unaware of this and has pursued violence for her own ends (10:5–19). As for Israel, Isaiah injects a ray of hope. A remnant will survive and turn to Yahweh (10:20–23). Another oracle predicts the end of Assyrian oppression. God will punish her as in the past He punished Egypt (10:24–27). A poem conjures up the terror an Assyrian army would have roused as it advanced on Jerusalem before Yahweh cut it down (10:28–34). The book of Immanuel ends fittingly with a song of praise to Yahweh 'God of my Salvation' (12:1–6).
Appendix 3 refers

Proclamations about foreign nations (13:1 – 23:18)

Babylon will fall to the Medes (13:1–22). Israel will one day be resettled on her own soil along with foreigners who will be her slaves (14:1–2). A mocking song about the ignominious death of a king of Babylon (14:3–23) is followed by an oracle in which Yahweh promises to break Assyria[10] (14:24–27). For Philistia, already under the rod, worse is yet to come (14:28–32). Isaiah describes a devastating invasion of Moab and the heart-rending plight of her people (15:1 – 16:14). He predicts the ruin of Damascus and (the northern kingdom of) Israel (17:1–11).
Appendix 4 refers

God saves Judah from invasion by a 'vast horde' (17:12–14). Cush will be laid waste by invasion. However a time will come when she will be converted to Yahweh[11] (18:1–7). Egypt faces civil war and ruin (19:1–15). Egypt will one day be converted and reconciled with Assyria and Israel. All three peoples will then be blessed (19:16–25).

Isaiah goes around naked and barefoot in an acted parable to indicate how Assyria will humble Egypt. Judah should place no reliance on help from that quarter (20:1–6). A vision of the fall of Babylon (21:1–10) is followed by a prophecy that after a brief respite Edom will be subjected to yet more suffering (21:11–12). Kedar, a town in Arabia, will be destroyed (21:13–17). Judah is condemned for ignoring Yahweh when she was under attack and never acknowledging His help in saving her (22:1–14). Shebna, a court dignitary, is condemned for building himself such a magnificent tomb (22:15–25). In a fine poem Isaiah prophesies that Tyre will fall but will eventually be restored to her former splendour when the profits from her trading will be consecrated to Yahweh (23:1–18).

The Apocalypse of Isaiah (24:1 – 27:13)

In a catena, or chain, of poems, as florid as they are obscure, and shot through with visions of tribulation and cosmic catastrophe, Isaiah portrays the future downfall of God's enemies, the end of death and the final felicity of the just. He hammers home the relentlessness of God's judgement. None of those who have defiled the earth by flouting His laws will escape, neither people below nor powers above.[12] The earth will be swallowed up in ruin and joylessness.

Nature itself will share man's fate. Yet hope glimmers. A few will be left, crying for joy as the vision ends with the brilliance of sun and moon eclipsed by the radiance of Yahweh reigning from Zion (24:1–23).

A canticle of thanksgiving blends into a vision of God preparing a banquet of succulent food and fine wines for the nations to celebrate His victories over tyranny, pride and death. Tears and sadness will be no more. Man's shame is expunged, trust in the Lord finally vindicated (25:1–12).

Another hymn of thanksgiving culminates in one of the few references in the Old Testament to bodily resurrection.

> Your dead will come back to life, your corpses will rise again.
> Wake up and sing, you dwellers in the dust.

Meanwhile God's people are invited to shelter for 'a little while' until the wicked are punished[13] (26:1 – 27:1).

In the end days God will lovingly tend His vineyard (Israel). His wrath will be only against the 'thorns and briers' that overran it and even then He invites repentance. Israel will blossom to a vast harvest and be gathered in from the ends of the earth to worship in Jerusalem (27:2–13).

Diverse oracles (28:1 – 33:24)

Isaiah contrasts the fading splendour of the northern kingdom of Israel and her drunken leaders, soon to be overthrown, with the glory awaiting the remnant (28:1–6). Judah too had better beware. Drunken prophets and priests who treat God's word as if it were something in a strange tongue will soon get taught a lesson by foreigners (the Assyrians) speaking a strange tongue (28:7–13). Addressing Judah's rulers Isaiah declares that relying on an alliance with 'Death' is as stupid as trying to sleep in a bed too short to stretch out in. The God who helped them in the past at Gibeon will just as surely act against them now as He pursues His mysterious ways. But all is not lost. He is at the same time laying a foundation stone of justice and uprightness[14] (28:14–22). A farming parable draws out how God treats everyone according to their own special needs (28:23–29).

Isaiah foresees a devastating attack on Ariel (Jerusalem). However when all seems lost God will rescue her and her enemies will feel like someone who dreams of quenching his thirst only to wake up parched (29:1–8). He next turns to obdurate people who are blind to God's teaching and to whom worship is mere lip-service.[15]

Their cleverness will avail them nothing (29:9–14). How absurd it is for people to try to keep their thoughts hidden from the same God whom they will soon be honouring when, in a short time, He replenishes the earth, succours the sick and lowly, and banishes villains and scoffers (29:15–24).

Isaiah denounces the despatch of envoys to negotiate an alliance with Egypt without first consulting Yahweh (30:1–7). The people of Judah are a rebellious lot. All they want is to be rid of the Holy One of Israel and live with their illusions. They have spurned repentance and God's help in favour of their own ways and are wedded to violence and deceit. They will be shattered like a pot of clay (30:8–17).

God is waiting to take pity on His people. After they have been refined by suffering He will heal their wounds. They will see Him with their own eyes and He will answer their cries for help. Idols will be discarded in disgust. There will be rich harvests and pasture. Streams will gush from every hill. Then, in awesome verse, Isaiah depicts God's destruction of Assyria watched by an Israel rejoicing in music and song (30:18–33)

The prophet again condemns Judah's soliciting Egypt for protection rather than God. Just as a lion is not deflected from its prey by the shouts of shepherds so nothing will stop Yahweh from protecting Jerusalem. A day will come when Israel will repent and discard her idols. Assyria will fall by the sword but it will not be by human agency (31:1–9).

Isaiah looks ahead to a king whose reign is just. Fools and scoundrels will be seen for what they are (32:1–8). He warns the haughty ladies of Jerusalem of the day of reckoning that is fast approaching. Vineyards will give way to brambles and the teeming city will become the haunt of wild donkeys (32:9–14). All will be transformed when God pours out His spirit to usher in an age of justice and peace (32:15–20). A chapter of changing moods brings in succession denunciation of some unspecified enemy, a plea for God's mercy, praise, lamentation at the disaster that has overtaken the land, God's withering judgement on sinners, and examples of virtues that are pleasing to God. It climaxes in a vision of Yahweh ruling in splendour over a land stretching far and wide. A land where sins are forgiven and His people enjoy peace and abundance, living in His very presence (33:1–24).

From judgement to bliss (34:1 – 35:10)

The Assyrian crisis is left far behind as Isaiah looks to the end of the world, to judgement and salvation. He begins with a scene of grisly carnage as God exterminates the nations in general and Edom, the incarnation of profanity, in particular (34:1–17). However this is but a prelude to a paean of hope and joy in which he envisions the wilderness carpeted in flowers and intones the bliss and perfection of salvation for those whom Yahweh has redeemed.

> Then the eyes of the blind will be opened,
> the ears of the deaf unsealed,
> then the lame will leap like a deer
> and the tongue of the dumb sing for joy.

An historical appendix (36:1 – 39:8)

These chapters largely replicate 2K 18:13 – 20:19 and round off Isaiah's oracles by recording his historical role during the reign of Hezekiah. They recall the advice he gave Hezekiah during Sennacherib's siege of Jerusalem in 701 B.C., Hezekiah's illness, and a prophecy that Babylon would one day carry Judah into captivity. However 2K 18:14–16 is omitted while Is 38:9–20, the Canticle of Hezekiah, part lamentation, part a psalm of thanksgiving and praise inspired by Hezekiah's recovery from his illness, is additional.

Deutero Isaiah

With Deutero Isaiah we awake in a different world. Gone are the storm clouds of menace and threat that have so far cast their shadows. Now we are in the sunlit uplands of salvation and peace on the far side of judgement. Cyrus is on the march and will soon free the exiles from Babylon's yoke. Liberation is in the air and the style modulates accordingly to poems that soar like a hymn in an exultant crescendo of praise.

Yahweh is the only God. Worshipping idols is absurd. He has not rejected Israel and still loves her. Her punishment is over and one day all nations will acknowledge Him. In a lyrical effusion of joy the poet describes the exiles' homecoming to a new Eden and a Jerusalem ringing with joy.

Four 'Songs' (which we gather together at the end) tell of a Servant, someone of supreme holiness who is destined to be a light to the nations and to reconcile man with God through His suffering. From the earliest times Christians have seen the Servant as foreshadowing Christ.

The coming liberation (40:1 – 48:22)

Israel has been amply punished for her sins. Her guilt has been atoned for and God will lead His people home across the desert in triumphant procession, like a shepherd gathering His lambs. Grass may wither and flowers fade but nothing could be more certain where God is concerned (40:1–11).

A hymn extols the majesty of God, Creator of heavens and earth, omnipotent, omniscient, eternal, incomparable, beyond all understanding. What a contrast with idols, mere pieces of wood fashioned so as not to topple.[16] How could Israel ever imagine that God had forgotten her? He does not grow tired or weary and those who trust Him will regain their strength, 'sprout wings like eagles', and never tire (40:12–31; 41:6–7).

In the first of a number of speeches cast in the mould of judicial debate Isaiah reveals that it is Yahweh, 'the first and the last' who has raised up the conqueror from the east before whom the 'coasts and islands', peoples of distant lands, are trembling[17] (41:1–5).

Has God rejected Israel? No, far from rejecting her He has chosen her as His servant. She need not be afraid. He is her God. Weak and despised like a worm though she may be, He will redeem her and confuse her enemies. She will become His tool and the desert will bloom to meet her every need (41:8–20).

Isaiah now voices the first of many denunciations of idolatry. Can idols interpret the past or foretell the future? Did they predict the coming conqueror? Can they do anything, good or bad? No! They are wind and emptiness (41:21–29; 42:8–9).

A victory song leads into a question. If Yahweh loves Israel so much why has He allowed her to suffer war and plunder? It is because she was deaf and blind and persisted in disobedience (42:10–25).

Israel is assured that there is nothing to be afraid of, nothing will prevail against her. Yahweh, her Creator, has redeemed her. He is her God, her Saviour and He will gather her from the ends of the earth. He loves her and will always be near her.

Yahweh is the only God and Saviour, eternal, all powerful. Israel is His witness that He can tell the future and save. What other nation could make such a claim of its gods? (43:1–13).

Appendix 5 refers

Yahweh will more than shatter the prison bars of Babylon. He will eclipse the miracle of the Sea by making a road in the desert and bringing rivers to wastelands. This despite the fact that Israel, far from honouring Him, rebuffed Him from the very start. (43:14–28).

Yahweh confirms Israel's election. He formed her in the womb to be His servant and great things are in store. He will pour out His spirit on her descendants and there will be pagan converts too. He alone is Israel's king and redeemer, the only God. Idols are nothingness. Carvers who chisel them out use the same wood to warm themselves and cook their meals (44:1–20).

Appendix 6 refers

Israel is Yahweh's servant. He will not forget her. He has forgiven her sins and wants her to return for He has redeemed her. He created heavens and earth and humankind and is Lord of history. He has empowered Cyrus and will direct his steps even though he does not know that he is God's instrument for releasing the exiles and effecting the restoration of Jerusalem and the Temple. Yahweh's wisdom is not to be questioned any more than the clay questions its potter[18] (44:21 – 45:13).

Isaiah now looks beyond the coming liberation to a time when all nations will reject their gods for Yahweh, the hidden Saviour God of Israel (45:14–25).

In a vision of the fall of Babylon Isaiah contrasts Babylon, whose idols he sees being carried on beasts of burden into a captivity from which there will be no release, with Israel. She does not carry her God. He carries her (46:1–13). A taunt song intones Babylon as a once elegant hedonistic queen who has since become a slave, grinding the flour and being forced to lift her skirts to cross streams. She showed no mercy to Israel and thought the good times would never end. Now the day of reckoning has come (47:1–15).

Yahweh, the only God who laid the earth's foundations, predicted Israel's future long ago. He did not want her claiming that idols were responsible! And it has all happened. Now He has news He has never revealed before. He has chosen a man to release her from Babylon. Not because she deserves it, for she is an impious rebel. No, He is holding His anger in check and doing it for the honour of His name.[19] If only she had listened before, what blessings she would have enjoyed! The chapter ends with a triumph song (48:1–22).

The joyful homecoming (49:8 – 55:13)

Has Yahweh abandoned His people? No, He can no more forget her than a woman her baby at the breast. He will lead her home in a joyful procession. The best days are yet to come. Israel will overflow her former bounds. The nations will be cowed, her oppressors destroyed. Can a tyrant's captive be freed? Yes! And it is God Himself who will do it (49:8–26). Israel was punished not because God 'divorced' her or was too weak to save her but because of her disloyalty (50:1–3).

Just as God blessed Abraham so too He will restore Zion to an Eden overflowing with joy and gladness as sorrow and sighing take flight. Heavens and earth may disappear but God's salvation will last for ever. Israel has no need to be afraid since Yahweh will protect her (51:1–16). Jerusalem's suffering is over. The cup of God's anger has passed to her enemies (51:17 – 52:6).

Isaiah visualises guards on the ruined ramparts of Jerusalem rejoicing as messengers arrive proclaiming salvation and peace as God leads His people back to Jerusalem in triumphant procession. Unlike the Exodus, when Israel left as fugitives, this is to be a victory march (52:7–12).

Isaiah likens Jerusalem to a repudiated barren wife who becomes incredibly fertile as Yahweh, who forsook her for a brief moment, takes her back in compassion and everlasting love. She will not be shamed again but live in boundless peace and splendour. No attack against her will ever succeed (54:1–17).

In a glorious finale Yahweh invites the (spiritually) thirsty and poor to a sumptuous banquet. It is life-giving and free for He is rich in forgiveness. All that is necessary is thirst for God. So let the wicked abandon their ways and grasp God's offer while there is time! He will make an everlasting covenant with Israel in pursuance of His promises to David and the nations will hasten to join her.[20] He will achieve His aims just as surely as the rain fertilises the earth. Nature herself bursts into song at Israel's homecoming (55:1–13).

The Servant songs

The Servant has a divine mission. Quickened by God's spirit He will teach the nations with patient gentleness and persevere until his mission is complete. He will bring light and justice, opening the eyes of the blind and freeing those who live in darkness (42:1–7).

Yahweh chose His Servant while He was still in the womb. He will make God's name known with teaching that will be held back until the appropriate time like arrows in a quiver. It will be sharp as a sword. He will restore Israel and bring salvation to the ends of the earth. He will end up despised and hated. Yet final glory will be His. (49:1–7).

The Servant is Yahweh's disciple, ever attentive to His will, ever eager to comfort the weary. Spite and insults do not deflect Him because God sustains Him and eventually His enemies will disappear like moth-eaten cloth. Let all who walk in darkness lean on God for the wicked will be engulfed by their guilt (50:4–11).

The Servant will be exalted and triumphant. The nations will marvel that One whom men rejected and despised, and who suffered so terribly, could be doing Yahweh's will. A despised 'man of sorrows', the punishment He endured was not for His own sins but ours. We had all gone astray like sheep. But by taking our sins on His shoulders and stoically suffering the punishment we deserved, 'like a lamb led to the slaughter', He opens the way for reconciliation with God (52:13 – 53:12).
Appendix 7 refers

Trito Isaiah

After the exhilaration of Deutero Isaiah these next chapters, set in the early years of post-exilic Jerusalem, begin in sombre mood. Trito Isaiah is forced to appeal for justice and right conduct. He commends the humble and contrite but at the same time pleads for Sabbath observance and denounces apostasy and self-justifying piety. It is all too familiar. Where Deutero Isaiah was content to ridicule idols Trito Isaiah is forced to condemn them.

But then the clouds lift and deliverance shines again. God Himself will shoulder arms against evil. He will 'wed the virgin Jerusalem' and make her a city of beauty and purity where the upright will dwell forever with new heavens and a new earth.

It would be comforting if this most magisterial of books were to end on this consoling note. But the unknown prophet of the restoration is just as insistent as the son of Amoz two centuries before on God's abhorrence of sin. So the wheel turns full circle. Where Isaiah began by promising 'the good things of the earth' to the virtuous but 'the sword' to rebels Trito Isaiah, in a brief coda, contrasts the fellowship God offers the faithful, Gentiles as well as Jews, with the eternal torment of the damned.

The shame of Zion (56:1 – 59:21)

Blessed are those who act justly, eschew evil and observe the Sabbath. Yahweh welcomes foreigners and eunuchs to His fold provided they observe the Sabbath and adhere to the covenant.[21] As for Israel's leaders they are uncaring and eaten up with self-interest. Worthy people die and no one cares. Death is a happy release (56:1 – 57:2).

The prophet launches a fierce invective against people who participate in sexual fertility rites, child sacrifice, idolatry and other abominations. It is the humble and contrite that God is drawn to. He has punished Israel but this will pass and then He will heal her. But there is no peace for the wicked (57:3–21).

God is not interested in fasting that is mere outward observance devoid of inner spirituality, nor in a person inflicting pain on himself. What He wants is justice and charity backed up by love of God and respect for the Sabbath (58:1–14).

Isaiah was clearly alive to people who were wondering why life was still so hard and the promised blessings so slow to materialise. In a penitential psalm he attributes the delay to sin still distancing them from God (59:1–15a). God's answer is forthright. Only a divine initiative can bridge the gulf between Zion's shame and the glories He wants to bestow on her. So He will buckle the sword and don the helmet of salvation Himself.

Yahweh's spirit and words will always be with Israel to guide her (59:15b–21).

The glory of Zion (60:1 – 66:24)

A new and glorious Jerusalem will arise. Nations will be drawn to her light. She will enjoy the wealth of the nations. Foreigners will rebuild her walls. Those that do not serve her will perish. Those that do will approach her in humble respect. The upright will live in God's everlasting light in justice, peace and splendour. Violence and mourning will be no more 'when the time is ripe' (60:1–22).

In a passage echoing the Servant songs Isaiah announces that Yahweh has good news for the afflicted and broken-hearted and release for those held captive (by sin).[22] The ruined cities of Judah will be rebuilt. Foreigners will attend to Israel's every need. She will at last become a kingdom of priests and abide in everlasting joy. The oracle ends with a hymn of thanksgiving (61:1–11).

A poem depicts God 'wedding' the new virgin Jerusalem. Prayer must be ceaseless until He restores her. No more will she suffer invasion and marauders. The reapers themselves will enjoy the bread of their toil and the harvesters their wine (62:1–12). However Isaiah tempers these visions of glory with a terrible warning as he depicts God ruthlessly slaughtering His foes, here symbolised by Edom, Israel's archetypical enemy (63:1–6).

Filled with a deep longing for the fulfilment of His promises, and recalling God's former mercies, Isaiah pleads for God to 'tear the heavens open' and come once more to the aid of His recalcitrant people, not holding their guilt against them for ever or letting them suffer more than they can endure. Jerusalem is a wasteland, the Temple a burnt-out ruin. Admittedly they are sinners but He is their Father (63:7 – 64:11).

God wants to help His rebellious people but they never approach Him. They prefer illicit worship on high places and in sacred groves, eating unclean food and dabbling in necromancy. But a few 'good grapes' will survive and from them will be born a new Israel. They will sing for joy. The rest will become a byword for cursing (65:1–16).

God will create new heavens and a new earth. The past will be forgotten. There will be no more sadness or premature death but long life, gladness and a peace in which everyone will be able to enjoy the fruits of his labours. God will anticipate every need[23] (65:17–25).

For all the effort being put into rebuilding the Temple, God would prefer more people of humble and contrite spirit. He is disgusted by those who practise pagan rites alongside lawful worship (66:1–4). Scoffers are in for a surprise. The new Jerusalem will be born suddenly like a woman giving birth without labour. The faithful will be comforted like a child at its mother's breast and peace will flow like a river in spate. But the guilty will suffer God's flaming fury (66:5–17).

God will gather every nation. Gentile converts will evangelise other lands and bring the scattered Jews back to Jerusalem. The new heavens and earth will endure for ever. God's own will honour Him but for the wicked 'the fire will never be put out' (66:18–24).

Appendix 8 refers

Jeremiah

According to the book's opening verses Jeremiah was of priestly lineage, hailed from Anathoth, a small town some four miles north east of Jerusalem, and prophesied from 627 to 587 B.C. However chapters 42 to 44 indicate that his ministry continued for a few more years while he was a refugee in Egypt.

Historical background

By the time Jeremiah began his ministry Assyria, under whose shadow Judah had lain for so long, was on the wane. Babylon was the emergent power and, after Nineveh was sacked in 612 with the help of the Medes, Assyria was virtually finished. An attempt by Pharaoh Necho of Egypt in 609 to revive her fortunes by going to her aid against Babylon was unsuccessful and when the Babylonians under Nebuchadnezzar crushed the Egyptians at Carchemish in 605 Babylon's ascendancy was put beyond doubt.

Meanwhile in Judah Josiah had begun his religious reforms following the discovery of the Book of the Law. It is likely that Jeremiah supported these reforms but there is no direct evidence. Josiah was killed in battle in 609 at Megiddo in an abortive attempt to stop Necho's errand of mercy to the stricken Assyria. His son Jehoahaz was king for a mere three months before Necho replaced him with his brother Jehoiakim. In 598 Nebuchadnezzar marched on Judah. Jehoiakim died soon afterwards and it was his son Jehoiachin who surrendered Jerusalem early in 597. Jehoiachin was deported to Babylon together with the nobles and craftsmen and the weak vacillating Zedekiah, another of Josiah's sons, was installed as king of what was by now no more than a Babylonian puppet.

Despite her defeat at Carchemish, Egypt was not quite a spent force and for most of his reign Zedekiah seems to have presided over an almost continual tussle between those of his advisors who, like Jeremiah, favoured a peaceful accommodation with Babylon and a pro-Egyptian party who advocated revolt. When Zedekiah did eventually opt for revolt it was disastrous. Egypt's intervention on Judah's behalf soon petered out and in 587 a rampaging Nebuchadnezzar sacked Jerusalem, burned down the Temple and carried most of the remaining citizens off to exile in Babylon.

Judah was now incorporated into the Babylonian empire and after the governor Gedaliah was assassinated many of the remaining inhabitants, fearful of retaliation, fled to Egypt taking a reluctant Jeremiah with them. Apart from a few final oracles no more is heard of Jeremiah and he probably died in Egypt after a life that spanned the most turbulent period in Judah's history, from the high hopes of Josiah's reforms to her inglorious end.

Structure

Jeremiah is difficult. Critics often disagree on where one oracle ends and the next begins. It is hard to discern any rationale in the way material is organised. It is certainly not chronological. Episodes from different periods of the prophet's life are juxtaposed with rare abandon. Many oracles are undated and can only be ascribed to a particular historical setting with hesitancy. Although Jeremiah's mission was primarily to Judah it is possible that some of his earlier utterances were directed at the people of the long defunct northern kingdom of Israel in the hope that repentance might still bring restoration. Fortunately these ambiguities do little to obscure the prophet's general drift. However they do mean that any attempt to subdivide the book to make it more digestible must be somewhat subjective.

Having said that, Jeremiah does break quite naturally at 25:13 with the first part of the book being largely an anthology of oracles warning Judah of the fate that awaited her unless she mended her ways and repented. However from these we can segregate: Jeremiah's call; a collection of five musings with God known as 'Jeremiah's confessions' in which the prophet reflects on his mission and bares his innermost soul; and a small scattering of oracles and wisdom sayings that do not naturally fit elsewhere. Thus part one of Jeremiah, 1:1 – 25:13, may be taken to comprise:

- Jeremiah's call (1:1–19)
- prophecies of judgement and doom (most of 2:1 – 25:13)
- Jeremiah's confessions (11:18 – 12:6; 15:10–21; 17:14–18; 18:18–23; 20:7–18)
- other oracles and wisdom sayings (embedded in 2:1 – 25:13)

The second half, 25:14 – 52:34, divides more straightforwardly into: a book of consolation and hope in which Jeremiah unveils the New Covenant and prophesies a future where Israel and Judah will be restored to God's blessing; a set of biographical and historical memoirs mostly set in Zedekiah's reign; oracles against the nations; and a brief historical appendix taken mainly from 2 Kings. Thus:

- a book of consolation and hope (chapters 30, 31, 33)
- biographical and historical narratives (chapters 26–29, 32, 34–45)
- oracles against the nations (25:14–38; chapters 46–51)
- an historical appendix (chapter 52)

Exceptionally the book of consolation and hope also contains three short prophecies from the first half of the book, 3:14–18; 16:14–15; 23:1–8.

Teaching

In the litany of reproaches and pleas that dominates the first part of his book Jeremiah ruthlessly exposes the inroads paganism had made into Judah's faith. She had rebelled against Yahweh. Her love had grown cold. Injustice was rife. But it was idolatry that drew the prophet's keenest censure. How could blocks of wood, the quintessence of futility, be compared with the Creator God of heavens and earth?

Steeped in sin Judah had learned nothing from past punishment and Josiah's reforms had failed to strike a deep enough chord. She was stubbornly set in her rebellious ways and was ripe for judgement. Hence her present war-scarred plight and the inevitability of worse to come. Sheltering behind the Temple liturgy and mechanically offering sacrifice was no substitute for moral probity and a heart true to God. Not even the Temple would be spared when God used Babylon as the sword of His cleansing wrath.

At the same time Jeremiah never failed to mingle his denunciations of depravity with calls for repentance. God was loving and merciful and yearning to be gracious if only Judah would confess her guilt. In the book of consolation and hope, the centrepiece of the second half of his book, this comes to the fore as the erstwhile prophet of doom turns to extol God's love and prophesy that after the purging of exile Yahweh would regather His scattered flock and resettle them in their ancestral land under a king of the House of David. Sorrow and mourning would give way to tears of joy. Yahweh would be their God and they His people.

Jeremiah realised that none of this could happen while the chasm between God's holiness and human frailty remained as it was. For God to relax His norms was unthinkable. And it was clear that his rhetoric for repentance was falling on deaf ears. The only alternative therefore was for God to build up His errant creatures so that they could meet His ideals. This would come about through a New Covenant whereby in some way men's hearts would be implanted with the desire and will to obey and sins would be forgiven. Jeremiah's prophecy of this New Covenant is one of the high peaks of Old Testament theology and the measure of its significance is that the Christian Scriptures claim by their very name to be the record of its fulfilment (New Testament can equally be rendered New Covenant).

JEREMIAH'S CALL (1:1–19)

Yahweh calls a hesitant Jeremiah to be a prophet to the nations. His mission is both to knock down and to build, to warn but at the same time to convey hope. He will meet great opposition but he is to proclaim God's word fearlessly for God will make him a 'pillar of iron'. He was chosen before he was even formed in the womb.[1] Yahweh used Jeremiah's sighting of an almond tree to convey that He would be watching to see that the words He gave him were fulfilled.[2] When Jeremiah saw a cooking pot on the boil with its mouth tilting (and thus the steam issuing) from the north Yahweh explained that disaster was about to boil over and that He would punish Judah for her sins with an invasion from the north.[3]

PROPHECIES OF JUDGEMENT AND DOOM

Israel's disloyalty (2:1–37)

Yahweh recalls Israel's bridal love after He had rescued her from Egypt. Disaster befell anyone who troubled her. Why has she deserted the God who shepherded her through the pitiless desert, a land of drought and shadow dark as death? It was not He who broke faith but Israel. She defiled the rich country He brought her to, oblivious of His protection and His presence in her midst. Priests, prophets, experts in the Law, civil leaders – all were culpable. Unlike pagans who are at least loyal to their gods Judah abandoned her God. And for what? For useless idols that are not gods at all! That is why her towns are gutted ruins. She has brought it all on herself. Courting Egypt or Assyria will get her nowhere. Wickedness brings its own retribution (2:1–19).

Israel's iniquity is ingrained. In her insatiable yearning for idols she is like a she-donkey on heat. She is totally wedded to her idolatrous practices. The people call a piece of wood 'father' yet come crying to Yahweh for help when they are in trouble. They have as many gods as towns. Past punishment, intended to correct, has been ignored. Prophets sent to help her have been murdered. Does a bride forget her wedding dress? Yet Judah has forgotten Yahweh time and again. Her hands are stained with the blood of the poor yet she still protests her innocence. That is why God has passed sentence on her (2:20–37).

Repentance (3:1–13; 3:19 – 4:4)

For Judah with her many 'lovers' to expect Yahweh to take her back is like a man wanting to remarry a wife he had previously divorced.[4] With her brazen lusting after other gods she is no better than a harlot (3:1–5). However where Law offers no solution, God's love and mercy does. He wants to cure (even) Israel's disloyalty and will respond to the first sign of repentance provided it is genuine[5] (3:19 – 4:4).

Yahweh asserts that Judah has learned nothing from Israel's fate and is worse in her shameless apostasy than Israel ever was. He orders Jeremiah to appeal to Israel to admit her guilt so that even now she can be forgiven (3:6–13).

The foe from the north (4:5 – 6:30)

In a long poem Jeremiah imagines that Judah is already being invaded. The invader approaches from the north like a scorching desert wind, a ravaging lion, his horses swifter than eagles, to reduce her to desert.[6] Prophets and priests stand aghast. Even now she could be saved if she chose to repent but her wickedness is too deeply entrenched. She has only herself to blame.

Jeremiah is overcome with anguish at the impending doom and likens it to some cosmic cataclysm. Mountains reel, birds flee, towns are abandoned. The earth is a barren waste, terror and panic everywhere. Judah will end her days with piercing screams like a woman in first labour (4:5–31).

There is not an honest person in the whole of Jerusalem. They are rebellious and obdurate to a man, refusing to repent, rushing to the brothel, lusting after their neighbours' wives like roving stallions, trusting in gods that are not gods at all. The people might be excused through ignorance but the prophets and priests are every bit as bad. They prey on the weak and defenceless and have no fear of God. They treat His warnings with contempt, cherishing the fond hope that He will look the other way. That is why a foe from afar, foraging like a wild animal, will banish Judah to exile and burn her like wood in the fire. Her misdeeds deprive her of God's blessings. Yet He will not annihilate her completely[7] (5:1–31).

Still in poetic vein Jeremiah sees the invader at the gates of Jerusalem, the daughter of

Zion. There is still time to repent, to take the ancient paths of righteousness, but who will listen? The people sneer at Yahweh's word and are impenitent, shameless, greedy for gain. Incense and sacrifice will get them nowhere. So the destroyer is on his way, cruel and pitiless, spreading terror in his wake. Jeremiah's mission was to refine Judah's 'metal'. But though the furnace burns fiercely there is no silver. All is dross (6:1–30).

The Temple sermon (7:1 – 8:3)

Of all Jeremiah's prophecies this was the most dramatic.[8] It was believed that the Temple was sacrosanct, God's earthly home, inviolable. It is not hard therefore to appreciate the bombshell Jeremiah delivered when he prophesied that unless Israel mended her ways – excising idolatry, stealing, murder, adultery, perjury, exploitation and injustice – she would face not only exile but the destruction of the Temple itself, just as Shiloh had been razed centuries before.[9] Those who imagined the Temple would protect them while they were still pursuing their godless ways were deluding themselves (7:1–15).

So intense was Yahweh's anger, fuelled by the people's appetite for idolatry, that Jeremiah was told that it would be fruitless for him to intercede.[10] Did they not realise that it was not God they spited with their infidelity but themselves? Sincerity and obedience was the answer not sacrifice.[11] But no one listened. So a heavy price would be paid. So terrible would be the destruction that the tombs of the dead would be desecrated and their corpses exposed to the heavenly bodies they once worshipped so avidly. Survivors would prefer death to life (7:16 – 8:3).

Further oracles of judgement and doom

As the main themes of Jeremiah's extensive repertoire of oracles of judgement and doom have already emerged, the remainder are now summarised more briefly.

Judah rushes into wickedness like a horse wildly charging into battle. Her unwillingness to repent is as unnatural as a bird forgetting its migratory habits (8:4–7). Her sins have turned her into a withered vine. An invader is on his way to trample on her (8:13–17). Judah's moral degeneracy leaves Yahweh no option but to purge her (9:1–8). A dirge spells out what happens when Yahweh is ignored: ruin, mourning, wailing, death, an end to bird-song and the bleating of flocks (9:9–21). Those, including pagans, whose circumcision (dedication) is merely of the flesh and lacks inner commitment, will be punished (9:24–25).

The people of Judah had better pack their bags. They are about to be evicted from their land. The destroyer from the north is on the march (10:17–22). Jeremiah prays for God's guidance and that He may vent His anger on Judah's oppressors (10:23–25). He is ordered to proclaim the covenant which God concluded with His people when He led them out of Egypt.[12] There seems to be a conspiracy against keeping it as a result of which Judah faces disaster. Her worthless idols will not save her nor will it do any good for Jeremiah to intercede (11:1–14). Vows and sacrifice cannot make amends for wickedness (11:15–17). Yahweh laments the way His people have behaved and the bitter harvest of thorns they have reaped (12:7–13). Judah's evil neighbours will also be uprooted but they will be saved if they turn to Yahweh (12:14–17). Jeremiah acts out a parable. His waistcloth was once as close to him as anything could be but it became useless after it was rotted by the waters of the Euphrates. Likewise Israel was once close to Yahweh but is no longer any use to Him now that she has been corrupted by the Euphrates (i.e. its pagan religion)[13] (13:1–11).

The people will be filled with the wine of God's wrath and destroyed like wine jugs smashed together (13:12–14). Judah's only hope is to swallow her pride and honour Yahweh (13:15–17). Jerusalem can no more change her godless ways than a leopard its spots. The enemy from the north is on his way to strip her (13:20–27). Yahweh declines to end a drought despite the people confessing their sins, and will not accept either their sacrifices or Jeremiah's intercession, even though it is false prophets who have led them astray. Indeed they will suffer invasion and captivity as well (14:1 – 15:4). Jerusalem will have more widows than the sands of the sea (15:5–9). Yahweh tells Jeremiah to remain celibate and to avoid mourning and merrymaking to symbolise the barrenness of a land under judgement (16:1–13). Jeremiah envisions God sending both fishermen and huntsmen to harry Judah, making the point with this two pronged assault that no one will escape[14] (16:16–18). Judah faces enslavement because her sin is engraved on her heart as indelibly as etchings from an iron stylus (17:1–4).

Jeremiah observes that as a potter can always reshape his clay into a different vessel, so too God can refashion the 'clay' of His creation, withholding punishment where He finds repentance and suspending blessings where He finds disobedience. However Judah's obduracy means there is little hope of her escaping disaster (18:1–12). Perennial sources of water can be depended upon. Yet Israel spurns the ever reliable Yahweh to worship a Nothing! That is why she will be scattered (18:13–17).

Jeremiah breaks an earthenware jug to illustrate how Babylon will 'break' Judah as punishment for her blatant apostasy. As a result he is beaten and imprisoned in the stocks for a day (19:1 – 20:6). Jeremiah tells Zedekiah that there is no hope for Jerusalem. The Babylonians will burn it down. However there is a choice for the people. They can either leave the city and surrender, in which case they will escape with their lives, or fight on and die 'by sword, famine or plague' (21:1–10). Addressing the House of Judah Jeremiah insists that the only way to escape God's wrath is to rule justly and attacks the complacency that assumes Jerusalem is inviolable (21:11–14). He tells an unnamed king of Judah that unless he rules fairly and with compassion his palace will become a ruin (22:1–9). In a prophecy made between the first and second deportations Jeremiah likens the exiles already in Babylon to good figs whom God will one day restore as His covenant people. Those left in Jerusalem are as doomed as bad figs (24:1–10). Since Judah will not repent she will be subject to Babylon for seventy years after which Babylon herself will be destroyed (25:1–13).

JEREMIAH'S CONFESSIONS

In the first of five 'confessions' Jeremiah tells how the townsfolk of his native Anathoth hatched a plot against his life. He was like a trustful lamb being led to the slaughterhouse. He prays for vengeance and asks why wicked people are allowed to prosper. Yahweh's response is that he must be prepared to endure even greater trials in the future. Even his own family will betray him (11:18 – 12:6).

In his second confession Jeremiah laments his birth and the commission from God which once gave him such delight. He has done his best but is arraigned for his uncompromising message. He calls for vengeance. Why must he suffer so much? In his anguish he comes close to accusing God of deception.[15] God's reply is blunt. Jeremiah is a free agent. If he wishes to continue as His mouthpiece his remedy is the one he has been advocating to others: to repent, by rejecting his rebellious thoughts, and devoting himself wholeheartedly to God's word. He need have no fear. God will be with him (15:10–21).

Later Jeremiah complains that because his prophecies remain unfulfilled he has become an object of derision. He himself had never wanted disaster to overtake Judah and begs God to silence his mockers (17:14–18). Jeremiah's fourth confession is a trenchant call for revenge on people who are even now hatching another plot against his life: the very people he had earlier commended and prayed for (18:18–23).

Finally Jeremiah protests that God has tricked him. His incessant prophecies of doom have made him a laughing-stock. Unfortunately there is no escape. Every time the burden seems more than he can bear God's word burns deep within him like a fire he cannot resist. He knows he will be vindicated in the end because Yahweh is on his side. Nevertheless he pleads for vengeance and, in the midnight of despair, rues the day he was born (20:7–18).

OTHER ORACLES AND WISDOM SAYINGS

Jeremiah castigates scribes who falsify Yahweh's Law and prophets and priests who preach a false sense of security[16] (8:8–12). He grieves over godless prophets who lead the people astray (23:9–40) and in deep sorrow laments the people's suffering during a famine (8:18–23). He launches a scathing polemic on the fatuity of idols. Blocks of wood, carved by human hand, embellished with gold, as lifeless as a scarecrow in a cornfield; how can they be compared with the one true God? (10:1–16) He prophesies that Gentiles will one day acknowledge Yahweh as God (16:19–21) and calls for strict observance of the Sabbath (17:19–27).

Jeremiah calls for humility on the part of an unnamed king and his mother (13:18–19). He urges his listeners not to weep for Josiah but for his son Jehoahaz (here called Shallum) who will die a captive far from his native land (22:10–12). He inveighs against the self indulgent, unscrupulous Jehoiakim, contrasting him unfavourably with his pious father[17] (22:13–19). And He prophesies that Jehoiachin (here called Coniah) will die in exile and that none of his descendants will ever occupy David's throne (22:20–30).

Three wisdom sayings teach that true wisdom lies in knowing Yahweh (9:22–23); that those who rely on Yahweh are blessed while those who depend on human strength are cursed (17:5–8, 12–13); and that Yahweh probes the heart, that most devious and depraved of things, to give everyone his just deserts (17:9–11).

THE BOOK OF CONSOLATION AND HOPE

The restoration of Israel and Judah (30:1 – 31:28; 31:35–40)

Jeremiah moves from the winter of doom to the springtime of hope. A day will come when Yahweh will snap the chains binding His people and return them to their ancestral home, their towns rebuilt.[18] Their wounds might seem incurable now but paradoxically it is they who will be restored to health and their enemies who will perish. Once again Israel will enjoy prosperity and peace and ring with laughter and thanksgiving. And so will be fulfilled God's great covenant promise 'You will be my people and I shall be your God' (30:1–24).

God's love for Israel is never ending. He will gather her like a shepherd from the ends of the earth. A mighty throng, the blind, the lame, women in labour; all will be there. They will worship on Zion and feast on God's lavish gifts, dancing with tears of joy. Mourning will be turned into gladness and sorrow banished forever.

Jeremiah pictures Rachel weeping for her children until Yahweh orders her to stem her tears with the promise that they will one day be regathered in their homeland. The loving relationship between Israel and Yahweh will be renewed.[19] The Yahweh who destroyed will once again be Yahweh the Creator, architect of a new Israel and a new Judah that will endure as long as the stars in the heavens. Jerusalem will be built anew, consecrated to Yahweh and inviolable for ever (31:1–28, 35–40).

Individual responsibility (31:29–30)

The time is coming, Jeremiah declares, when people will be punished for their own sins and no one else's. Everyone will be personally responsible for his own conduct.[20]

The new covenant (31:31–34)

Jeremiah now unveils his vision of a New Covenant in which Yahweh will implant His Law in people's hearts. No one will need to be instructed in the Law. Everyone, from least to greatest, will know God. God will forgive His people's sins and never call them to mind.[21]

Appendix 1 refers

The restoration of Israel and Judah continued (33:1–26)

In an oracle dating from shortly before Jerusalem's fall in 587, when he was held in custody in the guard house, Jeremiah prophesied that although Jerusalem was about to be destroyed, the future held only blessings. God would forgive His people's sins and regather them to live in peace and plenty in a new Jerusalem vibrant with shouts of joy and mirth. Moreover 'the days were coming' when a Branch, a Davidic king, would rule over Israel and Judah along with priests to offer sacrifice.[22] This would endure in perpetuity and happen as surely as night follows day.

Other oracles of hope

In other oracles of the end days Yahweh pleads with Israel to repent. He will take those who respond – one here, two there – to Zion. Shepherds will rule over them and no one will miss the Ark of the Covenant because Jerusalem itself will be Yahweh's throne.[23] All the nations will flock there and abandon their sinful ways. Israel and Judah will return to their ancestral land and be reunited (3:14–18). As their present shepherds have failed His flock, Yahweh will Himself regather the remnant of His people. Then He will raise up new shepherds to pasture them with a Branch of David to be their king[24] (16:14–15; 23:1–8).

BIOGRAPHICAL AND HISTORICAL NARRATIVES

These have been reordered to put them as far as possible in their likely chronological order.

Events in Jehoiakim's reign (26:1–24, 35:1 – 36:32, 45:1–5)

Four unrelated incidents are recorded. The first is Jeremiah's narrow escape from death when in 609 he prophesied the destruction of the Temple unless Judah repented, 7:1–15. He owed his life to the recollection that the prophet Micah had made a similar prophecy in Hezekiah's day, Mi 3:12, without being put to death notwithstanding that more recently a certain Uriah was murdered after he spoke out in similar vein (26:1–24). The second took place in 605 and recalls how, after Jeremiah had dictated his prophecies to Baruch, Jehoiakim ostentatiously had the scroll burned when it was read to him and ordered Jeremiah and Baruch to be arrested. Forewarned they escaped and Jeremiah was able to dictate a second and longer version[25] (36:1–32).

The third was Jeremiah's advice to Baruch when he was feeling downhearted in 605. He reminded him that Yahweh's grief greatly exceeded his own for, in punishing Judah, He was effectively destroying His own work. Baruch should not expect special treatment but his life would be spared[26] (45:1–5). The fourth contrasts the Rechabites' constancy in maintaining their ancestral ascetic lifestyle with Judah's rampant infidelity (35:1–19).

Events in Zedekiah's reign (27:1 – 29:32)

In a letter written shortly after 597 Jeremiah urged the exiles in Babylon to maintain a normal lifestyle. God had a plan and they would return after 70 years. But for those left behind in Jerusalem the future was bleak (29:1–23). The remainder of the chapter is difficult. It seems that one of the exiles, Shemaiah, was disenchanted by Jeremiah's letter and wrote to Zephaniah, the priest in Jerusalem, demanding that he be disciplined. Apparently Zephaniah read this letter to Jeremiah but took no further action whereupon Jeremiah sent a second letter to the exiles denouncing Shemaiah (29:24–32).

In the next episode Jeremiah put thongs and yokes on his neck in token of servitude and proclaimed that the only hope for Judah and her neighbouring states lay in subjection to Babylon. The reason was simple: Nebuchadnezzar was Yahweh's servant. False prophets who advised otherwise must be ignored. The alternative was oblivion[27] (27:1–22). Shortly afterwards a certain Hananiah flatly contradicted Jeremiah by declaring that the exiles would return in two years and pressed his point by snatching the yoke from Jeremiah's neck. However his death only two months later, as prophesied by Jeremiah, soon proved that Jeremiah, and not he, was the true prophet (28:1–17).

Jerusalem's last days (34:1–22, 32:1–44; 37:1 – 40:6)

Nebuchadnezzar's final invasion had now begun and Jeremiah went to advise Zedekiah that he faced certain defeat. Jerusalem would be burned down and he would be exiled to Babylon. Yet he would die a natural death and even receive a ceremonial funeral (34:1–7).

When the Babylonians surrounding Jerusalem heard that Egypt was on the march and lifted their siege, Jeremiah warned that this would only bring a temporary respite. They would return and burn the city down (37:1–10). Zedekiah ignored him. He assumed that all would now be well and rescinded a pledge he had made in the Temple to free all Hebrew slaves.[28] Jeremiah's response left him in no doubt as to Yahweh's fury. The Babylonians would return. Judah would be laid waste and Jerusalem gutted while Zedekiah and his cronies would suffer 'sword, famine and plague' and become objects of horror (34:8–22).

During the time the siege was lifted Jeremiah attempted to leave Jerusalem to attend to some property business. He was arrested as a deserter and imprisoned in an underground dungeon. When Zedekiah came to consult him he merely affirmed what he had said before namely that he, Zedekiah, would be handed over to the king of Babylon. Jeremiah was moved to better quarters in the guard house after he reminded the king that, unlike his other advisers, his prophecies were being proved right (37:11–21).

While he was still under arrest for continually preaching doom, Jeremiah was ordered by Yahweh to buy a field at Anathoth from his cousin as a token that life would one day return to normal.[29] Indeed the future was bright. Despite their past iniquities Yahweh would restore His people to their land and conclude an everlasting covenant (the New Covenant) so that, with singleness of heart, they would never reject Him again (32:1–44).

Infuriated by Jeremiah's continual prophecies of defeat, which they regarded as undermining morale, Zedekiah's ministers persuaded the king to have him thrown into a well to die.[30] However after languishing in the mud Ebed-Melech, a Cushite, heard of his plight and got Zedekiah's permission to have him returned to the guard house (38:1–13). In desperation Zedekiah then consulted Jeremiah for the last time.[31] He was told that he had two choices: to surrender and survive or fight on and face certain disaster (38:14–28).

After a siege of eighteen months the city walls were finally breached and Jerusalem fell. Zedekiah was captured trying to escape, blinded and deported to Babylon along with all but the poorest people. The city was razed and its walls demolished.[32] Jeremiah, who had been held in chains at Ramah awaiting deportation, was freed and entrusted to the care of Gedaliah, the newly appointed governor of the region[33] (39:1 – 40:6).

Events after the fall of Jerusalem (40:7 – 44:30)

When Gedaliah was assassinated the people remaining in Judah fled to Egypt taking Jeremiah and Baruch with them, in blatant disregard of Yahweh's word that He would protect them from any Babylonian reprisals whereas only further calamities awaited them in Egypt.

Jeremiah buried some stones near the entrance to Pharaoh's palace to indicate where Nebuchadnezzar would one day erect his throne after conquering Egypt (40:7 – 43:13). Meanwhile the people made it clear that they had no intention of forsaking their alien gods, particularly the Queen of Heaven.[34] When they had worshipped her in the past they had prospered. As soon as they forsook her there was nothing but trouble. In his last recorded prophecy Jeremiah tried to refute this twisted logic. It was the opposite of the truth and the consequences were dire. Apart from a few refugees who would return to Judah, all those who came to settle in Egypt would perish. As a sign of this Jeremiah prophesied the death of Pharaoh Hophra (44:1–30).

ORACLES AGAINST THE NATIONS (25:14–38, 46:1 – 51:64)

After Judah has been punished the cup of the wine of God's wrath will pass to the nations (25:14–38). Oracles then follow: on Egypt's defeat at Carchemish (46:1–12); on her invasion by Nebuchadnezzar (46:13–26); on Israel's ultimate salvation (46:27–28); on Philistia's calamitous defeat at the hands of Egypt (47:1–7); against Moab (48:1–47), Ammon (49:1–6) and Edom (49:7–22); against Damascus and other Aramaean towns (49:23–27); against Kedar and the Arabs (49:28–33) and Elam (49:34–39). A final oracle describes the fall of Babylon and contains a brief reference to Israel's restoration. It also relates how Jeremiah arranged for a sheet recording this prophecy to be tied to a stone and thrown into the Euphrates so that in sinking it would prefigure the way Babylon would one day sink never to rise again (50:1 – 51:64).

An Historical Appendix (52:1–34)

This describes the fall of Jerusalem and the fate of Zedekiah and is almost identical with 2K 24:18 – 25:30. It omits the assassination of Gedaliah but records the numbers involved in three distinct deportations to Babylon.[35] Verses 52:4–16 are also found, in abbreviated form, at Jr 39:1–10.

Lamentations

Lamentations consists of five elegies mourning the destruction of Jerusalem, a city that was God's own and thought to be inviolable. Yet the poet is under no illusions. She had played the rebel and fully deserved her fate. All the same embers of hope remain. Yahweh is near, His mercy not spent.

The poet is unknown. A tradition that Lamentations was composed by Jeremiah no longer commands wide support. However the poems' vivid descriptions have a freshness that does suggest an eyewitness.

First lament[1] (1:1–22)

Jerusalem is desolate and forlorn like a widow given over to grief and mourning, her splendour gone. She is starving, her children driven into captivity, the Temple defiled, an object of scorn. Yahweh is making her suffer for her crimes (1:1–11). Zion herself takes up the cry bewailing the terrible calamities Yahweh has flailed her with.[2] There is no-one to comfort her. Yahweh is in the right for she rebelled against Him. May her enemies be punished as she is (1:12–22).

Second lament (2:1–22)

Zion's plight results from the torrent of Yahweh's anger. He has behaved like an enemy. The suffering, the starving children, are heart-rending. False prophets bear a heavy responsibility. Her enemies may gloat but what has happened is Yahweh's doing. He has executed the threat of punishment made long ago. Let her pour out her heart and appeal to Yahweh's compassion.

Third lament (3:1–66)

The poet voices the nation's misery through the window of his own suffering. Yahweh is like a huntsman using him as a target for his arrows (3:1–20). Yet His mercy is surely not spent. Maybe it is salutary to have to endure suffering. The Lord is good to those who trust Him and in His love will not reject anyone for ever. If He brings grief, He will also have pity for it is not for His own pleasure that He torments and grieves the human race (3:21–39).

The poet invites his audience to examine their consciences and repent. Despite the present tribulation he knows that Yahweh is near to console him. At the same time he calls on Yahweh to repay His enemies as their deeds deserve (3:40–66).

Fourth lament (4:1–22)

How Zion has fallen! People dying in the streets clawing at rubbish heaps. Yahweh Himself has humbled the city that not even her enemies thought could ever be taken (4:1–12). Prophets and priests are the guilty ones and now they are shunned as lepers. Zion's sin is atoned for. Edom's punishment is still to come³ (4:13–22).

Fifth lament (5:1–22)

The poet beseeches Yahweh to relieve their pitiful state. They have lost homes and loved ones. They have to pay extortionate prices for water and wood and are starving. Women are raped, youths herded into forced labour. They are suffering for their forebears' sins. May Yahweh remember them and restore them as they were before.

Baruch

Baruch is one of the Deutero-Canonical books. It purports to be from the hand of Jeremiah's secretary.[1] However it is almost certainly a much later work, composite, and set against the backdrop of the Babylonian exile and attributed to Baruch to give it greater weight. Its purpose would probably have been to encourage its readers during a later tribulation. It has five quite separate sections.

Introduction (1:1–15a)

A narrator records how the book was written in Babylon five years after Jerusalem was burned down. It was sent to Jerusalem along with money for the Temple liturgy and the return of certain Temple vessels.[2]

The exiles pray for deliverance (1:15b – 3:8)

The exiles admit their guilt. They have been disobedient and served alien gods. Their plight is fully deserved and exactly what Moses forewarned if they persisted in sin (1:15b – 2:10). They pray that God may douse His anger and deliver their little remnant so that they may honour Him and the whole world know that He is God. The dead in Sheol cannot do it! After confessing their obstinacy in not yielding to Babylon (as advocated by Jeremiah, Jr 27:12), and recalling promises of restoration, the prayer ends with a plea for pity (2:11 – 3:8).

A wisdom poem (3:9 – 4:4)

Baruch presents wisdom as a woman, distinct from humankind and God. She is a treasure house, the key to life and peace, beyond man's reach, known only to God. She is the eternal Law. Those who keep her shall live. Those who desert her shall die. Israel forsook her. That is why she is in exile.

A message of hope (4:5 – 5:9)

After the poet explains that Israel's punishment was intended to be medicinal (4:5–9) personified Jerusalem speaks as a widow whose children have been sent into captivity for ignoring God's precepts. She expresses confidence that God will rescue her children and bring them to eternal joy (4:10–29). The poet replies that Jerusalem should take heart, discard her 'dress of sorrow and distress' and put on 'the beauty of God's glory'. God will comfort her. Her enemies will be vanquished. Every nation will see her splendour as her children are regathered to a city restored to glory for evermore: a Jerusalem to be called Peace-through-Justice, Glory-through-Devotion (4:30 – 5:9).

Jeremiah's letter (6:1–72)

A long rambling letter, ostensibly written by Jeremiah but almost certainly from another hand, warns those about to be deported to Babylon against the idols they will find there. They are powerless, useless, insensible, helpless, unconscious, lifeless: the work of men's hands, utterly worthless.

Ezekiel

According to his own dates (and there is no reason to doubt them) Ezekiel ministered to his fellow exiles in Babylon between 593 and 571 B.C. This was a climactic time for the Covenant people. We have the evidence not only of Ezekiel but also of Jeremiah that it was a period of spiritual bankruptcy when idolatry, immorality, violence, injustice and extortion were rife.

Nor was the political scenario any brighter. Nebuchadnezzar had captured Jerusalem in 597, plundering the Temple and deporting Jehoiachin and the leading citizens to Babylon. Jehoiachin's uncle Zedekiah, who succeeded him on the throne, fared no better. An ill-judged rebellion rekindled Nebuchadnezzar's ire and this time there was no reprieve. In 587 Jerusalem and the Temple were gutted, the people were exiled to Babylon, and Judah ceased to exist as a sovereign state. Standing astride the catastrophe of 587, Ezekiel's ministry thus has one foot in the vortex of Judah's last turbulent years, the other in the calmer waters of restoration yet to come.

Apart from the prophet's call, the first half of the book, which predates 587, is a sustained expose of Jerusalem's apostasy and the fate that awaits her. In fiery language, muted with only rare gleams of hope, and designed to shock a people desensitised by lives of spiritual adultery, Ezekiel drags her sins to the light of day and warns of approaching doom. Transported by the spirit back to Jerusalem in 592, he is given a vision of the future in which he sees the profanities that defiled the Temple in its dying days, the slaughter of the guilty, Jerusalem engulfed by fire, and Yahweh's departure from His Temple.

It may seem odd that Ezekiel, whose solicitude was to his compatriots in Babylon, should be hurling threats and reproaches at a city far away across the desert. However his purpose was clear enough: to maintain the exiles' faith and prepare them for restoration by convincing them that the debacle of 597, and the worse catastrophe yet to come, happened not because the Babylonian gods were more powerful than Yahweh, but out of the nation's unrelenting addiction to sin. God's chastisement was both just and inevitable and must be seen as an object lesson. For it was the exiles in Babylon, not those left in Jerusalem, who would be the seedbed of future resuscitation.

The fall of Jerusalem was a turning point in Ezekiel's ministry. With his earlier prophecies vindicated, people thronged to hear him and in part two of his book the erstwhile courier of doom becomes a messenger of hope, focusing on God's mercy and grace. After oracles predicting the downfall of Judah's neighbours and denouncing Israel's former rulers, he prophesies a glorious restoration powered by a New Covenant whereby God would refashion men's hearts so that they would willingly keep His commands.

Yahweh Himself will shepherd His people and they will live in the glow of His abiding presence. Israel and Judah will be reunited under a scion of David's House to live in idyllic peace. Victory over Gog, a supernatural invader from the north, symbolises God's final victory over evil at the end of time. Ezekiel ends with a vision of the future community, albeit one constrained, for all its high ideal of holiness, to the Jewish and material rather than the universal and spiritual: a new Temple, a new cult, a Promised Land even more fertile than the old.

Ezekiel breaks down as follows:

Oracles before the fall of Jerusalem

- Ezekiel's call (1:1 – 3:27)
- The fate awaiting Judah and Jerusalem (4:1 – 7:27)
- Yahweh abandons His Temple (8:1 – 11:25)
- Threats and reproaches (12:1 – 14:23)
- Allegories against Jerusalem (15:1 – 17:24)
- Personal responsibility (18:1–32)
- Threats against Jerusalem (19:1 – 24:27)

Oracles after the fall of Jerusalem

- Prophecies against the nations (25:1 – 32:31)
- The restoration of Israel (33:1 – 39:29)
- The New Israel (40:1 – 48:35)

Unlike the shorter oracles typical of many prophets, Ezekiel's style is more verbose. However what would otherwise be a dry presentation is enlivened by extraordinary visions, symbolic actions and colourful allegories. His writings are liberally peppered with the motif 'and they will know that I am Yahweh', a not so subtle reminder of the certainty of God's judgement. He alone has the power to punish and restore and His deeds will ultimately force people to recognise His omnipotence, holiness and wisdom.

ORACLES BEFORE THE FALL OF JERUSALEM (1:1 – 24:27)

Ezekiel's call (1:1 – 3:27)

Ezekiel, a priest, received his commission to be God's spokesman in 593 in a theophany in which he saw the glory of Yahweh enthroned in majesty on a heavenly chariot-throne borne by four living creatures. Addressed as 'son of man' he was to be God's envoy to the rebellious Israelites living near Babylon by the river Chebar.[1]

Ezekiel ate the scroll God gave him and found it 'sweet as honey' thereby making its message – 'lamentations, dirges and cries of grief' – his own. Although his audience would be stubborn and obstinate he must not be alarmed. God would make his resolve hard as diamond. It was an awesome assignment. Ezekiel would be held accountable if he failed to pass on God's warnings.

He was told he would be struck dumb and ordered to remain at home and to refrain from preaching except when God specifically opened his mouth.[2]

The fate awaiting Judah and Jerusalem (4:1 – 7:27)

Ezekiel performs a series of acted parables to dramatize the fate awaiting Jerusalem. He etches an image of the city on a brick and uses an iron griddle to depict a besieging army. He lies on his left side for three hundred and ninety days and on his right side for forty days to indicate the number of years Israel and Judah must suffer punishment.[3] He restricts himself to a near starvation diet to emulate the privations the inhabitants of Jerusalem will have to endure. He bakes his bread on cow dung to illustrate that living in exile will mean eating unclean food. Finally he shaves his head and beard – a sign of total catastrophe – and divides the hairs to symbolize how the siege of Jerusalem will end in fire, massacre, scattering and exile.[4] Few will escape the carnage[5] (4:1 – 5:4).

Ezekiel now reveals the reason for these dire omens. Jerusalem had responded to God's trust with abominations and wickedness that far surpassed anything the nations had perpetrated. That is why she will be reduced to a ruin, made an object of derision, scattered to the winds and harrowed by famine, wild beasts, pestilence and the sword[6] (5:5–17). He addresses the mountains, seats of pagan worship, as the personification of Israel's rampant idolatry as he blazes out the terrible judgement and slaughter soon to be meted out. He claps and stamps to drive his message home (6:1–14).

Doom, the end, is near.[7] Violence and pride are at their peak. Yahweh is about to vent His fury and sate His anger. No one will escape (7:1–27).

Yahweh abandons His Temple (8:1 – 11:25)

In the summer of 592 Ezekiel is carried in vision to Jerusalem where he witnesses the perversions that defile the Temple: a 'statue of jealousy'; men worshipping idols and swarms of sculptured animals; women weeping before Tammuz; men with their backs to the Temple adoring the rising sun[8] (8:1–18). Judgement is swift. The idolaters are hacked down by six men armed with deadly weapons while the innocent, marked with crosses on their foreheads by a seventh man dressed in linen, are spared.[9] The city is destroyed with fire from God's throne while the glory of Yahweh leaves the Temple in the same chariot-throne that Ezekiel saw in his inaugural vision[10] (9:1 – 10:22).

Ezekiel is instructed to condemn the notables who mislead the people of Jerusalem by complacently assuring them that the city's walls will save them much as meat in a saucepan is protected from the fire.[11] No! They will not escape God's justice but perish by the sword. And not only that. It is to the exiles in Babylon that the future belongs. They will return to Palestine and Yahweh will replace their hearts of stone with hearts of flesh so that, with a new spirit, they will keep His laws and truly become His people and He their God.[12] (In quoting this old promise Ezekiel is signifying the restoration of the communion between God and man that God always intended but which Israel shattered by her faithlessness.)

The glory of Yahweh now leaves Jerusalem and as the vision fades Ezekiel is returned to his fellow exiles in Babylon (11:1–25).

Threats and reproaches (12:1 – 14:23)

Ezekiel dons a backpack and breaks out of his house at night to mime how Jerusalem's prince will be forced to flee the city and face deportation.[13] He trembles and shudders as he eats and drinks to depict the horror of the coming siege. Scoffers should beware. These prophecies will be fulfilled very soon (12:1–28).

Ezekiel condemns false prophets who invent things to mislead people with their oversanguine forecasts. They are like labourers who plaster over a wall to hide the cracks. Women who base prophecies on divination and magic are just as bad (13:1–23).

Idolaters who seek guidance from Yahweh through a prophet must first mend their ways (14:1–11). When Yahweh pronounces sentence He spares only the righteous. And they can save no one but themselves. Not even Noah, Daniel or Job can do that.[14] (14:12–20). A few people will escape from Jerusalem and when the exiles see the sort of people they are they will be able to judge for themselves the fairness of God's judgement (14:21–23).

Allegories against Jerusalem (15:1 – 17:24)

A poem portrays the wood of the vine as no better than that of a wild forest tree and fit only for the fire.[15] Both ends of the vine (the kingdoms of Israel and Judah) have already been burnt (punished). Only the charred (partly punished) middle (Jerusalem) remains. Jerusalem has escaped once but fire will devour her yet (15:1–8).

Yahweh lovingly rears a homeless waif (Jerusalem) and she grows up to become a beautiful queen. He marries her and showers her with gifts.[16] But she is unfaithful and becomes a whore, bestowing her favours on the gods of Egypt, Assyria and Babylon. She never remembers the love that had been lavished on her. So she will be treated like a harlot, stripped and stoned to death by the very lovers she once lusted after with such abandon. Her sisters Sodom and Samaria were upright by comparison! Yet despite all this Yahweh will not forget His promises of old and one day will restore her, along with Sodom and Samaria, with a New Covenant that will never end[17] (16:1–63).

In the allegory of the eagles Ezekiel condemns Zedekiah's fateful alliance with Egypt and his subsequent rebellion against Babylon in violation of his oath of allegiance to Nebuchadnezzar[18] (17:1–21). He then switches to the Messianic future in a poem in which the shoot from the cedar tree represents a future king who will bring rest and felicity to all nations (represented by the winged creatures) (17:22–24).

Personal responsibility (18:1–32)

Everyone will be judged according to his own conduct. A son does not bear his father's guilt nor a father his son's. Furthermore if a good man lapses into sin, or a sinner renounces his sins, neither the former's previous virtue nor the sinner's evil deeds will be remembered.[19]

Threats against Jerusalem (19:1 – 24:27)

An elegy laments two rulers of Judah under the guise of young lions.[20] A second poem foretells Jerusalem's fiery end (19:1–14).

Ezekiel castigates Israel for her ingrained infidelities, particularly her profaning the Sabbath.[21] Yahweh had resolved to destroy her in Egypt and only stayed His wrath then to prevent His name being dishonoured among the nations.[22] All the same He will not be angry with her for ever. He will rescue her from exile, purge the ungodly, and reign over her Himself. Then not only Israel but all nations will acknowledge Him (20:1–44).

Ezekiel likens the massacre that will soon devastate the people of Judah, just and unjust alike, to a fire that consumes every tree, the green as well as the dry.[23] No one will escape. He drives home his message with bitter groans as he contemplates Yahweh readying His sword (the Babylonians) for the slaughter. He apes Nebuchadnezzar at a crossroads deciding by divination whether to attack Jerusalem or Ammon. The lot falls on Jerusalem because her sins are so flagrant. But Ammon's turn will come[24] (21:1–37).

In a ferocious assault Ezekiel catalogues Jerusalem's manifold sins: idolatry, violence, self-interest, lack of parental respect, social injustice, profaning the Sabbath and the Temple, sexual immorality, bribery, usury, extortion. Judah has become dross, worthless and impure, and will be melted down in the furnace of God's anger. Every strata of society is guilty; princes, priests, leaders, prophets, ordinary people (22:1–31).

In another powerful allegory Ezekiel reviews the fortunes of Samaria, the northern kingdom of Israel, and Jerusalem in the story of two sisters, Oholah and Oholibah. They belonged to Yahweh but became whores. Oholah (Samaria) lusted after Assyrian lovers but when Yahweh eventually handed her over to them they stripped and killed her. Oholibah (Jerusalem) learned nothing from this. She was even more debauched than her sister and took Babylonian and Egyptian paramours as well. So she too will be ravaged by her former suitors: stripped naked, disfigured, her family victims of the sword[25] (23:1–49).

When, in January 588, Ezekiel heard that Babylon's final assault on Jerusalem had begun, he likened her to a pot of meat that will be cooked until the bones are boiled and even the rust on the pot burns away. Nothing less can purify her. When his wife – 'the delight of his eyes' – died Yahweh forbade him to exhibit any grief as a sign to the exiles not to mourn Jerusalem's end. Her fate was fully deserved (24:1–27).

ORACLES AFTER THE FALL OF JERUSALEM (25:1 – 48:35)

Prophecies against the nations (25:1 – 32:31)

These prophecies, in which Ezekiel's poetic inspiration reaches its peak, were made between 587 and 571. Their position here is significant. Before Ezekiel could record his subsequent prophecies of an Israel living in peace after judgement, it was necessary to show how her neighbours would reap the fruits of their arrogance and be humbled to the point where they could never again pose a threat.

Ammon will be wiped out and occupied by Arabs for gloating over Israel's fate (25:1–7). Moab too will suffer invasion (25:8–11). Edom will be laid waste for crimes against Israel (25:12–14), likewise the Philistines (25:15–17). Tyre will be destroyed by Nebuchadnezzar for rejoicing at Jerusalem's downfall (26:1–21). A lament on Tyre likens her fate to a ship floundering far out at sea (27:1–36). Two oracles condemn her pride and corruption (28:1–19). Sidon will fall by the sword (28:20–23). With her hostile neighbours quelled, Yahweh will restore Israel to her homeland where she will live safe and secure (28:24–26).

Egypt will be devastated for her insufferable pride. She will be restored later although not to her former greatness (29:1–16). Nebuchadnezzar will conquer and plunder Egypt[26] (29:17–21). A terrible fate awaits Egypt on the Day of Yahweh (30:1–19). Egypt will be defeated by Babylon[27] (30:20–26). Egypt is likened to a great cedar tree that is suddenly cut down for its overweening pride (31:1–18). Egypt, cast as a crocodile, will be overthrown by Babylon (32:1–16). Pharaoh and his warriors will join the rulers and armies of other past empires in the netherworld (32:17–31).

The restoration of Israel (33:1 – 39:29)

Ezekiel's credentials and responsibilities as God's watchman are reaffirmed. So too is the principle of individual responsibility. The only new feature is a call to repentant sinners to repair the wrongs they have done. Again there is stress on God's desire for repentance and conversion and on the importance of present rather than past dispositions. An upright person who turns to sin will die. The sinner who repents will live (33:1–20).

The day Ezekiel had anticipated for so long finally dawns. A fugitive arrives with news of Jerusalem's fall. Ezekiel's freedom of speech is restored. Straightaway he rejects the claims of the survivors living in ruins in Jerusalem to be the true inheritors of the land promised to Abraham. On the contrary they are doomed. People now flock to hear Ezekiel but their enthusiasm is shallow. They listen to his words as they might an entertainer singing love songs but do not take the slightest notice of any of them[28] (33:21–33).

Ezekiel denounces the rapacious 'shepherds of Israel' who have preyed on their flock and led it astray. All they cared about was feathering their own nests. Now Yahweh Himself will shepherd His scattered flock. He will re-gather them, segregate the good sheep from the bad, and lead them to rich pastures where they will live in peace. He will raise up a shepherd of David's line to rule over them. He Himself will be their God[29] (34:1–31).

Ezekiel prophesies the destruction of Mount Seir i.e. Edom. Edom stabbed Israel in the back when she was under attack (from Babylon) and still covets her land[30] (35:1–15).

As in chapter 6 Ezekiel addresses the mountains of Israel but this time promising blessings and prophesying the New Covenant.[31] Israel will be repopulated and live in greater prosperity than ever before. She will be spiritually regenerated as Yahweh cleanses her of her sinful ways. He will replace her heart of stone with a heart of flesh and infuse her with His spirit so that she will henceforth respect His laws and reject her past behaviour. This would not be for the sake of an Israel that defiled the land He gave her but for His own name's sake, to demonstrate His holiness and power to the world[32] (36:1–38).

The celebrated vision in which Ezekiel saw a valley of dry bones resuscitated with new sinews, flesh, skin and breath does not teach personal resurrection (although it may incidentally prepare the ground for that) but is another assurance that the defunct nation of Israel, as lifeless as any dry bones and bereft of hope, will one day come back to life.

Ezekiel follows this with an acted parable in which he joins two sticks together to symbolise the future reunification of Israel and Judah. Cleansed from their former apostasy they will live for ever in their ancestral territory with a scion of David as shepherd and prince. God will enact a covenant of peace and dwell among them for ever (37:1–28).

Ezekiel now reveals a vision of the last days when a restored Israel living peacefully in 'towns without walls' suffers a massive invasion from Gog of the land of Magog in the far north. With florid gory detail – indescribable carnage, birds and beasts glutting on the dead – he describes how Yahweh will inflict a crushing defeat. Gog's forces will be annihilated[33] (38:1 – 39:20). Ezekiel summarises God's promises of restoration. They sanctify His name and proclaim His glory to the nations (39:21–29).

The new Israel (40:1 – 48:35)

Ezekiel concludes his prophecies of the new Israel by describing how in 573 B.C. he was transported in vision to a high mountain where an angel showed him a new Jerusalem. He was given a specification for a new Temple (40:1 – 42:20; 43:13–17); directions for the consecration of the altar (43:18–27); notified of a ban on anyone entering the east gate and on aliens entering or serving in the Temple (44:1–9); regulations for Levites and priests[34] (44:10–31); instructions on how the land was to be shared between the Temple, priests, Levites, the people and the prince (45:1–8); regulations on weights and measures, offerings and feasts[35] (45:9 – 46:24); details of the boundaries of the new Israel (47:13–23) and for Jerusalem's gates (48:30–35); and directions for the division of the land between the tribes and resident aliens (48:1–29).

These prescriptions raise many problems given that it is clear, especially from 47:1–12, that Ezekiel has the Messianic age in mind. We mention just two. Who is the prince who is introduced without explanation at 44:3? What is the continuing role of animal sacrifice in general and the sacrifice for sin in particular found at 43:18–27? The prince is obviously not the Messiah since he is enjoined to refrain from oppression, 45:8, to make burnt offerings, 46:12, and is given instructions on how to bequeath his property to his sons, 46:16. (The New Testament affirms that Christ's perfect sacrifice removed the need for Old Testament forms of sacrifice for ever, Heb 10:1–18.)

The presence of these and many similar difficulties makes the interpretation of Ezk 40 – 48 unusually difficult. But the general thrust is clear enough. Ezekiel has earlier witnessed Yahweh's departure from the Temple, its subsequent ruin and the scattering of Israel. Now he has envisioned the glory of the Messianic kingdom yet to come and with his priestly background it is his joyful task to complete his earlier prophecies with detailed directives for a new Temple and the reorganisation of national life in readiness for Yahweh's return.

Whatever the obscurities in these closing chapters with their rich Jewish colouring (for nowhere does his insight extend to the nations), nothing can hide Ezekiel's sense of the presence of God and his insistence on the centrality of worship and holiness. With his minute attention to detail he knows that nothing must be left to chance as Man stands before God. Nothing is too much trouble when the objective is the right relationship between God and a new Jerusalem to be named 'Yahweh is there', 48:35.

Two passages in particular provide a fitting climax. In one Ezekiel sees the glory of Yahweh returning in splendour to His Temple and hears His promise to dwell forever among His people (43:1–12). In the other, a text reminiscent of the paradisiacal conditions of Eden and the living water of Jesus, Ezekiel is shown a river streaming from the Temple bringing health and life wherever it flows, teeming with fish, sweetening the Dead Sea, and sustaining trees that fruit every month with leaves that heal and never wither[36] (47:1–12).

Daniel

Daniel is one of the most important books in the Canon but at the same time one of the most puzzling. With its lavish use of symbols it has long been a happy hunting ground for religious cranks who have trivialised it in attempts to relate its details to modern history and predict dates for the end of the world. However while there are admittedly obscurities, and legitimate grounds for different interpretations of detail, the core message is not in doubt and the reader would therefore be well advised to focus on the big picture and avoid becoming swamped in a deluge of minutiae the keys to which lie buried in the distant past. As Daniel takes in a swathe of history from the Babylonian empire to Antiochus Epiphanes some four centuries later, we shall begin with a brief historical resume.

Historical resumé

With the overthrow of Assyria in 612 B.C. hegemony in the fertile crescent passed to Babylon whose armies under Nebuchadnezzar captured Jerusalem in 597 and again ten years later, deporting all but the poorest people. In 539 Babylon fell to the Persian king Cyrus, who had earlier gained control over the Medes, Babylon's former ally against Assyria. In 538 Cyrus issued an edict allowing any Jew who wished to do so to return home to Judah. Many but not all did so. The Persian empire, of which Judah was now a province, then held sway for two centuries before being overthrown by Alexander the Great.

Alexander's empire barely survived his early death in 323. Within a few years it split in four: Thrace, Macedonia, Ptolemaia (Egypt) and Seleucia (Syria). For a century or so Palestine lay under Ptolemaic tutelage but in 200 it became a Seleucid fiefdom. The troubles which Daniel prophesies erupted in 167 during the reign of Antiochus IV Epiphanes. He embarked upon an aggressive promotion of Hellenistic culture and tried to purge the Jews' ancestral faith with a persecution that threatened its very survival. The Temple was desecrated and observance of the Law banned resulting in the Maccabean uprising.

Content

According to chapter 1, Daniel was a native of Judah who was carried off to Babylon while still a boy to be trained for service at Nebuchadnezzar's court. He remained in Babylon for the rest of his life which included the early years of Persian rule.

Chapters 3 – 6 are simple tales about Daniel and three companions. They project their heroes as personifications of virtue utterly devoid of sin or doubt. God is in control and they revel in His power to humble the proud and mighty and sustain those who like themselves stay loyal to their faith despite every affliction, even death. Chapters 13, 14 and 3:24–90 are deutero-canonical additions in similar vein.

Chapters 2, 7 – 12 are very different. They claim to look forward from Babylon to probe the future in a series of elaborately coded visions and angelic revelations. Ch 2 sets the scene by revealing how the kingdoms of this world will one day be supplanted by a universal and everlasting kingdom of God. Ch 7 adds flesh to these bones. After a review of the rise and fall of empires from Babylon to Alexander, it focuses on Antiochus Epiphanes. He will persecute the Jews until, following his death, God's kingdom will come as sovereignty is devolved on a 'son of man' whose rule will embrace all nations and never end.

The death of Antiochus and the coming of the future age are thus presented as contiguous events. Chs 11, 12 correct this perspective. After another historical digest building up once again to the maleficent Antiochus Epiphanes, the tone modulates from the Antiochus of history to a figure of godless evil who, at some indeterminate time in the future, will precipitate a tribulation of which Antiochus' was but a shadowy foreboding. God's people will be tested to the very limit. Then, at the height of his villainy, this monster will die to be followed by the end of sorrows and resurrection, some to 'shine as bright as stars for all eternity' others to 'shame and everlasting disgrace'. Only then, with the fell power of evil itself finally laid low, will God's kingdom dawn.

Daniel's references to resurrection and everlasting life are the most explicit of any in the Old Testament, albeit couched in selective and not universal terms. Moreover where other prophets give episodic glimpses of a future time when God will rule, with Daniel the idea is sustained. And where other prophets promise a glorious future with God reigning over a restored Israel in history in this world, Daniel's great contribution to salvation history is to show that these promises relate to a new creation outside history beyond the grave.

Date of composition

As we have seen, the dream of chapter 2 and the visions of chapter 7 onwards purport to date from the sixth century and to see into the future including the baleful reign of Antiochus Epiphanes. They become more detailed the nearer they get to Antiochus but have nothing to say of events after his death and are not always accurate on events immediately preceding it. This has led a majority of commentators, disinclined to accept the likelihood of divine revelation spanning a time horizon so far forward, to argue that Daniel was actually composed shortly before Antiochus' death by an unknown author who presented what was actually past history as future prophecy and concealed his identity by putting his message into the mouth of a well-known seer named Daniel.

By recounting stories of how, long ago, Daniel and his companions had remained loyal to God in the face of similar trials, proponents of this view maintain that it was intended to encourage the Jews of Antiochus' day, some of whom must have come to doubt divine providence in the face of the intense persecution they were facing, similarly to maintain their faith. Likewise, by presenting as 'prophecy' events that had already happened, it was hoped to kindle confidence that other prophecies that had so far not been realised, such as God's reign following closely upon Antiochus' death, would also shortly come to pass.

DANIEL AT THE BABYLONIAN COURT (1:1 – 6:29)

Daniel's deportation and education (1:1–20)

During the reign of Jehoiakim, Nebuchadnezzar plunders the Temple vessels and deports some boys to be educated in Babylon for service at court, among them Daniel and three companions.[1] Determined not to compromise their faith, they insist on a diet of vegetables and water rather than claiming their entitlement to rations from the royal table.[2] Despite this they thrive and at the end of their training are second to none in wisdom.

Nebuchadnezzar's dream of the great statue (2:1–49)

Daniel makes his mark and is rewarded with high rank when, alone among the king's sages, he is able not only to interpret one of Nebuchadnezzar's dreams but also to underwrite his credibility by telling the king what the dream was.[3]

Daniel's interpretation, received in a night vision after prayer, was that the four parts of the statue Nebuchadnezzar saw represented four empires that would successively rule the world. They would all pass away without trace, shattered by (God's) 'stone', and upon their ruins, without human aid, God would inaugurate His own everlasting kingdom.[4]

Daniel's companions in the furnace (3:1–23; 91–97)

Daniel's three companions surrender themselves to God's providence when they elect to be thrown into a fiery furnace rather than to submit to idolatry by obeying Nebuchadnezzar's command that they should worship a golden statue. A 'child of the gods' (presumably an angel) joins them in the furnace and they emerge unscathed.

Nebuchadnezzar's dream of the great tree (3:98 – 4:34)

Daniel interprets another dream in which Nebuchadnezzar is warned that he will be punished for his pride by imagining himself to be an animal and acting like one. As such he will be banished from society for seven 'times' until he learns humility and recognises God as Lord. A year later, having refused to repent, this is exactly what happened.[5]

Belshazzar's feast (5:1 – 6:1)

Belshazzar, king of Babylon, appropriates the Temple vessels for use as drinking cups when he throws a banquet.[6] At the height of the carousing a mysterious hand writes a message on the palace wall. Only Daniel is able to interpret its portent of doom, that God is about to put an end to Belshazzar's reign and divide his kingdom. That same night Belshazzar is murdered and his throne passes to Darius the Mede.[7]

Daniel in the lions' den (6:2–29)

Daniel is thrown to the lions after he refuses to obey an edict, designed by his enemies to trap him, forbidding prayer for thirty days to anyone except the Persian king Darius. When the next morning the king finds Daniel unharmed, an angel having sealed the lions' jaws, he is released and restored to favour.[8]

APOCALYPTIC VISIONS (7:1 – 12:13)

The four beasts (7:1–28)

Daniel has a dream in some ways similar to Nebuchadnezzar's of chapter 2 in which he sees four great beasts emerging from a stormy sea.[9] The fourth beast was unlike the others. It had ten horns with another horn, a little one, sprouting among them. This little horn had eyes like human eyes and a mouth full of boasting. Three of the original horns were pulled out by the roots to make room for it.

As with Nebuchadnezzar's dream, most commentators believe that the four beasts symbolise the empires of Babylon, the Medes, the Persians, and Alexander the Great. It is probable that the ten horns stand for Alexander's successors on the Seleucid throne while the little horn that sprouts from them represents the Seleucid king Antiochus Epiphanes who only came to power after displacing three rival claimants, hence the three horns that were extracted by the roots. The angel who interprets the vision for Daniel explains that this last horn is a king who will torment 'the holy ones of the Most High', i.e. God's people, for three and a half 'times' marked by blasphemy and attacks on their observance of the cult and the Law.[10]
Appendix 1 refers

This vision then blends with another of God sitting in judgement. The fourth beast with its boastful horn is put to death and kingship over all nations is conferred for ever on one like a son of man coming on the clouds of heaven.[11] In other words after Antiochus' death will come God's everlasting and universal kingdom.

The ram and the he-goat (8:1–27)

In another vision of the rise and fall of Antiochus Epiphanes interpreted by the angel Gabriel a he-goat with a great horn symbolizing the king of Greece (Alexander the Great) comes from the west and slaughters a ram with two horns, standing for the kings of Media and Persia.[12] At the height of the he-goat's strength its horn snaps and is replaced by four horns representing the four kingdoms into which Alexander's empire split after his death. From one of these springs a horn which grows to a great size (Antiochus Epiphanes). He will attack God's holy people, abolish the perpetual sacrifice, profane the Sanctuary and even challenge God Himself.[13] This will go on for two thousand, three hundred evenings and mornings and then, without human intervention, he will be broken and the sanctuary restored.[14]

The prophecy of the seventy weeks (9:1–27)

This chapter, in which after a prayer for mercy, Gabriel came to explain to Daniel the meaning of Jeremiah's prophecy, Jr 25:11; 29:10, that God's people would be captive in Babylon for seventy years, is obscure and interpretations are legion. Suffice to say that with its allusions to putting an end to transgression, placing the seal on sin, expiating crime and introducing everlasting uprightness, it is hard to see verse 24 as anything but a foreshadowing of Christ. Nevertheless it is perhaps significant that the New Testament nowhere alludes to this cryptic prophecy.

History from Persia to Antiochus Epiphanes (10:1 – 11:35)

An angel comes to give Daniel a preview of the future. But first he tells how he is fighting the angel for Persia and will soon have to contend with the angel for Javan (Greece) aided only by Michael, Israel's guardian angel[15] (10:1 – 11:1).

After a mention of four Persian kings and a mighty king (Alexander) whose empire will be divided into four on his death, the angel concentrates on what is effectively a resume of the intrigues and wars of the 'kings of the north and the south' (the Seleucid and Ptolemaic dynasties of Syria and Egypt) before narrowing at 11:21 to a 'wretch' of a king (Antiochus Epiphanes): his rise to power, his two Egyptian campaigns, his banning of the perpetual sacrifice and his desecration of the Temple with the 'appalling abomination'[16] (11:2–35).

From Antiochus to Antichrist (11:36–45)

The king will grow ever more arrogant and blasphemous. His pride will know no bounds. Disrespectful of the gods of his fathers he will magnify himself above every god. He will overrun many countries but then at the very moment when he seems to be carrying all before him he will die.

Reflection on 11:36–45

At first glance this seems like a continuation of the saga of Antiochus from 11:35. But although some of the facts still fit, the strikingly accurate prophecy of history from Cyrus to Antiochus that characterised the angelic revelation of 11:2–35 no longer holds.[17] The explanation is that from verse 36 the vision transcends history and jumps to the end days. For some time now the language has been welling up mightily to suggest more than mere human perfidy. The exalted tones in which Daniel introduces the son of man in chapter 7, condemns the wanton behaviour of the tyrant of chapter 8, and prophesies the end of sin in chapter 9, all suggest a significance beyond the straightforward application of the words to a purely historical scenario.

Increasingly, and it comes to a head in 11:36–45, we are in the company not of the 'wretch' Antiochus but of an embodiment of evil (Satan or 'Antichrist' as some would dub him) whose frenzied onslaught brings a tribulation of which Antiochus' was but a pale foreshadowing. In chapter 7 Daniel had 'telescoped' together the death of Antiochus, the prototype Antichrist, and the end of the world. He had been seeing the near and the distant in a single view. Now, in chapter 12, he steps clear of time to give the two events their proper separation. Antiochus' trials are but the precursor of a far greater tribulation to come at the end of history and not until then, following the end of evil and (as we see below) resurrection and judgement, will God's kingdom finally come about.

The final triumph of the just (12:1–13)

These troubles of the last days will be without parallel in the history of the world. But just as they are at their peak Michael, the defender of God's people, will arise and those whose names are found written in the Book will be spared,[18] to be followed by resurrection. Many will awaken, some to shame and everlasting disgrace, others to everlasting life (12:1–4). *Appendix 2 refers*

Daniel learns that the great tribulation will last for three and a half 'times' and drive God's people to the very brink of defeat. Many will be purged by their suffering but nothing will convince the truly wicked. Details of the final denouement must remain a mystery until the time of the End.[19] Daniel is promised that he will rise again to receive his reward (12:5–13).

DEUTERO-CANONICAL ADDITIONS

Daniel's companions in the furnace (3:24–90)

Three enhancements to the earlier story comprise: a prayer by Azariah confessing the nation's sin and praying for Israel to be restored to God's favour (3:24–45); an account of how an angel protected Daniel's friends from the heat of the furnace (3:46–50); and a hymn of praise sung by the three friends while they were entombed in the furnace (3:51–90).

Daniel saves the virtuous Susanna (13:1–64)

In this tale of the triumph of virtue over vice Susanna was a God-fearing woman of great beauty who was falsely charged with adultery by two elders after she declined to satisfy their carnal desires. She was condemned to death but exonerated following a cross-examination by Daniel of the libellants in which they gave inconsistent testimony.

Bel and the dragon (14:1–42)

The book concludes with two satires on the veneration of idols. In the first Daniel exposes an idol named Bel by showing that the food it 'ate' was actually consumed by the priests and their families overnight. In the second Daniel is thrown into the lions' pit after slaying a dragon which the Babylonians revered as a god. God protected Daniel and sent an angel to carry the prophet Habakkuk to him with food. After seven days the astonished king of Babylon released Daniel and acknowledged God as Lord.

Hosea

Hosea's mission was to the northern kingdom of Israel of which he was almost certainly a native. He was a contemporary of Isaiah and a little later than Amos during a period of religious decline and social decay in the second half of the eighth century, not long before the fall of Samaria and Israel's deportation to Assyria.

The opening chapters are enacted prophecy aimed at giving a fresh insight into the nature of God's love. The text is not unambiguous but it would appear that Hosea's wife Gomer betrayed him by taking lovers, and that he divorced her. Yet he still loved her and eventually bought her back out of slavery. Similarly Yahweh 'betrothed' Israel. Then when she became 'promiscuous', paying court to other gods as Gomer had pursued her paramours, He cast her off. But He still loves her. 'Divorcing' her was intended to bring her to her senses and one day He will take her back.

In the sequel Hosea arraigns Israel for the corruption that was leading her over the precipice of judgement to disaster. Yahweh alone could heal her, indeed was yearning to save her, but she was ignoring Him in favour of idols and foreign alliances. Rather than this he pleads for 'faithful love' and 'knowledge of God'.[1]

However reproof is not the end. From his experience with Gomer, Hosea knew what it was like to love, to be rebuffed and to go on loving and he saw God in a similar light. So in chapter 11 he complements his tale of woe by portraying God as an anguished parent recoiling in distress at the thought of separation from His beloved Israel. In a way which He cannot articulate he knows that God will somehow cure Israel of her disloyalty. Then there will be a joyful homecoming and she will abide with Him for ever.

Amos preached that punishment was inevitable. So did the more warm-hearted Hosea. But where Amos saw sin stemming from disobedience, Hosea saw it as the spurning of God's love with the cloth of judgement sewn in love and mercy.

Apart from his prophetic calling Hosea was clearly a poet of the highest rank with a gift for metaphor and colourful imagery few can match.

Hosea's marriage (1:1 – 3:5)

Yahweh tells Hosea to marry a whore as a reflection of His own 'marriage' to a 'whore' in faithless Israel.[2] So he marries a woman named Gomer. The names of the three children she bears him, and especially the last, Lo-Ammi, meaning 'not-my-people', point to Israel's coming estrangement from God[3] (1:1–9).

Israel's misfortunes will be reversed on the Day of Jezreel when Israel and Judah will be reunited and again become 'Children of the living God'[4] (2:1–3).

Failing repentance Yahweh resolves to 'divorce' His adulterous 'wife', Israel. He will stop providing her with grain and wool in the hope of bringing her to her senses and the realisation that it is He and not some 'lover' (some other god) whom she has to thank for her blessings (2:4–15). But that is not His final word. A time will come when He will seduce her, lead her into the desert and betroth her again, this time for ever in loyalty, 'faithful love' and the 'knowledge of Yahweh'.[5] Israel will respond with the ardour of her first love. Baal will be banished forever. Yahweh will restore His favours and usher in an era of peace, justice and righteousness in which even nature will respond[6] (2:16–25).

In like mode, Yahweh tells Hosea to take Gomer back. Although she is an adulteress he must love her as He loves the faithless Israel. So he buys her back.[7] However there must be a trial period before the relationship is fully restored just as a long time must elapse before Israel is fully reconciled with Yahweh in the latter days (3:1–5).

Israel's depravity (4:1 – 10:15)

Israel is consumed with violence and corruption, bereft of loyalty, love and knowledge of God. People drift aimlessly in a world where even nature suffers from man's sin. (4:1–3). Priests do not instruct the people but play on the fact that the more they sin the more they stand to gain from their (sin) offerings (4:4–11a). Hosea ridicules men who seek solace in a block of wood and denounces idolaters who desert Yahweh for the high places. Because of the bad example set by the men, young women who stray will not be punished (4:11b–14). Judah is warned not to follow Israel's shameful example (4:15–19).

Hosea condemns priests and the royal family for not upholding justice (5:1–2). While she is in her present wilful frame of mind sacrifice will gain Israel nothing. And Judah is no better (5:3–7). Israel faces certain dismemberment and Judah is condemned for encroaching upon her land. Israel's and Judah's troubles are not ailments amenable to political medicine. Only God can effect a cure and He is waiting for them to confess their guilt. Until they do He will rend them like a lion (5:8–15).

Hosea imagines an apparently penitential Israel returning to God confident that He will bind her wounds. But God rejects her plea as mere lip service, as fleeting as the morning mist. Only root and branch conversion will do: faithful love not sacrifice, knowledge of God, not burnt offerings.

God is keen to heal Israel but she has broken the covenant and crime in the shape of ambushes, marauders and deceit stare Him in the face wherever He looks (6:1 – 7:2).

Hosea mocks Israel – a half-baked cake, a silly witless pigeon – for ignoring God and turning to Egypt and Assyria for protection. Yahweh has rescued her times beyond recall yet she persists in spurning Him, trusting instead in foreign alliances and gods who are like a faulty bow. She will not escape His net when it comes to punishment (7:3–16). Hosea mercilessly exposes Israel's faults: violation of the covenant; appointing kings without Yahweh's consent; sham worship; reliance on foreign alliances, fortresses and gods made by human hand rather than God. Since she sows the wind she will reap the whirlwind (8:1–14).

Hosea condemns Israel's festive merrymaking since it is not God she is honouring but pagan deities. She is headed for Assyria and there will be no merrymaking there. To God, finding Israel was like finding grapes in the desert but it was not long before it all turned sour as Gibeah, Baal-Peor and Gilgal all too clearly revealed[8] (9:1–17).

The more blessings Israel enjoyed the more altars she built. But it was all two-faced. Soon the worthless idols she thanks for her harvests will be on their way to Assyria. Far from sowing righteousness and reaping love as God intended Israel has ploughed wickedness and reaped iniquity. Since she relies on her own strength rather than Yahweh's, punishment is inevitable (10:1–15).

God's love triumphant (11:1–11)

Israel's disloyalty to the God who weaned and nurtured her in tender motherly love leaves Him no option but to send her to captivity in Assyria. But He cannot bear to be parted from her and so in the end there will be a wonderful reunion when He will gather His people from the ends of the earth and resettle them in their homes like birds returning to their nests.[9]

Further admonishments (12:1 – 14:1)

This passage is difficult. The general drift is that Israel is steeped in a web of lies and deceit that goes right back to Jacob (12:1–15). Hosea ridicules men who kiss calves and honour images they themselves have made. He mocks the ineffectual monarchy Israel insisted on having. Chastened by the spectre of doom, now is the time for her to repent and grasp the opportunity of new life. But like a stupid child repentant Israel refuses to be born. So she must suffer the sword of Assyria (13:1 – 14:1).

Blessings for Israel (14:2–10)

Hosea ends on a note of hope. A call to Israel to mend her ways is followed by promises that God will cure her disloyalty and shower her with love and blessings. She will bloom like the lily and live in His shade. The upright will walk in Yahweh's ways while sinners stumble.

Joel

When Joel (about whom nothing is known) observes a plague of locusts devastating the land, he sees it as God's judgement on His people and as a portent of the Day of Yahweh. When the people repent and prosperity returns he interprets it as a sign that they may similarly expect deliverance and blessings on the Day itself provided they repent. But first will come the gift of God's spirit.

The locust plague (1:1 – 2:27)

Joel describes a country ravaged by locusts. Vines are fleeced, fig trees stripped to the bark. Drought and bush-fires are everywhere. Winebibbers, farmers, priests, wild animals: all are afflicted. Even the Temple offerings have had to be suspended. Joel sees this as a premonition of the Day of Yahweh and calls for public prayer and penance (1:1–20).

The swarming insects, as remorseless as any marauding army, darken the sun and turn the burgeoning land into desert waste (2:1–9). Joel's thoughts turn to the actual Day itself when it will be Yahweh before whom the stars lose their light (2:10–11). Back to the present, God invites repentance.[1] Provided it is genuine and not mere lip-service (tearing hearts rather than clothes) further calamity can be averted for He is slow to anger and rich in love. So Joel summons the nation to fast and pray. Everyone must join in: elders, children, infants, even brides and bridegrooms (2:12–17).

Yahweh does indeed take pity on His people. The deprivations of the blighted years are made good. The desert blooms, granaries are filled and vats overflow with wine and oil. God is with His people (2:18–27).

The outpouring of the Spirit and final victory (3:1 – 4:21)

Joel now prophesies that a time will come when God will pour out His spirit on all humanity regardless of age, sex or status.[2] A remnant, who call on His name, will be saved (3:1–5).

When the Day comes Judah and Jerusalem will be restored. The nations (i.e. God's enemies) will be treated as they treated others. They may muster for war, hammering their ploughshares into swords, but Yahweh will be sitting in judgement and they will be scythed down like corn at harvest time (4:1–14).

God's people are promised a glorious future. Jerusalem will be inviolable and Judah transformed from wilderness to fruitfulness, the mountains running with new wine. As for Egypt and Edom, archetypes of Israel's enemies, they will be devastated (4:15–21).

Amos

Amos is the first prophet whose oracles have been preserved in writing. He was a shepherd from Tekoa just south of Jerusalem in Judah and ministered in the eighth century B.C. He was also a herdsman and dresser of sycamore figs while the power of his poems suggests a man of some education. He prophesied in the northern kingdom before being ordered back to his own country.

Amos lived during a period of great prosperity for both Israel and Judah. Yet it was also a time of social decay. The growth of international trade had created a profligate merchant class that was bent on luxury and wealth and had little sympathy for the poverty of the peasants they exploited. Violence and fraud were rampant. And while on the surface religion seemed to prosper it was only skin-deep.

Amos is scathing on the ostentatious pomp of the liturgy. It had become an end in itself, an elaborate veneer beneath which sin romped on unabated whereas what God wanted was an inner spirituality based on justice and uprightness. Punishment was inevitable. The northern kingdom of Israel would be wiped off the face of the earth. No one would escape. No misdemeanour escapes God's gaze.

Punishment was not God's choice. He had given Israel every chance to mend her ways but His warnings had fallen on deaf ears. Even so a remnant who repented would be spared and a time would come when she would be restored to peace and prosperity. So in the end, although Amos only allows love a muted role, he does see justice married to mercy and a road left open for God's saving grace.

Prelude (1:1–2)

Amos' opening words set the tone of judgement. There is no escape, neither in the pastures nor on Carmel's bare mountain top.

Oracles against the nations (1:3 – 2:5)

Amos condemns Damascus for her ruthless attacks on Gilead; Gaza and other Philistine cities for deporting entire peoples as slaves to Edom; Tyre for handing prisoners-of-war over to Edom. He arraigns Edom for pitiless cruelty against Israel; the Ammonites for atrocities against Gilead; Moab for desecrating the corpse of a king of Edom; and Judah for deriding Yahweh's Law.

Against Israel (2:6 – 3:2)

Finally Amos attacks Israel for bribery and corruption; for abusing the downtrodden; for father and son sleeping with the same girl, and for profanity.[1] All this in defiance of the God who gave her the Promised Land and sent her prophets and Nazirite holy men to teach her. Yet she gagged the prophets and treated the Nazirites with contempt, forcing them to drink wine against their vows. No one will avoid Yahweh's judgement but Israel is particularly culpable because of her special relationship with Him.[2]

Amos' motivation (3:3–8)

There is no effect without a cause (does the lion roar if it has no prey?), equally every cause has an effect (does the trumpet sound without the people being alarmed?). Therefore since Yahweh has spoken, he has no option but to prophesy.

Warnings (3:9 – 4:13)

Violence and extortion are rife. That is why Israel will be plundered by an enemy. The luxurious ivory-embossed mansions of the indolent rich and the shrine at Bethel will be destroyed with no more left than a marauding lion leaves of a sheep (3:9–15). The pampered ladies of Samaria, 'cows of Bashan', bent on sensual gratification at the expense of the weak and poor, will be herded off as captives[3] (4:1–3). In ironic tones Amos pours scorn on people who make a display of their worship while persisting in their godless ways and acting as if the cult were a matter of 'the more the merrier'. 'Go to Bethel and sin, to Gilgal and sin even harder, bring your sacrifices every morning'[4] (4:4–5).

Yahweh has warned Israel repeatedly: with famine, drought, blight and mildew, locusts, plague, war, earthquake; all in the hope of eliciting repentance. But to no avail. So Israel 'prepare to meet your God' (4:6–12).

The first of three doxologies proclaims God's sovereignty over creation[5] (4:13).

A call to repentance (5:1–15)

After a lament that the virgin Israel will fall never to rise again (5:1–3) Amos condemns perverted justice and the disdain in which uprightness is held. The wealthy who have gained their vineyards and houses of dressed stone from exploiting the poor will not enjoy their ill-gotten gains. For those who repent there is hope although more is required than simply attending the shrines. It needs a change of heart, renouncing evil for good and espousing justice. Then maybe God 'will take pity on the remnant of Joseph'[6] (5:4–7, 10–15). A doxology extols Yahweh's power to humble the mighty (5:8–9).

More warnings (5:16 – 6:14)

Amos returns to the threat of impending punishment. Those longing for the Day of Yahweh are in for a surprise.[7] It will bring not light but darkness as when someone runs away from a lion only to meet a bear (5:16–20).

God cannot be placated by mere ritual and ceremonial, by festivals, chanting and sacrifice. What He wants are justice flowing like water and uprightness like a never-failing stream. Failing this Israel will be driven into captivity beyond Damascus[8] (5:21–27).

Appendix 1 refers

The day of the complacent self-indulgent upper class, wallowing in luxury on ivory beds, dining on the choicest cuts and imbibing wine by the bowlful, is over.[9] Because of Israel's pride and moral dubiety, her twisting of justice – as perverse as getting horses to gallop over rocks or oxen to plough the sea – Yahweh is raising a nation to oppress her (6:1–14).

Visions and more warnings (7:1 – 9:10)

Amos successfully intercedes following two visions in which locusts and fire threaten total destruction. God will not destroy His people utterly (7:1–6). A vision of Yahweh standing by a wall with a plumb-line conveys that just as a town with non-upright walls will fall so too will Israel for her impropriety (7:7–9).

When Amaziah, the priest at Bethel, stung by Amos' strictures, orders him back to his native Judah, Amos (described here as a herdsman and dresser of sycamore figs) vouches his credentials to prophesy and predicts Amaziah's bereavement and ruin (7:10–17).

Israel is like a basket of ripe fruit: ripe for punishment. Yahweh will not overlook her offences indefinitely (8:1–3). The first of three short oracles condemns dishonest merchants who can hardly wait for the Sabbath to pass before getting back to their fraudulent scales (8:4–8). The second paints the Day of Yahweh as 'the bitterest of days, like the mourning for an only child' (8:9–10). The third predicts a famine in God's word. People will search for it but not find it. But those who give up and resort to idolatry will perish (8:11–14).

In another vision Amos compares the coming doom to a sanctuary crashing down on the heads of the congregation inside. Escape is impossible. God will hunt down survivors whether they be on mountain tops, in the depths of the sea or crouching in the recesses of Sheol (9:1–4). A doxology extols Yahweh's might (9:5–6).

Israel should not regard herself as a favoured people. Yahweh cares for all nations. Those who complacently assume nothing unpleasant could happen to them are gravely mistaken. Israel will be 'shaken out' among the nations, wiped off the face of the earth. But not completely (9:7–10).

Restoration

For when the Day comes Israel will be restored and never uprooted again. There will be such abundance that the ploughman starting to prepare the ground for sowing will find the previous year's crop still being harvested (9:11–15).

Obadiah

Obadiah, the shortest book in the Old Testament, is in two parts.[1] First a prophecy of the oblivion awaiting Edom for her aggression towards Judah. Then, on a broader canvas as Obadiah looks to the Day of Yahweh, a prophecy that not only Edom but all God's enemies (represented as the nations) will be laid low while Israel and Judah, God's people, will be restored with God as king.

Judgement on Edom (1:1–15)

Edom is beneath contempt and will be humbled for her pride (1:1–4). Deserted by her allies, she will be ransacked and massacred to the last man[2] (1:5–9). This is because of her despicable behaviour when she stood gloating on the sidelines as Jerusalem was sacked and even joined in the slaughter and plunder herself[3] (1:10–15).

The Day of Yahweh (1:16–21)

On the Day of Yahweh the nations will suffer God's wrath and be crushed. Edom will be burned up like stubble while those who have escaped (the remnant) from the House of Joseph (Israel) and the House of Jacob (Judah) will recover their ancestral land and live with Yahweh as king.

Jonah

Jonah is unique in being a story about a prophet rather than a set of oracles by a prophet. Its historicity is unimportant. Nor is it important to know if Jonah was the prophet of 2K 14:25 or someone else. The identity of the author and its date are also problematic. Although the book is set in Nineveh before its fall in 612 it was probably composed much later as its tone resonates with the racially exclusive society that followed Ezra.

It teaches that Yahweh's mercy is free and universal; for the repentant citizens of Nineveh, a byword for infamy, as much as Israel. Even animals attract the concern of a God who delights in repentance rather than retribution. It is a warning against religious bigotry. In many ways Jonah was an admirable man. He offered to sacrifice himself to save his shipmates. But he was reluctant to carry the missionary torch to Nineveh that God proffered him. And even when he did he felt that Nineveh should be left to her fate, repentance notwithstanding. Neither his own rescue from the fish nor the response of the Ninevehites softened his heart. He was more worried about his own well-being. Love and the world beyond Israel lay outside his vision.

The book was a stern rebuke to Israel. She was reminded that far from being a light to the nations she had lost touch with God's ways. Unmoved by her own escape from the 'belly' of exile she could still not bring herself to wish mercy on others.

Jonah flees from being God's messenger (1:1–16)

When Yahweh orders Jonah to go and warn the people of Nineveh that He will no longer tolerate their wickedness, he pointedly boards a ship sailing in the opposite direction. While at sea Yahweh stirs up a violent storm that threatens the boat. After appeals by the sailors to their gods and lightening the load by jettisoning cargo are of no avail, lots are cast among the crew to see who is to blame for the storm. Jonah is singled out. He admits his guilt in running away from Yahweh and volunteers to be thrown overboard. The crew demur at first but when conditions worsen, and having first prayed to Yahweh for exoneration, they cast Jonah into the sea. The storm subsides and the crew offer sacrifice to Yahweh.

Jonah's prayer from the belly of the fish (2:1–11)

Jonah is swallowed by a great fish but after three days and nights, during which time he prays to God from the fish's belly, he is vomited on to dry land.

Nineveh repents (3:1–10)

The command to go to Nineveh is repeated and this time Jonah obeys. On arrival he proclaims that in forty days time the city will be overthrown. The response is dramatic. All the people from greatest to least acknowledge God, put on sackcloth, fast (even the animals are included) and renounce their evil ways. Yahweh lifts the threat of destruction.

Jonah's grievance and God's response (4:1–11)

Jonah is appalled. It was fear that God's compassion would lead Him to spare Nineveh that prompted him to try to evade his call in the first place. He sits outside the city to see what will happen. Yahweh arranges for a castor-oil plant to shelter him from the blazing sun. However next morning He sends a worm to attack it so that it withers. At the same time He summons up a scorching easterly wind. Overcome by the heat Jonah grows angry and wishes he were dead. God's responce is devastating. If Jonah is so vexed about the withering of a mere castor-oil plant and his own comfort, why should He not be concerned with the salvation of a hundred and twenty thousand people in Nineveh, not to mention their animals?

Micah

According to the inscription at 1:1 Micah, a native of Moresheth in south-west Judah, was active in the second half of the eighth century. He was thus a contemporary of Isaiah and Hosea and a little later than Amos. Politically it was a time of menace as Assyria increasingly flexed her muscles in the direction of Palestine. Domestically the very fabric of society was being torn apart. Affluence had created a two-tier society, one that became increasingly polarised as the merchant and ruling classes, who enjoyed a life of hedonistic luxury and pleasure, mercilessly exploited the poor whose plight grew ever more pitiable.

Whatever his book may lack in orderly arrangement, Micah compensates with an elevated style that is colourful, fervent and concise. He is keenly aware of his calling and with fiery rhetoric is fearless in denouncing injustice, moral turpitude and complacency. On the other hand he exhibits scant interest in the cult and only once targets idolatry.

He sees Samaria's coming fall as the wages of sin and a pointer to the equally dire fate awaiting Jerusalem. Even the Temple is not inviolate. But doom is not the end. Yahweh will rescue a remnant and humble their enemies. A king from Bethlehem will rule in everlasting peace from a Jerusalem to which the nations of the world will all be drawn. For Yahweh is a loving merciful God who requires: 'only this, to do what is right, to love loyalty, and to walk humbly with your God', 6:8.

Judgement on Samaria and Judah (1:1–16)

Yahweh is coming to deliver judgement against Samaria and Judah, Micah begins. Because of her sins, notably idolatry and sacred prostitution, Samaria will become a ruin (1:1–7). He continues with an anguished lament for the towns of Judah that face a similar fate and serves notice that even Jerusalem will not escape[1] (1:8–16).

Corruption and complacency (2:1–11)

Micah condemns covetous land-grabbers and rebukes his complacent compatriots who refuse to believe that Yahweh could ever turn His face against them. These are the self-same people who even now are cheating the underprivileged and heartlessly depriving helpless women and children. All they are interested in is their wine bibbing.

The remnant saved (2:12–13)

Despite the moral decay Micah foresees the day when Yahweh will gather His remnant and lead them to freedom.

Corruption and complacency continued (3:1–12)

Micah rebukes rulers who act like cannibals, stripping the people of all they have. In vain will they call upon Yahweh in their hour of need (3:1–4). He singles out venal prophets who are only too ready to tailor their message if it helps feather their nests. That is not his way. Driven by the spirit of Yahweh he will go on denouncing crime and sin whatever the cost (3:5–8). He next attacks the complacency of the civic leaders, priests and prophets who, guilty of injustice, violence and avarice, assert that no disaster can befall because 'Yahweh is with us'. On the contrary, it is because of people like them that not only Jerusalem but the Temple itself will be reduced to rubble (3:9–12)

Oracles of hope (4:1–13)

From such dire depths Micah switches to oracles of hope. In days to come the nations of the world will hasten to the Temple to learn of Yahweh and walk in His ways. There will be peace as swords are hammered into ploughshares[2] (4:1–5). Yahweh will gather His remnant – 'the lame and the strays, those whom He has treated harshly' – like a shepherd. He will forge them into a mighty nation and reign over them for ever from Jerusalem (4:6–8).

Micah then reverts from the glory of the future back to the present. Jerusalem is destined for exile in Babylon. However a time will come when God will rescue her and the enemies that now gloat over her will be crushed (4:9–13).

A ruler from Bethlehem (4:14 – 5:5)

Micah tells of a king, who will be humiliated by being struck on the cheek.[3] This leads in to a (Messianic) prophecy of a future ruler of Israel from Bethlehem whose origins go back to the distant past.[4] He will shepherd His people with the power of Yahweh, save them from their foes and bring enduring peace.

The future role of the remnant (5:6–14)

As dew revives grass so will the remnant bring life to the nations. Like a lion mauling sheep it will also trample on their enemies[5] (5:6–7). The day will come when Israel will have to forgo the supports she has so often lent on in the past – military prowess, divination, false gods – and learn to rely on Yahweh. His wrath will fall on those who still disobey Him (5:8–14).

The proper response to Yahweh's love (6:1–8)

We now hear the gentle protest, without rancour, of a God whose love and saving deeds, from the days of Moses and Balaam onwards, have so far fallen on stony ground. He does not want extravagant sacrifices, 'rams by the thousand', in return for the blessings He lavishes on His people; simply justice, brotherly love and humility.[6]

Further admonishments (6:9 – 7:7)

Micah denounces swindlers, violence and deceit: Ahab all over again! He laments a moral morass where integrity and honesty are all but unknown, where crime is rampant, everyone is on the make, officialdom is riddled with corruption and even families are at odds. Now, from the north, their punishment approaches.[7] Yet his faith in God remains resolute.

Further oracles of hope (7:8–20)

Israel must endure Yahweh's anger for a time because she has sinned. But He has not forsaken her. She will rise again and it will then be the enemy who now gloats over her who will be trampled underfoot (7:8–10). A day will come when converts from many nations will flock to an enlarged Jerusalem while judgement falls on the wicked (7:11–13). Micah prays for God to repeat the wonder of the release from Egypt by leading His people to lusher pastures and confounding their enemies. He concludes with a plea to the God who is so wonderfully forgiving to take pity on His people once more (7:14–20).

Nahum

Nahum has only one aim: to prophecy the grisly fate awaiting Nineveh the arch-oppressor and long-standing scourge of God's people. And this the book does with the vividness of an eyewitness in poems of ferocious intensity and a beauty of wordplay that is in sharp contrast with the harshness of the message.

Christians who are troubled that Nahum relishes the annihilation of Assyria so trenchantly should remember that he had probably witnessed the horrors Assyria perpetrated and was longing for the triumph of right over wrong. Because they hate cruelty and wickedness many Christians sometimes feel like Nahum. Today the significance of Nahum lies in its foreshadowing of God's final victory over evil at the end of time.

Prelude (1:1 – 2:1)

An (incomplete) alphabetic psalm sings the majesty of God and extols Him as judge of the wicked and protector of His people. He is slow to anger but when He does who can withstand His wrath? He takes vengeance on His foes and never lets evil go unpunished (1:1–8). Assyria will be lost without trace and Judah suffer her yoke no more (1:9 – 2:1).

The fate of Nineveh (2:2 – 3:19)

Nahum envisions the sack of Nineveh, chariots jostling in the streets, slave-girls beating their breasts, plunder everywhere (2:2–11). What price now for the den where the (Assyrian) lion used to tear up prey (booty) for his cubs (2:12–14)? Corpses litter the harlot city's streets (3:1–7). She has no more hope of survival than Thebes[1] (3:8–11).

Her fortifications will fall like ripe figs. Like women, she has no stomach for the fight and is wide open to her enemies. She may lay in a water supply and bolster her defences but fire will consume her and the sword cut her down nonetheless (3:12–15a).

The merchants and officials who used to swarm there will disappear as suddenly as locusts when the sun shines (3:15b–17). There will be no reprieve, merely effusions of joy that her barbaric cruelty has at last come to an end (3:18–19).

Habakkuk

Habakkuk was most likely written during Judah's last days. The prophet clearly has the Babylonians in mind when he asks why the wicked continue to prosper. He receives no more direct a reply than did Job. God merely assures him that in the long run justice will be done. In the second part of his book Habakkuk calls down curses on evil-doers and in stirring stanzas beseeches the Warrior God to save His people.

Why does lawlessness go unpunished? (1:1–11)

Habakkuk asks Yahweh why He remains silent before lawlessness and injustice. God replies that chastisement is coming (meaning to Judah!), and He is enlisting the Chaldaeans, fiercer than wolves, swifter than leopards, as violent as eagles swooping down to feed, as His rod.[1] This unexpected response sparked another question in Habakkuk's mind.

How can God possibly use the Chaldaeans? (1:12 – 2:1)

How can God, who is holy and abhors evil, allow the wicked (the Chaldeans) to swallow up those more righteous than themselves (Judah)? Are they to continue to live in arrogant luxury, treating other people like fish impaled on their hooks or caught in their dragnets? Habakkuk repairs to his watchtower to await God's response.

Life through faithfulness (2:2–4)

God replies that in the end justice will be done. Those who are evil will not survive while the upright will live through faithfulness.[2]

Five woes (2:5–20)

After a brief (and obscure) prelude Habakkuk intones a litany of woes against evil-doers. Woe betide those who succumb to cupidity, who amass ill-gotten gains, who perpetrate violence and wrong-doing, or who humiliate their fellow men or venerate man-made idols. They will reap as they have sown and work their own ruin.

Habakkuk's canticle (3:1–19)

In a poetic *tour de force* intended as a canticle for liturgical use, and drawing on mythological elements and events from Israel's history, the prophet extols Yahweh's power and prays for mercy and deliverance.[3] He describes Yahweh, His brightness like the day, mounting His charger and uncovering His bow as He marches to save His people. Trusting in the Lord he can await the outcome in the calm confidence born of faith. He feels as if he is walking on air.

Zephaniah

Zephaniah ministered in the reign of Josiah under whose two immediate predecessors, the infamously apostate Manasseh and Amon, religion in Judah plumbed new depths of degeneracy. The time was therefore ripe for a clarion call to alert a sinful nation that it was heading for catastrophe. With his forthright tone and tireless vigour this is what Zephaniah supplied. He was ideally suited to this task. He penetrated to the root cause of Judah's plight – indifference to Yahweh – and it is possible that the white-hot fury and urgency of his message was instrumental in encouraging Josiah to pursue the reforms he instigated following the discovery of the Book of the Law.

The Day of Yahweh (1:1–18)

A warning of universal judgement leads into a blistering attack on Judah and Jerusalem: on people who still cling to Baal; on dissolute courtiers and princes, traders and merchants; on unbelievers who complacently think they can treat Yahweh with indifference. All will be wiped out on the Day. It is near and hastening fast.

A call to conversion (2:1–3)

Even so those who humbly seek uprightness and Yahweh may still escape His wrath.

Against the nations (2:4–15)

Oracles depict the death throes of Philistia, Moab and Ammon, Ethiopia, and Assyria.[1] The once proud carefree Nineveh will be reduced to a ruin, a lair for wild beasts to rest in.

Against Jerusalem (3:1–8)

Jerusalem has not bowed to God's correction and is doomed. She is riddled with corruption. Her rulers and judges are driven by greed and avarice. Prophets and priests profane their calling. The fate of other nations has taught her nothing. If anything it seems to have encouraged her to sin all the harder.

Deliverance (3:9–20)

Despite his largely uncompromising stance so far Zephaniah ends in a victory song. When the Day comes the nations will be purged and converted while, with the proud and haughty rooted out, a chastened and humble Israel will live in peace (3:9–13). Jerusalem's sentence will be repealed. Fear and sorrow will yield to effusions of joy as Yahweh restores her fortunes, gathers His people and dwells as King in their midst (3:14–20).

Haggai

Haggai is the first of the post-exilic prophets. We first hear of him with Zechariah at Ezr 5:1 some eighteen years after the first exiles returned to Jerusalem from Babylon. Although the altar of burnt offering had quickly been restored, thus permitting some form of worship to resume on the site of the old Temple, work to restore the Temple itself had been suspended and it fell to Haggai along with his fellow prophet Zechariah to be the driving force behind its resumption, Ezr 6:14. His short book bears eloquent testimony to the zeal he applied to that task. Failure to act sooner had already cost the community dear in God's withholding of harvest and rain. Diligence would be quickly followed by God's support for the Temple and His long awaited intervention in history, heralding the overthrow of earthly powers, the appointment of Zerubbabel as His viceroy on earth, and the onset of the Messianic age.

However all of this, and Haggai's vision, was ahead of its time. Although the Temple was completed God's rule and the subjection of His enemies lay in the distant future with the Messianic hope vested not in Zerubbabel but in a later and greater descendant of David.

A call to rebuild the Temple (1:1–15)

Haggai urges Zerubbabel the governor of Judah and Joshua the high priest to press ahead with rebuilding the Temple.[1] The people have been dragging their feet, concentrating on their own homes and neglecting God's. That is why they have suffered drought and a run of poor harvests. Haggai's preaching must have struck a chord because only three weeks later the entire community set to work.

The future glory of the Temple (2:1–9)

However it seems that disillusionment began to creep in at the size of the task facing them. Haggai's response was an assurance that God was still behind the project and would soon make his decisive move into history. The glory of the new Temple would surpass the old.

Future blessings (2:10–19)

Haggai draws out the principle that whereas contact with something holy cannot make other things holy, contact with anything unclean does make other things unclean. The inference is that the people's neglect of God as revealed in the languor of their work on the Temple had tainted their offerings, thereby making them displeasing to God, and it was this that had led to their crop failures. However now that they had started work in earnest blessings were assured.

Zerubbabel, God's signet ring (2:20–23)

Haggai looks forward to the Day of Yahweh when God will intervene to subdue the nations and make Zerubbabel His servant, 'like a signet ring'.[2]

Zechariah

It is likely that Zechariah, son of Iddo was one of the earlier exiles to return from Babylon, Ezr 5:1. With his contemporary Haggai he was the inspiration behind the rebuilding of the Temple, Ezr 6:14, and according to the dates they quote chapters 1–8 of his book refer to events around that time. Few commentators believe that the same hand composed chapters 9–14. The style and interests are quite different and they are usually dated much later and ascribed to an unknown prophet known as Deutero Zechariah.

The core of chapters 1–8 is a set of eight visions. The first three visions relate to the restoration of Jerusalem and of the Temple. The later ones describe the steps that God will take to bring that about. Israel's guilt will be removed, and sinners and wickedness will be banished. God will bring in His servant the Branch (a Messianic title) who will rebuild the Temple, found a dynasty and reign as king alongside Joshua the high priest. Zechariah thus brings together Nathan's prophecy of a Davidic king with Ezekiel's vision of a community fostered by the priesthood.

Zechariah saw these things happening in his own day with Zerubbabel, the Head of David's House, as the Branch. Like Haggai he was ahead of his time and from the vantage point of the Gospels we can best see these visions as foreshadowing One who will later combine in His own person, perfectly and for ever, the offices of King and Priest that Zechariah saw separately fulfilled in the Branch and Joshua.

If chapters 1–8 are difficult, chapters 9–14 are even more intractable. Only the general drift, the restoration of Israel and Judah, God's rule over all nations in an age of perpetual light, and the frightful tribulation that must precede these terminal events, is not in doubt.

Beyond that much is deeply mysterious: the enigmatic reference to a king victorious yet humbly riding a donkey; the allegory of the shepherds; the one who was pierced; the fountain that washes away sin; Yahweh striking His shepherd and scattering the flock. Were these sparked in the prophet's mind by contemporary events or were they the fruits of divine revelation? Or both? Suffice it to say that in the death of the 'pierced one' and in Yahweh striking His shepherd we have echoes of Isaiah's Servant while the New Testament sees all these mysteries consummated in Christ: Mt 21:5; 27:3–10; 26:30–31; Jn 19:37.

Zechariah Son of Iddo

A call for repentance (1:1–6)

Yahweh invites the people to repent. Only then can they hope to avoid the fate of their ancestors. Men come and go but God's word remains for ever.

Eight visions (1:7 – 6:15)

In the first of eight visions Zechariah sees four horsemen. They have just returned from patrolling the world which they found still and at peace. Then in 'kind and comforting' words Yahweh reveals that He has returned to Jerusalem and the Temple will be rebuilt[1] (1:7–17). In his second vision Zechariah observes four horns and four craftsmen. The horns represent the nations that have scattered Judah while the craftsmen (suggested by the rebuilding of the Temple) represent the forces that will defeat them (2:1–4).

Zechariah then sees a man measuring Jerusalem (preparatory to rebuilding her walls). He is told that the new Jerusalem will be too big for conventional walls. Yahweh Himself will dwell there and He will be a 'wall of fire' to protect her (2:5–9).

A poem interrupts the visions to exhort the Jews still living in Babylon to return home. Yahweh will take possession of the Holy Land and live there among His people and converts from many nations[2] (2:10–17).

Zechariah witnesses the purification of Joshua the high priest prior to his being confirmed in an office he will retain as long as he walks in God's ways.[3] God then gives a glimpse of the future. He is going to introduce His servant the Branch, remove the country's sin in a single day and bring peace (3:1–10).

The fifth vision, a golden lampstand bearing seven lamps flanked by two olive trees discharging oil, is obscure. All the Bible tells us is that the lamps represent God's watchful presence in the world while the trees are the two anointed ones in attendance on God[4] (4:1–6a, 10b–14). The vision is followed by the promise that Zerubbabel, who began rebuilding the Temple, will see it through to completion. Inspired by God's spirit he will move mountains (4:6b–10a). The sixth vision, an immense flying scroll with curses on thieves and perjurers etched on its sides, announces God's judgement on sinners. They may hide in their homes but there is no escape (5:1–4). Zechariah next sees a woman representing wickedness rammed into a barrel that is sealed with lead and carried off to the land of Shinar[5] (5:5–11).

The four chariots of the eighth vision take us back to the first as they depart at God's behest to patrol the world. The message is that everything is under God's control even in the north where the chariot with black horses brings His spirit to rest[6] (6:1–8). In a concluding oracle Yahweh calls for Joshua to be crowned and relates how a man named Branch will 'branch out', i.e. establish a dynasty. He will rebuild the Temple and reign as king in harmony with a priest[7] (6:9–15).

On fasting (7:1–14; 8:18–19)

When the people ask whether a fast should be continued Zechariah suggests that they would be better served concentrating on love and justice. It was because they had neglected these that they had suffered so many hardships (7:1–14). Nevertheless the fast should continue along with three others with all becoming joyful occasions[8] (8:18–19).

Promises of blessings (8:1–17; 20–23)

A collection of short prophecies with Messianic overtones promises that God will regather His people to dwell with Him in Jerusalem in paradisiacal bliss. This may sound too good to be true but it is nothing to God! All that God requires is honesty and fair judgement. The passage ends with a reminder of Israel's missionary role as the prophet foresees a day when men from every nation will take a Jew by the sleeve since 'we have learnt that God is with you'.

Deutero Zechariah

The future of the nations (9:1–8)

Yahweh will vanquish Aram, the city states of Phoenicia, and the Philistines.[9] Once they have been purged of their abominations they will be assimilated into Judah like the Jebusites of old. God will protect His country against every foe.

The coming king of peace (9:9–10)

Zechariah foresees a king, victorious yet humbly riding a donkey, whose realm will embrace the whole world. He will banish war and bring peace.

Future blessings (9:11 – 11:3)

The exiles are urged to return to an Israel that is promised a glorious future once God has routed her enemies (9:11–17). Yahweh is the One to look to for help. Idols and diviners are delusions (10:1–2). Israel and Judah will be victorious over their foes and restored to the Land of Promise as if they had never been expelled (10:3–12). A poem taunts Israel's enemies – here cast as trees with their kings portrayed as shepherds and lions – with the downfall that will destroy their power and pride (11:1–3).

The allegory of the shepherds (11:4–17)

It is difficult to interpret this allegory, with its strong Messianic overtones, in detail but the general sense seems to be that God casts Zechariah in the role of good shepherd to a flock that does not appreciate him and which in the end detests him and pays him off for a derisory thirty shekels.[10] He then orders Zechariah to mime a worthless shepherd.[11]

New life and the smitten shepherd (12:1 – 13:9)

In the end days Yahweh will rescue Jerusalem and Judah from the nations massed against them and restore the House of David (12:1–9). He will pour a spirit of grace and prayer over His people so that they will turn to Him and mourn most grievously for 'the one who was pierced' (12:10–14). There will be a fountain for washing away sins and impurity. Idols will be expunged and the institution of prophecy, having been discredited by false prophets, will cease (13:1–6).

Yahweh will strike the shepherd who is close to Him and the sheep will be scattered.[12] There will be a sifting out. Two thirds of the flock will be lost while the remainder will be refined like silver in a fire and accept Yahweh as Lord (13:7–9).

God's final victory (14:1–21)

In lurid detail Zechariah describes the horrors that must befall Jerusalem in the latter days before the age of peace begins. All will seem lost with Jerusalem in enemy hands. But then God will sally forth to deliver His beleaguered people. Their enemies will be struck by plague and start to slaughter one another in their panic (14:1–5, 12–15). Victory will usher in an age of perpetual light and living waters. Jerusalem will stand high and many will live there totally secure. God will be king of the whole world, all in all (14:6–11). Survivors among the nations will worship Yahweh. Recalcitrants will have their blessings withheld. Everything will be holy, even such everyday objects as horses' bells and cooking pots (14:16–21).

Malachi

Whether 'Malachi' is a proper name or merely a pseudonym (meaning 'my messenger') is unknown. Either way the book is set in cheerless times after the return from Babylon. Doubts about God's love, the apparent lack of justice in the world, poor crops; all fuelled an air of scepticism. The end of the exile should have made the Jews realise that God still loved them. But their impoverished conditions left them unsure. Where were the lush pastures, gushing streams and freedom from foreign rule, Isaiah and others had promised?

The querulous tone of his listeners, bordering on hostility, can be sensed in the dialectical style Malachi adopts. Faith was at a low ebb. Priests had lost their sense of vocation. The laity, cheating over tithes, were no better. Foreign marriages and divorce had become a problem. It was almost as if Israel had lost heart.

Malachi assures his audience that God's love is undiminished. But if they still want to enjoy His favours they must abandon their casual, delinquent ways and repent. For however it may appear now, justice will be meted out. God will send a messenger, Elijah, and then will come the Day of Yahweh and judgement.

Yahweh still loves Israel (1:1–5)

Malachi answers Israel's doubts about God's love by pointing out that she has been spared the devastation visited upon Edom.

Irreverence to God (1:6 – 2:9)

Israel's worship is casual and perfunctory. Sacrifice is debased by offering blemished animals. They would not treat their governor like that! Better to shut the Temple doors and dispense with sacrifice altogether. Gentiles at least show the right disposition in their worship.[1] Priests find their duties a burden. It is a far cry from how it should be. They should hold God in awe, be models of truth, uprightness, peace and justice. They should help people avoid sinning, be well versed in the Law and teach it. Instead they lead people astray and apply the Law with partiality. If God is indeed Father He surely deserves better than this.

On marriage and divorce (2:10–16)

Malachi roundly condemns both marriages with foreign women and divorce.[2]

Judgement is coming (2:17 – 3:5)

The wicked seem to fare as well as the just. Has justice been forgotten? No! Yahweh will send a messenger to prepare the way and then come Himself to purify the priests, restore the liturgy, and judge evil-doers, adulterers, perjurers; all who exploit the downtrodden.

Israel's dishonesty about tithes (3:6–12)

Yahweh has not changed. Nor has Israel! She is still Jacob's child (an allusion to Jacob cheating his brother Esau), as disobedient as ever, cheating over tithes.[3] If only she would reform her fields would burgeon again untroubled by drought or locusts.

Justice on the Day of Yahweh (3:13–21)

Cynicism based on evil-doers who prosper leads to the revelation that there is a book of remembrance containing the names of the upright. They are the ones who will be spared on the Day God acts 'coming out leaping like calves from the stall' while evil-doers will be trampled underfoot and set ablaze like stubble.

Elijah will prepare the way (3:22–24)

Malachi ends with a reminder to keep the Law of Moses and a promise that Yahweh will send Elijah to bring reconciliation before the Day of Yahweh dawns.[4]

The New Testament

THE GOSPELS

The Synoptic Gospels

'Gospel' is a word meaning 'good news' and in revealing it in the life and teaching of Christ the Gospels are the centrepiece of the entire Bible. John's summing up of the purpose of his own work 'so that you may believe that Jesus is the Christ, the Son of God, and that believing this you may have life through His name' may be taken as applying to all. Of the four Gospels John's stands apart while because they present the same general view (or synopsis), the Gospels of Matthew, Mark and Luke are known as the synoptics.

Tradition ascribes authorship of the first Gospel to the apostle Matthew, a former tax collector otherwise known as Levi; the second to John Mark a co-worker at various times with Peter and Paul; and the third to Luke the physician who accompanied Paul on parts of his missionary journeys and who, together with Mark, was with him during his imprisonment in Rome. Whereas the traditions concerning Mark and Luke are widely accepted Matthew's claim to the Gospel that bears his name is less secure although it must be confessed that even those who deny it concede that at the very least he probably played a leading role in collecting the material from which it finally emerged.

The relationships between the synoptics have fuelled voluminous research. Did one borrow from another? Was there a common source or sources that fed all three? These and similar questions constitute the so-called 'synoptic problem'. To delve into this, fascinating though it is, would take us far beyond what is necessary for an understanding of the Gospels and so beyond the bounds of this work. Suffice to say that after allowing for stylistic variations and occasional changes of emphasis there is relatively little of Mark that does not appear in either Matthew or Luke. And that as well as depending on Mark and material that is unique to each of them, Matthew and Luke also drew upon a further common source or sources. There is no evidence that either used the other.

Equally vexed is when the synoptics were written. The issue is complicated by the possibility that there may have been several versions before the final canonical texts emerged and so it is difficult to do more than point to the second half of the first century.

Matthew targets a Jewish audience. He omits any explanation of Jewish customs. Christ's mission is to the lost sheep of Israel alone. He is preoccupied with final judgement and retribution. From the very first verse Jesus is the Christ, Son of David, Son of Abraham. In the infancy narratives He is portrayed as the new Israel, the new

Moses. He delights in showing how Jesus fulfils the Old Testament and binds Old to New. In no other Gospel are the religious leaders condemned so harshly for rejecting Him, for their hypocrisy and for their pedantic reading of the Law.

Where Matthew parallels Mark he is more concise. He refines the style, adjusts the sequence to group like subjects together and tends to remove human touches and signs of emotion in Jesus. Where the other evangelists speak of the Kingdom of God Matthew opts for the more reverential Kingdom of heaven.

In contrast to Matthew's measured tones Mark has the vividness of an eyewitness and the bustle of the market place. Tradition has it that much of his material came directly from Peter's lips. Where Matthew concentrates on Jesus' teaching Mark stresses His miraculous powers, His rejection and the ever lengthening shadow of the Cross. Mark's is a gentile audience, possibly the church in Rome. He explains Jewish customs and Aramaic words.

Luke's Gospel is for the whole world. When Jesus is presented in the Temple it is as 'a light of revelation for the gentiles'. He traces Jesus' ancestry back to Adam the common ancestor of the human race rather than to Abraham the father of the Jews. Luke is unique in being, with the Acts of the Apostles, the first part of a two-volume work which traces the beginnings of Christianity from the birth of Jesus to the rise of the early Church. Like Matthew, Luke omits or tones down anything from Mark that his readers might find offensive or which portrays the disciples in an unfavourable light.

Luke was blessed with fine literary gifts and his Gospel, less intimidating than Matthew's, is superabundant in Jesus' gentleness and humanity, the need for repentance, the abundance of forgiveness and God's mercy 'for the Son of Man has come to seek out and save what was lost'. He contrasts God's love of those who seemed least worthy of it, sinners and the outcasts of society, with His severity towards the proud and haughty. More than the other evangelists Luke brings out the presence of the Holy Spirit.

All four Gospels are faith documents intended to drive home the significance of Jesus; to convert the unbeliever and to deepen the faith of the believer. Far from being biographies even the details of Jesus' ministry are incomplete and sparing. Nor are they necessarily chronological as comparisons between them soon make plain. History is always subordinated to theology and it is not always easy to distinguish contemporary fact from later interpretation.

Matthew

The Birth and Infancy of Christ (1:1 – 2:23)

The ancestry of Jesus (1:1–17)

The opening of the New Testament resonates with hope and prophecy. In designating Jesus as Christ, son of David, son of Abraham, Matthew proclaims Him as the long awaited Messiah (Christ is the Greek equivalent of Messiah). As Son of David He is the inheritor of the promise that David's House would reign forever. As Son of Abraham He is heir to the covenant promises and the consummation of all Scripture. A genealogy shows Jesus' descent from Abraham and David through Joseph the husband of His mother Mary.[1]

Joseph takes Jesus as his son (1:18–25)

As the story of Jesus' birth begins Mary and Joseph are betrothed. This was something like a modern engagement but more binding. Unfaithfulness was regarded as adultery and the fiancé was often, as here, referred to as 'husband'. A formal act of dissolution was needed to end the relationship. This was what Joseph was minded to obtain when he heard that Mary was pregnant. But then, having been told by an angel in a dream that Mary was with child by the Holy Spirit and would give birth to a son whom he must name Jesus because He would save His people from their sins, he at once married Mary.[2] Mary was still a virgin when Jesus was born.[3]

The Virgin Birth is a stumbling block for some Christians. But is it any more remarkable than the belief that God created the whole cosmos or raised Jesus from the dead? Is it not fitting that He who, at the end, triumphed over death and reconciled man with God should also enter the world uniquely?

If Joseph was not Jesus' human father how could He be Son of David and Son of Abraham? Jewish law and custom at the time provide the answer. A child formally adopted and named by a Jewish man became that man's son. So when Joseph named and adopted Mary's child, Jesus legally became his son with all his hereditary rights.

Visit of the wise men (2:1–12)

The story of the three wise men coming to pay homage to Jesus, coupled with Herod's anxious enquiries, prepares us for the gentiles' readiness to accept the Gospel and the suspicious wariness of the Jews. There is significance in the gifts the wise men bore: gold (symbolising royalty); frankincense (divinity); myrhh (used in preparing bodies for burial).

Sojourn in Egypt (2:13–23)

Feeling threatened by the birth of a possible king of the Jews Herod ordered the slaughter of all male children under the age of two. However Joseph was forewarned by an angel and fled to Egypt where the Holy Family remained until after Herod's death. On returning, and following a further angelic warning, they settled in Galilee to avoid Herod's son.

THE BAPTISM AND TEMPTATION OF CHRIST (3:1 – 4:25)

John the Baptist (3:1–12)

Matthew introduces John the Baptist who was urging people from all over Judaea to repent prior to baptising them in the Jordan as they confessed their sins.[4] He had strong words for the Pharisees and Sadducees. Relying on their descent from Abraham was not enough. Unless they genuinely repented and bore fruit they would be cut down and thrown on the fire like a rotten tree.
Appendix 1 refers

John proclaimed that a greater One than he was coming. His would not be a mere ceremonial baptism with water symbolically washing away sins but one that purified men's hearts through the Holy Spirit. He would gather the wheat of the righteous into his barn but burn unrepentant chaff in an endless fire.

Jesus is baptised (3:13–17)

Before long Jesus Himself came from Galilee to be baptised, humbly submitting Himself to the reluctant John who immediately recognised his spiritual superior.[5] As He came out of the water Jesus saw the Spirit of God descending on Him like a dove while a voice from heaven proclaimed His Sonship. And so the first time in the New Testament all three members of the Trinity appear together: Father, Son, Spirit.

Jesus is tested in the desert (4:1–11)

In preparation for His ministry the Spirit led Jesus into the desert to be tested by the devil.[6] After a fast of forty days and nights the first test was the suggestion that He turn stones into loaves to satisfy His hunger. Jesus' response made plain that man is more than a physical creature and that his real nourishment comes from God.[7] The devil's second test, that Jesus throw Himself down from the parapet of the Temple and let the angels save Him, brought another sharp riposte. It would be tantamount to doubting God.

By accepting the kingdoms of the world from the devil in the third test Jesus could have established His rule without the Cross but only at the cost of accepting the world as it is with all its sin, and that would have been the negation of all He came to achieve.

Appendix 2 refers

Jesus begins His ministry in Galilee (4:12–25)

Hearing of John the Baptist's arrest Jesus left Nazareth and withdrew to Capernaum beside the lake of Galilee, a town He seems to have made the headquarters for His Galilean ministry.[8] There he began to proclaim His core message: 'repent, for the Kingdom of Heaven is close at hand.' Matthew records how He enlisted His first four disciples, all of them fishermen whom He invited to become 'fishers of men'. He went round the whole of Galilee healing and teaching and His fame spread far and wide.

THE SERMON ON THE MOUNT (5:1 – 7:29)

The Beatitudes (5:1–12)

Matthew begins his resumé of Jesus' teaching with an arresting series of paradoxes known as the Beatitudes. These are not rules so much as guiding principles to live by, expositions of attitudes and value systems to put man in a right relationship with God.

It is the poor in spirit, those who know their limitations and submit to God, who are blessed (not the self-reliant, who find no place for God in their lives). It is the gentle, the unassuming and undemanding, who will inherit the earth (not the proud and powerful). Those who mourn, because of the lost glory of a fallen world, will be comforted. (Not so those whose vision extends no further than satisfying their own desires.) Blessed are those who hunger for righteousness; the merciful, the pure in heart, the peacemakers. Blessed too are those who stand up for uprightness and their Faith whatever the cost (not those whose spiritual convictions bend in the wind).

Salt and light (5:13–16)

Jesus tells His followers to be like salt. (Salt was used both to improve food quality and preserve it from decay.) They must shine like beacons to show the way to God.

Jesus and the Law (5:17–19)

Jesus states that He had come not to abolish the Old Testament Law but to complete it. Clues to what He means come in the following verses where He gives the Law a new and deeper thrust, shifting the emphasis from visible conduct to inner desires, from rules and behaviour to principles and motives. It is the Law in this more general sense, which He will later sum up as love of God and love of neighbour, that Jesus has in mind when He stresses that no detail however small may be ignored.

Jesus' Law higher than the old (5:20–48)

Jesus now illustrates His completion of the Law with six antitheses each of which takes the form 'You have heard . . .' accompanied by an extract from an Old Testament law followed by 'But I say to you . . .' followed by His extension of that law.
Appendix 3 refers

It is not only murder that is a sin but its precursors, anger and insults too. So anyone involved in a quarrel should resolve it without delay even if it means delaying making an offering to God. Disputes should never be allowed to drag on as far as the courts.

Lustful thoughts are as much adultery as the physical act itself. It is the inner desire that counts. Therefore anything that besmirches a person's character must be ruthlessly excised. Anything is preferable to being cast into hell. The next two injunctions forbid divorce (except in the case of an illicit marriage) and swearing oaths.[9] A man's word should be such that a plain 'yes' or 'no' is enough without the need for anything more.

Jesus quotes the Old Testament law 'an eye for an eye . . .' to introduce his teaching that we must not react impulsively in disputes but turn the other cheek, responding to evil with good. We must try to break the cycle of pride, meanness and revenge and hopefully shame those who are attacking us into a change of heart.[10] We must love our enemies, not hate them, and pray for them. Our love must be as boundless as God's.

Secrecy in religious observance (6:1–6, 16–18)

Almsgiving should be performed quietly and without ostentation. The same is true of prayer and fasting. Those who make a great show have their reward (in human esteem) but those who do it in secret get their reward from God.

The Lord's Prayer (6:7–15)

Jesus warns against confusing quantity with quality in prayer. God knows what we want even before we ask. The prayer He gives as a model is in two parts. The first centres on God, the second on our needs.

In teaching us to address God as 'Our Father' Jesus introduces us to the same intimate relationship that He Himself enjoys. Then we acknowledge His holy nature, pray for His Kingdom to be established in all its plenitude and ask that the perfection that flows from His will being carried out in heaven be extended to earth. In the second half of the prayer we petition for our physical and spiritual welfare: for bread and forgiveness and to be delivered from the power of evil.[11] The prayer underlines that we can only expect God's forgiveness if we in our turn forgive those who offend us.

On right priorities (6:19–24)

Earthly possessions are transient, Jesus warns. So do not store up treasure on earth but in heaven where it endures for ever. Anyone with a diseased eye lives in darkness. That is bad enough. But how much worse it is for those whose spiritual sight is warped. Everyone must decide between God and money. You cannot serve both.[12]

Trust in providence (6:25–34)

Do not worry about things like food and clothing. Can you increase your lifespan by worrying? There is so much more to life. If God feeds the birds and adorns flowers so beautifully how much more will He care for His children? So trust God for your material needs and live for His Kingdom. The rest will follow.[13]

On judging and criticising others (7:1–6)

Jesus cautions against being censorious. As people judge others, so will God judge them. With His call to remove the log from our own eye before offering to remove the splinter in our brother's He is urging self-criticism and avoidance of a 'holier than thou' position of moral superiority. His use of 'splinter' and 'log' is typical of the exaggeration He so often employed to make His point. He goes on to counsel discretion in preaching the Gospel, saying that some people, like pigs trampling on pearls, may be incapable of appreciating it or even abuse it.

Approaching God in prayer (7:7–11)

'Ask and you will receive.' These words of Jesus teach us to pray to God with complete confidence. If we, with all our failings, give our children what they ask for, is it conceivable that God would be any less generous with His children?

The golden rule (7:12)

'Always treat others as you would like them to treat you.' This maxim, the golden rule, was well known in the ancient world in its negative form 'do not do to others . . .'. Jesus uses the more demanding positive form as a summary of the Law and Prophets.

Deciding for or against God (7:13–27)

There are two ways in life.[4] The road to destruction is wide while the path of life is hard with only a narrow gate. We must be on our guard against false prophets, wolves in sheep's clothing. Like a tree they can be distinguished by their fruit.

Performing spectacular acts and prophesying in His name are not necessarily signs of divine authentication, Jesus goes on. Nor is it enough merely to listen to His words, make a confession of faith or indulge in passive acquiescence. People who do that are building their houses on sand. No, it is those who act on His teaching, turning words into deeds, who will enter the Kingdom. Their houses are built on rocky foundations.

Jesus teaches with authority (7:28–29)

Matthew concludes the Sermon on the Mount by noting how Jesus' teaching 'made a deep impression on the people because He taught them with authority, unlike their own scribes.'

Works of Christ (8:1 – 9:34)

A number of cures (8:1–17)

A man with a virulent skin disease approached Jesus asking to be cleansed. The disease was probably leprosy which was not only a terrible physical affliction but also made sufferers virtual outcasts. Jesus did not need to touch the man to cure him – a look or word would have sufficed – but He did and in so doing demonstrated a sensitivity to the man's psychological need no longer to be treated as a 'reject' but welcomed back into God's family.[15]

A centurion now approached Jesus to beg Him to cure his servant back at home. With his words 'Sir, do not put yourself to any trouble because I am not worthy to have you under my roof', he showed himself to be a man of acute discernment, humility and faith. He quite clearly believed that Jesus could quell disease by a simple order (given at a distance too) just as he himself could command his subordinates. Indeed he virtually implied that just as he had authority from a higher source (his Emperor) so Jesus had authority (from God). Jesus was astonished and exclaimed that while gentiles would find a place in the Kingdom many Jews would be left in the darkness outside. After this cure Jesus went on to heal Peter's mother-in-law and many others – some possessed by devils.

The demands of discipleship (8:18–22)

Jesus stresses the insecurity ('foxes have holes . . .') and urgency ('leave the dead to bury their dead . . .') of the apostolic life. This last remark has sometimes given an impression of harshness on Jesus' part. But, setting aside the possibility of the hyperbole which characterised so many of His remarks, it may well have referred not literally to someone waiting to bury his father that very day but to someone who felt obliged to look after his father until after he died before he could follow Jesus. Jesus is making it clear that He wants 'today' disciples not 'someday' disciples who will always find reasons for prevarication.

At 8:20 Jesus, for the first time, refers to Himself as Son of Man. This was His favourite name for Himself and was suitably enigmatic for a ministry where for many reasons (people's expectation of a warrior Messiah, the need not to come into conflict with the religious authorities too soon) He did not wish to be too explicit. While the title emphasises Jesus' humanity it arises out of Dn 7:13 which uses it in the context of someone on whom everlasting Kingship is conferred by God and therefore points to something more.

Calming the storm (8:23–27)

The story of Jesus calming the storm as He crosses Lake Galilee shows Him exercising the Creator's power over nature and rebuking His disciples for their lack of faith.

The demoniacs of Gadara (8:28–34)

See Mk 5:1–20.

Cure of a paralytic (9:1–8)

This cure differs from others in that Jesus began by forgiving the man's sins. He sensed that the watching scribes regarded this as blasphemous (forgiveness of sins was a divine prerogative) and that they doubted His authority by doing the 'easier' thing. 'Forgiving sins is all very well,' they probably thought, 'after all who can tell whether they are forgiven or not? Why does He not heal the man so that we can all see what authority He really has?' And that is precisely what Jesus then did, thereby giving undeniable proof in the visible act of healing of His authority for His invisible act of forgiving sins and thus of His divinity.[16]

The call of Matthew: eating with sinners (9:9–13)

Jesus enlists Matthew, a tax collector, as a disciple.[17] Tax collectors were seen as hardened sinners in Jesus' day, with swindling and extortion their stock in trade. They were also despised for collaborating with the Romans. Jesus' invitation and His subsequent socialising with other tax collectors and sinners would therefore have scandalised the religious leaders. Challenged on this Jesus' response was succinct. It is not the healthy who need the doctor but the sick. Let them learn the meaning of the words: 'mercy is what pleases me, not sacrifice'.[18] He had come to call not the upright but sinners.

On fasting: the old and the new (9:14–17)

Questioned by John the Baptist's disciples on why His own disciples did not fast, Jesus compared His ministry to a wedding. His presence and message of salvation was something to rejoice about not an occasion for gloom. There would be plenty of time for fasting when He, the bridegroom, was taken away. Jesus then used a pair of similes to underline the freshness of His teaching. The 'new garment' of Christianity cannot be grafted on to the 'old cloth', the rigid legalism, of Judaism any more than people put new wine in old skins. There must be no clinging to old prejudices.

Further healings (9:18–34)

For the cure of the woman with a haemorrhage and the raising of the official's daughter see Mk 5:21–43. Jesus rewards the faith of two blind men by restoring their sight. The healing of the dumb demoniac is noteworthy for the Pharisees' icy rejoinder that Jesus must have been using Satan's power.

THE MISSION OF THE TWELVE (9:35 – 10:42)

A rich harvest (9:35–37)

Touring the towns and villages, healing the sick and teaching, Jesus likened the distress of the people to sheep without a shepherd or a harvest lacking labourers to gather it in.

The mission of the twelve (10:1–25)

Matthew names Jesus' twelve disciples (his first explicit mention of the Twelve) and describes how He sent them out to evangelise.[19] They were to minister only to Jews (not gentiles or Samaritans) proclaiming that the Kingdom of Heaven was close at hand, curing the sick and casting out devils. Just as they received spiritual gifts free from Jesus, so they must pass them on free. They were not to worry about money or creature comforts but to travel light and rely on God and charity.

If people rejected the Gospel they were to move on and leave judgement to God. They should have no illusions about the world they were being sent into. They would be like sheep among wolves. So although they must be innocent as doves they must be cunning as snakes, shrewd and worldly wise. They must expect persecution and vilification but the Spirit would help them defend themselves. Families would be torn and they would be hated. But anyone who held fast would be saved. If Jesus Himself received ill treatment and was thought to be an agent of Beelzebul (Satan) why should they fare any better.[20]

Words of encouragement (10:26–33)

They must not be afraid. The truth will come out in the end so let them shout it from the housetops. It is not men who can only kill the body they should worry about but God for He can destroy both body and soul. God's care extends even to sparrows so He will certainly look after them. Anyone who defends Him before men, Jesus continued, will find that He will defend them before God.

Dissension and loyalty (10:34–42)

Jesus insists that far from bringing peace to the world families will be torn apart over Him. A man's first loyalty is to Himself, before family. There will be suffering but anyone losing his life for His sake will gain eternal life while anyone saving his life in this world by denying Him will lose it in the next. The tiniest kindness will not be forgotten.

INDIFFERENCE AND OPPOSITION (11:1 – 12:50)

Jesus and John the Baptist (11:1–19)

Two of John's disciples came to enquire whether Jesus was the Messiah.[21] Jesus referred them to His healings and proclamation of the good news. He then spoke to the people about John. He neither bowed to popular opinion nor sought a life of luxury. More than a prophet, he was the messenger about whom Malachi had prophesied as preparing the way for Himself. Even so the least in the kingdom of heaven is greater than he.[22]

Jesus compared His contemporaries to petulant children who refuse to play at either weddings or funerals (they would listen to neither good news nor bad). Nothing fits their preconceived ideas: neither John with his ascetic lifestyle nor Himself who led a normal social life and befriended sinners. So they ignored both. Yet God's wisdom is proven by those who accept it.

Lament over the lake towns (11:20–24)

Jesus reproaches the Galilean towns where He had performed most of His miracles for their obduracy. Their fate on Judgement Day will be worse than that of Sodom whose people would certainly have repented if they had seen similar signs.

The good news revealed to the simple: the Father and the Son (11:25–27)

Jesus blesses God for revealing the mysteries of the Kingdom to people with open minds who are willing to be taught when to the learned and clever (people who take pride in their erudition and learning) it remains hidden. His prayer culminates in a towering affirmation of His Oneness with the Father.

Jesus, source of rest and comfort (11:28–30)

Jesus offers comfort and support to all who find the trials of life or the demands of discipleship too great to bear. He will give them rest for His yoke is easy, His burden light.[23]

Jesus and the Sabbath (12:1–8)

Jesus was taken to task by the Pharisees because in their view His disciples broke the Law by plucking ears of corn to assuage their hunger as they walked through the cornfields one Sabbath day. (The plucking was tantamount to work.) In His rebuttal Jesus reminded His accusers that David and his followers once ate bread that had been offered to God when they were hungry, something the Law only permitted priests to do.[24] Also, if priests can work on the Sabbath without infringing the Law, why should it be any different for the Master of the Sabbath? Jesus again quoted Hosea's 'mercy is what pleases me, not sacrifice' to underline that the Law must never become a harsh taskmaster.
Appendix 4 refers

Cure of the man with a withered hand (12:9–14)

Challenged for healing a man with a withered hand on the Sabbath, Jesus pointed out the absurdity of it being acceptable to rescue a stranded sheep on the Sabbath but not to heal a man. At this point the Pharisees began to plot to destroy Him.

Isaiah's prophecy (12:15–21)

Aware of growing opposition Jesus withdrew to work elsewhere. Matthew shows how Jesus was fulfilling Isaiah's Servant prophecy before their very eyes.

Jesus and Beelzebul (12:22–37)

When Jesus healed a blind and dumb demoniac the crowds wondered if He was the long awaited Son of David. The Pharisees however claimed that His power derived from Beelzebul (Satan). Jesus ridiculed this. It would be tantamount to Satan destroying himself. Why would they not admit that His exorcisms were God's work and that the Kingdom had caught them unawares? His exorcisms of demons proved that His power was greater than Satan's.

Jesus followed up with three warnings. Anyone not with Him was against Him. Secondly any sin, even speaking against Himself, could be forgiven bar one. The exception was blasphemy against the Holy Spirit. That would not be forgiven either in this world or the next.[25] Finally Jesus warned the Pharisees that every calumny they uttered would have to be answered for on Judgement Day. For as a tree can be judged by its fruit so too their words betrayed their hearts.

The sign of Jonah (12:38–42)

Despite His wondrous works the scribes and Pharisees asked Jesus for a sign to prove His credentials. He replied that the only sign they would get would be one like Jonah's three day entombment in the sea monster, a veiled reference to His resurrection. He went on to criticise His contemporaries lack of response. When Jonah preached, the men of Nineveh repented. Similarly the Queen of Sheba listened to Solomon. He is greater than either Jonah or Solomon but they take no notice.

Partial repentance (12:43–45)

Jesus warns against partial conversion. Unless the void left by the removal of unclean spirits is filled trouble can return that is even worse than before.

Jesus' family (12:46–50)

On being told that his mother and brothers were asking to see Him Jesus responded by stating that anyone who did the will of God was His kinsman.[26]

PARABLES OF THE KINGDOM (13:1–58)

Parable of the sower (13:1–9, 18–23)

Matthew introduces the parable of the sower scattering seed by telling us how Jesus taught from a boat, slightly offshore, to escape the pressure of the crowds. The parable distinguishes four ways in which people react to news of the Kingdom: those who do not understand it or who do not let it penetrate their hearts so that it is soon forgotten; those who welcome it initially but lack spiritual depth and fall away; those who are too wrapped up in the world to take heed; and finally those who hear it and yield a rich harvest.

Why Jesus speaks in parables (13:10–17, 34–35)

Jesus tells His disciples that they have been given the gift of understanding the mysteries of the Kingdom and have learned what the prophets of old longed for. But the people's minds are closed, as Isaiah foretold, so He teaches them in parables instead.

Parable of the darnel (13:24–30, 36–43)

The point of this parable is that the devil is never idle. Sinners and saints live side-by-side in the world and only at the end will they be separated into evildoers 'cast into the fiery furnace' and the righteous who will 'shine like the sun'. (Darnel is a weed that looks very much like wheat, its roots tangling with the wheat's.)

Parables of the Kingdom (13:31–33, 44–52)

Just as the tiny mustard seed germinates into a huge plant and only a small amount of yeast levitates a large mass of dough, so the Kingdom will grow to an enormous size from its small beginnings. The parables of the treasure and the pearl register that gaining the Kingdom is worth any sacrifice. The parable of the dragnet reminds us of the inevitability of judgement. Finally Jesus used the idea of a housekeeper bringing new and old things out of his storeroom to show that anyone who became a disciple had both His own new teaching and the wealth of the Old Testament to sustain him.

Jesus pays a visit to Nazareth (13:53–58)

When Jesus returned to Nazareth people were astonished at His wisdom and miraculous powers but would not accept Him. Was He not the boy next door getting above Himself? Because of their lack of faith He did not work any miracles there.[27]

FORMATION OF THE DISCIPLES (14:1 – 17:27)

John the Baptist beheaded (14:1–12)

Jesus' fame had reached King Herod who told his court that Jesus was John the Baptist risen from the dead.[28] This may well have been the pangs of a guilty conscience for Herod had only recently used the pretext of a rash promise made at a party to have John beheaded.[29]

The feeding of the five thousand (14:13–21)

Jesus' feeding of the five thousand from five loaves and two fishes by Lake Galilee opens our eyes in several ways. One is to see Him exercising in a speeded up way the power the Creator uses every day to provide our daily bread, something which through familiarity we too often take for granted. The blessing and breaking of the bread also suggests Jesus anticipating the Last Supper while the thought of God's people gathered together in peace and enjoying a meal transposes our thoughts to the banquet that Scripture associates with the inauguration of the Messianic age.[30]

Jesus walks on the water (14:22–36)

Jesus sent His disciples on ahead to cross Lake Galilee while He stayed behind to be alone to pray. When evening came He set out to catch them up, walking on the sea which was by then quite rough. The disciples were terrified when they saw Him, thinking they were seeing a ghost, and when Peter attempted to join His Master by walking across the sea to join Him his faith failed and Jesus had to rescue him. As they got into the boat the wind dropped and the disciples acknowledged Jesus as Son of God. When they landed at Gennesaret all the people brought their sick to Jesus begging merely to touch the fringe of His cloak. All that did so were healed.

Controversy over ritual purity (15:1–20)

See Mk 7:1–23.

The healing of the Canaanite woman's daughter (15:21–28)

Jesus withdraws to the region of Tyre and Sidon. When a Canaanite woman begs Him to heal her daughter He points out that His mission is to Israel and not 'little dogs'. But because of her faith He grants her wish nonetheless.[31] (It was left to Paul to drive home most clearly that Jesus' mission was to the whole world. In the Gospels the idea is largely confined to Jesus' instructions to His disciples after His resurrection, Mt 28:19.)

Many cures by the Lake of Galilee (15:29–31)

Jesus returns to Galilee where He performs many healings of the lame, the crippled, the blind and dumb.

The feeding of the four thousand (15:32–39)

This is possibly a doublet of the feeding of the five thousand.

The Pharisees ask for a sign (16:1–4)

When the Pharisees and Sadducees again ask for a sign Jesus contrasts their ability to read the weather signs with their inability to see signs (His miracles) that are before their very eyes. The sign of Jonah was all they would get.

The yeast of the Pharisees and Sadducees (16:5–12)

Jesus warns His disciples to be on their guard against the yeast of the Pharisees and Sadducees.[32]

Peter's profession of faith (16:13–20)

Near Caesarea Philippi Jesus invited His disciples to say who He was. Peter spoke for them all when he acknowledged Him as the Christ. Jesus responded by appointing Peter as the rock on which He would build His church. Evil would never prevail against it. Peter would be given the keys of the Kingdom. Whatever he bound on earth would be bound in heaven; whatever he loosed on earth would be loosed in heaven.[33]

First prophecy of the Passion (16:21–23)

With His identity revealed Jesus begins to brace the Twelve for the future, explaining that He must suffer and die before being raised up on the third day. Peter is appalled and starts to rebuke Him bringing Jesus' sharp riposte that he is thinking in human terms not God's.

The discipleship of the Cross (16:24–28)

Jesus explains that following Him means a life of self-renunciation. What would be the point of gaining the whole world if it meant losing heaven? He promises that everyone will be rewarded according to how he has behaved when He returns in glory.[34]

The transfiguration (17:1–8)

Six days later Peter, James and John were given a preview of Jesus in glory.[35] On a mountain top He was transfigured so that His face shone like the sun and His clothes became dazzling as light. They saw Him talking with Moses and Elijah and heard a voice from heaven saying 'this is my Son'.

The question about Elijah (17:9–13)

Jesus confirms that the prophecy that Elijah would precede Him, Ml 3:23, had been realised in John the Baptist. John was the 'Elijah' and as John had suffered so would He.

The healing of the epileptic demoniac (17:14–20)

See Mk 9:14–29.

Second prophecy of the Passion (17:22–23)

Jesus reminds his disciples of what lays ahead: resurrection and glory but first suffering.

The temple tax (17:24–27)

Jesus accepts the half-shekel temple tax as a proper obligation but explains that as God's Son He is exempt. Nevertheless He pays it rather than cause possible misunderstanding.

LIFE IN THE MESSIANIC COMMUNITY (18:1–35)

Who is greatest: leading others astray (18:1–10)

Jesus explains that Heaven will see a complete overturning of worldly standards. The greatest will be those who become like little children and anyone who despises or misleads such people is in grave peril.[36] Nothing is worth risking hell for so anything that could lead to sin must be avoided like the plague.

Lost sheep (18:12–14)

God does not want any of His 'little ones' to be lost and, like a shepherd, gets untold joy when anyone who strays returns to the fold.

Brotherly correction (18:15–18)

If a brother does wrong the first step should be to try to resolve the problem in private, one to one. The next step should be to call witnesses (to present evidence and help conciliate). If that too fails it becomes a community matter with possible disciplinary proceedings. Whatever the Church decides is final.[37]

Communal prayer (18:19–20)

Jesus promises that the prayers of two or three gathered together in His name will be answered for He will be among them.

Forgiveness (18:21–22)

Forgiveness must be unlimited: not seven times but seventy-seven.

Parable of the unforgiving debtor (18:23–35)

God will forgive more than we can ever imagine so we should be unsparing in our own forgiveness. Otherwise we exclude ourselves from God's forgiveness.

TOWARDS THE PASSION (19:1 – 22:46)

The sanctity of marriage (19:1–9)

Jesus confirms the sanctity of marriage. A man and wife become one flesh and no one may undo what God has put together. When Moses allowed divorce it was a concession to the hardness of men's hearts, not what God intended. Divorce is tantamount to adultery.

On celibacy (19:10–12)

To some it is given not to marry but to embrace a life of celibacy to serve God. 'Let anyone accept this who can.'

Jesus and the children (19:13–15)

Jesus blesses little children the people bring to Him. In their humility and trust they are models of the sort of people who will inherit the Kingdom.

Rewards and riches (19:16–30)

Jesus warns of the danger of riches. It is easier for a camel to pass through the eye of a needle than for a rich man to enter the kingdom of Heaven. Even so everything is possible for God.[38]

Jesus promises the Twelve that their self-sacrifice will earn them places of honour 'when everything is made new again'. No one who forsakes loved ones or home for His sake will fail to be repaid a hundred fold in the age to come and also inherit eternal life. But there will be surprises. 'Many who are first will be last, and the last, first'.

Parable of the labourers in the vineyard (20:1–16)

Those who only turn to God at the eleventh hour are welcomed into the Kingdom as much as those who have given a lifetime's devotion. There is no injustice in this. No one loses out. God's gifts are bestowed not because they are earned but because He is gracious.[39]

Third prophecy of the Passion (20:17–19)

For the first time Jesus speaks of being handed over to the gentiles prior to mocking, scourging and crucifixion.

Leadership in the Kingdom (20:20–28)

Through their mother, James and John ask Jesus for the top places in His Kingdom. Jesus replies that they are not His to give but His Father's. But they will share His cup of suffering.[40] Later He explains that true greatness lies not in pomp and power but in humility and service. It was better to serve than to be served and He Himself was the supreme example, giving His life a ransom for many.

The two blind men of Jericho (20:29–34)

As Jesus was leaving Jericho for Jerusalem He healed two (physically) blind men who had the (spiritual) insight to recognise Him as the son of David, the Messiah.

Jesus enters Jerusalem (21:1–11)

Jesus enters Jerusalem on a donkey revealing Himself as a man of peace. Enthusiastic crowds hail Him with the Messianic title 'son of David' and cries of 'Hosanna'.[41]

Jesus cleanses the Temple (21:12–17)

Jesus drives the money-changers and dealers selling doves (for sacrifice) out of the Temple. Their (quasi-commercial) activities were making it a den of thieves.

The barren fig tree (21:18–22)

When Jesus cursed a fig tree that was in leaf but bore no fruit He was making the point that Israel abounded in the leaves of religious observance but was barren of the fruits of righteousness. He then used the speed with which the tree withered to drive home that faith can move mountains. With faith everything asked for in prayer will be granted.

Jesus' authority (21:23–27)

The religious leaders set a trap by querying Jesus' authority. If He claimed it was divine He could be accused of blasphemy, otherwise He would be branded as an impostor. His response, asking whether John's baptism (i.e. ministry) was of heavenly or human origin was masterly. If they said heavenly, then why did they not believe him? If they said human they would expose themselves to the wrath of the crowds who revered John as a prophet. (Jesus was not being evasive. The correct answer on John would have answered their question on Himself because John pointed to Him as coming from God.)

Parable of the two sons (21:28–32)

Jesus used a tale of two sons, the first representing sinners who initially turn their backs on God but later repent, the second symbolising people who promise to serve God but do nothing about it, to bring home to the religious leaders that people who were once regarded as the dregs of society will enter the Kingdom before them.

Parable of the wicked tenants (21:33–46)

In this allegory the landowner is God, the vineyard His chosen people while mention of the owner providing a winepress indicates God's loving care. The tenants are the faithless Jews. The owner's servants who came looking for the fruits (of righteousness) were the prophets followed by the owner's Son, Jesus. The allegory is therefore saying that as a result of the tenants killing the prophets and then Jesus the vineyard (the role of God's chosen people) will be taken from the Jews and given to new tenants (the gentile Church). What is more, the Jesus who was rejected is now the cornerstone (of God's plan).

Parable of the wedding feast (22:1–14)

In this parable the king represents God, the wedding feast the Messianic banquet that Jesus sometimes used to portray the joys of the Kingdom. Despite invitations from the king's servants (the prophets and apostles) the first invitees (the Jews) were not interested. They even killed some of the servants. So the king punished them. He next sent His servants to invite anyone who could be found, good or bad. The hall was filled to overflowing. However one of the guests who had not taken the trouble to dress appropriately was thrown out into the darkness. Entry into the Kingdom does not depend simply on responding to God's call but on accepting its standards as well. Many are called but few are chosen.

Paying taxes to Caesar (22:15–22)

A deputation of Pharisees and Herodians tried to trap Jesus by asking whether it was right to pay taxes to Caesar or not.[42] By asking to see the Roman coinage they used Jesus forced His interrogators to answer their own question. Since they relied on Roman administration they had an obligation to pay for it. He then elevated the discussion to the spiritual plane. Just as Caesar should be paid his rightful due so too should God.

The resurrection of the dead (22:23–33)

The Sadducees, who denied resurrection, attempted to ridicule it by quoting a case where a woman married each of seven brothers. Whose wife would she be at the resurrection? Jesus explained that there is no marriage in the next world. People will be like the angels. He then showed the Sadducees how wrong they were on resurrection by quoting God's words at Ex 3:6: 'I am the God of Abraham'. God said this hundreds of years after Abraham died but Abraham was still alive to Him! 'He is God, not of the dead, but of the living.'

The two great commandments (22:34–40)

By summing up the Law and prophets as love of God and love of neighbour Jesus gave them a generality and clarity that transcends the detailed provisions that so often obscured them before. (Both commandments are found in the Old Testament, Dt 6:4–5; Lv 19:18.)

Christ, Lord of David and son of David (22:41–46)

Jesus next used Scripture to show that the Messiah was more than a son of David. The argument ran like this. In Psalm 110:1 David, the author, moved by the Spirit, said 'The Lord (God) declared to my Lord (the Messiah), take your seat . . .' The second 'Lord' is clearly superior to the author, David. How can this be so if the Messiah is merely a son of David?

WOES AND LAST DAYS DISCOURSE (23:1 – 25:46)

The hypocrisy and vanity of the scribes and Pharisees 23:1–12

Jesus warns the crowd that although they must observe what the scribes and Pharisees teach (presumably it accurately reflected Scripture) they must not copy what they do because they do not practise what they preach. They place a terrible burden on people (by insisting on minutiae of the Law) without (unlike Himself) doing anything to help them. They delight in showing off. He cautions His disciples against adopting such lordly airs. There is only one Father, God, and only one teacher, Himself. True greatness lies in humility and service.

The seven woes 23:13–36

Jesus launches into a scathing indictment of the scribes and Pharisees. They hinder people getting into the Kingdom (by opposing Jesus' teaching). Their efforts to make proselytes (converts to Pharisaism) are leading people to hell.[43] With their pedantic distinctions they make a nonsense of oath-taking. They worry about trivia like tithes on herbs while ignoring honesty and mercy. Like whitewashed tombs they are spotless so far as outward appearances go but riddled with corruption inside. They protest that they would never have persecuted the prophets. Yet they are the heirs of those who did and so might as well finish the job off (with His own death). For that and the murder of all upright men from Abel to Zechariah they will pay a heavy price.[44]

Jesus laments over Jerusalem 23:37–39

In a poignant lament Jesus recalls how He had so often longed to gather His people as a hen gathers her chicks under her wings. But they refused. Now they will not see Him again until He returns in glory.

Jesus' Olivet discourse (24:1–44)

Matthew follows Mark's closely, see Mk 13:1–37. However Mark's story of the absent master, Mk 13:33–37, is replaced by Matthew's story of the burglar, Mt 24:42–44, although exactly the same point is made: Christ will return when He is least expected, so be prepared.

Matthew has two passages not paralleled in Mark. The Second Coming will not be hidden but like lightening for all the world to see. People will be drawn like vultures to a corpse (24:26–28). The second is a warning not to be caught unawares like the people in Noah's day who went about their daily pursuits oblivious to the deluge that was about to engulf them. Of two people working together one will be taken, the other left (24:37–41).

Parable of the conscientious steward (24:45–51)

The good servant who assiduously does what the Lord requires of him will be richly rewarded. But anyone who thinks there is plenty of time to 'reform' and that a little carousing and debauchery in the meantime will do no harm could be in for a nasty surprise when Jesus returns unexpectedly.

Parable of the ten wedding attendants (25:1–13)

This parable also teaches preparedness for Christ's coming but in telling us that the five sensible attendants were unable to help the five foolish ones it goes further. Spiritual preparedness is not transferable. The foresight of the wise cannot stand in for the indolence of the fool.

Parable of the talents (25:14–30)

The lesson here is that God expects everyone to make full use of the gifts He endows them with, great or small, in the service of the Kingdom. Those who do will be rewarded while the rest face rejection.

The Last Judgement (25:31–46)

This awesome picture of the last judgement depicts the separation of the sheep, who will inherit the Kingdom, from the goats who face hell. The division is absolute and will be decided on the basis of deeds of loving kindness to one's neighbour which Jesus equates as acts done to Himself.

THE PASSION AND DEATH OF CHRIST (26:1 – 27:66)

The anointing and betrayal (26:1–16)

Two days before the Passover Jesus reminds His disciples of His coming crucifixion. Even as He does so the authorities are plotting how to carry it out without sparking a popular uprising. Meanwhile at Bethany a woman anoints Jesus with a jar of expensive ointment. The disciples are indignant at what they see as waste but Jesus interprets the woman's act as preparing His body for burial and praises her kindness. Judas meanwhile agrees to betray Jesus for thirty pieces of silver.[45]

The Last Supper (26:17–29)

Jesus has His disciples make preparations for the Passover meal.[46] Later that evening at table He discloses that one of them will betray Him. Then He institutes the Eucharist using words that both anticipate and interpret His death.

> Now as they were eating, Jesus took bread, and when He had said the blessing He broke it and gave it to the disciples. 'Take it and eat,' He said, 'this is my body.' Then He took a cup, and when He had given thanks He handed it to them saying, 'Drink from this, all of you, for this is my blood, the blood of the covenant, poured out for many for the forgiveness of sins. From now on, I tell you, I shall never again drink wine until the day I drink the new wine with you in the kingdom of my Father'.[47]

The covenant is the New Covenant prophesied by Jeremiah. Where the Old Covenant was sealed with the blood of animals, this is sealed with the blood of Christ, Lamb of God.[48]

Gethsemane (26:30–56)

Jesus makes His way towards the Mount of Olives where He tells His disciples that they will desert Him and that Peter will deny Him three times before the cock crows. Yet darkness is tempered with light. After His resurrection they will meet again in Galilee.

At Gethsemane, a small olive grove at the foot of the Mount of Olives, Jesus asked His disciples to stay awake as He went on a little way to pray.

> My Father, if it is possible, let this cup pass me by. Nevertheless, let it be as you, not I would have it.[49]

Returning He found them asleep. Twice more He prayed in similar vein while they slept on.

Jesus' prayer was answered not in release but in His being given the strength to go forward, calm and serene, in willing acceptance and total command.

> Look, the hour has come when the Son of man is to be betrayed into the hands of sinners. Get up! Let us go! Look, my betrayer is not far away.

Events now moved quickly. Judas arrived with an armed posse and betrayed Jesus with a kiss. Jesus was arrested. A scuffle ensued in which the high priest's servant had one of his ears cut off.[50] Jesus forbade further violence. His disciples ran away.

Jesus before the Sanhedrin (26:57–75)

Jesus was brought before the Sanhedrin and accused of threatening to destroy the Temple.[51] He remained silent to this charge but when Caiaphas, the high priest, asked if He was the Messiah He responded with a quotation from Dn 7:13

> It is you who say it. But, I tell you that from this time onward you will see the Son of man seated at the right hand of the Power and coming on the clouds of heaven.

a clear allusion to His coming exaltation and eventual return in glory. To the Sanhedrin this was blasphemy and merited death. He was struck and taunted while outside in the courtyard Peter denied Him three times.

Jesus before Pilate (27:1–31)

Next morning the Sanhedrin met again. Jesus was bound and brought before Pilate, the Roman governor.[52] Judas meanwhile, overcome by remorse, had hanged himself.[53]

Apart from indirectly acknowledging the title 'king of the Jews' when questioned by Pilate Jesus said nothing.[54] Pilate was amazed. He could see that the charges against Jesus were baseless and that he was being manipulated. His wife's dream that Jesus was innocent can only have fuelled his troubled mind. He clearly hoped that the Passover custom of releasing a prisoner chosen by the people would resolve his dilemma.

But the same people who had so recently cast their cloaks before Jesus now allowed themselves to be swayed into choosing Barabbas, a notorious criminal.[55] When Pilate protested Jesus' innocence they became increasingly insistent that He be crucified.

Fearful of having a riot on his hands Pilate gave in. Ostentatiously washing his hands of Jesus' fate he handed Him over, knowing Him to be innocent, to be scourged and crucified.[56] But first the Roman soldiers mocked Him, dressing Him in a scarlet cloak and a crown of thorns, spitting on Him and striking Him.

Jesus' crucifixion and death (27:32–56)

Jesus was led away to Golgotha, 'the place of the skull', a certain Simon of Cyrene carrying His cross. There, having refused an offer of drugged wine to deaden the pain, He was crucified beneath a sign 'This is Jesus, the King of the Jews'. As He hung on the Cross He was mocked by passers-by; by the bandits being crucified either side; even by the religious leaders who ridiculed Him: 'He saved others; He cannot save Himself'.[57]

Darkness covered the land from the sixth hour until the ninth (noon until three in the afternoon) at which time Jesus cried out:

My God, my God, why have you forsaken me?

After a further loud cry Jesus then yielded up His spirit.[58]

The veil of the Sanctuary was rent from top to bottom.[59] There was an earthquake and many holy people rose from the dead and, after Jesus' resurrection, left their tombs to enter Jerusalem.[60] Moved by all they saw the Roman centurion and his guards acknowledged Jesus as Son of God. Watching from a distance were a number of the women who had been with Jesus in Galilee.

Jesus' burial (27:57–66)

When it was evening a disciple of Jesus, Joseph of Arimathaea, a rich man, went to Pilate to ask for Jesus' body.[61] He wrapped it in a clean shroud and buried it in his own new tomb hewn out of rock, rolling a large stone across the entrance. Mary of Magdala and the 'other Mary' watched, sitting opposite the tomb.[62] Next day at the instigation of the chief priests and Pharisees, Pilate had seals set on the stone and a guard mounted to ensure that none of Jesus' followers could remove His body and claim that He had risen from the dead as He had prophesied.

THE RISEN CHRIST (28:1–20)

The empty tomb (28:1–10)

Early on the Sunday morning Mary of Magdala and the 'other Mary' went to visit the tomb. As they arrived there was a violent earthquake and an angel rolled the stone away and invited them to see where Jesus had lain. For the tomb was now empty. The angel told them that Jesus had risen from the dead. As they were running back to tell the disciples Jesus Himself appeared to them saying 'tell my brothers to meet me in Galilee'.

The bribing of the guard (28:11–15)

Matthew recounts how the guards were bribed to say that Jesus' body had been stolen by His disciples in the night.

The great commission to the world (28:16–20)

Jesus meets the eleven disciples on a mountain in Galilee. When they see Him they fall down in worship although some hesitate.[63] He explains that He has been given all authority in heaven and on earth. The disciples are to proclaim the Gospel to all nations baptising them in the name of the Father and of the Son and of the Holy Spirit and teaching them to observe all His teaching.[64] He ends with the promise of His abiding presence

'I am with you always; yes, to the end of time.'

Mark

PRELUDE TO MINISTRY (1:1–13)

Jesus' baptism and testing (1:1–13)

Mark presents his work as the Gospel of Jesus Christ, the Son of God. He says nothing of Jesus' birth or infancy, introducing Jesus at His baptism and subsequent testing in the desert and he cites the Old Testament to show how John the Baptist had prepared the way.
Appendix 1 refers

THE GALILEAN MINISTRY (1:14 – 10:52)

Jesus proclaims His message (1:14–15)

After John was arrested Jesus began His own ministry in Galilee calling on people to repent and believe the Good News (the Gospel). The Kingdom of God was close at hand.

The first four disciples are called (1:16–20)

See Mt 4:18–22.

The early ministry in Galilee (1:21–45)

Jesus began His ministry in Capernaum. His teaching in the synagogue made a deep impression as He clearly spoke with authority. He healed the sick and cast out demons. Among those He treated was Peter's mother-in-law.[1] Mark recounts how the unclean spirits recognised who Jesus was, one even hailing Him as the Holy One of God.[2]

The whole town came crowding to see Him and it was the same as He progressed throughout Galilee, preaching in the synagogues and healing every manner of complaint. When a man with a virulent skin disease disobeyed His stern instruction not to speak about his cure Jesus was forced to avoid the towns and stay outside.[3] But people kept coming.

No matter how busy He was, Jesus always found time to pray. Mark tells how He would get up early, long before dawn, to find a quiet place where He could be alone. Verses 21–38 probably depict a typical day in Jesus' ministry.

Cure of a paralytic (2:1–12)

This is similar to Mt 9:1–8 except that Mark accentuates the faith of the paralytic's friends by describing how, when they could not get to Jesus through the jostling crowds, they stripped the roof from the room where He was teaching in order to lower his stretcher down to Him.

The call of Levi (2:13–14)

See Mt 9:9 where the new disciple is named Matthew.

Eating with sinners (2:15–17)

See Mt 9:10–13.

On fasting: the old and the new (2:18–22)

See Mt 9:14–17.

Jesus and the Sabbath (2:23–28)

See Mt 12:1–8. Mark additionally quotes Jesus as saying 'the Sabbath was made for man, not man for the Sabbath' in an attempt to convey a sense of priorities.

Cure of the man with a withered hand (3:1–6)

When Jesus went into the synagogue one Sabbath and saw a man with a withered hand, the Pharisees waited to see if He would heal him and so give them something to charge Him with. However before effecting the cure Jesus asked them: 'is it permitted to do good or evil on the Sabbath; to save life, or to destroy it?' His meaning was clear. As the Sabbath was given by God for man's good, surely it is legitimate to use it for works of love and mercy. Wilfully to prolong suffering would be an act of evil. Discomforted, the Pharisees began to plot with the Herodians how to destroy Him.[4]

Jesus appoints the Twelve (3:7–19)

So numerous were the crowds that thronged to Jesus from all over Palestine that He took care, while by the lakeside, always to have a boat ready to jump into if there was ever any danger of His being crushed as they surged forward in their eagerness to touch Him and be healed. It was at this time that Jesus withdrew to a mountain where He appointed the Twelve disciples who would eventually carry on His mission.[5]

Jesus' family are concerned about Him (3:20–21)

Jesus' family thought He was beside Himself and needed help. The demands of the crowds meant it was difficult even to take a meal together.

Jesus and Beelzebul (3:22-30)

See Mt 12:22–32. It would appear that scribes had come down from Jerusalem specifically to see what Jesus was up to.

Jesus' family (3:31–35)

See Mt 12:46–50.

Parable of the sower (4:1–9, 13–20)

See Mt 13:1–9; 18–23.[6]

Why Jesus spoke in parables (4:10–12, 33–34)

See Mt 13:10–17; 34–35. Mark adds that Jesus explained everything to His disciples when they were alone together.

Four short parables (4:21–32)

Jesus made it clear that His teaching must not be hidden but spread far and wide like light from a lamp. The more people responded to His teaching, the sooner they would receive further enlightenment and conversely.[7] The Kingdom will grow in human hearts through its own power, quietly and mysteriously, just as a seed quietly and mysteriously produces grain. Just as the mustard seed is small but grows into a huge plant, so the Kingdom, small to begin with, will grow to an enormous size and provide shelter for all in its shade.

The calming of the storm (4:35–41)

Mark now shows Jesus' power over nature by describing how He calmed a storm that almost swamped the boat that was ferrying Him across the sea of Galilee. Matthew and Luke describe the same incident but it is Mark who adds touches that reveal Jesus' humanity. When we read how He slept in the stern of the boat, His head on a cushion, His weariness after a long day's teaching almost leaps from the page.

The Gerasene demoniac (5:1–20)

Mark next recounts how Jesus cast unclean spirits out of a howling demoniac who lived among the tombs. Why Jesus permitted (He did not order) the unclean spirits to go into a herd of swine that subsequently stampeded down a cliff to be drowned in the lake is problematic as it seems to attribute destructiveness to Jesus. Possibly it was intended as visible proof that the evil spirits really had been cast out. Possibly it was meant to show that to Jesus one man was worth more than many swine and so highlight the lengths to which He was prepared to go in order to quell evil. We do not know.

Despite the miracle – or maybe because of it, since the loss of so large a herd must have been a crippling blow to the local economy – the local people implored Jesus to leave. The cured demoniac begged Jesus to be allowed to join Him but He would not agree urging him instead to broadcast 'all that the Lord in His mercy has done for you' in the neighbouring towns.[8]

Cure of the woman with haemorrhage and the raising of Jairus' daughter 5:21–43

Back on the lake's western shore Jesus performed two more miracles. The lesson of both is faith. The woman with the haemorrhage would have been reckoned ritually unclean and so reluctant to approach Jesus direct. This makes her faith, based on a mere touch of Jesus' garment, all the more striking.

The raising of Jairus' daughter demanded a different type of faith; a persistent unyielding faith that had to surmount not only what must have been an agonising delay when Jesus broke-off to talk to the woman with the haemorrhage but also the dire news that the girl was already dead. Perhaps in Jesus', 'The child is not dead, but asleep' as He entered her room we are meant to see a hint that to God death is merely a sleep to which, like any other sleep, there is an awakening.[9]

Jesus visits Nazareth (6:1–6)

See Mt 13:53–58.[10]

The Twelve go out on mission (6:7–13)

Jesus sent the Twelve out in pairs to preach.[11] They were to take a staff and wear sandals but no spare tunic and they were to rely on God for food and accept hospitality wherever it came. If they were not welcome they were to move on. One thing the Twelve must have learned was that Jesus' power could be delegated for they were able to cast out devils and heal many sick people.

John the Baptist beheaded (6:14–29)

See Mt 14:1–12.[12]

The feeding of the five thousand (6:30–44)

After the disciples return from their mission Jesus takes them away to a lonely place for a short rest. But the crowds soon find them and Jesus takes pity and begins to teach them 'because they were like sheep without a shepherd.' This leads into the miracle of the feeding of the five thousand, the only one described in all four gospels, see Mt 14:13–21.

Jesus walks on the water (6:45–56)

See Mt 14:22–33. Where in Matthew the disciples acknowledge Jesus as Son of God, Mark refers to their bewilderment. Even after the miracle of feeding the five thousand they still could not make Him out. Mark omits the story of Peter stepping from the boat.

Jesus on outward show and inner purity (7:1-23)

A party of Pharisees and scribes came from Jerusalem to question Jesus. They began by asking why His disciples did not follow the custom of ritual washing before eating.[13] Jesus wasted no time in exposing their hypocrisy. They ignored God's commandments in favour of their own traditions. He then gave a concrete example. The Law clearly taught 'honour your father and your mother' but the Pharisees allowed a person to circumvent it by placing anything that might have helped their parents under a sacred vow to God.[14] Jesus then addressed the people. It is not what goes into a person like food that makes him unclean. That simply goes into his stomach.[15] No, it is what comes out of his mouth that defiles him. For that reveals what is in his heart where all evil intentions originate.

The daughter of the Syro-Phoenician woman healed (7:24–30)

See Mt 15:21–28.

The healing of the deaf man (7:31–37)

On His way back to Galilee Jesus healed a deaf man with a speech impediment. Mark notes that once the man's ears were opened his tongue was loosened too while the people marvelled at Jesus' ability to 'make the deaf hear and the dumb speak'.[16]

The feeding of the four thousand (8:1–10)

See Mt 15:32–39.

The Pharisees ask for a sign (8:11–13)

See Mt 16:1–4. There is a poignancy in Mark reporting how Jesus responded 'with a profound sigh' and 're-embarked and went away' when the Pharisees demanded a sign, as if He could now see that nothing He ever did would open their obdurate hearts.

The yeast of the Pharisees and Sadducees (8:14–21)

Jesus warns His disciples about the evil inclinations of the Pharisees and Herod. Unfortunately the disciples completely misunderstood the yeast (a symbol for evil) metaphor He used thinking He was referring to their shortage of bread, see Mt 16:5–12.

The blind man of Bethsaida (8:22–26)

The main point of the story is the two stage healing involved, a detail that would not have been highlighted unless it had something to tell us. The lesson is that if we have faith Jesus will open our eyes, not instantly but in stages. We may see things hazily at first but in time everything will become clear. Once He has started to work on us Jesus will see the job through to the end and not settle for anything less than perfection.

Peter's profession of faith (8:27–30)

See Mt 16:13–20.

First prophecy of the Passion (8:31–33)

See Mt 16:21–23.

The implications of discipleship (8:34–9:1)

See Mt 16:24–28. Mark adds that if anyone is ashamed of Jesus He will likewise be ashamed of that person when He returns in glory.[17]

The transfiguration (9:2–8)

See Mt 17:1–8.

A question about Elijah (9:9–13)

See Mt 17:9–13.

The healing of the epileptic demoniac (9:14–29)

This miracle is memorable for the exchange that was sparked by the sick boy's father asking Jesus to help 'if you can' (prompting Jesus' retort that with faith anything is possible) and his subsequent recognition that his faith was mixed with doubt and that he needed Jesus' help to sustain it.

At once the boy was healed. When the disciples enquired why they had been unsuccessful Jesus explained that such a cure could only come through prayer.[18]

Second prophecy of the Passion (9:30–32)

See Mt 17:22–23. Jesus was now concentrating on instructing His disciples. Even so they still could not understand what He meant by rising again on the third day.

Who is greatest: leading others astray 9:33–37, 42–50

See Mt 18:1–10. Mark adds that true greatness comes through service to others. Verses 49–50 are also additional. Verse 49, 'everyone will be salted with fire' is most likely a reference to the sustaining value of suffering. Salt was a preservative while fire was often used as a metaphor for suffering. Verse 50, Jesus' injunction to His followers not to lose their 'saltiness', is probably a call for them not to lose the spirit of devotion and self-sacrifice, 'the flavour', that set them apart for the sake of the Gospel. (As well as a preservative salt was widely used in the ancient world to give flavour.)

Lessons in discipleship (9:38–41)

The incident of the man casting out devils who was not one of Jesus' disciples shows that no one has a monopoly in serving God. No-one who fights evil in Jesus' name is to be hindered. Jesus' pithy epigram – 'anyone who is not against us is for us' – seems to rest uneasily with the 'anyone who is not with me is against me' of Mt 12:30 but there is no contradiction. The first governs our attitude to people who have not yet heard the Gospel. Matthew's relates to those who have heard it but have not responded positively. To be indifferent to the Gospel once you have heard it is to be against it.

Even the smallest act of kindness done in Jesus' name will have its reward.

Jesus on divorce (10:1–12)

See Mt 19:1–9

Jesus and the children (10:13–16)

See Mt 19:13–15.

Rewards and riches (10:17–31)

See Mt 19:16–30.

Third prophecy of the Passion 10:32–34

See Mt 20:17–19. Mark's picture of Jesus walking ahead, the disciples following in a daze and everyone apprehensive, shows not only that Jesus knew what awaited Him but that a presentiment of something dreadful about to happen pervaded His entire entourage.

Leadership in the Kingdom (10:35–45)

See Mt 20:20–28.

The blind man of Jericho (10:46–52)

See Mt 20:29–34. Matthew mentions two blind men.

THE JERUSALEM MINISTRY (11:1 – 13:37)

Jesus enters Jerusalem (11:1–11)

See Mt 21:1–11. Where Matthew refers to Jesus borrowing a donkey and a colt Mark mentions only a colt.

The barren fig tree (11:12–14, 20–25)

See Mt 21:18–22. In Matthew the tree withers the instant it is cursed whereas in Mark the incident extends over two days. Mark adds Jesus' teaching that prayer should be offered in a spirit of forgiveness.[19]

Jesus cleanses the Temple (11:15–19)

See Mt 21:12–17. Mark omits the healings that Matthew records. He adds that Jesus stopped the Temple being used as a short cut (probably between the city and the Mount of Olives) and that the chief priests and scribes were now determined to be rid of Him. Significantly he also adds 'for all peoples' to the end of Matthew's, 'My house will be called a house of prayer' thereby stressing the universalism of the Messianic age.

Jesus' authority is questioned (11:27–33)

See Mt 21:23–27.

Parable of the wicked tenants (12:1–12)

See Mt 21:33–46.

On tribute to Caesar (12:13–17)

See Mt: 22:15–22.

The resurrection of the dead (12:18–27)

See Mt: 22:23–33.

On the first commandment (12:28–34)

See Mt 22:34–40. Mark supplements Matthew by quoting the scribe's comment that the commandments to love God and neighbour are far more important than any burnt offering or sacrifice, a theme dear to the prophets.

Christ, Lord of David and son of David (12:35–37)

See Mt 22:41–46.

A warning against the scribes (12:38–40)

Jesus warns against the ostentation, avarice and hypocrisy of the scribes. They love their long robes and the respect of the people but their punishment will be severe (for they of all people should know God's will), see Mt 23:6–7.

The widow's mite (12:41–44)

Nothing could contrast more sharply with the mindset of the scribes than the story of the poor widow who gave two tiny coins as her Temple offering. Jesus saw her gift as the greatest of all since she contributed not just what she could spare but all she had.

Jesus' Olivet discourse (13:1–37)

As Jesus was leaving the Temple His attention was drawn to the grandeur of its buildings. His response was startling. For all their seeming stability they would be razed to the ground. Questioned later (while sitting on the Mount of Olives) about when this would happen and what signs there would be, Jesus embarked on His Olivet discourse. This blends the short term prophecy of the destruction of the Temple with the more distant future of His own return in glory[20] (13:1–4).

Jesus begins by warning that there will always be false messiahs, wars and natural disasters but none of these are signs of the end. His disciples must first proclaim the Gospel to all nations, a task for which they will be reviled and persecuted. However the Holy Spirit will support them and those who endure will be saved (13:5–13).

Jesus then describes a crisis when everyone in Judaea must flee to the mountains without delay. The signal for this will be 'the appalling abomination set up where it ought not to be'. This is an expression from Daniel 9:27; 11:31; 12:11 where it refers to the profanation of the Temple by Antiochus Epiphanes. Here it is pointing to the Romans' destruction of the Temple in A.D. 70 (13:14–18).

The perspective changes as Jesus now speaks of a tribulation unparalleled since the world began but which God in His mercy will not allow to go on for too long. Again there will be false messiahs but then, after the tribulation, and heralded by cosmic wonders, He will return Himself, coming in the clouds in power and glory to gather His elect from the ends of the world to inaugurate the beginning of the age of blessedness (13:19–27).

Just as leaves on a fig tree mark the onset of summer, so these signs will show that Jesus is near. But only the Father knows when that will be[21] (13:28–32). That being the case people must remain alert so as not to be caught unawares, a point underlined by the parable of the master of the house (13:33–37).

In this discourse Jesus was not just satisfying curiosity about the future but giving practical advice. He was preparing His disciples, and beyond them the Church, for a hostile world, counselling them not to be misled by confusing claims or speculative interpretations and to stand firm as their proclamation of the Gospel drew opposition and persecution.

THE PASSION AND DEATH OF CHRIST (14:1 – 15:47)

The general thrust of Mark's narrative is similar to Matthew's. But there are variations in detail. At 14:1–11 Mark omits Jesus telling His disciples of His coming crucifixion and of the precise amount Judas would be paid for betraying Him, both found in the parallel passage at Mt 26:1–16. At the institution of the Eucharist, Mark at 14:24 omits the phrase 'for the forgiveness of sins' after Jesus' words 'this is my blood, the blood of the covenant, poured out for many' quoted at Mt 26:28. Mark does not mention the possibility of angels being sent to Gethsemane to defend Jesus as does Matthew, Mt 26:53. He omits any reference to the death of Judas, Mt 27:3–10, to Pilate's wife's dream, Mt 27:19, and to Pilate washing his hands, Mt 27:24. He makes no mention of an earthquake and tombs opening following Jesus' death, Mt 27:51b–53; and knows nothing of the guard on the tomb, Mt 27:62–66.

On the other hand Mark's account of the preparations for the Passover supper, 14:12–16, is more detailed than Matthew's, Mt 26:17–19. At 14:61–62 he reports Jesus as saying 'I am' in response to the Sanhedrin's question, 'Are you the Christ?' whereas Matthew gives His response as, 'It is you who say it', Mt 26:64. Mark alone records that it was the third hour (9 AM,) when Jesus' crucifixion began, 15:25. He also gives a fuller account of Joseph of Arimathaea's burial of Jesus' body than Mt 27:57–61.

Unique to Mark, 14:51–52, is the account of the young man who ran away naked as Jesus was arrested. It is generally assumed that he was Mark himself otherwise the inclusion of the incident seems pointless.

THE RISEN CHRIST (16:1–20)

The empty tomb (16:1–8)

Early on the Sunday morning Mary of Magdala, Mary the mother of James, and Salome went to the tomb to anoint Jesus' body. To their amazement they found the stone guarding the entrance rolled back and the body gone. A young man in a white robe told them that Jesus was risen and that they must tell Peter and the disciples that He had gone on to Galilee to meet them there.

Appearances of the risen Christ (16:9–20)

Jesus Himself first appeared to Mary Magdala, then 'under another form' to two disciples as they were on their way into the country.[22] Finally He appeared to the Eleven, who had not believed earlier reports of His appearances, and reproached them for their lack of faith. He then gave them the great commission to preach the Gospel to all creation. Those who believed and were baptised would be saved. Those who did not would be condemned. He was then taken up into heaven to sit at the right hand of God while the disciples began proclaiming His name.

Luke

JOHN THE BAPTIST AND JESUS' EARLY LIFE (1:1 – 4:13)

The birth of John the Baptist foretold (1:1–25)

Luke begins with the events leading up to the birth of John the Baptist.[1] The angel Gabriel appeared to Zechariah, a priest, to announce that his wife Elizabeth would bear a son who was to be called John,[2] and who would be endowed with the power of Elijah and be filled with the Holy Spirit.[3] He would bring many back to God and prepare for the coming of the Lord. Zechariah was sceptical – both he and Elizabeth were getting on in years – and for this lack of trust he was struck dumb until after the birth.[4]

The birth of Jesus foretold (1:26–38)

In the sixth month of Elizabeth's confinement Gabriel appeared again, this time in Nazareth to a virgin named Mary, a cousin of Elizabeth, who was betrothed (engaged) to a man named Joseph, a descendant of David. She too would conceive a son, not by normal means but by the power of the Holy Spirit, and He was to be named Jesus.[5] He would be called Son of God. He would inherit the throne of His ancestor David and His reign would have no end. Mary's response – 'You see before you the Lord's servant, let it happen to me as you have said' – sets her apart as the epitome of obedience and faith.

Mary visits Elizabeth (1:39–56)

Mary went to visit Elizabeth. As soon as she heard Mary's greeting Elizabeth's child leapt in her womb. She was filled with the Holy Spirit and acknowledged Mary as 'the mother of my Lord.' Mary replied with the Magnificat, a hymn of praise and thanks in which she rejoices in her unworthiness and blessing and extols God's love, His greatness and holiness, His humbling of the rich and mighty, and His care for the poor and lowly.

The birth of John the Baptist (1:57–80)

After John was born Zechariah's speech returned and, filled with the Holy Spirit, he voiced the Benedictus, a poem praising God for bringing deliverance to His people through a scion of David in accordance with the prophecies, and proclaiming John as the one who would prepare the way. John grew up and lived in the desert until he was ready to begin his ministry.

The birth of Jesus (2:1–20)

Luke now recounts the birth of Jesus in Bethlehem, Joseph's ancestral town, to which the Holy Family had returned to be registered for a census. He was born in humble surroundings in an outhouse usually occupied by animals, their manger serving as His crib. An angel heralded Him as a Saviour, Christ the Lord, to the local shepherds while a heavenly host sang in praise. Mary, meanwhile, 'treasured all these things and pondered them in her heart.'

Jesus is presented in the Temple (2:21–38)

After Jesus was circumcised the Holy Family went up to Jerusalem to make the prescribed offering for Mary's purification and for Jesus, as a first-born son, to be consecrated to God in accordance with the Law.[6]

While they were in the Temple a devout man named Simeon recognised Jesus as the Christ and, in the *Nunc Dimittis*, proclaimed that He would bring salvation to all nations, and glory to Israel. But He would arouse great opposition and bring Mary deep anguish. A prophetess, Anna, also recognised Jesus as the future deliverer of Jerusalem.

Jesus in His Father's house (2:39–52)

We next hear of Jesus when He was twelve. He had stayed behind to be with the teachers in the Temple after His parents, having come to Jerusalem to celebrate the Passover, had left for home. His reply to His anxious parents when they found Him – 'Did you not know that I must be in my Father's house? – shows that even at that tender age He was aware of a relationship with God that transcended the norm. He returned to Nazareth to live under His parents' authority while Mary 'stored up all these things in her heart.'

John the Baptist (3:1–18)

The story resumes when Jesus was about thirty years old and John had begun to preach a baptism of repentance for the forgiveness of sins.[7] It was no good relying on descent from Abraham to avert retribution, John warned the people. Repentance meant a complete change of heart and a life based on honesty and charity. Otherwise they would be cut down and thrown on the fire like a rotten tree. When people began to wonder whether he might be the Messiah John was quick to correct them. He only baptised with water whereas One greater was coming who would baptise with the fire and power of the Holy Spirit.

Jesus' baptism and ancestry (3:19–38)

After reporting John's imprisonment, Luke tells of Jesus' baptism with the Holy Spirit descending on Him like a dove and a voice from heaven proclaiming Him Son of God. He then traces Jesus' ancestry back through David to Adam.[8]

Jesus is tested in the desert (4:1–13)

See Mt 4:1–11

THE GALILEAN MINISTRY (4:14 – 9:50)

Jesus begins His Galilean ministry at Nazareth (4:14–30)

Jesus taught throughout Galilee and before long came to preach in the synagogue of His home town, Nazareth, taking as His text Isaiah's, 'The spirit of the Lord is on me, for He has anointed me to bring the good news to the afflicted'. This text was being fulfilled even as they listened, Jesus added (i.e. He Himself was the anointed One, the Messiah).

The people were astonished but their amazement turned to hostility when they remembered that it was the local carpenter's son talking to them. What especially roused their ire and led them to attempt to kill Him however was Jesus' reference to Elijah and Elisha who, when faced with similar disbelief, turned to minister to heathens instead. The moral was clear. Unless the Jews opened their hearts the Gospel would go to the Gentiles.

Jesus teaches in Capernaum (4:31–44)

See Mk 1:21–39.

The call of the first disciples (5:1–11)

The call of Simon (i.e. Peter), James and John, occurred while Jesus was teaching by Lake Gennesaret (Galilee). Peter's eyes were opened through an act of faith. A professional fisherman, he knew very well that daytime fishing was unlikely to be fruitful after an unprofitable night and yet he unhesitatingly obeyed Jesus' advice to cast his net once more. His response to the ensuing miracle, a catch so heavy that the nets began to tear, changed his life. He confessed himself a sinful man, only to hear Jesus' words of forgiveness and new life, 'Do not be afraid; from now on it is people you will be catching'. The new disciples left everything to follow Jesus.

Cure of a man with a virulent skin disease (5:12–16)

See Mt 8:1–4. Luke notes how Jesus, though besieged by large crowds, always made time to escape to some lonely place to pray.

Cure of a paralytic (5:17–26)

See Mt 9:1–8; Mk 2:1–12.

The call of Levi: eating with sinners (5:27–32)

See Mt 9:9–13.

On fasting: the old and the new (5:33–39)

See Mt 9:14–17. Verse 39, 'the old is good' is probably an ironic comment on Jews who were determined to hold on to their old ways at the expense of the Gospel.

Jesus and the Sabbath (6:1–5)

See Mt 12:1–8.

Cure of the man with a withered hand (6:6–11)

See Mk 3:1–6.

The choice of the twelve (6:12–16)

After praying all night on a mountain Jesus made the momentous choice, from among all those who had followed Him, of the Twelve who would be the close witnesses of His life, death and resurrection in preparation for carrying the Gospel to the entire world.

The beatitudes (6:17–26)

Coming down from the mountain Jesus was faced with a great multitude who had come from afar to hear Him and be healed. He delivered something like a modern 'keynote' address beginning with a catena of blessings (recalling the Sermon on the Mount in Matthew) and woes. The blessings are best understood spiritually, as applying to those who are poor in the sense of acknowledging their dependence on God; hungry in yearning for spiritual fulfilment; weeping as they long for justice and peace. Blessed too are those who are reviled and persecuted for Christ's sake. Great will be their reward in heaven.

In the woes Jesus was not condemning affluence or pleasure as such. His strictures were directed at those who for whatever reason became blind to their social responsibilities and spiritual realities. With worldly values devalued as they are it is scarcely surprising that He also threw out a warning to those of whom the world speaks well.

Norms for living (6:27–49)

Jesus then turned to human relationships. His followers must love their enemies, abstain from retaliation, give unstintingly and treat others as they would like to be treated themselves. But mere reciprocity was not enough. They must be prepared to make the first move without thought of return, exercising compassion and forgiveness and never being judgemental. As they treated others so God would treat them.

The (spiritually) blind cannot lead the (spiritually) blind. So a disciple must learn before he can teach. He must eradicate his own shortcomings before finding fault in others (Jesus makes the point with humorous exaggeration; the plank in the disciple's eye, the splinter in his brother's). Just as a tree can be judged by its fruit so a man's words and actions reveal the state of his heart. Jesus stressed that His teaching was not just to be listened to. It must be acted upon. Anyone who did that would be building his life on solid foundations while the passive listener was like a man who built his house on sand.

The cure of the centurion's servant (7:1–10)

See Mt 8:5–13.

The raising of the widow's son at Nain (7:11–17)

Nearing the village of Nain Jesus was roused to compassion by the sight of a funeral cortege for the only son of a widow. Ignoring the law which said that touching a bier incurred ritual impurity He restored the young man to life and 'gave him to his mother'. Luke deliberately used this phrase to draw a parallel with a similar miracle by Elijah, a point not lost on the people who proclaimed that a great prophet had come among them.[9] Even death's dark abode was no match for Jesus.

Jesus and John the Baptist (7:18–35)

See Mt 11:2–19.

The woman who was a sinner (7:36–50)

The story of the sinful woman who wiped her tears off Jesus' feet with her hair, and kissed and anointed them with ointment while he was dining with a Pharisee, needs care.[10] Verse 50 makes it clear that the woman's sins were forgiven on account of her faith. The point of the parable of verses 41–43 is to show that forgiveness generates love. The statement in verse 47 that the woman's sins were forgiven because of her love should therefore be read in the sense that her love was an outward sign of her faith and that love was all the greater because of the forgiveness her faith told her would soon be hers.

The women accompanying Jesus (8:1–3)

As Jesus went around with the Twelve proclaiming the good news He was accompanied by a number of women who provided the necessities of life. All of them had been healed of evil spirits and ailments and included Mary of Magdala, Joanna and Susanna.[11]

The parable of the sower (8:4–8; 11–15)

See Mt 13:1–9; 18–23.

Why Jesus spoke in parables (8:9–10)

See Mt 13:10–17.

The parable of the lamp (8:16–18)

See Mk 4:21–25.

Jesus' family (8:19–21)

See Mt 12:46–50.

The calming of the storm (8:22–25)

See Mt 8:23–27.

The Gerasene demoniac (8:26–39)

See Mk 5:1–20.

Cure of the woman with haemorrhage and the raising of Jairus' daughter (8:40–56)

See Mk 5:21–43.

The Twelve go out on mission (9:1–6)

See Mk 6:7–13.

Herod and Jesus (9:7–9)

News of Jesus' ministry had by now come to the ears of Herod, the tetrarch of Galilee. He was curious to meet Jesus following rumours that John the Baptist, Elijah or one of the other prophets might have come back to life.

The feeding of the five thousand (9:10–17)

See Mt 14:13–21.

Peter's profession of faith (9:18–21)

See Mt 16:13–20.

First prophecy of the Passion (9:22)

See Mt 16:21–23.

The implications of discipleship (9:23–27)

See Mt 16:24–28; Mk 8:34 – 9:1.

The transfiguration (9:28–36)

See Mt 17:1–8. Only Luke reveals that Jesus was talking to Moses and Elijah about His coming Passion.

The epileptic demoniac (9:37–43)

See Mk 9:14–29.

Second prophecy of the Passion (9:44–45)

See Mk 9:30–32.

Who is greatest (9:46–48)

See Mt 18:1–5.

On using the name of Jesus (9:49–50)

See Mk 9:38–40.

JESUS' JOURNEY TO JERUSALEM (9:51 – 19:27

Jesus sets His face towards Jerusalem (9:51–62)

Jesus now began the journey to Jerusalem that would end in Calvary. His route took Him through Samaria. When a certain village refused to receive Him, James and John suggested calling down fire from heaven to punish it. But Jesus rebuked them.[12]

A trio of proverbs, steeped in hyperbole, stress the insecurity ('foxes have holes . . .'), the urgency ('leave the dead to bury their dead . . .') and the commitment ('once the hand is laid on the plough . . .) of the apostolic life, see Mt 8:18–22.

The mission of the seventy-two disciples 10:1–16

Jesus now sent seventy-two disciples out in pairs to towns He would soon be visiting Himself.[13] Although the harvest was rich, He warned, it would not be easy. They would be like lambs among wolves. Recognising their dependence on divine providence and the urgency of their mission they were to travel light – no purse, no haversack, no sandals – and not spend time on elaborate civilities. They were to take whatever hospitality came their way without shopping around and regard it as their wages. They were to heal the sick and announce that the kingdom of God was very near. Any town that did not welcome them must be warned of the consequences. Then they should move on to the next.

Jesus then warned of the fate awaiting (Jewish) towns like Chorazin that had been unmoved by His miracles. If (heathen) towns like Tyre and Sidon had witnessed them they would have repented long ago. He reminded His disciples that they were His personal representatives and hence God's too.

The disciples return (10:17–20)

When the disciples returned rejoicing at their success in casting out demons Jesus remarked that even more important for them was the fact that their names were inscribed among the elect in heaven.

The good news revealed to the simple: the Father and the Son (10:21–22)

See Mt 11:25–27.

The privilege of the disciples (10:23–24)

Jesus reminded His disciples how privileged they were to experience what the prophets and kings of old had longed for.

The two great commandments (10:25–28)

See Mt 22:34–40. Luke adds 'do this and life is yours'.

Parable of the good Samaritan (10:29–37)

In this well known parable Jesus might have depicted a Jew helping a fellow Jew he did not know or even a Jew ministering to a Samaritan. Instead He sharpened its impact on His Jewish audience by allotting the all-revealing act of love to a Samaritan, a member of a race Jews despised and ridiculed. The obvious point is that a man's neighbour is literally anyone needing help. But there is more to it. In verse 36 Jesus turns from the original question, 'Who is my neighbour?' to, 'What does being a neighbour mean?' The first implied a limitation. The second is meant to show that love should not be constrained by its object but be proactive and free flowing and, as Jesus' final bidding makes clear, acted upon.

Martha and Mary (10:38–42)

When Jesus was welcomed into the home of the sisters Martha and Mary, Martha complained that Mary sat listening to Him while she was left to prepare a meal all by herself. Jesus gently rebuked her. Listening to Him was more important than serving supper. The word of God must have first claim on our time.

Jesus on prayer (11:1–13)

Luke gives a shortened version of the Lord's prayer quoted at Mt 6:9–13. The point made by the ensuing parable of the nocturnal visitor is that if men will respond to a friend's request if it is pressed persistently enough, God will surely do the same.

The allusions to a father giving his son a snake when he asks for a fish or scorpions for eggs illustrate the absurdity of thinking that God could have anything but our best interests at heart. How could He who is perfect do less for His children than an earthly father, evil as he is? We have only to ask and we shall surely receive, even the gift of the Holy Spirit.

Jesus and Beelzebul (11:14–22)

See Mt 12:22–29.

Positive repentance (11:23–28)

Jesus presses the point that there is no middle ground: 'anyone who is not with me is against me.' Worse, unless the void left by the expulsion of unclean spirits is filled (by the nourishment of God's word) they will return stronger than ever. A conversion that casts out evil without positively replacing it with good will soon turn out to be no conversion at all. Veneration of Jesus is not enough. More important is to hear the word of God and keep it.

The sign of Jonah (11:29–32)

See Mt 12:38–42.

Light and darkness (11:33–36)

The Gospel must not be hidden any more than a lamp is put under a tub but broadcast abroad. Only when a man has a healthy mind, one sincerely seeking the truth and free of prejudice, will Jesus' teaching really take hold.

The Pharisees and lawyers denounced (11:37–54)

Prompted by the surprise of a Pharisee who had invited Him to dinner that He had not washed before sitting down at table, Jesus launched into a stern indictment of the Pharisees' way of life.[14] They were like people who only cleaned the outsides of their cups and plates. Their insides needed cleaning too: of extortion and wickedness. Let them clean their hearts by giving alms. They concentrated so much on tiny details of tithing that they forgot about justice and love. They were besotted with their own importance and misled people like unmarked tombs.[15] The lawyers were no better with their pettifogging rules, rules they did not even keep themselves. They built tombs for the very prophets their ancestors killed. Far from enlightening people they were a hindrance.

Open and fearless speech (12:1–12)

Every hidden word and thought will eventually come out into the open. It is God who should be feared not men. Men can only kill the body. God can cast you into hell. Yet there is no need to be afraid. Not even a sparrow is forgotten in God's sight and we are worth more than many sparrows. Every hair on our heads has been counted.

As His followers publicly confessed or disowned Him, Jesus went on, so He would declare for or against them before God. Speaking against Himself was pardonable but those who blasphemed against the Holy Spirit would not be forgiven.[16] No true believer need worry about how to defend himself when challenged. The Holy Spirit would guide him.

Material possessions (12:13–21)

Jesus next gave a warning against avarice, illustrating it with the story of a rich man who hoarded his crops so that he could look forward to a life of ease and luxury. Then suddenly he died. What use were his possessions then? Sadly they had so absorbed his mind that He had forgotten about the true riches of a right relationship with God.

Trust in providence (12:22–32)

See Mt 6:25–34. Luke adds Jesus' 'sell your possessions and give to those in need'.

On right priorities (12:33–34)

See Mt 6:20–21.

On being ready for Jesus' return (12:35–48)

Jesus drew a picture of servants waiting for their master's return, belts tightened and lamps lit, to bring home to His followers that they must always be prepared and ready for His return (as Judge). He would come unexpectedly like a thief in the night.

Those in authority will be well rewarded if they perform but treated the same as unbelievers if they abuse or neglect their responsibilities.[17] The severity of punishment of those who fall short will be tempered according to how much they understood of what Christ expected of them. The more a person is entrusted with, the more will be required of him.

Jesus on His Mission (12:49–59)

Jesus explained that His coming was meant to set the world on fire (people opting for or against Him) and He wished it was blazing already. There was a 'baptism' He must receive (His passion) and until then His power (in His humanity) was restrained. He warned that He would be a source of dissension, even splitting families. He marvelled that people who were so clever at recognising changes in the weather could not see that the Messianic age was being inaugurated before their very eyes. Just as it paid to settle disputes without going to court and getting a severe sentence, so people would be well advised to repent and make their peace with God without delay.

Repent while there is time (13:1–9)

Jesus used two news stories – the butchering of some Galilean pilgrims by Pilate, and an accident when a tower collapsed at Siloam – to explain that such disasters are not punishment for sin. But they should give people occasion to pause and think. For unless they repented they too would assuredly perish. And just as a vinedresser will only give a fig tree so long to bear fruit before cutting it down, so it is with God and judgement.

The healing of a crippled woman (13:10–17)

When Jesus healed a crippled woman the Pharisees were aghast because it was the Sabbath. But He threw them into confusion by pointing out that if it was right to water animals on the Sabbath surely it was right to relieve suffering.

Two parables of the Kingdom (13:18–21)

See Mt 13:31–33.

Entry to the Kingdom (13:22–30)

En route to Jerusalem Jesus was asked if only a few would be saved. He replied that many would not. The door was narrow and once it was shut it would be too late (so seize the opportunity now). Mere acquaintance with Him, hearing His teaching without responding, was not enough. There would be surprises. Many (like Jews) who thought they would be first in line would be excluded while people from 'east and west . . .' (meaning gentiles) would get in.

Jesus continues on to Jerusalem (13:31–35)

Jesus refused to be deflected from continuing on to Jerusalem because of a report that Herod was out to kill Him. His mission overrode all else. But as His thoughts turned to Jerusalem He was overcome by sorrow: 'How often have I longed to gather your children together, as a hen gathers her brood under her wings, and you refused'.

Healing a man with dropsy (14:1–6)

This story makes the same point as that of the crippled woman, 13:10–17.

Against self-exaltation (14:7–11)

The moral of this parable on choosing places at table is in the last verse: 'For everyone who raises himself up will be humbled, while one who humbles himself will be raised up'.[18]

Choosing guests (14:12–14)

Favours should not be done in the hope of being repaid. Instead they should be extended to the poor and needy who are unable to respond leaving the question of repayment to God.

The parable of the heavenly banquet (14:15–24)

With this parable Jesus made the point that, notwithstanding their spiritual heritage and advantages, Jews (the original invitees) who refused to respond to His teaching and treated His invitation with derision would find themselves excluded from the (heavenly) banquet in favour of the outcasts of society, the poor and sick, and people from the 'open roads and hedgerows' (gentiles) who would respond. More generally those who are too engrossed in this world may find themselves excluded from the next.

The price of discipleship (14:25–35)

Jesus warned that being a disciple was no easy option. It meant foregoing family and possessions and could even lead to death.[19] The would-be disciple must therefore think carefully before setting out just as a builder or a king marching to war first makes sure he has the resources to finish the job. Giving up half way through would be like salt that has lost its saltiness. And what good is that?

The lost sheep and the lost drachma (15:1–10)

Surrounded by tax collectors and sinners – people whom the self-righteous religious leaders shunned – Jesus now delivered three of His most moving parables. The parables of the lost sheep and the lost drachma reveal God's joy at recovering repentant sinners. He cannot bear to lose a single one. But moving as these two stories are, they are eclipsed by the parable of the prodigal son.

The prodigal son (15:11–32)

Again the moral is God's joy at a repentant sinner. The depths to which the younger son had sunk are abundantly conveyed by his feeding pigs, work that would have been repugnant to a Jew since Jews regarded swine as unclean animals. But no matter. When desperate straights led him to repent and he returned home it was to find his father (God) running out to greet him in his eagerness to be reconciled. He could hardly blurt out his remorse before he was cut short and, without recrimination, his father welcomed him back into the family and ordered a feast, because, 'This son of mine was dead and has come back to life'.

Sadly the elder brother would not join in the festivities and stayed out in the fields sulking at the lavish rejoicing over his brother's return. He had always been obedient but never once had his father thrown a party for him. The parable ends with his father reminding him that all he has is his but we are not told how he responded.

The omission is deliberate. For the elder brother represents the Pharisees and other self-righteous people who bridle at God's goodness. Jesus was inviting them in this secondary theme to accept repentant sinners as their brothers and was still awaiting their response.

The crafty steward (16:1–9)

The interpretation of this parable is difficult because it could give the impression that Jesus was condoning dishonesty. It tells of a steward who, having mismanaged his master's estate and facing dismissal, resorted to what looks like sharp practice by allowing his master's debtors to settle their accounts for less than they owed.

However all is not what it seems. It was normal practice in Jesus' day for stewards to earn a living from commission on sales of their master's produce or, as here, on interest levied on loans from his capital. In reducing the debts the steward was therefore only foregoing some of the interest due to him and not giving his master's money away. This was a clever move because not only would the alleviation of the debts enhance his master's reputation (people at large would not know how much was the steward's doing) but he would establish a fund of good will for himself for the time when he would be out of a job. His master could view the matter objectively since he was not losing out in any way (he would have known the steward was charging interest). Indeed the master praises the steward for his astuteness.

Jesus used the story to contrast the ingenuity and wiliness men employ in their secular affairs with the lacklustre way God's work is sometimes tackled.

On money (16:10–15)

Tainted though money may be, people must make responsible use of their wealth. If a man is a poor steward of money how can he be trusted with spiritual riches? But it must not go too far. No one can serve both God and money. The Pharisees' avarice makes them an abomination in God's eyes.

The Law remains (16:16–18)

The teaching of the Kingdom did not mean that the Law was superseded. Far from it. Every detail still stood. Indeed in stating that divorce followed by remarriage was tantamount to adultery Jesus showed that He even sharpened it, see Mt 5:17–19, appendix 3.

The parable of the rich man and Lazarus (16:19–31)

The message is stark. Failure to practise love and charity in this life leads to loss in the next. And once death comes it is too late to do anything about it. An unbridgeable gulf prevents anyone moving from the rich man's hell to Lazarus' heavenly bliss or vice versa. Sadly not even a spectacular sign like someone returning from the dead will persuade people whose hearts are set against God's word.

Four sayings on discipleship (17:1–10)

Lapses in faith are bound to occur but woe to anyone who causes another's downfall. If a brother strays he should be corrected and forgiven, again and again provided he is truly sorry. Even a little faith can achieve great things. No disciple is doing more than his duty as a servant and should therefore guard against spiritual pride.

The healing of ten lepers (17:11–19)

This miracle is another example of the power of faith. It also foreshadows the contrasting responses of Jews and gentiles to Jesus and the Gospel.

The day of the Son of Man (17:20–37)

In response to the Pharisees' question about when the Kingdom would come Jesus said that it did not admit of visible signs but was already (present and active) in their midst. Then He addressed His disciples. First He must suffer and be rejected. As for His Second Coming they must take care not to be misled by false signs for there will be no mistaking it. Just as lightning illumines the whole sky so will the glory of the Son of Man. It will be sudden and unexpected with people getting on with their lives just as they were at the time of the flood and Sodom. So let them beware of the attractions of this world and remember what happened to Lot's wife. For when the Day comes families and workmates will be split, some taken, others lost as the vultures gather for judgement.

The parable of the unjust judge (18:1–8)

In this parable Jesus is impressing on His followers the need to persist in prayer and never lose heart. If a judge who neither fears God nor cares for his fellow men is moved to act by sheer dogged persistence, how much more will God answer prayer even if He does sometimes appear to delay? But having said that, Jesus muses, how many people with faith will He find when He comes again?

The Pharisee and the tax collector (18:9–14)

This story contrasts the self-righteous person who thinks he deserves well of God with the humble sinner who knows his unworthiness all too well and throws himself on God's mercy. The one, childlike in his dependence on God, is justified in God's eyes (his sins forgiven). The other, proud and contemptuous, is not. There is no suggestion that the Pharisee in the parable was leading other than a good life according to the Law but he was eaten up by spiritual pride. He did not even ask for forgiveness. 'Everyone who raises himself up will be humbled, but anyone who humbles himself will be raised up.'

Jesus and the children (18:15–17)

See Mt 19:13–15.

Rewards and riches (18:18–30)

See Mt 19:16–30.

Third prophecy of the Passion (18:31–34)

See Mt 20:17–19.

The blind man at Jericho (18:35–43)

See Mt 20:29–34. Unlike Matthew, Luke mentions only one blind man. Also he places this incident as Jesus was approaching Jericho rather than leaving it.

Zacchaeus (19:1–10)

Zacchaeus saw Jesus and became a new man. He is the perfect example of a rich man passing through the eye of the needle, 18:24–27, for not only was he wealthy but, as a tax collector, his riches would have been acquired by dubious means.[20] Yet eager as he was to see Jesus, Jesus was even keener to see him, inviting Himself into Zacchaeus' home for the night: 'for the Son of man has come to seek out and save what was lost'.

The parable of the pounds (19:11–27)

In this parable the man of noble birth represents Jesus. He travelled to a distant country (heaven) to be appointed king (by God). Sometime later He returned (the Second Coming). While He was away His compatriots (the Jews), who did not want Him as king, did all they could to run Him down while His servants (His disciples) were given money (natural gifts and abilities) with which to make a profit (they were to announce God's kingdom).

When in due course the nobleman returned He sent for His servants to see how they had fared. Those who had done well and made a profit were rewarded, each according to how he had performed but all generously. One however had done nothing. He was rebuked. Surely he could have done something simple.[21] His money was given to the servant who had done best in his Master's absence, thereby prompting Jesus' maxim: 'everyone who has will be given more, but anyone who has not will be deprived even of what he has.' Those who did not want Jesus as king were judged accordingly.

TEACHING IN JERUSALEM (19:28 – 21:38)

Jesus enters Jerusalem (19:28–44)

See Mt 21:1–17; Mk 11:1–11, 15–19. Additional to Matthew and Mark, Luke records Jesus' refusal to reprove His disciples for their joyous acclamation as He approached the city from the Mount of Olives and also His lament on its coming destruction.[22]

Jesus cleanses the Temple and teaches there (19:45–48)

See Mt 21:12–13, Mk 11:15–19.

The authority of Jesus (20:1–8)

See Mt 21:23–27.

Parable of the wicked tenants (20:9–19)

See Mt 21:33–46.

On tribute to Caesar (20:20–26)

See Mt 22:15–22.

The resurrection of the dead (20:27–40)

See Mt 22:23–33.

Christ, Lord of David and son of David (20:41–44)

See Mt 22:41–46.

A warning against the scribes (20:45–47)

See Mk 12:38–40.

The widow's mite (21:1–4)

See Mk 12:41–44.

Jesus' Olivet discourse (21:5–38)

Luke follows Mark with some omissions. The general drift is the same. Verse 24, which tells of the Jews suffering until 'their time is complete', is peculiar to Luke.[23] Mark's parable of the master of the house, on the need to be prepared for Jesus' return, is omitted in favour of an exhortation to people to pray for strength to sustain their faith and avoid succumbing to worldly temptations while they await the Master's return.

THE PASSION AND DEATH OF CHRIST (22:1 – 23:56)

Luke agrees with Matthew and Mark in the main but there are differences in both ordering and content. He omits mention of Jesus' anointing at Bethany, Mt 26:6–13; the death of Judas, Mt 27:3–10; the soldiers' mocking of Jesus, Mt 27:27–31; Jesus' refusal of wine as He was nailed to the Cross, Mt 27:33–34; the earthquake and the tombs of the holy people opening after Jesus' death, Mt 27:51–53; the guard on the tomb, Mt 27:62–66; and all reference to Jesus meeting His disciples in Galilee after His resurrection, Mt 26:32.

Unique to Luke is Jesus' prayer that Peter recover his faith and so be able to help the others, and His advice that the disciples would now have to carry money and swords.[24]

Luke's rendering of Gethsemane is brief but emotionally charged. He augments Matthew and Mark by relating how an angel strengthened an anguished Jesus, 'His sweat falling to the ground like great drops of blood', and how Jesus healed the high priest's servant's ear.

Luke differs from Matthew and Mark in the sequence of events surrounding Jesus' trial. Whereas Matthew and Mark have Jesus arraigned before the Sanhedrin twice – an unofficial enquiry at night in the high priest's house followed by a brief but more formal meeting in council early the next morning – Luke only records the latter although the dialogue he reports is substantially the same. Also proper to Luke is the story of how Pilate, clearly unimpressed by the allegations against Jesus, passed Him over to Herod for a second opinion. Herod hoped to see Jesus perform a miracle and when He did not comply made fun of Him and handed Him back to Pilate.

Luke is alone in recording how Jesus, as He was led away to Calvary, returned a lament from some women with the prophecy, 'If this is what is done to green wood (i.e. wood not meant for burning – the innocent), how much worse will it be for dry wood (i.e. wood meant for burning – the guilty).

Only Luke recounts Christ's words of forgiveness from the Cross

> Father, forgive them; they do not know what they are doing.

and His promise to the brigand who was being crucified alongside who turned to Him in faith

> today you will be with me in paradise.[25]

Luke does not mention the cry of dereliction testified by Matthew and Mark but instead gives Jesus' last words as

> Father, into your hands I commend my spirit.

According to Luke not only the centurion but the crowds too were deeply moved by what they witnessed and went home 'beating their breasts'.

THE RISEN CHRIST (24:1–49)

The empty tomb (24:1–12)

On the Sunday morning a party of women, among them Mary of Magdala, Joanna and Mary the mother of James, found the stone sealing Jesus' tomb had been rolled away and the body gone. They were reproached for their puzzlement by two men in brilliant clothes. 'Why look among the dead for someone who is alive. Had not Jesus said He would rise again on the third day?' The Eleven thought the women's story pure nonsense when they heard it although when Peter went to see for himself all he saw, to his astonishment, were the linen clothes.[26]

The road to Emmaus (24:13–35)

Later the same day two of the disciples were joined by the (unrecognised) risen Lord as they were walking to Emmaus. They told this 'stranger' about Jesus: how their hopes had been dashed and the rumour that He was still alive. The 'stranger' gently rebuked them for being so slow to believe what the prophets had foretold – that the Messiah must suffer before being glorified – and explained the relevant Scriptures to them.

As night drew near they pressed Him to stay with them and when later at table He blessed and broke the bread their eyes were opened. They recognised the stranger as the risen Christ. But by then He had vanished from their sight. They hastened back to Jerusalem and their companions only to find that Jesus had also appeared to Peter.

Jesus appears to the apostles (24:36–49)

As the Eleven were discussing this momentous news Jesus came and stood among them. They thought they were seeing a ghost but when He showed them His hands and feet and ate a piece of grilled fish they were overjoyed.[27] He again explained how He was fulfilling the Scriptures and then commanded them to preach the Gospel to all nations. But first they must remain in Jerusalem until they received the Holy Spirit.

Jesus ascends into heaven (24:50–53)

Taking them out to Bethany Jesus blessed them. As He did so He was carried up to heaven.[28] Transported by joy the disciples returned to Jerusalem where 'they were continually in the Temple praising God.'

JESUS' LIFE AND TEACHINGS IN THE SYNOPTIC GOSPELS

Apart from the stories of His birth and the time He spent in the Temple when he was twelve years old, virtually nothing is known of Jesus' childhood and early manhood. When He emerges from obscurity it is to receive baptism from John the Baptist who recognised in Jesus the One whose coming he had anticipated. With the descent of the Spirit and the heavenly voice this must have been the time when Jesus first became fully aware of who He was. The temptations then led Him to explore what it meant to be Son of God and to define the nature of His mission.

Accompanied by a band of disciples, all of whom like their Master severed their ties with the past and trusted in providence to supply their needs, Jesus embarked upon an itinerant preaching and healing mission, addressing synagogues and open air crowds. He taught with an authority that amazed His hearers. His call for repentance, leading to forgiveness and the promise of God's Kingdom (God in some sense ruling powerfully as King), was at first warmly received. Attracted by His wondrous cures crowds flocked to hear Him. But then, as it became clear that His was not a kingdom of this world and that His gentle approach would not satisfy their hopes of a warrior Messiah who would release them from the Roman yoke and bring material prosperity, their enthusiasm waned.

It was not long before Jesus was at odds with the religious authorities. Although He was not directly concerned with social reform or political agitation they saw His claim to forgive sins and interpret the Law, and His strong denunciation of their own hypocrisy and self-righteousness, as undermining their authority and the status quo. When, stung by His fearless teaching, their animosity turned to outright hatred and a resolve to kill Him, Jesus realised that His mission was to be more than teaching and healing. He saw that His life was to be patterned on Isaiah's Servant and that He was destined to suffer an agonising death, a death that was at the very heart of God's plan for redeeming the world, before rising again. Accordingly He turned more and more to instructing His disciples so that, quickened by the Spirit He promised to send them and inspired by the resurrection He never doubted would follow the death He now saw as the inevitable climax of His mission, they would be the spearhead for carrying the Gospel to the ends of the world.

And so it was that in His last spring the sinless Jesus journeyed to Jerusalem (before this the synoptics, unlike John, present a largely Galilean ministry) where, in the agony and glory of the Passion and the crowning triumph of the resurrection, He inaugurated the New Covenant, laying down His life for the forgiveness of sins, conquering evil, overcoming death and opening the portals of heaven to all who believed.

Jesus the man

Though more than human Jesus was also very human: working as a carpenter; having no fixed abode; at times hungry, thirsty, tired, wrathful, sorrowing, socialising, liking children, befriending sinners, being exposed to temptation and human frailties, wishing to avoid his own awful death. At ease not only with the poor but with middle class fishermen and the well-to-do, He overrode taboos and social convention. He mixed with the marginalised and outcasts of society; lepers, sinners, tax collectors, people of doubtful morals. He was no ascetic and had an easy approach to women including them in His teaching and travelling entourage.

Though He rarely spoke openly of His own status, reacting to Messiah with reserve because of its political overtones, and preferring the enigmatic 'Son of Man' to describe Himself, He was invariably the pivotal figure of the drama He was living out. He had a clear sense of destiny, an air of command, authority in teaching, an irresistible and effortless control of evil spirits and a calm foreknowledge and direction of events. He made total demands on His followers, speaking with assurance on forgiveness and judgement and making obedience to His teaching and faith in His person the sole criterion of their eternal destiny.

Jesus' teaching

Jesus' teaching is characterised by His use of parables, proverbs, maxims, and aphorisms, all intended to rouse a sinful Israel to decision, to destroy complacency, to tease minds and open eyes. It is based on principles rather than detailed recipes and claims a unique authority: 'You have heard how it was said . . . but I say this to you . . .' He regarded the Old Testament as creedal. Even so He purged the Law of its formalism and legalism, rejecting its fragmentation into a host of minor prohibitions. He deepened its thrust by cutting to the thought behind the act and elevating it to a more searching critique of motives culminating in the supremacy of love: love of God and love of neighbour, love marked not by sentimentality but by unselfish service. The standard He set was the perfection of God Himself; loving as He loves, forgiving as He forgives, mercy without measure. Far from portraying God as fearsome and remote Jesus delighted in revealing Him as a loving Father who rejoiced every time one of His errant children returned to the fold.

The centrepiece of His message was the Kingdom of God. Jesus never defined what He meant by this. He took it for granted that His audience would know from the Old Testament that though God had always been King rebellious man had fallen under the dominion of Satan and sin. Now, faithful to His promises, God was acting to overthrow Satan and establish His unchallenged rule once and for all. Indeed the Kingdom was already present in embryo. It had come quietly, devoid of drama or ostentation, sown in the lives of His followers like a seed. Nurtured by prayer, it had the power to grow silently but mightily. Eventually it will be all embracing with God's rule universally recognised as the consummation of the process begun in His earthly ministry. Meanwhile we are in an intermediate age with the Kingdom partly with us, partly to come.

Signs that the Kingdom was already present were afforded by the many wonders Jesus performed. His miracles over nature, of healing and of casting out devils, even over death itself (all of them dependent upon faith) were not just kind deeds but proof that the Messianic age really had dawned. They showed His power over darkness and evil in all its forms, physical and spiritual, and were foretastes of the age to come when, arising out of His redemptive death (a sacrifice that the resurrection showed God had accepted) the whole of fallen creation will be freed from Satan's grip. His raising of the dead, though not yet giving the new life of the world to come, was nonetheless a sign of that new life.

The gates of the Kingdom are open to all, gentile and Jew, pariah and saint. To all, that is, who repent, acknowledge Jesus as their Saviour and let Him transform their lives to holiness and love. The invitation is always there and those who turn to Him later will be welcomed no less fulsomely than those who have served longer. But delay is dangerous for no one knows when the end will come and with it judgement. And then it will be too late. So awareness, wakefulness and preparedness are key. Everyone must plough his own furrow.

Not all will qualify. If there is anything that excludes from the Kingdom it is pride and self-righteousness, love of possessions and the superficial attractions of this world. What benefit is there if success in this world comes at the expense of imperilling life in the next? There cannot be two masters, God and money. Present values will be turned completely upside down. The first will be last and the last first. Whereas the world values what the outer man does God values what the inner man is.

Jesus taught that no sacrifice is too great for the kingdom's sake. Anything that risks our spiritual well-being must be ruthlessly excised. All that is necessary is to respond in childlike trust, in humility and faith (the faith that can move mountains) to His call by renouncing self, committing to Him unconditionally, listening to His words and acting on them, using whatever gifts we have been given to perform works of love in His name. He will do the rest. For 'His yoke is easy and His burden light'.

Jesus was under no illusions regarding the future. Having commissioned His followers to proclaim the Gospel to the ends of the earth He knew it would draw opposition and persecution in a hostile world. There would be false messiahs and false prophets, confusing claims and speculations, wars and disasters. And then suddenly without warning, like a thief in the night, following one last great tribulation, He would come again.

John

The objective John sets himself in writing his Gospel – to foster belief in Jesus as the Christ, the Son of God, so that in believing his readers might have life through Him, 20:31 – could apply to any of the Gospels. And indeed the broad sweep of John is familiar, from the Synoptics: the preparatory ministry of John the Baptist, the call of disciples, Jesus' dual ministry of word and miracle, the growing enmity of the religious authorities, and as Jesus' life reaches its climax, the same pattern of betrayal, trial, crucifixion and resurrection. But dissimilarities are also marked. John identifies three Passovers to the Synoptics' one. He focuses on Jesus' activity in Jerusalem and has little to say of the Galilean ministry. He omits the parables, includes little of the Synoptics' teaching and records fewer miracles.

Stylistically John is worlds apart. In place of the short crisp episodes in the Synoptic Gospels, worldly parables and pithy proverbs revolving around the Kingdom of God, John paints longer scenes often accompanied by closely knit dialogues and discourses that touch more on Jesus' mission and relationship with His Father than life in this world.

The distinctive character of the Gospel is evident from the outset. John is not content to begin with a child in Bethlehem or Jesus' baptism. He introduces Jesus as the Word, the creative power behind the universe and life, the essence of divine energy. A sense of destiny is never far away. Jesus' assertion of a special relationship with the Father and His claim to be the divine Son sent by God to save the world become stumbling blocks that generate conflict and rejection from the start. As the divine light grows, darkness becomes ever more impenetrable. If the Synoptics show man as God by contrast John reveals God as man.

But although John's Jesus is human and humble He is always fully conscious of His divine sovereignty and power, in the world but not of it, His mind moving on a plane more of eternity than of time. He uses a new vocabulary with words that assume new shades of meaning. He is the bread of life, the new manna, the living water, the light of the world, the good shepherd, the resurrection and the life, the true vine, the Way, Truth and Life.

The Father and He are one. He is the agent of His Father's will and the revelation of His nature. He was sent by the Father not to judge but so that all who believe might live. The Father has entrusted everything to Him: judgement, the gift of life. Everything the Son does derives from the Father's abiding power. Laying down His life for His friends and glorified on the Cross He conquers death and opens the gates of heaven for those born anew of the Spirit. The Spirit will continue His work in a world for which He prays for unity and peace and to which He bequeaths the supreme commandment of love.

Structure

As an aid to memory John can be broken down as follows:

> The prologue (1:1–18)
> The inaugural week in Galilee (1:19 – 2:12)
> Jesus in Jerusalem and Judaea (2:13 – 3:36)
>   dialogue with Nicodemus in Jerusalem
>   John the Baptist's final witness
> Jesus in Samaria and Galilee (4:1–54)
>   dialogue with the Samaritan woman at the well
> Jesus' second visit to Jerusalem (5:1–47)
>   the cure at the pool of Bethesda and discourse
> Jesus in Galilee (6:1–71)
>   the bread of life dialogue
> Jesus in Jerusalem for the feast of Shelters (7:1 – 10:42)
>   dialogue
>   the woman taken in adultery
>   dialogue
>   the cure of the man born blind
>   the good shepherd allegory
>   dialogue
> Jesus goes up to Jerusalem for the last time (11:1 – 12:50)
>   the raising of Lazarus
>   Jesus foretells His death
> The Last Supper and farewell discourse (13:1 – 17:26)
> The Passion of Christ (18:1 – 19:42)
> The Risen Christ (20:1 – 21:25)

THE PROLOGUE (1:1–18)

> In the beginning was the Word:
> the Word was with God
> and the Word was God.
> He was with God in the beginning.

Without preamble John presents the central figure of his Gospel as the pre-existent Word. His opening 'in the beginning' recalls creation and sets Jesus in a timeless eternity. The Word did not become. He was. He was God and He was with God. Everything came into being through Him. In Him was life and a light that darkness could not dispel.[1] God sent John (the Baptist) to testify to the light. But although John came first the light was One who came after him yet existed before him (1:1–8, 15). The Word was the true light but when He came into a world that owed its being to Him He was not recognised, even by His own people. But to those who did accept Him He gave the power to become children of God, children born not from human stock but of God (1:9–13).

So the Word became flesh and dwelt among us revealing His glory as the only Son of the Father.[2] Moses brought the Law. Jesus Christ replaced it with grace and truth.[3] No one has ever seen God except the Son who has made Him known (1:14, 16–18). *Appendix 1 refers*

THE INAUGURAL WEEK IN GALILEE (1:19 – 2:12)

John the Baptist's testimony (1:19–34)

John begins his account of Jesus' ministry with the Baptist's admission that he was neither the long awaited Christ nor Elijah nor the Prophet but only a herald sent to prepare the way for One whose sandals he was unworthy to unstrap.[4] When John saw Jesus walking towards him near Bethany he recognised Him at once as the One on whom he had seen the Spirit descending like a dove, exclaiming that 'He was the lamb of God that takes away the sin of the world'.[5] Where John baptised with water He would baptise with the Holy Spirit.

The first disciples (1:35–51)

Jesus recruits His first disciples: Andrew and an unnamed companion (both of whom were previously followers of John the Baptist); Andrew's brother Simon Peter (whom Jesus dubbed Cephas meaning Rock); Philip, and Nathanael to whom Jesus (despite his initial jest that nothing good could come from Nazareth) promised that he would 'see heaven open and the angels of God ascending and descending over the Son of Man'.[6]

The wedding at Cana (2:1–12)

Jesus' first miracle, transforming water into wine at a wedding in Cana, occurred before the beginning of His public ministry at the Passover in Jerusalem. It may have been that which prompted His remark 'my hour has not come yet'. By performing it Jesus not only gave a blessing on marriage but also an indication that His was to be no ascetic religion but one of fellowship and joy.[7]

JESUS IN JERUSALEM AND JUDAEA (2:13 – 3:36)

Jesus cleanses the Temple (2:13–25)

Jesus went up to Jerusalem for the Passover. Entering the Temple He expelled the money changers and the pedlars selling cattle, sheep and doves.[8] His Father's house was not to be used as a market place.[9] When the authorities asked for a sign to prove His authority His reply was both enigmatic and challenging: 'tear down this Temple and in three days I will build it up'.[10] John notes Jesus' uncanny insight into human nature.

Jesus' dialogue with Nicodemus (3:1–21)

One night a Pharisee named Nicodemus came to see Jesus.[11] Jesus told him that no one could enter the Kingdom of God without being (re)born from above through water and the Spirit. In other words unless he allowed himself to be spiritually reborn and led by the Spirit (of which the water of baptism is the outward symbol). How this happens is as mysterious as the wind which you can hear without having any idea where it will blow next. Jesus then recalled how, long ago, Moses had made a bronze serpent and lifted it up as a standard so that anyone who looked upon it might be saved, Nb 21:4–9. In like manner the Son of Man must be 'lifted up' so that all who believe in Him may have eternal life[12] (3:1–15).

John now muses on what is effectively the core Gospel message.[13]

> For this is how God loved the world:
> He gave His only Son,
> so that everyone who believes in Him may not perish
> but may have eternal life.
> For God sent His Son into the world
> not to judge the world,
> but so that through Him the world might be saved

No one who believes will be judged while those who do not believe are judged already by virtue of their disbelief.[14] People who do wrong shrink from the light because they do not want their evil ways exposed. But those who live by the truth relish the light because it shows quite plainly that what they do is through God (3:16–21).

John the Baptist's final witness (3:22–36)

Moving on to the Judaean countryside Jesus soon began to attract more followers than John the Baptist, who was nearby. Questioned about this John explained that he was not the Christ but only His forerunner, the bridegroom's friend, not the bridegroom Himself. He was overjoyed to hear Christ. Now he must fade into the background (3:22–30).

John reflects on how Jesus' heavenly origin raises Him above anyone on earth. His words come from God who has filled Him with the Spirit. Yet no one accepts His message. The Father loves the Son and has endowed Him with full authority. He is the touchstone of eternal life and divine wrath (3:31–36).

JESUS IN SAMARIA AND GALILEE (4:1–54)

The Samaritan woman at the well (4:1–42)

Jesus' popularity had come to the ears of the Pharisees and so, to avoid a confrontation that He did not want at this stage of His ministry, He decided to return to Galilee. On the way He passed through Samaria and, tired by the journey, stopped by a well to rest. There he encountered a Samaritan woman who had come to draw water. He told her of the living water He could provide, 'a spring of water, welling up for eternal life'. The woman probably had no idea what He was talking about but Jesus urged her to return with her husband. It then emerged that she had been married five times and was now living with a paramour.

Probably feeling uneasy at this focus on her private life the woman diverted the conversation to whether God should be worshipped in Jerusalem or, as the Samaritans held, on the mountain where they now stood.[15] Jesus explained that the Samaritans' worship was deficient. Salvation came from the Jews. But what really mattered was not where God was worshipped but that He should be worshipped in spirit and truth.[16] When the woman alluded to the Messiah as someone who would explain everything Jesus openly confessed that He was the Messiah.[17]

Jesus was now joined by His disciples while the woman returned home to encourage her townsfolk to come and meet Him for themselves. When the disciples pressed Jesus to eat He replied that the only sustenance He needed was to complete the work of the One who had sent Him. The fields were white, ready for harvest.[18] One sows, another reaps, Jesus went on; His disciples could reap the fruits of those who had laboured before them. The Samaritan woman was a keen witness and many Samaritans became believers.

Jesus in Galilee (4:43–54)

Back in Galilee Jesus again visited Cana where His word, given in response to faith, instantaneously healed a court official's son at Capernaum some miles away.[19]

JESUS' SECOND VISIT TO JERUSALEM (5:1–47)

The cure by the pool of Bethesda (5:1–18)

Some time later when Jesus was again in Jerusalem He healed a man who had been sick for thirty-eight years, warning him 'to sin no more lest worse befall you'.[20] Meanwhile the religious authorities were less interested in the miracle and more with the fact that since it happened to be the Sabbath both the sick man and Jesus had (in their eyes) transgressed by 'working' on what the Law regarded as a day of rest, the man by picking up his sleeping-mat after he was cured, Jesus by effecting the cure. Jesus defended His action by saying that as His Father carried on working so did He.[21] But this only made matters worse. Not only was Jesus breaking the Sabbath, now He was talking of God as His Father and equal. So they grew even more determined to kill Him.

Jesus' defence of His Sonship (5:19–47)

In a discourse intended to demonstrate the unity of Father and Son, Jesus began by declaring that the Father loves the Son and that the Son is entitled to the same honour as the Father. The Son's authority comes from the Father who has delegated to Him both judgement and the power to raise the dead and give life. The time has now come when the (spiritually) dead will hear the Son and all who listen and believe will pass from death to eternal life without judgement. The (physically) dead will come back to life at the sound of His voice: the good to life, evil-doers to judgement. The Son's judgement is just because it is based on the Father's will[22] (5:19–30).

Jesus then summoned 'witnesses' to vouch for Him. He discounted His own witness but cited four others: John the Baptist, the wonders He had performed, the Father Himself and the Scriptures. However, although they pored over the Scriptures, His critics failed to see that it was Himself they were pointing to. They were only interested in peer approval and more likely to accept someone claiming to act on his own authority than God's. They revered Moses but did not see that it was Himself he was writing about[23] (5:31–47).

JESUS IN GALILEE (6:1–71)

The feeding of the five thousand (6:1–15)

This is the only one of Jesus' miracles recorded in all four Gospels. However only John relates how Jesus was subsequently forced to take to the hills when the people wanted to make Him king there and then.[24]

Jesus walks on the water (6:16–21)

That evening the disciples left for Capernaum by boat while Jesus followed later, walking across the water to catch them up.

The discourse in the synagogue at Capernaum (6:22–59)

Next morning, when the people who had witnessed the feeding miracle caught up with Him at Capernaum, Jesus urged them to set their priorities not on bread to eat (which was why they were following Him) but on the food that leads to eternal life, food He could give them by the power God had vested in Him. All they needed was to believe in Him (6:22–29).

This prompted them to ask for a sign to justify their trust, something akin to the manna their ancestors ate in the desert.[25] Jesus explained that the bread Moses provided was not the life-giving bread from heaven He was talking about. That came not from Moses but from the Father. Indeed it was Himself. For He was the bread of life and no one who accepted Him would ever hunger or thirst.[26] Jesus went on to promise that He would never reject or lose anyone who came to Him.[27] He had come down from heaven to do His Father's will which was that all who believed in Him would have eternal life and be raised up on the last day (6:30–40).

At this the Jews started murmuring.[28] What had got into this man, with His humble origins, to claim that He had come down from heaven? But Jesus was undeterred. No one could come to Him and believe unless they were drawn by God.[29] Only He had seen God.[30] Those who ate the manna were all dead but those who eat the bread of life which comes down from heaven will live for ever. And that bread is His flesh. At this the Jews started arguing among themselves: 'How could they eat His flesh?' But Jesus persisted. Not only must they eat His flesh, they must also drink His blood. Only then would they be raised up on the last day to eternal life[31] (6:41–59).

Division among the disciples (6:60–71)

When many of His followers complained that these were outrageous ideas Jesus tried to reassure them. To think of ordinary human flesh was to miss the point. He belonged not just to earth but to the heavenly spiritual realm as they would see from His ascension and it was as spirit, not in terms of literal flesh, that what He had said gave life. Even so this was the parting of the ways. Many could not accept such radical ideas and left Him. This prompted Jesus to question the Twelve about their intentions. Peter's response affirmed their deepening faith that He was indeed the Holy One of God. Even so Jesus perceived that one of the Twelve, Judas Iscariot, would one day betray Him.

Jesus in Jerusalem for the Feast of Shelters (7:1 – 10:42)

Jesus teaches at the feast of Shelters (7:1–52)

Jesus remained in Galilee as the Jews in Judaea were bent on killing Him. However as the feast of Shelters drew near He decided, after some hesitation, that He would go up to Jerusalem after all, not publicly as His brothers were urging, but secretly[32] (7:1–13).

Halfway through the festival He began to teach in the Temple. He began by asserting that any God-fearing person would know that His teaching was from God and not His own. He then charged the Jews with breaking the Law. They wanted to kill Him for healing on the Sabbath! Circumcision was allowed on the Sabbath so why not healing?[33] They should stop making superficial pronouncements about His work and judge it objectively (7:14–24).

The crowd was perplexed. Why were the authorities taking no action? Could it be that they now recognised Him as the Christ? Surely not, because when the Messiah came His origins would be unknown whereas everyone knew where this man came from.[34] Jesus was quick to pick this up. They might know His earthly origins but they did not know His true origins because they did not know the One who sent Him.

At this the authorities wanted to detain Him but were providentially restrained because 'His hour had not yet come'.[35] However when it became apparent that people were beginning to accept Jesus as the Messiah the Pharisees despatched the Temple guards to arrest Him. Jesus meanwhile continued with an oblique allusion to His coming death: in a little while He would return to the One who sent Him (7:25–36).

On the last day of the feast Jesus returned to the metaphor of living water.[36] Let anyone who was thirsty and believed in Him come and drink! In an aside John explains that Jesus was speaking of the Spirit that believers would receive once He had been glorified.[37]

The people were confused. They knew the Messiah would come from Bethlehem but thought in their ignorance that Jesus hailed from Galilee. As for the Temple guards, they returned empty-handed, overawed by Jesus' presence. This ruffled the Pharisees but one of their number, Nicodemus, defended Jesus' right to a fair hearing (7:37–52).

The woman taken in adultery (7:53 – 8:11)

Next morning the scribes and Pharisees brought before Jesus a woman who had been caught in adultery.[38] They were trying to trap Him. If He upheld the Law and the woman was stoned He would lose His reputation for compassion and could be denounced to the Romans.[39] If He advocated mercy He would be criticised for flouting the Law. Jesus took neither course. In saying 'Let the one among you who is guiltless be the first to throw a stone at her.' He roused His opponents' consciences so that all they could do was slowly drift away. In His final words to the woman, 'Sin no more', He tempered mercy with warning, neither condemning nor condoning.

Jesus the light of the world (8:12–30)

When He next spoke to the people Jesus used the analogy of light.[40] He was the light of the world and anyone who followed Him would not be walking in darkness but have the light of life. When the Pharisees objected to His self-testimony Jesus replied that (in contrast to 5:31) it was valid in His case because He knew His heavenly origin. But if they wanted to press the Law's ruling that two witnesses were required then He had the Father to back Him up. But where was His Father, they asked, obviously thinking of a natural father whose witness would not be valid in his absence? Jesus replied that they knew neither Him nor His Father and would die in their sin. He was going where they could not follow. When the Jews wondered if this meant suicide Jesus again alluded to His heavenly home.

When they then asked who He was Jesus replied that He had been sent by God and that after He had been lifted up they would understand who He was, a reference to His coming crucifixion and resurrection. God was with Him and all He did was the Father's will. At these words many came to believe in Him and it was those He now addressed.

Jesus and Abraham (8:31–59)

If they believed, Jesus continued, they would come to the truth and as the Son He would set them free[41] (8:31–36). Yes, they were physically descended from Abraham but if they were truly his children as they claimed they would behave like Abraham instead of which they wanted to kill Him for speaking the truth that came from God.[42] Nor was God their father otherwise they would love the One He sent. No, their father was the devil, a murderer and liar. That is why they could not bear the truth. Stung by these rebukes the Jews accused Jesus of being possessed but He ignored their taunts. He was not looking for His own prestige but to honour His Father[43] (8:37–50).

Jesus made one final appeal. Anyone who kept His word would never see death. The Jews took this literally. Was He claiming to be greater than Abraham and the prophets who were all dead? Who was He? Jesus reminded them that the God they claimed as theirs was His Father before declaring that 'Abraham rejoiced to see My Day'.[44] The Jews took this literally as a claim that He had seen Abraham. Jesus' reply 'before Abraham ever was, I am' was the last straw. It implied absolute existence and divinity both in its timelessness and in His appropriation of God's name, 'I am'.[45] To the Jews this was blasphemy and they made to stone Him. But once again He eluded their clutches (8:51–59).

The cure of the man born blind (9:1–41

When Jesus came across a man who had been blind from birth He first had to correct His disciples' assumption that his affliction was punishment for sin.[46] It was not. Rather it should be seen as an opportunity to do God's work (9:1–3).

However it was time for action not speculation. His time was limited so as long as He had the chance He must let His light shine on the darkness around Him by doing God's work. With this Jesus restored the man's sight. Later in the day the man's declaration of faith showed that his spiritual eyes had been opened too. The Pharisees were incensed. Once again Jesus had broken the Law by 'working' on the Sabbath and their stubborn attempts to discredit Him were unavailing (9:4–38).

Jesus was scathing. His restoration of physical sight was but a symbol of His wish to give (spiritual) sight to the (spiritually) blind. Unfortunately those who thought they could see turned out to be blind (blinded by prejudice and pride: all they could think about was keeping the Sabbath). If the Pharisees had confessed their ignorance they would not have been guilty. But as it was (their closed minds leaving no room for the light of the world) their guilt remained. It was in that sense that He brought judgement into the world (9:39–41).

Jesus the good shepherd (10:1–21)

In this beautiful allegory Jesus is the gate to the sheepfold. There is no other way in. He is also the shepherd. The sheep follow the sound of His voice and His alone, ignoring strangers, as He leads them to pasture and life. Bandits who try to climb in to the pen some other way only come to kill or destroy[47] (10:1–10).

The good shepherd is dedicated to His sheep and lays down his life for them whereas the hired hand abandons them at the first sign of trouble. He knows His sheep and they know Him just as He and the Father know one another. There are other sheep in other folds but only one flock and only one shepherd to lead them.[48] Jesus is that shepherd. And as He lays down His life of His own free will, so He has the power to take it up again (10:11–21).

Jesus Son of God (10:22–42)

A little later during the feast of Dedication, as He was walking in the Temple precincts during the feast of Dedication, Jesus was asked by the Jews if He was the Christ.[49] He replied that His works were sufficient answer. But they did not believe because they were not His sheep. His sheep believed and would be given eternal life. They could never be wrested away from Him since they were the Father's gift and He and the Father were one.

As the Jews made to stone Him for blasphemy Jesus observed that if the scriptures could speak of ordinary mortals as gods then surely they could not object to someone the Father had sent into the world being called Son of God.[50] They had only to consider His miracles to see that He was doing God's work and that 'The Father is in me and I am in the Father'. Faced with the threat of further violence Jesus then withdrew across the Jordan.

JESUS GOES UP TO JERUSALEM FOR THE LAST TIME (11:1 – 12:50)

The raising of Lazarus (11:1–44)

The raising of Lazarus, four days after he had died and was already in the tomb, is the greatest of Jesus' miracles recorded by John and unimpeachable proof that God had given Him power over life and death. Jesus had tarried for two days before journeying to Bethany in response to Lazarus' sisters' cry for help.[51] This was to be no mere healing miracle but one that fortified the disciples' faith and gave the clearest proof possible that in Jesus death had met its match.

> I am the resurrection.
> Anyone who believes in me, even though that person dies, will live,
> and whoever lives and believes in me
> will never die.
> Do you believe this?

The question, to Martha, shows again that faith is paramount. Martha had already affirmed that God would grant Jesus anything He asked. Now she confessed Him the Christ, the Son of God. Such was Jesus' bond with His Father that He was able to thank Him for the miracle even before it happened.

The Jewish leaders condemn Jesus to death (11:45–57)

Jesus' greatest sign was also the occasion for the Jews' greatest hardness of heart. Although many who witnessed Lazarus' raising came to believe in Jesus the chief priests and Pharisees resolved that He must be killed. They were frightened that His growing popularity might lead to the Romans seeing it as the start of an insurrection to which they would have to respond with force. Little did Caiaphas the high priest realise how prophetically he was speaking when he told the ruling council in these words that it was better for one man to die for the people than for the whole nation to perish. Jesus meanwhile withdrew to be near the desert, while in Jerusalem people gathering for the Passover began to speculate whether He would attend it or not.

The anointing at Bethany (12:1–11)

This is the same incident as Mt 26:6–13; Mk 14:3–9 albeit with variations in detail: John puts it six days before the Passover, Mark two; only John names Lazarus and his sisters; John has Mary anoint Jesus' feet rather than His head as in Mark; John alone identifies Judas Iscariot with the grumbling at the waste of money and reveals the chief priests' plot to kill Lazarus.[52]

Jesus enters Jerusalem (12:12–19)

Jesus' hour had come. Humbly mounted on a donkey He entered Jerusalem to the acclaim of a large crowd waving palms, crying Hosanna and hailing Him as the Lord's anointed and King of Israel. The Pharisees began to wonder if it was not already too late to stop Him.

Jesus foretells His death and glorification (12:20–36)

Some Greeks who were in Jerusalem for the Passover asked to see Jesus. He told them that the climax of His life was now at hand. As a seed falling into the ground yields a rich harvest so, He implied, His death was the key to a spiritual harvest. Anyone who loved his life in this world would lose it while anyone who hated it would gain eternal life. Serving Him meant following in His footsteps with all that entailed but with the certainty of recognition by His Father[53] (12:20–26).

Jesus now revealed the strain He was under. Should He pray to be spared the horror of the death that was now imminent? No. For it was for this hour that He had come into the world. At this a voice from heaven proclaimed that God's name had been glorified and would soon be glorified again.[54] Judgement was coming on the world, Jesus continued. Satan, the prince of this world, was about to be crushed and in being lifted up He would draw people everywhere.[55]

Bystanders were perplexed at the idea of the Son of Man being 'lifted up'. Surely the Christ was eternal? Jesus responded with one final appeal. His light would not be with them much longer so let them embrace it while they still had the chance lest darkness envelop them. Then 'He was hidden from their sight'. It was the end of His public ministry (12:27–36).

John's evaluation (12:37–50)

John observes that despite Jesus' many signs the people as a whole did not believe Him. Their hardness of heart made it impossible as Isaiah had foreseen.[56] And those that did believe would not admit it for fear of being ostracised. He then quotes Jesus confirming His oneness with, and commission from, God. He had come as light to dispel darkness. Those who rejected His word judged themselves for everything He said was commanded by the Father for the sake of eternal life. He had come not to judge but to save the world.

THE LAST SUPPER AND FAREWELL DISCOURSE (13:1 – 17:26)

The Last Supper: humility and treachery (13:1–30)

John differs from the Synoptic Gospels in his account of the Last Supper. He omits any reference to the institution of the Eucharist including instead the story of Jesus washing His disciples' feet and a long farewell discourse neither of which features in the other Gospels.

Jesus' washing of His disciples feet is to be interpreted at two levels. In not disdaining the role of a menial servant Jesus was illustrating the way of humility and love. But His rejoinder to Peter, 'If I do not wash you, you can have no share with me', gave the act a wider spiritual significance too. Not to be cleansed by Jesus was to have no place in the Kingdom.[57] It was after this that a deeply disturbed Jesus indicated that Judas would betray Him. John records that 'it was night'.

Jesus then began the most profound of all His discourses, the most sublime of all farewells. In it He declares Himself the gateway to eternal life, establishes the supremacy of love, promises to send the Spirit, and prays for the unity of His Church.

Prelude: the hour has come (13:31–38)

The time was near, Jesus began, that would bring glory to both Father and Son.[58] Soon He would be going where His disciples could not follow. But first He gave them a new commandment: to love one another even as He loved them. Let that be their hallmark.[59] At this Peter avowed that he would lay down his life for his Master. Jesus allowed that he would eventually follow Him.[60] Yet he would disown Him three times before morning broke.

Jesus the Way to the Father (14:1–14)

Having heard of Judas' betrayal, Peter's denial and Jesus' own impending departure, the disciples must have been deeply dismayed so Jesus now sought to console them. They must trust. He was going ahead to prepare places for them. Then in due course He would return so that they might be 'where I am'.[61] They knew the way. When the literal-minded Thomas pointed out that they did not know the way Jesus replied that He was the Way, Truth and Life.[62] No one could come to the Father except through Him. When Philip asked to be shown the Father Jesus explained He was in the Father and the Father was in Him. It was the power of God that was responsible for His works. Whoever believed would produce even greater works and whoever asked in His name would never be denied.[63]

Jesus promises the Holy Spirit (14:15–26)

True love meant keeping His commandments, Jesus went on. He would therefore ask the Father to send another *paraclete*, the Spirit of truth, to be with them and in them for ever.[64] Although the world at large would not recognise the Spirit, He would teach them and remind them of what they had already learnt (14:15–17, 25–26). The time was approaching, Jesus continued, when the world would no longer see Him. Yet they would not be left orphans. They would know in their hearts, 'that I am in my Father and you in me and I in you'. He would indwell all who kept His words and loved Him and they would know He lived through the inward vision of faith (14:18–24).

Peace and consolation (14:27–31)

Jesus then bequeathed a peace the world could never know.[65] He had promised to return and rather than being sad they should rejoice that He was going to the Father who was greater than He.[66]

At this juncture Jesus made to leave. The prince of darkness was on his way, the final denouement close at hand. However the discourse continues and it is a while later before they actually set out for the garden where Jesus will be arrested.[67]

Jesus the true vine (15:1–8)

Jesus Himself gave the key to this lovely allegory. He is the vine, His Father the gardener, His followers the branches.[68] God wants every branch to yield fruit so He prunes the good branches to make them even more fruitful (by promoting their spiritual growth) while branches that bear no fruit are cast aside and burnt.[69] Just as a branch withers unless it draws life from the vine so His disciples are powerless unless He and His words remain in them, in which case nothing asked for in prayer is beyond their reach.

Love one another (15:9–17)

Jesus again commanded His disciples to love one another as He had loved them and as the Father loved Him. No one can have greater love than to lay down his life for his friends. To remain in His love they must keep His commands. But that did not make them servants. On the contrary they were His friends as evidenced by the way He had told them everything He had learned from His Father, a privilege not granted to mere servants. They did not choose Him. He chose them. And for a purpose: to go out and bear fruit.[70]

The hatred of the world (15:18 – 16:4)

Jesus warned His disciples that they would attract the same hostility as Himself because they were no longer part of a world that, despite His teaching and miracles, did not recognise who had sent Him. But when the Spirit, whom He would send from the Father came, He would support their witness with His own. He was saying all this to forewarn them of the trials they would face in the difficult days ahead.

The Holy Spirit as teacher (16:5–15)

Jesus then explained that His departure would actually benefit them for only then would the *paraclete* come. And when He did He would show the world the error of its ways and make clear who He was, the true nature of His mission and the significance of His death in defeating Satan. He would teach them things they had not previously been mature enough to understand including enlightenment on the future, all the while building on what He had already taught them to further glorify His name.

Jesus' departure and return (16:16–33)

For a short time they would be plunged into sorrow while the world rejoiced. But then, like a woman giving birth, they would experience a joy that would never fade. All their questions would be answered. There would be no more need for the veiled language He had used in the past.[71] Praying in His name they would be able to approach the Father directly for anything they wanted because the Father loved them for loving Him.[72] He came into the world from the Father and it was to the Father that He would now return.

With the scales at last beginning to fall from His disciples' eyes Jesus warned them again of difficult days ahead. They would be scattered and desert Him. However He would not be alone because God would be with Him. Then He raised their hearts.

> I have told you all this
> so that you may find peace in me.[73]
> In the world you will have hardship,
> but be courageous:
> I have conquered the world.

Jesus prays for Himself (17:1–5)

Jesus now prayed that just as He had glorified God in His earthly mission so might He now be restored to the glory that was His before the world began and give eternal life to all who were entrusted to Him.[74]

Jesus prays for His disciples (17:6–19)

Jesus next prayed for His disciples. They had accepted His teaching and knew that like Himself it came from God. May they be protected from the Evil One and preserved in truth and unity just as He and the Father were one. They no more belonged to the world than He did. But as God had sent Him into the world so now He was sending them.

Jesus prays for future believers (17:20–26)

Finally Jesus prayed for all future believers. May they be one as He and the Father were one so that, out of their unity, the world might come to believe that the Father sent Him and loves them as He loves the Son. May they always be with Him to see the glory that was His from the beginning. Addressing the Father Jesus promised that His redemptive work would never cease.

THE PASSION OF CHRIST (18:1 – 19:42)

Jesus is arrested (18:1–27)

Jesus now set out for Gethsemane. John's account of His subsequent arrest and interrogation and Peter's denial is broadly similar to that found in the Synoptic Gospels. However he omits mention of Jesus' anguish in the garden although 12:27–28 is reminiscent of it. And, in place of the proceedings before the Sanhedrin later the same evening, reported by Matthew and Mark, he briefly describes an interrogation before Annas, the high priest's father-in-law.

Jesus before Pilate (18:28 – 19:16)

John treats this at more length than the Synoptics and paints a Pilate even more reluctant to condemn Jesus. Indeed it was only when the Jews insisted that Jesus was professing to be king in defiance of Caesar that he authorised His crucifixion.[75]

Jesus' crucifixion and death (19:17–37)

Unlike the Synoptic Gospels, John omits to record Simon's help in carrying the cross, that the two men who were crucified beside Jesus were criminals, the mocking as Jesus hung on the cross, the darkness that came over the land, Jesus' cry of desolation and the rending of the veil of the Temple. Instead he describes three incidents not found in the Synoptic Gospels.

First, besides casting lots for Jesus' clothes, he relates how the soldiers played dice for Jesus' seamless undergarment. Then he describes how a group of women, including Jesus' mother, stood with 'the disciple whom Jesus loved' near the cross. Seeing them together Jesus told His mother to take the disciple as her son and the disciple to accept her as his mother.[76]

The third event proper to John is one to which he clearly attached singular importance. When the soldiers deputed to break the victims' legs found that Jesus was already dead they pierced his side with a spear instead, resulting in an issue of blood and water.[77]

John gives Jesus' last words as 'it is fulfilled' after which He 'gave up His spirit'. He reminds us that no one took Jesus' life. He remained in control until the end and surrendered it willingly: prophecy fulfilled, sacrifice offered, salvation achieved.

Jesus' burial (19:38–42)

John parallels the Synoptic Gospels while adding that Nicodemus also assisted with Jesus' burial.

THE RISEN CHRIST (20:1 – 21:25)

The empty tomb (20:1–18)

John's account of the discovery of the empty tomb bears all the freshness of an eye witness: the 'other' disciple sprinting ahead of Peter, the head cloth neatly rolled up. (Compelling evidence that the body had not been stolen. Thieves would either have left the grave clothes in a heap or taken them with the body.)

A little later when Mary of Magdala encountered the Risen Lord she at first mistook Him for the gardener.[78] However when Jesus called her by name she was transported with a joy that led Jesus to exclaim

> Do not cling to me, because I have not yet ascended to the Father. But go ahead and find my brothers, and tell them: I am ascending to My Father and your Father, to My God and your God.

What does this mean? Possibly Jesus was indicating that their relationship had changed. He was no longer the Jesus of Galilee. More likely, following Mt 28:9, He was not declining to be touched but gently telling Mary that she must not detain Him because she had work to do: to tell the brothers.[79] He had not ascended so would be around for a little while yet!

The significance of 'I am ascending' is probably that Jesus saw 'ascension' as a sequence of events beginning with His rising from the tomb and ending with His final ascension from the Mount of Olives forty days later. His reference 'to My Father and your Father, to My God and your God' is illuminating. Nowhere does Jesus ever address God or the Father as 'our God'. His relationship is unique. He is the Father's eternal Son from before the world began. Christians become the Father's children by receiving Him in faith.

Appearances to the disciples (20:19–31)

That same evening Jesus mysteriously appeared to His disciples in a closed room and showed them the wounds in His hands and side. He commissioned them to continue His work, breathed the Holy Spirit into them and gave them authority to forgive and retain sins.[80] A week later He reappeared in similar circumstances and singled out Thomas who had missed the earlier gathering and had refused to believe without seeing for himself. His ecstatic reaction when he set eyes on his Risen Lord – 'My Lord and my God' – prompted Jesus', 'Blessed are those who have not seen and yet believe'.

Appearance in Galilee (21:1–25)

Jesus' appearance to the disciples, cooking breakfast while they were fishing in the sea, quickly leads into the account of how Peter was given the opportunity to rescind his threefold denial the night before the crucifixion with a threefold avowal of love. His reward was Jesus' commission to feed His lambs, a path that would eventually lead to his own martyrdom. However his curiosity about the beloved disciple's future brought a rebuke. It was none of his concern. Let him concentrate on serving his Master with his own life.

Appendix 2 refers

ACTS OF THE APOSTLES

Acts is a sequel to the third Gospel and ascribed to the same author. It reveals the birth pangs of the early Church and shows in colourful vignettes how Christianity spread from Jerusalem, first to Judaea and Samaria, and then across the Mediterranean. It carries the story from the mother church in Jerusalem to Paul's detention in Rome and the Gospel proclaimed in the heart of the Roman Empire. It exudes the essence of early Christian preaching, the inspiration and activity of the Holy Spirit, the Gospel's transforming power and the sacrifices and triumphs of its early adherents.

It begins with Jesus' ascension and the bestowal of the Holy Spirit at Pentecost. This is followed by gallery portraits of the early Christian community, portraying it as evangelical, fearless, vital, brimming with joyful fellowship, taking harassment in its stride. A loving community, caring and sharing, working many signs and miracles, led by the Spirit.

With the martyrdom of Stephen a new era began. The ensuing persecution sparked a dispersion that took the Gospel to Samaria, Phoenicia, Cyprus and Antioch. Shortly after came another epoch-making event, the conversion of Saul (later Paul) of Tarsus from the Church's most rabid opponent to her most potent evangelist. Then, with the descent of the Holy Spirit in the household of the Roman centurion Cornelius, God showed Peter that the Gospel was for gentiles as well as for Jews.

Before long the spotlight moves from Peter to Paul. Acts leaves the sheltered confines of Palestine and Jewish tradition to breathe the fresh air of the vast expanses of the gentile world. In three foundational missionary expeditions Paul evangelised Cyprus, Galatia, Macedonia and Greece. Between the first and second of these he went up to Jerusalem to attend a special council called to settle once and for all the vexed question whether gentile converts must be circumcised and subject to the Law. The answer was 'no'. No longer was Christianity to be seen as a variant of Judaism with belief in Jesus as the Messiah added to traditional belief but a new faith in which salvation comes through Christ and in no other way.

Acts ends by recording Paul's last visit to Jerusalem, the two years he spent in custody in Caesarea, and his final journey to Rome where he is placed under house arrest but still left free to proclaim the good news.

Paul always began by taking the Gospel to the Jews in their synagogues. He felt he owed it to them because of their ancient heritage. A scattering accepted it but most did not and increasingly his mission was to the gentiles. Indeed the Jews soon became the greatest hindrance to Paul's work. In city after city they deeply resented the way he brought gentiles to accept a Christ they could not countenance themselves.

Strictly speaking 'Acts of the Apostles' is a misnomer as the book is mainly concerned with Peter and Paul. Even then there is no mention of Peter after the Council of Jerusalem and Acts needs to be merged with the epistles even to get an adequate picture of Paul's journeys. It does not attempt a balanced history of the early Church so much as highlighting some of the more important events. Nothing is said about the foundations of the churches in Galilee or Rome, nor does it shed any light on church procedures such as baptism.

Prologue (1:1–11)

Acts begins with a resume of the events leading up to Jesus' ascension. He taught the apostles for forty days and instructed them not to leave Jerusalem until they had received the Holy Spirit. They were not to concern themselves with when the kingdom would be restored to Israel but, once they had received the Spirit, to concentrate on proclaiming the Gospel to the ends of the earth.[1] With this He was lifted up into a cloud and ascended into heaven while two angels questioned the apostles' staring into the sky and revealed that when Jesus returned it would be in the same way.[2]

THE CHURCH IN JERUSALEM (1:12 – 8:3)

Judas is replaced by Matthias (1:12–26)

The apostles returned to Jerusalem where they were joined in prayer by Mary and Jesus' brothers.[3] Peter addressed a congregation of about a hundred and twenty to tell them of Judas' death and to elect Matthias in his place.[4]

Pentecost (2:1–13)

Pentecost found the apostles again gathered together. Suddenly, with a sound like a mighty wind and with tongues of fire resting on their heads, they were filled with the Holy Spirit.[5] They were given the power to speak different languages and the Jews and proselytes from many nations who were in Jerusalem at the time were astonished when they heard the apostles proclaiming the marvels of God in their own tongues.[6]
Appendix 1 refers

Jesus is Lord and Christ (2:14–36)

Peter took the opportunity of this polyglot audience to deliver a powerful address. These men were not drunk as some of them thought. What they had witnessed was the outpouring of the Holy Spirit and the beginning of the last days prophesied by Joel (2:14–21). Peter then turned to Jesus. That He came from God was clear from the miracles God performed through Him. Even when they had Him crucified it was not the end. God raised Him to life.

Peter then proceeded to show that Jesus was the promised Messiah, quoting Ps 16:8–11:

for you will not abandon me to Hades
or allow your holy one to see corruption.

The psalm was attributed to David but, with its hope of avoiding the corruption resulting from death, Peter continued, it obviously could not refer to David himself since everyone knew he was dead and where his tomb was. The only person it could refer to was that descendant of David's whom he knew (through Nathan) would one day succeed him on the throne, in other words the Christ or Messiah. It is His body that would not see corruption. But they had all just witnessed Jesus raised to life and saved from corruption. Hence Jesus is the Christ (2:22–33).

For good measure Peter next quoted from Ps 110:1

The Lord declares to my Lord,
take your seat at my right hand,

to give another demonstration that Jesus was the Christ. Since David, to whom the psalm is attributed, never went up to heaven himself to be at God's right hand, the only person it could refer to is, again, the Christ. But Jesus has just ascended into heaven. Therefore Jesus is the Christ[7] (2:34–36).

Appendix 2 refers

The first Christian church (2:37–47)

The people were conscience stricken. What were they to do? Peter assured them that if they repented and were baptised in the name of Jesus forgiveness and the gift of the Holy Spirit would follow. About three thousand came forward. They joined together in prayer and praise, attending the Temple and meeting in their homes for the breaking of bread.[8] They shared food and owned everything in common while the apostles worked many miracles. Day-by-day the Lord added to their number.

The healing of a cripple (3:1–26)

When Peter and John cured a cripple they used the occasion to explain to a crowd that the miracle was not due to their own power but to faith in the Jesus whom they had allowed to be crucified and whom God had raised from the dead. Now they must repent so that their sins could be expunged. Then God would send Christ and the time of restoration (the Second Coming). Moses and the whole prophetic tradition had predicted there would be this opportunity for conversion and warned of the dire consequences of ignoring it. They were all heirs of the covenant God made with Abraham to bring blessings to all nations.

Persecution and prayer (4:1–31)

Exasperated by all this talk of resurrection the religious authorities hauled the two apostles before the Sanhedrin. Filled with the Holy Spirit Peter spoke out fearlessly. It was the power of Jesus Christ that had healed the cripple, he exclaimed; the same Christ whom they had rejected and who was now the cornerstone of (God's plan of) salvation. The authorities were astonished at such boldness and could find no grounds for punishment, especially in the presence of the (now cured) cripple and with the people all praising God. Peter and John were dismissed with a warning and the whole community joined in prayer. As they prayed the house they were in rocked and they were filled with the Holy Spirit.
Appendix 3 refers

The early Christian community (4:32–37)

The community now numbered some five thousand. It was totally united. No one claimed private possessions and no one was ever in want. Everything was shared. Barnabas, a Cypriot, was one of many who sold land he owned and gave the money to the apostles.

Ananias and Sapphira (5:1–11)

Ananias and his wife Sapphira sold some property with the stated intent of giving the proceeds to the common fund. However they secretly retained some for themselves. When the enormity of their sin was made apparent to them both dropped dead. (Their sin was not failure to share, which was voluntary, but hypocrisy, trying to appear more generous than they really were, a lie to the Church and the Holy Spirit.)

Further healings and persecution (5:12–42)

The apostles worked many signs and miracles and the sick were laid in the streets in the hope that at least Peter's shadow might fall on them. More and more became believers and a second attempt by the authorities to curb them was no more successful than the first. When they were thrown into gaol an angel released them the same night, and when they were caught preaching in the Temple the next morning and again interrogated by the Sanhedrin Peter was uncompromising: obedience to God comes before obedience to men.

The Sanhedrin was minded to put them to death but Gamaliel, a Pharisee, urged restraint. If their enterprise was of human origin it would fail of its own accord. If it came from God they would be powerless against it whatever they did. His advice prevailed. The apostles were flogged and released to continue teaching the good news.

The Seven and Stephen (6:1–15)

Seven men were appointed to safeguard the interests of the Hellenist widows after they complained that they were being overlooked in the distribution of food from the common pool. This was done to prevent the Twelve being distracted from their ministry. Among the seven were Stephen and Philip. The community now included a number of priests.

Appendix 4 refers

Stephen began to perform miracles and became such a formidable debater that some of his fellow Hellenists, realising that he was more than they could handle, turned the people against him and had him arrested and brought before the Sanhedrin for blasphemy.[9]

Stephen's speech and martyrdom (7:1 – 8:3)

Stephen's polemic (it can scarcely be called a defence) began with a resumé of God's stewardship of Israel from Abraham to Moses, intended to show how the major events of divine revelation had occurred outside Palestine (7:1–34). He followed this by declaiming that the same Moses who was chosen by God to rescue His people from Egypt was later pushed aside and disowned (7:35–43). Then he attacked the Temple as the focus for worship comparing it unfavourably with the Tent that had served in the desert days (7:44–50). He was trying to draw a clear distinction between Judaism and Christianity by demonstrating how neither the land of Palestine nor the Temple need be seen as central to the new faith while at the same showing how the Jews had just re-enacted their ancestors' rejection of Moses.

In a withering crescendo he indicted his accusers with resisting the Holy Spirit, breaking the Law, murdering the prophets and finally Christ Himself. When Stephen described seeing a vision of Jesus at God's right hand he was hustled out of the city and stoned, his dying words of forgiveness echoing Christ's own.[10] His execution was approved and watched by a young man named Saul who joined in a persecution that scattered all except the apostles throughout Judaea and Samaria[11] (7:51 – 8:3).

Up to now, despite a gradual build up of opposition in the form of warnings, 4:17,21, murderous intent, 5:33, and floggings, 5:40, the Twelve had attended Temple services and carried on as devout Jews differentiated from others only in their belief in Jesus as the Messiah. Now a new note emerges. We are at a turning point with Christianity beginning its separation from the shackles of Judaism and entering a world where, as we shall shortly see from Paul's missions, Jews would prove to be its most implacable enemy.

THE EARLIEST MISSIONS (8:4 – 12:25)

The mission to Samaria (8:4–25)

Philip, one of the Seven who was forced to leave Jerusalem, went to a town in Samaria where he was singularly successful in evangelising the local population. When they heard of this Peter and John paid a visit during which the new converts, who had earlier been baptised, received the Holy Spirit. When Simon, a former magician, naïvely offered to pay for the power to impart the Holy Spirit, Peter gave him a stinging rebuke. Money cannot buy what is a gift from God.

Philip and the Ethiopian courtier (8:26–40)

The Spirit next led Philip to an Ethiopian eunuch whom he found sitting in his chariot puzzling over one of Isaiah's Servant passages and wondering whom it referred to. After he heard about Jesus the Ethiopian asked to be baptised and went on his way rejoicing while Philip continued up the coast to Caesarea proclaiming the good news as he went.

The conversion of Saul (9:1–43)

Saul meanwhile was *en route* to Damascus to stamp out the Way when suddenly he was blinded by a brilliant light and heard the voice of the risen Christ directing him on to the city. There a disciple named Ananias, to whom the Lord had appeared in a vision, told him that he was God's chosen instrument to bring His name 'before gentiles and kings and before the people of Israel'. At once his sight returned as if scales had fallen from his eyes. He was baptised and filled with the Holy Spirit.[12]

Saul lost no time in beginning to preach that Jesus was the Son of God both in Damascus and (according to Ga 1:17) in Arabia. However some time later (three years according to Ga 1:18) he fell foul of the local Jews and had to be smuggled out of the city by being lowered down the outer wall in a basket to escape a plot on his life. He returned to Jerusalem where Barnabas vouched for his sincerity to the not-unnaturally wary apostles. But his time there was short lived. He fell out with the Hellenists and for his own protection was sent back home to Tarsus (from where according to Ga 1:21 he preached in Syria and Cilicia).

There was now a lull during which, left in peace, the churches in Judaea, Galilee and Samaria continued to grow. Peter evangelised the coastal plain of Sharon. He cured a paralytic in Lydda and moved on to Jaffa where he lodged with a leather-tanner and restored to life a disciple named Tabitha.[13]

Peter baptises the first gentiles (10:1 – 11:18)

Cornelius, a God-fearing Roman centurion stationed in Caesarea had a vision telling him to send for Peter.[14] Next day Peter also had a vision telling him that all foods were fit to eat. By the time he arrived at Cornelius' house Peter had come to appreciate that the vision meant far more than the abrogation of the Jewish dietary laws distinguishing clean from unclean foods. It applied to social relationships in general. No one was profane or unclean. As a result he was no longer precluded from mixing with gentiles, and Cornelius' household in particular, as he would have been before.

Peter's sermon in Cornelius' house is the fullest summary of the Gospel in Acts. As he was speaking the Holy Spirit came down on the little congregation and they began speaking in strange tongues and praising God. Moved by this signal mark of God's favour Peter gave orders for them all to be baptised.[15]

Peter faced a critical audience from the elders in Jerusalem on his return. Their charge was a serious one for at the time it was believed that acceptance into the Christian Church and social fellowship with Jews were only available to gentiles who were willing to embrace Judaism by undergoing circumcision and observing the Law in its entirety. However once they learned that Peter had acted under divine guidance their concerns melted away and they all praised God for His grace to the gentiles. *Appendix 5 refers*

Founding of the church in Antioch (11:19–30)

The dispersion following Stephen's death carried the Gospel to the Jews as far afield as Phoenicia, Cyprus and Antioch. In Antioch there was also a mission to the gentiles. Barnabas, who was sent from Jerusalem to investigate, was overjoyed at what he found and sent for Saul to help him succour the infant church.[16] They worked together for a whole year before travelling to Jerusalem with money to help tide the mother church over a famine (during which visit Paul's meeting with Peter recorded at Ga 2:10 took place). It was at Antioch that believers first came to be called Christians.

The persecution of Herod (12:1–25)

Herod launched a new wave of persecution. James the brother of John was beheaded and Peter imprisoned in chains. Peter escaped with the help of an angel and after going to the house of John Mark, a Christian meeting place, to make sure James, the Lord's brother, and the others knew of his good fortune, he left for an undisclosed destination.[17]

Herod died. Barnabas and Saul returned to Antioch taking John Mark with them. *Appendix 6 refers*

PAUL'S FIRST MISSION: THE COUNCIL OF JERUSALEM (13:1 – 15:35)

Paul's first missionary journey (13:1 – 14:28)

Barnabas and Saul set out on what was to be the first of the latter's great missionary journeys taking John Mark to assist them. Making landfall at Salamis in Cyprus they trekked the length of the island to Paphos, proclaiming the Gospel to the Jews in their synagogues. When a Jewish magician tried to rubbish his teaching Paul struck him temporally blind. This so impressed the Roman proconsul that he became a believer himself[18] (13:1–12).

From Paphos they sailed to Perga in Asia Minor where John Mark returned to Jerusalem while Paul and Barnabas continued overland to Antioch in Pisidia. On the Sabbath Paul was invited to address the synagogue. His resumé of Israel's history, culminating in Jesus, clearly struck a chord and there were many converts from among the Jews and 'devout converts'.[19] The following Sabbath virtually the whole town turned up to hear him. This made the Jews jealous and they began contradicting everything he said. Paul's response was unequivocal. He had felt bound to proclaim the Gospel to the Jews first but since they rejected it he would now turn to the gentiles.

Many gentiles became believers. But the Jews stirred up more trouble and Paul and Barnabas were forced to leave[20] (13:13–51).

Their next stop was Iconium where they gained both Jew and gentile converts. But opposition from both camps, with the threat of stoning, meant that once again they were forced to beat a hasty retreat. They moved on to Lystra where Paul's healing of a crippled man led them to being taken for gods themselves. In his sermon Paul appealed to the evidence of God in nature and providence (14:1–18).

Jews from Antioch and Iconium now appeared and turned the people against them. Paul was stoned and left for dead but was sufficiently recovered the next day to accompany Barnabas to Derbe where they won more converts. Then they retraced their steps to Perga, encouraging the new disciples they had gained on their outward journey, and appointing elders.[21] From Perga they took ship back to Antioch (14:19–28).

The Council of Jerusalem (15:1–35)

Back in Antioch Paul was soon immersed in controversy over whether circumcision and keeping the Law were necessary for gentile converts. In view of their growing numbers this was a live issue and Paul and Barnabas were sent to Jerusalem as part of a delegation to thrash the matter out with the apostles and elders at a gathering now known as the Council of Jerusalem.

After much debate Peter pointed out that God did not distinguish between Jew and gentile. Both had been given the Holy Spirit and both were saved through faith in Christ. So why impose on gentiles a burden even they themselves could not sustain.[22]

After Barnabas and Paul had reported on their gentile ministry James began his summing up. He alluded to Peter's conversion of Cornelius and quoted Amos to show that a gentile mission was fully in accord with God's will. His verdict was that gentiles should merely be told to abstain from anything polluted by idols, from illicit marriages, from the meat of strangled animals and from blood. These scruples must be respected to avoid giving offence to devout Jews.[23] Nothing more.

Paul and Barnabas returned to Antioch accompanied by Silas and with a letter giving the Council's decision which was warmly received.

PAUL'S SECOND AND THIRD MISSIONS (15:36 – 20:38)

Paul's second missionary journey (15:36 – 18:23)

Some time later Paul and Barnabas disagreed over John Mark whom Paul felt had deserted them on their earlier mission. So when Paul set out again he chose Silas to accompany him while Barnabas took John Mark with him to Cyprus.

Paul's route took him through towns he had evangelised on his earlier journey. He passed on the findings of the Jerusalem council and at Lystra engaged Timothy, whom he had circumcised, as an additional travelling companion.[24] The Holy Spirit then guided him to Troas where, in a night vision, he was urged to cross into Europe and Macedonia.[25] At Philippi, the principal city, there being no synagogue, he preached beside the river and baptised a purple-dye trader named Lydia along with her household (15:36 – 16:15).

On another occasion Paul's exorcism of a slave fortune-teller so annoyed her masters, who could no longer make money out of her, that they had both Paul and Silas charged with proselytising.[26] They were flogged and imprisoned but released the next morning to Lydia's house after an eventful night in which an earthquake opened the prison gates. Paul's gaoler and his household were converted, and Paul received an abject apology from the authorities when he revealed his Roman citizenship[27] (16:16–40).

They next stopped at Thessalonica where they won over many gentiles but also a few Jews. Unfortunately other Jews incited a mob and they were forced to leave under cover of darkness for Beroea. Jason, with whom Paul had been staying, and some of the brothers were forced to put up bail against his returning.

In Beroea some Jews joined with the gentiles in becoming believers. However it was not long before troublemakers arrived from Thessalonica and Paul again had to be hustled out of town. This time his escort took him as far as Athens before returning with instructions for Silas and Timothy to join him as soon as possible (17:1–15).

Paul was appalled at Athens, a city given over to idolatry. In his preaching he took as his point of departure an inscription he had seen 'To An Unknown God'. That was the very God he had come to proclaim! Since this God created everything and was Lord of heaven and earth He did not live in man-made shrines nor need anything men could provide. On the contrary He was the provider, giving the earth for a dwelling place and the seasons to ensure sustenance, and it was in these manifestations of His goodness that He should be sought. We are His children so it is folly to think of Him in terms of gold or stone, Paul went on. God was prepared to overlook a past based on ignorance but now it is different. He is calling for repentance because a day is coming when everyone will be judged by a Man He has already appointed and who is vouched for by His having raised Him from the dead. Unfortunately this fine rhetoric made little impact. Any mention of resurrection was met with flippancy and scorn (17:16–34).

Paul next proceeded to Corinth where he lodged and worked with Aquila and his wife Priscilla, tentmakers like himself, who had recently been expelled from Rome. Soon Silas and Timothy rejoined him. Although the president of the synagogue and his household became believers the Jews were largely antagonistic and Paul again turned to the gentiles. With the Lord's encouragement in a vision he stayed in Corinth for eighteen months during which an attempt by the Jews to prosecute him for propagating a religion contrary to Roman law was contemptuously dismissed by the Roman proconsul Gallio.

When Paul eventually left Corinth it was to sail via Ephesus, which he promised to return to on a later occasion, to Caesarea. Then he went 'up to greet the church' (almost certainly Jerusalem) before continuing on to Antioch where, after a brief respite, he set out through Galatia on his third missionary journey (18:1–23).

Apollos (18:24–28)

Meanwhile when Aquila and Priscilla arrived in Ephesus, having accompanied Paul that far on his homeward journey, they found an Alexandrian Jew named Apollos preaching there. Although he was well versed in the Scriptures and knew about Jesus he was only aware of John's baptism. So they took him under their wing. Later he moved to Achaia where he became a tower of strength.[28]

Paul's third missionary journey (19:1 – 20:38)

When he reached Ephesus, having trekked overland, Paul found some believers who had only received John's baptism of repentance. So he baptised them in the name of Jesus whereupon the Holy Spirit came down on them and they began to speak with tongues and to prophesy.[29] Paul remained in Ephesus for over two years teaching the Way first to the Jews and then, after they had rejected it, to the gentiles.

So vibrant was Paul's ministry that even napkins and aprons that he had touched could cure the sick. However when a band of Jewish exorcists tried to cast out evil spirits in the name of 'Jesus whose spokesman is Paul' they were cruelly exposed. Seeing this some Christians who had themselves practised magic burned their manuals on a bonfire (19:1–20).

Towards the end of Paul's stay in Ephesus the peace was disturbed by a riot by the silversmiths in the town's great open-air theatre. Ostensibly it was sparked by concern for the prestige of the goddess Diana but behind it was the silversmiths' concern that if Christianity became too popular their lucrative business from the sale of silver images of Diana would be at risk.[30] Faced with a baying mob the town clerk restored order by pointing out that Paul and his friends had done no wrong and that anyone with a genuine grievance had recourse to the courts (19:23–40).

Paul now began his homeward journey. He had intended to travel via Macedonia and Achaia and thence onwards by sea but after three months in Greece, just as he was about to set sail for Syria, he got wind of a plot against him by the Jews. He therefore decided to return overland, via Macedonia to Troas, where he was joined by Luke and where he restored to life a young man who had been killed after falling from a window[31] (19:21–22; 20:1–12).

Paul continued overland to Assos and then boarded ship. :anding at Miletus he sent for the elders of the church at Ephesus to bid them farewell. He told them how he had devoted himself to the Gospel through thick and thin, to both Jew and gentile. Now, in captivity to the Spirit, he was on his way to Jerusalem to face persecution and imprisonment. They would see him no more. They must be vigilant for false teachers would prey on them, even from within their own ranks. Paul reminded the Ephesians that he had always provided for his own needs and those of his companions.[32] They too must help the weak for 'there is more happiness in giving than in receiving'[33] (20:13–38).

PAUL A PRISONER: THE JOURNEY TO ROME (21:1 – 28:31)

Paul in Jerusalem (21:1 – 23:35)

Paul made landfall at Tyre where he stayed with Philip. Ignoring warnings of danger he pressed on to Jerusalem where James and the brothers gave him a warm welcome and alerted him to a problem. Thousands of Jews had become Christians while remaining staunch upholders of the Law and they were troubled by rumours that during his recent missions Paul had charged Jews that this was no longer necessary. They suggested that the best solution was for Paul publicly to prove his dedication to the Law by sharing the purification ceremony of four men who had taken a vow and paying their expenses.[34]

Unfortunately some Jews who saw Paul in the Temple accused him not only of preaching against the Law but of taking gentiles into a part of the Temple restricted to Jews. A riot ensued and only prompt action by the Roman garrison prevented a mob lynching. Paul was arrested but given permission to address the crowd (21:1–40).

He reminded them how he was brought up a devout Jew and as a young man persecuted Christians with matchless zeal. He described his conversion and how God had chosen him to be His witness to the gentiles, a calling later confirmed by Christ in a vision in the Temple.[35] Up to this point Paul had been heard in rapt attention. But the word 'gentiles' set the spark to the tinder of the crowd's wrath and uproar broke out. The Roman authorities took him inside the fortress to scourge him in the hope of getting at the truth but had to desist when he revealed his Roman citizenship. Next day they brought him before the Sanhedrin where he cleverly played off the Pharisees, who believed in resurrection, against the Sadducees who did not. The proceedings ended in confusion and Paul was returned to the fortress for his safety. That night the Lord appeared to reassure him: just as he had borne witness in Jerusalem so now he must do the same in Rome.

After the Jews were found to be hatching a plot against Paul's life he was transferred to Caesarea, the seat of Felix the governor of Judaea (22:1 – 23:35).

Paul in Caesarea (24:1 – 26:32)

Five days later a delegation from the Sanhedrin arrived in Caesarea to present the case against Paul, essentially that he was a ringleader of the Nazarene sect and a troublemaker who had profaned the Temple. Paul refuted each charge admitting only that he was a follower of the Way. However that was in no way incompatible with being a strict Jew.

Felix adjourned the proceedings and kept Paul in custody while allowing him to have his friends attend to his needs. He apparently hoped that Paul might offer him money in return for his release and was reluctant to do anything that might antagonise the Jews. With his wife Drusilla he took advantage of Paul's presence to learn more about the Way. But when Paul began to talk about uprightness and judgement they wanted to hear no more. After two years Felix was succeeded by Porcius Festus (24:1–27).

One of Festus' first acts was to turn down the Jews' request to have Paul returned to Jerusalem for trial. (They planned to ambush him on the way.) Instead he arranged a hearing in Caesarea where the Jews made charges they could not substantiate and which Paul easily rebutted. Anxious to curry favour with the Jews, Festus then asked Paul if he would be willing to be tried before himself in Jerusalem. But Paul, knowing that he could easily be handed over to the Jews once he was back in Jerusalem, opted instead to exercise his right as a Roman citizen to be tried before Caesar[36] (25:1–12).

A little later King Agrippa arrived to pay his respects. When Festus outlined Paul's case Agrippa asked to see Paul himself. So the next day Paul was brought before the two of them to make his defence (25:13 – 26:1). Paul argued that he was on trial for proclaiming no more than the hereditary Jewish faith including resurrection. He had once persecuted Christians but then came Damascus and his missionary career. When he came to mention Christ's suffering and rising from the dead Festus expostulated that he was mad. Undeterred Paul intimated that Agrippa believed the prophets and must surely support him. Agrippa made light of Paul's remark but was obviously impressed. After retiring to confer Festus and Agrippa agreed that Paul was innocent and but for his appeal to Caesar could have been released (26:2–32).

On to Rome (27:1 – 28:31)

When Paul eventually set sail for Italy it was winter and progress was slow due to heavy seas. Off Malta his ship ran aground and began to break up but, as promised in an angelic vision, no lives were lost. Everyone got ashore either by swimming or drifting ashore on pieces of wreckage (27:1–44).

After wintering in Malta where Paul survived an encounter with a viper and was able to effect a number of cures, they set sail for Italy, disembarking at Puteoli where Paul spent a week with the Christian community before carrying on overland to Rome, the brothers hastening out (some forty miles) to greet him. Arriving in Rome Paul was allowed to stay in his own lodgings with a guard (28:1–16).

After three days Paul met with the Roman Jews to explain the circumstances of his arrest and to try to persuade them that Jesus was the fulfilment of their ancestral faith. Not for the first time some believed but the majority did not. Seeing this he quoted Is 6:9–10 on Israel's spiritual blindness before pointing out how, in stark contrast, the gentiles were responding. Israel's rebellion was complete.

A brief epilogue records that Paul spent two years in Rome in his own lodging proclaiming the Gospel without hindrance of any kind (28:17–31).
Appendix 7 refers

THE PAULINE EPISTLES

Paul

Paul's life

Paul, a member of the tribe of Benjamin, a Pharisee, Ph 3:5, and a Roman citizen, Ac 16:37, was born in Tarsus, Ac 9:11, a provincial capital in what is today south eastern Turkey. As a youth he was initiated into tentmaking, the craft from which he always insisted on earning his living even while actively preaching the Gospel. He studied the Scriptures and the Law at the feet of the famous rabbi Gamaliel, Ac 22:3 and, while still a young man, was deputed to harry Christians, a task he performed with burning zeal, Ac 8:3; 26:10.

He witnessed Stephen's martyrdom when it is hard to believe that the manner of Stephen's dying – with a prayer for his assassins on his lips – did not have a profound impact upon him, Ac 7:55 – 8:1. In any event it was not long afterwards, when on the road to Damascus and still in the midst of his persecuting frenzy, 'breathing threats to slaughter the Lord's disciples', that he encountered the risen Lord and was instantly transformed from the new faith's arch persecutor to its ardent apostle to the gentiles, Ac 9:1–19.

Paul spent three years preaching in Damascus and Arabia before the Jews hatched a plot to kill him, which he only evaded by being let down from Damascus' city walls in a basket. He fled to Jerusalem where Barnabas took him under his wing and vouched for him to the not unnaturally suspicious elders. However, after only about two weeks opposition from the Hellenist Jews forced him to flee again, this time back to his native Tarsus from where he ministered in Syria and Cilicia, Ac 9:20–30; Ga 1:15–24.

Some ten years later Paul was sought out by Barnabas to help foster the newly founded church at Antioch. The two worked together for a whole year before being sent to Jerusalem on a famine relief mission, Ac 11:22–30. There Paul met the church leaders and reached agreement that Peter's apostolate should concentrate on Palestine, while his own would be overseas, Ga 2:1–10.

Some time after returning to Antioch Paul set off on the first of his missionary journeys. He traversed Cyprus and southern Galatia preaching, as became his established pattern, first to the Jews in their synagogues and then, when they did not respond, to the gentiles.

It would seem that soon after returning home news reached Paul that a body of Jewish Christians were insisting that gentile converts must be circumcised and obey the Law if they were to be saved. This idea had already reached the Galatian churches he had recently founded as a result of which he hurriedly despatched the first of his epistles, GALATIANS, to remind his readers that salvation came only through faith in Christ. (There are differing views regarding the sequence of events in Paul's life, including when and where some of his letters, such as Galatians, were written. So although the chronology assumed here commands wide support the reader should always be aware that others are possible).

But the dispute was too fundamental to be left there. Unresolved it would have relegated Christianity to a branch of Judaism and denied the centrality of Christ. The matter was settled at a special council held in Jerusalem where it was ruled that gentiles need not be circumcised and observe the Law but merely refrain from illicit marriages and certain dietary practices out of respect for the feelings of Jews in mixed communities.

Paul returned to Antioch to embark on his second missionary tour. He revisited southern Galatia and then, guided by the Holy Spirit, moved on to Philippi, Thessalonica and Beroea in Macedonia before proceeding down to Athens and Corinth from where, after a stay of some eighteen months during which time he wrote 1 and 2 THESSALONIANS, he set sail back to Palestine, making a brief stopover at Ephesus on the way.

After only the briefest of respites Paul then set out on his third missionary journey, making his way overland to Ephesus where, despite opposition from the Jews and devotees of Diana, the city's patron goddess, he soon gained many followers. It was here that 1 CORINTHIANS was composed.

Paul remained in Ephesus for over two years and then left for Macedonia (where he dictated 2 CORINTHIANS) en route for Greece where it seems he visited Corinth again and wrote ROMANS. He then retraced his steps to Miletus, a port near Ephesus, where he bade farewell to the elders of the church there. Setting sail he disembarked at Caesarea whence, disregarding warnings, he went up to Jerusalem bearing a collection for the poor that had long been dear to his heart. There some Jews from Asia accused him of denigrating the Law and in the riot that followed he was only saved by the timely intervention of the Roman garrison.

He was arrested and transferred for his own safety to Caesarea where Felix, the Roman governor, held him in custody for two years. When Festus, Felix's successor, hoping to curry favour with the Jews, suggested that Paul should stand trial before him in Jerusalem, Paul, wary of the probable outcome of any such 'trial', appealed to Caesar. He was taken to Rome and spent the next two years under house arrest during which time he probably penned EPHESIANS, PHILIPPIANS, COLOSSIANS and PHILEMON. At this point the account of Paul's life in Acts comes to an abrupt end.

Tradition however does not. According to non-canonical sources Paul was released for lack of evidence and carried the Gospel into Spain. Also, if the epistles 1 and 2 TIMOTHY and TITUS are from Paul's hand, they would also date from this time and imply that he undertook a fourth mission that embraced Crete and led to his revisiting Asia Minor, Greece and Macedonia before ending his days once again in Rome with death not far away. Tradition has it that he was beheaded a few miles outside the walls of Rome and that friends buried him in a cemetery near the city.

Paul's character

Paul was fervently dedicated. Whether persecuting the Church or preaching Christ he pursued his ideal with matchless courage and perseverance and with no regard to cost or his own discomfort. Indeed he welcomed sharing his Master's suffering. Only God and preaching Christ as Saviour mattered. While his unique pioneering role made him ambitious, it was only for Christ, never for himself, and he was never arrogant. He always attributed whatever he achieved to God working through him. Though he could be fiercely outspoken with those he disagreed with, or who for whatever reason stood in his way – stubborn Jews, rabid Judaizers, jealous detractors – he was by nature sensitive, tender, fatherly and protective.

Paul's style

As a writer Paul displays great power and vitality. He thought fast and emotionally and usually dictated his letters, hence a tendency to a superfluity of words and a literary style that, in the absence of revision, can sometimes be convoluted if not near impenetrable. His writing is full of asides, digressions, afterthoughts and not always transparent metaphors. The argument can disconcertingly jump abruptly from one topic to another. He is steeped in the Scriptures but his liking for arguments and allegories based on Old Testament quotations that are not always in context, and which he sometimes arbitrarily links together, is not one that the modern mind can easily adjust to. (His opponents would have used similar methods and so he was doing no more than turning their own style of exegesis against them.)

Our problems in getting to the heart of what Paul meant are compounded by the fact that he wrote his epistles to address specific issues arising out of the life of particular churches. Often we not only have to infer what those issues were but also have to try to recover the earlier oral teaching that Paul had given his readers and which he takes for granted in his letters without more ado. Quite often therefore we are in no better position than that of an intruder eavesdropping on a conversation between teacher and pupil.

Paul and belief

Although ROMANS comes close at times, Paul nowhere gives a systematic exposé of his theology. However he frequently draws wider implications from particular issues so that his letters have a depth and generality beyond their immediate occasion and all the key tenets of the faith are there.

Paul had a lofty conception of God without ever seeing Him as remote. He is near in Christ. He was deeply aware of God's demand that His creatures be holy as He is and of His boundless love. Hence His initiative to save us, an initiative that was His alone, an act of grace and unmerited favour springing from that love.

We owe our redemption entirely to Christ who died for our sins to give us life. We can no more earn salvation by our own efforts than we can square the circle. Only by faith appropriating the fruits of Christ's death to our own situation can we ensure our own salvation. Faith in this context means letting Christ take charge of our lives so that our old sinful selves are killed-off and we gradually grow in His likeness. Delivered by Christ from the power of sin (for all men are sinners) we are then reconciled with God to become children of God.

Paul affirms Christ's pre-existence. He is Head of all creation. He marvels at Christ's heavenly glory and His condescension in the voluntary act of humiliation that was the Incarnation. He is at once son of David and Son of God. Paul is in no doubt of Christ's divinity and equality with the Father and gives Jesus the title, Lord, that the Old Testament reserved for God alone.

He preaches the Trinity even if he does not declaim it explicitly. It is the Holy Spirit implanted in us through whom God reveals Himself, who pours God's love into our hearts, who witnesses to our destiny as children of God, who endows us with many gifts and who leads us to sanctification. Our bodies are temples of the Spirit, His outpourings a well of hope. Father, Son and Holy Spirit are one: Creator, Redeemer and Sanctifier.

The epistles are full of practical advice for godly living, charity and brotherly love, for practising self-denial and leading peaceful, orderly, disciplined lives in which idleness and moral laxity find no home. Faith cannot be confined to the shadow of the Temple. The follower of Christ must promote justice in every corner of life and society. It is in Paul that Christian altruism finds its noblest expression.

To Paul the faithful constitute one body with Christ as its Head. So he deplored divisions and abhorred enmities. Love is supreme, greater than faith and hope. The resurrection is the one fact on which all else hinges. He yearns impatiently for the end of history, Christ's return and the conversion of Israel. To the great apostle there was but one Master, Christ; one Gospel, the Cross; one Wisdom, Christ. He longed to be with Christ and his love for Him inflames, even now down the ages.

CHRONOLOGY

The sequence of events assumed in this book is approximately as follows:

A.D. 30   Ascension of Jesus
       30   Pentecost
       34   Stephen martyred, Paul converted
       34–37 Paul in Damascus and Arabia
       37   Paul flees Damascus and makes his first visit to Jerusalem
       37–47 Paul in Tarsus, Syria and Cilicia
       ?   Peter in Samaria; the conversion of Cornelius
       47   Paul's second visit to Jerusalem (with Barnabas) where he agrees his
              mission with the Church leaders
       47–49 Paul's first missionary journey
       49   Council of Jerusalem
       49–52 Paul's second missionary journey
       53–58 Paul's third missionary journey

58–60 Paul imprisoned in Caesarea
61–63 Paul imprisoned in Rome
63–67 Set free, Paul makes further missionary journeys?
67   Paul is martyred in Rome?

Romans

The epistle to the Romans was written from Corinth towards the end of Paul's third missionary journey. It is the first great work of Christian theology, a towering treatise, the most doctrinal of all Paul's epistles, dealing not with special problems in the style of most of his other works but with universal truths that are foundational to the Christian faith and essential to an appreciation of the Christian life.

It has been suggested that Paul wrote Romans so as to leave for posterity a definitive account of his teaching. But for all the nobility and depth of its themes it is not a complete exposé of his credo. It is more likely that he wrote it to introduce himself to the Roman church prior to his planned visit there in the hope of forestalling any misunderstandings over his cardinal beliefs.

Romans is in three parts. It begins with, and is dominated by, the great theme of salvation by faith. Then it wrestles with the problem of Israel's tardy response to the Gospel before concluding with counsel to guide Christians in their daily lives. As the exposé of salvation by faith is closely argued we begin by summarising its main threads.

Salvation through faith: the main concepts

Everyone needs salvation because everyone is a sinner. Fortunately God has provided the answer. He promises salvation to all, Jews and gentiles alike, through faith in Christ. This is an act of pure grace on His part, i.e. a gift, unmerited and unearned, completely free, made possible by Christ's sacrificial death on the Cross.[1]

As soon as we commit to Christ we are justified, acquitted of past sins and given a fresh start. The slate is wiped clean. The righteousness man could never achieve himself is credited to him though faith in Christ. But although justification declares us righteous it does not make us righteous. It is only the first step on the road to salvation.

For though we are revitalised the urge to sin remains and must be fought every day. But now we are no longer alone. For just as Jesus died for our sins, so now the risen Lord empowers us with the Holy Spirit to help us fight the ungodly desires that would otherwise result in death. Gradually we grow in holiness and likeness to Christ, a process of sanctification that reaches completion only when we are raised from the dead as Jesus was raised to receive glorification as children of God and the blessedness of perfect existence. Thus salvation follows justification and sanctification in this life and results in glorification in the next.

Paul is at pains to stress that salvation cannot be earned (as the Jews believed) by obeying the Law. No one can make himself innocent in God's eyes through keeping the Law. For although the Law makes us aware of what sin is, it does not give us the inward strength to obey it. We are powerless to save ourselves from the tyranny of sin and death. Only Christ and living a new life in the Spirit can do that.

INTRODUCTION (1:1–15)

Paul introduces himself as an apostle called by Jesus Himself to preach the Gospel promised by God through the prophets. The Gospel concerns One who in human terms was a descendant of David but who by His resurrection was shown to be Son of God. He hopes that he will soon be able to visit Rome in person.[2]

MAIN THEME: SALVATION THROUGH FAITH (1:16–17)

Paul states the letter's main theme. It is about God's saving justice: the way He offers salvation to all who have faith, Jews and Greeks alike.[3]

HUMANITY'S PLIGHT: THE NEED FOR SALVATION (1:18 – 3:20)

The default of the pagan world (1:18–32)

Before developing his theme Paul pauses to explain why it is necessary for God to act. He begins with pagans. They incur God's wrath for closing their minds to the truth. God's existence is clear from Creation yet they refuse to honour Him. They think they are wise but by worshipping dumb idols they show how stupid they are. So God has abandoned them to their abominations and rottenness.[4] They know they are in the wrong and deserve to die 'yet not only do they persist in their folly but encourage others to do the same'.

The default of the Jews (2:1 – 3:8)

Paul next addresses an imaginary Jew. By berating others he condemns himself for he commits the very same sins. He should not misinterpret God's patience. It is intended to encourage repentance so by refusing to repent he is storing up trouble for himself on the Day.[5] God is impartial and rewards everyone according to their just deserts: eternal life for the good but for evil-doers retribution.

It is not people who have heard the Law whom God justifies but any who have kept it. Gentiles who do not have the Law will be judged according to the natural Law written in their hearts and voiced in their consciences. When a Jew transgresses the Law he so proudly boasts of he brings God's name into contempt. His circumcision counts for nothing unless he keeps the Law. Indeed an uncircumcised man who kept the Law would be better off than a Jew who broke it.[6] True circumcision is not external but in the heart and of the spirit (2:1 – 29).

Is there any advantage then in being a Jew? Yes! It was to the Jews that God entrusted His revelation. If some Jews are unfaithful will God still be honour His promises? Yes, God will always be true. Is it fair for someone to be punished if his iniquity highlights God's righteousness? What a question! You might as well suggest promoting evil that good might come of it, a maxim Paul says he has already been slanderously accused of (3:1–8).

No one is righteous (3:9–20)

Everyone is in the grip of sin. No one is innocent in God's eyes through keeping the Law. All the Law does is tell us what sin is, what is right and what is wrong.

JUSTIFICATION: THE IMPUTATION OF RIGHTEOUSNESS (3:21 – 4:25)

Justification is by faith (3:21–31)

Paul now embarks on his main theme. God's plan for salvation was foreshadowed in the Old Testament and depends upon faith in Christ. It has nothing to do with keeping the Law and applies to both Jews and gentiles. All have sinned but all can be justified by the free gift of God's grace, made possible by Christ sacrificing Himself on the Cross to reconcile us to Him. All this demonstrates God's justness both in respect of the past when He held His hand over sins that were committed and now.[7] No one can boast since we are justified solely by faith and not by obeying the Law.[8] So was the Law pointless? No! We are placing it on its true footing.[9]

Abraham was justified by faith (4:1–25)

Justification by faith is grounded in the Old Testament: 'Abraham put his faith in God and this was reckoned to him as uprightness', Gn 15:6. Moreover this happened when Abraham was uncircumcised. So justification by faith is open to all whether circumcised or not. God's promise to Abraham (of blessings for all nations) would have been worthless had it been based on the Law since no one can avoid breaking it. Instead the promise was a free gift dependent on faith and so is assured for all of Abraham's descendants who share that faith.

The supreme example of Abraham's faith was his belief that God would produce life (Isaac) from his and Sarah's virtually dead (aged) bodies. Our faith will similarly be reckoned to us for justification if we believe in He who raised Jesus from the dead.

FROM JUSTIFICATION TO SALVATION (5:1 – 8:39)

Faith opens the door to salvation (5:1–11)

Justified by faith we have a new standing before God. We are at peace with Him. We are admitted into His favour and can exult in the hope of sharing His glory. We can even rejoice in hardship because hardship develops character, perseverance and hope, a hope that we can depend upon since God has poured His love into our hearts through the Holy Spirit we have now been given[10] (5:1–5). The proof of that unfathomable love is that Christ died to reconcile us with God while we were still sinners. Given that, how much more so, now that we are justified by His death, can we be sure that (the risen) Christ will save us by His life[11] (5:6–11).

Christ brings life as Adam brought death (5:12–21)

Paul now uses Adam, representing the old fallen humanity, as a foil to exult in the renewal that God has wrought in Christ, head of the new reborn humanity. As sin and death came into the world through the disobedience of one man (Adam), so the free gift of justification and life comes to humanity through the obedience of one man, Christ. Not that there is any comparison between the two when one takes account of the number of people and the many offences the free gift atones for. Moreover however much sin increased after the Law was given God's grace (the key to eternal life) was always more than sufficient.[12]

New life in union with the risen Christ (6:1–11)

Paul now defends the idea of justification by faith against a possible misconception. If we are living under grace, God's undeserved but freely given favour, why should we not go on sinning to give the divine grace all the more opportunities to display itself? He uses the analogy of baptism, the initiation ceremony into the Christian Church, to show how absurd such a notion is. For when we go under the water our old sinful unregenerate selves are crucified with Christ and share in His death. Equally when we rise out of the water we are united with Christ in his resurrection and reborn to new life. Where before we were dead to God and slaves of sin, afterwards we are new people alive in Christ.[13]

The choice: sin or uprightness (6:12–23)

That being so Christians must not allow themselves to succumb to sin's enticements any more but surrender to God. Then sin will no longer have any power over them and they will become beacons of uprightness. But let there be no misunderstanding. The fact that they are living under grace rather than the prohibitions of the Law is no licence to sin. On the contrary they have a clear choice: either to be slaves of sin, leading to shame and death, or slaves of uprightness leading to sanctification and eternal life.

Freedom from slavery to Law (7:1–6)

Paul employs a marriage analogy to show that Christians are no longer bound by the Law. Effectively what he is saying is that dying with Christ in baptism ends the (Jewish) Christian's former 'marriage' to the Law and frees him to 'marry' the risen

Lord. Previously, sinful cravings aroused by the Law made us fit only for death. Now we are released from lives spent observing the Law and a catalogue of rules to lead lives nurtured by the Spirit. The focus of our lives has moved from Law to Christ.

The role of the Law (7:7–13)

Does this mean that the Law is sinful? No! What the Law does is show us what sin is. True, it also stimulates our desire to sin thereby setting us on the road to death, but that is sin's doing not the Law's. The Law itself is good and holy.

Man's struggle against his natural inclinations (7:14–25)

Paul paints a harrowing picture of the conflict that results when people try to overcome sin by themselves. It cannot be done. The battle between obeying the Law and yielding to sin issues in despair and defeat. Human nature is simply not up to it. Only Christ can defeat sin.

Life in the Spirit (8:1–17, 26–27)

Living in Christ we need no longer fear condemnation because the Spirit which gives us life frees us from the tyranny of sin and death.[14] What the Law could not do because of the weakness of human nature God did by sending his son as a sacrifice for sin (8:1–4).

Those who follow their natural inclinations are opposed to God and can never be pleasing to Him. They do not, indeed cannot, observe God's precepts and have nothing to look forward to but death while those who live by the indwelling Spirit are promised life and peace. People who do not have the Spirit do not belong to Christ. But with Christ in them, though their bodies die because of sin, He who raised Jesus from the dead will also raise their mortal bodies through His Spirit living in them[15] (8:5–13).

All who are guided by the Spirit are not slaves in fear of God but sons of God, entitled to call Him 'Abba, Father'. And if children, heirs of God, fellow heirs with Christ, sharing His glory provided they share His suffering. The Spirit also helps us to pray with prayers that are in accord with the mind of God (8:14–17; 26–27).

The glory to come (8:18–25, 28–39)

Present sufferings are nothing compared with the glory to come. All creation is eagerly waiting for God's children to be revealed. And just as we are waiting in hope for our bodies to be set free, so too all creation is groaning as in labour pains as it waits to be transformed from decay into the same glorious freedom as God's children.[16]

God works for the good of those who love him. He decided beforehand those who were to be moulded like his Son. Having called them He justifies them and having justified them He will glorify them. The chapter ends with a paean of praise for God's love. With God on our side who can be against us? Nothing can separate us from God's love.
Appendix 1 refers

THE PROBLEM OF ISRAEL (9:1 – 11:36)

God has not failed in his promises to Israel (9:1–13)

Paul agonises over his fellow Jews' recalcitrance but denies any suggestion that God has reneged on His promises. The singling out of Isaac and Jacob from the rest of Abraham's descendants to propagate the covenant promises means that it is God's choice rather than physical descent that determines the true Israel. The fact that Jacob was preferred to Esau before they were even born strengthens the argument because it rules out any question of character or achievement influencing the choice.[17]

God's sovereign will (9:14–24)

Does this mean that God is unjust? Paul rules such a question out of court. God is sovereign and free to act as He sees fit. The pot has no right to question the potter. Paul must have realised that just saying this was not very helpful for, in a passage that is difficult to interpret, he seems to go on to suggest that God has directed everything for the glory of His people, gentiles as well as Jews, and destruction only comes to those who spurn every opportunity to repent.

Israel has only herself to blame (9:25 – 10:21)

Paul quotes Scripture to show how the gentile's warm response, compared with Israel's, was prophesied long ago, a situation for which Israel has only herself to blame.[18] She has tried to win God's favour by keeping the Law whereas the gentiles have relied on faith. Paul next invokes texts originally used by Moses in connection with the Law to show Israel that salvation does not involve 'scaling the heights or plumbing the depths' but is easy and open to all. Christ has already done the hard work by coming down from heaven and being raised from the dead. All people have to do to be saved is to believe that and accept Him as Lord. So Israel has no excuse. She was given the good news and cannot pretend that she did not hear it or understand it.

Israel's rejection is only temporary (11:1–36)

Paul rejects any idea that God has totally forsaken Israel. He, himself a Jew, is a Christian. There is a faithful remnant just as there was in Elijah's time. But apart from those who were chosen Israel's heart is hardened. So is this the end for her? No! Her loss is the gentile's gain and will stir her to envy. Imagine the joy when she does respond: it will be like life from the dead (11:1–15).

Paul next uses the metaphor of a (gentile) wild olive grafted on to a cultivated (Jewish) olive tree with deep roots but with some of its branches broken off (unbelieving Jews) to warn the gentiles against feelings of pride. They must never forget that it is Jewish roots that sustain them and remember God's severity. He did not spare His own people and they will suffer the same fate if they do not persevere. And if Israel does repent, how easy it will be to graft the natural branches back on again (11:16–24).

Now for a mystery. Part of Israel has its mind hardened but this will only be until

the gentile conversion is complete. Then all Israel will be saved. God still loves her. Just as the gentiles were disobedient in the past but have now been shown mercy, so it will be with Israel. God has made all humankind disobedient only to show mercy to all.[19] The chapter ends with a hymn to God's wisdom (11:25–36).
Appendix 2 refers

CHRISTIAN LIVING (12:1 – 15:13)

Personal and political ethics (12:1 – 13:14)

Paul urges his readers to dedicate themselves not to the world but to God. They must eschew self-importance and take a measured view of themselves. As our bodies have their various organs, each with their own jobs to do, so we all form one body in Christ, each with our own roles to perform according to the gifts God has given us (12:1–8).

In a list of moral precepts Paul commends generosity, conscientiousness, genuineness, sincerity, unpretentiousness, virtue, brotherly love, humility, enthusiasm, perseverance, prayer, charity, sharing joys and sorrows, overcoming evil with good (12:9–21).

Everyone should obey the civil authorities. Their authority comes from God and there is nothing to fear if one is honest. Apart from the penal consequences it is also a matter of conscience and for the same reason it is right to pay taxes. The only debt anyone should owe is love, for love is the fulfilment of the Law. Let there be no indecency or licentiousness. Christ must be the role model (13:1–14).

Consideration for the weak in faith (14:1 – 15:13)

Welcome brethren of weaker faith but do not get into arguments over doubtful points like what food to eat and observing holy days, Paul continues. Be tolerant because it is not for us to judge but God to whom we are accountable for our convictions. No food is unclean but if what you eat upsets your brother then abstain out of consideration for him. Never put obstacles in your brother's path for if anyone eats with a troubled conscience he is condemned at once. Serving God is so much more important than eating and drinking. It is about peace and the joys of the Holy Spirit. So do not sow dissension over things like food[20] (14:1–23). The strong in faith should have regard for the weak and not just please themselves. Each of us must consider his neighbour's good so that we accept and support one another as Christ accepted us (15:1–13).

EPILOGUE (15:14 – 16:27)

With consummate tact Paul opens his closing address by telling the Christians in Rome that his intention is merely to refresh their memories. He bases his authority on the success of his apostleship to the gentiles. With Christ working in him he has set up new missions from Jerusalem to Illyria, all in places where the Gospel had never been preached before.[21] After returning to Jerusalem with a contribution for the poor from the faithful in Macedonia and Achaia he plans to visit Rome en route to Spain. Aware of the danger he will face in Jerusalem he appeals for their prayers (15:14–33).

Among the many people in Rome to whom Paul sent greetings we may single out Phoebe, whom it is believed was the bearer of the letter, and Prisca and Aquila, the married couple with whom he had earlier lodged in Corinth, Ac 18:1–3. The epistle ends with an admonition against false teachers, greetings from Timothy and Gaius his scribe, and a doxology (16:1–27).

1 Corinthians

1 Corinthians was written towards the end of Paul's stay in Ephesus on his third missionary journey. It appears that visitors from Corinth had told him of problems in the church he had only recently founded there. Then, while he was digesting that news, a letter arrived from the Corinthians themselves seeking guidance on various matters. 1 Corinthians is Paul's response. He begins by addressing the problems that were brought to his notice:

- divisions in the Church
- a case of incest
- court cases between fellow Christians
- sexual immorality (1:1–6:20)

And then takes up issues raised in the Corinthians' letter

- on marriage and celibacy
- on eating food that had been offered to idols
- on decorum in worship (7:1 – 11:34)

The letter ends in a stirring crescendo as his thoughts turn to the spiritual gifts, the Body of Christ, love and resurrection. (12:1 – 16:24)

Factions in the Church: God's wisdom and man's (1:1 – 4:21)

After greetings and thanksgiving Paul opens with an appeal for unity. He had heard from Chloe's people that various factions had formed.[1] People were saying that they belonged to Paul or Apollos or Cephas or to Christ Himself.[2] At least, Paul observes, no one could excuse him of trying to found a sect. He had only baptised one family in Corinth (1:1–16).

Paul contrasts human wisdom, which demands signs and proofs and looks to experts and intellectual debate, with the wisdom of a God which, to those who are on the way to ruin, looks like foolishness. The foolishness of the Cross, a foolishness which seems to run contrary to human experience but which, if they did but accept it, would be their salvation. The riddle of God's ways was before their very eyes. How many of them were wise or influential by human norms? No, God works through the weak and lowly to show that He alone, rather than human endeavour, is responsible for our new life in Christ (1:17–31).

In his preaching in Corinth Paul had relied not on flights of oratory or persuasive argument but on the fact of the crucified Christ and the power of the Spirit so that their faith might be based not on human wisdom but on the power of God. It was not that he discounted wisdom. Rather that Christian wisdom was beyond this world, something mysteriously conveyed through the Spirit of a God who had prepared for man's glory even before the world began. The man who has no time for the Spirit is unable to recognise spiritual things. They look to him like folly. The man who is led by the Spirit on the other hand sees with the mind of Christ while remaining an enigma to others[3] (2:1–16).

The Corinthians' jealousies and rivalries show they are spiritual babes. Paul and Apollos are mere servants, gardeners who planted new growth. But the growth itself is God's work alone and the Church has only one foundation, Christ. When the Day (of judgement) comes every teacher's work will be shown for what it is although even those whose work does not stand the test of time will still be saved.[4] But be warned. The Church is God's Temple and anyone who attempts to pull it down will himself be destroyed. Rather than clinging to any one teacher they should remember that all teachers are God's servants; servants who have been entrusted with the divine mysteries to bring men to God (3:1 – 4:5).

Paul asks why his readers adopt such superior airs when they owe everything to God. There they are, acting as if they were already in the Kingdom without any help, while the apostles are beaten up and treated like tramps. He was saying this not to shame them but to get them to take himself as their role model. That is why he was sending Timothy to remind them of his teaching. He hoped to visit Corinth himself before long and then he would find out whether the arrogant people who were throwing their weight about were all talk or really had any power.[5] Will it be the rod of discipline he has to wield when he comes or the spirit of gentleness? (4:6–21).

Incest in Corinth (5:1–13)

Paul turns to the case of a man living with his stepmother. He must be expelled from the community in the hope that the experience would bring him to his senses. The old yeast of corruption must be cast out lest it taint the fresh dough of the whole community. Paul now corrects a misunderstanding from an earlier letter.[6] When he told them to cease fellowship with people living immoral lives he meant fellow Christians not pagans. Pagans are for God to judge.

On litigation (6:1–11)

Paul chides the Corinthians for using pagan courts to settle petty matters they should as Christians be able to resolve themselves. Better still, why not simply suffer the wrong?

On sexual immorality (6:12–20)

No evil doer will inherit the Kingdom of God but sexual immorality is especially grave since our bodies are members of Christ's Body and the temple of the Holy Spirit. They have been bought at a price and should therefore be treated with reverence for the glory of God.[7]

On marriage and celibacy (7:1–40)

Paul now turns to the questions raised by the Corinthians in their letter beginning with marriage and celibacy.[8] He would like everyone to remain celibate as he was but if they could not control their desires then they should marry. Married couples should not withhold sexual relations save by mutual consent and then only for limited periods for prayer. Divorce is forbidden even for those married to unbelievers (7:1–11).

So far he has given the Lord's rulings. What follow are his own personal judgements. If the non-Christian partner in a mixed marriage wishes they may separate. But it would be better to stay together. The believer might convert the other to Christ. Normally a Christian should stay in the station in life he was in when he was called, whether circumcised or not, slave or freeman. But none of these things is of any consequence compared with the obligation to keep God's commandments (7:12–24).

It is not a sin if a virgin gets married. What is important, since time is short, is for people not to get so engrossed in the cares of married life, or any other distractions for that matter, that they leave too little time for God.[9] If a man feels strongly about marrying his fiancé then he should do so. But if he decides to remain single that is better still. Finally Paul makes the point that a wife is free to remarry if her husband predeceases her. But it must be to a Christian and again she would be better off remaining single (7:25–40).

Food offered to false gods (8:1–13)

Paul now considers whether Christians were free to eat food that had earlier been offered to pagan gods. (The custom was that only part of such food was given to the idols or their priests. The remainder was either eaten at a sacred banquet or sold in the market). He begins by emphasising that the gods in question simply do not exist and in any case eating food cannot affect our standing with God one way or the other. But the real point is that if the sight of a mature Christian eating such food were to lead astray a fellow believer, whose conscience was uneasy about it, that would clearly be wrong because it would be starting him on the road to spiritual disaster. Liberty must recognise self-denial and be tempered by love and regard for others.

Paul's own example (9:1–27)

This reference to self-denial leads Paul to cite his own lifestyle as an example. He has never exercised his right as an apostle to be accompanied by a wife or to be provided by the Church with sustenance. He has endured privations galore for the sake of the Gospel.

Nor is he seeking to avail himself of any rights now, adding with a touch of humour that he would rather die than give up his one ground for boasting! The truth is that preaching the Gospel is not a matter of choice. He is impelled to it and is prepared to become all things to all men if that is what it takes to win souls for Christ.[10] Like an athlete training for the victor's crown he is straining every sinew to make sure that, having proclaimed the good news to others, he is not denied a heavenly prize himself.

Lessons from Israel's past (10:1–13)

To show that the possibility of failure was very real Paul cites Israel's past. Although their ancestors were miraculously sustained by spiritual food and drink (the manna and water from the rock) they perished nonetheless for they were guilty of idolatry and immorality. So no one should ever presume that he is in good standing with God but always be alive to the possibility that he might fail. All the same God never tests a man beyond his strength.

No compromise with pagan rites (10:14–22)

The thought of Israel's idolatry brings a condemnation of participation in pagan worship. For just as joining in the Eucharist means sharing in the Body and Blood of Christ, so joining in pagan rites is tantamount to communing with demons.

More on food (10:23 – 11:1)

Paul adds a footnote to his earlier teaching on food. There is no need when shopping at the butcher's or when invited out to a meal to enquire where the meat came from. Only if a fellow believer raises a point of conscience should one refrain from eating it.

Decorum in worship: women and the veil (11:2–16)

The reasoning Paul employs to rule that men should pray with their heads uncovered but that women should be veiled is obscure. It was probably given to prevent squabbling over the different traditions that Jews, Romans and Greeks would have brought to the Church.

Decorum in worship: the Lord's supper (11:17–34)

It appears that celebration of the Eucharist at Corinth was preceded by a communal meal as at the Last Supper and that word had reached Paul that, far from this being a fraternal gathering, cliques had developed. Some people ate excessively while others went hungry. Some even got drunk. This was quite unacceptable, Paul warned. Commemorating the Lord's death must be approached with reverence and only after rigorous self examination.[11] As for the preliminary meal they should exercise restraint and eat together. Anyone who was really hungry should first eat at home.

Spiritual gifts (12:1–30)

The Spirit gives people different gifts to enable them to serve the Lord, among them wisdom; knowledge; faith; healing; working miracles; prophecy; the ability to distinguish good and evil spirits; the gift of tongues; the ability to interpret speaking in tongues. And just as the human body has many organs each with their own special roles, so too Christians form one Body in Christ, each with their own complementary and vital parts to play. Furthermore just as the weaker parts of our bodies are the most indispensable, and the least comely receive the most attention, so too God has fashioned the Body of Christ to give greater recognition to its more humble and inconspicuous members so that everyone will feel involved and readily join in its joys and sorrows. Paul concludes with lists of Church offices and spiritual gifts to drive home the church's diversity and how its members all depend on one another.[12]

A hymn to love (12:31 – 13:13)

Paul's ineffably beautiful hymn to love needs little comment.

> Love is always patient and kind; love is never jealous; love is not boastful or conceited, it is never rude and never seeks its own advantage, it does not take offence or store up grievances. Love does not rejoice at wrongdoing, but finds its joy in the truth. It is always ready to make allowances, to trust, to hope and to endure whatever comes.

Without love we are nothing. Prophecy and tongues will disappear, Paul goes on.[13] Knowledge will be superseded by fuller understanding. Imperfection will give way to light and we shall see not dimly as now as reflections in a mirror but face to face. But faith, hope and love will remain and the greatest of these is love.

The gift of tongues and orderly worship (14:1–40)

Although speaking in tongues is a spiritual gift it is less important than prophecy.[14] For whereas prophecy edifies the whole community, speaking in tongues is unintelligible and benefits only the speaker. So anyone who speaks in tongues should pray to be given the gift of interpretation too. There is another point. If the whole congregation spoke in tongues an unbeliever would think they were raving whereas prophecy could lead to his conversion (14:1–25).
Appendix 1 refers

Assemblies should be aimed at building the community. So speaking in tongues should be confined to three people at the most at any one gathering, speaking one at a time with one of them interpreting. Anyone may prophecy but again there should be no more than three on any one occasion speaking one at a time with the rest weighing their words.[15] As always women should remain silent.[16] Why do these Corinthians think it is only they who know God, cries Paul, when anyone with spiritual insight would recognise that he was speaking for God[17] (14:26–40).

The resurrection of the dead (15:1–58)

In this stirring chapter Paul confounds those who profess Christianity while denying the resurrection of the dead. He begins by recalling Jesus' post-resurrection appearances: to Peter; to the Twelve; to a gathering of over five hundred; to James; to all the apostles; and finally to himself. He then presents his argument. If there is no resurrection of the dead then Jesus was not raised. And if Jesus was not raised we are not released from our sins and the whole edifice of our faith crumbles in ruins making us the most pitiable of men.

But Christ *was* raised from the dead, the first-fruits of all who sleep in death. And just as death came into the world through one man, Adam, so the resurrection of the dead comes through one man, Christ, who at the end, having abolished death and quelled every hostile power, will present the Kingdom to His Father. If death were the end, Paul goes on, what would be the point of being baptised on behalf of the dead?[18] Or the perils and privations he endures for the Gospel? One might as well enjoy oneself regardless (15:1–34).

But how will the dead rise? Like a seed that by 'dying' in the ground produces new life in a new 'body'. Just as there are different kinds of flesh and just as the heavenly bodies vary in their splendour, so the body that is now perishable, dishonoured and weak will be raised imperishable, in glory and power.[19] As we now have a natural earthly body like Adam so we shall then be given a spiritual heavenly body like Christ[20] (15:35–49).

Nothing perishable can enter the Kingdom of God so at the end, when the last trumpet sounds, the bodies of those who are alive at that time will be transformed, in the twinkling of an eye, without experiencing death, while those who are already dead will be raised imperishable to receive their new bodies. Death, where is your sting? (15:50–58)

Conclusion (16:1–24)

Paul ends with practical and personal matters: arrangements for a collection for the poor of Jerusalem; plans to revisit Corinth after he leaves Ephesus and has passed through Macedonia; a request to the Corinthians to receive Timothy warmly; and the news that Apollos was delaying his projected visit.[21] The epistle concludes with exhortations, greetings, best wishes from Aquila and Priscilla and a final Maranatha, come Lord.

2 Corinthians

Paul wrote 2 Corinthians in Macedonia while en route from Ephesus to Greece towards the end of his third missionary journey. It appears that while in Ephesus some problems had caused him to pay a 'painful visit' to Corinth and that after his return he sent Titus to Corinth with a 'severe letter' calling for an unknown offender to be disciplined.

The letter begins with Paul giving us the background to this 'painful visit' and his 'severe letter' and revealing his joy when Titus brought him the news of the Corinthians' friendly response (1:1 – 2:17; 7:5–16). This is split by a long digression in which the apostle answers criticisms and describes the nature of the apostolate, its wonder and joys (3:1 – 7:4). In the remaining two sections Paul urges a collection for the mother-church at Jerusalem (8:1 – 9:15) and makes a spirited defence of himself against detractors (10:1 – 13:13).
Appendix 1 refers

2 Corinthians was clearly written at a time when relationships between Paul and the infant church at Corinth were having their ups and downs. If in Romans we see Paul the professor of theology, and in 1 Corinthians the pastor of his little flock, 2 Corinthians shows him very much in the dock, forced to defend himself and his ministry against opponents who were twisting the Gospel and questioning his credentials and motives.

Who these adversaries were and what motivated them is not entirely clear. They were almost certainly Jews and may have wanted to impose at least a modicum of Jewish practice on Paul's gentile converts (although Paul nowhere alludes to this). Some at least proclaimed a variant Gospel. Bad blood may have been whipped up during Paul's 'painful visit' and by his 'severe letter' while jealousy may also have fuelled the agitators' bile.

2 Corinthians was difficult for Paul to write as to do himself and hence the Gospel justice he had, to some extent, to sing his own praises. But he succeeds magnificently. In the most personal of his letters he bares his soul and with outbursts of passion and studied irony vehemently counters the slander that was hurled against him, thereby bringing us face-to-face with the perils and frustrations that were his daily lot.

We can only marvel at his love of the Church and his resilience as he is assailed on all sides. Despite disappointments that would have felled lesser men his resolve never fails. He rejoices in his hardships for then he knows he is near the Lord who alone must take credit for whatever he achieves. He is content to be judged solely on his success in building the Church. God's commendation is what counts and His alone.

BACKGROUND (1:1 – 2:17)

Greetings and gratitude for divine comfort (1:1–11)

Paul greets his readers and praises God for His unfailing support in every adversity. Christ's encouragement suffuses our lives no less than His suffering. He himself had just been in such desperate straits that he feared for his life, but God saved him.

Paul's change of plan and the 'painful visit' (1:12 – 2:17)

Paul assures the Corinthians that he has always been open and honest with them. When he changed his plans for visiting them it was not that he was vacillating. It was simply his desire to spare them a repetition of the distress of his 'painful visit'. So, in agony of mind, he sent a letter (the 'severe letter') instead. The troublemaker had now been disciplined enough and should be forgiven and encouraged lest he became disheartened[1] (1:12 – 2:11).

Paul describes how he could not settle in Troas (a stopover on his way to Macedonia) even though his preaching was warmly received. He was worried at Titus' non-arrival so pressed on to Macedonia. At this point he must have recalled the good news that awaited him there for he breaks off to praise God for the Gospel's triumphant advance in which he has played a part[2] (2:12–17).

THE APOSTOLIC MINISTRY (3:1 – 7:4)

The glory of the New Covenant (3:1–18)

Paul dismisses any idea that he lacks letters of commendation. Surely his readers' lives in Christ resulting from his ministry are testimony enough. All his competence comes from God who has empowered him to be minister of a new covenant. If the Old Covenant that was engraved on stone and which led to death was so glorious despite being transitory, how much more glorious is the New which is of the Spirit, brings saving justice, and lasts for ever. Unlike Moses who had to wear a veil after he had been speaking with God so that the people could not see the fading of the radiance that illumined his face, in token of the Old Covenant's transitory nature, he can speak out fearlessly. Regretfully the Jews still have a veil covering their hearts. For while Christians are being transformed into images that reflect their Lord, the Old Testament they study can never fully become intelligible without Christ.

The steel of earthenware pots (4:1–18)

He had never been devious or manipulative in proclaiming the word of God, Paul continues. If the Gospel message seems blurred it is only because the distractions of this world blind men to its light. Why is it that such treasure has been entrusted to someone as fragile as himself (an earthenware pot)? It is to show that the power behind it can only be God's. That power and his own weakness are apparent every day. Yet though he faces hardship he is never distressed, though cornered never beaten. Sharing in Jesus' death he also shares in His life. Faith sustains him in the knowledge that physical decay is offset by spiritual renewal and that present trials will be eclipsed by the eternal glory of the world to come.

Earthly decline, heavenly renewal (5:1–10)

We would prefer to be with the Lord, Paul continues, for in this life we are guided only by faith, not yet by sight. At the same time we hope that we shall be alive when Christ comes again so that we shall be able to put our heavenly home, the new glorified body which the Spirit pledges, over the top of the 'tent' that is our present mortal body. (In other words we would like to be transformed from mortality to immortality without having to die.) But whatever the outcome our desire must always be to please Christ because one day we must appear before His judgement seat.

The ministry of reconciliation (5:11 – 6:2)

It is that fear, Paul continues, that spurs him on to win people for Christ unlike others who are only interested in appearances. God can see that and he hopes his readers can too. He is telling them this not to commend himself but to give them ammunition to counter his critics. If he has been unreasonable it was for God, if reasonable for them.[3] But there is something else that drives him. Christ's love, revealed in His dying for all, really leaves Christians no option but to turn from living for themselves to serving Him. Anyone in Christ is a new creation, a new person, thanks to God who reconciled us to Himself through Christ. Now is the time to avail oneself of that grace without delay.

The resilience of mission (6:3–10)

We put no obstacles in your way, Paul maintains.[4] Rather we prove ourselves genuine servants of God both in the way we endure hardship – floggings, imprisonment, starvation – and in our projection of the power of God through purity, patience, truth, love and the Holy Spirit. Whatever befalls we keep bouncing back, 'dying' yet still alive, in pain yet full of joy.

Avoid ungodly attachments (6:11 – 7:4)

Paul appeals to the Corinthians to distance themselves from unbelievers. How can uprightness and wickedness cohabit any more than light and darkness? There can be no compromise with false gods. Anything that defiles either body or spirit must be ruthlessly excised.[5]

PAUL'S JOY (7:5–16)

Paul now resumes where he left off at 2:17. Even in Macedonia he was still beset with problems but everything changed once Titus arrived from Corinth with the reassuring news that the Corinthians were sorry for past differences and looking forward to seeing him.[6] He was overjoyed. He no longer had any regrets about sending the 'severe letter' because although it had caused distress it was not the sort of distress that ends in death but the kind that leads to repentance and salvation. Now they were blameless.

THE COLLECTION FOR THE POOR AT JERUSALEM (8:1 – 9:15)

With good relationships restored Paul turns to a project dear to his heart, namely a collection for God's holy people.[7] To encourage the Corinthians to be generous he cites the example of the Macedonians who had contributed beyond their means. However there was no need for hardship. What mattered was a fair balance so that no one had either too much or too little (8:1–15).
Appendix 2 refers

His assistant Titus and two colleagues had already left for Achaia to get it moving.[8] Having already told the Macedonians that Corinth had been ready for a year he did not want to run the risk of anyone who happened to visit Corinth finding them lagging behind. The collection needed to be completed in good time in any case so that it did not become a last minute imposition. Having the three brothers administer the collection would preclude anyone being able to accuse him of impropriety in what promised to be a large sum of money (8:16 – 9:5).

Paul reminds the Corinthians that those who sow sparsely will reap sparsely and vice-versa. God loves a cheerful giver and will enrich him both materially and with spiritual gifts. Their generosity will testify to their faith and when they hear of it the recipients' prayers will overflow with thanksgiving and love (9:6–15).

PAUL DEFENDS HIMSELF (10:1 – 13:13)

In view of the way the sarcasm and anger of chapters 10–13 jar with the friendly tone of chapters 1–9 many critics believe that these concluding chapters are an extract from Paul's 'severe letter' tacked on later by an editor. However they never allude to any incident that could have given rise to the 'severe letter', being concerned instead with the intrigues of sham apostles and Paul's self vindication. A more likely explanation is that after composing chapters 1–9 Paul received news of further problems in Corinth whereupon in the heat of anger he wrote the stormy chapters 10–13 in a renewed effort to reimpose order on his recalcitrant church.

Paul refutes accusations of weakness (10:1–18)

Paul ironically quotes a charge that though he was bold at a distance he was weak and subservient when present in the flesh. He adroitly turns the slur on his detractors by hoping that when he arrives there will be no need for him to act harshly.[9] They should remember that the weapons he deploys to demolish the specious arguments that people use against the Gospel are not his own but God's. He was quite prepared to root out dissidents for he yielded to no one in his dedication to Christ and when he arrives will soon give the lie by his actions to the sneer that despite his fine letters he was unimpressive and lacked eloquence[10] (10:1–11).

He disdains to measure himself against his critics. They merely preen themselves whereas he has founded the Corinthian church and hopes to achieve even greater things rather than claiming credit for other men's labours as they do (10:12–18).

False apostles and further defence (11:1–33)

Paul now decides, with some diffidence, to indulge in a little boasting. Having arranged their 'marriage' to Christ he is dismayed to find the Corinthians so gullible when some chance comer starts preaching a different Gospel. He may not be the best orator yet when it comes to spiritual knowledge he was more than a match for their 'super-apostles'.[11]

Had he been wrong in not charging for his preaching and relying on the brothers from Macedonia for sustenance?[12] No. He would never be a burden on them. But nor was he inclined to keep quiet about it. It showed his love and undermined his rivals' claims to be working on the same basis as he was. Counterfeit apostles! Agents of Satan! (11:1–15).

Since these 'wise' Corinthians have allowed themselves to be duped and bullied by these false apostles, perhaps he had been too lax with them. So let them remember that he is every bit as much a descendant of Abraham as his detractors. And as a servant of Christ much more so! The hardships he has endured – imprisonment, floggings, shipwreck, brigands, traitors, lack of food and sleep, not to speak of the anxiety he endures every day for the fledgling churches he has founded – are all the proof anyone needs. He is utterly distraught when anyone stumbles. With a touch of humour he recalls the time when he escaped from Damascus by being let down from a widow in a basket (11:16–33).

Vision and thorn (12:1–10)

Possibly to counter opponents who boasted about their spiritual experiences Paul reveals a mystical encounter of his own fourteen years before when he was 'caught up into Paradise'. He reports it briefly and with some restraint – referring to himself impersonally as a man in Christ – because he wants to be accepted for what he is rather than for this revelation. He also mentions a 'thorn in the flesh', an affliction he had long had to suffer lest he get above himself. Three times he had prayed for release only to be told that the Lord's power was sufficient, indeed was realised to perfection, in human weakness.[13]

The third visit (12:11 – 13:13)

With bitter sarcasm Paul gives vent to his feelings. All his boasting is the Corinthians' fault for not backing him up. Non-entity he may be but he has the measure of these 'super-apostles' and has all the hallmarks of a genuine apostle. The only thing he has not done is to become a drain on them! He is about to make his third visit, not to be a burden, not for gain, but out of love. They seem to think he has filched money by trickery. But where is the evidence that either he, or Titus, has ever defrauded them?[14] (12:11–18)?

His forthcoming visit may result in quarrels and bad temper and he is worried that they may not all have yet repented of their sexual libertinism. If so he warns that they will not be spared for he shares not just Christ's weakness but His power too. He prays that they may pass their test even if that means he is precluded from passing his own test of showing how strong he is. They have been warned (12:19 – 13:10).

Paul concludes by wishing his readers joy and hoping they will grow in godliness, mutual support, peace and harmony (13:11–13).

Galatians

Galatia covered a swathe of the central mountainous area of what is now modern Turkey. Paul founded a number of churches there on his first missionary journey and (although alternative chronologies have been pressed) it seems likely that Galatians was written shortly after his return when news reached him that agitators had subsequently been undermining his work. These were most likely Judaizers, Christian Jews who denied his doctrine of salvation by faith, maintaining instead that Christians must observe the Law and be circumcised. They were also questioning Paul's authority. *Appendix 1 refers*

Galatians is Paul's response. Stirred to his depths and writing in great stress as he sees the success of his recent mission being put in jeopardy, he begins by asserting his authority as an apostle of equal standing with the Twelve in Jerusalem. He follows this with a mighty polemic which in many ways foreshadows his later epistle to the Romans. The only way to be reckoned upright before God is through faith in Christ. The Law is powerless to give life and was only a temporary expedient until Christ came. It is Abraham's spiritual descendents by faith, not his physical progeny, who will inherit God's promises. Finally lest his call to be led by faith rather than Law should be seen as an invitation to loose living, Paul underlines that Christians are new people, bound by the Gospel of love under the guidance of the Spirit.

Opening address and warning (1:1–10)

In an unusually brusque opening Paul underlines that his apostolic commission comes directly from Christ and the Father. He is amazed at the Galatians deserting the true Gospel for a perversion promoted by some trouble-makers. There is no other Gospel and anyone who tries to concoct one is under God's curse. Who am I trying to please now, men or God?[1]

Paul's call and mission (1:11 – 2:10)

Paul recalls how the Gospel came to him by direct revelation from Christ. Despite having previously persecuted Christians with tireless zeal he learned that he had been chosen to take the Gospel to the gentiles and such was the sufficiency of his encounter with the risen Lord that he saw no need to hurry to Jerusalem to confer with the other apostles.[2] Instead he spent time in Arabia and Damascus and only after three years journeyed to Jerusalem to meet Peter and James the Lord's brother. He then returned to Syria and Cilicia (1:11–24).

Years later, inspired by another revelation, he went up to Jerusalem again, this time accompanied by Barnabas and Titus. There he met the Church leaders, James, Peter and John. When he went through his message to the gentiles with them they had nothing to add and accepted that he had been entrusted to take the Gospel to the gentiles as Peter had to the Jews.[3] All they asked was that he should remember the needy[4] (2:1–10).

(In the notoriously difficult passage beginning at v 3 Paul is making the point that no one queried his assistant Titus, a gentile Greek, not being circumcised thereby showing that no one considered it necessary for Church membership.)

Peter's vacillation (2:11–14)

Paul describes an occasion in Antioch when he publicly rebuked Peter for yielding to pressure and withdrawing from table fellowship with gentiles. The rest of the Jewish Christians present and even Barnabas had followed his example.[5]

Paul's credo (2:15–21)

Paul now summarises his message. The only way to be reckoned upright, even for Jews, is by faith in Christ. No one can do it by keeping the Law. Since we are justified through (faith in) Christ and not by the Law, does that mean we can go on sinning?[6] Of course not! That would make Christ an agent of sin which is unthinkable. On the contrary, Paul continues, although (as a Christian) I am dead to (outside) the Law, by being crucified with Christ I become a different person, alive to God through Christ living in me.[7] If salvation comes through the Law, then Christ died needlessly.

The Christian experience (3:1–5)

Paul sharply reproves his readers. Stupid people! What was it that changed their lives and gave them the Spirit with its many signs and favours? Was it the Law? Or the Gospel?

Faith saves, Law condemns (3:6–18)

Paul now turns to Scripture to support his thesis. Abraham was reckoned upright because of his faith. So it is people of faith who will receive the blessings promised in his name. Those who depend on the Law are under a curse because no one can live up to it. What Christ did by His death was to take that curse, which should have been ours, upon Himself thereby enabling the blessings God promised Abraham to be appropriated by all (who bond with Him) through faith. Paul bolsters his argument with two further points. Firstly God's promise was to Abraham's progeny in the singular, not the plural. This means, he argues, that it was addressed to Christ and so by implication to all who are with Him in faith. Secondly there can be no question of the promise depending on obedience to the Law since the Law was not given until four hundred and thirty years after Abraham's time.

The function of the Law (3:19–24)

So what was the point of the Law? It acted as a benchmark to reveal what sin was and only applied until the progeny (Christ) came. Indeed the very manner of its bestowal through angels and an intermediary indicates its subordinate position because the promise to Abraham was made directly by God.[8] Does the Law run counter to God's promises? No. Before faith it acted like a guardian, keeping us in check until God sent His Son. But it had nothing to do with giving life. That only comes through faith in Christ.

The coming of faith (3:25 – 4:7)

With faith all who are baptised are clothed in Christ and become children of God, one brotherhood irrespective of race, sex or status. And, being in Christ, they become Abraham's progeny and so heirs to the promises made to him. An heir to property is like a slave for until the time appointed by his father he is under the control of guardians. Similarly we were slaves, slaves to the wiles of the world, until God sent Jesus to redeem us and enable us to be adopted as His sons and receive the Holy Spirit.

Paul appeals to the Galatians (4:8–20)

Why, having known God, do you want to go back to paganism, Paul demands. It does not make sense. Already you are celebrating pagan festivals and feast days. Why have you changed? You used to be so contented and would have done anything for me. Have I offended you simply by telling the truth? I am going through the pain of giving birth all over again, Paul continues, and I am at my wit's end.

The allegory of Hagar and Sarah (4:21–31)

Paul makes one final effort to drive home what is at stake with an allegory comparing Hagar and her son Ishmael with Sarah and Isaac. Hagar a slave girl represents the old covenant with Jerusalem in slavery (to the Law) while her son Ishmael, born according to human nature, represents Judaism. Sarah, a freewoman, stands for the new covenant and the heavenly Jerusalem rejoicing in the freedom of the Gospel while her son Isaac, born through the Spirit, stands for Christians. Scripture says that Hagar and Ishmael are to be driven out and not to share Isaac's inheritance. Therefore, Paul concludes, it is not those born under the Law of the old covenant who will inherit God's promises but those who embrace the Gospel of the new covenant and are born of the Spirit.

The danger of falling from grace (5:1–12)

In another impassioned plea Paul reminds the Galatians what they have to lose. Christ set you free, he begins. So do not allow yourselves to become slaves again. Remember that if you opt for circumcision you must keep the whole Law and will then have turned your backs on Christ and God's grace (His free unmerited favour). The salvation Christ offers has nothing to do with circumcision but issues solely from faith working through love. 'If only those teaching circumcision would go and mutilate themselves' an exasperated Paul bemoans.

Godly living (5:13 – 6:10)

Having preached freedom from the Law Paul now insists that this must not become a licence for indulgence. The Gospel must be lived. Christians must serve one another and love their neighbour. They must allow themselves to be guided by the Spirit in love, peace, kindness, gentleness and self-control and never forget that sexual vice, idolatry, jealousy, malice and quarrelling have no place in God's Kingdom.

If anyone does wrong gently correct him. Carry one another's burdens. Worry about your own achievements and stop comparing them with everybody else's. Those who plant in the field of natural desires will reap the harvest of death whereas life in the Spirit brings eternal life.

Postscript (6:11–18)

The people who are trying to force circumcision on you, Paul concludes, are only out to make a good impression (on their fellow Jews). They do not keep the Law themselves and simply want to be able to boast that they have won you over to Judaism. Never forget. What matters is not circumcision or uncircumcision but being part of a new creation.

Ephesians

There is a strong case for believing that Ephesians was composed as a circular to all the churches in Asia Minor. In support of this thesis the opening greeting is notably non specific. Indeed the attribution 'in Ephesus' after 'to God's holy people' in verse 1 is missing in the most ancient manuscripts which suggests that the verse may well have been left with a blank space for a particular church's name to be inserted as its copy was delivered by a courier.
Appendix 1 refers

Unlike Paul's other letters it lacks local colour and does not address specific problems, rising above the heat of controversy to more exalted themes and reading more like a homily than a letter. We know from his farewell, Ac 20:17–38, how attached Paul was to the Ephesian church yet the epistle contains no personal greetings. Indeed when we read 1:15; 3:1–4, far from suggesting close ties with his readers, we are left with the impression that the author had never met them.

Ephesians is a hymn to God's eternal purpose, a font of encouragement and hope. God has chosen His people for an unimaginable destiny: through grace to be adopted sons; through Christ to be redeemed from the shadow of sin; to be quickened by the Spirit and showered with blessings. Paul marvels at God's bounty in extending His promises to gentiles as well as Jews. He ends by addressing the practical demands of living as the Body of Christ in a world besotted with sin. A battle that can only be won with the Lord.

Greetings and opening hymn (1:1–14)

After the briefest of salutations the letter begins with an anthem of praise that echoes from eternity to eternity. Blessed be God the Father who chose us in grace and love before ever the world began to be adopted sons, one family, holy and faultless, thanks to Christ whose blood gained us freedom and forgiveness of sins. All the spiritual blessings of heaven are ours in Christ under whom everything in the heavens and on earth will be perfected when God's mysterious plan has run its course.[1] We (Jews) were chosen to be His people from the very beginning before He came. Now you (gentiles) too, having accepted the Gospel, have become God's people and received the Spirit, the guarantor of our inheritance.[2]

Paul's prayer (1:15–23)

Paul tells his readers how he thanks God unceasingly for their faith and love. May they grow in knowledge of God and come to understand the full glory of the heritage He offers and the power He exercises on their behalf. That power was seen when God raised Christ from the dead and enthroned Him at His right hand far above all other principalities, ruling forces, powers and sovereignties as the head of the Church which is his Body.[3]

Salvation is a free gift (2:1–10)

In the past both Jews and gentiles were spiritually dead through following the world's godless ways. But God's love is so great that He brought us to life with Christ for a place in heaven. This is not on account of anything we have done but by God's grace through faith. We are God's work of art, created to do the good works He has already assigned us.[4]

The unity of the Church (2:11–22)

There was a time when gentiles were excluded from God's promises and without hope. But with His blood Christ made Jews and gentiles one Body, reconciled with God and at peace. He abolished the Law that had previously kept them apart so that everyone now has free access to the Father by the Spirit. Gentiles are no longer aliens but fellow citizens of a family of God with Christ Himself as the cornerstone, the whole edifice growing into a dwelling place for God in the Spirit.

Paul's apostleship (3:1–21)

Paul realises that his gentile readers may not all be aware of the background to his ministry. He therefore explains how God had revealed to him something that was hidden from previous generations, namely that gentiles are members of the same Body and share the same inheritance as the Jews. Furthermore God has given him the task of proclaiming this news to the gentiles and shedding light on how God's plan works so that, through the Church, the (malevolent) cosmic powers may see how many-splendoured God's wisdom is and how it achieves its purpose in Christ.[5] Resulting from this, and united with Christ in faith, we can now approach God in complete confidence. He prays that the Spirit may strengthen them so that Christ may live in their hearts and they come to know the fathomless depths of His love and be filled with the fullness of a God who can do vastly more than we can ever imagine.

A call for unity (4:1–16)

Paul now turns from doctrinal to practical concerns. Christians must lead lives worthy of their calling, supporting one another in humility and love and working to preserve unity. There is but one faith and one Body. They must use their God-given gifts, diverse as they are, for the common good until they reach that maturity where they are no longer tossed hither and thither by every new fad and deception but have grown in the image of Christ in truth and love to form the perfect Body of which He is the Head and they the joints.

Life as God's children (4:17 – 6:9)

Christians must discard the old unregenerate way of life that led to alienation from God and become new people grounded in righteousness and holiness. They must never lie, persist in anger, steal, use foul language or offend the Holy Spirit. Instead of yielding to bad temper and malice they must be generous, sympathetic and forgiving (4:17–32).

Christ must be their model, especially in love. There must be no impurity, coarse language or greed. These are all forms of idolatry. They must not allow themselves to be taken in by specious arguments. Having cast off darkness they must behave as children of light projecting goodness, uprightness and truth and showing up wickedness for what it is. They must discover what the Lord wants of them and make good use of their time. Instead of wine let them drink of the Holy Spirit and always give thanks to God (5:1–20).

Wives should be subject to their husbands for the husband is head of his wife as Christ of His Church. Husbands should love their wives as Christ loves His Church and died for it. Children must obey their parents while parents for their part must take care not to exasperate their children. Slaves must serve their masters loyally while masters must treat their slaves humanely. Neither must ever forget that they both have the same Master in heaven and He has no favourites (5:21 – 6:9).

Spiritual war (6:10–24)

There is a battle to be won. Not against human enemies but the malign forces of evil. Only by donning the armour of God with truth, uprightness and in faith can Christians prevail. Paul asks for prayers for all God's people and for himself, so that in proclaiming the Gospel he, an ambassador in chains, may speak as fearlessly as he ought.[6]

Philippians

Philippi was an important Roman colony strategically situated astride one of the Empire's main highways. It was the site of the first church Paul founded in Europe and the only one from which he accepted any payment for his work.

Despite being written while he was under house arrest in Rome this is a warm chatty letter in which Paul thanks the Philippians for a gift and implores them to stay united in their faith. Christ Himself must be their role model. He reminds them that no one can become righteous by obeying the Law, but only through faith in Christ. The power and love of God are never far away. Paul clearly had a warm relationship with the church in Philippi while his desire to be close to his Master influences his every thought. He seems relaxed and at peace, radiant despite all the storms and stress life tosses his way.

Thanksgiving and prayer (1:1–11)

Paul includes Timothy in his initial salutation. He offers thanks for the Philippians' devotion to the Gospel and prays that they may continue to grow in love and discernment.

Paul's circumstances (1:12–26)

He begins on a happy note. His chains are proving to be a help rather than a hindrance.[1] They have brought him into prominence and emboldened the local church by his example. It was true that some of its members were not acting out of the highest motives, preaching out of rivalry or jealousy rather than love, but what did it matter so long as Christ was being proclaimed? But he was torn. While on the one hand he looked forward to death and being with Christ, on the other hand there was a lot more he could do in this life and that was how he thought it would all work out. In which case he would see them again.

Fight for the faith (1:27–30)

Paul tells the Philippians that they must live up to the high ideals of the Gospel and fight as a team undeterred by opponents who will thereby be given a sign that they are lost while the Church will prevail. Like himself they have been granted the privilege not only of believing in Christ but also of suffering for Him.

Unity in humility (2:1–11)

Make my joy complete, Paul continues, by your being one in love, heart and mind. Be done with jealousy, vanity, selfishness and think instead of humility and serving others. In short copy Jesus, who though He had the nature of God, emptied Himself of glory and took on our humanity even to the extent of dying on a cross. For which God exalted Him, all creation worships Him and every tongue confesses Him Lord.

Live the faith (2:12–18)

Remain obedient and continue to work out your salvation in fear and trembling.[2] You can depend on God to give you the will and strength. Do it cheerfully so that you shine like stars in the darkness of the depravity around you. Then at least, Paul continues, he will not have run the race and toiled in vain. If he is to be put to death he will rejoice and so must they.[3]

Timothy and Epaphroditus (2:19–30)

Paul promises that he will send Timothy to visit them as soon as his own position is clarified. Indeed he is hopeful that he will be able to come himself before too long. Epaphroditus who had been sent from Philippi to help him, and who had recently recovered from a severe illness, would also be returning to them.

The true way to salvation (3:1–21)

Just as he is about to end Paul breaks into a long diatribe against proponents of circumcision and the Law. He should know! He was once as fervent a champion of the Law as anyone and blameless as far as it went. But now he knows how mistaken he was. True circumcision is of the spirit and uprightness comes not from the Law but from faith in Christ. So now, moulded to Christ, He is striving to share in the power of His resurrection and win a new glorious resurrected body for himself. He has not got there yet but, like an athlete, is racing all out for the finishing line. He urges them to do the same and not follow people whose god is their stomach and whose minds are rooted in earthly things.[4]

Thanks for help and final wishes (4:1–23)

Paul follows a plea for two women to settle their differences with calls for the congregation to be joyful. They should never worry but tell God of their needs and always be grateful. They should hold to all that is true and honourable. Then the peace of God which is beyond all understanding will guard their hearts and thoughts.

Paul acknowledges a gift the Philippians' have given him while at the same time making plain that, strengthened in Christ, he has learned to take life as it comes living in plenty or poverty as fortune dictates. They were the only ones to help in the early days of his ministry. Now he is fully provided for.

Colossians

Colossae was a small town a hundred miles east of Ephesus on the trade route to the interior of Asia Minor. There is no evidence that Paul ever went there himself and the church there may have been founded by one of his disciples, a Colossian named Epaphras, 1:7; 4:12.

The letter seems to have been prompted by reports that false teachers were threatening to undermine the true faith. Colossians is Paul's response but since he rises to the challenge by positive teaching rather than refuting specific heresies the best we can hope for is to try to reconstruct the false doctrine from that.

At the heart of the problem seems to have been a denial of Christ's pre-eminence as God and Saviour. The purity of the Gospel was being tainted by imports from secular philosophy, from some sort of belief in supernatural powers, angel worship and dietary taboos, and from observance of pagan festivals and a leaning to asceticism. The danger was acute and if left unchecked would have threatened the infant church with a faith that was man-made rather than Christ-centred. Paul attacked these perversions by stressing Christ's deity and supremacy, His work in reconciling man with God and His subjection of every authority and power. He alone was the fount of salvation. Everything else, human rules and wisdom, was a distraction and delusion. Christ is God incarnate. In the second half of the epistle Paul follows up this uncompromising message with guidelines for a Christian lifestyle.

Address, thanksgiving and prayer (1:1–14)

Paul includes Timothy in his greetings and gives thanks for the Colossians' faith, love and their hope of heaven. He prays that, divinely quickened, they may be brought to full knowledge of God and so be able to lead a life worthy of the One who had delivered them from darkness and redeemed them from sin.

Christ the head of all creation (1:15–20)

Paul extols the glory and majesty of Christ. Pre-existent, He is the image of the invisible God and in Him everything visible and invisible, every sovereignty and power, was created and has its being.[1] By His death on the Cross He brought peace and reconciled everything to God both in heaven and on earth. He is the first-born from the dead and the head of His Body, the Church. All fullness of deity is found in Him.[2] He is supreme in every way.

Salvation for the Colossians (1:21–23)

Paul now explains the implications of this for the Colossians. Where they were once estranged from God now, because of Christ's death, they will be able to stand before Him holy and faultless: provided only that they hold fast to the Gospel faith.

Paul's ministry (1:24 – 2:5)

In a brief digression Paul tells how happy he is to endure suffering for a mission conferred on him by God Himself.[3] This is to reveal what had only recently come to light, namely that gentiles too are called to salvation. Infused with Christ's power his aim is therefore to bring everyone to faith in Christ. He strives even for those he has never met to ensure that they are not beguiled by specious arguments but bound together in love and led to a full understanding of the mystery of God in which all wisdom and knowledge resides.

Fulfilment is only in Christ (2:6–15)

Paul now declares that to acknowledge Christ is only the beginning. You must go further, he goes on. Root yourselves in Him and do not be deflected by hollow human philosophies that ignore Him. For Christ in bodily form is divinity in all its fullness and it is in Him, as head of every sovereignty and power, that you find your own fulfilment[4] (2:6–10).

Christ has circumcised you, not physically, but by stripping away your old sinful selves. In baptism your old sinful self was buried with Him and you were then raised up to new life with Him with your sins forgiven.[5] He has stripped the sovereignties and ruling forces of their power and wiped out your debt to the Law by nailing it to the Cross[6] (2:11–15).

False trails (2:16–23)

Do not give way to outworn and ineffective rules about food and festivals. These are mere shadows of the reality that is Christ. Likewise be wary of people who profess humility by worshipping angels or who harp on about visions they have seen. In their spiritual pride they have lost touch with Christ.[7] If you are really committed to Christ you should not be worrying about rules on what you can eat or touch. They might appear to help in cultivating self-discipline and humility but they are completely useless when it comes to quelling the fires of self-indulgence.

Raise your sights to Christ (3:1–4)

Since you have been raised to share Christ's life, Paul continues, raise your sights and focus on heavenly rather than earthly things, for you have died to this life and are already living in Christ. That life may be hidden now but when Christ returns it will come out into the open and you will appear with Him in glory.

Christian conduct (3:5 – 4:6)

Cast-off everything in your old self that incurs God's wrath: sexual lusts, evil desires, and especially greed because it is tantamount to idolatry. Purge yourselves of anger, bad temper, malice, abusive language, dirty talk, lying. You have discarded your old self and its old habits and put on a new self which will gradually grow in the image of God. In that new self there is no room for social or ethnic distinctions. Christ is in everyone. As God's people you must be clothed in compassion, generosity, humility, gentleness, patience, tolerance, forgiveness, but above all in love. Live by the Gospel. Teach and counsel one another. Always be grateful and give thanks to God in Christ's name.

Wives are to be subject to their husbands. Husbands must love their wives. Children must obey their parents. Parents should not irritate their children. Slaves should always work conscientiously as if for the Lord knowing that He will repay them. Masters should treat slaves fairly because they too have a Master in heaven.[8] Persevere in prayer. Make the most of your time with unbelievers, expressing yourself pleasantly and sensitively.

Personal news and final wishes (4:7–18)

It seems that Tychicus and Onesimus, a Colossian, were deputed to deliver the letter. We learn that Mark was a cousin of Barnabas and that Luke was a doctor.[9] From his exclusion from the list of 'the circumcised' we may also infer that Luke was a gentile. Paul is fulsome in praise of Epaphras and asks that this letter be passed on to Laodicea in return for another letter the Laodiceans already have.[10] He ends with a poignant reminder of 'the chains he wears' and his usual benediction 'grace be with you'.[11]

1 Thessalonians

According to Acts 17 Paul's missionary activity in Thessalonica was cut short by Jewish trouble-makers after which he made his way via Beroea to Athens and Corinth. While in Athens he became concerned about the infant Thessalonican church's welfare and sent Timothy back to investigate. When Timothy rejoined him in Corinth it was with encouraging news.[1] Although some people were running him down and there was perhaps some moral laxity, the little church was thriving. However the Thessalonians had a couple of questions. What happened to people who died before Christ came again? And when would the *parousia* (His Second Coming) take place? 1 Thessalonians is Paul's response and it is reasonable to suppose that it was written in Corinth shortly after Timothy's return.[2] In it he congratulates the Thessalonians, defends the purity of his motives, urges them to even greater holiness and answers their questions. 1 Thessalonians is thus not doctrinal but a warm letter of encouragement to a flock from a pastor who rejoices in their faith and is deeply concerned for their spiritual welfare.

Opening address (1:1–10)

Paul rejoices at the way faith, love and hope shine through his readers' lives. God's favour in choosing them was evident from the Gospel coming to them not only from himself but with the power of the Holy Spirit too. Their faith and the way they had overcome adversities and abandoned pagan gods was talked about everywhere. They were a model church and were now waiting for Jesus to come from heaven and save them from the coming wrath.[3]

Paul's defence (2:1–12)

In a spirited defence of his ministry Paul maintains that despite every obstacle he had preached fearlessly and, thanks to God's support, his campaign had been fruitful. His motives had always been of the highest order. He had never tried to deceive anyone. He had slaved night and day not to be a burden on them.[4] He had not laboured for his own gain but for God's and was dedicated to getting them to live good Christian lives.

The Thessalonians' steel (2:13–16)

As for the Thessalonians they had proved enthusiastic and doughty converts withstanding similar persecution from their own countrymen as their fellow Christians in Judaea suffered from the Jews. The Jews were stopping at nothing to prevent his taking the Gospel to the gentiles but retribution had finally overtaken them.[5]

Timothy's visit (2:17 – 3:13)

Paul tells how he had yearned to see them again when he was in Athens but Satan always stood in the way. So he sent Timothy back to help them surmount the hardships that inevitably came their way. When Timothy returned it was with the wonderful news that they were in good heart. Now he was praying for the day when he would be able to see them again himself and plug any gaps in their faith.[6] Meanwhile may they grow in love and holiness in readiness for Christ's return.

An exhortation to holiness (4:1–12)

For all their virtues Paul urges the Thessalonians to even greater spiritual heights especially in brotherly love and sexual relations for immorality was nothing less than a rejection of God. It was also important that everyone should carry on earning his living and not become a nuisance by sponging on others.[7]

The Second Coming (4:13 – 5:11)

Paul reassures his readers about the Second Coming. Those who have already died in Christ will be at no disadvantage. They will be the first to rise and only then will those who are alive be taken up in the clouds, along with them, to meet the Lord in the air. This Day, the Day of the Lord, will come when it is least expected. So vigilance and mutual encouragement must be their watchwords as they 'put on faith and love for a breastplate, and the hope of salvation for a helmet'.

Concluding exhortations (5:12–28)

Be considerate and respectful to your church leaders, Paul concludes. Live peaceful orderly lives. Build up community spirit by encouraging the wary and supporting the weak. Be patient and see that no one repays evil with evil. Be joyful, pray constantly, and always give thanks. Be open to new ideas. Neither stifle the Spirit's promptings nor discount prophecy but at the same time exercise discernment, holding on to what is right and discarding what is wrong or evil.

2 Thessalonians

It would appear that Paul's statement in 1 Thessalonians that Christ would return when He was least expected did not satisfy his readers. They wanted to know when. So he wrote this second letter shortly after, and again from Corinth, to reveal that it was not imminent because the final effusion of evil that must precede it had not yet taken place.

Justice will prevail (1:1–12)

The epistle begins with thanksgiving for the Thessalonians' faith and mutual love. The hardships they are bearing so steadfastly mark them out as worthy of the Kingdom of God. Relief will come when Jesus appears from heaven when those who now harass them will reap the consequences. Anyone rejecting the Gospel will be lost eternally, excluded from the presence of the Lord and the glorification of His followers.

Apostasy in the Last Days (2:1–12)

Do not be misled by rumours that the time for Christ's return, the Day of the Lord, has already arrived. Paul begins. That is not so. There must first be certain signs. It cannot happen until after the great tribulation (or revolt) has taken place and the 'wicked One' has begun to flaunt himself as God. Although the 'mystery of wickedness' was already at work there was 'something' (as in verse 6) or 'someone' (as in verse 7) stopping the 'wicked One' from appearing at the moment. However once this restraint was removed the 'wicked One' would appear whereupon the Lord would make His Second Coming and destroy him (2:1–8).

While the 'wicked One' was at large Satan would take every opportunity to do his worst. He would use every trick and deception in the book, all kinds of signs and wonders, to delude people who were already on the path to destruction for rejecting the Gospel (2:9–12).

Reflection

The above passage is not easy to follow. Paul had already discussed the whole matter with the Thessalonians in person, 2:5–6, and therefore saw no need to explain every detail again now. It seems that the 'mystery of wickedness' is Satan and the 'wicked

One' an agent of his yet to come. Whatever (or whoever) Paul may have had in mind as the restraint on the 'wicked one', today it is natural to see it as the Holy Spirit holding back the final denouement until the Gospel has been proclaimed to the entire world.

With these identifications, and consistently with the rest of Scripture, the passage can be decoded as follows. The Gospel will never have an easy passage. Wickedness (Satan) will always be at work beneath the world's veneer of decency even though the Holy Spirit is for the moment restraining it. But the battle is of cosmic proportions and just before the end of the world it will rise to a climax. The arrival of the 'wicked One', an agent of Satan, will precipitate a major crisis which will lead many astray. There will be mass defections and Christianity's very survival will seem to be in doubt. But when all seems lost Christ will return and win the final victory.

Whether the 'wicked One' will be an individual anti-Christ, a succession of anti-Christs, a political institution or some other personification of evil that will temporarily seem to gain the upper hand we do not know.[1] All we can say with certainty is that final victory is assured.

Prayers for God's help (2:13 – 3:5)

Paul thanks God for the Thessalonians. He urges them to stand firm in their faith and prays that they will receive the same encouragement from God as he has. He asks for their prayers both for the rapid spread of the Gospel and for himself to be preserved from wicked people. The Lord can be relied upon to protect His own and so he has every confidence that the Thessalonians will hold fast.

Against idleness (3:6–15)

Paul urges the brothers to dissociate themselves from any of their number who live undisciplined lives and in particular those who refuse to work.[2] Such people should not be allowed to eat. Even so they are not to be regarded as enemies but as brothers in need of correction. He himself, who always earned his keep when he was with them by dint of sheer hard work, should be their role model.

Finale (3:16–18)

Paul ends with a prayer for peace and points to the final greeting being in his own hand.[3]

1 Timothy

The epistles to Titus and Timothy, to place them in their probable chronological order, form a closely knit trio. Since they are addressed not to churches but to pastors they are collectively known as the Pastoral epistles. Consistent among themselves in style and theology, they diverge sufficiently from Paul's other letters to lead many scholars to ascribe them to a different hand.

However to each objection to Pauline authorship there is a counter argument of equal plausibility and all that is certain is that if the Pastorals are accepted as Pauline it is necessary to assume that Paul was released from the captivity in Rome, where ACTS leaves him, and then undertook another tour of the eastern Mediterranean (taking in Crete, Asia Minor, Macedonia and Greece) before being re-arrested and taken back to Rome where tradition has it he was martyred. It is impossible to fit the movements reported in the Pastorals into the Acts framework in any other way. It seems probable that Titus and 1 Timothy were written in Macedonia and 2 Timothy in Rome. In any event 2 Timothy is Paul's swan song.

One of the Pastorals' chief concerns is to safeguard the Gospel against false doctrine. What this was is not clear. Paul did not tell Timothy and Titus what they already knew and rather than refuting it point by point dismisses it *en bloc* as an aberration. However there are signs that some of it was of Jewish origin to do with the Law, 1Tm 1:6–7; Tt 3:9. There was certainly an interest in myths and genealogies, 1Tm 1:4; Tt 1:14; 3:9, a leaning to an asceticism that opposed marriage and certain foods, 1Tm 4:3, and not least a denial of anything other than a purely spiritual resurrection, 2Tm 2:18. Whatever it was Timothy and Titus are charged to defend the Gospel uncompromisingly and not waste time on intellectual speculation and wrangles over words.

The Pastorals also address the practical problems faced by a growing church: the qualities required of church leaders, the role of women, care of widows, slaves and so on. In the two letters to Timothy Paul is also at pains to bolster his young protégé's confidence so that he may exploit to the full the talents he was so amply endowed with.

Opening remarks (1:1–20)

Paul reminds Timothy that when he left him in Ephesus it was to put a stop to deviant teaching and a fascination with myths and genealogies that was deflecting people from what really mattered: love, a pure heart and faith. As for certain self-styled students of the Law, they were out of their depth and should remember that the Law was not intended for profitless speculation or the upright but to restrain evil-doers.

Paul thanks the Lord for his calling, for showing him mercy and giving him strength, love and faith. Once the greatest of sinners he is now the living proof that Christ came into the world to save sinners and lead those who trust him to eternal life. He charges Timothy to fight like a soldier, with faith and a good conscience. Those who ignore their consciences wreck their faith.

Prayer (2:1–8)

Paul now embarks on his main charge, the ordering of the community beginning with worship. Prayers should be offered for everyone, especially those in authority, in the interests of peace and harmony. God would like everyone to be saved. There is only one God and only one mediator, Christ Jesus, a human being who gave Himself as a ransom for all. Pray men should be offered reverently and free of ill-will.

Women in church (2:9–15)

Women should dress modestly. Their best adornment is good deeds and it becomes them to be quiet and self-effacing. They may not teach or have authority over a man for that would be to violate the created order. After all Adam was created before Eve and it was Eve who was the first to sin. Devoted motherhood is a woman's way to salvation provided she maintains the Christian virtues.

Qualifications for the ministry (3:1–16)

Elders must be of impeccable character and good home managers. How can you manage a church if you cannot run a home? They should not be newly converted lest they become swollen with pride, and must be beyond reproach in the eyes of outsiders. They should be temperate, courteous, hospitable, gentle, neither avaricious nor quarrelsome, and good teachers. Similar qualities are required of deacons and their wives.[1]

False teaching (4:1–6)

The Holy Spirit says that in the last days people will be deceived by false teaching and that some will abandon their faith altogether. Two current examples are the embargoes against marriage and certain foods. However what the people who preach this nonsense forget is that everything God created is good and no food is taboo provided it is received with thanks.

General advice to Timothy (4:7 – 5:2)

Paul tells Timothy that he is to have nothing to do with myths and old wives' tales but must train like an athlete to be spiritually fit. If physical exercise is beneficial how much more so is spiritual training that prepares not just for this life but for the next.

He must conduct himself so as to be an example to all and so that no one can look down on him because of his youth. He has a natural gift for the ministry and must put it to good use. Then he will save both himself and those who listen to him. In all his dealings with people he must be respectful and gentle and exercise sober restraint.

Advice on widows, elders and slaves (5:3 – 6:2)

When widows have relatives it is their Christian duty to look after them. Otherwise widows over sixty who are alone but who have been diligent in prayer and are of good Christian character should be enrolled.[2] Younger widows are best left off the list however. Then if they want to remarry they cannot be accused of breaking their pledge. Indeed as there is the risk of their becoming idle busybodies it is probably best if they do remarry.

Elders who perform well deserve double pay. Never uphold an accusation against an elder, Paul continues, unless it is supported by two or three witnesses in which case the guilty party must be reprimanded publicly. Have no favourites. Do not be hasty in making appointments. Keep yourself pure. Take a little wine for the sake of your digestion. Slaves must respect their masters so as not to bring the faith into disrepute.[3] Those with Christian masters should serve them all the better knowing it is fellow believers who will benefit.

False teaching (6:3–10)

Paul roundly condemns teachers who do not reflect the words of Christ. Such people are conceited and crave nothing more than to engage in endless argument. All this leads to is constant wrangling and insults from men who are devoid of the truth and think religion is a way of making money. Religion does bring gains but only to people who are content with their station in life. Love of money on the other hand is at the root of all evil and its pursuit an entrapment that can obscure the faith and kill the soul.

Final instructions (6:11–21)

Timothy must avoid these snares. He must apply the Christian virtues, fight the good fight and so win the eternal life to which he was called. He must press doggedly on until the coming of the Lord. He must teach the rich not to be high-minded but to be rich in generosity and good works, setting their sights on God who alone can give them the only riches that matter. Guard the truth that has been entrusted to you, Paul concludes, and do not get side tracked on to godless half-baked ideas that are falsely called knowledge. For that can be one's undoing.

2 Timothy

See 1 Timothy

Paul encourages Timothy (1:1 – 2:13)

After a warm greeting Paul sets out to stiffen Timothy's resolve by reminding him that God saved us, not for anything we have done, but for His own purpose as an act of unmerited grace. That has now been revealed in Christ who has replaced death with immortality. Timothy must never therefore feel ashamed of the Gospel, nor of Paul's captivity, but share in his hardships, conquer his timidity, trust in the power of God, and let the Spirit fan his God-given gift to witness into flame. This is all the more necessary as he himself is now a prisoner and forsaken by virtually all his friends (1:1–18).

Paul exhorts Timothy to draw strength from Christ and accept whatever hardships come his way. As the Gospel was entrusted to him so he must teach others so that they too can pass it on. He must be as dedicated as a soldier who sacrifices everything to gain his commanding officer's approval; as punctilious as an athlete who knows he cannot win the victor's crown unless he sticks to the rules; and as industrious as a farmer. Let him be inspired by Christ's rising from the dead and from his own example: chained up like a criminal for spreading a Gospel that cannot be stifled in order that others might live (2:1–13).

False teaching (2:14–21)

Stick to the basic Gospel, Paul continues. Avoid arguments over words and senseless philosophical discussion that only sows dissension and upsets people's faith. There was an example of this recently with all the talk of resurrection having already happened.[1] Just as the dishes in a mansion vary in what they are suitable for, so it is in the Church. So distance yourself from false teaching and be like one of the better dishes: fit to serve the Master.

Personal advice to Timothy (2:22–26)

Paul warns Timothy to shun the passions of youth and pursue the virtues of uprightness, faith, love and peace. He must steer clear of theorising that only spawns divisiveness. He must be kind and patient, a good teacher, and gentle when correcting people who oppose the truth in the hope that God may open their minds to it.

Moral decay in the last days (3:1–9)

Difficult days lay ahead. People will become wilful, swollen with pride, putting love of pleasure before love of God, effecting an outward piety without allowing their faith to rule their hearts. Such people must be avoided. So too must men who prey on silly women who are obsessed by their sins and prepared to clutch any straw without ever coming to the truth. Eventually their folly will give them away.

Paul charges Timothy (3:10 – 4:5)

Paul cites his own life as evidence that a life lived for Christ is certain to attract persecution from impostors who deceive themselves as much as others. But what does it matter? Christ has rescued him every time! So let Timothy take heart, hold to his beliefs and remember the Scriptures he has known since a child, the Scriptures that are inspired by God and show the way to salvation through faith in Christ Jesus (3:10–17).

Paul charges Timothy to proclaim the Gospel and stick to it whether it is welcome or not, encouraging and correcting falsehood as the case may be. It will not be easy. The time is sure to come when people will be looking for anything that tickles their fancy and prefer fiction to truth; anything to satisfy their own agendas. So he must keep his head, stay with the Gospel and take suffering in his stride (4:1–5).

Paul's personal epilogue (4:6–22)

The time has come for me to depart. I have fought the good fight to the end; I have run the race to the finish; I have kept the faith; all there is to come for me now is the crown of uprightness which the Lord, the upright judge, will give to me on that Day; and not only to me but to all those who have longed for His appearing.

With these words, hauntingly sad yet pregnant with hope and joy, Paul, incarcerated in chains in a hostile Rome, makes his final farewell. Save for Luke he is all alone. No one was with him when he recently had to defend himself in court. Titus is in Dalmatia, Tychichus on his way to Ephesus. He left Erastus in Corinth and Trophimus in Miletus. He urges Timothy to come and see him and to bring Mark along with a cloak and some parchments he left behind in Troas. He sends greetings to his old friends Prisca and Aquila. There is no self-pity, no regrets. He is not downhearted for he knows that the Lord will bring him safely to His heavenly Kingdom.

Titus

See 1 Timothy

Titus' commission (1:1–16)

Paul introduces himself as a servant of God, an apostle of Christ chosen by God to proclaim the truth that gives the hope of eternal life. He reminds Titus that he was left in Crete to consolidate the church there and in particular to appoint overseers. As God's representatives these must be men of impeccable character fully capable of presenting and defending sound doctrine. At this very moment there are people going around spreading false doctrine and myths, especially Jews. They must be stopped. Their own actions give the lie to their claim to know God.

Christian conduct (2:1 – 3:2)

Paul insists that sound doctrine must be matched by good behaviour. He therefore instructs Titus in the conduct to be expected of older men, older women, younger women and younger men. Love and moderation must reign supreme. Slaves must be obedient and honest at all times. Everyone must respect civil authority, seize every opportunity to do good, eschew slander and be peace abiding, polite and gentle (2:1–6, 9–10; 3:1–2). Titus himself must set an example by his sincerity and earnestness and by preaching that leaves his opponents lost for words. He must get across that God's saving grace is for all men. People must therefore reject worldly passions and live upright godly lives as they wait in hope for the Saviour who has ransomed them from their sins (2:7–8, 11–15).

The gift of salvation (3:3–11)

We too were once slaves to our passions, Paul goes on, and full of hate. But God in His love changed all that and saved us. Not because of anything we had done but purely out of love so that, justified by grace and renewed in the Holy Spirit we might become heirs in hope of eternal life. Titus must be quite uncompromising in driving this message home so that people devote themselves to good works and avoid fractious arguments about genealogies and minutiae of the Law.[1] Anyone who stubbornly persists in disputing the Gospel should be left to his own devices.

Finale (3:12–15)

Paul concludes by asking Titus to join him in his winter quarters at Nicopolis as soon as he has been relieved and by stressing that Christians must always make themselves useful.

Philemon

This, the shortest of Paul's epistles to have survived, is a private note to a man of some standing named Philemon. He had a home large enough for the local church to meet there, v2, and owned a slave, Onesimus. According to v19 it was Paul himself who won him over to Christianity.

It would appear that Onesimus had fled from his master and absconded with some of his valuables. He subsequently met up with Paul in Rome where he was converted to Christianity, v10. (He may have already met Paul in Philemon's house.) Paul would have liked to have kept Onesimus to help him but did not want to presume upon Philemon's generosity whose property as a slave he legally still was. So he decided to send him back to Philemon and wrote this letter as a plea for lenience on Philemon's part. (Runaway slaves were liable to severe penalties which even a Christian master might not entirely waive.)

In fact, in what is a masterpiece of discretion and tact, Paul pleads for far more. He asks that Philemon receive Onesimus, now a fellow Christian, not as a slave but as a brother, indeed as if he were the apostle himself. Whether he also wanted Philemon to free Onesimus is uncertain. Perhaps Paul was deliberately vague on this point, not wishing to invoke his apostolic authority or play on the debt Philemon owed him for converting him, but preferring to leave it to Philemon's conscience.

We can only marvel at the unlikely trio caught up in Philemon in a common allegiance to Christ. Paul, a Pharisee and itinerant Jewish preacher now in prison; Philemon a well-to-do gentile; Onesimus, a fugitive slave and one time thief.
Appendix 1 refers

Hebrews

Hebrews is more a sermon than a letter. It begins without the customary greetings and yields no clue regarding either its author or its intended recipients. The most likely theory is that they were a group of Jewish Christians contemplating a reversion to Judaism, possibly under pressure of persecution, possibly because they found that the interior promptings of the Spirit could not compete with the regular outward ritual of the Law, or possibly again because they saw no sign of the promised Kingdom.

Hebrews tells us that the pillars of the Old Covenant – Law, the levitical priesthood, the sacrificial system – were only temporary expedients until the coming of Christ who alone, higher than the angels, greater than Moses, as perfect priest and perfect offering, could shatter the shackles of sin and restore fellowship with God in a New Covenant. In short Hebrews signals nothing less than the eclipse of the old dispensation.

The levitical priests were mortal sinful men offering sacrifices that were quite incapable of expiating sin. In contrast Christ is blameless and divinely appointed. Far from ministering in a man-made sanctuary He is seated at God's right hand and His priesthood is everlasting. His once-only sacrifice of His own body sealed a New Covenant and enabled forgiveness of sins as animal sacrifices, endlessly repeated, never could. In place of the Promised Land of Canaan, Christ offers life in God's own presence in the Promised Land of heaven.

Hebrews is reassuring. Having shared our humanity Christ understands our frailties and so is the perfect advocate on our behalf. Against that it is punctuated with warnings to those who reject the Gospel.

Hebrews is not easy. It is closely reasoned and leans heavily on arguments from Scripture that modern readers may find unconvincing even though the methods the author employs would have raised no eyebrows in his own day.

THE SUPREMACY OF CHRIST (1:1 – 3:6)

The majesty of the Son of God (1:1–4)

In a regal opening the author proclaims the deity, supremacy and sufficiency of the Son. He is both heir and agent of Creation, the reflection of God's glory, the impress of His being. Everything is sustained in Him. And now having purged our sins He sits enthroned at God's right hand far above the angels.

The Son greater than the angels (1:5–14)

That supremacy is what the author now sets out to demonstrate using quotations from Scripture in which he attributes the words directly to God.[1] Thus speaking of the First-born (i.e. the Son) he quotes God saying

Let all the angels of God pay Him homage,

proof of His ascendancy over angels. Again, addressing the Son, he quotes God saying

Your throne, God, is for ever and ever,

proof that He, the Son, is divine and reigns in glory. Angels are servants used by God to help bring men to salvation.

A warning (2:1–4)

If a message (the Law) given by angels was so binding that every infringement was punished, how can we expect to escape punishment if we ignore the promise of salvation from the lips of the Lord Himself? Especially as it has been attested by signs and miracles and the gift of the Holy Spirit.[2]

Man's destiny in Christ (2:5–18)

Man has a wonderful destiny. For a little while he is to be less than the angels but God's plan is that ultimately everything will be subject to him. This is certainly not the case at the moment. But we can see what it means in Jesus who was for a time lower than the angels but is already crowned with glory and honour because of the death He endured for us. He shared our humanity and took us as His brothers so that in overcoming the devil He could free us from our sins and death. The suffering and temptations He experienced make Him the perfect person to help us when we are tested.

Christ greater than Moses (3:1–6)

Jesus is greater than Moses. Moses worked faithfully in God's house. But Jesus was the builder of that house. Again Moses was a servant in God's household. But Christ is the faithful Son in charge of that household. And we Christians are that household so long as our hope never wavers.

THE PROMISED REST (3:7 – 4:13)

Because of their disbelief God would not allow the Israelites, whom Moses led out of Egypt, to find their place of rest, the Promised Land of Canaan (3:7–19). Nor did they find it under Joshua. But God's promise still stands as was made clear when He inspired

David to say 'If only you would listen to Him today; do not harden your hearts', words that imply the door is still open. The key to opening it is the Gospel although merely hearing is not enough. It is necessary to respond with faith. Those who do, enter God's very own place of rest while those who do not will be lost. Nothing is hidden from God. His gaze penetrates our most secret thoughts (4:1–13).

In stating that Israel did not find her place of rest under Joshua, Hebrews is saying that Canaan, which Israel occupied under Joshua, was never the Promised Land God ultimately intended for His people. It goes on to make plain that this was to be something incomparably more wonderful, repose with God in His very own abode outside of space and time. Thus the Promised Land of Canaan in the Old Testament is to be seen as merely a dim foreshadowing of the heavenly homeland God would unveil in the New.[3]

THE HIGH PRIESTHOOD OF CHRIST (4:14 – 10:18)

Christ the perfect high priest (4:14 – 5:10)

The author now embarks on his core theme, the high priesthood of Christ. We must persist in our faith, he begins, because in Jesus we have a high priest who is in the presence of God yet who understands our weaknesses because He has been tested exactly as we are. We should therefore never be afraid to ask for mercy or help.

He next shows how Jesus exceeded the qualifications required of other high priests. They were chosen to offer sacrifices for sins, to empathise with the people and had to have been called by God as Aaron was. Now Christ was not only appointed by God but His is an everlasting priesthood of the order of Melchizedek. Furthermore in His life on earth He learned from His suffering the full cost of (human) obedience and so reached a perfection (in His human character) that enabled him to become the source of salvation for all who obey Him.

A call to progress (5:11 – 6:20)

Before going on to explain the significance of Melchizedek the author pauses to say that his readers will find what he now has to say difficult because they are such slow learners. He begins by reminding them that people who turn their backs on the Holy Spirit are headed for doom. They cannot repent again.[4] Not that things have got to that stage, he assures them. God will not forget their love and works. If they persevere and do not become complacent they will have every reason for confidence. Not only did God confirm His promise to Abraham with an oath but Jesus has already passed through the curtain that guards God's presence.[5]

Christ is higher than the levitical priesthood (7:1–28)

Melchizedek is both king and priest. His life has neither beginning nor end.[6] He remains a priest for ever. Priests normally take tithes from ordinary people but Melchizedek took a tithe from no less a person than Abraham. Furthermore he blessed

Abraham. Since tithes pass from an inferior to a superior and a blessing is given by a superior to an inferior this means that Melchizedek is superior to Abraham and thus to his descendant Levi. From this it follows that Christ's priesthood (which is of the order of Melchizedek) is superior to the old priesthood that was descended from Levi (7:1–10).

That levitical priesthood and the Law were powerless to bring anyone to perfection and have now been cast aside. That is why we have been given in Christ a new priesthood, and with it the abolition of the Law, in favour of something (the New Covenant) that really can bring us close to God. That we have a complete break with the past is evident from the fact that Christ came from Judah, a tribe from which priests had never been chosen from before. Christ's priesthood is perpetual and sealed by God on oath and that makes the (New) Covenant of which He is the guarantor all the greater too.

Such is the high priest who meets our needs: holy, free from sin, raised above the heavens, perfect, eternal. Unlike other priests who offer sacrifices every day, first for their own sins and then for the people, He needed to offer Himself but once (7:11–28).

The new covenant (8:1–13)

This new priesthood has several implications. To begin with Christ is enthroned at God's right hand and His sanctuary is the true one in the heavens not some man-made shrine. Then unlike earthly priests who merely offer the sacrifices laid down by the Law, His offering of Himself is the heavenly reality of which theirs were but pale shadows. Finally the New Covenant of which Christ is the mediator is far superior to the Old Covenant it supersedes and which failed because men could not live up to its demands. Under the New Covenant men will be guided by the spirit of obedience God will implant in their hearts and everyone will know Him. He will forgive their sins and never call them to mind.

The old and new covenants compared (9:1–28)

Under the old covenant priests regularly worshipped in the Holy Place in the outer part of the Sanctuary but only the high priest, and he only once a year, was allowed to pass through the veil into the Holy of Holies where God dwelt. In this way the Holy Spirit was showing us that the old liturgy, which focused on externals like eating and washing, could never cleanse hearts and consciences sufficiently to allow access to God. However all that was only temporary until the time was ripe for God to establish a new order (9:1–10).

That new order arrived with Christ who entered the heavenly Sanctuary taking with Him not the blood of animals but His own blood, the blood that won our redemption. If the blood of animals was able to restore bodily purity, how much more will the blood of the blameless Christ purge us of guilt and set us free to serve the living God[7] (9:11–14).

Just as the Old Covenant was sealed in blood, so too is the New that Christ inaugurated. It is, as it were, His legacy and since legacies only become operative when the legatee dies so the New Covenant only became effective with Christ's redeeming death. His self-sacrifice to release people from their sins is valid for all time including sins committed under the Old Covenant. It completely transcends the old Mosaic system where priests had to sacrifice animals over and over again and even then could do no more than purify shadows of the heavenly realities. Christ is not ministering for us in some man-made sanctuary but in heaven in God's presence. When He comes again it will not be to deal with sin – He has already done that – but to bring salvation to those who are waiting for him[8] (9:15–28).

A summary (10:1–18)

The Law was only a foretaste of better things to come. The fact that its sacrifices had to be repeated shows how ineffective they were in removing sin. So Christ came in obedience to God's will to offer His own body. Having done that He is seated at God's right hand awaiting the time when His enemies will be made His footstool. He has established the New Covenant under which God will no longer recall anyone's sins. There is no need for any more sin offerings.

FAITH AND ENDURANCE (10:19 – 13:25)

Perseverance (10:19–39)

Christ's death means we can approach God with confidence. So let us do so with pure hearts, steadfast in faith, firm in hope, fruitful in love and good works. Anyone who tramples on Christ or insults the Spirit faces God's fiery wrath.[9] So having endured so much already, the author declaims, do not fail now. Persevere.

Faith (11:1–40)

The inspired author insists that only faith can guarantee the blessings we hope for or prove the existence of realities yet unseen. He goes on to give examples of faith in the lives of Abel, Enoch, Noah, Abraham, Sarah, Isaac, Jacob, Joseph, Moses and Rahab with allusions to many more including Daniel, the Maccabees and Isaiah. None of these received what was promised (in this life) because God has made provision to give them something better in the heavenly realm along with us.[10]

Fortitude (12:1–11)

The writer exhorts his readers to be done with sin. Let them remember Jesus and persevere as He did. As a loving Father God uses the vicissitudes of life, harsh though they seem at the time, to train us as His sons for spiritual maturity and life.

Dangers to be avoided (12:12–17)

So cast off despondency and fear and support the (spiritually) lame lest they stumble. Seek peace and holiness. Let no one spurn God's grace and become so embittered that he disrupts the whole community. Avoid immorality and let no one behave like Esau and become so worldly minded that he forgets his spiritual destiny.

The old and new covenants contrasted (12:18–29)

The author now contrasts Christians under the New Covenant with Israel under the Old. Instead of the terror of lowering storm clouds and blazing fire that Israel experienced at Mount Sinai, where not even an animal could approach the mountain on pain of death, Christians have come to Mount Zion, to God Himself and a joyful assembly of angels and the faithful, all enrolled as citizens of heaven. There too is Jesus whose blood made it all possible. But be warned. If those who ignored the Old Covenant did not escape punishment, how can those who ignore the New? Soon this transient order will pass away and only the eternal will remain. Let us therefore be thankful and worship in reverence and fear.

Final exhortations and epilogue (13:1–25)

Continue in brotherly love and always welcome strangers. You may be entertaining angels. Remember those in prison or suffering ill-treatment. Preserve the sanctity of marriage and replace covetousness with contentment. God will not fail you. Copy the faith of those who taught you, remembering that Christ is the same now as He always was and always will be.

Verses 9–15 seem to be a warning against reverting to Judaistic rituals. Christians have their own liturgy and should rely on God for strength rather than looking to strange dietary rules that have never helped anyone. Jesus made His sacrifice for sin outside the city walls just as the animals whose blood was used to atone for sin were burned outside the camp.[11] Let us therefore also join Jesus outside the camp (of Judaism).

Keep on performing good works and sharing. Obey your leaders cheerfully and with a good grace. The letter ends with greetings, a reference to Timothy having been set free, and a prayer to the God of peace who brought Jesus back from the dead.

THE GENERAL EPISTLES

James

The author presents himself as James servant of God and of the Lord Jesus Christ and most scholars uphold the traditional view that this is the James who was Jesus' brother and leader of the early Church in Jerusalem.

The letter is addressed to the twelve tribes of the Dispersion. Although this would seem to indicate Jewish Christians living outside Palestine, the possibility that 'twelve tribes' is a symbolic designation for the whole Christian Church as the new Israel cannot be ruled out. The author was clearly addressing believers who were experiencing difficulties: an unscrupulous upper class, discrimination, internal bickering. There are signs too that their faith was becoming a superficial formality. Having been released from the cloying shackles of the Jewish Law perhaps they did not yet understand that their new faith also made demands albeit of a different kind.

James addresses these problems in a series of crisp, staccato and only loosely connected imperatives or sermonettes. The dominant theme is his insistence that Christianity is not some abstract passive faith but one that demands 'doing' rather than merely 'hearing': love in action.

Without works faith is an empty shell. He is vehemently opposed to anything that smacks of hypocrisy, pretence or insincerity. James is sometimes criticised for being light on theology. He has nothing to say about Christ's redeeming work for example. But these matters are dealt with elsewhere, in the Gospels and by Paul. James is content to take them for granted and lay his emphasis on day to day duties and practicalities.

Trials build character (1:1–4)

After the briefest of salutations James plunges straight into his first point. Trials should be seen as a blessing for they build spiritual maturity.

Pray for wisdom (1:5–8)

Anyone who lacks wisdom must seek it from God who will respond generously provided the supplicant has faith and prays in confident expectation without wavering.

On poor and rich (1:9–11)

The poor should be glad that their faith has lifted them up: the rich that it has taught them humility and that wealth is as fleeting as a wild flower.

On trials and temptation (1:12–18)

Happy the man who weathers life's trials. He will receive the crown of life. When a person is tempted it is not God's doing but his own evil desires from within, desires that give birth to sin which, if unchecked, leads to death. What comes from God is good and perfect. He has given us (re)birth through the (Gospel) truth so that we might become first-fruits among all His creatures.[1]

True religion (1:19–27)

Be a good listener, slow to speak and slow to anger. God's cause is never served by human wrath. Have done with filthiness and welcome the Word. It can save you. But only if you act on it and do not simply listen to it. Anyone who takes no action is like someone who glances at himself in the mirror and then hurries away.[2] Bridle your tongues. True religion means helping the needy and steering clear of the world's pollution.[3]

Against discrimination (2:1–13)

Partiality such as favouring the rich at the expense of the poor contravenes the command to love one's neighbour and is thus a sin. Remember that falling foul of the Law on one point makes you guilty of breaking it all.[4] Bear in mind that you are to be judged and remember that he who acts without mercy will be judged without mercy.

Faith and deeds (2:14–26)

Faith without deeds is dead. Unless faith expresses itself in works of love like clothing the poor and feeding the hungry it will not bring salvation. James presses his point with examples. Even the demons believe in one God. Yet they tremble with fear.[5] Abraham's faith was perfected when he offered Isaac for sacrifice and it was this, faith and deeds working together and not faith alone, that led to his justification. It was the same with Rahab when she helped Joshua's spies.
Appendix 1 refers

On sins of the tongue (3:1–12)

James cautions against over eagerness to take up teaching. Teachers carry a heavy responsibility and will be judged particularly strictly. Everyone must learn to control his tongue. The tongue is a pest full of deadly poison and difficult to tame. Tiny though it is, it can inflame one's whole being just as a bit can control a horse, a rudder a ship, or a small flame ignite a forest fire. Yet we use it both to curse our fellow men and to bless God. This cannot be right. Does salt and fresh water come out of the same pipe?[6]

True wisdom (3:13–18)

True wisdom comes from above and reveals itself in gentleness and mercy, in people who are kind and considerate and whose lives are marked by good deeds. Anyone whose wisdom is purely human is consumed by jealousy or selfish ambition and sows disharmony and wickedness.

On submitting to God (4:1–17)

Why is there all this quarrelling among you, James thunders at his readers? It is all about gratifying your selfish desires and passions! No wonder your prayers are not answered. Do you not realise that to adopt the world's values is to be God's enemy? So humble yourselves before the Lord and give Him the chance to lift you up so that you can put the devil to flight. The closer you get to God the closer He will get to you. So see yourselves for what you are and turn from the laughter of ungodliness to the grief of repentance (4:1–10).

Do not speak evil of one another for by so doing you are putting yourself above the Law rather than under it. There is only one judge. As for the self-confident (business) man, let him remember that he is like mist, here today and gone tomorrow. So instead of his self-confident loud-mouthed bragging let him base his plans around 'if it is the Lord's will'. Anyone who knows what is the right thing to do but does not do it commits a sin (4:11–17).

A warning to the unscrupulous rich (5:1–6)

James fulminates like an Old Testament prophet as he castigates the complacent rich, not inviting their repentance but announcing their impending doom: people who have hoarded so much wealth that it is rotting away; who cheat the harvesters in the fields of their wages; who murder the innocent. Their lives of luxury and insulated self-indulgence have merely been fattening them for the slaughter of judgement. The very fact that their gold and silver is corroding away unused bears witness to their selfish greed and lack of social conscience.

On patient endurance and swearing (5:7–12)

Be patient for the Lord is coming, like a farmer waiting for the rains. He will not be long. Do not complain about one another. Let God do the judging. Bear persecution with patience like Job and the prophets. Do not use oaths when making a promise, just say 'yes' or 'no.'

On prayer (5:13–20)

Anyone in trouble should pray while those in good heart should sing songs of praise. Let the elders anoint the sick with oil in the name of the Lord and pray over them. Prayers offered in faith will save them and remit their sins. All Christians should confess their sins and pray for one other. Elijah showed how effective prayer was. James ends with a reminder that anyone who brings a lapsed believer back to God saves him from (spiritual) death and ensures his sins will not be held against him.

1 Peter

Although its authenticity is often called into question it is by no means improbable that 1 Peter was written by the apostle Peter shortly before his martyrdom in Rome around A.D. 64. In any event it is a message of hope and encouragement to Christians facing persecution. They must never forget the glorious heritage awaiting them in heaven and accept trials with patience and fortitude as tests of their faith. Indeed they should rejoice because those who share Christ's suffering will also share His glory. So let them take Christ as their model, live blamelessly, and set an example to pagans.

Opening address: salvation (1:1–12)

Peter addresses himself to Christians in the Roman provinces of Asia Minor. He thanks God that through faith in a Christ they have never seen they have been given new birth and a heritage in heaven that can never fade. Despite trials to test their faith they are filled with joy at the certainty of their salvation. It is this salvation, now revealed in the Gospel, that the prophets were searching for when the Spirit revealed to them the sufferings of Christ and the glory to follow.

A call for holiness (1:13–25)

Prepare yourselves, Peter goes on. Break out of your old sinful mould and be holy even as God is holy. Live your lives in reverential awe of the Father who impartially judges everyone by what he has done. Never forget that your redemption was bought with the precious blood of the blameless Christ. It is because of Him that you now have faith in God. Reborn and purified by the Word of God, you must excel in love.

The new people of God (2:1–10)

Rid yourselves of spite and hypocrisy, Peter continues, and since you are spiritual babes grasp the spiritual milk that will help you grow up to salvation. Stay close to Christ, the cornerstone, so that you may become living stones and together form a spiritual house, a holy priesthood offering spiritual sacrifices.[1] To unbelievers Christ is a stone to stumble over but you have been called from darkness into light to be a chosen race, a holy nation.[2]

Christian conduct (2:11 – 3:12)

As strangers and nomads Christians must forswear bodily passions and set such an example that even gentiles (meaning here non-believers) sit up and take note.[3] They should submit to civil authority and let their good deeds quash any foolish gossip about them. They must never let their freedom become a cloak for wickedness.[4] Rather let them show respect to everyone, love their fellow Christians, fear God and acknowledge the emperor.[5]

Slaves should respect their masters and accept their lot even when they were treated unfairly. They should find inspiration in the patient suffering of Christ who, though totally innocent, bore our sins on the Cross and thereby brought us lost sheep back to the flock of which He is the shepherd (2:11–25).

Wives should be obedient to their husbands so that any who were unbelievers might be won over by their reverence and purity. Rather than doting on the latest fashions they should cultivate that gentle and tender demeanour that is so precious in God's sight. For their part husbands should treat their wives with consideration and respect as equal heirs of the gift of life. Let everyone be of one mind, full of love and compassion, self effacing, never repaying wrong with wrong but always with a blessing (3:1–12).

Persecution (3:13–17)

No one can hurt you if you only do what is right.[6] But if you have to suffer for righteousness sake how blessed you are! Never be afraid. Simply acknowledge and honour Christ as Lord and have your answer ready for anyone who challenges your hope. But do it courteously so that your detractors are shamed into silence. If you are to suffer, better for it to be for doing right than wrong.

Christ preaches to the dead (3:18–22)

This next passage is compact to the point of obscurity. Peter begins by reminding his readers that Christ died for our sins to lead us to God; the upright dying for the guilty. He then reveals how, between His death and resurrection, Jesus preached to the dead, the 'spirits in prison'.[7] Although Noah's generation is singled out this is probably meant to be representative of all who died before Christ, thus affording them also the opportunity to accept Him and appropriate the fruits of His redeeming death. Picking up on Noah Peter then draws a parallel. As in olden days the water bearing the Ark saved Noah and his family, so the water of baptism saves men now through the power of the risen Christ.[8]

Through suffering to life (4:1–6)

Peter returns to suffering. Accept it as Christ did, he resumes, because you will then no longer be susceptible to the pull of sin but only to God's will. People will be amazed when they see how you have renounced the licentious ways that are still driving them to ruin and will revile you for it. But that is something they will have to answer to God for. Now you can see why the Gospel was preached to the dead: to give them the same chance to enjoy life with God as everyone else.

Live for each other (4:7–11)

The end is near. So persevere in prayer and love and use the special gifts God has given you for the common good.

On suffering (4:12–19)

Do not be perturbed by the suffering you are experiencing. If you share Christ's suffering or are insulted for His name's sake be glad. For as you share in His suffering so you will share in His glory. Suffering as punishment for being a criminal is one thing but there is no shame in suffering for being a Christian. If Christians are suffering, what will it be like for people who reject the Gospel? If it is hard for the upright to be saved, what will happen to sinners? So stick with God and continue your good works.

Instructions to elders and the young (5:1–11)

Peter calls on the elders to nurture their flock like shepherds, not as a duty or for money but willingly and eagerly. They should lead not by lording it but by example and then when the chief shepherd appears they will be given the unfading crown of glory. Younger people should subject themselves to the elders by wearing the apron of humility. Let them unload their troubles on to God and always be on the look out for a devil who is like a roaring lion, ceaselessly on the lookout for someone to devour. Have faith and stand up to him, Peter continues, knowing that your brothers throughout the world are undergoing similar trials and that it will only last a little while. God will support you.

Final greetings (5:12–14)

Peter ends by explaining that he has written the letter to encourage his readers to persevere. Along with Mark he ends with greetings from 'your sister in Babylon'.[9]

2 Peter

Very few critics today believe that 2 Peter stems from the pen of the apostle whose name it bears. Most consider it to be a pseudonymous work written after his death. Its purpose however is clear. It is a rebuttal of false teachers and people who scoff at God's apparent inactivity. Do not be misled, the writer warns. God will act in His own good time and then those who have falsified His word will be judged accordingly. Meanwhile Christians should be guided by Scripture and live pure and holy lives as they patiently await the Lord's return. There are a number of similarities with Jude and it is probable that 2 Peter drew on Jude rather than the other way round.

Salutation and exhortation to spiritual progress (1:1–11)

The writer introduces himself as Simon Peter, servant and apostle of Jesus Christ. Through His divine power and knowledge of Christ, God has given us all we need to enable us to live godly lives so that, free from the corruption of sin, we may become partakers of the divine nature.[1] Therefore it behoves us to supplement our faith with goodness, understanding, self-control, perseverance, piety, kindness and love. With these qualities there will be no danger of our faith becoming unfruitful or so short-sighted that we forget how our sins were washed away. We must never waver. Then we will avoid stumbling and be sure of a warm welcome into the Lord's eternal kingdom.

Apostolic witness (1:12–18)

Peter tells his readers that he is writing this as a memoir for after his death. Make no mistake, he continues, he is not dealing in fantasies. He witnessed Christ's glorification with his own eyes.[2]

The inspiration of prophecy and Scripture (1:19–21)

Given this confirmation of prophecy we would do well to let prophecy guide us in the future too.[3] But we must be careful. Just as prophecy is inspired by the Holy Spirit so the interpretation of Scripture is not a matter for the individual.[4]

False teachers (2:1–22)

The reason for this cautionary note soon becomes clear as Peter goes on to say that there will be false teachers in the future just as there have been in the past. They will deny Christ and bring the Truth into disrepute. They will even try to make money out of their fabrications. Yet their doom is assured for God has clearly shown, with sinful angels and the way He punished evil-doers in the days of Noah and Lot, how He delivers His own while destroying the ungodly[5] (2:1–10a). Insolent rogues! They are as dissipated and as avaricious as Balaam.[6] With their fine talk they prey on new converts by appealing to their lower instincts and offering so-called freedom.[7] Yet they are slaves themselves, slaves of depravity. Far better never to have become a believer than for someone who has accepted Christ to revert to his previous godless ways (2:10b–22).

Scoffers and the Day of the Lord (3:1–10)

Peter reminds his readers that this is the second letter he has sent to encourage them.[8] He warns them of people who will scoff because Christ has not yet returned and everything still seems to go on much as it always did. Such people would be well advised to remember how the flood came unexpectedly out of the blue to destroy sinners. It will be the same with the Day of Judgement. God is not being slow in meeting His promises but patiently holding the door of repentance open as long as possible because He does not want anyone to perish. No, when the Day of the Lord does come it will come like a thief, without warning. And then the whole world will be consumed by fire.
Appendix 1 refers

A call to holiness (3:11–18)

In the meantime while you are waiting for God's promise of new heavens and a new earth where uprightness reigns, Peter concludes, take advantage of His patience and lead pure and holy lives. This, after all, is what Paul taught. Some of the things Paul wrote about, like the rest of Scripture, are difficult to follow and some unscrupulous people have distorted their meanings.[9] So be careful not to be deceived and continue to grow in the grace and knowledge of Christ.

1 John

1 John contains neither greetings nor blessings, neither names nor clear references to concrete situations. It seems to have been written to bolster its readers against a rash of false teaching but what this was is difficult to tie down as John refutes it without ever spelling out precisely what the heresies were. However there are clues.

John's opponents seem to have been of a persuasion that saw the physical world as inherently evil. Only things of the spirit were pure. As a result they denied that Jesus the human being and Christ the divine Son of God could possibly be one and the same. If matter was evil how could the Son of God possibly appear in human flesh? They appear too to have claimed insight that went beyond the Gospel. Such was their detachment from the material world that they saw salvation as having little to do with morality or brotherly love. Thus they appear to have regarded themselves as free of sin and in no need of redemption. All of these were beliefs which if unchecked would have torn the heart out of Christianity.

But there is of course no need to read the epistle as a rebuttal of error. We can take it as it stands, as a devotional critique drawing out the implications of belief so that 'our joy may be complete' and 'you may know that you have eternal life', 1:4; 5:13. It is dominated by two great aphorisms, God is light, God is love, that rightly stand alongside the evangelist's other great recognition that God is spirit, Jn 4:24. The letter has a strong pastoral flavour as John addresses his readers with fatherly solicitude and tender concern. His aim is to sustain and encourage yet also, without harsh admonition, to warn.

1 John can be difficult to follow. More a poem than an essay, themes recur again and again, mingled in diverse ways like the views from a meandering river. It begins by portraying God as light. Believers must therefore turn to Jesus to cleanse them from their sins and dispel the darkness that would otherwise exclude them from His company and eternal life. The way to please God is by keeping His commandment and being rich in brotherly love. Love is supreme, leading to life as children of God. John warns against false prophets. The proof of a true teacher is that he believes Jesus is God in human nature. He rounds off as he began with eternal life. Life and the Son go together. It is impossible to have the one without the other.

On authorship see Jn appendix 2.

Prologue (1:1–4)

Our theme, John begins, is the Word of life which has existed from the beginning and which we have heard, seen and touched.[1] The life we are talking about is eternal life with the Father and His Son Jesus Christ and we are revealing what we know so that you too may share it. Then our joy will be complete.

God is Light (1:5 – 2:28)

Walk in light (1:5–7)

God is light. There is no darkness in Him at all.[2] Therefore we delude ourselves if we think we can share in God's life while walking in darkness. For that to be possible we must live in light as He does. Then we will enjoy fellowship with one another and Jesus' blood will cleanse us from every sin.

Break with sin (1:8 – 2:2)

Whoever says that sin has no hold over him, or that he has never sinned, is deceiving himself. So let us acknowledge our sins. Then God will forgive us and purify us because in Jesus we have an advocate whose sacrifice expiates the sins of the whole world.

Keep the commandments especially that of love (2:3–11)

Whoever says he knows God without keeping His commandments is a liar. On the other hand people who obey God by walking in Christ's footsteps find that love is thereby brought to perfection. No one can walk in light while hating (i.e. not loving) his brother. But anyone who loves his brother remains in light.[3]

Be detached from the world (2:12–17)

After assuring his readers that their sins have been forgiven, that they know God and have overcome the devil, John urges them not to fall into the trap of worldliness: gratification of bodily desires, greed, pride in possessions. None of these are from God. All are transient and will pass away. But whoever does the will of God abides for ever.

Beware of antichrists (2:18–28)

Christians must be on the alert. They know the Antichrist will come in the final days but many (lesser) antichrists are already at work rejecting Jesus (the man) as the (divine) Christ and therefore denying both the Father and the Son.[4] They must stick to the Gospel they were reared on with its promise of eternal life.[5] With the Spirit that is all they need. They do not need any other teacher and can await Christ's return unafraid.

GOD'S CHILDREN (2:29 – 4:6)

God adopts His own (2:29 – 3:2)

John marvels at God's love. He has already adopted the righteous as His children. What this means has not yet been unveiled. Suffice to say that they will be like Him and see Him as He is. But the world at large cannot relate to this any more than it could accept Jesus.

Break with sin (3:3–10)

Whoever treasures this hope must be pure like Christ. People who sin are not Christ's but the devil's and the two are implacably opposed. The whole point of Christ's coming was to release people from the devil's spell. No child of God goes on sinning because God's seed remains in him.[6] What distinguishes a child of God from a child of the devil is that he lives uprightly and loves his brother.

Keep the commandments, especially to love (3:11–24)

Love one another, John continues. Do not be like Cain who murdered his brother because he was upright. At the same time do not be surprised if the world hates you. Life and love go together. The one implies the other and no one who hates his brother will enjoy eternal life. True love means not just talk but action as when Jesus laid down His life for us. We must be prepared to do the same or at the very least help our brother in need (3:11–18).

Love proves that we belong to God and even if our consciences reproach us for not doing enough we can take heart from the fact that God knows everything.[7] When our conscience is clear we can approach God knowing that our prayers will be answered because we are keeping His commandments to believe in Jesus and love one another. If we are faithful to these we remain in God and He in us.[8] And the proof is the Spirit within us (3:19–24).

Beware of Antichrist (4:1–6)

Not everyone who claims to speak under inspiration is genuine. The acid test is whether a prophet acknowledges that Christ, the Son of God, came in human flesh in Jesus. If so his message is from God. If not he is a false prophet and his message is from the Antichrist whose spirit is already at large in the world. But there is no need to worry. Christians have already won the battle against these false prophets because God who is in them is greater than the devil who is in the world. The world listens to false prophets because they reflect its values. But the true believer, John says, listens to us. So when people deny us we know that the spirit of falsehood is at work.

THE SUPREMACY OF LOVE (4:7 – 5:5)

God is love. He revealed His love by sending His Son to expiate our sins and give us life. It was not that we loved God but that He loved us.[9] Since He loves us we must love one another. By so doing we become His children and His love for us then reaches perfection. No one has ever seen God but as long as we love one another and acknowledge Jesus as His Son we remain in Him and He in us, as evidenced through the Spirit (4:7–16).

Love is perfect when judgement holds no terrors because it means we will have become like Christ. Perfect love drives out fear.[10] It was Christ Himself who said that whoever loves God must also love his brother. If we do not love our brother whom we can see how can we love God whom we cannot see? Whoever believes that Jesus is the Christ is a child of God and he will love his brothers because they are also children of God. Loving God means keeping His commandments.[11] This is not burdensome because every child of God is assured of victory through faith in Jesus as Son of God[12] (4:17 – 5:5).

THE SOURCE AND FRUITS OF FAITH (5:6–13)

John now proceeds to counter a heresy that Jesus was not the Christ, the divine Son of God. He presents three arguments all of which point to the same conclusion and are attested not by human witness but by God Himself. The first is water (alluding to the divine commission Jesus received at His baptism). The second is blood (His death and, by implication, His subsequent resurrection). The third is the Spirit (with His inner promptings). It was crucial to have this testimony because belief in the Son (i.e. that Jesus the man was also the divine Son of God) is the key to eternal life. To believe in the Son is to have life. Not to believe in the Son is not to have life.

SUPPLEMENTS (5:14–20)

Believers can be sure that when they pray for something that is in accord with God's will it will be granted. In particular if they pray for a brother who has sinned, then provided it is not a deadly sin he will be forgiven.[13] All evil-doing is sin but not all sin leads to death.

John concludes by summarising some of his main points. No child of God can go on (habitually) sinning because Christ protects him from the Evil One. Christians belong to God but the world is in the grip of the Evil One. Christ came so that we might know God. We are in God and we are in His Son, Jesus Christ. He is the true God and eternal life. Be on your guard against false gods.

2 John

This short letter is addressed to the Lady, the chosen one, and her children, probably a church and its congregation. It makes just two points. Let them abide by the command to love one another. And let them have no truck with deceivers (the Antichrist) who deny the Incarnation – that Jesus Christ, the Son of the Father, came in human nature – and whose teaching deviates from or even goes beyond the orthodox faith that came from Christ.

3 John

It seems that Gaius, to whom this letter is addressed, had been helping some itinerant missionaries (presumably sent by John) and that someone had reported this back to John thus prompting the apostle's commendation and his hope that Gaius would keep up the good work. Unfortunately the minister in charge of Gaius' congregation, Diotrephes, was not so agreeably disposed. Not content with preventing the church from getting a letter John had sent it, he also spread false innuendos about John, refusing to welcome his envoys and expelling from his church anyone who offered to help them.[1] In this difficult situation John urges Gaius to follow the good example rather than the bad, in other words to keep on supporting the missionaries. He assures him of Demetrius' credentials and soon hopes to pay a visit himself when he will take the whole matter up in person.[2]

Jude

The author introduces himself as Jude, brother of James, and explains that his aim is to encourage his readers to uphold the faith against infiltrators who are perverting it and rejecting Christ.[1] He reminds them how in bygone days Israel was punished for her lack of faith and how God disciplined deviant angels and struck Sodom and Gomorrah[2] (1–7).

Undeterred these present day heretics are acting in the same mould, indulging in immorality, spurning God and abusing angels in language that not even the archangel Michael used in his argument with the devil.[3] They abuse anything they do not understand. The only things they do understand are the sensual passions that will be their downfall. They follow in the unworthy tradition of Cain, Balaam and Korah and will share the same fate.[4] They behave shamelessly at the community meals caring only for themselves.[5] They are barren and useless and it was they Enoch had in mind when he prophesied God's judgement on godless sinners[6] (8–16).

The apostles had warned that the end days would bring mockers who would sow discord. So, Jude concludes, build up your faith and keep praying to stay within God's love as you wait for Christ to give you eternal life. Be compassionate to those who are wavering under the influence of this false teaching, snatch others from the fire, to others again be compassionate but wary (17–23).

Jude concludes with a doxology in praise of the God who can keep His people from stumbling and bring them safely to His glorious presence innocent and joyful (24–25).

THE REVELATION TO JOHN

Revelation, a book of climactic grandeur and devastating power, brings the Bible to a triumphant conclusion. As it draws back the veil to reveal the serene majesty of God in heaven we are transported through the travails of history to the final overthrow of Satan and the establishment beyond space and time of God's everlasting Kingdom. In the end there is only Christ who lives for ever and Satan who dies for ever. Where GENESIS shows God creating, Revelation shows Him recreating. All the promises of life in glory coalesce in the vision of man living with God in a new creation, a new Jerusalem where Christ is enthroned as King of kings. It is the conclusion of God's revelation to men. The age-long conflict is over.

Without Revelation the Bible would end leaving us with hope yet in an atmosphere charged with tempest and suffering and with a Church under threat. Christ conquered evil on the Cross but its power is not yet finally spent so that, through the centuries, ever more monstrous powers, godless and evil, have appeared on the world stage. Darkness has deepened so that today in a world riven by discord and inequality, where man has acquired powers beyond his moral competence, and where honour is accorded the profane and trivial, humanity is enveloped by a pall of foreboding. It is against this sombre background that Revelation, never more relevant and even now still being played out, assures us that history is in God's hands and that He will ultimately prevail.

However, although its promise to reveal the future attracts readers like a magnet, few persist and Revelation must rank among the least understood books in the Canon. It is steeped in Scripture with perhaps two-thirds of its verses containing Old Testament allusions. But the main difficulty facing the modern reader is a succession of visions that can appear to lack a common thread and an apocalyptic style abounding in imagery, some of it mythological in origin and much of it perplexing and obscure.

Accordingly, before proceeding to our synopsis, we begin by showing the reader how to navigate a course through this challenging book. We start by placing it in its historical context and discussing the four principal schools of interpretation. From there we then go on to outline its core message: the trunk without the branches.

Authorship/date

According to tradition Revelation was written by the author of the fourth Gospel. Today many scholars dispute this on grounds of style and opt for an otherwise unknown John. The arguments are not compelling and it is best to accept that we do not know. In any case the question of authorship has no bearing on the book's interpretation.

It seems likely that Revelation was written at a time when the Church was weathering a storm of persecution, either under Nero who was emperor of Rome from A.D. 54 to 68 and whose onslaught was confined to Rome, or under Domitian, A.D. 81 to 96, who attacked it throughout the empire. Most scholars favour a date around A.D. 95 although a case can be made for at least part of Revelation being composed shortly after Nero's death, say around A.D. 70.

The four principal schools

Historicists see Revelation painting a panorama of history from Christ's advent to the end of time. However as they can rarely agree among themselves on which historical events John's visions portray this view is largely discredited. The preterist confines it to events in the author's own day under the Rome of Nero, viewing it as a tract of hope for the faithful during a time of vicious persecution. To the futurist all but the first three chapters relate to the times surrounding the Second Coming. The idealist sees Revelation as poetic and symbolic, affirming the sure outcome of the great cosmic battle between good and evil, God and Satan, but otherwise declining to identify any of its images with specific future events whether to do with history or the last days.

There is certainly a level of meaning in Revelation that relates to Rome and passages that John's readers would have seen as pointing to contemporary events. They would have recognised the travails that John describes and the Church crying out for vindication as their own. But this cannot be the whole story any more than it seems likely that John's visions focus purely on the end days. On the contrary, in so far as Revelation addresses the battle between Christ's sovereignty and satanic power, it is timeless and universal, encompassing the whole of history, a beacon of hope for all ages. To confine it to Rome or the last days is to force it into a mould too small for the grandeur of its conception and the cosmic sweep of its themes. It is significant that whenever John alludes to Rome he does so obliquely so as to leave open the possibility of a wider meaning as well.

This work therefore leans towards the idealist interpretation while admitting a futurist element and recognising that some of John's visions can certainly be interpreted as relating to Rome as well as having a more universal dimension. However, to avoid complicating an already difficult analysis, we have generally excluded references to Rome from our main text and gathered them together separately in appendix 4.

Outline

Pared down to its core Revelation is a drama in seven acts:

1. John tells of a revelation in which he was told to write down all he saw, both about current events and the future (1:1–20). He begins with current events, writing letters at Jesus' dictation to the seven churches of Asia about their spiritual welfare (2:1 – 3:22).

2. The visions of the future begin with John seeing God enthroned in heaven and a Lamb (the risen Christ) about to break the seven seals of a book of destiny (4:1 – 5:14). As the seals are broken we are shown a world riddled with warfare, famine, disease and death and a Church crying out for justice (6:1–17). But God will protect His own, and one day they will stand before His throne in heavenly bliss (7:1 – 8:1).

3. Trumpet blasts herald seven more visions, contemporaneous with the seals, depicting environmental disaster, demonic torment and suffering (8:2 – 9:21). John is confirmed in his prophetic role (10:1–11) before more visions promise that, whatever happens in the meantime, the Church's final triumph is assured (10:1 – 11:19).

4. Revelation now pauses to reveal what lies behind the world's suffering and strife. Although Satan has been defeated he remains at large until Christ's return (12:1–17), striving until the very end through his henchman, the beast, to entice the world into his clutches (12:18 – 13:18). In further visions John sees the joy of the redeemed in heaven while the godless are harvested for oblivion (14:1–20).

5. The pouring of the seven bowls triggers more portents of the future, paralleling the seals and trumpets, and culminating in the powers of evil mustering to engage God in battle (15:1 – 16:21).

6. Events move to their denouement. After a final intense tribulation Babylon, the home of rebel man, is utterly destroyed (17:1–18). Heaven rejoices as the world mourns (18:1–24). Heaven opens to proclaim the marriage of the Lamb to His Church (19:1–10). Christ rides out at the head of the heavenly hosts and the beast is hurled into a 'lake of burning sulphur' where it is joined, after a final effusion of his malevolent power, by Satan and death. Then comes the last judgement (19:11 – 20:15).

7. John sees a new heaven and a new earth where, free from pain and death, mourning and sadness, God's people will abide in His presence for ever (21:1 – 22:5). Revelation concludes by assuring us that Jesus, the morning star, is coming soon. Meanwhile the water of life is freely available to all who have washed their robes clean (22:6–21).

Act 1 is introductory and, in so far as it deals with the state of individual churches, stands apart. Acts 2, 3 and 5 give three parallel prophecies of the world's dire plight and prospects. At the same time acts 2 and 3 assure us that no matter what else may befall the Church will ultimately prevail while acts 2 and 4 give glimpses of the heavenly joy that awaits the faithful. Act 4 also explains why there is so much trouble in the world. Although Christ's victory on the Cross means that Satan's ultimate oblivion is assured he is free to roam the world until Christ returns in glory. Act 6 describes that return, the death of Satan and the last judgement. Act 7 reveals the new creation where God's people will dwell with Him forever.

In short Revelation tells us that, despite the problems and disasters that will continue to afflict the world, and an outpouring of apostasy and evil in the latter days more terrible and virulent than anything ever seen before, God's triumph is assured. Christ will return. Evil, sadness and death will be no more. Everything will be made anew and God's people will live in His presence forever. Paradise regained to Genesis' paradise lost.

Aids to understanding

The reader is advised to familiarise himself with the above outline and to use it as a guide to avoid getting lost in the thickets of detail in which Revelation abounds. Equally, until he has grasped one self-consistent interpretation, it is probably best to resist the temptation to explore the variant meanings of which almost every chapter seems capable. Then, when he does pursue alternatives, he will have a yardstick to measure them against.

It must never be forgotten that Revelation is about visions: some of events in heaven; some conveying divine truths; others portraying history, the last days or the world to come. As such it is telling us not what will actually happen next but what John *saw* next. This distinction is crucial and as a result, although the book does have a broad chronological drift, from the seals' preview of history to the new Jerusalem, not everything is in sequence.

In particular it is vital to appreciate that the seals, trumpets and bowls give us three parallel snapshots of history, each taking us up to the last days. They are not to be read as the seals visiting one set of disasters on the earth, the trumpets another and the bowls yet more again. All three are variations on the same theme: the catastrophes that will afflict a fallen world until Christ's return.

Sometimes the Seer's vision leaps ahead. Visions of the redeemed in heaven in chapters 7 and 14 anticipate Christ's return and the last judgement in chapters 19 and 20. In chapter 18 people are urged to flee a Babylon whose fall was related in both of chapters 16 and 17, and so on.

The reader will have divined by now (and it becomes clearer the more we read it) that Revelation, with its array of visions, is highly symbolic. We do not, to state the obvious, have to believe in a literal 'beast' as the devil's henchman. Nor are we called upon to accept a literal 'lake of burning sulphur' or to expect the Second Coming to involve Christ riding ahead of the armies of heaven on a white horse.

On the other hand Revelation's lush imagery should not delude the reader into believing that every symbol has an inner meaning capable of being decoded. Some are purely decorative. Nor must he be disappointed if he cannot harmonise every detail or expect every allegory to yield a simple correspondence between symbol and object. John was a theologian, not a logician, and to ignore this misses the spirit of a book that was never intended to provide a timetable or blueprint but rather, like poetry, to lift the soul and nourish the spirit.

Revelation is best regarded as a working over in colour of a picture with which we are already broadly familiar in black and white. And although not every tint or shadow may stand out the overall picture is clear, bringing Scripture to a towering climax in an epic of hope, the victory song of the Church.

ADDRESS AND OPENING VISION (1:1–20)

John addresses his revelation to the seven churches of Asia and begins with greetings from the triune God: from He who is (God the Father), from the seven spirits before His throne (the Holy Spirit in each of the churches) and from Jesus Christ, the First-born from the dead who has washed away our sins with his blood and made us a kingdom of priests.[1] He will come again on the clouds when everyone will see Him, even those who pierced Him, and mourn.[2] Finally God Himself is quoted as the eternal Alpha and Omega[3] (1:1–8).

John received his vision one Lord's Day while he was on Patmos on account of the Gospel.[4] He saw One like a Son of man, the First and the Last, the Living One who was once dead but is now alive forever, the One who holds the keys of life and death. In other words the risen Christ who told him to write down all he saw of 'present happenings' and of 'what is still to come' and send it to the seven churches.[5]

He was surrounded by seven golden lampstands, representing the seven churches, and was holding seven stars standing for the angels of the churches.[6] He wore a long robe (symbolising His priesthood) tied with a belt of gold (His royalty). His head and hair were white (symbolising eternity) and He had burning eyes (to probe minds and hearts) and feet of burnished bronze (denoting permanence). His voice was like the sound of the ocean, like a trumpet, and His face shone like the sun (calling to mind His transfiguration). Out of his mouth (denoting judicial authority and might) came a sharp double-edged sword (1:9–20).

LETTERS TO THE SEVEN CHURCHES (2:1 – 3:22)

The letters are cast in a set pattern. Christ introduces Himself, followed by words of commendation (except for Sardis and Laodicea), rebukes and warnings (except for Smyrna and Philadelphia), and promises of heavenly reward for those who are victorious.[7]

Ephesus is commended for perseverance in the face of suffering and for combating apostasy and the Nicolaitans but is warned that its love has grown cold.[8] The faithful of Smyrna may be poverty stricken but spiritually they are rich. Jews who persist in slandering them are no better than disciples of Satan. More persecution is on the way but it will be brief and they must persevere. Then they will receive the crown of life.

The congregation at Pergamum has largely kept faith despite living where 'Satan is enthroned'.[9] However some have followed Balaam and succumbed to adultery while others have embraced Nicolaitanism. They must repent.[10] Thyatira is commended, apart from tolerating a prophetess called Jezebel who ate food that had previously been offered to idols.[11] Unless she repents she will be punished along with her followers.

Although there are a few believers, Sardis is spiritually dead, withering on the vine. She must rekindle her faith. Philadelphia has been faithful and escapes rebuke. She will be protected when the time comes for the whole world to be tested.[12] Laodicea, materially rich but spiritually naked, is admonished for the apathy born of complacency.[13] She is neither hot nor cold and is called upon to wake up and repent by One who is eager to help.

A Vision of God in Heaven (4:1 – 5:14)

John is summoned up to heaven to be told about the future. He sees God seated in glory in His heavenly court on a throne encircled by a rainbow and emitting peals of thunder and lightning.[14] Before the throne is a crystalline sea and seven flaming lamps, the seven Spirits of God.[15] Surrounding it are twenty-four elders arrayed in white robes and golden crowns and four living creatures, each with six wings, studded with eyes, and resembling a lion, a bull, a human face and an eagle respectively; all engaged in ceaseless adoration.

The Seer does not attempt to describe the indescribable God. He is content to convey majesty and awe, power and glory. The rainbow recalls the covenant with Noah and mercy while the crystalline sea reflects the calmness and peace of God's rule. What the twenty-four elders symbolise is conjectural, perhaps the twelve tribes and the twelve apostles, the old Israel and the new, the totality of God's people. The four living creatures possibly stand for the created order in general and animate nature in particular; God's world as the elders stand for His Church[16] (4:1–11).

The focus changes to a Lamb that appears to have been sacrificed. It has seven horns and seven eyes symbolising power and knowledge and, taken together, the seven Spirits that God sends out to all the world.[17] As John watches all creation – the four living creatures, the twenty-four elders, myriad angels, every living thing – join in a hymn of praise. For it is the Lamb that has won people for God with His blood. And because of that only the Lamb, in heaven or on earth, is worthy to break the seven seals of a scroll (a book of destiny) that God holds in His right hand[18] (5:1–14)

The Seven Seals (6:1 – 8:1)

The Lamb breaks the first six seals (6:1–17)

As the first four seals are broken four horsemen, the notorious Four Horsemen of the Apocalypse, appear representing powers hostile to Christ; warfare and strife; poverty and famine; pestilence and Death.[19] A quarter of the whole earth is stricken by sword, famine, plague and wild beasts.[20]

The fifth seal shows those who have died for their faith crying out for vengeance on the ungodly.[21] They are given white robes in pledge of the joy that will one day be theirs. But for now they must be patient. History must run its course. With typical apocalyptic imagery the breaking of the sixth seal announces the Last Day.

The seals, like the trumpets and bowls that come later, present an overview of history up to Christ's return. They are not confined to any one age. The four horsemen ride-out every day to scourge the world and will continue to do so until the end of time.

God's servants will be preserved (7:1–17)

Two visions now temper the grim prospect we have just seen with promises of preservation and ultimate victory. The four angels holding back the four winds are ordered not to release them until God's servants, all one hundred-and-forty-four thousand of them from all the tribes of Israel, have been sealed on their foreheads for protection.[22] God's people have nothing to fear.[23]

John then saw a countless multitude of all races standing before God's throne and the Lamb, clothed in white (symbolising resurrection and glory) and waving palms.[24] They are the ones who have survived the great trial and washed their robes white again in the blood of the Lamb.[25] With the angels, the elders, the four living creatures-all creation-they are worshipping God and the Lamb for their salvation is effected through His blood and He will lead them to springs of living water. They will never hunger or thirst again and God will wipe away their every tear.

The seventh seal (8:1)

The breaking of the seventh seal brings silence, a solemn prelude to the further catastrophes yet to be unleashed.

THE SEVEN TRUMPETS (8:2 – 11:19)

John next saw seven angels bearing seven trumpets that will soon bring more omens of the future. But before they could be blown he saw the prayers of the faithful rising up to God. Thunder, lightning and earthquakes showed that they had been heard (8:2–5).

The first six trumpets are sounded (8:6 – 9:21)

The first four blasts depict environmental disaster. Even the heavens are dimmed. But the devastation is partial, limited to a third, indicating that it is not final but intended to bring man to his senses and give him the chance to repent. A lone eagle warns of the three woes yet to come with the remaining three trumpets (8:6–13).

The fifth trumpet brings hideous stinging locusts with orders to torment, but not to kill, anyone not branded with God's seal. What they signify is uncertain. Physical pain certainly but probably also mental anguish and the enmities, lost opportunities to do good, and pangs of conscience that bondage to Satan carries in its wake and which sometimes makes death seem preferable to life[26] (9:1–12).

The sixth trumpet unleashes an army from the Euphrates and with it plagues of fire, smoke and sulphur. Once again the slaughter is limited to one-third offering survivors the chance to repent.[27] But to no avail (9:13–21).

The end is near (10:1–11)

John sees an angel descend from heaven carrying a small open scroll. At the same time a heavenly voice gives him a message he is forbidden to divulge. The angel declares that when the seventh trumpet sounds the time of waiting will be over and the mystery of God (the inauguration of His Kingdom) will be fulfilled.[28] Told to eat the scroll prior to prophesying again John found it both bitter and sweet.[29]

What this means is that the final act of the divine drama is about to begin in preparation for which John (in the secret message) is told more about God's plan than can generally be revealed. By eating the small scroll, which probably contained the remaining visions, he is confirmed in his prophetic role.

The two witnesses (11:1–14)

John is told to measure (mark-out for protection) the Temple (representing the Christian Church) but to leave the outer court (the world outside the Church) for the gentiles (non-believers) to trample over, which they will do for forty-two months (the time between Christ's first and second Comings).[30] The survival of the Church is assured (11:1–2).

Two witnesses appear. They are divinely protected and, with the ability to withhold rain, 1K 17:1, and turn water into blood, Ex 7:14–25, have the attributes of Elijah and Moses. Being likened to Zechariah's two olive trees, Zc 4:3–14, confirms that they represent the Church proclaiming the Gospel.[31] This they will do for twelve hundred and sixty days, i.e. until Christ's return. Then the beast from the Abyss (Satan's henchman) will slay them and people will rejoice, leaving their corpses unburied for three-and-a-half days (a relatively short time) in the great city where their Lord was crucified, a city also known as Sodom and Egypt.[32] Then God will breathe new life into them and they will be taken up to heaven (11:3–14). In other words the Church will continue until the very end when, after a brief but virulent persecution, it will appear to go under before God revives it and awes the world.

Appendix 1 refers

The seventh trumpet (11:15–19)

With the seventh trumpet voices in heaven announce the Kingdom of God as heaven opens to reveal the Ark of the Covenant.[33]

THE CONFLICT BETWEEN GOOD AND EVIL (12:1 – 14:20)

John is now about to learn that the world's tribulations are but a shadow of the stupendous battle between the forces of good and evil.

The allegory of the woman and the dragon (12:1–17)

A woman (old Israel) gives birth to a Son (Christ). A dragon, who is identified as Satan, the devil, the primeval serpent, and whose tail sweeps a third of the stars from the sky, tries to devour the child to nip God's salvic plan in the bud.[34] But he is thwarted. The child is taken up to God while the woman (now representing the new Israel of the Church) escapes to the desert where God protects her for twelve hundred and sixty days, i.e. until Christ's return[35] (12:1–6).

The scene changes. War breaks out in heaven. Michael and his angels defeat the dragon and hurl him out of heaven down to earth. A heavenly voice proclaims God's kingdom. Christ is king and the faithful share in the victory won with His blood[36] (12:7–12).

Defeated at the heavenly level, aware that his time is limited (until Christ comes again), and failing once again to hurt the woman (the Church) in the face of divine protection (the earth rescuing her from the torrent of deception spewing from his mouth), the dragon now vents his fury against her other children, i.e. individual members of the Church[37] (12:13–17).

Satan attacks the Church (12:18 – 13:18)

John next saw a beast emerging from the sea. It was part-leopard, part-bear, part-lion, and the dragon had delegated all its power to this beast. One of its heads had received a deadly wound which seemed to have healed.[38] It mouthed blasphemies, defied God and attacked the Church. The whole world marvelled and worshipped it, all that is except God's servants who suffered death and persecution for their faith.[39] This was allowed to go on for forty-two months, i.e. until Christ's return[40] (12:18 – 13:10).

A second beast emerged from the ground, part dragon, part lamb, (the arch-priest of false religion, 'a dragon in lamb's clothing'). It exercised the same malevolent powers as the first beast and used fake miracles like calling down fire from heaven to deceive people into worshipping it. It erected a statue to the first beast that was so life-like it was able to talk and anyone who refused to conform by being branded with its emblem or worshipping it was ostracised or put to death.[41] Its number was 666[42] (13:11–18).

Revelation is warning against 'tinsel' religion that superficially attracts but has no substance. With the statue it is also cautioning against worshipping counterfeit gods such as materialism. People who spurn such snares must not be surprised if society rejects them.

Salvation and judgement (14:1–20)

Three visions now contrast the bliss of the faithful with the fate of the damned. In the first John sees the redeemed standing on Mt Zion with the Lamb singing a hymn only they could learn.[43] Then three angels proclaim Babylon's fall and urge the beast's cronies to abandon him and glorify God before it is too late to escape the torments of the damned. The third pictures judgement as a harvest for the winepress of God's anger.[44]

THE SEVEN BOWLS (15:1 – 16:21)

As the saints in heaven sing a triumphant hymn of praise, seven angels leave the heavenly sanctuary bearing the seven golden bowls that contain the plagues with which God will now exhaust His wrath.[45] The first plague afflicts unbelievers with virulent sores. The second and third turn the sea and fresh waters to blood. The fourth brings a scorching sun. The fifth plunges the beast's empire into darkness. With the emptying of the sixth bowl foul demonic spirits muster the forces of evil from across the Euphrates to confront God in battle at Armageddon.[46] With the seventh bowl Babylon, the great city, is rent in three.[47]
Appendix 2 refers

THE FALL OF BABYLON (17:1 – 19:10)

The prostitute and the beast (17:1–18)

John now saw the arresting figure of a woman riding a scarlet beast with seven heads and ten horns and with blasphemous titles written all over it.[48] The woman was garishly dressed and on her forehead was written: 'Babylon the Great, mother of all the prostitutes and filthy practices on earth.' She was drunk with the blood of the saints and martyrs. She represents the gaudy seductiveness of a world wallowing in immorality and steeped in violence. Yet despite her debauchery the world rushes to patronize her and drink the wine of her (spiritual) adultery (17:1–7,15, 18).
Appendix 3 refers

The beast's heads represent seven emperors. Since seven symbolises completeness and as the emperors may be taken as representing dominant worldly systems – political, economic, social – what this means is that the beast, as the life force behind the heads, is the driving force behind all history as one worldly regime follows another.

Only one regime is yet to come, v10. We know that the beast is one of the seven that is to rule, v 11, and that he is still to come, v 8. Therefore the regime still to come, which will only last for a short while, v 10, is the beast's. The beast is also the eighth, v11. This not only reaffirms that the beast's reign will come at the very end but that it will be something outside the usual pattern. In fact as the beast will be reigning as one of the seven heads as well as being the life-force behind them, he will no longer be bringing his malevolent influence to bear from 'behind the scenes', but 'up front', as a ruler in his own right. As such we can expect to see naked undisguised evil in all its stark pent-up power and horror.

In short the last days will see the world in the grip of a regime of unsurpassable wickedness, evil incarnate. Fortunately its time will be brief but whatever tyrannies and depravities the world experiences before will be as nothing compared with the horrors and abominations that will be visited upon it then in the great tribulation. This will astonish all except Christians.[49] Then the beast will be destroyed. The description of it as 'once alive, alive no longer and yet to come', v 8, is clearly intended as a parody on the titles of God and Christ[50] (17:8–11).

The beast's ten horns are ten kings who for a short time will join with the beast to bring Babylon, his own empire of vice and violence, crashing to its doom as God lets evil work for Him by destroying itself.[51] But when the unholy alliance take up arms against the Lamb it is defeated[52] (17:12–14, 16–17).
Appendix 4 refers

The fall of Babylon (18:1–24)

As an angel announces Babylon's fall a voice from heaven calls on God's people to abandon her before it is too late. For all her pride she is powerless before God's might and will be utterly razed (18:1–8). Kings join merchants and mariners in bewailing her fate as they recall the good times they shared there. Their dirge is interrupted by heavenly jubilation as an angel hurls a boulder into the sea to demonstrate how the source of so much misery and bloodshed must disappear never to rise again. As her lights go out and the bustle and sounds of revelry and industry fade away only a ghostly stillness remains (18:9–24).

Songs of victory in heaven (19:1–10)

The heavenly hosts erupt in a paean of praise to God for meting out justice on the evil system that has corrupted the earth and killed the saints. Then all the redeemed join in to hail the betrothal of the Lamb to a bride dressed in white. God's reign has begun.[53]

THE SECOND COMING (19:11 – 20:15)

The death of the beast (19:11–21)

John now saw Christ riding forth on a white horse as Captain of the armies of heaven: the Second Coming. Ranged against Him were the beast and all the kings of the earth with their armies. Birds were summoned to gorge themselves on the slain.[54] No details of the hostilities are given for the decisive battle has already been won on the Cross. We are simply told that that the beast and the false prophet are taken prisoner and hurled to destruction in 'the fiery lake of burning sulphur'.[55] All the rest fall by the sword of Christ.

The millennium (20:1–10)

This is one of the most disputed passages in the Bible. It tells how Satan will be chained up for a thousand years (i.e. for a long time) to prevent his leading the nations astray. All those who have been martyred or refused to acknowledge the beast will then be resurrected to reign with Christ in 'the first resurrection'. But the rest of the dead will not be restored to life until the thousand years have elapsed at which time Satan will be released for a short while. Unfettered he will launch an all-out attack on the Church.[56] Then God comes to her aid and he perishes in the fiery lake.

The difficulty lies in deciding whether this prophecy should be taken literally. Some think it should though they differ widely on how it would fit into the Bible's other chronology. Others, following Augustine, see the thousand years as symbolic of the Christian era between Christ's first and second Comings. The first resurrection is then the believer's rising to new life as he accepts Christ in baptism while Satan's binding is the restraint he labours under in the life of a believer energised by the Holy Spirit.[57] In fact no explanation of the millennium is free of difficulties and it remains a mystery.[58]

The last judgement (20:11–15)

Heaven and earth fall away to leave the dead standing before God on a great white throne. All are judged according to their deeds and those who are not saved are cast into the burning lake, the second death, to be joined finally by Death and Hades.[59]

THE NEW JERUSALEM (21:1 – 22:5)

John's vision now passes from space and time to eternity with a new heaven and a new earth. The sea, the home of the Satanic beast, is no more. A new Jerusalem comes down from heaven dressed as a bride as a heavenly voice proclaims that God will make His home among His people and wipe away their every tear. There will be no more death, mourning, sadness or pain. The world of the past has gone. He will be their God. But for cowards and renegades there is only the second death in the burning lake (21:1–8).

The new Jerusalem, glittering with diamonds and gold, each gate a single pearl, its walls encrusted with precious stones, reflects the glory of God. High walls bearing the names of the twelve apostles on their foundation stones denote security. Angels guarding gates that are never closed and that bear the names of the twelve tribes on their portals commemorate Israel. Measurement reveals the city to be a perfect cube.[60] Filled with the radiance of God and the Lamb there is no need for a Temple for worship nor sun nor moon for light. Nothing impure will ever enter her gates. Trees of life proliferate, each bearing twelve crops a year. The throne of God and the Lamb are in the city and the redeemed will see them face-to-face reigning for ever and ever[61] (21:9 – 22:5).

CONCLUSION (22:6–21)

An angel assures John that all he has witnessed comes from the Lord God and Jesus Himself. Because time is short it must not be kept secret but (it is implied) blazoned abroad while taking care not to distort it in any way. Jesus, the morning star, is coming soon.[62] He will reward everyone as their deeds deserve when only the pure, those who have washed their robes clean, will be entitled to feed on the tree of life.[63] Revelation closes by inviting those who thirst to avail themselves of the free water of life, and a yearning for Christ's return.

APPENDICES

The Bible: A Survey

1: CHRIST FULFILS THE SCRIPTURES

The gospels miss no opportunity to show how Christ fulfilled the scriptures. For example He was of Davidic descent, 2S 7;11–17; Is 11:1; Jr 23:5; Mt 1:1–17, born of a virgin, Is 7:14; Mt 1:23, in Bethlehem Mi 5:1; Mt 2:6. Like Moses He was called out of Egypt, Mt 2:15, and like Israel He was tested and began His mission in the desert, Mt 4:1. He ministered in Galilee, Is 8:23 – 9:1; Mt 4:15. On His last journey He entered Jerusalem on a donkey, Zc 9:9; Mt 21:5, where He was betrayed for thirty pieces of silver, Zc 11:12; Mt 26:14–16; 27:9, and His disciples deserted Him, Zc 13:7; Mt 26:31. None of His bones were broken -- as was the usual custom – when He was crucified, Ex 12:46; Jn 19:36. Instead His side was pierced with a lance, Zc 12:10; Jn 19:37.

The reader may also be interested to have references for the examples of Jesus fulfilling prophecy quoted in the main text. For example He gives hearing to the deaf, sight to the blind and makes the lame walk, Is 29:18; 35:5; Mt 11:5. He is the light of the world, Is 49:6; 60:19–20; Jn 1, 3:19; 8:12, and the living water, Ex 17; Is 55:1; Jn 4:1–15; 7:37–38. He frees prisoners and soothes the broken-hearted, Is 61:1–2; Lk 4:18–19. He epitomises the lowly who will be exalted, Is 29:19; Jn 13:12–15. He is the new manna, the bread of life, Ex 16; Jn 6:22–58. Like Moses' bronze serpent He would be 'lifted up' to save, Nb 21:4–9; Jn 3:13. Jonah's entombment in the belly of the sea-monster prefigured His own burial, Mt 12:40. He was the cornerstone the builders rejected, Is 28:16; Mt 21:42.

In addition it is instructive to note that Jesus Himself alludes to the Servant at Mt 16:21; 20:28; Mk 8:31; 10:45; 9:12 and identifies with him at Lk 22:37. Mt identifies Jesus with the Servant at 8:17; 12:18–21.

2: TWO TESTAMENTS, ONE BIBLE

There is sometimes a tendency for Christians to downplay the Old Testament as of little relevance in the light of the New whereas in fact they fit together like hand and glove. The Old sets the stage for the New but, being preparatory in paving the way for Christ, is incomplete without it. Equally the New cannot fully be understood without the Old.

We are indebted to the Old Testament for revealing God's holiness; for showing why man needs redemption; for driving home the deadly insidious stamp of sin; for revealing God's never flagging love as He takes it upon Himself to save man despite every obstacle and ingratitude placed in His way; and for giving the first hints of the plan God would employ to do that. Only after all other means had failed did God send His own Son to do for man what man could not do for himself.

Jesus expressly spoke of the Old Testament pointing to Himself and He being its fulfilment, Mt 5:17; Lk 24:25–27, 44; Jn 5:39. He was steeped in the Old Testament. It was His guide and mentor and His teaching was anchored in it, His recorded words containing some forty direct quotations, around sixty clear allusions, and over one hundred possible allusions. (The New Testament as a whole contains roughly two hundred and fifty Old Testament quotations, around one thousand clear allusions and many more unconscious ones.)

The essence of the Gospel message – the need for reparation for sins, love of God, love of neighbour – is already taught in the Old Testament. The Spirit of Christ is alive in its ideals. The two Testaments are inexorably linked and it is God who links them for throughout the Bible there is but one God, one plan of salvation, one theology.

> To the Old Testament belongs more fear, just as to the New Testament more delight; nevertheless in the Old Testament the New lies hid, and in the New Testament the Old is exposed (St Augustine)

> The Old Testament to the New is like a seed to a tree (Aquinas).

3: MYSTERIES OF THE ATONEMENT

Jesus made abundantly clear what He had come to achieve: victory over evil, forgiveness of sins, restoration of fellowship with God, the offer of eternal life:

> For this is my blood, the blood of the Covenant, poured out for many for the forgiveness of sins, Mt 26:28

> I have come so that they may have life and have it to the full, Jn 10:10

> The Son of man must be lifted up so that everyone who believes in Him may not perish but may have eternal life, Jn 3:14–16

> Now sentence is being passed on this world; now the prince of this world (i.e. Satan) is to be driven out, Jn 12:31

Elsewhere in the New Testament we read that Jesus died in our place, that he paid the price for our sins, that He made satisfaction for them, that He ransomed us, that His death was a sacrifice.

At the risk of repetition two cardinal facts stand out.

- By living a life free of sin Jesus conquered evil and thereby overcame death, the wages of sin. As such He was the antithesis of Adam.
- By His sacrificial death Jesus made it possible for our sins to be forgiven and for us to be reconciled with God, the prelude to eternal life.

With his selfless, sinless life of obedience and love, defying evil even at the cost of His own life, we can perhaps begin to see how Jesus overcame Satan and conquered evil but it is not so clear how His death freed us from our sins with all that flows from that. Following on from the Old Testament sacrificial system it naturally comes across as some sort of judicial *quid pro quo* that God required before releasing us from our sins, Jesus' death substituting for our own and thereby assuaging God's sense of justice. But many find that this concept of a 'judicial' God requiring reparation for our sins sits uneasily alongside the God of love that Jesus revealed. Theologians have debated the problem for centuries without reaching any final resolution and it is probably best to accept it as a mystery and acknowledge that it is more rewarding to concern ourselves with 'what' Jesus achieved rather than 'how'.

But two things are certain. If we are ever led to think of God 'using' Jesus' death in some way, we must always remember that Jesus is God and that it was therefore God Himself who suffered for us, as a supreme act of love. (And this of course provides us with a possible answer to the difficulty highlighted in the previous paragraph.) Secondly, only Jesus, who as man led a perfect blameless life, but who was already united with the Godhead – 'the Atonement before the Atonement' – could atone for our sins. For if on the one hand it was appropriate that it should be a man, free from sin, who should offer an act of obedience and perfect selfless love to counter the flawed self-love and rebellion that lies at the heart of man's sin, on the other it needed the infinite power that only God's love could provide to conquer the might of evil and roll back the frontiers of sin.

There are many other mysteries surrounding Jesus' death. What was in His mind as He went up to Jerusalem for the last time? Did He sense that His destiny, like the Servant's, was to die and that the time was nigh? There is plenty of evidence for this, e.g. Lk 18:31, but taken by itself it leaves the impression that Jesus was actively seeking death. Or, did He take the view that, having preached in Galilee and other areas, His mission would not be complete until He had taught in the religious capital as well, and confronted in those who wanted to put Him to death the very heart, the very depths of evil, the obvious danger notwithstanding? It is more than likely that both elements were active in His mind.

Why did God redeem us the way He did? Again we do not know but there are pointers. The way God chose shows, perhaps as no other way could, the depths of His love and His hatred of sin. What else could lead us to take sin quite so seriously? Perhaps also we are led to accept, a little more readily than we might otherwise, the mysteries of faith and suffering. Even Jesus' faith was tested at Gethsemane and Calvary, and though we may still find the problem of suffering as intractable as Job did, at least we can be sure that if even God had to suffer in His earthly existence then it must be intrinsically woven into the fabric of life itself. How God would have redeemed us had Jesus' teaching met a more ready response, or if Israel had remained faithful, is yet another puzzle.

4: TYPOLOGY

The reader will probably have noticed by now instances where earlier characters or events in the Bible foreshadow or suggest, albeit incompletely, what is revealed in fullness and perfection later on. Indeed, as is perhaps best brought out in Hebrews, the Old Testament as a whole prefigures in the shadowy realm of earthly life the spiritual essence of the age of ultimate reality yet to come.

Although these correspondences between different parts of God's revelation can be expressed as simple parallels they are infinitely richer. The same event can sometimes be paralleled in different ways so that what we have are not simple one-to-one relationships but multi-dimensional. As analogies they help to make spiritual truths more intelligible. As underpinning threads they demonstrate the consistency of God's purpose. In their harmony, their secret affinities, they are more than illustrations. They point the way to proof, indeed to the eye of faith they already are proof. From many examples we cite the following.

Adam, the representative first man, attempted to grasp equality with God and because of his pride fell, bringing sin and death. Jesus, the first-fruits of a new humanity, emptied Himself of His divinity, trod the path of humility and was exalted, paying the price for sin and becoming the source of life. Adam was tempted in a garden and failed. Christ was tested in a garden and prevailed.

As the uprightness of one man, Noah, led to mankind being given new life in a world cleansed of sin by the waters of the flood, so the uprightness of one man, Jesus Christ, brings new life in a creation cleansed from sin by the waters of baptism.

Isaac, the obedient son, was miraculously conceived as the first-fruits of the Old Covenant. He was offered in sacrifice but delivered from death to become the father of a new race. Likewise Christ, the obedient Son, was miraculously conceived. He offered Himself as a sacrifice and came back from the dead to become the first-born of the New Covenant.

Christ is foreshadowed in Joseph, who suffered humiliation and was left for dead only to 'come back' to be exalted and save his people.

Christ is the second Moses. He inaugurated the New Covenant and sealed it in His own blood as Moses mediated the Old Covenant through the blood of animals. As the great Lawgiver He completed the Law given on Sinai with the Sermon on the Mount.

We first hear of Moses in the ark, Jesus in the manger. Both renounced a royal court to share their people's tribulations and save them. Both were saved from infanticide and called out of Egypt. Moses spent forty days with God on the mountain after crossing the waters that led to freedom. Jesus spent forty days in the desert listening to God after experiencing the waters of baptism. The radiance of Moses' face after he had seen God prefigures Jesus' transfiguration. Moses created the old Israel of history, Jesus the new Israel of faith.

In the Exodus God rescued from slavery all those who put their trust in the blood of a lamb. He did this by a miraculous crossing of the waters of the Sea. In a new Exodus He redeems from sin all who commit to the Blood of the Lamb through the waters of baptism.

God rescued His people from 'death' as slaves in Egypt so that as Israel they might carry His name to all nations. He rescues Christians from 'death' through sin so that they can become the new Israel of His church and witness to all nations.

Redeemed, the Israelites of old were no longer slaves but first-born sons of God with an inheritance, the Promised Land of Canaan. However they still had to endure a long struggle in the desert, with countless temptations and distractions along the way, in order to learn that they still depended on God for survival and to put their trust in Him. And in the end it was only a new reborn generation that entered the Promised Land. Redeemed, Christians are no longer in bondage to sin but have an inheritance as children of God and the hope of eternal life in the Promised Land of the age to come. However they still have many trials and tribulations to overcome in the 'desert' of this earthly pilgrimage as they learn to put their trust in God and accept their total dependence on Him. And it will only be those who are born again in Christ who will enter the Kingdom. (In short Israel's trek from Egypt to the Promised Land prefigures our own journey to eternity.)

In the wilderness God gave the people His Law, lived among them in the Sanctuary, and fed them with the manna. Today He has given Christians the law of love, He indwells them as the Holy Spirit and feeds them with the Bread of Life in the Eucharist.

The Jews ate an unblemished lamb on each (Passover) anniversary of their release from slavery, a release effected with the help of the sacrificial blood of a lamb. Christians eat the Body and Blood of the sinless Lamb of God in the Eucharist each time they commemorate Jesus releasing them from their sins through His own blood offered in sacrifice.

There are many other examples. The twelve tribes of Israel parallel the twelve disciples of the church, the new Israel. Christ's sacrifice is prefigured in the ancient rite of the Day of Atonement when animal sacrifices removed the sins of the whole nation. And just as Christ made His sacrifice for sin outside the city walls so the animals whose blood was used to atone for sin on the Day of Atonement were burned outside the camp.

Nor are the examples necessarily confined to Christ. There are parallels between Moses and Elijah, Elijah and Elisha (2K Appendix 1 refers) and also between Moses and Joshua.

It is common in the literature to find these correspondences described in terms of 'types' and 'antitypes' and the whole subject referred to as typology. Thus Moses is seen as a 'type' of Jesus; Jesus as the 'antitype' of Moses. In this vein Jesus is thus a 'type' of the sort of person a true Christian will eventually become.

Genesis

1: GENESIS AND SCIENCE

It is a pity that right at the outset the Bible is so often seen as being at odds with science. At the root of the problem is the failure to realise that the Genesis accounts of creation are not meant to be taken literally. They are more akin to poetry. 'Day' in Genesis 1 for example does not mean a period of time but is used as a pictorial way of punctuating conceptual stages in the creative act. (Day seven, with its portrayal of God resting after six days labour, is also used to explain the seven day pattern of our lives.)

More fundamentally the sacred author was not interested in the way God went about creation and has little to say about it. He was not concerned with physics and biology, the mechanisms that brought the cosmos and life into being, but with theology. What he was at pains to establish was that God is the ultimate cause behind existence. It was at God's behest and under His direction that creation came about as a purposeful act whose designs, conceived in love, are temporarily thwarted by sin. Otherwise the Bible leaves science to the scientists and concentrates on theological concerns beyond their remit. Calvin summed it up: 'He who would learn astronomy, and other recondite arts, let him go elsewhere'.

There is no conflict. Whatever theory of the origin of the universe eventually prevails will be no more, and no less, than an expose of the processes God employed to bring it about. The laws of physics that govern it will be God's laws, the fruit of His mind. Should the 'big bang' theory with its concept of creation from nothing (as Genesis teaches) eventually hold the ring, it will be tempting to see the hand of God in the spark that ignited the bang. Nor would God be denied by deeper theories that purport to explain the source of the big bang in terms of quantum fluctuations or cosmic inflation. These concepts still rest on the laws of physics – God's laws – and merely push the debate one step further back.

Likewise with theories based on evolution that purport to explain the origins and nature of life. What science is doing is trying to unravel the way God went about fashioning the animal world and man *in so far as man is a physical being*. But there is more to it than that. For Genesis reveals that, unlike other living creatures, God created man in His own image. Man is not just a biological specimen but has a supernatural dimension too. Although therefore the human body may have evolved from lower life forms in the way that evolution theory suggests that cannot be the whole story. At some point in the process Genesis insists that God intervened to add a spiritual dimension as well. In other words Genesis tells of a discontinuity in the evolutionary chain. What had previously been an animal, an animal with a body like the human body, suddenly became a creature of a different order altogether: a fusion of the material and the spiritual, whole man, man in God's image.

2: CREATION IN GOD'S IMAGE

What does being created in God's image mean? Not that we resemble God physically for He is an infinite spirit, but that we reflect – however slightly – a little of God's own nature in having free will, in being rational creatures with an intellect, and in the spiritual dimension where we have a moral sense, a conscience, and the ability to appreciate abstract concepts like goodness, truth, faith, beauty and love. Indeed it is only because our minds are dependant on His that we can conceive of the very idea of God. However much he may resemble animals physically man is of a different order of creation altogether.

3: CREATION AND MAN

We live in a universe where God is the ultimate reality. Life and the cosmos are no accident but the conscious act of a loving God who, in a supreme manifestation of His love, created us and created for us so that, immortal, we might live with Him forever. All this was done out of love, as a gift, an act of grace. We did nothing to deserve it. How could we merit our own creation?

Creation involves self expression. So the glory of the universe and its beauty not only provide compelling proof of God's existence but also gives us a glimpse, however fleeting, of His own majesty.

The universe is personal. Life has a meaning. Man is not a cipher, lost in the vastness of space, not just another animal, but in the image of God Himself without whose fellowship he is incomplete. God is intimately involved in His universe and we are meant to work with Him, and even to co-create with Him, by creating life. Not any life, remarkable though that would be, but life in His image.

Notwithstanding his high spiritual standing man should never undervalue the rest of creation; neither the material world nor the animal world; not his own body, least of all his fellow beings. All are God's creation and God Himself said they were good. As God's appointed custodian of the earth man has a responsibility for all of them and must care and respect, never abuse them. Created in God's image humanity is one, equal, irrespective of race, sex or social status.

But despite his marvellous endowments man must never forget that in the last resort he is a creature and as such but a pale finite image of the infinite Creator on whom he depends for life and all that sustains it.

4: SIN, FALL AND FREE WILL

What was the sin that led to the Fall?

What is the sin that leads to man's estrangement from God? Stated simply it is disobedience, man rebelling against God, man abusing the freedom God has given him. And that says it all. What could be more foolish than man, the finite creature, disobeying God, the infinite Creator?

But we can go further. Denying access to the tree of the knowledge of good and evil is the Bible's way of saying that God reserves to Himself, with the wisdom He alone as Creator possesses, and with man's best interests at heart, the right to set standards of behaviour. Man, a creature, does not enjoy moral independence. But when he eats of the tree he is striving to achieve just that: to decide for himself what is right and what is wrong. In other words he is aspiring, as the Bible says, to 'be like gods', to be a law to himself, and, oblivious of God's infinite wisdom and the fact that it is God's universe not his, to challenge God's right to determine the moral code in His own creation.

The root of such overweening vanity is the most fundamental sin of all: pride. Man snatching at equality with God, resentful of higher authority; man wanting to be his own master and to play God. He cannot accept that God, who has given him everything, even his very existence, knows best. Self-surrender, dependence on God, is anathema. He has to assert himself, feed his pride, challenge God, 'do it his way'.

Is God punishing us because of the Fall?

We should not see the consequences of the Fall as God inflicting punishment but rather as the workings out of an inexorable process whereby a sin-ridden world inevitably spawns degeneration and incurs its own retribution. Sin spreads like a plague once it has taken root. Lies breed more lies. Adultery leads to abortion, broken homes, stunted children. Yesterday's deprivation feeds today's conflict. Excessive concentration on profit may incur environmental catastrophe. Sin has a massive head of steam behind it. That is why the world is the sad tarnished place it is. A world where mankind is at loggerheads with itself, spending more on hurting than healing. A world of discord and drudgery, injustice and inequality, warfare and persecution, famine in the midst of plenty.

What about death?

We should not even think of death as punishment. Of course it is in a way. If man had been obedient from the start there would have been no need for banishment and death. He could have enjoyed God's company as he was. But that was never the case and man's sinful bent means that if God allowed him into heaven as he is life in heaven would soon be no better than life on earth. The discord and strife sin carries in its train is incompatible with the perfect and mutual all-embracing love God wants His children to enjoy.

The lesson of history and experience is that man cannot overcome evil and conquer sin by himself. That is why God's plan is that he will be reborn with a new heart so that, although he still retains free will, he will always (freely) exercise it as God would wish. In a nutshell man must be reborn to become 'sin-resistant' like Christ. Such rebirth can only be partial in this world and it is physical death, followed by resurrection to a new world, that offers the opportunity for this to happen and for the last vestiges of our sinful natures to be subdued. So death, far from being the great enemy, is also the door to rebirth and eternity.

How terrible it would be if we were allowed to live on in this world, witnessing all the wars, injustice and suffering that flow from man's perfidy and, not least, the full ramifications of our own wilfulness. Imagine the anguish of Adam and Eve had they witnessed their own descendants drowning in the flood.

Why did God give us free will?

Why did God give us free will when it is the cause of so many problems? Creating us in His image it could scarcely be otherwise. Without it God would have created little more than toy robots and in His love He wanted to create children not slaves. He wanted beings who could freely choose and love and enjoy the blessings He planned for them. There is all the difference in the world between forced love, which is not really love at all, and the love that, freely given, cannot contain itself because of the infinite God-given love it receives.

Why do we sin so easily?

Why do we succumb to sin so easily? We are in the realm of mystery. The Bible reveals we have a proclivity to sin right from infancy, Gn 6:5; 8:21; Ps 51:5; Jr 16:12; 17:9; 18:12. Then as we grow up we are further 'infected' by what we see around us: quarrelling and selfishness, pride and disobedience, lovelessness and lust. Right and wrong become hard to tell apart and before long we make our own contribution to the burgeoning stockpile of sin in the world. Thus on top of our inherent tendency to sin is the accumulated sin of humanity, past and present, relentlessly weighing down on us to corrupt us even more.

5: GENEALOGIES

Genealogical lists in the Bible are often selective. Several generations may be subsumed under a single 'he begat'. Even 'father of' can encompass remote ancestry and by-pass generations. They are sometimes used, as in Genesis 10, to show relationships between peoples since names of tribes or geographical locations can be substituted for individuals just as today we might refer to Britain as the father of America. In addition the ancient authors were sometimes more interested in connecting different historical episodes or showing how number patterns recurred in generations than in strict biographical detail. The three sets of fourteen generations highlighted in Jesus' ancestry in Matthew 1 is a case in point. For all these reasons Biblical lists are often more symbolic or theological than biographical and can only rarely be taken as historical.

6: ORIGINS OF THE PROLOGUE STORIES

It would be a mistake to see the stories of Cain, Noah and the rest fitting neatly together as in a modern history book. The story of Cain for example cannot immediately follow the Fall because it presupposes, not least in Cain's wife, a more populous earth than could ever have been possible at that time. Rather they are snapshots at different points in time, each intended to make its own religious point, and it may even be that they originally circulated independently and had their origins in events that had nothing to do with the theological reasons for which the editor of Genesis later pressed them into service.

The story about Cain may have started as nothing more than a simple tale to extol the virtues of the shepherd's life. The brief about Noah's drunkenness may have begun as an attempt to explain Israel's later enmity with, and dominance of, the Canaanites, Israel being descended from Shem. The Babel story may have begun as a primitive attempt to explain the origin of language. And so on.

7: ABRAHAM AND FAITH

Abraham was the man of faith *par excellence*, a man for whom faith bridged the gap between promise and fulfilment. He was unfailingly true to God even though situations kept cropping up where it was hard for him to see how God could ever fulfil His promises, most of which related to the future and could never be fulfilled in his own lifetime anyway.

The statement that Abraham 'put his faith in Yahweh and this was reckoned to him as uprightness' is a cornerstone in St Paul's doctrine of justification by faith as set out in Romans. It means that Abraham put his complete trust in God. He was content to leave matters in His hands and in humble submission cast aside all doubts and anxieties. It was because of this, and not on account of any merit he may have possessed (and notwithstanding his human frailties) that God credited him with uprightness. As a result he became pleasing to God and was able to enjoy a personal relationship with Him.

Faith leaves God free to act in our lives and so lift us beyond our inadequacies. Indeed St Paul teaches that once righteousness is credited to us through faith God then uses that faith to produce actual righteousness. Faith is crucial because God remains hidden in this world. Arguments for His existence can never completely remove the possibility of doubt.

8: ANGELS

The mention of angels in the Bible is sometimes no more than a literary device, adopted out of reverence by the inspired author, to refer to God in a deferential way or to avoid giving the impression of God talking directly to man. In such cases alternation between 'Yahweh' and 'angel of Yahweh' is common and it is sometimes hard to tell whether it is God Himself or the angel who is speaking. The angel may become virtually identified with God with 'Yahweh', 'angel of Yahweh', and 'angel of God' being used almost synonymously, Gn 16:7–13; 21:17–19; 22:11–18; 31:11–13; Ex 3:2–6; Jg 6:11–24.

In other instances angels are clearly seen to be acting as God's agent; involved with Sodom, Gn 19; deputed to lead Israel, Ex 23:20; 32:34; 33:2; barring the way to Balaam, Nb 22:23–35; conveying His word, Ezk 40 – 48; explaining visions, Zc 1 – 8; or delivering a message, Lk 1:11–20, 26–38.

In Daniel, Dn 10; 12:1, angels are seen as heavenly representatives or guardians of earthly powers on behalf of whom they fight in heaven. Even pagan nations have them. Finally Mt 18:10, Ac 12:15 indicate that people have guardian angels while Rv 1:20 suggests that the same is true of churches.

9: Doublets in the Pentateuch

Readers will be struck by likenesses in the two stories of Abraham passing Sarah off as his sister, Gn 12; 20. A similar story about Isaac occurs at Gn 26. There are several other instances of doublets such as: two accounts of God's covenant with Abraham, Gn 15;17, two stories of Abraham dismissing Hagar, Gn 16;21, and of negotiations with Abimelech, Gn 21; 26, two versions of Moses' call, Ex 3;6, two descriptions of quails providing food for Israel, Ex 16; Nb 11, and of water being obtained by striking a rock, Ex 17; Nb 20.

These doublets are often explained as being renderings of the same story but this is far from proven and it is best to keep an open mind. Gn 20:13 suggests that passing-off Sarah as his sister was a ploy Abraham frequently employed when travelling abroad. If so there is nothing surprising in more than one incident being reported. The supporting details are in any case different. In Gn 12 Abraham is ordered out of Egypt by Pharaoh. In Gn 20 Abimelech invites him to stay. In Gn 20 Sarah is taken into Abimelech's household. In Gn 26 Rebekah is not.

Close reading reveals little overlap between the two covenant passages. The latter could be a reaffirmation of the former with circumcision and the name changes added. Abraham's attitude is quite different in the two accounts of Hagar's banishment. In the first Hagar runs away of her own accord while in the second Abraham banishes her. As regards the provision of quails and water from rocks, there need be nothing surprising in this happening more than once in a desert trek extending over forty years.

Exodus

1: God's name

Possible renderings of God's name at Ex 3:13–15 include 'I am', 'I am he who is', 'I am who I am', 'I am the one who exists', 'He who causes what is', 'I am who I will be'. While these are all mysterious, they all convey the idea of active presence, creative activity. We shall not be far wrong therefore if we take these different interpretations of God's name as connoting the personal, eternal and all-sufficient aspects of His nature and as implying that He is the very apotheosis of existence, the underlying transcendent reality, God of the eternal 'now'. From the context in which the name was disclosed they also tell us that He is a God ready to act and to help, a God who will reveal Himself by His actions.

According to Gn 4:26 the name Yahweh was made known to Enosh, a grandson of Adam, and in fact 'Yahweh' occurs quite frequently in Genesis. However the alternative account of Moses' call in Ex 6 supports Ex 3 by telling us that God had not previously revealed the name 'Yahweh' but had hitherto been known as El Shaddai.

2: EVERYTHING ATTRIBUTED TO YAHWEH

The statement at Ex 4:21 that Yahweh would make Pharaoh obstinate so that he would not let the Israelites go rings strange to modern ears. Yahweh wanted the Israelites released so if He had influenced Pharaoh to take a contrary course He would have been instrumental for no apparent reason in subjecting the hapless Egyptians to the ten plagues.

The explanation is that the Old Testament writers tended to attribute everything to Yahweh as Creator and the ultimate cause of all there is. So when some passages such as Ex 4:21; 10:1,20,27 speak of God hardening Pharaoh's heart while others refer to Pharaoh being obstinate or stubborn, Ex 8:15, 28; 9:35, exactly the same thing is meant. Nowhere is there any suggestion that God forced Pharaoh to act against his will. In every instance God allowed Pharaoh to exercise his free will and be himself.

Similar remarks apply to the initiatives attributed to God at Jos 11:20; Jg 14:4; 1S 2:25; 16:15 and elsewhere. Once again the sacred author is attributing to Yahweh motives freely conceived in the minds of the perpetrators. God is painted as causing what He merely permits. Eventually Israel's spiritual growth raised her above this primitive way of thinking and the confusion over God's moral nature to which it must occasionally have given rise.

3: MIRACLES IN EXODUS

Various theories have been suggested to explain the plagues Yahweh inflicted on Egypt. One is as follows. The Nile sometimes acquires a reddish hue from flood waters bringing down red marl from its source in the Ethiopian highlands. Micro-organisms harmful to fish are deposited at the same time, hence the first plague. Decomposing fish driven ashore would attract frogs. Mosquitoes and flies are both endemic in Egypt and would breed easily in humid flood conditions. The fifth plague that killed off the Egyptian livestock could have been due to anthrax contracted from dead frogs while the boils of the sixth plague could have been the result of infection from the flies. Hail and locusts are not unknown in Egypt in early spring while the darkness of the ninth plague might have arisen from winds blowing masses of fine dust from the mud deposited by the floods. The Israelites would have been spared these afflictions because they were domiciled some way off at Goshen.

The death of the Egyptian first-born is not easily explained. However it may have taken little more than a localised epidemic, including the death of Pharaoh's eldest son, to start a rumour going. The escape across the Sea of Reeds could have been due to unusually strong winds creating a temporary channel across one of the lakes north of present day Suez before subsiding to allow the waters to return and engulf the pursuing Egyptians. But whatever view we take of how these miracles occurred, what is undeniable is the miraculous element in their timing. The plagues sowed confusion and fear in Egyptian hearts at the very time Israel was bent on leaving.

As regards the wilderness miracles, manna could have been the sweetish secretion produced by the tamarisk tree. Quails regularly pass over Sinai while migrating between Europe and Africa and often land in large droves for respite. Sweetening brackish water by other natural agents is relatively unremarkable while springs of water can be found in mountain rocks to this day.

There is of course nothing in the nature of miracles that compels natural causes. God is greater than His Creation and has the freedom to transcend the natural laws He Himself ordained if He so wishes. Having said that we should at the same time never discount an element of folklore especially in stories like those of the miraculous powers attributed to Moses at Ex 4:1–9. These would have been passed down by word of mouth for centuries before being written down and there would have been a natural tendency for them to become larger than life in the retelling.

4: THE FIRST-BORN

Exodus tells us that all male first-born, humankind and animal, are to be consecrated to God in commemoration of His rescuing Israel from Egypt and adopting her as His first-born son. With animals consecration meant being offered to God in sacrifice but God decreed that human first-born were to be redeemed instead. NUMBERS tells us that this was effected by the Levites substituting for them and serving God by helping the priests in the Dwelling, Nb 3:12–13, 41–46.

Clean animals of the flock and herd – sheep, goats and cows – were offered up on the eighth day after their birth, Ex 22:29. Nb 18:15–18 speaks of the meat reverting to the priests. According to Nb 3:41–46 the Levites' cattle came to substitute for all Israel's first-born cattle.

Different rules applied to unclean animals which could not be offered in sacrifice. Ex 13:13, using a lamb or a kid as an example of a clean animal and a donkey as an example of an unclean animal, shows (presciently) that an unclean animal was either redeemed through a clean animal being sacrificed in its place or it faced death. Lv 27:27 and Nb 18:15–18 stipulate other ways in which redemption might be handled (probably at different times in Israel's history).

5: THE HISTORICAL BACKGROUND TO EXODUS

The Exodus poses difficult chronological and geographical problems and the dearth of independent sources, coupled with the text's overriding theological concern, mean that little can be stated with certainty. However a date of around 1250 B.C. seems to fit what evidence there is best, in which case the Pharaoh would have been Rameses II.

The most likely location for the crossing of the Sea of Reeds is somewhere in the vicinity of the Bitter lakes and the present day Suez canal. Unfortunately the route the Israelites subsequently followed may probably never be known. They left behind no sedentary population, nor were there any other residents, to perpetuate names for most of the places they passed through. However there is no reason to doubt the tradition that equates Mount Sinai with Jebel Musa, the awesome granite peak that towers over the Monastery of St Catherine near the southern tip of the Sinai peninsula.

Although doubts have been cast, few seriously doubt that the Exodus really did happen. What testifies to it most eloquently is the unlikelihood of a proud nation glorying in its formation from slavery and powerlessness in so unflattering a manner unless it were by the hand of God. As the story of the birth of a nation it is unique. Liberation happened almost against Israel's will. Her faithlessness and lack of fibre reverberate throughout the narrative. The litany of murmurings and scarcely stifled rebellions against Moses, notwithstanding a backdrop of miracles, paints a picture so lamentable that only the fact that it was true could possibly account for it. Clearly something quite momentous happened to weld a bunch of dispirited slaves into the genesis of nationhood. To deny the Exodus would be to make the history of Israel quite inexplicable.

6: FEASTS AND FIRST-FRUITS

Ex 12:1–28, 43–51; 13:3–10 describe the feasts of Passover and Unleavened Bread as family feasts to be held in one's own home to commemorate Israel's escape from Egypt. Ex 23:14–17 introduces two further feasts. The feast of Harvest, or Weeks, was the occasion for offering the first-fruits of the wheat harvest to God, Ex 34:22. The feast of Ingathering, otherwise known as the feast of Shelters, Tabernacles or Booths, was held in the autumn to celebrate the completion of all harvesting including the fruit harvest. Both these festivals were acts of thanksgiving acknowledging man's dependence on God's bounty.

Lv 23 presents a liturgical calendar. We learn that the Feast of Weeks was held fifty days after Passover (hence its Greek name Pentecost) and that the Feast of Shelters lasted for seven days and was a colourful, joyful occasion when people lived in huts made of palm branches and the boughs of trees and shrubs to remind them of their tent-dwelling days in the desert. We also hear for the first time, Lv 23:23–25, of a feast at the start of the seventh month known elsewhere, Nb 29:1, as the Feast of Acclamation or Trumpets. Nb 28, 29 set out the sacrificial prescriptions for the various feast days and introduce a new feast at the start of each month, the feast of New Moon.

There were two other feasts not mentioned in the Pentateuch: the Feast of Purim celebrating the Jews' deliverance many years later from slaughter by the Persians, Est 9:20–32; and the Feast of Dedication mentioned at Jn 10:22 which marked the purification of the Temple after its desecration by Antiochus Epiphanes, 1M 4:36.

First-fruits were offered to God to thank Him for the harvest. They were a token symbolising consecration of the entire harvest to God and not until they had been offered were the people permitted to partake of the harvest, Lv 23:14. Ex 22:28 tells us that people must offer their first-fruits willingly while Ex 23:19 stipulates that only the best is acceptable. Lv 2:12–16, backed up by Lv 23:13, suggests that the cereal offering may have been the rite used for giving first-fruits.

Lv 23: 11–14 describe a first-fruits offering during Passover week. This would be too early for wheat so it is usually assumed that it refers to the barley harvest which ripens several weeks earlier. Nb 15:17–21 mentions a first-fruits offering of bread.

As a result of worship henceforth being confined to just one Sanctuary chosen by God, Dt 16:1–17 stipulates that the feasts of Passover, Unleavened Bread, Weeks and Shelters are in future to be pilgrimage feasts celebrated at the chosen Sanctuary (in effect Jerusalem) rather than at a local shrine or, as in the case of the feasts of Passover and Unleavened Bread, as family occasions at home as hitherto. Dt 26:1–11 makes the same point for offering first-fruits. It also refers to first-fruits being returned to God in commemoration of His rescuing Israel from Egypt and giving her the Promised Land. Nb 18:12–13 prescribes that first-fruits are to revert to the priests for their upkeep.

7: THE DWELLING

The courtyard surrounding the Dwelling had a single gateway just in front of which, where it could not be avoided, was the bronze altar of burnt offering. It was here that sacrifice was offered and the food was eaten nearby. Between the altar and the Dwelling was a bronze basin where priests washed themselves before performing their sacred duties.

Three of the Dwelling's sides were a framework of acacia wood strengthened by crossbars overlaid with gold. They were dressed in linen woven in violet-purple, red-purple and crimson and embroidered with great winged cherubim signifying God's presence. The eastern side was open apart from a curtain similarly dressed and carried on poles of acacia wood overlaid with gold. Sheets of goats' hair, red dyed rams' skins and fine leather served as a roof and overhang the sides and back.

The Dwelling was divided by a veil into an outer Holy Place and an inner Holy of Holies. The Holy Place contained a golden lampstand and a gold table for the loaves of permanent offering. According to Lv 24:5–9 there were always twelve of these (as a reminder that God was the provider of food and all good things) and they were replaced every Sabbath. From the reference to cups and bowls it is probable that the table also carried oil or wine. Seven lamps, burning continuously from dusk to dawn, provided the only source of light within the Dwelling. Still in the Holy Place, but in line with the Ark, was the golden altar where incense was burned every morning and at twilight.

Inside the Holy of Holies was the Ark, the centrepiece of Israel's worship. This was a gilded wooden chest containing the two tablets on which God had inscribed the Law. It was carried by means of two golden shafts each of which passed through two golden rings on either side. On top of the Ark was the Mercy seat. This was made of pure gold and adorned with golden cherubim protecting it with their upstretched wings. It was above the Mercy seat that God's Presence resided. Only priests were allowed to enter the Holy Place while the Holy of Holies was only entered once a year, by the high priest on the Day of Atonement, Lv 16. It was the veil separating the two that was rent at the moment of Jesus' death, symbolising that man, hitherto barred through sin, now had access to God's presence.

The court surrounding the Dwelling was enclosed by finely woven linen curtains carried on bronze poles with bronze sockets held together by silver hooks and rods. In the middle of the eastern facing side was the gateway, screened by a curtain of violet-purple, red-purple and crimson. The court was probably one hundred and fifty by seventy five by seven and a half feet high with the gateway thirty feet wide while the Holy of Holies was most likely a fifteen foot cube.

When Israel was on the move the Dwelling occupied the centre of the camp. Once she was settled in the Promised Land most of what we know concerns the Ark. It was housed in a variety of locations in pre-monarchial times until David finally brought it to Jerusalem where his son Solomon installed it in the newly built Temple. It is usually assumed that it remained there until it was destroyed when the Babylonians sacked Jerusalem in 586 B.C. However 2 Mc 2:1–12 reports that Jeremiah hid the Ark on Mount Nebo shortly before.

Although there are almost certainly elements that go back to Moses' time, it is widely held that this description of the Dwelling is a retrojection of either Solomon's Temple or the second Temple after the Exile. The elaboration that is described here would clearly have been hard for nomadic desert wanderers to sustain. In Moses' day it is possible that the Ark was no more than a simple wooden box and the Dwelling a conventional bedouin tent.

Leviticus

1: SACRIFICE, THEORY AND SYMBOLISM

The theory of sacrifice

The Bible never explains in so many words how the deaths of innocent animals were thought to expiate sin. However it is possible to piece together an outline of the probable rationale.

A holy God cannot countenance sin. Sin separates man from God. And separation from God means death. To counter this, and as a temporary measure, God in His mercy allowed the lives of perfect and blameless animals to be offered in sacrifice in place of the human lives that in strict justice should really have been given up.

It is best explained at 17:11. An animal's life-force resided in its blood. So when an animal was offered in sacrifice and its blood was shed, that life-force was liberated and could be offered to God by being applied to the altar in place of the sinner's own guilt-stained life which would otherwise have been forfeit. It is because of its central role in atonement that Lv 17 insists so strongly that blood must be treated reverently and never eaten.

The symbolism of the sin sacrifice

Although there are variations in detail a number of common threads run through the sacrificial rituals that Leviticus describes so exhaustively. Every detail has significance and so we now explain some of them using the sacrifice for sin, 4:1–35, as an example.

1. The stipulation that the sacrificial victim be unblemished was in deference to God's sanctity and perfection. Only the best could be offered to God.
2. In laying his hands on the animal's head the supplicant showed that he identified with the victim. It was his sacrifice. Whatever happened to the victim thereafter was done in his name. In other words the animal became a substitute for the supplicant, and its life was offered in place of his, so that his sins might be forgiven and he be reconciled with God.
3. By killing the victim himself the supplicant was reminded that the penalty for sin was death and that, were it not for God's mercy, he would merit nothing better himself.
   (Hereon it is a priest who acts because only a priest could approach the altar.)
4. In the case of a sin sacrifice for the high priest or the whole community, sprinkling the victim's blood in front of the Dwelling curtain, and daubing the horns of the altar of incense with it, cleansed the Dwelling from the profanity to which sin had subjected it.
5. In pouring the animal's blood round the foot of the altar of burnt offering, and in the case of a sin offering for a secular leader or a private individual also smearing some of the blood on the horns of the altar of burnt offering, the priest symbolically offered the sinner's life, represented by the animal's blood, to God as the sinner petitioned God for forgiveness and the restoration of friendly relations. It was as the sacrificial blood came into contact with the altar (i.e. as the life in the blood was returned to God) that forgiveness was granted.
6. By placing what was regarded as the choicest and most vital parts of the animal's body on the altar of burnt offering and burning them (typically this meant the kidneys and fat attached to vital organs such as the entrails, loins, liver and kidneys) the priest offered them to God. The victim was not regarded as food for God as in many primitive religions but, as it went up in flames, seen as being assimilated to the smoke and thereby ascending to God along with the penitents' prayers and worship.
7. To understand who could join in eating the rest of the animal it is necessary to appreciate that the victim could not be eaten by anyone on behalf of whose sins it had been offered up. In the case of a sacrifice for the high priest or the whole community what was not burned for God on the altar therefore had to be wholly burned to ashes outside the camp. (Any sin of the high priest, as the nation's representative before God, necessarily involved the whole community, 4:3.) In the case of an offering for a secular leader or a private individual on the other hand what was not offered to God could be eaten by the priests in which case, being holy, it was eaten in the court surrounding the Dwelling.
8. Saying that a sacrifice was burned 'as a smell pleasing to Yahweh' implied God's acceptance of the offering.

A bizarre practice?

With its macabre and detailed instructions for the ceaseless slaughter of dumb animals and the daubing of their blood, Leviticus seems a strange, repugnant, even bizarre book to many people. Yet compared with the religions of neighbouring tribes Israel's faith, with its emphasis on holiness, obedience and forgiveness, shone brightly. There was none of the sacred prostitution, orgiastic fertility rites, child sacrifice, self mutilation, superstition, and magic that characterised Canaanite religion. Instead sacrifice in the Old Testament, despite the bloody slaughter, was dominated by the ethical; by a recognition of the awfulness of sin and the need for atonement; with the need to give thanks; and above all, with God's transcendent holiness.

An easy option?

Israel's sacrificial system is sometimes seen as an easy option, a mechanical way of appeasing God that encouraged a lax, easy going attitude to sin. It was all too easy to assume God's acceptance. By stressing the external in making amends for sin, so the argument runs, there was inevitably a tendency for sin's seriousness to be played down.

That there were abuses is clear from the prophets' many strictures, Is 1:11; Am 4:4; 5:21. However three points need to be made. Firstly, sacrifice was expensive. Animals commanded a high price. Secondly, in the case of a reparation offering where the wrong could be valued, as well as the cost of the sacrificial animal, the sinner also had to make good the loss plus a one fifth surcharge. Thirdly the emphasis on blood and death emphatically underlined the seriousness of sin and the need for obedience.

2: SACRIFICIAL, CLEAN AND OTHER ANIMALS

Apart from instances of poverty where turtledoves or young pigeons could be substituted in burnt offerings and sin offerings for private individuals, only animals from the herd (bulls and calves) and the flock (lambs and goats) were acceptable for offering to God in sacrifice. These could also be eaten as food along with other clean animals such as deer, gazelle and certain types of fish and bird defined in Lv 11.

Unclean animals were not permissible as food. Thus out of the whole animal kingdom a subset was defined as clean. These could be eaten as food. Out of all the clean animals a further subset was defined of animals suitable for offering in sacrifice to God.

3: TITHES

Tithing was a form of land tax levied in recognition of the fact that the land really belonged to God. Our knowledge of it rests on three main texts. Lv 27:30–33 tells us that tithing applied to produce of the soil and livestock. The rate quoted for animals is one tenth (picked out as they passed by the recipient in single file without any substitutions allowed) and so far as is known the same rate applied to soil tithes as well. Tithes could be redeemed by a cash payment of their market value plus one fifth.

According to Nb 18:20–32 tithes were remitted to the Levites who then passed on a 'tithe of their tithe' (i.e. one tenth part of their tenth part) to the priests for their upkeep. Although this only refers to the soil tithe it is likely that similar arrangements for livestock were taken for granted. Gn 14:20; 28:22 are possibly early instances of tithing.

Numbers

1: LARGE NUMBERS

Many of the numbers recorded in the Old Testament such as those in Moses' census appear impossibly large. Exodus speaks of 600,000 men escaping from Egypt, not counting their families, and many similar problems crop up in the historical books.

There is evidence that numbers were difficult to transmit accurately in writing. For example 2S 10:18 refers to seven hundred chariots where 1Ch 19:18 mentions seven thousand. In addition it has been conjectured that numbers above a thousand were used to convey no more than 'a very large number'. Other theories hold that the word for 'thousand' is sometimes confused with the word for 'family', 'chief', 'commander' or 'soldier'. However none of these hypotheses seems capable of resolving the problem entirely and uncertainty remains.

2: THE HIDDEN, MYSTERIOUS GOD

Ex 33:20 tells us that no human being may see God and live. Lv 16:2, 11–13 make the same point. Moses hides His face when God calls to him from the burning bush, Ex 3:6, while at Sinai the people are told to purify themselves and keep their distance, Ex 19:10–13; 20:18–21. The Ark is to be carried on shafts to avoid anyone touching it, Ex 25:14. The Levites must pitch camp around the Sanctuary to prevent ordinary people approaching it, and so incurring death.

Why is this? Because God's holiness is so far above human unworthiness, His majesty so far above human comprehension, that the full force of His presence would overwhelm us. Only by remaining hidden and limiting His power to what can be achieved through normal human activity, and allowing the possibility of a natural explanation, can God protect our free will and bring us to genuine maturity. Otherwise our relationship would be built on awe and fear and denied the chance to grow into one willingly entered into where our wills, freely expressed, are at one with His.

It is for similar reasons that God has revealed Himself gradually in history and why the Bible is as it is rather than providing a fully comprehensive treatise. To reveal Himself more openly would be to base belief on knowledge rather than the faith that God demands.

* * *

God is deeply mysterious: take the choice of Abraham, a tent-dwelling nomad with an elderly barren wife, to be the father of Israel; the long wait for Isaac, the son on whom God's promises depended; the centuries in Egypt; the long wait for the Advent of Christ.

Then there is the mystery of divine election when God disregards human convention: the choice of Isaac over Ishmael, of Jacob over Esau, even while they were still in the womb, of Joseph and David over their elder brothers. Choices based not on man-made laws of inheritance but on God's sovereign will and power.

God's strange workings are also revealed in Isaac, Jacob, Joseph, Samson, Samuel and John the Baptist all being born of women who were previously childless until God opened their wombs. All these births occurred at pivotal points in the unfolding of God's plan thereby pressing home that the lives in question were His gift and that the divine plan is in His hands demanding His intervention.

That there is mystery is scarcely surprising. Mystery is part of the awe and wonder we naturally feel before an infinite, transcendent Being who is beyond human understanding. God's ways, as mysterious as they are gratuitous and inscrutable to human gaze, are not our ways. We must learn to expect the unexpected and not rule anything out where God is concerned. So much seemingly unlikely prophecy has already been fulfilled that we should never discount anything for the future. That is why it is best to lean towards accepting Biblical events as historical unless there are compelling reasons to do otherwise. We should never forget that Jesus repeatedly confirmed the authority of the Old Testament.

3: SHEOL

Sheol, or Hades, was the underworld, a pit under the earth to which both the righteous and unrighteous went after death. There were no punishments or rewards. It was a land of forgetfulness and darkness, of silence, stillness and dust, where men existed as shadowy replicas of their former selves, separated from the God they could no longer praise, Ps 6:5; 88:5, 10–12; 115:17; Qo 9:5–6,10; Is 14:9–11; 38:18. Rather than a form of survival it was a denial of survival. Yet enigmatically it was not entirely without hope for God's power extended even there, 1S 2:6; Ps 139:8; Am 9:2.

Deuteronomy

1: SANCTUARIES IN ISRAEL

Dt 12 calls for Israel's worship to be confined to just one sanctuary (in effect Jerusalem) once she was settled in the Promised Land, in place of the multiplicity of shrines permitted by Ex 20:24. The aim was to keep her faith pure by ensuring that worship took place in a hallowed setting under strict priestly supervision, free from the risk of contamination from the many depravities of the Canaanite religion she would soon be living alongside: child sacrifice, temple prostitution, orgiastic fertility rites etc. However this did not come about for many years. Local sanctuaries flourished, among them Beersheba, Bethel, Dan, Gilgal, Mizpah, Ophrah, Shechem and Shiloh.

These shrines would doubtless have assimilated much of the liturgy prescribed for the Dwelling with the sanctuary housing the Ark being regarded as the main sanctuary. We know that the Ark moved between shrines in the early days and that it was not until David's day that Jerusalem became its permanent home. Even then the outlying sanctuaries remained and as a result the dangers Deuteronomy had foreseen became a reality. Israel's history is riddled with condemnations of idolatrous worship.

Indeed it was not until Hezekiah's reign centuries later that any serious attempt was made to close outlying shrines, some of them little more than ancient Canaanite sites, 2K 18:4,22. However this bore little fruit. Hezekiah's successor, the impious Manasseh, reversed his reforms, 2K 21:3–4, and it was not until the next king Josiah who, energised by the discovery of a 'Book of the Law' during repair work on the Temple, instituted more drastic reforms, that Jerusalem finally became established as the sole sanctuary, 2K 23.

Not long after Josiah's death the Jerusalem Temple was destroyed and Judah went into captivity in Babylon. With the return from exile the Deuteronomic ideal was at last fully realised. Israel never again had any sanctuary except the rebuilt Temple.

Why did it take so long? The most likely explanation is that Deuteronomy lay hidden and forgotten until coming to light centuries later as the 'Book of the Law' that sparked Josiah's reforms. This prescribed a series of reforms so similar to those in Deuteronomy that the correspondence of the two books cannot reasonably be in doubt. The fact that prior to Hezekiah and Josiah the Bible nowhere suggests that multiple sanctuaries were invalid (Jos 22 is a possible exception) is further evidence that Deuteronomy was lost and forgotten. But how and why is a mystery. (The 'Book of the Law' was probably an early version of today's Deuteronomy. The once prevalent view that Deuteronomy was a pious fraud, written in Josiah's day, attributed to Moses to confer authority, and hidden in the Temple so that it could quickly be 'discovered' to lend legitimacy to reforms which had already been decided upon, is no longer widely held.)

2: THE PRIESTHOOD AND THE LEVITES

God's establishment of the priesthood in the family of Aaron, a Levite, is recorded at Ex 28:1. Lv 8 describes the ordination ceremony. Aaron was succeeded by his son Eleazar, Nb 20:22–28, shortly after which, Nb 25:12–13, Yahweh promised the priesthood to Eleazar's son Phinehas and his descendants in perpetuity in recognition of Phinehas' zeal in curbing an affair between an Israelite and a Midianite woman.

Various texts enable us to piece together the priests' duties: to lead worship and the sacrificial rituals; to care for the sanctuaries; to interpret the Law; to teach; and in certain circumstances to act as judges. In addition the high priest entered the Holy of Holies once a year to enact the rites of the annual Day of Atonement, Lv 16. Post-exile priests also had an important political role.

The whole tribe of Levi was also consecrated to Yahweh. Ex 32:25–29 attributes this to the help the Levites gave Moses in quelling the golden calf rebellion. According to Nb 3:12–13; 8:16–18 they were to substitute for human first-born all of whom would otherwise have been dedicated to God's service in remembrance of His mighty act of deliverance from Egypt. Their duties were to assist the priesthood and to look after and transport the Dwelling, Nb 1:48–53; 3:6–9; 8:19.

Unlike the other tribes neither the priests nor the Levites as a whole were given a territorial allocation in the Promised Land. Instead the other tribes were ordered to cede forty eight towns with surrounding pasture for the Levites to dwell in, Nb 35:1–8, thereby dispersing them, as their role demanded, throughout the length and breadth of Israel.

Having no land to support them the priests were entitled to everything dedicated to God for their upkeep. This meant sacrificial offerings (except the portions specifically set aside for Yahweh or to be shared in a communion offering as prescribed in Leviticus 1–7); first-fruit and first-born offerings and gains from the curse of destruction, Nb 18:8–19. The Levites were supported by tithes. However they, in their turn, were required to remit 'a tithe of the tithes' they received (i.e. one tenth of their own one tenth share) to the priests, Nb 18:20–32.

With the single sanctuary ruling of Dt 12 a new situation arose. Levites in the outlying sanctuaries became redundant and so Dt 18:1–8 allowed them to move to Jerusalem to minister on equal terms with the existing incumbents (an option that would have been quite impractical if taken up in any strength). The redundancies that were anticipated no doubt account for Deuteronomy's repeated calls commending the Levites to the people's charity and for Dt 18:1–8 allowing them to share in the priestly entitlements.

3: THE LAW

The Pentateuch contains an extensive caucus aimed at regulating the lives of God's people and collectively known as the Law. Best known are the two versions of the Decalogue, the Ten Commandments, Ex 20:1–17; Dt 5:7–21. Building on these are three major codes:

> the Book of the Covenant, Ex 20:22 – 23:19
> the Law of Holiness, Lv 17:1 – 25:55
> the Deuteronomic code, Dt 12:1 – 26:15

plus two more specialised collections:

> the Law of Sacrifice, Lv 1:1 – 7:38, Lv 16:1–34
> the Law of Purity, Lv 11:1 – 15:33

and a number of briefer compilations: Ex 34:14–26; Nb 5:1 – 6:21; 8:1 – 9:14; 15:1–41; 18:8 – 19:22; 27:1–11; 28:1 – 30:17; 35:1 – 36:13; parts of Ex 12:1 – 13:16.

How the Law evolved

According to the Bible the Law was all promulgated during Moses' lifetime. However, modern scholarship is predominantly of the view that the Law evolved over centuries. For example the Book of the Covenant, with its presupposition of a sedentary lifestyle seems more suited to a settled community of shepherds and peasants than a nomadic desert existence while there are indications that the Deuteronomic code is, in part at least, a derivative to reflect later economic and social conditions and a more enlightened view of morality. (From many possible examples compare Dt 14:21a with

Ex 22:30; Dt 15:1–11 with Ex 23:10–11; Dt 15:12-18 with Ex 21:2–6; Dt 16:18-20 with Ex 23:1–3,6–8; Dt 23:20–21 with Ex 22:24.)

More generally, like the Pentateuch as a whole, the Law is best seen as a vast mosaic, a compendium of laws of different ages ranging from Sinai to the monarchy or beyond with retrojections from the days of the Temple mingled with items of great antiquity, the whole subsumed under the Mosaic umbrella to confer authority. It is the evolution to meet changing lifestyles and a growing awareness of what God required that accounts for what might otherwise be seen as inconsistencies.

The nature of Israel's Law

The Law covers civil and criminal affairs, moral and religious prescriptions, details of ceremonial and ritual. Everything, religious and secular, is encapsulated in one code and ascribed to God. The sacred pervades the profane. The entire fabric of society is brought under God's sovereign will and, with its inexhaustible attention to detail, the Law drives home as nothing else could God's loving concern with every scintilla of His creatures' existence.

At first glance the Law's diversity and its apparent lack of structure – Lv 19:26–30 deals with avoidance of blood, magic, mourning customs, prostitution, and keeping the Sabbath, in five consecutive verses – seems to preclude logical analysis. General imperatives like those in the Decalogue ('you shall not . . .') that brook no argument and imply severe consequences if they are disobeyed lie alongside laws hedged around with conditions: 'if someone does this and this then the consequences are such and such'.

However certain themes stand out. Human dignity is held in high regard. It is not permitted to go into a borrower's home to seize whatever he is offering as collateral for a loan. He must be allowed to bring it out himself, Dt 24:10–11. Physical punishment must never cause injury or humiliation, Dt 25:1–3. Slaves must be treated humanely and freed every sabbatical year loaded with gifts, Dt 15:12–18. Women taken in war still had rights, Dt 21:10–14. The labourer must be paid his wages promptly, Lv 19:13. Nothing must be taken in pledge that would cause undue hardship, Dt 24:6.

Despite occasional severity the overarching impression is of humanity and a high moral tone. Justice, fairness, compassion, concern for widows, orphans and aliens: these are the leitmotivs. If an enemy's beast of burden strayed or fell under its load he was to be helped, Ex 23:4–5. The better off must show a generous heart by not charging brother Israelites interest on loans, Ex 22:24. There was one Law for everyone irrespective of status.

But the line was drawn sharply at anyone attempting to entice people away from the one true God. Whether an individual or a community, the guilty party must be utterly destroyed, Dt 13. The relatively humane rules of war of Dt 20:10–14 are specifically set aside for Canaanite foes, Dt 20:15–18. They must be annihilated since they pose a direct threat to faith.

Some laws were intended to teach a general point by example. The injunction of Lv 19:9–10 not to reap to the edges of fields and to leave fallen grapes teaches regard for the poor and there are many similar examples where the reader must distil the essence and look for the comprehensiveness of spirit that underlies the literal words.

Other laws were aimed at distancing Israel from her neighbours as befits a nation that was Yahweh's personal possession. The purity laws of Lv 11–15 are of this kind. Sometimes, with prohibitions against cattle cross-breeding, sowing two sorts of grain in a field, wearing a garment woven from two kinds of fabric, or boiling a goat in its mother's milk we seem to be in the world of superstition. And that is precisely where we are. For these were all pagan practices that figured in Canaanite fertility rites and for that reason alone, to keep its own religion pure and unsullied, Israel was forbidden to copy them.

The impact of the Law

The Law made a tremendous impact. It revealed, perhaps more clearly than anything else, God's character, His constant insistence on His rights over His own creation, His righteousness, the standards of morality He expects of His people, the nature of sin. By hammering home the idea of God as pure and holy the Law moved Israel forward from early perceptions of a God inspiring feelings of awe and transcendence, and demanding ritual purity, to the imperative for man to be both physically and morally pure, sovereign of a clean conscience. With the Law embracing every facet of life, every moment gave an opportunity to praise God, every detail a chance to be holy. The Law made it impossible to forget God for He was to be found not just in the Temple but pervading every aspect of existence. Loyalty to God was paramount. Transcending all else are Jesus' two great commandments: love of God, Dt 6:4; and love of neighbour, Lv 19:18,33.

Joshua

1: MIRACLES IN JOSHUA

Israel's dry-shod crossing of the Jordan and the fall of Jericho may both have natural explanations. We know that the flow of the Jordan was interrupted by landslides in 1267 and again in 1927, while the collapse of Jericho's walls may have been due to one of the many earthquakes to which the region is prone. In neither case, however, is Divine intervention ruled out. The timings of the two events were undeniably providential.

2: THE CURSE OF DESTRUCTION

The curse of destruction (*herem* in Hebrew) presents a problem to Christians. How can we reconcile such bellicose fanaticism and pitiless slaughter with the God of love we know today?

The *herem*'s rationale was that in a war fought on behalf of God (it was only invoked in a holy war) all the spoils belonged to the deity that won the war. No profit must accrue to the human victor. Therefore all living things, animal and human, irrespective of age or sex, must be 'devoted' to Yahweh, i.e. killed with booty being made over to the Sanctuary. (This is the ruling of Jos 6:17–21. On the other hand Jos 8:2, 26–28; 11:10–14 say that Israelites could keep booty and livestock for themselves while Dt 13:15–19 rules that booty must be burnt.)

One approach to an answer compares Yahweh with a surgeon who does not hesitate to remove a limb if life itself is at risk. In Canaan life (in the deepest sense) was at risk. Only if Israel remained morally pure, unsullied by the abominations of Canaanite religion, would she be fit to fulfil her mission. Therefore, the argument goes, the Canaanites had to be utterly wiped out for the greater good. (In sympathy with this Dt 20:10–18 only applies the herem to cities 'in the land Yahweh is giving you' i.e. to Canaan. Other cities, 'cities that were far away', were to be treated more humanely with the lives of women and children being spared.)

Another possibility is that Israel misunderstood what was meant when Yahweh ordered her not to become embroiled with Canaanite religion and to destroy its religious emblems. Perhaps in misplaced zeal she extended this to extermination in common with the way her neighbours practised holy war.

Although it does not affect the moral issue we do know that the *herem* could not have been widely applied. There are many signs that the Canaanites were far from being exterminated. So it may be that when the history of how Israel won the Promised Land came to be written up many years later, the authors exaggerated the application of the *herem* in order to highlight the zeal they mistakenly thought their forebears ought to have displayed.

We must never forget too that the *herem* reflects the brutality and religious culture of the harsh times in which Israel grew to nationhood, an age waiting for, but not yet ready for, the fuller revelation of Christ's Gospel of love.

3: COLLECTIVE AND INDIVIDUAL RESPONSIBILITY

Early in Israel's history it was believed that a whole family, a tribe or even the entire nation could be contaminated and incur guilt on account of the sin of a few of its members, perhaps only one. The stories of Korah, Dathan and Abiram in Nb 16 relate how whole families were punished for their leaders' rebellion. And not long after the capture of Jericho the entire nation suffered humiliation at Ai due to one man's avarice.

As time went on this idea of collective guilt gave way to the realisation that individuals were responsible for their own sins and theirs alone. The first glimmerings are found at Dt 7:10; 24:16 and we see them applied by Amaziah when he refused to kill the children of his father's murderers, 2K 14:6. But the change only really came into focus with the prophets, Jr 31:29; Ezk 18.

Before long it was realised that this teaching presented problems. God is fair and just yet justice in this world is far from perfect. Job highlighted the dilemma but could do no more since it is only with the later revelation of rewards and sanctions beyond the grave that the tension can be resolved.

In his intercession for Sodom at Gn 18 Abraham was trying to apply the principle of collectivity in reverse, pleading that the delinquent many should be saved on account of the upright few. And this way round the principle works. For it is on this basis, that one Man's virtue can merit forgiveness for many, that the entire Christian hope of salvation rests.

4: JOSHUA, JUDGES AND THE CONQUEST OF CANAAN

Superficially Joshua suggests a quick outright conquest of the Promised Land with the tribes acting in unison and the Canaanites virtually annihilated, Jos 10:40; 11:16,23; 18:1; 21:43. However this is inconsistent with Judges which, set in the period after Joshua's death, paints a more piecemeal subjection involving tribal wars fought on local fronts with Israel settling among her Canaanite neighbours, sometimes reducing them to forced labour, on other occasions intermarrying, Jg 3:5. Closer reading shows that Joshua is nearer to Judges than first impressions might suggest. There are many references in Joshua to territory still to be won and to Canaanite communities living alongside Israel, some but not all subject to forced labour, Jos 13:1,13; 15:63; 16:10; 17:12–18;23:4,12–13.

The truth probably lies somewhere in between. Joshua probably won battles without necessarily subduing the Canaanites for good and once they got their second wind the Canaanites may well have counter-attacked. Hence the need for follow-up operations like those at Hebron and Debir which were sacked by Joshua, Jos 10:36–39, but subsequently had to be recaptured, Jg 1:10–11. Most likely Israel only held the hill country initially as she would have been no match for the well defended cities of the plains where the defenders could deploy the iron chariots that Israel did not yet possess, Jos 17:14–18; Jg 1:19,34. The rest of the land would then have been won by a series of local wars extending over many years in the way Judges suggests together with intermarriage and natural assimilation.

Viewed in this light, where Judges recounts history in the raw – defeats and servitude as well as victories – Joshua presents a foreshortened and coloured account extolling Yahweh the warrior and highlighting the fulfilment of His promises by emphasising the supernatural element. Not so much what happened in strict accuracy but theologised history, the meaning behind the events in the wide embrace of God's providence.

(Archaeology offers little help. Although there is evidence of violent destruction at many of the sites Joshua is reported to have put to the sword, in other cases there is none at all and even where there is there are difficulties in reconciling the dates suggested by archaeology with those generally accepted for the Israelite invasion.)

Judges

1: Baal and Canaanite religion

Although the Bible sometimes uses 'Baal' to denote pagan gods generally, it was more properly the name by which the head of the Canaanite pantheon was known. Lesser gods within the pantheon, who watched over local communities, were worshipped under different names or known simply as the 'Baal of . . .'. as at Nb 25:1–18.

Canaanite religion was a nature religion with scant concern for morality. Baal was the god of soil fertility while his consort Astarte, or Asherah, was the goddess of fecundity and love. It was common for Baal to be represented by sacred stones and stone pillars flanking an altar while wooden poles provided emblems for Astarte.

Baal's power was thought to depend on his sexual relationship with Astarte. As a consequence festive occasions were often marked by riotous drinking and sexual incontinence because it was hoped that intimacy with a temple prostitute would remind Baal to enjoy intercourse with his consort and so ensure fertility.

What was the attraction of all this for Israel? The explanation lies in Baal's supposed power to influence fertility. Life's very existence depended on plentiful crops and sheep and when Israel arrived in Canaan it seemed from the indigenous people's lifestyle that Baal could be depended upon to provide them. Yahweh had proved Himself in the desert and in war but was He able to control the weather and fertility as well as Baal? Rather than take a chance why not insure against famine by worshipping Baal too? So some Israelites forsook Yahweh for Baal. Others worshipped both. Others still worshipped Yahweh but at Canaanite shrines. The result was that in many instances Yahweh worship became subsumed within the Canaanite cult and largely forgotten.

2: Cruelty in the Old Testament

The Yahweh of the Old Testament sometimes seems a far cry from the God of love of the New. Humanity is engulfed by a great flood; Sodom is incinerated; Egypt stricken by plagues. The Bible attributes all these disasters and many more directly to God.

The first point is that in ancient days everything was ascribed to God as the ultimate cause, see Ex appendix 2. Today we see things differently, as God acting through people and events in the natural unfolding of history. The flood may have arisen out of climatic change, the Sodom firestorm because of volcanic activity, both of which God harnessed, when they occurred, to suit His purpose.

Likewise we do not necessarily have to believe that God caused the deaths of Aaron's sons, Lv 10:1–2, or of the unfortunate Uzzah who steadied the ark with his hand, 2S 6:6–7. These and similar tragedies could also have had natural explanations and been attributed to God either through superstition or to make a didactic point.

But mystery remains. We cannot easily understand the mental anguish God inflicted on Abraham when He was asked to sacrifice Isaac. We cannot explain (even after Job) why the innocent suffer along with the guilty. We can only remember that we live in an imperfect fallen world brought about by man's own folly. We must remember too that God can 'even-up' justice in the next world and that when He punishes it is, like a loving parent, to correct and warn, never to inflict hurt for its own sake. At other times 'punishment' is no more than leaving us to the consequences of our own actions.

*   *   *

Much of the violence in the Bible is man-made: Joshua hanging his enemies, Jos 10:26; Saul's massacre of the priests at Nob, 1S 22:6–23; David's brutal treatment of his Moabite prisoners, 2S 8:2. At other times we read of bizarre customs like cutting up a dead concubine, Jg 19, for the pieces to be sent as messages for vengeance.

The fact is that the characters in the Bible were not saints but men of their time and that God acts in history as He finds it using people with strengths and weaknesses like anyone else. We must remember too that while reporting it the Bible never commends behaviour that falls below what God desires.

Dominant in Israelite thought was their unique status as God's people. Opposition to them was opposition to God. Vengeance was therefore not a personal matter but vindication of God's honour. Often it went too far. But at least the perpetrators could never be accused of a lazy or spineless indifference.

2 Samuel

1: THE DAVIDIC COVENANT

Although the Davidic covenant, in its enigmatic oracular style, refers to David's immediate successor its significance, as David was quick to realise, lay in the distant future with God's promise of a home where His people would live in freedom and peace with a king of David's House reigning over them forever. Its whole tenor is futuristic. It is the start of the Messianic hope, the golden thread that runs through the Old Testament and reaches its apogee in Christ.

Its timing was providential. Under David and Solomon Israel enjoyed the trappings of empire. She had vanquished her traditional enemies – Aram, Ammon, Edom, Moab, Philistia – and enjoyed material prosperity. It seemed as if God's promises were at last being realised. Then, following Solomon's death, there began the long decline that led to captivity and exile. Hopes were dashed. Supported by the prophets, it was the promise that David's House would reign for ever that helped prevent Israel plunging into despair and losing her faith.

1 Kings

1: HIGH PLACES AND CANAANITE WORSHIP

High places, hills and spreading trees, often accompanied by pillars and sacred poles, were among the most popular sites for Canaanite worship because of their coolness and numinous qualities. So much so that in the Bible 'high places' is almost synonymous with pagan religion. That is why worshipping on 'the high places' is so vehemently condemned as a perversion. It was the main reason for Deuteronomy's call for worship to be confined to just one sanctuary of God's choosing. However pious the intent there was always the risk that frequenting former Canaanite shrines would expose Israel's spiritual life to the danger of assimilating something from the depraved rites that were practised there – child sacrifice, sacred prostitution, fertility rites, self mutilation and so on.

2 Kings

1: PARALLELS INVOLVING ELIJAH

There are many parallels between Moses and Elijah, the prophet whose stature is indelibly underscored by his presence with Moses at Jesus' Transfiguration. Moses saved Israel from oppression under Pharaoh; Elijah saved Yahweh worship from persecution under Ahab. Moses parted the Red Sea as Elijah the Jordan. Both experienced God on Mt Sinai, sheltered in a cave, and covered their faces as God passed by. Both possessed miraculous powers and had mysterious deaths. The manner in which Moses was followed by Joshua resembles the way Elijah was succeeded by Elisha. (There are also parallels between Elijah and Elisha. Both parted the Jordan, replenished a widow's oil and restored a child's life by stretching themselves over it.)

Nehemiah

1: THE CHRONOLOGY OF EZRA–NEHEMIAH

The chronology of EZRA–NEHEMIAH has given rise to much debate. However taking the Bible's own sequence of events the first exiles left Babylon in 538, Ezr 1:1. The foundations of the new Temple were laid in 536, Ezr 3:8, whereupon everything ground to a halt until 520, Ezr 4:24, when work was resumed and the Temple completed in 515, Ezr 6:15. Ezra came to Jerusalem in 458, Ezr 7:8. Nehemiah followed and rebuilt the city walls in 445, Ne2:1,11–18; 6:15. (The dates of the reigns of the Persian kings used in these deductions are: Cyrus 559–530, Darius 522–486, Artaxerxes 465–424. However Cyrus's reign as king of Babylon, which the Bible takes as his starting point, only commenced in 538.)

Ezra's reading of the Law and the renewal that followed also seem to belong to 445 since they are sandwiched between Nehemiah's rebuilding of the walls and their dedication which it is reasonable to assume also took place in 445. Nehemiah's second visit to Jerusalem must have begun somewhere between 433 and 424 because we know from Ne 5:14; 13:6 that his first governorship lasted from 445 to 433 and that his second visit also began in the reign of Artaxerxes who died in 424.

Arguing that it seems unlikely that Ezra would have waited 13 years, from 458 to 445, before the reading of the Law recorded at Ne 8, some scholars believe that the events recorded in Ezra and Nehemiah should be reordered. However although many alternative chronologies have been proposed none succeeds in explaining this and other perceived anomalies without creating as many new problems as they solve. There therefore seems no compelling reason to abandon the traditional reading.

Job

1: JOB'S LIVING DEFENDER

Amidst his suffering Job's thoughts momentarily transcend the barrier of mortality. Despairing of vindication on earth his vision jumps to a witness in heaven, a Defender on high, to plead his cause with God, 16:19–21. The idea recurs a little later but now the possibility occurs to him that God would no longer be a Stranger, the remote mystery God of chastisement, but a Friend on whom, after awakening, he would look from his flesh, 19:25–27. That Job saw all this happening after his death is evident from the context. He thought his death was fast approaching and that he would die without vindication.

The same ideas are latent in an earlier text, 14:13–17, where, in another insight, Job imagines a situation in which, after a spell in Sheol during which God's anger would be assuaged, he would in some way be reconciled with God and his sins forgiven.

It is possible to read into these texts a hint of resurrection but the verses in question are so difficult to interpret that dogmatism is precluded. What does seem clear however is that, while he would not have been fully conscious of the seed encased in his words, Job's thoughts were in some way stumbling, straining, towards what would one day be revealed in Christ. Certainly no Christian could read his words without calling to mind:

> He (Christ) lives for ever to intercede for them, Heb 7:12

> We have an advocate with the Father, Jesus Christ, the upright, 1Jn 2:1

Psalms

1: VENGEANCE IN THE PSALMS

Some of the laments call for vengeance on the wicked: e.g. at Ps 10:15; 31:17–18; 54:5; 58:6–11; 69:22–28; 109:6–20; 137:7–9. The most extreme instances occur in Ps 109 and in Ps 137 which, despite the beauty and poignancy of its opening verses, contains some of the most vengeful language in the Old Testament and has long been a source of concern to Christians. There is no denying the problem but it should be tempered with the realisation that the psalmists were men of their day who, carried away by hunger for justice and for evil to be destroyed, confused the sinner with the sin. They were motivated by their conviction of God's detestation of evil and, in their righteous zeal, saw retribution as something demanded by His holiness. Moreover justice demanded that retribution be proportionate to the wickedness. So drastic punishment was the psalmist's way of asserting just how wicked God's enemies really were. It should also be borne in mind that the calls for vengeance are all prayers. There is never any suggestion of the psalmist calling for summary justice. Everything was left to God's providence.

Isaiah

1: THE DAY OF YAHWEH

Isaiah's prophecy at 2:1–5 of the advent in the final days of God's universal rule is an example of the way the prophets sometimes turn, often quite abruptly, from contemporary events to a time in the future when Yahweh will break decisively into history. This may be introduced potently as the 'Day of Yahweh', the 'Day of the Lord', or simply as the 'Day' but more often by an emphatic 'that day!', or some more subdued phrase like 'in the final days', 'when that day comes', etc. Without an explicit 'Day' these waymarks may sometimes be so deeply embedded in the text that only the most careful reading spots them.

Chronologically the Day is first mentioned by Amos, Am 5:18–20, where it is apparent from the context that Israel had hitherto looked forward to it as a time when Yahweh would intervene to deliver Israel and scatter her foes. Amos turned this idea on its head. Far from being a Day of victory and light it would be a Day of mourning and lamentation marked by cosmic convulsions as Israel was judged for her sins. Zephaniah saw it as a Day of retribution against sinners involving the whole earth, Zp 1:14–18.

At other times, in contrast, the Day is invoked in prophecies of God establishing His universal dominion with a return to the paradisiacal world of Eden, Is 2:1–5; Hos 2:18–25; Am 9:11–15. To Joel it was the Day when God would pour His spirit on all humanity, Jl 3:1–5.

After the exile the Day modulated into a time of both rewards and retribution when evil-doers would be destroyed and the upright healed and renewed, Ml 3:19–21. Elsewhere it is seen as the time of a battle when God will defeat evil before settling His people forever in peace, Ob, Jl 4:1–16; Ezk 37 – 38; Zc 14.

The prophets, telescoping events of the present age with those of the world to come, saw the Day in history. To Christians it is associated with Christ's two Comings culminating beyond history in the Day of Judgement, see 2 P appendix 1.

2: PROPHECY AND THE FUTURE

To Christians with the eye of faith, the prophecies of Is 7 – 11 point to Christ. Does this mean that Isaiah and other sages foresaw the future? It would be presumptuous to be dogmatic where divine revelation is concerned so we cannot rule it out. On the other hand it is possible to see how these prophecies and others like them could have originated out of contemporary events with God enabling them to assume a significance for later events which the prophet himself need not have been aware of.

For example Isaiah doubtless saw that Ahaz, having spurned God, was an unworthy king who dimmed the glory of the Davidic dynasty. The original meaning of his Immanuel oracle may therefore have been that Yahweh would raise a worthy successor to revive its tarnished fortunes, perhaps the child of Ahaz and a court virgin. The child would be a sign that God was still with His people. He would create an empire, establish justice and peace and so on. In chapters 9 and 11 Isaiah may simply have employed poetic licence to inspire his audience rather than trying to portray an idealised reality.

Nathan's prophecy of 2S 7 that David's dynasty would endure for ever may have originated simply as an assurance that David's House would continue to provide Yahweh's viceroy on earth with it only later assuming the spiritual significance we see in it today.

Certain psalms, notably Pss 2, 72, 110, have long been taken as foreshadowing Christ. But the idealised hopes of peace, justice, prosperity and worldwide dominion they promise, together with references to the king's divine Sonship and everlasting reign, may well have originated in addresses to the king on state occasions when they would have reflected, in the stilted symbolic language of the court, no more than pious hopes for long life and victory over his enemies and the king's status as guardian of God's covenant promises.

When we come to the prophecies in Daniel and the predictions of exile in Leviticus and Deuteronomy, it is widely held that these were made after the events they purport to prophesy. But even if this is the case it does not deny them, in God's providence, the additional deeper meanings they have since assumed.

Other texts, such as God's judgement on the snake at Gn 3:14, with its premonition of evil's eventual defeat, are not so easily explained and in the last resort we have to accept that we are faced with the inscrutable ways of a hidden God to whom nothing is impossible. There is one other point we cannot possibly ignore. Christ openly spoke of Himself as the fulfilment of Old Testament prophecy, Lk 24:25–27.

3: THE REMNANT

'Remnant' is a recurring theme in Isaiah. Whatever disasters befell Israel God would preserve a remnant as the seed of a new and more faithful community to inherit His promises. He would never leave His people without a witness to the true faith. At a stroke the 'remnant' idea resolved the tension between a God whose chosen people had disqualified themselves by infidelity from being guardians of His covenant promises and the same God who had promised that same people blessings.

It is like a two-sided mirror. On the one hand 'remnant' carries a note of despair. Only a remnant will survive God's judgement on recalcitrant Israel. At the same time it is a window of hope. At least a remnant will survive and so preserve the hope that somehow God's choice of Israel as His vehicle for bringing light to the world will eventually bear fruit.

Isaiah does not always speak of the remnant in so many words. At 1:9 he speaks of a few survivors, at 4:2 of Yahweh's seedling, and at 6:13; 11:1 of Israel being cut back to a stock that will be a holy seed. (Other references to the remnant theme in Is include 10:20; 28:5; 37:31. There are also references in the minor prophets: Ba 2:13; Mi 2:12–13; 4:7; 5:2; Zp 2:7; 3:12–13; Ob 17 = Jl 3:5; Hg 1:12; Zc 8:11–12; see also Ezr 9:8, Ne 9:31).

As crisis followed crisis the successive survivors constituted the remnant. To Amos, following the demise of the northern kingdom, the remnant would have been the southern kingdom of Judah. To Isaiah at Is 37:31 it would have been the survivors from Sennacherib's invasion. To Jeremiah and Ezekiel it was the exiles in Babylon and the rump that later returned to Jerusalem. Ultimately it was narrowed down to the one upright sinless man, Jesus Christ, before widening out into His Church.

It is possible that vestiges of the remnant theme go back to the earliest times, possibly to Noah's family who alone escaped the flood, and to God's election of just one man, Abraham, after the excesses of Babel.

4: EDOM: ISRAEL'S ARCHETYPAL ENEMY

Several of the prophets voice oracles against foreign nations forecasting their punishment or doom. This is only to be expected. If Israel, God's chosen people, deserved censure how much more so must nations that did not recognise Yahweh at all and even oppressed His elect. They must be humbled so that they could never again threaten the divine plan.

Edom is particularly singled out. Is 34:5–17; 63:1–6 are but two of many fulminations against her. Others include Lm 4:21–22; Ezk 35:1 – 36:5; Jl 4:19; Ml 1:2–5. Obadiah is given over almost entirely to a tirade against Edom.

Enmity between Israel and Edom originated in the days of Jacob and Esau, their founding fathers, and the final breach came during Nebuchadnezzar's campaign of 587 when Edom not only rejoiced over Jerusalem's fall, Ps 137:7, but, as Obadiah shows, ravaged Judah herself.

As time went on Edom came to personify the profane, the figure par excellence of enmity to God and His people's persecutor and adversary. The oracles against Edom, many of which with their ferocity and burning hatred carry the stamp of a cosmic element, should therefore be read as directed against evil in all its guises and therefore as prefiguring the ultimate end of everything that opposes God. Nahum, with its invective against Assyria, and similar texts, may be read in similar vein.

5: MONOTHEISM

Deutero Isaiah repeatedly affirms that Yahweh is the only God, 43:8–13; 44:6–8; 45:5–6, 14, 18, 21–22; 46:9; 48:12. Earlier prophets had taught that there was only one God whom Israel ought to worship and implied that He was the only God but they did not state it in so many words. Elijah showed that Baal was powerless, not that he did not exist. With the sole exception of Dt 4:35 (and possibly Dt 6:4, though the meaning is disputed) the Pentateuch merely forbade the worship of other gods although it could be argued that the relationship between God and His Creation as painted in Genesis was so close as to leave no room for other gods.

Deutero Isaiah positively delights in denying other gods and poking fun at idols. His argument that Yahweh can do what no idol can do, namely foretell the future and interpret the past, 41:21–29; 48:1–11, would have been particularly telling since the Babylonians set great store by their gods' prophetic ability. His stress on the vacuity of idols would have been a key element in preventing the exiles in Babylon, deprived of the Temple and their traditional liturgy, from abandoning Yahweh for the local gods.

6: THE SPIRIT OF YAHWEH

The spirit (or breath) of Yahweh was active throughout the Old Testament. It blew life into the first man's nostrils, Gn 2:7, as it later did into Ezekiel's army of dry bones, Ezk 37:5–14. It guided Joseph, Gn 41:38, and enabled the craftsmen working on the

Dwelling, Ex 31:3, 35:31. It inspired Moses, Nb 11:16–30; Balaam, Nb 24:2; the judges Othniel, Gideon and Jephthah, Jg 3:10; 6:34; 11:29; Saul, 1S 10:6,10; 11:6; and David, 1S 16:13.

It energised the prophets generally, Zc 7:12; Elijah, 2K 2:9; Isaiah, Is 48:16; Micah, Mi 3:8; Zechariah, Zc 4:6b. It was promised to Israel, the people of God, Is 32:15; 44:3; 59:21; Ezk 39:29; Zc 12:10. Nehemiah acknowledged its instruction, Ne 9:20,30. The spirit is vexed by sin just as God is, Is 63:10. Where the spirit is present God is present, Ps 139:7.

It would be the spur to inward renewal and moral regeneration under the New Covenant, Ezk 11:19; 36:26–27. It would be poured out on Isaiah's Son of David, Is 11:2, and on the Servant, Is 42:1. Joel looked forward to the day when the Spirit would descend on all humanity, Jl 3:1–2. It is closely identified with Wisdom, Wi 1:6–7; 9:17.

In the Old Testament the spirit's role was limited. It came down upon individuals for a particular time and purpose: to empower charismatic leaders beyond their normal capabilities in times of crisis; to endow them with special graces; to equip men to be messengers of the divine Word. Except for Moses and Elijah these gifts were usually temporary.

In the New Testament, following Pentecost, it is different. Now, as promised by Jesus, the Spirit indwells God's people permanently as the source of spiritual strength and regeneration, see ACTS, Appendix 1.

7: THE SERVANT SONGS

No one knows who Isaiah had in mind as the Servant: the prophet himself, Cyrus, Jeremiah, Israel have all been suggested. Be that as it may. Christians, supported by the testimony of the New Testament, are united in seeing him as pointing to Christ, Mt 8:17; 12:17–21; Lk 22:37; Jn 12:38; Ac 8:32–35.

The Songs break new ground. Israel had long believed that suffering was the wages of sin. Not only do the Songs confound that idea but, more importantly, by attributing value, indeed immense value, to the Servant's suffering and death they show that it would not be despite suffering that the world would be reconciled with God but through it.

Isaiah recognised that Israel had disqualified herself through sin from being the 'holy nation' to proclaim His name to the nations that God chose her for. Instead that role would be filled by someone of supreme holiness, the Servant. He would be the perfect expression of what God always intended Israel to be.

> I shall make you a light to the nations
> so that my salvation may reach the remotest parts of earth. 49:6

In the second Song at 49:3 the Servant is Israel whereas at 49:5 He is sent to Israel to reunite her with God. How can Israel be sent to Israel? The puzzle is easily resolved. Christ, as the ultimate one man remnant of the old Israel, became the founder and head of the new Israel of His church. Christ therefore is (the new) Israel and it was to (the old) Israel that He was sent.

8: UNIVERSALISM

Isaiah ends on a universalist note. Every nation will be called upon to spread God's light and witness to His glory. As the only God and Creator of all that is, Yahweh's sovereignty over all nations had long been clear enough. It is manifest in the plagues inflicted on Egypt and in God's use of Assyria to discipline Israel. But not until Isaiah is the theme that God offers salvation to all articulated explicitly and at length.

It is implicit in God's mission call to Abraham – 'all clans on earth will bless themselves by you'. It is hinted at in Ruth and in the healing of the Aramaean army commander Naaman, 2K 5. But in Isaiah it comes to the fore. It first appears at 2:2–3 with the nations streaming to Zion to learn God's ways and wells up steadily thereafter. Egypt and Assyria are blessed along with Israel, 19:16–25. God is preparing a rich banquet for all peoples, 25:6. His Servant will be a light to the nations, 42:1–7; 49:6. The nations will one day discard their idols and acknowledge Yahweh as the one true God, 45:14–25. He welcomes foreigners who faithfully keep His covenant, 56:1–9. All nations will throng to the new Jerusalem, 60:1–7. See also Jr 3:14–17; 12:14–17; 16:19–21; Dn 7:13–14; Am 9:7; Jl 3:1; Zp 3:9–10; Zc 2:15; 8:20–23; 14:16.

Later on Jonah reinforced this message in no uncertain terms. Not even the cruel and vicious Assyrians, Israel's arch tormenters, are excluded from God's love. Even so the universality of salvation was only finally accepted in the New Testament with the baptism of the Roman centurion Cornelius and Paul's ministry to the Gentiles.

Jeremiah

1: THE NEW COVENANT

For a time Jeremiah seems to have hoped that Judah's conversion to godliness, her circumcision of the heart, would come about through self-propelled renewal. However he gradually came to realise that because of human frailty, the waywardness of the human heart, this was not going to happen. Judah would not listen to God. She was rebellious and stubborn. This led him to his supreme insight. Since the Law could not be relaxed, because it reflected God's unchangeable nature, there was only one alternative. If there were to be any hope for delinquent man his inner nature would have to be reshaped to enable him to measure up to what God required of him. Since man could manifestly not do this himself God would have to do it for him. And this He would do by writing His Law inwardly on his heart rather than externally on Sinai stone as before.

What this means is that instead of a nature that was devious, depraved and unresponsive God would infuse His creatures with a heart that was sensitive and responsive to His will, one that prompted obedience. More! He would sustain them with His spirit.

> I shall give you a new heart, and put a new spirit in you; I shall remove the heart of stone from your bodies and give you a heart of flesh instead. I shall put my spirit in you, and make you keep my laws, and respect and practise my judgements. Ezk 36:26–27.

No longer will man be alone as he struggles to live as God requires. Now God promises to offer His spirit in support to counsel, guide and uplift him. The overarching emotion has changed from a God to be feared to a God who loves and the end result will be what God always intended. Everyone, from least to greatest, will know Him personally.

This new covenant also contains the promise that sins (for sins there will still inevitably be in this life) will be forgiven and never more called to mind.

Jeremiah saw the New Covenant being fulfilled 'in the days to come'. We now know that it was inaugurated by Jesus at the Last Supper, Mt 26:26–28, when He died for the forgiveness of sins and prepared the way for the Holy Spirit to lift and rule men's hearts.

Daniel

1: APOCALYPTIC LITERATURE

Daniel, notably chapters 2; 7 – 12, is the prime example in the Old Testament of a type of literature known as Apocalyptic of which there are many examples outside the Canon. Its counterpart in the New Testament is the book of Revelation which indeed is sometimes known as the Apocalypse. 'Apocalyptic' stems from a Greek word meaning 'to unveil' and its *raison d'être,* as that name implies, is to unlock secrets that are normally hidden from human eyes, especially about the end of this age and God's kingdom of the world to come.

It differs from mainstream prophecy in substance and style. The classical prophets warned of divine judgement and preached repentance. They pointed to a future when, as a result of God's actions in the course of history, the good would prosper, the wicked perish and a righteous king would govern wisely and justly over a creation restored to the perfection of Eden. Suffering and evil would be no more.

Unfortunately life after the exile continued to be a bitter pill of servitude and want. The promised good times did not materialise. The faithful continued to suffer, sinners to flourish. Had God forgotten His promises? This was the seedbed from which Apocalyptic literature in general and Daniel in particular germinated. Eschewing calls for repentance – demonstrating, as it were, an impatience with history – the apocalyptist accepts judgement and focuses squarely on the end of time. He no longer looks for a turning point in history but a time, the Day of Yahweh, when God will break into history to deliver His promises in a new age beyond history. Preceded by a period of intense suffering, he typically sees history reaching a climax in a final titanic struggle between God and the massed cohorts of darkness, a battle that culminates in cosmic catastrophe, the collapse of the physical world and political institutions, judgement, the annihilation of evil, the triumph of God's kingdom, the vindication of the just and their endless felicity in a new creation beyond time.

It has been remarked that 'a prophet afflicts the comforted' (pricking consciences) while 'the apocalyptist comforts the afflicted' (teaching the coming of God's kingdom). Moreover where the prophet is an optimist who tries to bring about God's kingdom by reforming the present world through repentance, the apocalyptist is a pessimist to whom it is past mending. God's will can only be done in the next world after this one is removed. Where the prophet sees change coming through natural means the apocalypse sees supernatural.

The prophet typically preaches as well as writes and does so under his own name. The apocalyptist's work is wholly written, otherwise it would not be understood. He normally writes under an assumed name although Revelation may be an exception. In style the contrast is even more marked. More than the classical prophet the apocalyptist dreams and sees awesome cosmic signs in visions that sometimes border on the bizarre. He receives his inspiration from angelic mediators rather than directly from God. He revels in cryptic numbers and luxuriant weird symbolism: strange animals and monsters that depict the clash of mighty forces of good and evil.

The use of symbolism is no accident. The apocalyptist uses it as a way to shed light on mysteries that defy the bounds of ordinary speech, to paint the unpaintable. In times of persecution it also served as a code to prevent the message inflaming an ongoing situation by coming to the oppressors' attention. Antiochus Epiphanes is never mentioned by name in Daniel nor Rome in Revelation. (It would be a mistake, however, to assume that every symbol in an apocalypse has some hidden meaning. And even where it does it may well be indecipherable today. In a modern cartoon we have no difficulty in decoding a bear as Russia whereas we no longer have the 'code books' of old.)

Besides Daniel a number of other Old Testament texts exhibit apocalyptic features. These include Is 24 – 27; 34 – 35; elements of Is 65:17 – 66:24; Ezk 38 – 39; Zc 12 – 14. Unsurprisingly, since they are also concerned with God's decisive intervention into history, passages depicting the Day of Yahweh also carry apocalyptic hints notably Jl 2:1–2, 10–11; 3:1–5; Zp 1:14–18. In the New Testament, apart from Revelation, the supreme example is Christ's Olivet discourse, Mt 24, while others include 1Th 4:13 – 5:6; 2Th 2:1–12; 2P 3:10–13.

2: RESURRECTION

It was a long time before the realisation dawned that the old idea of the dead spending their days in Sheol, a joyless shadowy underworld, was incompatible with a God who otherwise poured out His love so bountifully. If God truly cared for His creatures how could He let His relationship with them fall away into nothingness? And so the idea of resurrection gradually began to take its place, reaching its climax in the Scriptures with Jesus' great revelation that it had been latent from the earliest times, as far back as God's revelation to Moses that He was the God not of the dead but of the living, Mt 22:31–32. The clearest affirmation of individual resurrection in the Old Testament occurs at Dn 12:2–3. Other relevant texts include Is 26:19; 2M 7; 12:38–45; 14:46; Ws 1:1 – 5:16 and possibly Jb 16:19–21; 19:25–27; Ps 16:9–11; 49:15; 73:23–28. Ezk 37, the well-known passage where Yahweh restores life to a valley full of dry bones, is usually interpreted as referring to Israel's corporate revival as a nation after the exile but it can certainly be taken as preparing minds for individual bodily resurrection too.

Amos

1: TRUE RELIGION STEMS FROM THE HEART

That the basis of a right relationship with God is justice and uprightness, avoidance of evil and an inward spirituality rather than ritual observance, goes right back to Moses' call to his followers to 'circumcise' their hearts, Dt 10:16. It comes out again in Samuel's admonishment of the chastened Saul: 'obedience is better than sacrifice', 1S 15:22.

However it was left to the prophets to drive the lesson home that sacrifice was not an automatic antidote to sin and that ethics count for more than cult. This is not to say that the prophets were hostile to liturgy, merely that they denied its efficacy apart from the interior commitment of a heart turned to God. It took a long time for Israel to realise that holiness was a moral ideal.

Amos was the first to stress the point, Am 5:14–15; 21–27, quickly followed by Hosea, Hos 6:6, Micah, Mi 6:8, Isaiah, Is 1:10–17; 58:1–8, Joel, Jl 2:13, and others. Jeremiah spoke in similar vein when he denied that the Temple could hold ruin at bay, Jr 7:1–15.

Matthew

1: NEW TESTAMENT PARTIES, SECTS AND INSTITUTIONS

The Pharisees were the spiritual descendants of the pious Jews who fought to preserve Judaism at the time of the Maccabees. They prided themselves on meticulous observance of the Law including its oral traditions. Unfortunately this eventually degenerated to a dry legalism that concentrated on the letter rather than the spirit and elevated ritual above love and mercy. Not least it gave rise to the arrogance born of pride and hypocrisy that Jesus so vehemently denounced. However though it is easy to criticise the Pharisees, their zeal is undeniable. They may have misunderstood the service of God but at least they believed in God. St Paul was a Pharisee.

The Sadducees were people of wealth and position. They were conservative in religion refusing to accept any of the Scriptures other than Pentateuch as authoritative. As a result they denied many later ideas, most notably any belief in resurrection. Many of the chief priests were Sadducees.

The Scribes were religious intellectuals ie judges, writers, teachers, skilled in interpreting the Scriptures, particularly the Law, and showing how to apply them to everyday life. They were sometimes known as 'doctors of the Law'. Most but not all were Pharisees.

2: JESUS' TEMPTATIONS

Jesus' temptations can be seen as options He had to weigh when deciding how to execute His mission. He could have miraculously turned stones into loaves and so produced a world of material plenty; or compelled belief by spectacular miracles that permitted no possible doubt about His divinity; or He could have satisfied popular demand by assuming political power and restoring David's empire. All these paths would have led to some good through an amelioration of worldly strife and hardship.

So why did Jesus reject these easier routes in favour of the Cross? Because they would have meant subordinating spirituality to materialism. Setting aside the way of faith in an omniscient God in favour of a superficial belief based on spectacle and glitter. Foregoing God's perfect Kingdom for one based on the values of this world. This might have brought peace of a sort to the earth but it could not have brought peace with God. Only by preaching the Gospel of love and following the path of suffering that led through Calvary to the outright conquest of evil and sin could Jesus reconcile man with his Creator and lead him to the sinless perfection God always intended and without which heaven would not be heaven.

3: JESUS SPIRITUALISES THE LAW

In His Sermon on the Mount, and later in His summing up of the Law as love of God and love of neighbour, Jesus penetrated the Mosaic Law's outer fabric to reveal an inner sanctum of spirituality and love. He deepened and broadened its thrust by calling into question the thought surrounding the act and by requiring not merely outward observance but changes in the confines of the human heart. Much of the detail of the original Mosaic Law (though not its underlying moral precepts) was attuned to a particular age and community. By stressing principles rather than precepts Jesus brought it to its full flowering so that in its more generalised form it would have eternal and universal validity.

It was this new dimension of the Law that Jesus had in mind when He said that He had come to complete it and that not even its smallest detail could be ignored. The Christian is no more bound to the detailed demands of the Mosaic Law than he is to its sacrificial rituals which Jesus rendered obsolete by His own perfect sacrifice on the Cross. But he is committed in entirety to the law of love.

4: THE LAW AND LATER TRADITIONS

By Jesus' day the Law had become not so much a guide to conduct as an oppressive despot spawning spiritual arrogance and religious pride. We get a clue what was wrong from Lv 19. There are no priorities. The command to love one's neighbour is immediately followed by the edict not to wear garments made from mixed materials. Tattooing is forbidden in one verse, prostitution in the next. When we realise that Leviticus was probably edited into its final form in the fifth century we can see how early the rot began to set in.

Worse was to follow. The original Mosaic Law as revealed in the Pentateuch gradually become hedged around with an extensive collection of 'oral traditions' which extended it by analogy to cover situations in every aspect of daily life in an effort to ensure that it could not be broken inadvertently. There were over thirty acts that were forbidden on the Sabbath for example. It was permissible to spit on a rock on the Sabbath but not on the dry earth. The spittle might move some of the dirt and thus be regarded as ploughing which was work and therefore forbidden! There were rules over which knots could be tied and untied on the Sabbath. On any day handling a non-canonical book made the hands unclean. And so on. As well as providing a happy hunting ground for the pedant and legal quibbler these and hundreds of similar restraints made it virtually impossible for anyone even to think they could keep the Law in its entirety.

Eventually these oral traditions were codified in written form and, since they were regarded as being 'implicit' in the Law, accorded the same standing. As a result the Law became a melange of divine revelation and human zeal and frailty and its observance degenerated into a fetish as it increasingly came to be seen as a stern rule book to be followed in order to please God and achieve righteousness. The tragedy was that Israel never understood that the Law did not impute righteousness so much as demonstrate the need for a contrite heart and forgiveness. Despite the urging of the prophets it was left to Jesus finally to bring home that what God desired was not a legalistic relationship but one based on repentance and love.

Several of Jesus' confrontations with the Pharisees arose out of His ignoring these oral traditions. When the Pharisees criticised His disciples for picking ears of corn on the Sabbath, Mt 12:1–8, it was not for picking someone else's corn as such (Dt 23:26

allowed it) but because it was done on the Sabbath and thereby constituted 'work'. Likewise when Jesus cured a man with a withered hand, Mt 12:10–14, it was the fact that it was done on the Sabbath that incensed them.

Mark

1: THE MESSIANIC SECRET

According to Mark (but rather less so in Matthew and Luke) Jesus frequently ordered people He cured not to speak about it, e.g. Mk 1:44; 5:43; 7:36 etc. He also forbade unclean spirits to name Him as the Messiah, Mk 1:34; 3:12 etc. Even the apostles were constrained, Mk 8:30; 9:9. This reticence is sometimes called 'the Messianic secret' and there were probably three reasons for it.

Firstly Jesus wanted people to follow Him because of His teaching and example and not because they saw Him as a miracle worker who could effect wondrous cures. Secondly, most people were expecting a Messiah who would evict the Romans and restore David's empire. If His fame had fuelled this idea it would have provoked the Romans into retaliatory action. Thirdly, until they had witnessed His suffering and resurrection and received the Spirit His disciples were in no position to speak meaningfully about Him anyway. There was also the practical side. The more publicity Jesus got, the more difficult it became for Him to get His teaching across, Mk 1:45.

John

1: WORD

'Word' has Old Testament roots suggesting God's active presence. It is God's Word that called the cosmos into being. The prophets repeatedly testify to the Word of God calling men to obedience and declaring His will to save. It is action, never returning to God without completing its mission, Is 55:11. John's 'Word' is in the same tradition but goes further assimilating the Old Testament notion of personified Wisdom. It is with God from eternity and His intimate at Creation, Pr 8:22–31; Jn 1:2–3, and the untarnished mirror of God's active power against which evil cannot prevail, Wi 7:30; Jn 1:5. However John does not stop there. He equates the Word with God, and with Christ, in a way the Old Testament, for all its suggestive allusions, never did with Wisdom. Other pointers to Jesus as the Wisdom of God are found at Mt 11:19, 1Co 1:24–30; Col 1:15–17; Heb 1:2–3.

2: The authorship of the Johannine Gospels and Epistles

The only clue the Gospel gives as to its author comes at 21:20–24 which suggests that it was written by 'the disciple whom Jesus loved', almost certainly the apostle John, brother of James and son of Zebedee. This accords with tradition and ties in with the fact that with his striking knowledge of Jesus' inner thoughts, and his ability to quote snippets of conversation and supply small details that betray an eye witness – all of them the stuff of treasured memory rather than literary licence – the author must clearly have been someone very close to Jesus.

Although 2 John and 3 John are both attributed to 'the Elder' (1 John is anonymous) similarities in style and thought make a strong case for all three coming from the same hand. Although this view is not undisputed none of the alternatives avoids posing as many new problems as old ones it solves, thereby leaving us with no compelling reason to abandon the traditional view of apostolic authorship.

Acts of the Apostles

1: The Holy Spirit

Acts is driven by the divine hand. The dominant motif is the presence of the Holy Spirit, so much so that Acts is sometimes described as the Gospel of the Spirit as a sequel to the Gospels of Christ. It was the Spirit that gave Christ's followers the power to witness to Him, Ac 1:8; 5:32. In particular it was the Spirit who inspired Peter and Stephen and Barnabas, Ac 4:8; 6:10; 11:22–24, who led Philip to the Ethiopian eunuch, Ac 8:26–40, who succoured the churches in Palestine, Ac 9:31, who guided Peter in his epoch making conversion of Cornelius, Ac 10:1 – 11:18, and who inspired the Church elders at the Council of Jerusalem, Ac 15:28. The Spirit guided Paul in his missions, Ac 13:1–12; 16:6–7, and ensured that his teaching was persuasive and well received, 1Th 1:4–5. Every believer receives the power of the Spirit when he is baptised, Ac 2:38; 5:32; 1Co 12:13.

2: Arguing from Scripture

It is probably fair to say that the mode of argument from Scripture exemplified in Ac 2:14–36 carries less conviction today than it did in apostolic times. The Scriptures are applied with a rare abandon. In particular it should be noted how the argument sometimes depends upon the Septuagint, the Greek translation of the Old Testament, rather than the Hebrew Scriptures themselves. We have an example at Ac 2:27 where Peter quotes Ps 16:8–11 in its Greek form as affirming that God will not allow His holy one to see 'corruption' whereas the original meaning in the Hebrew text was 'abyss' or 'grave', a distinction that is crucial in Peter's argument based on Christ's resurrection.

Another instance is at Ac 13:41. Paul warns his audience to take his message seriously by quoting Hab 1:5 from the Septuagint as 'cast your eyes around you, mockers . . .' The Hebrew rendering 'cast your eyes over the nations . . .' would not have supported his point at all.

* * *

The Septuagint was the earliest translation of the Hebrew Old Testament into Greek. Its origins are shrouded in antiquity along with the legend that seventy translators worked in isolation from each other yet produced translations that agreed verbatim. It seems to have originated from the Jewish community in Alexandria sometime between 250 and 100 B.C. and was the version used by Greek speaking Jews at the start of the Christian era. As the above examples show there are times when it varies significantly from the Hebrew.

3: THE EARLY GOSPEL MESSAGE

Peter's sermons in Ac 2, 3, 4, are of exceptional interest in revealing the earliest known Gospel message. In essence it was this. Jesus was an historical person. He was sent by God and attested by miracles and signs. He was put to death in contravention of the Law but with God's foreknowledge and as part of the divine plan. God freed Him from Hades and raised Him to life. He now sits at God's right hand. He was the promised Messiah. Only He can save, so men must repent and be baptised in His name for their sins to be forgiven and to receive the gift of the Holy Spirit. All this was foretold in the scriptures.

Peter also underlines that in so far as he and the other apostles were able to effect miraculous cures, they were all performed in Jesus' name through faith in Him.

4: THE DIASPORA AND HELLENISTS

The Assyrian and Babylonian deportations led to a large dispersion of Jews around the Middle East especially as many of the descendents of those who ended up in Babylon chose to remain there permanently rather than returning home to Judaea once the Persians eventually allowed them to do so. Later on Alexander the Great encouraged Jews to move to the recently founded city of Alexandria in Egypt and from that time on the dispersion of Jews gained momentum as opportunities for trade and commerce grew apace. Before long Jewish communities were to be found not only in Mesopotamia, Egypt and Persia but also throughout the eastern Mediterranean as far afield as Italy. These Jews are generally referred to as the Jews of the Dispersion or Diaspora.

Hellenists were Greek speaking Jews. Many lived outside Palestine as a result of the Diaspora but some were to be found in Palestine, either having returned from abroad to spend their last days there or temporarily on pilgrimage. They had their own synagogues in Jerusalem where the Bible was read in Greek rather than the Hebrew used in the synagogues of native born Palestinian Jews.

Hellenists generally had a cosmopolitan liberal outlook that set them apart from their more traditional and conservative Palestinian counterparts and, without compromising there faith, were more inclined to entertain Greek ideas and culture.

5: MAKE DISCIPLES OF ALL NATIONS

Early Jewish converts to Christianity simply added their belief in Jesus as the Messiah on to orthodox Judaism marked by circumcision and adherence to the Law. And they believed that any gentile converts must do the same: become circumcised and accept the Law.

The conversion of Cornelius is thus a landmark event and it is significant that the hand of God in the Holy Spirit is clearly seen directing both Cornelius and Peter. The outcome was climactic. Peter was brought to realise that God has no favourites. The Gospel is for everyone. There is no need for gentiles to be circumcised (and, by extension, to embrace the Law). Moreover, whereas the dietary laws of Lv 11 (and the rigorous way they were interpreted down the ages) had hitherto made it impossible for Jews to eat with, and by extension to mix with, gentiles without risking ceremonial defilement, that too was now all in the past. Social intercourse was open to all.

Such a break with tradition was unlikely to go unchallenged and Peter first had to convince his fellow apostles, Ac 11:1–18. Even then dissension rankled until some years later matters came to a head. Some Jews were still arguing that salvation was dependent upon circumcision and the Law and unless the matter was dealt with there was the likelihood of the Church splitting into separate Jewish and Gentile factions. What was at stake was quite fundamental: the pre-eminence of Christ and the recognition that He offered the only way to salvation. Only with the authority of a specially convened meeting in Jerusalem involving the apostles and all the elders, Ac 15, were the last vestiges of doubt finally removed. Church membership required neither circumcision nor adherence to the Law. Even then some Jews refused to conform and were a thorn in Paul's side for years to come.

*   *   *

It is curious in a way that this controversy was not resolved earlier. Although Jesus had instructed His disciples to carry the Gospel to the ends of the earth, for some years nothing happened even though the Old Testament had also taught that God offers salvation to all, Is appendix 8. Possibly there was some misunderstanding and they took it to mean converting Jews living abroad. Whatever the reason it was years before there was either an overseas mission or any drive to evangelise gentiles.

6: THE HEROD DYNASTY

Herod the Great, the Herod of Jesus' birth, ruled as king of the Jewish people in Palestine from 37 to 4 B.C. He served Rome well and rebuilt the Temple but was always unpopular at home. His son Archelaus succeeded him and ruled until deposed by the Romans in A.D. 6 following warnings of revolt against his repressive rule. He was followed by his brother, Herod Antipas, who married Herodias, his niece and wife of his half brother Herod Philip. Along with Herodias he was responsible for John the Baptist's death, Mt 14:3–12, and was also the Herod of Jesus' trial. He was deposed in A.D. 39.

The Herod who figures in the persecution of Acts 12 ruled from A.D. 39 to 44 and was a nephew of Herod Antipas and a grandson of Herod the Great as well as being a brother of Herodias (the family tree is extremely complex). It was his son, Agrippa, who was king at the time of Paul's imprisonment in Caesarea, Ac 25:13 – 26:32. He ruled until A.D. 100.

All were puppet kings who owed their positions to Rome and wielded what limited power they had within severe constraints.

7: WHY THE GOSPEL SPREAD

No one can deny Paul a major share of the credit for the remarkable way the Gospel spread in the decades following Christ's death. His strategy of founding churches on strategic highways and in large population and administrative centres of the Roman empire at a time when there was peace, excellent roads and communications, and when Greek was widely spoken, was unarguably sound.

Corinth is a case in point. Straddling the highway linking the north of Greece with the south, and the hub of east to west sea routes, it was ideally placed as a centre of commerce and communications. A large cosmopolitan city where Jews, Greeks, Romans, Egyptians and Asiatics all rubbed shoulders, it was also the capital of the Roman province of Achaia that covered much of Greece south of Macedonia. Once sown in Corinth the Gospel would therefore have every chance of spreading far and wide.

But there were other factors too. One was the Diaspora which meant that Jewish communities were to be found throughout the Mediterranean. Even though these rarely responded themselves they were often home to gentile proselytes and God fearers, gentiles who were already steeped in the Old Testament and who therefore already possessed a solid base for the new faith to build on.

Then again, because Judaism was regarded as harmless, and Rome saw early Christianity as no more than a deviant sect, it too was tolerated apart from intermittent persecutions which, though terrible at the time, were of relatively short duration and incapable of stemming the flood tide of the new faith. More widely there was a void waiting to be filled. It was a time of spiritual emptiness with no other religion capable of supplying the need. In the gentile world Christianity was therefore assured of a ready response.

Romans

1: SALVATION BY FAITH

Paul's teaching on salvation by faith is all about showing how Christians can appropriate Jesus' victory over death for themselves. For in His battle against evil Jesus acted as our 'champion'. All that is necessary is that we acknowledge our inability to save ourselves and, in simple trust, accept Him as Saviour and Lord. It is as simple as that.

For those who avail themselves of Christ's great gift (for gift it is, nothing is asked in return) three things follow. First we are justified. God takes us just as we are and forgives our sins. It is as if, having been on trial, we were acquitted.

Then we are indwelt by the Holy Spirit who gives us the strength gradually to subdue our sinful natures and grow in holiness. This is crucial because although we are no longer under the shackles of the Mosaic Law we are still subject to law, Christ's Law of love, and we will be faced with temptations and distractions that lure us away from it every day of our lives. Finally after death, victorious at last over evil and at-one with God, we will be glorified and raised to eternal life.

Notice that attaining holiness does not come overnight. Typically we stumble and need forgiveness again and again. The hidden God does not force the pace but wants us to accept Him freely because we see that His is the only way rather than being driven by some display of divine power. Like Israel in the wilderness the journey to the Promised Land, the Kingdom of God, is a continual battle against sin, and it will only be after death that our transformation into Christ's likeness is complete. After death, though we shall retain free will, sin will be a thing of the past. Our wills will be fully in accord with God's because, Christ-like, that is what we shall freely choose.

With this perspective even death can be seen in terms of mercy and hope. Mercy, because how terrible it would be if God had let man live for ever in a world estranged from Himself, the very fountain of Being; subject to a never-ending battle with evil. Hope because death gives the opportunity, with the help of the Holy Spirit, for recreation in Christ's image.

To the Jews Paul's doctrine of salvation by faith was shattering. They had been brought up to believe that the only way to good standing with God was by strict adherence to the Law and when Paul turned this on its head it seemed little short of blasphemous. Not only that, it opened the gates to gentiles and so destroyed at a stroke the Jews' privileged status.

Paul taught that the Law was only intended to be temporary, to reveal the nature of sin, and show man's need for God's help. It could never be a vehicle for salvation. The spiritual strength needed to keep it was just not there. Worse, hard taskmaster that it was, the Law's detailed demands tended to make the Jews lose sight of God and the need to build a personal relationship with Him. It challenged hope and left little room for love.

2: Predestination and Election

Predestination

The New Testament contains several texts that suggest predestination. For example Rm 8:29 says 'He decided beforehand who were the ones destined to be moulded to the pattern of his Son'. Others include Rm 9:1–24; 11:7; 11:25–32; Ep 1:4.

How anything like predestination can be consistent with free will and our individual accountability to God for our conduct is a mystery. But surely no more incomprehensible than some of the mysteries we accept from modern science: how electrons or light can behave as a stream of particles one moment while exhibiting wave-like properties the next; or how time goes slower the faster we travel. We accept those mysteries because the theories that underpin them accurately describe the workings of the material world. In the same way we should accept religious mysteries if the overall doctrines of which they form part accurately reflect the experience of our spiritual lives.

And that is precisely the situation many people enjoying the gift of faith find themselves in. They instinctively feel that they have gained it not by any act of their own but through something outside of themselves that will not be denied and which eventually possesses them. Accepting Christ in faith is something they experience rather than something they decide upon.

Having said that, by no means all exegetes agree that the texts we have quoted earlier imply predestination. It is sometimes argued for example that God did not decide or choose from the outset who would be saved but that in His omniscience He knew who would respond in such a way as to be saved. Others maintain that they are further instances of the tendency we find in the Old Testament to attribute everything to God as the ultimate cause and that it is therefore unnecessary to read predestination into them, see Ex appendix 2, Jn note 29.

In the end we have to confess ignorance. Scripture may support predestination of some form or it may not. But even if it does there is never any suggestion that God's choosing takes away man's responsibility. The tension between God's choice and man's free will remains and how the two can be reconciled is beyond our comprehension. As Paul says it is not for creatures to quiz the Creator but to fall back on the fact that He orders everything for their good.

Election

Predestination is not to be confused with election (although both terms are sometimes used rather loosely). Election is an act of sovereign choice whereby God chooses an individual or group of people for a particular purpose. For example Israel was elected to be a kingdom of priests, a holy nation, to evangelise the world; Isaiah and Jeremiah to be prophets. As election is a privilege the fact that people like Ishmael and Esau were not chosen to propagate the covenant promises, where Isaac and Jacob were, says nothing about their eternal destinies.

1 Corinthians

1: SPEAKING IN TONGUES

The gift of speaking in tongues, or glossolalia, is first mentioned at Mk 16:17. It was bestowed on Cornelius and his household at Caesarea, Ac 10:44–46, and on some disciples Paul baptised in Ephesus, Ac 19:6, in both cases following the descent of the Holy Spirit. Paul mentions it at 1Co 12:10, 28–30 with an extended discussion at 1Co 14.

It was a way of praising God in ecstatic utterances that were not recognisable as any ordinary language. At Caesarea and Ephesus it was a group (and possibly temporary) phenomenon whereas at 1Co 14:27–28 Paul seems to describe a continuing gift possessed by individuals under their control. It would appear that (at least some) speakers in tongues could interpret their utterances, 1Co 14:13, 27.

What happened at Pentecost has similarities with glossolalia and this has led some commentators to regard this too as an early instance of the phenomena. But this is unlikely. Luke quite clearly tells us that the apostles were speaking in known foreign languages which bystanders could understand and which he then goes on to enumerate, Ac 2:1–13.

2 Corinthians

1: HOW MANY LETTERS AND VISITS?

The questions of how many times Paul visited Corinth, how many letters he wrote to the Corinthians, and how to reconcile what Acts tells us of his movements with the apostle's own commentary in 2 Corinthians raise difficult issues which the obscurity of many of the allusions in 2 Corinthians do little to resolve. Many reconstructions have been proposed and we are left to judge on a balance of probabilities. However the following commands wide support and is the peg on which our synopsis hangs.

1. Paul founds the church at Corinth on his second missionary journey, Ac 18:1–11.
2. While at Ephesus on his third missionary journey he hears about immorality at Corinth and sends an earlier letter than the two canonical ones, 1Co 5:9–13.
3. The Corinthians reply with questions, 1Co 7:1. Travellers also bring news, 1Co 1:11
4. Paul responds by despatching 1 Corinthians.
5. Some crisis leads Paul to make a 'painful visit' to Corinth, 2Co 2:1.
6. A further incident at Corinth causes Paul to send Titus to Corinth with a 'severe letter' calling for an offender to be disciplined, 2Co 2:3–11; 7:8–12.
7. This cleared the air but Paul only got the good news reported at 2Co 7:5–16

when he met up with Titus in Macedonia while on the journey from Ephesus to Corinth referred to at Ac 20:1–3 towards the end of his third missionary journey.

8. While in Macedonia Paul writes 2 Corinthians.

On this basis Paul made three visits to Corinth as against the two recorded in ACTS and wrote four letters to the Corinthians of which the second and fourth are in the canon while the first and third are lost. It is sometimes surmised that 1Co 6:14 – 7:1 is a fragment of the lost first letter and 2 Corinthians 10–13 an extract from the third.

Strictly speaking Ac 20:1–3 only speaks of Paul visiting Greece but there seems little doubt that the bulk of his time would have been spent in Corinth. That was certainly his intention, 2Co 9:5; 12:14; 13:1,10. The fact that this was his third visit to Corinth is confirmed by 2Co 12:14; 13:1–2.

2: THE COLLECTION FOR THE POOR OF JERUSALEM

Paul was keen to do all he could to help 'God's holy people', the poor among the Christians in Jerusalem, by means of an offering from the Gentile churches. Apart from an oblique reference at Ga 2:10 we first hear of it at 1Co 16:1–4 and it is treated at length at 2Co 8,9.

Living conditions for Christians in Jerusalem could not have been easy. Quite apart from the famine during the reign of the Roman emperor Claudius, Ac 11:27–30, as converts to a controversial minority faith they would have attracted both social and economic discrimination and possibly even been ostracized by their families. As the mother church Jerusalem would also have been obliged to support a large number of teachers and visitors. Not least, Palestinian Jews suffered double taxation, both Roman and Jewish.

Apart from seeing it as an expression of brotherly love and binding the nascent gentile churches in a common purpose, Paul probably hoped the collection would help bond the Jewish and gentile wings of the Church by bringing the gentile churches to recognise their indebtedness to the church in Jerusalem. By the time of Paul's last visit to Corinth when he wrote Romans it is clear that the collection had been successfully completed, Rm 15:25–27, 30–32 and, when he finally reached Jerusalem with it he was warmly received, Ac 21:17; 24:17.

Galatians

1: THE CHRONOLOGY OF ACTS AND GALATIANS

How to dovetail Paul's activities as reported in ACTS and GALATIANS, and the timing of his composition of GALATIANS relative to the Council of Jerusalem, are problems that have prompted fierce debate. One of the more likely sequences is as follows.

1. Following his conversion Paul begins preaching in Damascus and Arabia. After three years he is forced to flee to Jerusalem where before long he falls foul of the Hellenists and has to return home to Tarsus from where he preaches in Syria and Cilicia, Ac 9:20–30; Ga 1:15–24.
2. On visiting Cornelius Peter is shown that no one is unclean in God's sight. Jews and gentiles may enjoy normal social relations and gentiles may be received into the Church without recourse to the Law or circumcision, Ac 10:1 – 11:18.
3. Barnabas takes Paul under his wing and together they build up the church in Antioch. They travel together to Jerusalem on a famine relief mission. While in Jerusalem Paul agrees his gentile mission with Peter and the elders, Ac 11:22–30; Ga 2:1–10.
4. Paul returns to Antioch, Ac 12:25.
5. Peter visits Antioch and is rebuked by Paul for refusing to eat with gentiles, Ga 2:11–14.
6. Paul undertakes his first missionary journey in southern Galatia, Ac 13:1 – 14:28.
7. On his return, hearing that dissidents were denying his teaching on salvation by faith and were insisting that his recent converts observe the Law and undergo circumcision, Paul writes GALATIANS.
8. Paul attends the Jerusalem Council where the issues regarding gentile Church membership that were effectively resolved when Peter baptised Cornelius were debated anew and ratified, Ac 15:1–29.
9. Paul returns to Antioch, Ac 15:30–35, prior to embarking on his second missionary journey.

This would make Galatians the earliest of all Paul's epistles.

Ephesians

1: THE CAPTIVITY EPISTLES

Along with Philippians, Colossians and Philemon, Ephesians is one of the so-called captivity epistles. According to tradition all four were written while Paul was under house arrest in Rome awaiting trial, Ac 28:30–31, and despite much speculation that they may have been written while Paul was imprisoned in either Ephesus on his third missionary journey (a captivity of which Acts knows nothing), or in Caesarea as in Ac 23–26, or that they come from a different hand altogether (an argument advanced on grounds of style and theological content), this still remains the most likely scenario.

Philemon

1: SLAVERY

Slavery was widespread in New Testament times. But while on the farm and or down the mine slaves seem to have been treated little better than automated animals, conditions for domestic slaves in the home were much more humane and probably approximated to those enjoyed by servants in a Victorian Christian household. Some were well educated and received training in the arts, medicine or a trade. It was not unknown for slaves with good service to be freed and accepted into society with virtually equal rights as freeborn citizens.

Since Paul's ministry was mostly in cities it would have been these more tolerably treated urban slaves that he would usually have come across. Even so the fact that, along with the New Testament generally, he seems to have accepted the institution of slavery without question, and even given it tacit approval, is to many a cause of offence.

However not many options were open to a tiny Church in an entrenched and largely hostile society that took slavery for granted. Outright denunciation would certainly have led to the Church's suppression and probably to violence and bloodshed that would have achieved nothing. So rather than attacking slavery head on Paul tackled it obliquely as in PHILEMON, using gentle pressure to influence attitudes from within the prevailing social structure.

James

1: JUSTIFICATION, FAITH AND WORKS

Taken out of context Jm 2:21, 24 could be construed as James postulating a doctrine of justification by works in opposition to Paul's doctrine of justification by faith. But there is no contradiction. In view of the old Jewish belief that salvation could be won by obedience to the Law Paul was at pains to underline in the clearest possible terms, without ambiguity, that no Christian can earn his own salvation. The only way is through faith in Christ. He therefore stressed faith almost exclusively. But though he did not highlight it as much as James he was equally sure that faith must issue in good deeds. This comes across at Ep 2:10 and also at Ga 5:6, 13–15 where he speaks of 'faith working through love'. To Paul commitment to Christ without works of love was unthinkable. The one led into the other.

James approached the dichotomy of faith and works from the opposite direction. He wanted to ensure that no one could possibly think that bare unproductive faith – mere passive intellectual assent, lip service – was sufficient for salvation. True faith,

faith that saves, means far more than that. It so transforms a person that he cannot help but undertake good deeds and their absence would be proof that his faith was only skin deep. It is in this sense that at Jm 2:24 he says 'it is by deeds and not only by believing that someone is justified'.

In short faith and deeds go hand in hand. Faith leads to justification, rebirth and a new nature. Good works then follow as surely as day follows night through the promptings of the Holy Spirit and the commandment of love. But it is faith that saves. Works do not themselves earn salvation but are evidence that saving faith is present. In that sense deeds bring faith to perfection. Stated otherwise salvation does not depend upon good deeds; it results in good deeds.

2 Peter

1: THE DAY OF THE LORD

To the Old Testament prophets the 'Day of the Lord', or more simply 'the Day', was a future occasion when God would intervene in history with spectacular effect, Is appendix 1 refers. To Christians and the New Testament it is used in two slightly differing senses. Usually it denotes the whole span of time beginning with Christ's First coming and ending with His Second at the end of time. Elsewhere it means just the Second Coming and the Day of Judgement. So although in one sense it has already begun, in another it is yet to come. Either way, and particularly as the Day of Judgement, it is to be seen as the fulfilment of the 'Day' foretold by the prophets.

The Revelation to John

1: THE GREAT TRIBULATION

Scripture tells us that in the last days Satan will mount an all-out attack against the Church, one that will push it to the very brink of defeat. Known as the great tribulation or the great distress it will be a time of unparalleled suffering, evil and apostasy. But it will be brief. And then the Church will rise again to meet its Lord at His Second Coming.

This prophecy can be discerned in Revelation at 11:7–12; 20:7–10 but is also latent in the rather obscure symbolism of 17:8–11. Christ Himself refers to 'a great distress unparalleled since the world began' preceding His Second Coming in His Olivet discourse. It will not be allowed to go on for long but in the meantime there will be many false messiahs and prophets, Mt 24:21–24. Elsewhere in the New Testament the same idea is found in Paul, 2Th 2:1–12, and, more tangentially, in John's teaching that the latter days will see the coming of Antichrist. Indeed his 'antichrist' disciples are already among us, 1Jn 2:18–28; 4:1–6; 2Jn 7; see also 1Tm 4:1–2; 2Tm 3:1–5; 2P 3:3; Jude 18.

The idea of a great tribulation is by no means confined to the New Testament. Ezekiel's vision, Ezk 38:1–39:20, that Israel would suffer a final massive invasion at the hands of Gog before God destroys her enemies once and for all tells essentially the same story. But the closest parallels are provided by Zc 14 with its description of the plunder of Jerusalem prior to God's ushering in a new age of perpetual light and by Daniel in which the account of the horrors of Antiochus Epiphanes' attack on the Jews of his day is a clear foreshadowing of the greater onslaught that Satan will unleash in the end days, Dn 11:36–12:13. Other allusions are found at Zc 12:1–9; Is 24–27, 34–35.

2: The Bowls and the Moral Order

Although the afflictions stemming from the bowls are attributed to God's anger, we would do well (and likewise with the seals and trumpets) to see them as resulting from rebellious man's callous disregard of God's laws down the ages. They are the inevitable consequences of a humanity that has ignored its God-blessed origins, abused its power, and forgotten that it was meant to lovingly care for the beautiful plenteous world God created for it. Instead man's reverence of the false gods of self, materialism, and pleasure, together with his propensity for exploitation and short-termism, have created a world of hunger and strife with environmental catastrophe crouching at the door and ever more evil forces and agents of destruction waiting in the wings.

In short, defiance of God's will carries its own inexorable consequences in its train. The moral order exacts its toll. And in that sense, since the moral order is God's, we can say that it is indeed God who visits the bowls' disasters upon His creatures.

3: The Beast and its worldly empire, Babylon

The beast is the devil's henchman, the power of evil at work in the world. It is the apotheosis of satanic deception, the architect of every evil system opposed to God, a counterfeit image of God and Christ. No one is immune to its heady allures for it cannot be confined to any one place or time nor to particular historical events.

It operates on the grand scale through godless institutions and idolatries of whatever kind: religious, political, economic, social or cultural. The beast is at work wherever we find false religion, political regimes that promote tyranny and genocide, economic systems that squander wealth and deny opportunity, social repression and injustice and decadent art. It manifests itself in spiritual famine, aggression, corruption, inequality, misery and want, lives devoid of meaning. It is the malign power behind Babylon.

Babylon

Babylon is the repulsive epitome of godless society, the city of rebel man as the New Jerusalem is the abode of man redeemed. It represents the world as it is. A world which, dazzled by the beast's seductive charms, has forsaken God; a world drawn to the vulgar and garish, sated on salaciousness and with the blood of oppression and violence on its hands. Babylon is a byword for every society that is opposed to God. It revels in pride and vainglory, in self-indulgence, self-sufficiency and self-exaltation in place of God. Whenever the Church is persecuted we know we are in Babylon. Babylon is the beast's creation, his empire. All the evil that supports Babylon derives from the beast and its master, Satan.

4: INTERPRETING REVELATION IN TERMS OF CONTEMPORARY ROME

John's contemporaries would have read Revelation's message of God's ultimate triumph over Satan as applying to their own day. They were living in the last days. They were being tested in the great trial of 7:14. They were the martyrs of 6:9. They would have readily decoded Revelation's Babylon as Rome and the beast as Nero.

What would have encouraged them in this view more than anything else would have been chapter 17 and its setting against the background of the 'Nero redivivus' myth that arose after the emperor's death. The myth held that Nero, an arch-persecutor of the early Church who was eventually forced to flee and committed suicide, had not died but had fled to Parthia whence he would return at the head of a large army to regain his throne and take vengeance on his enemies. When this did not happen the legend modulated to the effect that Satan would appear as antichrist in the guise of Nero whom he would miraculously restore to life. (Parthia was a powerful military power beyond the Euphrates that Rome never subdued, a continual thorn in her flesh.)

With this in mind we can see how John's contemporaries would have interpreted chapter 17. A prostitute, Babylon, was sitting on seven hills. Rome was known for its seven hills. Therefore the woman and Babylon stood for Rome. The beast the woman was sitting on was once alive, is alive no longer, and is yet to come up from the Abyss. This fitted the Nero redivivus myth. Nero had once been alive and ruled. He was alive no longer, having committed suicide. According to the myth he would return from the underworld to regain power. Therefore the beast represents Nero.

Rome's days of empire are nearly over, Revelation continues. Only one of her seven emperors is still to come and his reign will be short. Then there will be an eighth who is at the same time one of the previous seven. This again suited the Nero myth. Nero had reigned (as one of the seven) but would return at the head of a Parthian army and reign again (as an eighth). The ten kings who join with the beast, Nero, to overthrow the woman, Rome, would have been seen as representing Parthia and her satellites. Their time is brief ('a single hour') because they are then defeated by the Lamb. In short Revelation would have been interpreted as saying that Rome was about to be humbled after which there would be a brief period of intense distress as antichrist, effectively incarnate in Nero in line with the myth, reigned for a short time. Then would come the final victory of the Lamb.

Nero would have been read into other passages too. At 13:3 the beast's 'fatal' wound that had since healed fitted Nero's 'recovery' from his supposed suicide. At 13:18 the number 666 effectively named Nero. How? Because the letters of the Hebrew alphabet doubled up as numerals and when this was done it so happened that 'Caesar Nero' could be made to produce 666.

The rider with a bow and a victor's crown at 6:2 would have been seen as heralding a Parthian victory over Rome since bows were the Parthians' tell-tale weapon. The army massed across the Euphrates at 9:13–21 would also have been identified with the Parthians, and the sting in the horses' tails as a reference to their tactic of firing a salvo over their horses' tails as they fell back. The drying up of the Euphrates at 16:12 would have suggested the removal of Rome's main line of defence against Parthia while the statue worship of 13:15 would have been taken as an allusion to Roman emperor worship.

NOTES

Genesis

1. This second account is not always consistent with the first but that is immaterial. Genesis is not interested in peripheral scientific detail but with theological truth expressed poetically and at that level the accounts are complementary.
2. Man enjoys free will but if he abuses that gift by rebelling against God he will exclude himself from life with God.
3. In Biblical times naming something signified ownership or authority over it.
4. The source of evil is a mystery. Perhaps it is a consequence of free will and has to exist in the nature of things as the absence of good rather as the absence of light implies darkness. We cannot say. However it is noteworthy that although we are told that God created light he is not attributed in Gn 1 with the origin of darkness, an ancient symbol of evil. Rv 12:9; 20:2 identify the snake with the devil, Satan, and the dragon of Rv 12.
5. Because of references to nakedness and loin-cloths, and the sexual overtones in v16, it is often assumed that the errant pair's sin was sexual in nature. However the narrative is pitched at a higher level, rebellion against the moral order in general, and meant to be read figuratively. For example we should take their feeling of nakedness as indicating spiritual nakedness, loss of the free uninhibited relationship they were meant to have with one another and with God, while their pathetic attempt to restore innocence with fig leaves represents the futility of man trying to repair the damage of a spoiled relationship with God by himself.
6. Because the struggle is willed by God ('I shall put enmity . . .') final victory over evil is assured and this verse is therefore a first hint of ultimate salvation. This thesis is supported by the fact that the snake is struck on the head whereas the woman's offspring are only injured in the heel, a less serious hurt. Indeed some translations actually speak of the woman's offspring crushing the snake's head while the snake is merely said to strike the woman's heel. Even more portentous are those renderings (not undisputed) that use a masculine or feminine pronoun instead of 'it' to denote the striker of the snake and which have led some commentators to see foreshadowings of either Jesus or Mary. A hint of salvation may also be seen in the fact that the man and woman are merely punished whereas the snake is cursed.
7. St Paul builds on this theme at Rm 8:18–22 maintaining that the whole of creation is subject to corruption and decay. It would seem that man and nature are so closely related that the Fall led to cosmic breakdown on a massive scale, affecting the animal kingdom and the material world as well. We can see how man's folly can account for some natural disasters but catastrophes like earthquakes and cruelty in nature are more difficult to understand leaving this teaching deeply mysterious.

8. The start of v22, 'now that man has become like one of us', should be read as irony.

9. In Eden man rebelled against God. Now he is at odds with his neighbour. Thus stand revealed the antitheses of Christ's two great commandments.

10. Only now at 4:25 is the man given his name, Adam.

   The way life spans gradually reduce to more normal levels as the Old Testament unfolds probably emphasises the growth of wickedness in the world since long life was thought to indicate divine favour. This view is supported by 6:3 where God restricts human life to one hundred and twenty years in view of man's sinfulness.

11. Note the contrast with Christ's seventy-seven offers of forgiveness, Mt 18:22.

12. This differs from Ex 3:13–15; 6:2–3 which maintains that 'Yahweh' was only revealed to Moses much later, Exodus appendix 1.

13. Like Elijah, 2K:2, Enoch did not die, perhaps a hint that obedience to God leads to victory over death. It is possible that highlighting Enoch's godliness is also meant to balance Lamech's violence by reminding us that although we all have Cain-like tendencies we nonetheless retain the seed of holiness too.

14. With Noah, where sin was 'washed away' by the waters of the flood and new life came through the uprightness of one man, we have a prefigurement of the cleansing waters of baptism and the new life offered by the one upright Man, Christ.

   We tend to take for granted the recurring cycle of sun and rain on which our welfare depends, forgetting our total dependence on the regularity of the seasons and man's puny strength when confronted with nature's elemental power.

15. The arcs of light in the rainbow recall God's love, the dark clouds His wrath subsiding in the retreating storm.

16. This story is not really meant to tell us about different languages and man being scattered but to show how, despite every warning, man persists in his quest to be his own master, 'to be God' if you like. But now, following His covenant with Noah, God responds less drastically. Viewed from another angle the Babel story shows us that when men try to ape God misunderstandings and disunity follow as surely as night follows day. Looked at in that way Babel is later reversed at Pentecost when, in another divine descent, humanity is united in the Holy Spirit, Ac 2:1–13.

17. Abram, Isaac and Jacob are known as the Patriarchs, a term sometimes used to include their forebears as well.

18. God's calls for obedience at 17:1; 18:19 are not conditions on which the promises depend but natural demands from a holy God for moral excellence from His servants. When later at Sinai God elected Israel to be His vehicle for fulfilling the covenant that commission was dependant upon obedience; to His Law. There is thus a distinction between the promises (unconditional) and the choice of the nation chosen to propagate them (conditional).

19. This comes across more clearly at Si 44:21; Ac 3:25; Ga 3:6-9.

20. Both here and in the similar incident at Gerar, 20:1–18, the inclusion of Sarai in a foreign ruler's harem could easily have jeopardized the birth of the heir on whom God's promises depended. But God was always in control. It would be wrong to judge this incident by modern norms. In Abram's day a husband's life was rated more valuable than a woman's honour.

21. Melchizedek figures in Heb 5–7 and at Ps 110:4 in allusions to Christ's priesthood. It is possible to see in his dual role of priest and king a foreshadowing of the Messiah and in his offering of bread and wine to Abram in thanksgiving for his victory an allegory of the Eucharist. However it has to be said that although Hebrews recognizes the first of these portents it is silent on the second. Following Ps 76:2 Salem is probably to be identified with Jerusalem.

22. This was not an unusual arrangement in ancient Mesopotamia when a wife was barren.

23. Circumcision signified consecration of the source of life to God. The new names signify new destinies.

24. Later repeated by Jesus, Mt 19:26.

25. Abraham asked God to save everyone rather than just the innocent because he was conditioned by the then prevalent principle of collective accountability. This usually came across in terms of retribution – if an individual sinned the entire community bore the punishment – but he was trying to apply it the other way round, to forgiveness, pleading for the many to be saved in return for the innocence of the few, see Joshua, appendix 3.

26. Lot is the typical fifty-one per cent believer. He had a modicum of decency. He was hospitable to his guests and his offer to sacrifice his virgin daughters should be judged against the backcloth that in his day hospitality was rated higher than a woman's honour. Yet when it came to the point his faith was lukewarm. He hesitated and was only saved by being hustled out of town by the angels. Nonetheless he was saved. God will not give up so long as goodness has the smallest foothold in the human heart. With Lot's future sons-in-law it was different. Given a last chance to escape the divine wrath they thought it was all a joke and were lost. Lot's wife was typical of those who can never wholly discard their past and grasp new life. She kept looking back and also perished.

27. God confirms that the covenant will be propagated through Isaac not Ishmael. This does not mean that He did not love Ishmael's side of the family. His promises to Hagar and Ishmael show that He did. The distinction was not about who God loved but between the people He elected to work through and the rest. But all were eligible to enjoy His blessings.

28. 2Ch 3:1 identifies Moriah with the hill upon which the Temple was later built.

29. Heb 11:17–19 tells us that in being willing to sacrifice the son on whom the covenant promises depended Abraham must have had faith in God's ability to raise the dead.

    In the anguish of Abraham, father of the people of God, and his beloved son Isaac, the first-fruits of the promise, the Church has long seen, in Isaac's miraculous birth and his proffered sacrifice, a prefiguring of that other Son who, born of grace rather than nature, and given up to a sacrificial death, became 'the first-fruits of all who have fallen asleep', 1Co 15:20.

30. The birthright was probably the elder son's traditional double share of his father's estate while Isaac's blessing, which Jacob also acquired later at Esau's expense, 27:1–29, would have conferred headship of the family.

31. It would be a good twenty years, 31:41, before the havoc wrought by Jacob's deceit would be played out and Isaac's family would be reunited although there is no record even then that Jacob ever saw his mother again.

32. Leah would have been veiled at the wedding ceremony.

33. Perez's descendants include David, and Joseph the husband of Mary, mother of Jesus, Rt 4:18–22; Mt 1.

34. We have at 37:10 an example of the sort of inconsistency that is not uncommon in the Bible due to its complex history of traditions being handed down by word of mouth, clerical errors, multiple authorship, etc. It implies that Rachel was alive whereas 35:19 had already reported her death. Sarah would have been 90 when she attracted Abimelech (reading 17:17 with 21:5) while Ishmael would have been at least 14 when Hagar carried him on her shoulder (taking 16:16 with 21:5,14). And so on. Fortunately such discrepancies relate only to peripheral matters, never to fundamentals.

35. Joseph was testing his brothers. Would they stand by Benjamin when the 'theft' was discovered? Had they truly repented? Clearly they had. Judah spoke for them all when he offered to be punished in Benjamin's stead.

36. Without God's assurance leaving Canaan would have strained Jacob's faith to the limit. Why move to Egypt when Canaan was their inheritance? The hand of God was at work. All the time Israel was in Egypt Canaan was a battleground for marauding armies and would not have provided suitable conditions for embryonic tribes to bond in nationhood. Egypt on the other hand was at peace, the ideal womb for the seed of Israel to grow.

37. The Egyptians had a prejudice against shepherds. Jacob and his family would therefore have been left largely alone in Goshen and so better able to retain their identity and avoid the lure of pagan gods.

    Gn 47:13–26 stands apart, explaining how land in Egypt gradually fell out of private ownership to become crown land.

38. Manasseh and Ephraim came to be treated as two separate tribes instead of a Joseph tribe. Jacob's unconventional blessing was borne out. Ephraim became the strongest of, and sometimes indeed a synonym for, the northern tribes.

Exodus

1. The Midianites were nomads descended from Abraham and his second wife Keturah, Gn 25:2. It may be that they retained some belief in Yahweh and that Moses' own faith was thereby rekindled at this time.

2. Zipporah's father is here called Reuel. Elsewhere he is named as Jethro, Ex 3:1; 4:18 or Hobab, Nb 10:29; Jg 1:16.

3. Moses found God in the desert as later on did Israel, Elijah and Jesus Himself. Horeb is another name for Sinai.

4. Pharaoh was asked to make a small concession initially so that if he agreed God could then open his heart to accede to the larger demand for Israel to leave Egypt altogether. By rejecting the small request Pharaoh was exhibiting the depth of the opposition God faced and hence the extraordinary measures needed to overcome it.

5. The Amalekites were descendants of Esau, Gn 36:12, 16.

6. Note that the first commandment does not deny the existence of other gods. That only came later at Dt 4:35; 6:4 and, most emphatically, with Deutero Isaiah. In saying that He was a jealous God Yahweh meant that He expected total commitment and exclusivity in Israel's relationship with Him. The reference at 20:5 to parental sins being punished in later generations is a poetic way of saying that sin's repercussions cannot be confined. Broken homes today scar society tomorrow. Today's lax pollution control is tomorrow's environmental disaster. Moses makes it clear at Dt 7:10; 24:16 that God holds people to account for their own sins and theirs alone, see also Ezk 18.

7. Dt appendix 3 refers.

8. This means places that had been made holy by some sort of divine manifestation as in a theophany, a vision or a dream. Shechem, Beersheba and Bethel all traced their origins as sanctuaries in this way; Gn 12:6–8; 26:23–25; 28:1–22.

9. This was in the interests of public decency since priests only wore simple loin cloths when offering sacrifice. 'Unhewn' implies stone unprofaned by human hand in keeping with God's holiness. It also points to simplicity in worship.

10. Many slaves were no more than debtors discharging their debts through their labours. Slaves were entitled to be fed and housed by their masters and this is why some preferred to remain in servitude when their time was up. Better to stay with a benevolent master who provided the necessities of life than face insecurity and possible starvation on their own.

11. This seems crude but its aim was to limit vengeance. It is also possible that it was never meant to be taken literally but to emphasise that punishment should fit the crime. Lv 19:18 urges forgiveness and explicitly forbids vengeance.
12. See Jos appendix 2 for possible explanations of such harsh action.
13. The stones symbolised permanence, twelve the twelve tribes.
14. What is here called the Dwelling is sometimes called the Tabernacle or the Sanctuary. The tablets holding the Law are sometimes called the Testimony while the Ark is at times referred to as the Ark of the Covenant, the Ark of the Testimony, or simply the Testimony.
15. Breaking the tablets symbolized the breaking of the Covenant.
16. This passage is problematical because whereas elsewhere the Tent is identified with the Dwelling here it appears as something quite separate. Also while Nb 1 – 3 speaks of the Dwelling being sited in the midst of the camp this text refers to the Tent being outside. A possible explanation is that the Tent was a temporary refuge until the Dwelling was completed.
17. Moses was conveying a trace of God's own glory and prefiguring Christ's Transfiguration.
18. The repetition is deliberate to make the point that although man may rebel God will not be deflected. The plan that was explained in such detail before the golden calf is here spelled out again, exactly the same. God's Will prevails.

Leviticus

1. Although much of Lv's ritual undoubtedly has ancient origins it is possible that some of it may reflect the liturgy of Solomon's Temple. It is difficult to see how the more elaborate ceremonial could have been enacted by a nomadic community.
2. Only unblemished animals were acceptable for sacrifice, 1:3, just as today only the best, not leftovers, in terms of our energy and wealth should be seen as good enough for God.
    Ex 29:38–42; Nb 28:4–8 both legislate for two lambs to be sacrificed in the Dwelling every day as burnt offerings, one at dawn the other at twilight. It is this that is referred to, somewhat obliquely, at Lv 6:1–6 where it is ruled that the altar fire must be kept burning at all times. There must never be a single moment when sacrifice is not being offered to God. This ritual changed later since 2K16:15 refers to a burnt offering in the morning with a cereal offering in the evening.
3. The exception to this was when the offering was made by a priest in which case, of course, none of it would be eaten. A priest could not both make and receive an offering.
4. Leaven and honey were barred from the cereal offering because of their association with fermentation and hence decomposition. Salt was always included because it was associated, as it still is in the Middle East, with friendship and so symbolised harmonious relations with Yahweh.
5. 7:35–38 are an epilogue to the sacrificial manual as a whole.
6. The reference to confession at 5:5 stands alone. However confession was a central feature of the all important Day of Atonement, 16:21, and is also stipulated at Nb 5:7 so it seems probable that it formed part of all expiatory sacrifices.
7. It is difficult to see how the lying, stealing and cheating of 5:21–22 could constitute 'inadvertent' sin. A possible explanation is offered by Nb 15:22–31 where 'inadvertent' sin is contrasted with sinning 'defiantly' leading to the thought that 'inadvertent' may mean not just unintentional sins but sins due to ignorance and human frailty too.
8. No sin is implied. It just happened that it was the sin form of offering that was prescribed for this particular form of uncleanliness.

9. These were what Mary offered when Jesus was born, Lk 2:24.

10. The Day of Atonement became Judaism's modern Yom Kippur.

11. When people wanted to eat one of the animals that was acceptable for sacrifice as food its slaughter must be carried out as a cultic act at the Dwelling under priestly supervision. And it must first be offered to Yahweh as a communion sacrifice. In other words there was to be no distinction between religious and profane killing in such cases. This was both to protect the sacredness of blood and to guard against the danger of superstitious practices creeping in if slaughter were allowed in unhallowed places. Verse 7 indicates that this had already begun to happen.

12. Molech was a pagan god associated with the sacrifice of children by burning them alive. That this practice had spread to Israel is evidenced not only by the prohibition recorded here but also by texts such as 2K 16:3; 21:6; 23:10; Jr 7:31.

13. All further attempts to distance Israel from her pagan neighbours and, in the case of divination and magic, to remind her to put her trust in God alone.

14. The reference to prostitution was probably primarily aimed at sacred prostitution which was one of many Canaanite customs Israel had to guard against. The Canaanites thought that an act of procreation between a worshipper and a temple prostitute paralleled the union between the fertility god and the earth and so 'reminded' the deity to fertilize the earth.

15. The command to love one's neighbour occurs twice in this chapter. The Old Testament conception of neighbour was normally restricted to fellow nationals but v34 is explicitly aimed at aliens.

16. Shaving beard edges and gashing the body, like disordering hair and tearing clothes, were all ways of expressing grief.

17. This last prohibition was probably based on the view that before eight days animals were too insubstantial for sacrifice. Alternatively it may have been felt that not until the eighth day could a life be regarded as having an independent existence. Circumcision was not performed until the eighth day, Gn 17:12. The injunction against slaughtering a mother on the same day as her young may have been a further attempt to distance Israel from pagan fertility rites although it has been argued that both this and the previous ruling reflect the high regard in which parental affection was held.

18. See Ex appendix 6.

19. The Jubilee year rules about the redemption of property and freeing slaves were intended to counteract the social inequalities that inevitably built up over time. Permanent loss of well-being and freedom has no place in God's norms.

20. Samuel is an example of a person vowed to God, 1S 1:24–28, while Jephthah's daughter was vowed unconditionally to God, Jg 11:29–40. Consecrating an animal could mean either offering it for sacrifice or using it to support the priesthood, perhaps by providing milk or acting as a beast of burden.

Numbers

1. Abstaining from alcohol signalled renunciation of a life of pleasure; hair indicated strength so leaving it uncut was a sign of God's ingrowing power; avoiding corpses marked a person apart. Samson and probably Samuel are the only known lifelong Nazirites although it is possible that John the Baptist was one too.

2. Confirming Ex 25:22.

3. Worship should never become a rigid taskmaster. God allows latitude when practical problems arise.

4. Israel left Egypt on the fifteenth day of the first month of the first year, Nb 33:3 and pitched camp at Sinai exactly three months later, Ex 19:1. Israel left Sinai on the twentieth day of the second month of the second year, Nb 10:11, giving therefore a stay there of just over ten months.

5. A slow grudging after-the-event faith is no faith at all.

6. We are reminded of the sin against the Holy Spirit, the deliberate closing of the heart to God, Mt 12:31–32.

7. On the curse of destruction see Jos appendix 2 and for tithes Lv appendix 3. Later on Dt 18:1-8 extends the priestly entitlements to the Levites as a whole.

8. The reason for this is unclear. According to Nb 20:12,24; 27:14; Dt 32:51 it is connected with this miracle, the 'Waters of Meribah'. Perhaps it was for disobeying Yahweh by striking the rock rather than simply ordering it to release its water as Moses had been instructed, thus implying a lack of faith, that mere words were not enough. (This miracle is not to be confused with the similar event at Ex 17:1–7 where Moses *was* ordered to strike the rock). On the other hand Moses' words 'listen now, you rebels . . . at v 10 suggest ill temper or impatience on Moses' part (see Ps 106:33) or even his assuming credit for the miracle himself rather than Yahweh.

   Dt 1:22; 37–38 suggest a different explanation asserting that it was the people and not Yahweh, as in Nb 13, who proposed reconnoitring the Promised Land before marching in. Moses' fault could then have been lack of faith in agreeing to this rather than relying on Yahweh's assurance that the Promised Land was theirs for the taking without more ado.

9. Jesus drew a parallel with Himself, Jn 3:14. Moses overcame the poison of serpents by lifting up something that had the form of a serpent but without a serpent's poison. God will overcome the poison (sin) of men by 'lifting up' someone in the form of a man but without a man's poison (sin).

10. An extraordinary sign signifying an extraordinary event. We do not necessarily have to believe that the donkey literally uttered human speech although all things are possible to God. This could be a poetic way of saying that Balaam was puzzled by the donkey's erratic behaviour and, as he pondered, everything suddenly became clear to him.

11. Balaam seems to be depicting a future king who will bring glory and vanquish Israel's foes. It is usually taken as an allusion to David but some expositors see it as pointing to Christ. The enemies referred to in the prophecy – Moab, Edom etc. – were among those conquered by David but may also be taken to symbolise the forces of evil Christ later overcame. Like the prophecy at Gn 49:10 some see it as having been composed in or after David's time to help confer legitimacy on his reign with God endowing the words with deeper significance.

   It would appear from Nb 31:8,16 that Balaam later lapsed.

12. The chief heathen deity worshipped at Peor.

13. The story is resumed at ch 31.

14. Thus the secular authority would in future be subordinate to the religious. On urim see 1S note 10.

15. It seems that the Midianites were more widely implicated in Israel's apostasy than 25:6 would suggest.

16. Manasseh later receives a second share of land west of the Jordan, Jos 17, hence the phrase 'half tribe of Manasseh'.

17. The battle against God's enemies leaves no room for half measures.

18. One effect of this would be to disperse the Levites among the other tribes. This was essential if they were to fulfil their role as ministers of Israel's worship.

Deuteronomy

1. The transit of Edom is at variance with Nb 20:14–21.
2. This Decalogue differs from Ex 20 only in presenting the Sabbath as a memorial of the Exodus rather than of Creation.
3. See Jos appendix 2.
4. Fearing God means holding Him in respectful awe, offering Him worship, honour and reverence, obeying His Law.
5. More than outward obedience is needed. Devotion to God must come from the heart and guide inward desires too.
6. Worship of other gods is the cardinal sin. If people forsake the true God and turn to other gods like money and materialism and so exclude God what hope can there be?
7. This was an important dispensation. Lv 17 had ruled that whenever a cultic animal, i.e. one suitable for sacrifice, was killed, even if only for food, this must be done under priestly supervision at the Dwelling. This would not have presented a problem when Israel was a close-knit community in the desert but would have been impractical with just one sanctuary in the wider reaches of the Promised Land.
8. For the people to eat the tithe, as reported here and earlier at 12:4–7, seems to contradict Nb 18:20–32 which says that the tithe was intended to support the Levites. However this probably refers to a small portion that was set aside to be dedicated in the sanctuary in the presence of the people to mark the sacredness of the whole. For the people to have eaten much of the tithe would obviously have gone against its raison d'être apart from which they could not possibly have eaten anything like a tenth of the whole harvest during a visit to the sanctuary.

   Every third year there was a variation, the people as a whole being denied this privilege in favour of just the poor, 14:28–29.

   Similar considerations may also explain the references at 12:4–7; 14:23, 15:20 to eating the first-born offerings. These were the priests' entitlement, Nb 18:15–18, but possibly a portion was again set aside for communal dedication. In any case the number of first-born animals was probably more than the priests alone could cope with.
9. This was no ordinary promise as evidenced by Peter, Stephen and Jesus Himself, Ac 3:22–24; 7:37; Jn 5:45. Like Moses, Jesus' life was spared in infancy. Like Moses, Jesus renounced a royal court to share the tribulations of his people. Like Moses, Jesus saw God face-to-face, revealed His will and reflected His glory. Like Moses, Jesus was a covenant-mediator and intercessor. Like Moses, Jesus brought salvation to Israel.
10. These dispensations were purely practical. The outcome of ancient battles often depended on which side panicked first so there was little point in conscripting men who had no stomach for the fight.
11. See Lv 19:19.
12. To remind Israel to obey God, Nb 15:37–41.
13. Gerizim and Ebal are two mountains overlooking Shechem from the north and south respectively.
14. It is difficult to know whether these threats were genuine prophecy or insertions by editors after the event.
15. We first hear of Joshua at Ex 17:9 as one of Moses' lieutenants. He was present at Sinai when Moses received the Law, Ex 24:13, and assisted in the Tent of Meeting, Ex 33:11. With Caleb he submitted the minority report urging Israel to trust Yahweh and occupy the Promised Land immediately following the reconnaissance, Nb 14:5–9.
16. Moses appears once more in the Bible, talking face-to-face with Jesus at His Transfiguration.

Joshua

1. Rahab, a Canaanite, was saved by her faith and the deeds that flowed from that faith, Heb 11:31; Jm 2:25.
2. It is unclear why the men were not circumcised. The ending of the manna marks the completion of an era. Henceforth Israel will be led not by sight but by faith.
3. This is one of several parallels with Moses. Another is Joshua's crossing the Jordan which parallels with Moses' passage of the Sea.
4. With Yahweh's reputation already well established, 5:1, this was further psychological warfare.
5. Mt 1 tells us that Rahab was an ancestress of Ruth, David and Joseph, the husband of Mary, mother of Jesus.
6. Achan was guilty of sacrilege by retaining what was rightfully Yahweh's. As a result the whole nation was reckoned to have sinned and could only be cleansed by the guilty party himself being 'devoted' to Yahweh, 7:10–15.
7. Joshua may have been praying for the sun not to shine too soon so as not to sap their energy. Alternatively, since he arrived after a night march, he could have been praying for more darkness to capitalise on the enemy's confusion.
8. Israel does not seem to have enjoyed the use of war chariots until the reign of Solomon, 1K 9:19; 10:26–29. Indeed 1S 13:19–22 informs us that when Israel was under the Philistine yoke she was not even allowed to employ blacksmiths. This would have put her forces at a crippling disadvantage on the plains.
9. For more details of the Danites' migration see Jg 1:34; 18:1–31.
10. Up to now only the three cities of refuge east of the Jordan have been named, Dt 4:41–43. The forty eight towns would not have been for the Levites' exclusive use but shared with the tribes on whose land they were situated.
11. It was apt that Joshua should urge Israel to reaffirm her commitment at this time. She had followed Yahweh when she was looking forward in hope to the Promised Land. Would she still be loyal now that she actually possessed it?

Judges

1. References to Judah and Simeon are examples of how the Bible often refers to tribes in terms of their founding forebears.
2. Later events show that any occupation of Gaza and other Philistine towns can only have been temporary. The capture of Jerusalem at 1:8 is contradicted at 1:21 and is probably a scribal error. Jerusalem was only taken under David, 2S 5:6–9.
3. The Danites are later obliged to migrate to an area north of Galilee, Jg 18.
4. Various reasons are given for Yahweh not expelling the Canaanites completely: to punish Israel; to test her fidelity; to teach her how to wage war. Elsewhere it is attributed to allowing time for her population to grow and prevent the country becoming a wilderness, Ex 23:29–30; Dt 7:22, and to allow time for repentance, Ws 12:3–22.
5. Jabin, the king of Canaan named here as reigning from Hazor, was reportedly killed by Joshua's forces who are also reported as having burned Hazor to the ground, Jos 11:10–11.
6. Leaving the relative safety of the hills for the plains where their chariots rendered the Canaanites virtually invincible was a bold act on Barak's part, only made possible because of his trust in Yahweh.
7. The key to Barak's victory may lie in 5:21 which suggests that a torrential downpour flooded the Wadi Kishon and trapped the Canaanite chariots in the ensuing mud.

8. Gideon possibly reasoned that the first sign was inconclusive because the ground would dry more quickly than the fleece.

9. In the dream the tent would have represented the nomadic Midianites, the barley bread cake would have represented the agricultural Israelites.

10. It is likely that Abimelech was only a local Shechemite chieftain rather than king of all Israel.

11. This is the only instance in Judges where Israel's repentance is explicitly stated.

12. Jephthah should have known that while it is a sin to break a vow, in this case it was an even greater sin to fulfil it.

13. Ephraim was perhaps jealous of Jephthah's growing prestige.

14. Significantly, as we shall see, the nazirite vows include a prohibition on cutting one's hair, see Nb 6:5.

15. Samson's marriage seems to have been of a type not unknown in the Middle East where the husband does not live with his wife but pays her occasional visits.

16. With the breaking of the nazirite vow, and especially in cutting the hair that symbolised God's power growing in him, Samson's strength deserted him. When his hair regrew his strength returned.

    Samson was not a liberator like the other judges and probably owes his position in the Bible to his exploits living in folklore and legend. He achieved next to nothing, playing tricks on the Philistines as if he was conducting a private feud but never defeating them; a wasted talent.

17. The Danites were migrating because they could not hold the land allocated them by Joshua, Jos 19:47; Jg 1:34.

Ruth

1. Esau, Joseph and Moses all had foreign wives. Later on mixed marriages were forbidden by the Law, Ex 34:15–16; Dt 7:3–4, but it is doubtful how rigorously this was enforced as David, Solomon and Ahab all had foreign wives while the denunciations of mixed marriages in Ezr, Ne and Ml show that they were also common in post-exilic times. It is sometimes conjectured that Ruth was written as a counterweight to the strict prohibitions in Ezr, Ne and Ml.

2. A near relative had a right of redemption over a widow, to preserve the deceased husband's name by marrying her. He had a similar right over other near relatives and over family land that was up sale.

3. When a man spread his cloak over a maiden it was a sign that he wished to marry her.

4. Any child Ruth bore the kinsman would be the legal heir of Ruth's first husband and hence Elimelech so any land he bought would eventually revert to the child. Thus if he exercised his redemption rights he would be paying for land that would eventually fall out of his own estate.

5. Thus Judah, Tamar, Boaz and Ruth were all forebears of David and hence, Mt 1:3–16, of Joseph the husband of Mary.

1 Samuel

1. 'Yahweh Sabaoth' probably meant Yahweh Lord of the hosts of heaven. Children were dedicated to Yahweh by serving in a sanctuary. The reference to Samuel not having his hair cut probably implies the nazirite vow, Nb 6.

2. Sheltered in a building rather than the Tent of old, 1:3,9; 3:3,15.

3. Taking the Ark into battle was tantamount to using it as a magic talisman. Victory required true repentance.

4. Yahweh was as much Lord in Philistia as in Israel.

5. The Philistines wanted to see if their afflictions were due to Yahweh or to chance. Cows without previous yoke experience and mourning their calves would not normally take a direct course.

6. Possibly some tragedy occurred which Israel attributed to lack of respect being shown to the Ark. The Ark could not be returned to Shiloh as it had been sacked by the Philistines shortly after the battle of Aphek. The Bible does not report this explicitly but it is implied by Ps 78:60; Jr 7:12.

7. Being given the spirit of Yahweh here means being given the power to perform extraordinary deeds.

8. It was wicked because it betrayed a lack of trust in God. He had always raised up leaders in the past – men of the stamp of Moses and the judges – so why could He not be relied on to do so in the future? Bypassing God, and wanting a king 'to be like the other nations' was a denial of Israel's special calling to be a holy nation.

9. Saul's transgression is unclear. He seems to have followed Samuel's instructions of 10:8 to the letter. Possibly his fault lay in not containing himself until the very end of the seventh day.

10. At 1S 14:41 Saul sought Yahweh's help with the 'urim' and 'thummim'. These were probably sticks or stones which, by a process of selection, were made to give a simple 'yes' or 'no' answer to a question. More complicated decisions were probably handled by some sort of elimination routine. Sometimes the word 'ephod' is used in place of urim and thummim as at 30:6–8. However 'ephod' could also mean a priestly vestment, 22:18 or some unspecified cultic object, Jg 8:27.

11. Israel had neither swords nor spears, much less chariots, as the Philistines would not allow her to employ their blacksmiths for this purpose, 13:19–22. This explains much of her difficulty in combating the Philistines.

12. Saul's rejection may seem harsh but he was told, 15:3, by Samuel, speaking for Yahweh, that the war was to be a holy war in which everything would be put under the curse of destruction, ie slaughtered, Jos appendix 2. In sparing Agag and the best of the animals, albeit for the people to sacrifice to Yahweh, Saul was therefore making a casual observance of a divine directive. Hence Samuel's comment that obedience takes precedence over an external rite like sacrifice. Probably Samuel saw this as the last straw in a series of incidents which together demonstrated Saul's unsuitability to be king.

13. In choosing an unproven shepherd boy as Israel's future king God shows once again that He 'does not see as human beings see; they look at appearances but He looks at the heart', 16:7.

14. It seems odd that Saul did not know his minstrel and armour bearer, 17:55. Possibly he was in one of his black moods. The reference at 17:54 to Jerusalem is an error. Jerusalem was only captured much later by David himself, 2S 5:6–10.

15. This incident is quoted by Jesus as an example of human need taking precedence over ceremonial, Mt 12:1–8.

16. David had Moabite blood through Ruth.

17. David spares Saul twice. Earlier Saul tries to spear David twice and Saul is rejected twice. Although these doublets can be made to fit harmoniously there are other inconsistencies and many scholars believe that two traditions have been interlaced.

18. Saul started well enough. Modest, valiant, he gave God the credit and was generous to those who had earlier opposed him, 11:12–13. But his impetuosity and melancholia made

him in the end a tragic, even pathetic figure. We may perhaps sympathise with him more than the Bible does; more victim of a job beyond his capabilities than a villain. But then the Bible judges him not simply as a king but as a servant of Yahweh.

2 Samuel

1. Since a king's harem usually passed to his successor this was tantamount to Abner laying claim to Ishbaal's throne.
2. David probably reckoned that a son by Michal would help rally Saul's former supporters to his side. Saul gave Michal away after David fled his court, 1S 25:44.
3. Having Meribaal at his court would prevent him becoming a rallying point for factions still loyal to Saul.
4. The prophecies are borne out in the deaths of David's sons Amnon, Absalom and Adonijah and in Absalom's public appropriation of his concubines, 16:20–23.
5. Ostensibly to gain revenge for Amnon's violation of Tamar. However Absalom's initial reaction to Tamar's distress was decidedly muted and he may also have been motivated by the thought of improving his chances of succeeding David.
6. For evidence of Ahithophel's standing see 15:12;16:23. It seems that he was a grandfather of Bathsheba, 11:3; 23:34.
7. Apart from defeated soldiers trying to evade capture the only other instances of suicide in the Old Testament are Abimelech, Jg 9:54; Samson, Jg 16:30; Saul 1S 31:4; Zimri, 1K 16:18; and Razis, 2M 14:41.
8. David may have been angry with Joab for his outspokenness following Absalom's death or possibly he hoped that the appointment of Amasa, who had previously been Absalom's army commander, would help win Absalom's supporters over to his side. From 2S 17:26; 1Ch 2: 13–16 it appears that Joab and Amasa were both nephews of David.

1 Kings

1. Taking a king's concubine was tantamount to claiming the throne.
2. It would be wrong to see this as simply paying off old scores. Joab's slaying of Abner and Amasa would have reflected on David's honour and left his heirs open to the threat of blood vengeance. Only by the culprit himself being slain could this be averted. David did not feel he could act himself against his old comrade-in-arms but there was nothing to stop Solomon. Shimei had cursed David, 2S 16:5–14, and it was believed that a curse remained in force unless countered in some way. David could not kill Shimei as he had promised to spare him, 2S 19:22–24, but again Solomon was not bound.
3. As Abiathar was a descendant of Eli this fulfilled the prophecy of 1S 2:27–36 that Eli's line would lose the priesthood. Like Abiathar, Zadok was a descendant of Aaron.
4. 1K 3:2 rationalises this on the grounds that the Temple was not yet built ignoring the fact that Israel had long had other sanctuaries. 2Ch 1:3–6 legitimises it as Gibeon, the principal high place, 1K3:4, was where the Tent of Meeting was now sited.
5. This does not contradict God's promise that David's House would reign forever, 2S 7. It is merely Solomon's immediate heirs who would be dispossessed if they were unfaithful.
6. 1K 5:27–28; 11:28 tell of Israelites also being conscripted.
7. Pressure must have been building for some time as people contrasted the opulence of Solomon's court (and his drift to paganism) with the heavy taxation needed to support it and their conscription into labour gangs.

8. Bethel and Dan were both existing shrines, Gn 12:8; Jg 17–18. Jeroboam probably hoped that the calves, Canaanite emblems associated with Baal, would appeal to the Canaanite elements in his kingdom and thus be a source of unity.

9. There are problems with this story, not least God's use of an elderly prophet living in Bethel who lies to the man of God thereby causing him to disobey God and lose his life. The prophecy was fulfilled some three hundred years later, 2K 23:15–18.

10. To avoid repetition we omit mention of the condemnatory epilogue that is the lot of every king of Israel – 'he did what is displeasing to Yahweh . . .' – and the adverse judgements meted out to every king of Judah apart from Hezekiah and Josiah.

11. It is evident from Ahab's denunciation of him as the 'scourge of Israel', 18:17, that Elijah must have been active for some time before we meet him in the Bible.

12. Would Ahab have been such an intransigent opponent of Yahweh without his wife egging him on, 1K 21:25? He clearly accepted Yahweh to a degree since Obadiah was a believer, 18:4,13, and his repentance over Naboth's vineyard, 21:27–29, seems sincere. Jezebel on the other hand was fanatical, 18:4, 13; 19:2; 21:4–7.

13. The thunderstorm that broke the drought and underwrote Yahweh's supremacy (for Baal was nothing if not a nature god) may have been no miracle in itself but its timing assuredly was.

   For all its drama the defeat of Baal on Carmel was not a total victory as evidenced by Jehu's later attack on Baalism, 2K 10:18–27, and the Baal cult objects that still remained in Josiah's time, 2K 23:4.

14. It seems that Elijah lost his sense of proportion after his triumph on Mt Carmel and gave way to self-pity. By manifesting His presence in a still small voice rather than the earthquake etc God tenderly reminded him that serving Him is not all high profile work but equally to be found in the quiet unrecognised routine of daily life. As we shall see in 2K Hazael became one of Israel's worst oppressors while Jehu butchered Ahab's entire family. In the event it was Elisha who faced up to Hazael and Jehu; 2K 8:7–15; 9:1–10. Using two such bloodthirsty individuals is best seen as God acting through history as He finds it and as it naturally unfolds.

2 Kings

1. Possibly from flash floods caused by overnight rain in the hills.

2. The superstitious Israelites probably thought that the sacrifice would lead to the intervention of the Moabite gods.

3. Miracles are not common in the Old Testament and most are clustered around three periods when the power of God was needed to sustain His people in times of extreme danger or stress. The deliverance from Egypt and the conquest of Canaan are two. The testing of Israel's faith by Baalism and its aftermath is the third.

   Some of Elijah's and Elisha's miracles seem to have a distinctive legendary character and may have got embellished in the telling. So an occasional modicum of scepticism may not be out of order.

4. Naaman was an admirable character: prepared to listen, even to a servant girl; quick to humble himself and bathe in the Jordan after his initial anger, born of the unfamiliar situation he found himself in, was spent; quick to recognise Yahweh; generous and humble when dismounting to converse with Gehazi.

5. Possibly Elisha had urged trust in Yahweh but the king thought he had been misled when relief did not come.

6. It was not unusual for defeated nations to be deported especially their artisans and potential trouble makers. Assyrian practice was to settle deportees in small scattered communities where they could be assimilated into the local populace. This is what happened with Israel. The Babylonians on the other hand settled their captives together in discrete colonies where they could maintain their national identities. This is what later befell Judah.

7. A mixed religion evolved because the Assyrians were keen to placate the local gods as well as their own, 17:25–28. It is unlikely that all the inhabitants of Israel were deported. The mixed race that resulted later became known as the Samaritans.

8. Plague was probably the reason for the catastrophe that afflicted the Assyrians but the threat of intervention by Egypt or unrest back in Assyria have also been surmised as reasons for their precipitate departure, 19:9. 2K 18:13–16 on the other hand record that Sennacherib was bought off.

9. Probably an early version of today's Deuteronomy as the reforms it calls for are so similar.

10. Necho was marching north to the aid of Assyria when Josiah, calculating that Assyria's downfall would profit Judah, made his fateful attempt to stop him. This was in 609. It was on his return journey, also in 609, that Necho deposed Jehoahaz. Egypt was now the dominant power in Syria and Palestine but this was soon to change. In 605 Nebuchadnezzar won a decisive victory over Necho at Carchemish and became master of the Middle East. It was in 604 shortly after this that he carried out his first invasion of Judah and exacted tribute. Jehoiakim's revolt took place in 601, Nebuchadnezzar's two strikes against Jerusalem were in 597 and 587.

1 Chronicles

1. We learn that the reason God forbade David to build the Temple was that he was a man of war, 22:8; 28:3–4.

2. The chronicler's attention to cantors and gatekeepers in chs 25, 26 bears ample witness to his interest in the Temple.

2 Chronicles

1. 2Ch 3:1 identifies the Temple Mount, Mt Zion, with Mt Moriah the site of Abraham's offering of Isaac.

2. 2Ch 21:12 gives the only reference to Elijah or Elisha in Chronicles. Their omission is probably because they ministered in the 'lost' northern kingdom.

3. This is not Zechariah the prophet but almost certainly the Zechariah to whom Jesus refers at Mt 23:35. Abel's is the first murder recorded in the Jewish scriptures, Zechariah's the last, since 2 Ch is the last book of the Jewish Canon.

4. Only priests were allowed to do this, Nb 17:5.

Ezra

1. Sheshbazzar is only referred to at Ezr 1:8–11; 5:14–16. Elsewhere Zerubbabel is named as leader. Possibly we have two names for the same individual. Or Zerubbabel may have been Sheshbazzar's successor.

2. Zerubbabel was a grandson of Jehoiachin (otherwise Jechoniah), Mt 1:12, and the heir to David's throne. Joshua was the grandson of the last pre-exilic chief priest, 2K 25:18; 1Ch 5:40; Hg 1:1.

3. Notice how cedar wood was imported from the Lebanon just as it had been for the First Temple.
4. The 'people of the country' or 'enemies' would have been composed of several elements: descendants of Jews who never left Palestine when Nebuchadnezzar carried off their compatriots and encroaching Samaritans, Arabs and Edomites who would have filled the void left by the deported Jews. The Jews and Samaritans would doubtless have felt that they were the heirs to the Mosaic tradition and therefore had a right to share in rebuilding the Temple. Zerubbabel and Joshua would have declined their offer because they wanted to keep the faith free from outside influences.
5. Artaxerxes, who forbade the rebuilding of the walls here, later gave leave to Nehemiah to do just that, see Ne 2.
6. Scribe originally meant a writer or clerk. However, beginning with Ezra it gradually came to acquire the meaning it had in Jesus' day, namely an official teacher and interpreter of the Law.
7. In the small community that Ezra inherited mixed marriages would easily have allowed pagan influences to creep in.

Nehemiah

1. It was risky because Artaxerxes had been warned that Jerusalem was a hotbed of rebellion, Ezr 4:11–16.
2. Sanballat was governor of the Persian province of Samaria. His opposition was probably political. Judah had formerly been his responsibility so he would not have welcomed it being given autonomy with Nehemiah as governor, 5:14.
3. This incident is misplaced since 5:14 shows it occurred at least twelve years into Nehemiah's term of office.
4. Had Nehemiah agreed he would have been discredited. Only priests were allowed in the inner sanctum, Nb 18:7.
5. Probably an early edition of the Pentateuch.
6. Jerusalem needed repopulating because she had suffered more than elsewhere from the Babylonian invasion.
7. This prohibition is based on Dt 23:4–7 and ignores the following two verses which permit a more liberal treatment of certain foreigners. Presumably it was thought that the situation called for the most stringent measures.

Tobit

1. See 1K 12:26–33.
2. We learn at 6:15 that this was because the demon loved her.
3. Raphael is one of only three angels identified by name in the Bible. The others are Gabriel, Lk 1:19, and Michael Jude 9.

Judith

1. For example Nebuchadnezzar was king of Babylon not Assyria and the return from captivity took place long after he was dead, 4:1–3. Holofernes and other names and turns of phrase are of Persian origin. The geography of 2:21–28 is confused.

Esther

1. Everything hinged on Vashti's indisposition. Then how 'lucky' it was that Esther was chosen over other candidates; that Mordecai heard of the plot to assassinate the king; that this was recorded in the Annals; that Esther concealed her identity; that the king was in a convivial mood when Esther petitioned him; that when the king could not sleep he had the Annals read to him and that Mordecai's role in thwarting the assassination attempt was part of the reading; that the king was alert enough to enquire if Mordecai had been rewarded. Luck indeed!
2. Usually taken to be Xerxes I who reigned from 485 to 465.
3. No reason is given. Was he party to the plot against the king?
4. Decrees of the Persian kings were regarded as irrevocable, 8:9. But although the previous decree could not be annulled it could be countervailed with a new one.
5. The best that can be said is that this is almost certainly unhistorical and that it is probably included to highlight by exaggeration the remarkable reversals of fortune that God can bring about.
6. This is the feast of Purim which is celebrated by Jews to this day. Although the Book of Esther is read at the feast it is mainly a secular carnival-like event with masquerade parties and copious feasting.

1 Maccabees

1. In 1M, 6:1–17 is inserted between 4:35 and 4:36. In 2M, 11:1–21, 11:27 – 12:1 are placed between 8:36 and 9:1, 10:9–13 is inserted between 9:29 and 10:1, and 11:22–26 is included with 13:1–26.

   In broad terms, for there is a little more to it, the dates quoted in Maccabees are relative to the start of the Seleucid era in 312 B.C. Thus the year 148 quoted at 1M 4:52 for the dedication of the Temple is 312–148=164 B.C. in the modern calendar. To avoid confusion over similar names we usually refer to the Seleucid kings by number as well as by name, e.g. Antiochus VI, even though the Bible itself does not do this.
2. According to the Roman historian Josephus this was an altar to the Greek god Zeus; see also 2M 6:2.

   Antiochus adopted the title Epiphanes meaning Manifest because he liked to think of Zeus as manifest in himself. His subjects countered with the nickname Epimanes meaning madman.
3. The Hasideans are usually thought to be forerunners of the Pharisees of Jesus' day.
4. Judas puts his trust in 'Heaven'. Out of respect 1M, unlike 2M, avoids the word 'God'.
5. The feast of Dedication, Hanukkah in Hebrew, is celebrated in December and resembles the older feast of Shelters.
6. Beth-Zechariah was the well known battle in which a follower of Judas named Eleazar killed one of the enemy's elephants by stabbing its underside thereby bringing it down on his own head and crushing him.
7. Antiochus V was only about nine at this time so Lysias would have been responsible for the actions recorded in his name.

2 Maccabees

1. The feast of Dedication, 1M 4: 59, is here described as the feast of Shelters in the month of Chislev.

2. This is one of three varying accounts of Antiochus' death: 1M 6:1–13; 2M 1:11–17; 9:1–29. On the fire see Lv 6:5–6.
3. On resurrection see also 12:38–45; 14:46. Note too the reference to creation from nothing, 7:28.
4. We have here one of several supernatural signs recorded in 2M. Others relate to the punishment of Heliodorus 3:25; Antiochus' pillaging of the Temple 5:1–4; Judas' victory over Timotheus 10:29; and Judas' dream of Onias and Jeremiah, 15:11–16.
5. Given the earlier account of Timotheus's death this passage must be out of sequence.

Wisdom literature

1. Wisdom-style excerpts also occur elsewhere in the Old Testament e.g. in a number of the psalms including Ps 1,15,32,34, 37,49,73 and at Is 28:23–29; Jr 17:5–11; Ba 3:9 – 4:4. On the three pillars see Jr 18:18.
2. See Pr 1:20–33; 3:16–19; 8:1 – 9:6; Si 1:1–10; 4:11–19; 14:20 – 15:10; 24:1–23; Ws 1:4–6; 6:12–16; 7:22 – 8:1; Jb 28; Ba 3:9 – 4:4.
3. St Paul sees Jesus as the wisdom of God at 1Co 1:24–30 and at Col 1:15–17 where he effectively picks up where Ws 7:22 – 8:1 leaves off. The language of Heb 1:2–3 also links Christ to Wisdom. It is possible that Jesus Himself does so at Mt 11:19.

Job

1. The idea that suffering was the fruits of sin persisted until Jesus' day, Lk 13:1–5; Jn 9:1–3. See Jos appendix 3.
2. It is important to remember that neither Job nor his friends know that he is being tested.
3. There is no reason to suppose that Job thought he was totally free from sin; see 7:21; 13:26; 14:16. Probably he meant that he was no worse than the common run of men and that his suffering was therefore disproportionate.
4. The reordering in chapters 24 to 27 is an attempt to make sense of what is otherwise a disordered text.
5. The remedial role of suffering was also alluded to by Eliphaz at 5:17–19.
6. See also 7:20.
7. They presumptuously thought they knew God's mind and set themselves up in judgement.

Psalms

1. The doxologies are: 41:13; 72:18–20; 89:52; 106:48. They do not form part of the psalm to which they are appended.
    From Ps 10 to Ps 147 the usual (Hebrew) numbering adopted here is one ahead of the Greek and Vulgate which combines Pss 9, 10 and Pss 114, 115 under one number but divides Pss 116, 147 into two. Despite having separate numbers under the Hebrew system Pss 9, 10 are nonetheless read as one psalm. The same is true of Pss 42,43.
2. Bibles vary in whether they number them or even include them, thereby leading to variations in verse numberings.
3. Korah and Asaph were cantors, 1 Ch 6:16–24.
4. Moreover a referral might not be to David personally but to his dynasty.
5. Among the few psalms that can be dated with some precision are Pss 74, 79, 80,

137 which clearly refer to the destruction of Jerusalem in 587 and the subsequent exile.

6. Pss 25, 34, 37, 111, 112, 119, 145 are 'acrostic' (or nearly so) in that each couplet begins with the next letter of the Hebrew alphabet beginning with the first. The same applies to Pss 9, 10 taken together. Poems were written in this way to aid memorization and to convey a sense of wholeness. Pr 31:10–31 is an acrostic as are several of the Lamentations, the 'wholeness' in these instances applying to the portrait of a perfect wife and mother in Pr and the totality of misery and grief following the fall of Jerusalem in Lm.

7. Ps 106, a lament, is a companion to Ps 105 showing how Israel repaid God's bounty with ingratitude and infidelity in a story of betrayal relieved only by God's mercy. Both psalms show affinities with Ps 78 in which their themes are interwoven.

8. Hymns of praise, thanksgiving psalms and songs of trust may also be individual or collective. It is not always easy to decide which since 'I' may represent a spokesman speaking on behalf of a community. Six of the individual laments, Pss 6, 38, 51, 102, 130, 143 along with Ps 32 are known as the penitential psalms.

9. We are reminded of Job in Pss 38, 39, 88. Ps 38 also has echoes of Isaiah's Servant.

10. This is one of the few hints of immortality in the psalms. See also Ps 16:9–11 and possibly the even more enigmatic Ps 17:15; 73:23–24 where the psalmist yearns for some indissoluble union with God.

11. As do Pss 75, 81, 82.

12. Ps 18 is virtually identical with 2S 22:2–51.

13. The risen Jesus' testimony at Lk 24:44 that everything written about Him in the Law, the Prophets and the Psalms was to be fulfilled is further evidence that the Psalter anticipated Him. It is true that by 'Psalms' Jesus probably meant the third part of the Hebrew canon including the Wisdom books but the point is still made.

14. There is no suggestion that the psalmists would have had the Messiah in mind when they composed these psalms. They would probably have been written to celebrate important occasions in the life of the contemporary king. As such they would have employed a stilted laudatory style – 'the king will bring justice and peace to all nations', 'the king will endure from age to age' etc. – of a kind thought to befit the king's status as Yahweh's viceroy on earth. Nothing more would have been implied. On other occasions the psalmist would have been reacting to events in his own day. Pss 48, 76 were probably inspired by the defeat of Sennacherib at the gates of Jerusalem in 701. Only later would the idea have gained ground that God was using these psalms to point to a greater king whose reign would be one of universal blessing.

15. Others include: Ps 8:2 = Mt 21:16; Ps 22:8 = Mt 27:43; Ps 31:5 = Lk 23:46; Ps 34:20 = Jn 19:36; Ps 35:19 = Jn 15:25; Ps 41:9 = Jn 13:18; Ps 69:4 = Jn 15:25; Ps 69:9 = Jn 2:17; Ps 78:2 = Mt 13:35; Ps 78:24–25 = Jn 6:31; Ps 82:6 = Jn 10:34; Ps 91:11–12 = Mt 4:6; Ps 110:1 = Mt 22:44; Ps 118:22 = Mt 21:42; Ps 118:26 = Mt 21:9.

Quotations from the Psalter occur throughout the New Testament. When Peter argues his case with the Jewish leaders at Ac 4 he caps his defence by quoting Ps 118:22. Indeed Psalms vies with Isaiah among Old Testament books for frequency of citation in the New.

Proverbs

1. This foundational theme is found at 1:32–33, 2:20–22, 3:33–35, 4:18–19, 8:35–36. We are reminded of the two ways identified by Jesus, Mt 7:13–14, and Moses, Dt 11:26–28; 30:15–20. Fear of Yahweh means that reverential awe which accepts Him

as the one supreme being and which expresses itself both in worship and obedience to His precepts.

2. For most of the time instruction is conveyed in the paternalistic style of a father teaching a child. However both here, 1:20–33, and at 8:1 – 9:6 it is personified Wisdom herself who speaks.

3. Wisdom is not mere knowledge but knowledge grounded in fear of God, reverence and awe.

4. The repeated warnings against adultery may have been aimed at spiritual impurity, the worship of false gods, as well as physical infidelity. Idolatry was often repudiated by the prophets in terms of adultery or harlotry e.g. Hos 1:2.

5. The 'silly woman' of 9:13–18, the antithesis of Wisdom, is often referred to as Folly.

6. The red-hot coals represent the pain of contrition which is more readily roused by kindness than animosity.

7. Many of the proverbs bear the imprint of life in the raw: e.g. the pictures of the drunkard 23:29–35, the cantankerous wife 21:19, 27:15–16, and the hen-pecked husband who takes to the roof of his house rather than submit to his wife's nagging 25:24.

8. In Hebrew the poem is an acrostic, see Ps note 6.

Ecclesiastes

1. 'Futility' is the leitmotiv of the whole book occurring over 30 times. Many texts use the word 'vanity' instead rendering the sage's opening proclamation as 'vanity of vanities, all is vanity' but the meaning would be the same for 'vanity' in this context means something transient, lacking in substance. Qoheleth employs two other catch-phrases: 'chasing after the wind', meaning a futile pursuit; and 'under the sun', meaning life without God.

2. Qoheleth drives home his 'futility' theme relentlessly: 1:14; 2:11,17,19,21,23,26; 4:4,7,8,16; 5:9; 6:9; 8:14, 12:8.

3. This refrain reverberates throughout the book: 2:24–25, 3:12–13, 3:22, 5:17–19, 8:15, 9:7–10, 11:9. It is not an invitation to strive for a life of luxury, as 2:1–11 makes plain, but a call to enjoy whatever good things come one's way. Notice how Qoheleth always attributes such pleasures to God.

4. Here, 3:17, as at 8:10–14, 11:9, 12:14 Qoheleth expresses confidence in divine judgement. In the first two instances he links this with the injustices of life, a theme he also alludes to at 2:17–23, 7:15, 9:1–2; 11–12. How he reconciled his vision of judgement with his strongly held view that death was the end is not clear.

5. The emphasis is on conscientiousness in prayer rather than the hasty recital of prayers unaccompanied by a repentant heart. 'Listen' has the sense of 'obey' as elsewhere in the Old Testament.

6. This is obscure. The first may be a warning against moral pride but the latter? Perhaps Qoheleth merely meant to convey that no one can steer clear of venial sin.

Song of Songs

1. Its attribution to Solomon at 1:1 is almost certainly a literary fiction.

2. Most modern Bibles have rubrics in the margins to indicate who is speaking.

3. The lover is idealised as a king. This, and similarly 'queen', was a common form of address between engaged couples.

   The subdivision of the Song into six poems is widely accepted. However ambiguities over pronouns and over who is addressing whom, together with other obscurities, mean that other readings are also possible.

4. This is their first appearance. They appear as a chorus here and at 5:9, 6:1, 7:1. The lover addresses them at 2:7, 3:5, 8:4; the beloved at 1:5, 5:8, 6:2 and the poet himself at 3:11.

5. This refrain, addressed to the daughters of Jerusalem at 2:7 and repeated at 3:5; 8:4, is a plea for restraint against false arousal. Love is not to be forced but left to its own delicate tempo.

6. Vineyards are a metaphor for their love, foxes for anything that could harm it.

7. This may be intended to remind us that the lovers are now married; at 4:8 the shepherd calls the maiden 'bride' for the first time. He also calls her 'sister' at 4:9, a word widely used in the east as a term of endearment between lovers.

8. 4:12. In other words she is a virgin.

9. 4:16. In other words to consummate the marriage.

10. 6:11 – 7:1 are obscure.

11. In the ancient world public affection was acceptable between siblings but not between lovers.

Wisdom

1. Wisdom is personified at 1:4–6; 6:12–16; 7:22 – 8:1 and associated with God's spirit at 1:5–7; 7:22–23; 9:17.

2. By 'visitation' at 3:7 the author means some kind of divine event like judgement; see also 3:13,18; 4:6, 20.

3. It was thought that fertility and long life were signs of God's favour.

4. As in Ecclesiasticus, Wisdom is associated with upholding the Law.

5. Identities have to be surmised as the author does not use proper names either here or, apart from the odd instance as at 18:1, in the following antitheses. Instead Israel and Egypt are referred to by such terms as 'the holy people', 'the godless' etc.

6. The antitheses take some liberties with the Pentateuch narrative. For example, according to 11:7 Yahweh turned the waters of the Nile into blood to punish Pharaoh for his infanticide whereas Ex 7:14–24 tells us that it was to induce Pharaoh to let Israel go. Also events are sometimes embellished, e.g. the statement that the manna was transformed into what each eater wished, 16:21.

7. See 11:5. In the first antithesis the common factor is water; in the second and third food: in the fourth light and its absence, darkness; in the fifth the Sea.

8. Ws 11:9; 16:18 imply that the plagues continued even after Israel had left Egypt.

9. A reference to the plagues of frogs, mosquitoes, horseflies and locusts. The agent of sin has become the agent of punishment, 11:16; 12:23.

10. God's mercy is open to all, a point made explicit by 11:23.

11. Some commentators see in 17:21 a hint that the darkness the Egyptians experienced was a subjective darkness, a darkness in the mind, and that the spectres that terrified them resulted from their own evil consciences. With this reading the antithesis would be between the darkness of sin and the light of the Law, see 18:4.

12. The reference is to the plague that followed the rebellions of Korah, Dathan and Abiram, Nb 16; 17:6–15.

Ecclesiasticus

1. Extra Biblical sources pinpoint this as 132 B.C. thus giving a date for the composition of the original book of around 180 B.C.. The translation he refers to would have been from

Hebrew to Greek for the benefit of the many Jews living outside Palestine who would have been Greek speaking.

2. Wisdom is also personified at 4:11–19; 14:20 – 15:10.

3. See also his eulogies of Aaron, 45:6–22, and of the high priest Simon, 50:1–21.

4. See especially 1:12; 7:8; 9:11–12; 11:21–22; 12:6; 16:12–14, 37:24–26.

Isaiah

1. The devastation could be the result either of the Syro-Ephraimite war or Sennacherib's invasion of 701.

2. Because so many men will have fallen in war.

3. The force of vv 9–10 is not that God willed the people's obstinacy but that He foresaw it and incorporated it into His designs. The Bible often expresses what God foresees as it were His will. Perhaps there is also a touch of irony.

4. Ahaz ignored Isaiah's advice and invited Assyria to intervene on his behalf against Aram and Israel, 2K 16.

5. The Hebrew speaks merely of a young woman of marriageable age. It was only later tradition that took her to be a virgin as understood by Matthew and Luke, Mt 1:23.

6. These were the first parts of Israel to fall to Assyria. Isaiah is contrasting that humiliation with the glory to come when the Messiah makes it the centre for His earthly ministry, Mt 4:13–16.

7. 'A shoot from the stock' suggests that this descendant of David would arise at a time when the Davidic dynasty appeared to be all but extinct. The mention of Jesse, David's father, rather than David himself also suggests a new beginning; a king like David but in some way different. All of which underpins the Messianic tone.

8. This probably refers to Sennacherib's invasion of 701 as do 14:24–27; 17:12–14; 22:1–14; 29:1–8. Shiloah was possibly a perennial stream that enabled Jerusalem to survive a siege.

9. Only here and at 17:1-11; 28:1-6 does 'Israel' refer to the northern kingdom as opposed to God's people in general.

10. The prophecies about Babylon, here and at 21:1-10, are almost certainly later than Isaiah.

11. Cush was the ancient name of Ethiopia but here it means Egypt which at the time was ruled by an Ethiopian dynasty.

12. These poems may have been inspired by a ruined city, the 'city of nothingness' as 24:10 puts it.

13. The wicked are symbolised here by Leviathan, a mythical sea monster.

14. According to Rm 9:30–33; 1P 2:4–6 the foundation stone is Christ. The background is the invasion of 701 and the alliance with 'Death' refers to Judah's attempts to get Egypt to come to her aid.

15. As so often the people's shortcomings are attributed to God.

16. This is the force of 40:19–20 read in conjunction with the misplaced 41:6–7.

17. The legal summons was a favourite literary device of Deutero Isaiah as was his use of 'coasts and islands' to denote the nations and 'the first and the last' to encapsulate Yahweh's eternal nature.

18. This is the first time Cyrus is referred to by name having been alluded to anonymously, and somewhat obliquely, at 41:1–7, 25; 45:13; 46:11; 48:12–15. The potter metaphor may have been used to counter criticism that the prophet saw restoration being effected through the agency of a pagan. God in His omnipotence is free to act in any way He chooses.

19. Yahweh is bound by His covenant promises which have not yet been fulfilled.

20. This is the New Covenant of Jr 31:31–34. See also 59:21; 61:8.

21. Dt 23:2–9 had placed severe restrictions on foreigners and others. Eunuchs had earlier been excluded from Judaism because it was thought inappropriate for someone deprived of the means to propagate life to associate with the God of life.

22. Jesus read vv 1–2 in the synagogue at Nazareth at the start of His ministry, Lk 4:18.

23. Despite prophesying a new heavens and earth, and earlier a new Jerusalem, the prophet cannot dissociate his thoughts from the world he knows. Life, though longer, would still be finite and he finds it necessary to assure his readers of freedom from marauders, 65:19–22; 62:8–9, and that foreigners would serve them and rebuild their city walls, chs 60, 61.

Jeremiah

1. Jeremiah's call reminds us of Moses' in that both were reluctant and of Isaiah's in that both had their mouths touched as a sign that they were accredited mouthpieces for God's word.

2. The words for 'watchful' and 'almond tree' are similar in Hebrew.

3. Apart from Egypt invaders invariably attacked Palestine from the north.

4. Something expressly forbidden under the Law, Dt 24:1–4.

5. Genuine in the sense of being a 'circumcision of the heart' defined at Dt 30:6 as loving Yahweh with all one's heart and soul. Repentance must be more than mere words and embrace inward devotion and moral rectitude.

   This is one of the few passages in Jeremiah where Israel means just the old northern kingdom rather than God's people as a whole. Jeremiah is citing it to make the point that God wants to forgive even Israel. If He can forgive Israel who was punished with deportment a century before, how much more so is He prepared to forgive Judah!

6. When Jeremiah prophesies 'disaster from the north' as here and at 6:1; 10:22; 13:20; 25:9 it is not always clear whether he means invasion by Babylon or is using the phrase as a metaphor for some unspecified disaster. But it matters little.

7. This, 5:18, is the remnant theme, see Is appendix 3. Other references include 4:27; 5:10; 23:3; 31:7; 50:20. The two figs vision of 24:1–10 shows that Jeremiah saw the remnant as emerging from the people carried off to Babylon in the first deportation of 597.

8. Ch 26 tells how Jeremiah was arrested and narrowly escaped death as a result of it.

9. Shiloh had once been Israel's main sanctuary and the place where the Ark was kept, 1S 4. However despite this it was later destroyed by the Philistines. This is attested by archaeology but only referred to in the Bible at Ps 78:60.

10. Jeremiah frequently interceded for his people but on three occasions, here and at 11:14; 14:11, God made it clear that it was pointless. Corruption had gone too far. Other references to Jeremiah interceding occur at 15:11;18:20.

11. Jeremiah is not denigrating sacrifice but insisting on proper priorities. Judah was wrongly putting sacrifice before obedience. Obedience was God's prime requirement. Sacrifice was secondary in the sense that it was only introduced after God's call for obedience as a path to forgiveness where obedience failed. Other instances of the inability of sacrifice to placate God's wrath occur at 6:20; 11:15; 14:12. The call at v 21 to 'eat all the meat', is ironic. So debased was the practice of sacrifice that the people might as well eat all the sacrificial meat, not just the portion that was theirs by right according to Lv's prescriptions, for all the good it would do.

12. It is likely that this was in support of Josiah's reforms, 2K 22, 23.

13. Jeremiah is rich in symbolic actions: the almond tree, chapter 1, the cooking pot on the boil, 1, the two wine jugs, 13, the potter, 18, smashing an earthenware jug, 19, the two baskets of figs, 24, wearing a yoke and thongs, 27, buying a field, 32, burying stones in Egypt near Pharaoh's palace, 43, casting a prophecy into the Euphrates, 51. In a way Jeremiah's whole life of celibacy and restraint was a symbolic act, chapter 16.

14. The Babylonians were renowned in both fishing and hunting.

15. Both here, 15:18, and at 20:7 Jeremiah's remarks border on blasphemy.

16. This is the first mention in the Bible of the scribes as interpreters of the Law.

17. The father was, of course, Josiah. Surprisingly, nowhere apart from possibly 11:1–14 does Jeremiah refer to Josiah's reforms although there can be little doubt, in view of his harsh invective against idolatry, that he espoused them.

18. Phrases like 'the days are coming', 'when that time comes', herald the fact that Jeremiah has the Day of the Lord in mind.

19. V22b, 'the Woman sets out to find her Husband again', is variously interpreted but it is natural to equate 'Woman' with Israel and 'Husband' with Yahweh especially as Jeremiah has earlier portrayed Israel as an adulterous wife, 2:20; 3:1,20.

20. Until now Israel had subscribed to a doctrine of collective responsibility, see Jos appendix 3, and these verses reflect the bitterness of people who traced their present plight to the sins of their ancestors and saw little justice in it. Ezk 18:1–4 teaches that this new principle already applies.

21. Other references to the New Covenant occur at Jr 32:39–40; Ezk 11:19; 16:60; 18:31; 34:25; 36:26; 37:26; Is 55:3; 59:21; 61:8. Sometimes it is called the everlasting covenant, the eternal covenant, the covenant of peace or something similar.

22. Branch, the fresh growth that emerges from a parent root, in this case the House of David, gradually became a Messianic title for the hoped for Davidic king who would rule for ever; see also Jr 23:3–6; Zc 3:8; 6:12. The idea is also implicit in Isaiah where he refers to a 'seedling', Is 4:2–6, and a shoot growing from the stock, Is 11:1.

23. The Ark had been the focal point of Israel's religious life from the desert days. It would lose that role in future because God would dwell in person among His people in Jerusalem. The old economy is to be replaced. Jeremiah also refers to Israel's rulers as 'shepherds' at 2:8; 10:21; 23:4.

24. Branch, meaning a branch of the Davidic dynasty, came to be used as a Messianic title.

25. Probably the basis of the book we have today. Note the contrast between the contemptuous way Jehoiakim treated Jeremiah's scroll and the respectful way his father Josiah reacted when the Book of the Law was read to him, 2K 22 – 23.

26. As Jeremiah's secretary, Baruch probably attracted as much disparagement as the prophet himself.

27. It seems likely that Jeremiah spoke out because an anti-Babylon alliance was in the offing, possibly sparked off by encouragement from Egypt and the fact that Nebuchadnezzar was beset with problems back home in Babylon. However his view was based not on political expediency but on his conviction that it was God's will. He had no illusions about Babylon but for the moment she was God's winnowing blade. The historical context and 28:1 imply a date of 594 or 593.

28. Zedekiah had probably been hoping to gain God's favour by freeing the slaves. Now he saw no need for it.

29. The property business mentioned at 37:11–12 possibly had something to do with this.

30. Jeremiah was not a traitor. His position was simple. Yahweh had abandoned His people and decreed Jerusalem's destruction. Why then invite further slaughter when their fate was sealed beyond human redress?

31. Zedekiah was a tragic figure. He knew in his heart that Jeremiah was right but lacked the courage of his convictions.
32. The burning of the Temple is not reported here but it is at 52:13; 2K 25:9.
33. Jeremiah was almost certainly on friendly terms with Gedaliah. It was his father Ahikam, 39:14, who had helped to save Jeremiah after his Temple Sermon, 26:24.
34. Probably Astarte, goddess of fertility.
35. The first two deportations were those of 597 and 587 as reported in 2K 24 – 25. The third, in 582, is not recorded elsewhere. The numbers Jeremiah gives for the first deportation differ substantially from 2K which does not give any details at all for the second deportation.

Lamentations

1. The first, second and fourth laments are acrostics with twenty-two verses each. The third is an acrostic with sixty-six verses in blocks of three. The fifth has twenty-two verses but without any alphabetic pattern. See Ps note 6.
2. Zion is personified at 1:9,11, 12–16,18–22.
3. Edom sided with Babylon when she attacked Judah and was rewarded with slices of her territory.

Baruch

1. Baruch first appears at Jr 36:1–4 around 604 as Jeremiah's scribe. After the fall of Jerusalem he was carried off to Egypt with Jeremiah, Jr 43:1–7, after which nothing else is heard of him.
2. It appears that the Temple was still in use, possibly as a shell with a makeshift altar, see Jr 41:5.

Ezekiel

1. The year 593 derives from 1:2 which is compatible with all the other dates in the book. The meaning of 'thirtieth year' in 1:1 is disputed. The vision may have grown out of a thundercloud. Notice how it came from the north, the direction from which tribulation usually came. By manifesting himself in Babylon Yahweh showed the exiles that He was not tied to Jerusalem or the Temple but omnipresent.
   In calling Ezekiel 'son of man' Yahweh was contrasting the frailty of the human bearer of the divine message with the greatness of its originator. Apart from Dn 8:17 where Daniel is addressed in the same way, and Dn 7:13 where it means much more, 'son of man' is not found in the Old Testament. As applied to Ezekiel it is unrelated to Jesus' use of 'Son of man' to refer to Himself.
2. Confirmation that Ezekiel initially preached from home is found at 8:1, 14:1, 20:1. It was some seven-and-a-half years before his 'dumbness', which may have been figurative rather than literal, and intended to signify that he was only to preach when told to do so by God, was removed, 33:21–22, having been foretold at 24:26–27.
3. Attempts to relate these figures to historical events have not proved successful.
4. Like Jeremiah, Ezekiel excelled in the acted parable. As well as the examples given here he mimes Zedekiah's flight from Jerusalem and trembles and shudders as he eats and drinks, 12:1–20; apes Nebuchadnezzar, 21:23–32; refrains from mourning when his wife dies, 24:15–24; and joins two sticks to symbolise the reunification of Israel and Judah, 37:15–22.

5. Ezekiel touches upon the 'remnant' theme here, 5:3, and at 6:8–9; 9:3–6 (those marked with crosses); 11:13; 12:16; 14:22.

6. On the four scourges see Lv 26:21–26; Rv 6:8.

7. Ezekiel seems to have the Day of Yahweh in mind at verses 7, 10–12, 19 and also later at 13:5, 30:3.

8. The statue of jealousy was probably a statue to Baal's consort the goddess Asherah; 2K 21:7 may refer. The animal carvings may have represented Egyptian deities. Tammuz was a Mesopotamian fertility god. Ezekiel is very clear, here and elsewhere, that idolatry is the cardinal sin. All other perversions begin there. If people forsake the true God and turn to other gods with their counterfeit standards and values what hope can there be?

9. The seven men may be the seven angels who stand in the presence of God, Rv 8:2.

10. The fact that Ezekiel exhibits such a detailed knowledge of affairs in Jerusalem has led to suggestions that, although his book places his ministry entirely among the exiles in Babylon, he may have begun it in Jerusalem or returned to visit it. There is not a shred of evidence for such theories which, if adopted, would pose other problems. Ezekiel would have known Jerusalem and the Temple intimately from living there as a priest before the deportation. We know too from Jr 27 that letters passed between Palestine and Babylon. In any case it is hard to see what would have been the point of placing any part of Ezekiel's ministry in Babylon if it had in fact been exercised in Jerusalem. None of this discussion is, of course, necessary for those who accept the authenticity of visions and the supernatural agency that Ezekiel claims transported him by the spirit, see 3:12,14; 8:3; 11:1,24; 40:1; 43:5.

11. Jeremiah noted Israel's inclination to derive comfort from the supposed inviolability of the Temple, Jr 7; 26, and Ezekiel deplores the same sentiment here. The proverb 'days go by and visions fade', 12:21–22, is similarly complacent.

12. Nothing prepares us for this sudden promise of reconciliation. God has not forgotten His promises to Israel even if Israel has forgotten Him. Restoration there will be! However if Israel is ever to live as God requires, men's inner dispositions must first be totally transformed. Here and at 36:26 Ezekiel parallels Jeremiah's New Covenant, Jr 31:31.

13. For Ezekiel, Israel had only one King and so here and elsewhere he refers to her human ruler as 'prince'. The prophecy was borne out in Zedekiah.

14. The general thrust of Ezekiel's teaching on personal responsibility as developed at 18:1–32; 33:10–20 is one of encouragement. No one is punished for the sins of others. God judges everyone on his own conduct and his alone and welcomes repentance. However there is a more sombre side. No one, however worthy, can save anyone else. It is problematic whether the Daniel mentioned here is the prophet of that name or a more ancient figure.

15. There are several examples in the Old Testament of Israel being likened to a cultivated vine that bears rich fruit: Is 5:1–7; Jr 2:21; Hos 10:1; Ps 80:8–15. Here the opposite view is taken.

16. Some people find the explicit sexual imagery of chapters 16, 23 offensive. Perhaps it was meant to be, to help make the point that God finds sin repugnant.

17. This is the New Covenant annunciated by Jeremiah at Jr 31:31–34 and by Ezekiel at 11:19, 36:26. Sodom and Samaria represent the Gentile nations who are all included in it.

18. The first eagle represents Nebuchadnezzar, the second Egypt. Lebanon symbolises Jerusalem, the cedar tree David's dynasty. The topmost branch of the cedar tree is Jehoiachin while the seed which later becomes the vine is Zedekiah.

19. Present dispositions are what count not a person's past. Yahweh is merciful, keener to pardon than to punish. He wants everyone to repent and live. Jeremiah saw the principle of individual responsibility as applying in the future. Ezekiel taught that it applied already.

20. Probably Jehoahaz and Jehoiachin though the precise identifications are disputed.

21. Ezekiel's emphasis on the Sabbath in this indictment may be due to the increased significance it acquired as a focus for unity during the exile when, with no Temple, Israel's traditional worship was not possible.

22. Yahweh's name would have been dishonoured if the nations thought that by destroying Israel He was unable to fulfil His promises to her.

23. How Ezekiel, knowing nothing of rewards and punishment beyond the grave, would have reconciled this indiscriminate slaughter with his recent rubric on personal responsibility is far from clear.

24. 'They will take away your diadem . . . until the rightful ruler comes' in vv 31–32 reminds us of Gn 49:10 and is sometimes seen as a Messianic portent to the effect that the royal succession will be in abeyance and God's people left in a sorry state until the Messiah comes.

25. Where chapter 16 stressed cultic infidelity, it is political infidelity that is more to the fore here. However since political alliances often involved the junior partner adopting the cults of the superior the distinction is a fine one.

    Judah entered into liaisons with Assyria 2K 16:7–18; Babylon 2K 20:12–19; and Egypt Jr 37:5

26. Given in 571, this is Ezekiel's last dated oracle.

27. This refers to Egypt's attempt to come to the aid of Zedekiah during the siege of Jerusalem, Jr 37:3–10.

28. Ezekiel must always have had something of a reputation as evidenced by the elders' visits to his home, 8:1, 14:1, 20:1. Now he definitely had one, 33:30–33. The fall of Jerusalem was a pivotal point. It established his credibility and from now on his message is increasingly infused with a hope that had hitherto only appeared intermittently.

29. 'Shepherd' was a common term for 'king' or 'ruler' and Jesus' allegory portraying Himself as the Good Shepherd, Jn 10:11–18, may have been suggested by this text. The 'shepherd' theme also occurs at Is 40:10; Jr 2:8; 3:15; 10:21; 23:1–4.

30. As so often in the Old Testament Edom should be taken as representative of all Israel's enemies.

31. As in chapter 11 and at Jr 31:31–34.

32. In the eyes of the nations Israel's degradation reflected upon Yahweh. What sort of a God was He if he could not control and protect His own people? Israel's rescue would demonstrate that He was a God of might, albeit one who acted out of holiness. In this way they would come not to ridicule but to revere Him, see also 39:21–29.

33. This prophecy is unique in depicting an attack on Israel after the inauguration of what is clearly the Messianic age. However it is not to be taken chronologically but as an allegory, shot through with symbolism, depicting the final triumph of good over evil and an assurance that in the fullness of time God will deliver His people from any foe however powerful and destroy evil for ever. Gog and Magog recur at Rv 20:8 where, in similar mode, they stand for the church's enemies ranged against her in the final days.

34. Ezekiel institutionalised the distinction between priests and the Levites in general. Because of past infidelities the Levites would be confined to acting as Temple servants e.g. guarding the gates and slaughtering the sacrificial victims. He confirmed what had been the case since Solomon's day, 1K 2:26–35, namely that the priesthood was vested in Zadok's descendants.

35. Occasionally Ezekiel's cultic prescriptions differ from the Pentateuch: e.g. compare Ezk 46:6 with Nb 28:11.

36. Ezekiel's vision points, in spirit if not in detail, and despite its inadequacies, to the Jerusalem of eternity, Rv 21:1 – 22:5.

Daniel

1. This expedition of Nebuchadnezzar's may be the one referred to at 2K 24:1.
2. They wanted to avoid any risk of violating the Lv dietary laws. Even meat from clean animals could be taboo if, as could well have been the case in Babylon, it had previously been offered to a pagan god.
3. Daniel reminds us of Joseph. Both were carried off as youths to a foreign land to attain high office at their captors' courts through their wisdom and ability to interpret dreams.
4. Exegetes usually take the four empires to be those of Babylon, the Medes, the Persians and Alexander the Great even though Media was never a separate empire apart from Persia. The feet of iron and clay signify the two parts of Alexander's empire that were of most significance to the Jews after his death, that is the Ptolemaic and Seleucid kingdoms of present day Egypt and Syria. A 'stone untouched by any hand' implies the absence of any human agency.

    Daniel is peculiar in that while 1:1 – 2:4a; 8:1 – 12:13 are written in Hebrew, like the rest of the Old Testament, 2:4b – 7:28 are in Aramaic. Chs 13 – 14, like all the deutero-canonical additions, are extant only in Greek.
5. 'Times' stands for an indefinite period. As used here and at 7:25 it means years.

    Daniel had no doubt that pride, as seen first in Nebuchadnezzar and later Antiochus Epiphanes, was the propellant that drives evil. Nebuchadnezzar had reason to be proud. His empire was the most civilised the world had yet seen and Babylon itself was a place of wonder. Unfortunately he forgot who made it possible and so succumbed to pride. So he had to learn that God is master of men's destinies and can humble even the greatest until they acknowledge Him.
6. Belshazzar's sin went beyond pride to contempt for God.
7. Daniel poses a number of historical problems. Darius the Mede is unknown to history. The appellation 'Mede' is unlikely in any case because Babylon fell to the Persian king Cyrus and he had conquered Media some years before. Among other difficulties we shall cite two. Firstly Belshazzar was the son of Nabonidus, the last Babylonian king, and not of Nebuchadnezzar as 5:11,18 state. Moreover he was never actually king himself although he did rule during his father's absence in voluntary retreat. Secondly there is no historical evidence for Nebuchadnezzar's affliction mentioned in ch 4. However the story could fit Nabonidus, so it may be that to make it more 'newsworthy' the author replaced Nabodinus by the better known Nebuchadnezzar. But of course none of this is important. The author's aim was to inculcate theology and hope not history and his narratives serve that end even if they do not always reflect exact historical truth.
8. Daniel's readers in Antiochus' day could hardly have failed to see parallels between their own trials and those suffered by their forebears in Babylon. Ch 1 would have taught them that even in the most difficult environment of a pagan court it is still possible to uphold the Law. They would readily have identified Nebuchadnezzar's golden statue in ch 3 with the statue of Zeus that Antiochus installed in the Temple, 2M 6:1–2. The story of Nebuchadnezzar's madness would have resonated with the popular belief that Antiochus was mad and fed hope that he too would be humbled by God just as Nebuchadnezzar had been. In Belshazzar's defiling of the Temple vessels they would have seen a parallel to Antiochus' pillaging of the Temple, 1M 1:20–24. Ch 6 would not only have inspired them to put their trust in God but brought home that there was nothing to be surprised at if some Jews collaborated with Antiochus, 1M 1:11. Daniel had also been plotted against.
9. To the ancients the stormy tossing sea would have conjured up visions of evil and primeval chaos and the brute strength of the beasts the malevolent power of paganism; both in sharp contrast with the heavenly visions that follow.

10. 'Three and a half times' means three and a half years, roughly the duration of Antiochus' persecution. Three and a half is half of the perfect number seven and was a symbol of evil. For Antiochus' attacks on the Jews' religion see 1M 1:41–64.

11. Whatever Daniel, writing under divine inspiration, may himself have understood by the enigmatic title 'son of man', we know from Jesus' own testimony, Mt 24:30; 26:64, that He is that Son of Man who is also Son of David and Son of God.

12. This is the first instance in the Bible of an angel being referred to by name.

13. Ex 29:38–42; Nb 28:4–8 decree that two sacrifices must be offered in perpetuity each day at dawn and twilight.

14. In other words for one thousand one hundred and fifty days, roughly the three and a half 'times' or years of 7:25.

15. It was believed that all nations had guardian angels who promoted their interests before God. The angelic struggles depicted here are therefore a reflection in the heavenly sphere of the strife between God's people and their oppressors on earth. Michael, one of the 'Chief Princes', 10:13, a great prince, 12:1, is the defender of God's people, 10:21b;12:1.

16. The statue of Zeus, 1M 1:54; 2M 6:2. Ch 11 gives added strength to the view that Daniel was composed in Antiochus' day. Nowhere else in Old Testament prophecy is there such a welter of minor and unnecessary detail.

17. For example it is not true that Antiochus considered himself greater than all the gods. His coins bore not his own imprint but that of the Greek god Zeus. Nor does the statement that he lacked respect for the gods of his fathers fit well. It was the Greek pantheon that he ordered the Jews to worship. He did not undertake a third campaign against Egypt as 11:42 suggests, nor die within the Holy Land as 11:45 implies but on campaign in Persia, 1M 6:1–16; 2M 9:1–28.

18. What may be termed the Book of Life in which human actions, good and bad, are recorded: Ex 32:32–33; Ps 40:8; 69:28; 139:16; Is 4:3; Dn 7:10; Ml 3:16; Lk 10:20; Rv 20:12.

19. Like the date of Jesus' Second Coming, which is known only to the Father, Mt 24:36. Attempts to explain verses 12, 13, where the suffering is predicted to last first twelve hundred and ninety and then thirteen hundred and thirty five days, have not been successful. The most likely explanation is that they are additions by scribes who, taking the passage to refer to the historical Antiochus Epiphanes, modified the original figures to make them conform with the actual duration of Antiochus' persecution once it was known.

Hosea

1. See 2:21–22, 4:1, 6:6. By faithful love Hosea means man's submission to the will of God and love of his fellow men as a reflection of God's love. By knowledge of God he means man's willing response to what God requires of him.

2. This passage defies neat analysis. Sometimes Hosea's private life with Gomer is to the fore as God uses it as a symbol of His own love for Israel while at other times God speaks directly of His relationship with Israel. The one is the image of the other as the focus alternates between the personal and the theological without it always being clear which is uppermost.

3. Favourable references to Judah at 1:7; 6:11; 12:1 are generally reckoned to have been added later after the fall of Samaria by disciples of Hosea who had emigrated to Judah. 'Judah' at 12:3 is thought to be an error in place of Israel.

4. These verses, with their abrupt change of mood, would come more naturally later as reinforcing 2:16–25. Day of Jezreel means the Day of Yahweh.

5. 'Seduce' is significant. It makes plain that it is Yahweh who takes the initiative.
6. Hosea saw all this happening on the Day of Yahweh, see vv 18,20,23.
7. As one might redeem a slave. Possibly Gomer fell into slavery after separation from Hosea and we have a foreshadowing of the way God would later 'buy' His people out of their slavery to sin.
8. For the shameful incident at Gibeah see Jg 19 – 21; for the sin of Baal-Peor see Nb 25:1–5; Gilgal probably refers to Saul's disobedience there culminating in the rejection of his kingship, 1S 13:8–15.
9. God is heart-stricken (in human terms) at the thought of losing Israel despite her faithlessness. In the event compassion and love quench the flame of anger so that, torn between justice and love, love proves the stronger.

Joel

1. Joel records God speaking at 2:12, 19–20, 25–27; 3:1–3; 4:1–8, 12–13, 17, 21; himself elsewhere.
2. Moses yearned for the bestowal of God's spirit, Nb 11:29. Ezekiel prophesied that God would give man a new spirit, Ezk 11:19; 36:26–27. Peter identified the fulfilment of Joel's prophecy with the miracle of Pentecost, Ac 2:16–21.

   In this second half of his book Joel is thinking in terms of the actual Day beginning with Christ's First Coming and concluding with His Second.

Amos

1. Either father and son sleeping with (say) the same servant girl or with the same temple prostitute. Amos's ire is further roused by worshippers in the Temple laying on clothes taken as pledges and by their drinking wine in God's house that had been acquired as fines.
2. Notice the masterly way Amos moves to his climax. Having carried his audience with him in condemning Israel's neighbours, he extends his tirade to their brothers in Judah and then, having roused their consciences, springs his trap, pointing the finger at Israel herself.
3. Bashan was a region in Transjordan renowned for its lush pastures and fat cattle.
4. Bethel and Gilgal were two of Israel's leading sanctuaries.
5. At first sight this doxology like the two others at 5:8–9; 9:5–6, seems to interrupt Amos's flow. However by highlighting God's boundless power all three augment His threats by leaving no doubt about His ability to carry them out.
6. For 'remnant' see Is appendix 3.
7. For Day of Yahweh see Is appendix 1.
8. Amos is not arguing for a purely ethical religion without cult but stressing that cult is meaningless without holiness. 'Beyond Damascus' is code for Assyria.
9. Amos makes no criticism of wealth as such, only how it is gained and its corrosive effect on character.

Obadiah

1. Ob 1b–9 resembles parts of Jr 49:7–22 though in a different order. There are also isolated parallels in Joel.
2. Edomites were evicted from their land between the fifth and third centuries first by Arab and then by Nabataean invaders. Some Edomites then settled in southern Judah in an area later known as Idumaea.

3. This refers to Nebuchadnezzar's capture of Jerusalem in 587. The vividness of the description suggests an eyewitness.

Micah

1. These prophecies were borne out by the fall of Samaria in 722, Sennacherib's invasion of Judah in 701 and Nebuchadnezzar's plunders of Jerusalem a century later.
2. This prophecy is virtually identical to Is 2:2–4.
3. Possibly a reference to the humiliation suffered by Hezekiah, king of Judah, during Sennacherib's invasion of 701.
4. Whose 'origins go back to the distant past' suggests that Micah had some supernatural figure in mind. Mt 2:6 confirms that this is a prophecy of Christ. In the following verse 'Yahweh will abandon them only until she who is in labour gives birth' implies that the birth will be delayed and that there will be a period of distress until it happens (as indeed there was until Christ was born).
5. The ultimate 'remnant', the Church, does indeed act as both dew to revivify and lion to warn.
6. In other words not empty mechanistic piety but a pure and loving heart.
7. The direction from which invaders usually came.

Nahum

1. An Egyptian city sacked by Assyria in 663.

Habakkuk

1. Chaldaeans is another name for Babylonians.
2. The germ of a theme developed by Paul in Romans.
3. The liturgical intent is shown by the three pauses and the instruction to the choirmaster at the end.

Zephaniah

1. Since these countries were west, east, south and north of Jerusalem it is likely that they were meant to illustrate the fate of God's enemies generally. Ethiopia really means Egypt which was ruled by an Ethiopian dynasty at the time.

Haggai

1. Zerubbabel was the grandson of Jehoiachin, head of the House of David and thus 'king-in-waiting'.
2. A signet ring bore its owner's mark and represented him and his authority. Through the veiled language he uses we can see that Haggai (mistakenly) saw Zerubbabel as God's elect on earth, the promised Messiah.

Zechariah

1. Yahweh's words were comforting because people were expecting Jerusalem's restoration to be accompanied by some dramatic upheaval and the Day of Yahweh, Hg 2:6,22. Without Yahweh's assurance they would therefore have been dismayed at the peaceful conditions reported by the horsemen.
2. This is chronologically the first appearance of 'Holy Land' in the Bible; see also 2M 1:7.

3. Satan's intervention is difficult to interpret. Perhaps Satan had been railing against Israel's sins being forgiven thereby prompting the angel's retort that it was a near thing: Jerusalem was like a 'brand snatched from the fire'.

4. Possibly the oil flowing from the trees (to service the lamps) indicates that God needs human assistance, represented here in the persons of Joshua and the Branch (the two olive trees) for His light to shine out in the world.

5. It is appropriate that wickedness is banished to Shinar, i.e. Babylon, the place where mankind's first organised revolt against God took place with the tower of Babel, Gn 11.

6. The north was the direction Israel's molesters usually came from.

7. Zechariah is following in the footsteps of Jeremiah who, at Jr 23:1–8; 33:14–18, prophesied that God would raise up a Branch from David's House who would rule in duo with a priest over a restored Israel. He saw Joshua filling the priestly office while, like Haggai, he looked upon Zerubbabel as the long-awaited Branch (this is borne out by his equating the restoration of the Temple with Zerubbabel at 4:6b–10 and with the Branch at 6:12–13). It is possible that the crowning ceremony at 6:9–11 originally named Zerubbabel and that Joshua's name was substituted later when hopes in Zerubbabel began to fade and political power passed to the priesthood.

8. The fast in the fifth month that prompted the question was probably a commemoration of the destruction of the Temple, Jr 52:12. The fast in the seventh month probably marked the assassination of Gedaliah, Jr 41:1–2, with those of the tenth and fourth months probably recalled the siege of Jerusalem and the breaching of her walls; 2K 25:1–4.

9. A prophecy possibly inspired by the campaigns of Alexander the Great.

10. The compensation for goring by an ox, Ex 21:32, and the same price as was paid for Jesus, Mt 26:14–16.

11. Foreshadowing the afflictions the Jews will suffer following their rejection of the good shepherd.

12. The one who was pierced and the scattering of the sheep are both seen in the Gospels as Messianic portents, Jn 19:37; Mt 26:30–31. Note the similarity between Yahweh striking His shepherd and crushing His servant, Is 53:6–10.

Malachi

1. Malachi may have been impressed by Persian religion.

2. Dt 7:1–4 forbade mixed marriages on the grounds that they would dilute dedication to Yahweh.

3. Tithes were a levy for the upkeep of the clergy, Lv appendix 3.

4. Jesus confirmed that Elijah, the messenger of 3:1, had indeed come before Him in the person of John the Baptist; Mt 11:10–14; 17:10–13. John was Elijah in the sense that he ministered with the spirit and power of Elijah.

Matthew

1. Of the four women Matthew mentions Tamar seduced her father-in-law Judah, Rahab was a Canaanite prostitute who helped with the capture of Jericho and Solomon's mother committed adultery with David. Only Ruth, another non-Jew, was a model of virtue. It seems that Matthew particularly wanted to highlight that the forebears of the Saviour of the world included both sinners and non-Jews.

2. Jesus is the Greek form of the Hebrew Joshua and means 'the Lord saves'.

3. Matthew is always keen to show how prophecy is fulfilled in Jesus. Here he links Jesus' birth to Isaiah's Immanuel prophecy, Is 7:14. See also 2:15, 17; 4:14; 8:17; 12:17; 13:15; 21:4; 26:31; 27:9.

4. John was an ascetic and prophet in the old style thus linking Jesus to the Old Testament traditions. Judaea was the Greek and Roman name for Judah. Repentance means renunciation of sin, regret for past conduct and turning to God to start a new life. Respecting Jewish sensitivities to the use of the divine name Matthew, alone among the four evangelists, uses 'Kingdom of Heaven' instead of 'Kingdom of God'.

5. That Jesus should have insisted on being baptised when He was sinless has troubled some Christians. However Jesus came in His humanity to identify with us and show us the Way and baptism is more than forgiveness of sins. It was to be the rite for entry into the Church that He would found and so here, as elsewhere, Jesus led by example.

6. Parallels with Moses and Israel abound. Like Moses and Israel, Jesus came out of Egypt. Jesus' birth like Moses' was accompanied by infanticide. Like Moses, Ex 34:28, Jesus fasted for forty days. After 'baptism' in the Sea the old Israel was tested in the wilderness for forty years and found wanting. After His baptism Jesus, the new Israel, was tested in the wilderness for forty days and emerged triumphant. Jesus is thus portrayed both as the new Israel and as a second Moses leading His people from the bondage of sin just as surely as Moses rescued the old Israel from slavery in Egypt.

7. Where the old Israel demanded bread and died in the wilderness Jesus denied Himself and lived.

8. Thereby fulfilling Isaiah's prophecy of the glory that awaited the northern region of Palestine, Is 8:23 – 9:1.

9. The meaning of 'illicit marriage' is unclear.

10. 'Turning the other cheek' does not imply pacifism or rule out self-defence. Jesus' thrust was on attitudes and, should our best efforts fail to elicit a suitable response, there may well be times when force becomes inevitable.

11. The petition for bread is not simply for ordinary food but for the bread of life.

12. Money can easily become an obsession that overrides the quest for God.

13. Jesus is not teaching abdication from worldly concerns, or denying foresight and industry, but underlining the need for proper priorities and trust in a God who already knows our needs and will provide the necessities of life.

14. See Pr note 1.

15. On Jesus cautioning the man to tell no one see Mk appendix 1.

16. Why did Jesus do it this way? Possibly to give an oblique hint of His divinity. But also, by forgiving the man's sins first, to demonstrate symbolically that spiritual health is the more fundamental. He was concerned to heal the whole man. It should not be inferred from this incident that physical ailments are due to sin. Jesus Himself refutes this, Jn 9:1–3, as does Job.

17. Matthew is called Levi in Mk and Lk.

18. This quotation from Hos 6:6 means that God prefers love and compassion to strict compliance with every formal requirement of the Law. To the Pharisees 'sinner' included every shade of misdemeanant from the truly morally degraded to those whose fault lay in no more than not observing every minor detail of the ceremonial Law.

19. The twelve are also named at Mk 3:16–19; Lk 6:13–16; Ac 1:13 with slight variations. 'Disciple' often means one of these Twelve but occasionally it means someone from the wider following Jesus attracted. The choice of twelve, after the twelve tribes, symbolises the start of a new reconstituted Israel of faith.

20. V 23, which says that they 'will not have gone round of the towns of Israel before the Son of Man comes' has occasioned much debate. It probably means that the preaching of the Gospel will barely be complete before Christ's Second Coming.

21. Jesus' low key approach seems to have caused even John to have doubts.

22. This was not a slight on John, simply recognition that membership of the Kingdom transcends any earthly existence. V 12 is an enigma to which we no longer have the key.

23. A yoke was a collar-shaped frame that enabled two animals to pull together as a team. Jesus is thus telling us that if we 'yoke' to Him He will be pulling alongside us and lightening the burden of our earthly pilgrimage.

24. The implication is that since Scripture did not condemn David, the Pharisees rigid interpretation of the Law cannot be correct. Even a custom of divine origin admits of exception. See 1S 21:2–7 with Lv 24:5–9.

25. While speaking against Jesus is excusable, blasphemy against the Holy Spirit is not. What this means is the stubborn and persistent refusal to entertain the Spirit's promptings, the deliberate quenching of conscience, the conscious choice of darkness over light, in short the refusal to admit the love and power of God. In this way, by his own free choice, by becoming so hardened that he wilfully rejects truth and refuses to heed God's promptings, a man can put himself outside the range of forgiveness because he is in effect deliberately shutting God out of his life.

26. Reference to brothers does not necessarily imply full brothers. In Jesus' day 'brothers' was often used to denote half-brothers, cousins or even more distant members of the family.

27. God will not act for blessing in the face of human rebellion.

28. This Herod, Herod Antipas, was the son of the Herod who was king of Judaea at the time of Jesus' birth.

29. Apart from not wanting to break his promise Herod was probably not sorry to see the end of John. He had been critical of him divorcing his wife to marry Herodias, his half-brother Philip's wife, while Philip was still living, Mk 6:17–29.

30. See Is 25:6; Mt 8:11; 26:29; Lk 22:30; Rv 19:9, and possibly Mt 22:2–14.

31. 'Little dogs' sounds harsh. But Jews spoke of gentiles as dogs and Jesus' use of the diminutive would have softened it.

32. Yeast was a symbol for evil. Also only a little was required to affect a whole batch of dough. Jesus was therefore making the point that the teaching of the Pharisees could lead many people astray. The fact that the disciples thought Jesus was referring to their being short of bread is a sad commentary on their perception, coming so soon after Jesus' feeding miracles.

33. This passage has varying interpretations. That by His reference to keys Jesus conferred some sort of authority on Peter is not disputed. Where opinions divide is whether this meant authority within the Church for administration, doctrine etc; whether it included forgiveness of sins; and whether whatever authority Peter was given applies to his successors too.

34. V 28 is difficult. Some think that Jesus was referring to His Second Coming and was mistaken. However in view of 24:36 this seems unlikely. More likely He meant either His transfiguration or resurrection.

35. The Gospel of faith usually leaves little room for clear signs but this was a time when something was needed to bolster morale. Peter, James and John formed an inner circle within the Twelve. Here they witness Jesus' glory as later they will witness His agony in Gethsemane and as earlier they were the only ones to witness the raising of Jairus' daughter, Mk 5:37. Moses and Elijah represent the Law and Prophetic tradition both of which Jesus fulfils.

36. Like little children in humility and childlike trust and in having no pretensions to status, power or pride.

37. The power given to Peter at 16:19 is here extended to the Church.

38. Riches can become an all-consuming passion that leave no room for love or neighbourly obligations. Thus abundance can fuel deficiency, and the most important deficiency of all, absence of God. The command to sell everything is not a universal requirement but one that fitted this particular case aimed at shattering the rich young man's covetousness. Abraham, Isaac, Jacob, David and Job were all rich men.

39. With their calling Jews would have expected better treatment than sinners and gentiles.

40. James was subsequently beheaded, Ac 12:2.

41. A word originally meaning 'please save' but which by now had simply become an acclamation.

42. The Herodians were supporters of the puppet Herodian dynasty that ruled Judaea on behalf of Rome. Jesus thus risked either acknowledging servitude to Rome and losing popular support or being charged with disloyalty to Rome.

43. Proselytes were gentiles who accepted Judaism in its entirety. They are to be distinguished from God fearers who accepted the main tenets of the Jewish faith, including attendance at the synagogue, but without subscribing to circumcision or the full panoply of the Law.

44. The Zechariah mentioned here is the one whose murder is reported at 2Ch 24:20–22. As 2Ch was the last book of the Jewish Canon the reference is thus to the first and last murders in the Old Testament.

45. Some see Zc 11:12.

46. Despite giving only the barest details Matthew manages to endow the preparations with a supernatural quality reminiscent of the arrangements for Jesus' entry into Jerusalem. Although the synoptics all indicate that this was the Passover meal John places it one day earlier, see Jn note 75.

47. Jesus links His death to life in the Kingdom symbolised by the idea of the Messianic banquet, see note 30.

48. The Israelites in servitude in Egypt were saved by the blood of a lamb and commemorated their deliverance in the Passover meal where lamb was eaten. The new Israel of Christ's Church is saved from slavery to sin through the blood of the Lamb of God, an event commemorated in the Eucharist where the Lamb of God is eaten.

49. Man earned death by asserting His will against God in the Garden of Eden. Jesus earned salvation by submitting His will to God in the Garden of Gethsemane.

50. Jn 18:10 identifies the assailant as Peter.

51. The Sanhedrin was the highest tribunal of the religious rulers within Judaism with the high priest at its head.

52. Only the Romans could authorise a death sentence.

53. Ac 1:15–20 gives an alternative account of Judas's death. Nothing highlights the religious leaders' hypocrisy so much as their dilemma about what to do with the silver Judas returned to them. They could not apply it to the Treasury as, being blood money, it would contravene the Law. But they could use it to get an innocent man put to death.

54. From Pilate's first question it is clear that the Sanhedrin's strategy was to portray Jesus as a political agitator who could threaten Roman rule. Arguments about Messiahship and blasphemy would have meant nothing to the Romans.

55. Perhaps the mob, seeing Jesus a prisoner of the Romans, now saw Him as an impostor.

56. Scourging meant flogging prisoners with leather whips laced with strips of metal or bone to weaken them and so alleviate some of the agony of crucifixion.

57. Little did they know that it was only by not saving Himself that He could save others.

58. Jesus was quoting Ps 22 which, after expressing trust in God during affliction, ends in vindication. The words convey the unimaginable sense of desolation Jesus must have felt on the Cross as, deserted by His friends and rejected by the people, God hid His face as, the sinner's substitute, He bore the sins of the world.

59. This was the curtain in the Temple that prevented access to God's inner sanctum. The way to God was now open to all.

60. This is best read as meaning that certain holy people were resurrected at the same time as Jesus thus making the point that people who died before Jesus benefit from His triumph every bit as much as those who come after.

61. According to Mk 15:43 Joseph was a member of the Sanhedrin.

62. The 'other Mary' was probably the Mary mother of James and Joseph of 27:56.

63. The failure to recognise Him immediately is common to almost all the risen Christ's post-resurrection appearances.

64. Jesus entrusts His disciples, and through them the Church, with the task previously entrusted to Israel at Sinai.

Mark

1. This is the only direct indication we have that any of Jesus' disciples were married.

2. The exorcism of unclean spirits is a clear demonstration of Jesus' power over evil. Noteworthy also is the way evil recognises its conqueror in Him.

3. More than the other evangelists Mark depicts a Jesus with human emotions. Here He speaks sternly, at 3:5 He is angry and grieved, at 8:12 He sighs profoundly, at 10:14 He is indignant. Matthew and Luke usually omit such observations.

4. This incident shows just how sour the old wine of Judaism had become. The man with the withered hand was merely a pawn in a plan to trap Jesus and when this failed thoughts turned to silencing Him.

5. It was no accident that Jesus chose twelve disciples, mirroring the twelve tribes of old. He was creating the new spiritual Israel of faith to replace the old unfaithful Israel of history that had signally failed in its mission to lead the world to God.

6. At 4:13 we have the first of several instances where Mark is critical of the disciples for their obtuseness and failure to understand. See also 6:52; 7:18; 8:14–21; 9:30–37; 10:35–45. Matthew and Luke sometimes but not always tone down such remarks. Compare Mt 13:51 (which refers back to Mt 13:18–50) with Mk 4:13, Mt 14:33 with Mk 6:52, Mt 17:23 with Mk 9:32.

7. Understanding is like a snowball. The greater it is, the more it grows. Let it stagnate and it will melt away.

8. This was a far cry from Jesus' usual call for secrecy but in this more remote area beyond the Jordan there would have been less danger than in Judaea of the miracle attracting the wrong sort of attention.

9. For the first time Jesus singles out Peter, James and John as a specially privileged Three within the Twelve. It is the same Three who will be with Jesus at His transfiguration and at Gethsemane.

10. Mark reports that Jesus could work no miracle in His home town. This is in contrast with Matthew's more reverential comment that He did not perform many miracles there. Luke omits mention of miracles altogether.

11. Possibly intended as a trial-run as part of their training.

12. Mark states that Herod had a great respect for John. Yet he still sacrificed him to satisfy the wife he had unlawfully married. He must have known that it was his wife who was behind her daughter's bizarre request.

13. A symbolic washing up to the elbows to remove defilement from contact with sinners, nothing to do with hygiene.

14. A son could declare that an asset such as property or money be considered 'Corban', i.e. devoted to God. As such it could no longer be passed on to support his parents. On the other hand he himself could live in the property or invest the money during his lifetime since it only reverted to God on his death.

15. Jesus is in effect declaring that all foods are clean.

16. Once our ears are open to God's word our tongues should be loosed to speak out about it.

'Making the deaf hear and the dumb speak' has echoes of Is 35:5 where it is part of a vision of Israel's glorious future. Its use here suggests that Jesus was indeed bringing the Kingdom of God in His wake.

17. To be ashamed of Christ is to deny Him in the hour of trial and take one's stand with the sinful world around. Jesus' followers need to know when to stand up and be counted.

18. God does not expect perfect faith all at once and he will help us deepen it, if we ask. The disciples' were unable to effect the cure because they forgot that the power Jesus had given them was not inherent but depended on God through prayer.

19. Mark's statement that it was not the season for figs fits awkwardly with Jesus' cursing of the tree. A possible explanation is that He was looking for an early immature crop that sometimes appeared before the leaves.

20. Following a revolt Jerusalem and the Temple were razed by the Romans in A.D. 70.

Mark may have combined two separate discourses. On the other hand the linkage would have seemed quite natural to Jews at the time. If God were to allow His Temple to be destroyed, how could the end of the world be far away?

21. V30, where Jesus says that all the things He has described will happen before His generation has passed away, is difficult. The most likely explanation is that that He was only referring to the events of A.D. 70.

22. See Lk note 27.

Luke

1. Luke addresses his Gospel to a certain Theophilus of whom nothing is known although by being addressed as 'your excellency' we may conclude he must have been a person of some standing.

2. Naming was a father's duty. When God took over the task it was a sign that something momentous was in the offing.

3. Ml 3:23 prophesied that Elijah would return before the Day of Yahweh.

4. It would seem from verse 62 that Zechariah was made deaf as well as mute.

5. Meaning 'God saves'.

6. See Lv 12:1–8; Ex 13:1, 11–16.

7. Luke uses the same quotation, Is 40:3–5, as Matthew and Mark to show that John was the forerunner to the expected Saviour but extends it by one line to bring out the universality of the salvation that Jesus offers.

8. Luke's genealogy differs from Matthew's. Apart from going back to Adam and being in reverse order, it contains a different and longer set of names. Various theories have been proposed to explain this. One suggests that as well as omitting generations Matthew traces the legal line of descent, Luke the physical. An example illustrates the principle. Joseph is listed as the son of Heli in Luke but of Jacob in Matthew. It is possible that Jacob died without leaving any children and that he had a brother Heli who then married his widow by whom he had a son Joseph. In that case Heli would be Joseph's actual father while under Jewish law Jacob would still have been regarded as his legal father. Dt 25:5 refers.

9. For similar wonders by Elijah and Elisha see 1K 17:17–24; 2 K 4:18–37.

10. There are no grounds for identifying the woman either with Mary of Magdala, 8:2, or Mary the sister of Martha, 10:39. Nor is there any reason to link the story with the anointment of Jesus at Bethany, Mt 26:6–13.

11. These women would witness Jesus' crucifixion 23:49, burial, 23:55, and resurrection, 24:1–11.

12. The Samaritans were descendants of survivors of the northern tribes who were left behind after the Assyrian deportation of 721, 2K 17:24–41. They intermarried with people from other parts of the Assyrian empire resulting in a mixed race that the Jews of the southern kingdom regarded as outside their heritage. They erected their own temple on Mt Gerizim although this was destroyed in 129 B.C. Like the Sadducees they only accepted the authority of the Pentateuch. Otherwise their religion differed little from mainstream Judaism and like the Jews they looked forward to a Messiah. The disdain that Jews and Samaritans felt for each other therefore sprang more from racial considerations than religious ones.

13. Seventy-two was the traditional number of gentile nations and so this mission foreshadowed the Gospel being taken to the whole world.

14. The washing would have been a ritual washing aimed at removing defilement from contact with gentiles and sinners rather than anything to do with hygiene.

15. Walking on a tomb made a person unclean, Nb 19:16.

16. See Mt note 25.

17. From verse 41 it would seem that Jesus had Church leaders in mind although the point is valid more widely.

18. Jesus is not advocating a clinging 'Uriah Heep' type humility nor denying self-promotion when it is done for the right reasons. As with much of His teaching a balance has to be struck. But what He emphatically condemns is the overweening sort of pride that exalts self before all else.

19. In saying that disciples must 'hate' their father, mother etc. Jesus meant that they must take second place to God.

20. The Romans deputed the task of collecting taxes in a locality to the highest bidder. Their was no salary, the appointee being free to demand more than the authorities required to leave a surplus for himself. It was therefore a job ready made for extortionists, which is why tax collectors were regarded as out and out sinners.

21. Serving God does not have to be high profile. Every missionary needs backup support.

22. By the Romans in A.D. 70.

23. According to Rm 11:11–32, Israel will eventually be converted.

24. Earlier, 9:3, 10:4, Jesus had told his disciples to rely on God's providence. Now it is different. The world is a hostile place. Unfortunately the disciples took Jesus' figurative language on swords literally.

25. To most onlookers Jesus was dying and His promises and teaching being proved hollow. This is therefore an outstanding example of how faith saves and that it is never too late to turn to God.

26. Although the four evangelists agree on the cardinal facts of what happened on Easter morning they differ on details. While some divergencies are only to be expected when different witnesses write up an event many years later, they are at the same time eloquent testimony to the genuineness of the accounts. It would have been so easy for editors to have harmonised the differences if there had been any intent to fabricate evidence of the resurrection.

27. Jesus' risen body was clearly modified in some way and not subject to the known laws of nature. He could materialise and vanish at will. However there is no doubting its

physical nature. He bore the scars of His crucifixion, could eat and be touched, and was recognisable although, in some strange way, not always immediately.

28. Luke seems to have condensed what actually took place over a longer period. Ac 1:1–11 tells us that the ascension took place forty days after the resurrection.

John

1. Jesus is the light that illumines the way to life as children of God, a light that evil can never dim.

2. A glory revealed in the moral splendour of His life and atoning death.

3. Only at verse 17 does John identify the Word with Jesus.

   In grace Jesus supplements the Law's emphasis on obedience and justice with His message of love and mercy. In becoming man and living on earth He conveyed the truth.

4. The Jews expected that Elijah would come again in advance of the Christ, Ml 3:23, and Jesus confirmed that this had indeed happened with John the Baptist, Mt 17:9–13. They also awaited a Prophet who would be a second lawgiver like Moses, Dt 18:14–19, a role that Jesus did indeed assimilate into His Messiahship.

5. These words recall the Passover lamb that commemorated Israel's release from slavery, Ex 12:1–14, and resonate with Is 53:11, 'My Servant will justify many by taking their guilt on Himself'.

6. An echo of Jacob's dream, Gn 28:12. The Son of Man would be the 'ladder' linking heaven and earth.

   Nathanael is not named as a disciple in the Synoptic Gospels but is commonly assumed to be Bartholomew whose name follows Philip's in their lists. The unnamed disciple may have been John, the author of the Gospel. The Synoptics locate the call of the first disciples in Galilee rather than 'beyond the Jordan' as John does.

7. Some see this miracle as symbolic: Jesus replacing the water of Judaism with the rich new wine of the Gospel. An abundance of wine had long been seen as a sign of the Messianic age, Am 9:13.

8. According to John, Jesus was in Jerusalem for three Passovers, 2:13, 6:4; 13:1. The Synoptic Gospels mention only one. John also differs in placing the cleansing of the Temple at the beginning of Jesus' ministry rather than at the end. However he may have deliberately transposed the incident to highlight the decadence in the Jews' religious life that Jesus was up against right from the start.

9. The sale of animals to pilgrims who needed them for sacrifice, and changing money into the currency needed to pay Temple dues, were not in themselves improper activities. However they were open to abuse through profiteering and so, along with the inevitable hubbub of commercial activity, unsuited to a hallowed place.

10. John notes that Jesus was referring to His eventual resurrection and the 'Temple' of His Body, the Church, that would eventually come to replace the Temple building as the dwelling for God's presence. The expulsion of the animals may also be seen to symbolise the coming replacement of animal sacrifice by Jesus' own perfect sacrifice.

11. Nicodemus probably came at night to avoid the opprobrium of his peers. Later, 7:50–52, he spoke out openly on Jesus' behalf and later still assisted at His burial, 19:39

12. Already, in talking of being 'lifted up', Jesus is conscious of the shadow of the Cross.

    'Believing in Christ' as the way to eternal life recurs again and again in John. It means not intellectual assent but complete trust in Christ to direct our lives with the confidence that He will save us. Nothing else can; not money nor cleverness nor good deeds; nothing. Salvation depends upon believing rather than doing.

13. Along with most commentators we take 3:16–21, 31–36 as John's reflections on what he has just reported.

14. John does not see judgement as something that takes place at the end of time before a divine tribunal. It belongs to the present. Men judge themselves according to whether they declare for or against the light.

15. It would appear that this was Mt Gerizim, see Lk note 12.

16. Worship should be led by the Spirit and grounded in the truth of God's revelation in Christ.

17. This is the clearest instance of Jesus openly confessing His Messiahship; but see also 9:35–37; 10:25.

18. The harvest of souls. The fields were white with the robes of the Samaritans streaming across the fields to hear Him.

19. By persisting in his request, and setting out for home on the strength of Jesus' word without any other evidence that his son would be cured, the official showed that he had the faith Jesus was looking for.

20. It would be wrong to infer from this that the man's ailment was due to sin. Rather it should be read at face value. Jesus was urging him to repent lest he went on to imperil his spiritual health.

21. Although the rabbis held that God rested on the seventh day after His act of creation, they also taught that He continued working every day, including Sabbaths, to sustain His creation.

22. This text needs care. 'The dead' usually means the physically dead but at verse 25 it refers to the spiritually dead. Again verses 28,29 allude to the traditional idea of a judgement at the end of time whereas verse 24 implies that eternal life begins without judgement the moment one accepts Jesus as Saviour. However there is no contradiction. For believers, judgement after death will only confirm what has already taken place in their lives and need hold no terrors.

23. Jesus had in mind Moses' prophesy that God would raise up a prophet like himself, Dt 18:14–19.

24. A kingdom of this world was one of the temptations to which Jesus was exposed by the devil, Mt 4:8–11.

   In mentioning that the Jewish Passover was near, 6:4, John may have been intending to lead his readers into seeing it as the precursor to the Christian Eucharist which this miracle and Jesus' subsequent discourse lead up to.

25. The previous day's miracle was apparently not enough. Perhaps they were angling for Jesus to provide a regular supply of food as had happened with the manna.

26. Jesus is the life-giving bread of the new age as manna was of the old.

27. He would not allow anyone who continued to believe to be overcome by Satan and lost.

28. 'Jews', in contexts like this, is virtually emblematic of disbelief. It generally means the religious leaders acting out of malice rather than the ordinary people.

29. The same point, that all who come to believe in Christ are 'drawn' by God or 'given' by God, is made at 6:37,39,65. This does not imply predestination. What it may mean is that belief begins with God awakening and prompting the heart, through the Scriptures and in other ways, and that those who exercise their free will and respond are then led to Christ. Belief would thus be the combination of an initial enabling gift from God followed by a faith whose nature is none the less voluntary by needing support in line with the 'Lord, I believe; please help my unbelief' of Mk 9:24. See Rm appendix 2.

30. Meaning that only He had the authority and knowledge to speak about God.

31. To be told to drink His blood seemed to contravene one of the Law's strictest prohibitions, not to drink blood, Lv 7:26–27; 17:10–14. Little did his opponents realise that by ordering them to do just that Jesus was in fact acting in complete accord with the Law, for Lv 17:11 goes on to explain that the reason for not drinking blood is because 'blood is what expiates for a life' and this is exactly what Jesus' blood would accomplish.

    Jesus' satisfaction of the physical hunger of the multitude with bread the day before was a pointer to the way the 'bread' of His body would fill their spiritual needs. And just as plenty of bread remained after the people had eaten their fill, 6:13, so Jesus' life-giving bread never runs out.

32. Jesus' brothers, probably meaning cousins or near relations, had little understanding of His aims and wanted Him to use the festival to enhance His reputation through miracles and healings. But to be seen as a wonder-worker was not Jesus' way. He wanted to capture hearts and minds. Moreover He knew that the time had not yet come for a confrontation with the authorities and so decided to go up quietly on His own.

33. Jesus was evidently referring to His healing at the pool of Bethesda, 5:1–18.

34. The Jews knew that the Messiah would be born in Bethlehem, Mi 5:1, but expected that He would remain concealed until He openly and unmistakeably revealed Himself.

35. Jesus' hour had not yet come and human agency was impotent to press it. As at 5:18; 7:2–9, 44; 8:20,59; 10:39; 11:53 John conveys a sense of destiny.

36. With echoes of Ex 17:1–7; Is 55:1. Jesus had first used it at 4:10–14 in conversation with the Samaritan woman.

37. The word 'glorified' occurs frequently in John. In a general sense it means the revelation of God's character, presence or power. In particular it is used of Jesus' exaltation, resurrection and ascension.

38. While it is widely agreed that this passage was not written by John it has ancient attestation and there are no grounds for doubting its authenticity.

39. Lv 20:10; Dt 22:22 stipulated the death penalty for adultery but 18:31 confirms that the Jews were not empowered by the Romans to impose a capital sentence on their own authority.

40. See Is 49:6; 60:19.

41. From the grip of sin.

42. What mattered was not physical descent from Abraham but spiritual.

43. The way this discourse develops, at least from 8:37, sits uncomfortably with the statement at 8:31 that it was delivered to new believers. Perhaps hecklers at 8:33, 39, 41 etc. threw it off course.

44. Abraham's life was inspired by God's promise that his seed would be the channel for bringing blessings to all mankind, Gn 12:3. In saying that Abraham rejoiced to see 'My Day' Jesus was claiming to be the means for bringing that about. Indeed in speaking of 'My' Day (not 'the' Day) Jesus was giving another hint of His divinity by assimilating to Himself the Old Testament Day of Yahweh, the Day when God would intervene decisively in human affairs, see Is appendix 1.

45. 'I am' or 'I am He', as at 8:24, 28, 58 is God's name as revealed to Moses, Ex 3:14, and when He uses it Jesus is identifying Himself quite unambiguously with Israel's God of the Old Testament.

46. Genesis teaches that suffering does result from sin at the cosmic level. But this does not carry over to a direct causal relationship at the individual level as Job also makes clear.

47. At night sheep were gathered into pens to protect them from thieves. The shepherd would often lie across the entrance so that no one could get in without his knowledge. In this

way he functioned as a gate and was the sole arbiter of who got in and who was excluded. In the allegory bandits and hired hands represent upstart Messiahs, fake prophets and false teachers. The role of the gatekeeper is unclear. The idea of a shepherd to lead Israel in the Messianic age goes back to Ezk 34 where the shepherd is also presented as a second David. In laying claim to be both the good shepherd and the lone gate that leads to the rich pastures of eternal life Jesus was again indicating that He was the Messiah.

48. The other folds hold the gentiles who, with the sheep in the Jewish fold, form one flock under the one shepherd.

49. A trick question. 'No' would discredit Him while 'Yes' could lead to denunciation to the Romans as a political agitator.

The Feast of Dedication commemorated the re-dedication of the Temple by Judas Maccabaeus after the sacrilege of Antiochus Epiphanes, 2M 10:1–8. It took place in the winter some two to three months after the autumnal Feast of Shelters which was the setting for the preceding events, 7:1 – 10:21.

50. Ps 82:6 refers to certain judges as gods because they acted as God's agents.

51. The sisters feature at Lk 10:38–42 and again at Jn 12:1–11 and it is to this that 11:2 refers.

52. It is not the same occasion as Lk 7:36–50. Though there are similarities, such as the anointess wiping Jesus' feet with her hair, these are more than outweighed by the many differences.

53. We must recognise the selfish striving for advantage and pleasure in this world as the destructive impermanent things they are and turn instead to the eternal values of love and justice espoused by Jesus.

54. Jesus had already glorified God with His teaching and healing. His atoning death would soon do so again by showing the unimaginable depths of God's love.

55. Judgement was coming since with God's supreme revelation people would have to elect either to be for Him or against Him. 'Lifted up' has an extended meaning here: not just Jesus' crucifixion but also His resurrection and ascension. Jesus' exorcisms of demons and evil spirits reported in the Synoptic Gospels bear eloquent testimony to the victory over evil He speaks of here.

56. On 12:40 see Is note 3.

57. The impetuous Peter, missing the symbolism, offered his hands and head to be washed as well as his feet. But what Jesus had in mind was the cleansing from sin that would be available to all through His conquest of evil on the Cross.

At 13:23 we have the first reference to 'the disciple whom Jesus loved' or 'the beloved disciple'. Other instances occur at 19:26; 20:2; 21:7,20. Together with 18:15; 19:35 the references are most likely to the apostle John himself.

58. Jesus, and through Him the Father, would shortly be glorified in His death, resurrection and ascension.

59. This new commandment demands a love to match Christ's own, a love unto death.

60. An allusion to Peter's own martyrdom.

61. Of all the definitions of heaven none is better than 'to be where He is'.

62. Jesus is the Way because He reveals the one true God. He is Truth because He is the answer to the riddle of life. He is life because those who believe will live forever. However although we can only be saved through Jesus, we cannot say that only those who explicitly know Him will be saved.

63. Energised by the Spirit Jesus' followers would produce great works like taking the Gospel to the entire world. To ask 'in Jesus' name' is to pray in complete faith for something that is in full accord with His nature and will.

64. *Paraclete* is a Greek word meaning 'counsellor', 'advocate' or 'supporter'. As the Holy Spirit it is the very presence of God dwelling in our hearts. In the Old Testament the Spirit empowered chosen individuals for specific tasks. But since Pentecost, Ac 2:1–13, His power is available for all believers to draw upon.

65. The peace of total trust in God.

66. In saying 'the Father is greater than I' Jesus was speaking from within the limitations of His humanity wherein He had been sent by the Father to perform His will, 3:17; 5:30; 12:49; 14:10. There is therefore no conflict with texts like 1:1; 8:24; 10:30 which are written from the heavenly perspective in which Jesus and the Father are one.

67. Not until 18:1 in fact. Some maintain that chs 15–17 are misplaced or that their words were spoken en route but there may have been some lingering until they were all ready to leave the supper room.

68. Jesus called Himself the true vine in contrast to the prophets' portrayal of Israel as a fruitless vine, Is 5:1–7; Ezk 15:1–5.

69. It is clear from the context and especially 15:9–14 that 'fruit' is to be interpreted as a life of love and obedience.

70. In this case 'fruit' means proclaiming the Gospel.

71. Because of the enlightenment the resurrection would bring and the guidance of the Holy Spirit.

72. United with Jesus in faith and love, and praying in His name, their prayers would be received as if from Jesus Himself.

73. Not simply peace in the midst of conflict but the inward peace that can only come from God.

74. Eternal life is described as entering into a personal relationship: to know the one true God and Jesus Christ.

75. Pilate's own future would have been in jeopardy if his superiors in Rome heard that he had released a dissident claiming to be king. It was here that Pilate voiced his two famous witticisms: 'Truth? What is that?' and 'Behold the man'.

At 19:14 John asserts that Jesus was condemned and hence crucified on the morning of the day during which the Passover meal was prepared implying that the Last Supper was held twenty four hours before the Passover meal would have been eaten. The Synoptic tradition on the other hand maintains that the Last Supper was the Passover meal, Mk 14:12; Lk 22:7. Many theories have been proposed to resolve this discrepancy, including confusion over different calendars that were in use at the time, but none has gained wide acceptance. It is possible that Jesus, knowing how events were shaping, arranged to observe the Passover a day in advance in order that Christ, the Lamb of God who was to save the new Israel from sin, would have been sacrificed at the very hour when the Passover lambs that commemorated old Israel's escape from tyranny were being slain in the Temple.

76. Matthew and Mark record that there were women watching from afar but do not mention Jesus' mother.

77. Breaking the legs of men being crucified was usually an act of mercy to induce death. Here haste was the motivation. The bodies could not be left hanging because that evening was the start of an especially solemn Sabbath, one that coincided with the Passover, Dt 21:23 refers.

Just as it was not permitted to break the bones of Passover lambs, Ex 12:46, so it was with Jesus, the Lamb of God. The piercing fulfilled a prophecy by Zechariah, Zc 12:10. The blood from Jesus' side can be seen as symbolising His atoning sacrifice and the Eucharist and the water the coming of the Spirit with Baptism.

78. Like Adam the first-born of the old creation, Jesus, the first-born of the new creation, first appears in a garden.

79. 'Cling', after all, implies a prolonged holding rather than a mere greeting.
80. We may compare Jesus' breathing the Holy Spirit with God breathing life into the first man, Gn 2:7.

Acts of the Apostles

1. The apostles still saw the kingdom as the earthly restoration of David's dynasty. Only after they had received the Holy Spirit were their eyes opened.
2. The angels' words imply that Jesus would return in due course but none the sooner for their standing and staring! There was work to be done so let them get on with it. Time must not be wasted in speculation about the *parousia*, the Second Coming. Jesus' own riposte had similar overtones.
3. Many take 'brothers' in relation to Jesus to mean close relatives, cousins perhaps. In other contexts 'brothers' has the connotation of fellow Christian disciples. This is the last time Mary, the mother of Jesus, is mentioned in the New Testament.
4. Mt 27:3–10 gives a different but equally ignominious account of Judas' death.
5. Pentecost was the Greek name for the ancient Festival of Weeks which was celebrated fifty days after the Passover, Lv 23:15. By now it also commemorated the giving of the Law at Sinai. Luke sees Pentecost, which came fifty days after the Christian 'Passover' of Crucifixion and Resurrection, as heralding a new era wherein it is no longer the Law but the Spirit that drives believers.
6. Babel reversed. For proselytes see Mt note 43.
7. In a nutshell Peter's argument is this. In his psalms David foretold that the Christ would be both raised from the dead and exalted. Both these things happened to Jesus. He fits the facts. Therefore Jesus is the Christ.
8. These early Christians were still practising Jews. Jews who also happened to accept Jesus as the Messiah.
9. We are not told what it was in Stephen's preaching that so antagonised his compatriots but it would appear from his speech in ch 7 that he was starting to tread the path that Paul would later blazon into a highway by asserting the supremacy of Christ and playing down the significance of the Holy Land and the Temple.
10. It looks as if Stephen's speech was cut short as the court rose against him in fury to carry out what was more a lynching than a judicial sentence. As the Jews had earlier rejected Christ so now they were turning their backs on Christianity.
11. Most commentators believe that the persecution was directed mainly against the Hellenist Christians. If the non Hellenists were forced to flee as well it is hardly likely that the apostles would have been exempt. Whatever its scope the persecution was providential in that it scattered the seeds of the new faith far and wide.
12. Saul's conversion is recounted twice more in Acts at 22:1–21; 26:9–23. Christians often spoke of their belief as the 'Way'.
13. Leather-tanning was regarded as an unclean profession so it is a sign of Peter's eyes being opened that he was prepared to lodge with a man engaged in such a business.
14. On God-fearers see Mt note 43.
15. This is the first 'pure' gentile conversion we know of. The Samaritans were partly of Jewish origin and still obeyed the Law. The Ethiopian courtier had been on pilgrimage to Jerusalem and was probably a Jewish proselyte.
16. Barnabas was a happy choice. As a Cypriot, 4:36, he would have been less parochial than his colleagues from Palestine. Antioch, a cosmopolitan city of half a million inhabitants, was the third city of the empire after Rome and Alexandria and, with its nearby port where European and Asiatic met, an ideal springboard for the spread of the Gospel.

17. Both James, Jesus' brother, and John Mark, a cousin of Barnabas, Col 4:10, feature again later on. This is the same John Mark that tradition names as author of the second Gospel.
18. Hereon Luke uses the Roman 'Paul' in favour of the Hebrew 'Saul'.
19. 'Devout converts' is an ambiguous term which may refer to proselytes or God-fearers or both.
20. Paul's policy was to appeal to the Jews first and only after they rebuffed him, as happened time and again because of his insistence on Christ as the sole source of salvation, to turn to the gentiles, 13:46–48; 18:5–8.
21. After the rough treatment Paul and Barnabas encountered on their outward journey it speaks volumes for their pluck that they returned home the same way to put fresh heart in the young churches they had founded.
22. This is the last appearance of Peter as an active participant and of the apostles as a body. The James who speaks shortly was Jesus' brother who now seems to have become the leader of the mother church. He must be distinguished from the James who was killed by Herod at 12:1 and who was one of the Twelve.
23. Gentile converts were not to be compelled to be circumcised and were to be free from the Law and were merely asked, as a courtesy in effect, to refrain from acts that Jews would find especially objectionable and which would therefore otherwise impede good relations.
24. After the recent debate it may seem odd that Paul should have had Timothy circumcised. But Timothy's mother was Jewish and so in Jewish law he was a Jew despite having a Greek father. As such Paul was probably keen not to flout Jewish scruples and give the impression that being a good Christian meant being a bad Jew.
25. Ac 16:11–17 is the first of the 'we' passages that imply Luke himself was present. The others are 20:5 – 21:18; 27:1 – 28:16.
26. It was unlawful for Jews to proselytise Romans.
27. We learn here that Paul and Silas were both Roman citizens for whom flogging was unlawful. The church at Philippi was founded on a business woman, a fortune-teller and a gaoler!
28. Achaia was a region covering much of Greece south of Macedonia and including the gulf of Corinth.
29. On speaking with tongues see 1Co 14 and 1Co appendix 1.
30. Diana (or Artemis) was a fertility goddess.
31. Luke's presence is evidenced by the start of the second 'we' passage at 20:6.
32. Paul delighted in always earning his keep and never having to rely on the support to which the missionary was traditionally entitled, Ga 6:6; 2 Th 3:7–9. He was determined never to be a burden and always practised a trade, Ac 18:3; 1Co 4:12; 1Th 2:9; 2Th 3:7–9. The only exception was with the Philippians from whom he did accept money, 2Co 11:9; Ph 4:10–18.
33. A saying Paul attributed to Jesus although it is not found in the Gospels.
34. Although Paul taught that it was faith in Jesus and not observance of the Law that led to salvation he did not seek to dissuade Jews from following the Law provided they also accepted the primacy of Christ.
35. The vision is the most important difference between this account of Paul's conversion and that at 9:1–19. It presumably happened during his first visit to Jerusalem after his conversion, 9:26–30.
36. Paul was confident of the Roman judicial system as it would be applied in Rome but feared that a local trial might well see the inexperienced Festus bending over backwards to appease the Jews.

Romans

1. Salvation means being made fit to share God's life in eternity. Faith in Christ means total trust in His promises with people admitting their insufficiencies and handing the direction of their lives over to Him. It is deeper and far removed from mere intellectual assent. The reader may sometimes see references to God's saving justice or simply His justice, justness or righteousness. These are all terms meaning God's way of restoring harmony between Himself and fallen man, getting mankind in the right relationship with Himself to permit his salvation.

2. Paul follows the custom of the day in beginning his epistles with his own name, the recipient's and a greeting but often, as here, extends the conventional formula with thanksgiving, prayer and doctrinal thoughts.

3. Greeks means gentiles.

4. Men have free will and can do as they please. But in the end wilful rejection of God reaps its own harvest. That is what Paul means by saying 'God has abandoned them'.

5. The Old Testament Day of Yahweh, now the Day of Judgement.

6. Circumcision, the seal of the covenant, Gn 17:1–14, was seen by the Jews as marking God's favour towards them.

7. God's justness is shown in that sin deserves punishment, and punishment there duly was: borne by Christ on the Cross. God held His hand over past sins in the sense that Christ's atoning sacrifice when it came would cover all sins, those committed before His time as well as those during and after.

8. We cannot alter our status before God by ourselves. Salvation is not about achieving but believing.

9. The Law makes people conscious of sin and thus their need for God and a Redeemer.

10. It is because suffering deepens character and hence trust in God that Paul can speak of it generating hope.

11. The risen Christ will sustain us after we have been justified and not allow us to slip back.

12. Sin multiplied because the Law increased awareness of it and so made its fruits more tempting.

13. Bonded to Christ we have a new spiritual vitality. We are reminded of Jn 3:3–8, being reborn through water and the Spirit.

14. Paul often speaks of being 'in Christ' meaning a Christian so welded to Him that Christ's experiences in this life become his own. Christ's death for sin is his, the death of the 'old man'. Christ's resurrection is his own rising to a new life, the 'new man', empowered by the Spirit. Likewise Christ's ascension to heaven is his own because his eternal destiny is assured.

15. The Spirit gives the person in faith-union with Christ the power to live righteously. Previously, ruled by his disordered nature, he was unresponsive to God. Now he is transformed. God's commands become God's enablings. What he 'ought' to do becomes what he 'wants' to do. The key event in our lives is not physical death but the moment we accept Christ. Thereon we are immortal by virtue of the Spirit living in us and life after death is a continuation of our life on earth in Christ.

16. The material world was also deformed as a result of man's fall, Gn 3:17. Like the human body it too is destined to be restored to its original perfection, Is 65:17; Mt 19:28; Rv 21:1.

17. Paul is saying that 'Israel', meaning God's people and the inheritors of His promises, has never meant the physical descendants of Abraham but an 'Israel' determined by God.

18. From here until 11:36 when Paul talks of Israel he means the stubborn unbelieving Jews.

19. The 'all' in 'all Israel' and 'show mercy to all' has led some to conclude that Paul was teaching that all mankind will be saved. This is certainly a possible interpretation. On the other hand 'all' could be read in the sense of 'Israel as a whole' or 'all except those who refuse to accept Christ and thus exclude themselves.' So no conclusions can safely be drawn.

20. In short respect conscience and do not sow discord over unessentials.

21. Neither Acts nor Paul's own writings indicate when he visited Illyria but it is most likely to have been on his third missionary journey after leaving Macedonia for Achaia, Ac 20:1–2.

1 Corinthians

1. Nothing is known of Chloe.

2. These factions seem not to have reflected doctrinal differences but to have arisen from people identifying with a particular teacher much as Greeks tended to attach themselves to philosophical schools or rabbis to particular scholars. We know that Apollos followed Paul's pioneering ministry in Corinth and his eloquence he may well have attracted a following, Ac 18:24 – 19:1. For all his other strengths Paul does not seem to have been a particularly polished speaker, 2Co 10:10, although he would obviously have had supporters as founder of the church in Corinth. Cephas was the Aramaic name for Peter. However it does not necessarily follow that Peter visited Corinth because it would have been natural for him to have had adherents among the Jewish Christians anyway. The Christ sect may have been those who realised that the true faith left no room for attachment to anyone else.

3. Nowhere does Paul condemn the genuine open-minded pursuit of knowledge and wisdom but rather the state of mind that leads to intellectual smugness and arrogance and a 'cleverer than thou' attitude that leaves no room for God.

4. Paul has in mind imperfect yet still dedicated teachers.

5. The power of the Spirit reigning in their lives.

6. Regarding the earlier letter see 2Co appendix 2.

7. There seems to have been a view that since it is permissible to indulge the appetite for food there need be no restraint on other physical desires. The idea of Christians as members of Christ's Body is developed in ch 12.

8. Paul alludes to the Corinthians' letter at 7:1, 25; 8:1; 12:1, 16:1.

9. Paul may have felt that the last days were imminent and that preparing for the end of this world must therefore take precedence over everything else. Alternatively he may have foreseen (as actually happened) a period of widespread persecution which made it all the more important for people to concentrate on proclaiming the Gospel.

10. This did not mean compromising his Christian beliefs but that where no real principle was at stake he would steer clear of positions that might make the task of conversion all the more difficult.

11. Paul's is the earliest of all the accounts of the Eucharist.

12. The Corinthians set great store by speaking in tongues, a gift that Paul twice places last, vv 28, 30, hinting that there were more important gifts, a theme he develops in ch 14.

13. Prophecy and tongues would have no purpose in the perfection of heaven and the presence of God.

14. Prophecy in this context means spreading God's word through preaching and teaching.

15. That is, testing them against Scripture. The early Church quite clearly had no formal ministry or settled order of service.

16. This seems to be at variance with 11:5 where Paul refers to women prophesying. A possible explanation is that he was forbidding women commenting aloud on what others were saying. The proper place for that was at home, v35. Corinthian society never allowed women to confront men in public so to have permitted it in church could have led to tensions.

17. Paul is ironically alluding to the Corinthians' reluctance to accept his teaching.

18. It is unclear what this was. Possibly a proxy baptism for relatives or friends who died unbaptised.

19. Paul is arguing that God is able to fashion His material in many different ways to accomplish His aims.

20. By a spiritual body Paul means an imperishable body designed for eternal life with God. It does not imply disembodiment. Jesus' resurrected body was no longer subject to the laws of physics but it was real nonetheless.

21. Timothy's journey referred to here must be the one mentioned at 4:17; Ac 19:22.

2 Corinthians

1. Paul must have heard of this when Titus met him in Macedonia, 7:5–7.

2. The narrative is resumed at 7:5.

3. Unreasonable in reflecting God's stringent demands; reasonable in trying to get them to accept Christ.

4. It is not our fault, Paul is saying, if you do not respond.

5. It is commonly held that 6:14 – 7:1 is out of context and once formed part of a letter to the Corinthians that has not come down to us and which Paul refers to at 1Co 5:9–13, see appendix 1. Certainly 7:2 seems to follow on smoothly from 6:13.

6. This was the Corinthians' reaction to his 'severe' letter.

7. The poor of the mother church in Jerusalem.

8. Corinth was the capital of the province of Achaia. Titus had already been involved with the collection in some way, 8:6.

9. He hopes the Corinthians will have dealt with the trouble-makers themselves.

10. Greece was noted for its orators so it is quite possible that Paul did not measure up to some of the Corinthians' expectations in that regard. If so he was in the good company of both Moses and Jeremiah, Ex 4:10–12; Jr 1:6.

11. A sarcastic reference to the trouble-makers. It seems from v 22 that they were Jewish Christians but we know no more.

12. Greek rhetoricians did charge a fee and Paul's opponents probably argued that the fact that he did not (implying that he could not) proved that he was second rate.

13. The strong are tempted to go their own way. The weak, those who know their limitations, look to God to lead them. Acceptance of weakness therefore opens the door for divine power to take the lead.

   We do not know what Paul's affliction was. Malaria, epilepsy and an eye problem have all been surmised.

14. Paul is answering insinuations that he was embezzling some of the money that had been collected for the poor. At 8:18–21 we saw how he had tried to forestall this calumny.

Galatians

1. Paul was reacting to accusations that he tried to ingratiate himself with potential converts by telling them that they did not need to observe the Law. Speaking so plainly now should leave no doubt where he really stood.

2. 'Apostle' gradually came to be used of Church leaders generally but, apart from Ac 14:4, 14, the Gospels and Ac restrict it to the Twelve. However Paul was always keen to assert that he too was an apostle like them, called by God in his own right, Rm 1:1; 11:13; 1Co 1:1; Ga 1:1. Like them he had seen and been commissioned by the risen Lord, Ac 22:21;

26:16; 1Co 9:1–2. Part of his opponents' charge against him was that he was not a *bona fide* apostle.

3. In practice the distinction was more geographical than racial. Paul always tried to approach the Jews first on his missions outside Palestine while Peter, after the conversion of Cornelius, could hardly ignore gentiles within Palestine.

4. The poor of the Jerusalem mother church, see 2Co appendix 2.

5. What was at stake was nothing less than the risk of the Christian community splitting into two factions that refused to eat together and which logically therefore could not share the Eucharistic Meal. The question of social relations between Jewish and gentile Christians had of course been effectively settled when Peter baptised Cornelius, see Ac appendix 5.

6. Paul is answering an objection to the doctrine of justification by faith that it encouraged godless living.

7. And therefore the question of behaving as you please simply does not arise. The Christian is 'crucified' with Christ in the sense that when he is united with Him in faith he gives up all pretensions to self-salvation and undergoes a 'death' that releases him from allegiance to the Law and gives him a new life animated by Christ. He is a new person.

8. All this is implied. Paul has earlier, v16, identified the progeny with Christ. The intermediary was Moses who, according to Jewish tradition, was accompanied by angels when the Law was given at Sinai.

Ephesians

1. All creation, now tainted by sin, will be restored in Christ to the beauty and purity God always intended.

2. The 'we' of v11 and at 2:3 indicates that Paul, a Jew, is addressing Jews. The 'you' of v13 and 2:19 shows he has the gentiles in mind. The 'our' of v14 means that the inheritance (life with God in heaven) is the same for both.

3. Paul does not explain what he means by principalities, ruling forces etc. It may be that here he meant no more than the mysterious forces that were then commonly supposed to influence human affairs. But when the terms recur at 3:10; 6:12 he clearly has in mind malevolent spiritual forces hostile to God of whatever shape or form.

4. Good works cannot earn salvation but they are a necessary ingredient in the Christian life. Having been reconciled with God through faith in Christ Christians see it as a natural part of their new life to perform good works.

5. The powers of evil can now see that they are doomed.

6. Paul also refers to his captivity at 3:1; 4:1.

Philippians

1. The fact that he is in prison is alluded to here, 1:12–14, and also at 1:7 and possibly 2:17,23.

2. When Paul tells the Philippians to 'work out' their salvation he does not mean they must try to earn salvation by good works but rather that they should persevere in their faith so that Christ can go on working in them. It must be in 'fear and trembling' because salvation must never be taken for granted but always approached in a spirit of awe and reverence.

3. Because it would be for the sake of the Gospel.

4. Paul is referring to Judaizers, Jewish Christians who, while accepting Christ as the Messiah, insisted that circumcision and observance of the Law, exemplified here by the dietary laws, were necessary for salvation.

Colossians

1. Every power of whatever kind owes its existence to Christ and is subject to Him. The Colossians would have seen in this an allusion to the supernatural spirit beings that figured in their heresy.

2. 'Fullness' here means that everything in God is equally to be found in Christ. Christ contains and represents all that God is. When Paul speaks of everything being reconciled he means that the whole of creation will be restored to the beauty and harmony that God always intended but which has been temporarily disrupted by the Fall.

3. Verse 24 is difficult. Paul is not saying that he is happy to be making up a shortfall in Christ's suffering as if Calvary was in some way inadequate for our redemption. A possible explanation is that the Church inevitably entails further suffering as it grows in the world. That is why Paul is suffering and he calls it Christ's suffering because it is borne on His account.

4. The incarnate Christ was fully God and in union with Him our every need is met.

5. Do not worry about circumcision, Paul is saying. You have been circumcised all right! Not by a minor physical operation but by a spiritual one in which your old sinful natures have been cut away and replaced by new ones.

   The fact that Paul brings up circumcision, and in v14 mentions the Law, suggests that some of the false teachers among the Colossians may have been Judaizers who insisted on them as preconditions for salvation. However the brevity of the references suggests that even if this were the case they were not the main points at issue.

6. Here 'sovereignties' means forces hostile to God. It is not just the debt to the Mosaic Law that is expunged by Christ but equally the gentiles' debt to the natural law to which they are bound by conscience.

7. Part of the Colossian heresy seems to have been that man could only approach God through the mediation of angels.

8. This is one of several instances where Ep and Col exhibit a close literary interdependence; see Ep 5:22–25; 6:1–9.

9. This is the first we hear of Mark since he parted company with Paul at Ac 13:13; 15:36–40. Whatever it was that led to that rupture now seems to have been happily resolved.

10. This may have been Paul's letter to the Ephesians.

11. Paul also draws attention to his imprisonment at 4:3,10.

1 Thessalonians

1. We can infer what the news was from Paul's response in 1Th.

   There is a discrepancy between Ac and 1Th. According to Ac, Paul arrived in Athens alone and although he sent for Silas (i.e. Silvanus) and Timothy to join him there it was not until Corinth that they were all together again, Ac 17:13–15; 18:5. However 1Th 3:1–2 indicates that Timothy was with Paul for a time in Athens.

2. Apart from probably Ga (about the dating of which there is some controversy) this would make it the earliest of Paul's epistles and the earliest book in the New Testament.

3. God's judgement.

4. As well as preaching Paul earned his own keep and did not look to his would be converts to provide his board and lodging.

5. Whether by retribution Paul meant the Day of Judgement or foresaw some catastrophe such as the A.D. 70 destruction of Jerusalem prophesied by Jesus, Mt 24, we cannot say. The harsh tone he employs here was doubtless inspired by the way he had been treated by the Jews in Macedonia not long before, Ac 17:1–15. So sure was he of the Jews' fate that he spoke of it as if it had already happened. Later on he adopted a more conciliatory attitude towards them: Rm 9–11.

6. Paul's precipitate eviction from Thessalonica had prevented him teaching there for as long as he would have liked.
7. A cautionary note to people who spent too much time speculating on when Christ would return and who even gave up their jobs in the expectation that it would be very soon.

2 Thessalonians

1. On the great tribulation in the end days see Rv appendix 1.
2. Because they thought Christ's return was imminent.
3. Paul used to dictate his letters to a secretary sometimes adding a few words in his own hand at the end to prove authenticity. At Rm 16:22 the secretary actually introduces himself. At Ga 6:11 Paul humorously refers to his own large handwriting. Other texts where Paul indicates that he is writing himself are 1Co 16:21; Col 4:18.

1 Timothy

1. 'Wives' can also be read as 'deaconesses'. The Greek is ambiguous.
2. Presumably to be looked after by the Church in which case it would appear that they pledged not to remarry but to consecrate themselves to God.
3. Otherwise their conduct could be seen as subversive.

2 Timothy

1. Probably a view that resurrection was merely a spiritual quickening that came with acceptance of the Gospel.

Titus

1. A warning against literalism and legalism. Regarding genealogies, people may have been doing fanciful research into their antecedents hoping to establish kinship with Old Testament heroes like David or even Jesus.

Hebrews

1. The author sees in the ancient texts new meanings that were not originally intended. The quotation from v6 about angels does not appear in the usual Hebrew translation of the Old Testament but is from the Greek Septuagint, see Ac appendix 2.
2. According to Jewish tradition God did not give the Law to Moses directly but through angels, Ac 7:53; Ga 3:19.
3. This is in any case clear from the Old Testament. Canaan was never free from strife for very long and was eventually lost anyway. When restoration came after the exile it was to a land under foreign tutelage, truncated and still subjected to violence and war.
4. The author has in mind someone who has wilfully rejected Christ and the salvation He offers. It is the sin against the Holy Spirit of Mt 12:31–32, a hardness of heart that leaves no room for God and His mercy.
5. The promise is God's oath to Abraham to shower blessings on his descendants, His promise of salvation, Gn 12:1–3.
   In the desert Sanctuary (or Dwelling) a curtain prevented people from entering the innermost Holy of Holies where God dwelt, Ex appendix 7. There was a similar curtain in Solomon's Temple, 1K 6:16, and it was the rending of this as Jesus died, Mt 27:51, that showed that His death had opened the way for man to have access to, i.e. to be reconciled with, God.
6. Gn 14:17–20 is silent on Melchizedek's background.

7. It was stated earlier that animal sacrifice could never remove guilt so it seems odd to read that animals could restore bodily purity. However the reference in v13 to the ashes of a heifer, with the obvious allusion to Nb 19, shows that all the author has in mind is removal of the ritual defilement that came from such things as touching a corpse. So there is no contradiction.

8. This passage, 9:15–28, covers much of the same ground as 8:1–13.

9. Again it is the deliberate calculated rejection of God and all He offers that the author has in mind, see note 4.

10. Note vv 13–16; 39–40 particularly.

11. Lv 16:26–28.

James

1. Under the Law the first-fruits of the harvest were consecrated to God. James sees Christians who have recently been reborn in the Gospel as the first-fruits of a mighty harvest the Gospel will ultimately draw in.

2. Without noticing, for example, that his clothes were dirty.

3. True religion means discarding a value system based on power, wealth, pleasure and self for one built around compassion, love and neighbour.

4. To fail in one point is to fail in love, the very essence of God's Law. If one link fails, the whole chain is broken. We cannot 'cherry pick' God's rules, keeping some while ignoring the rest. When James talks of Law as here and at 4:11 he means not the old Mosaic Law but Christ's Law as summed up as love of God and neighbour, what he sometimes calls the Law of liberty or freedom in contrast to the enslaving compulsion of the former Law.

5. James' point is that the demons know that their belief in God is insufficient by itself to save them, hence their fear. Mere intellectual assent without good works to back it up falls woefully short of the faith that saves.

6. It is hard to exaggerate the tongue's potency for evil. Careless words can besmirch character, split families and incite crowds to hatred, all leading to untold misery and suffering.

7. Otherwise his attitude is sinful because it excludes God.

1 Peter

1. The spiritual house is the Church. Believers form a holy priesthood because they are all called to God's service. The spiritual sacrifices are lives reflecting Christian values.

2. By his quotation from Ex 19:5–6 where God chose Israel to be His vehicle for bringing blessings to the world, Peter is showing that the Church is the new Israel and as such inherits the responsibility to witness implicit in that role.

3. Christians are strangers and nomads in this world because their true home is with God in heaven.

4. Unburdened of a myriad of detailed laws of conduct, such as the Jews had to contend with under the Mosaic Law, and subject only to self-discipline under Christ's law of love, there was always a danger that the unwary Christian could be lulled into profligacy or delude himself that the Spirit's guidance coincided with his own improper desires.

5. Peter was not of course calling on Christians to compromise their consciences but to render to Caesar what was his due. He was in no doubt where the line should be drawn, Ac 5:29. But he also knew that it was usually possible to live according to the law of the land without compromising one's faith and this is what Christians should do. They would gain nothing from a reputation for disorderly behaviour. If they were to be persecuted let it be for things that mattered, obedience to God, and not from flouting man-made laws that in no way contravened God's will.

6. The emphasis is on the spiritual life since there may certainly be suffering in this life as the following verses make plain.
7. Some exegetes interpret the spirits in prison as fallen angels. This leads into but one of many alternative interpretations to which this text has given rise.
8. To avoid any possible misunderstanding Peter emphasises in vv 21–22 that the efficacy of baptism has nothing to do with the outward act of washing the body but everything to do with what it symbolises internally viz the pledge made by a Christian at his baptism to follow Christ and keep a clear conscience.
9. 'Your sister in Babylon' is generally taken to mean 'the church in Rome'. Peter probably used this cryptogram either to ward-off possible persecution if the letter was couched too openly and came to the eye of the Roman authorities or to allude to Christians being exiles in a foreign land just as Israel had been in Babylon.

2 Peter

1. In faith-union with Christ the Christian is empowered to fight sin and grow more like Him until, fully perfected, he is ready to share in the divine nature, life with God Himself.
2. He is referring to the transfiguration. At v14 Peter alludes to the revelation Jesus gave him of his death, Jn 21:18–19.
3. The confirmation was the transfiguration which proved that Jesus was the Messiah.
4. This too must be guided by the Spirit.
5. There is an elaborate discussion of the fate of fallen angels in the non-Biblical Book of Enoch and Peter probably had this in mind when referring to sinful angels.
6. They even insult the angels, vv 10b–11. But though the angels are so much more powerful they do not denounce them in God's presence, presumably out of reverence.
7. Freedom from the restraints imposed by the Christian moral code.
8. The earlier letter was probably 1 Peter but could have been another letter that has not come down to us.
9. The linking of Paul's letters with the rest of Scripture shows that they were already being accorded the same standing as the Old Testament. Already the Christian canon of Scripture was in the making.

1 John

1. In John's Gospel Jesus is the Word. Here in an equally enigmatic but prescient opening He is the Word of life.
2. Light indicates moral perfection, holiness, purity; darkness the opposite.
3. John calls this an old commandment that has acquired new meaning. It is old because as love of neighbour it is in the Old Testament, Lv 19:18. It is new because Jesus gave love a deeper meaning.
4. The Father cannot be known without the revelation afforded by the Son.
5. The Holy One referred to at vv 20, 27 refers to the Spirit who opens hearts to God's word and the Truth.
6. When John says at 3:6,9; 5:18 that no one who is in God sins he is not talking about the occasional sinner who later expresses sorrow. He knows that all Christians sin, 1:8,10. He means that the true Christian cannot fall into habitual sin because God's power, or 'seed' as John puts it, is working within him.
7. God knows our heartfelt desire to love as well as our remorse at our imperfect actions. He knows what we truly are and it is this, rather than our own doubts that ultimately counts.

8. John often talks of God being 'in' us and we being 'in' Him. By this he means God's presence within us in the Spirit and the way Christians, even now in this life, begin to experience the life they will one day share with God for all eternity.

9. The love John speaks of is of divine origin. Love is what God is by His very nature. It is of His essence and not prompted because He finds things worthy of His love.

10. Perfect love implies full communion with God and hence that total awareness of His love that precludes fear.

11. Love finds its natural expression in the desire to please God.

12. At Mt 11:30 Jesus promised 'my yoke is easy and my burden light' and, given the support of the indwelling Spirit that faith in Jesus assures us of, that is how it is. Serving God becomes a delight.

13. By deadly sin, John probably meant the sin against the Holy Spirit, Mt 12:31–32.

3 John

1. We can only surmise why Diotrephes behaved in this unchristian way. Perhaps he had too high an opinion of himself, v 9, and wanted to escape from John's influence and be free to act in his own way.

2. Demetrius must have either been a member of Gaius' community or one of the missionaries.

Jude

1. James is generally assumed to be James the brother of Jesus.

2. Concerning the angels see 2P note 5.

3. A reference to an incident reported in the uncanonical Assumption of Moses where Michael was sent to bury Moses but was opposed by the devil claiming that the body belonged to him.

4. Cain was deficient in faith Heb 11:4; Balaam was guilty of avarice, Nb 22–24; Korah rebelled against Moses, Nb 16.

5. Community meals regularly preceded the Eucharist in the early church. Sometimes they got out of hand, 1Co 11:17–22.

6. A reference to the uncanonical Book of Enoch.

The Revelation to John

1. Seven implies perfection and completeness so although it is addressed to just seven churches Rv is intended for all.

2. The godless will mourn because it will be too late for repentance.

3. Alpha and Omega, the first and last letters of the Greek alphabet, express entirety. God is attesting that He is the source of all things and Lord of history.

4. He was probably exiled to Patmos for refusing to stop preaching the Gospel.

5. 'Present happenings' means the letters of chs 2–3; 'what is still to come' is revealed in chs 4–22.

6. Scripture indicates that both individuals and nations can have an angelic counterpart on the heavenly level, Mt 18:10; Ac 12:15; Dn 10:13; 12:1 and it appears from this that the same is true of churches.

7. The rewards are couched in symbolic language that is not always easy to interpret although the overall meaning is clear. The role of the Spirit is emphasised in all seven letters in words – 'let anyone who can hear, listen to what the Spirit is saying to the churches' – that suggest that they are meant for all churches down the ages.

8. Possibly the Ephesians bore down on false teaching with such zeal that it led to divisiveness and censoriousness. Virtually nothing is known of the Nicolaitans.

9. Pergamun was known as a hotbed of Roman Emperor worship.

10. Adultery is used in the spiritual sense of forsaking the true God for false gods. Balaam encouraged Israel of old to be unfaithful, see Nb 25:1-3 read along with 31:16.

11. Thyatira was an industrial centre and it is likely that many Christians would have belonged to trade guilds where such food was commonly eaten at social events. This was not censorious in itself but could easily become a slippery slope leading to licentiousness. Jezebel would also have been at fault in ignoring the sensitivities of fellow Christians, 1Co 8.

12. Possibly a reference to the great tribulation, appendix 1.

13. Laodicea was a wealthy city, a centre of banking and the clothing trade, and boasted a medical school. Christ alludes to all three. She is not rich but poor so He offers her (spiritual) gold tested in the fire (of suffering and martyrdom). He can provide white robes to hide her spiritual nakedness and ointment to cure her spiritual blindness.

14. Recalling God's revelation of Himself at Sinai, Ex 19:16. Flashes of lightning and peals of thunder, along with earthquakes and hailstones occur three more times in Rv as evidence of God's presence, at 8:5; 11:19; 16:18.

15. The Holy Spirit in all its plenitude.

16. We are reminded of Ezk 1 although there are differences.

17. The activity of the risen Christ through the Holy Spirit.

18. Someone 'worthy' is needed to open the scroll because opening it will bring about the events it portends.

19. The key to understanding the seals is to recognise their parallelism with the preview of the future given by Jesus in His Olivet discourse. Seal 1 corresponds to Mt 24:5, seals 2 to 4 to Mt 24:6–8, seal 5 to Mt 24:9–14 and seal 6 to Mt 24:29–30. (Mt 24:15–28 alludes to the fall of Jerusalem with which Rv is not concerned.) In particular this helps to identify the conqueror on the white horse of the first seal. Because Christ rides to victory on a white horse at 19:11–16 he has sometimes been identified with Christ even though that would put him at odds with the other three horsemen all of whom represent suffering and destruction. However by linking the prophecy of false messiahs in Mt 24:5 with the vision of the first horsemen as a victorious warrior the natural interpretation is to see him representing forces hostile to Christ (which are often victorious in this world).

   The exclusion of oil and wine from the excessive prices being charged for the necessities of life under the third seal is intriguing. Could it be that they stand for luxury items that the well-to-do continue to enjoy while the rest of the world goes hungry and thus highlight life's gross inequalities? The four horsemen are modelled on Zc 1,6.

20. We are reminded of Ezk 14:21. 'A quarter of the whole world' is probably meant to be read metaphorically. Even so it is by no means an unlikely figure when the whole span of human history and in particular the third world is taken into account.

21. Rv literally refers to 'the inhabitants of the earth'. However this, and similar terms like 'all the people who dwell on earth' are used in Rv as technical terms to denote, not all humanity but rather, those who are satisfied with the prevailing world order and the reign of evil as opposed to the rule of God. Vengeance is to be understood not in terms of vindictiveness but as the desire to suppress perpetrators of evil and see justice done.

22. The four winds represent the catastrophes that will be unleashed not just by the seals but by the trumpets and bowls too.

23. This does not mean they will be protected from everyday ills but that their eternal destiny will never be imperilled by the demonic forces at work in the world. We are reminded of the daubing of blood on the lintels of the houses of the Israelites to protect them during

the Exodus and the crosses marked on the foreheads of the righteous when Yahweh visited His wrath on the defilers of the Temple in Ezekiel's day, Ex 12:7–14; Ezk 9:4.

One hundred-and-forty-four thousand from all the tribes of Israel signifies a very large number from all parts of the Church, the new Israel. There is no justification for treating these as Jews and the multitude mentioned in the following vision as gentiles. No such differentiation is found elsewhere in Rv. Indeed v3 refers to the one hundred and forty-four thousand quite generally as 'the servants of our God'. What significance should be attached to the enumeration of the individual tribes is unclear unless it is meant to indicate the completeness of God's care and that no one will be overlooked.

24. Palms recall the joy of the ancient Feast of Shelters, Lv 23:39–44.

25. John's original readers would have identified the great trial with the ongoing Roman persecution. To the last generation of Christians it will mean the tribulation that will precede Christ's return, appendix 1. More generally it means the privations and suffering that afflict all believers down the ages.

26. The locusts recall Jl 1–2. The name of their leader, Abaddon in Hebrew or Apollyon in Greek, means Destroyer.

27. Mention of the Euphrates always struck a chord of fear. It was from across the Euphrates that armies from Assyria and Babylon used to attack Israel. The Euphrates was also the border with Rome's most formidable foe, Parthia.

28. Since the sixth trumpet showed man hardened beyond repentance there was no point in further delay.

29. Bitter and sweet because of the mixture of woes and blessings it contained, see Ezk 2:8 – 3:3.

30. Forty-two months occurs here, 11:2, and at 13:5. The equivalents, twelve hundred and sixty days and three and a half years or 'times', are found at 11:3; 12:6 and 12:14. They mark a period of intense suffering or tribulation as at Lk 4:25; Jm 5:18 and especially Dn 7:25; 8:14; 12:7,11. In Rv they encompass the period between Christ's first and second Comings, a time when unbelievers thrive but God's people maintain their witness nonetheless. The three-and-a-half days at 11:9, 11 signify a relatively short period of suffering. Three-and-a-half probably owes its significance to the fact that it is half seven, the perfect number, and therefore represents broken perfection.

31. At Zc 4:3–14 the olive trees stood for Joshua the priest and Zerubbabel, heir to the throne of David, whom the prophet thought would together restore true religion after Israel's return from Babylon.

32. This passage, v 8, is difficult. Since 'the great city' in Rv stands for Babylon, a synonym for godless civilisation as a whole, it means that God's witnesses will be rejected everywhere, just as they were in Jerusalem, in a world fouled by moral degradation (Sodom) and slavery (Egypt).

The Abyss, here and at 9:1; 17:8, is a mythological home for demons. We hear more of the beast in chs 13 and 17.

33. In the desert days the Ark was hidden from view in the Holy of Holies with access barred to all except the high priest on the annual Day of Atonement. Its sighting therefore heralds a new era in which access to God is open to all.

34. The serpent is the serpent of Gn 3, evil in all its hideous might, and the reference to its tail sweeping the stars from the sky an allusion to its power to wreak havoc.

35. The vision passes over Jesus' life, simply alluding to His nativity and ascension and thus implying His resurrection and the successful completion of His earthly mission on which v 11 depends.

36. According to Dn 10:21; 12:1 Michael is the guardian angel of God's people and his victory

over the dragon is a poetic way of saying that the battle between good and evil has already been won on the heavenly plane.

37. Christ's victory over Satan will not be complete until He comes again and finishes him off once and for all, 19:11 – 20:3; 20:7–10. Meanwhile, although the Church as an institution is secure, each individual still has his own battle to fight.

38. As at 11:7 the beast is the devil's earthly agent, the power of evil that manifests itself throughout history, appendix 3. Like its master the beast received a fatal wound at Calvary but to the extent that it is allowed to go on harrying the Church until Christ's return the wound may be said to have healed. The rejuvenated beast is thus a parody of the risen Christ.

39. When 13:7 speaks of the beast conquering the saints (believers), it means the destruction of their physical lives, not the subversion of their faith for which they persevere despite suffering, v 10.

40. God permits the beast to have its way, verses 5, 7. History must be allowed to run its course.

41. As the first beast caricatures Christ so the second apes the Holy Spirit. Together with the dragon they parody the Trinity.

42. For 666's possible link to Nero see appendix 4. Alternatively 6, in falling short of 7, the symbol of perfection, could stand for imperfection in which case 666 could depict the very pinnacle of foulness.

43. Because only they are imbued with the joy that comes from redemption. Mt Zion is prophetically the place where God's people will assemble one day, Jl 3:5; Ob 17. References in verses 4, 5 to the saved being virgins are to be interpreted metaphorically. Adultery was often used as a metaphor for infidelity. Here we have the reverse, virginity symbolising fidelity.

44. This vision is unusual in that an angel instructs 'one like a son of man', Jesus, what to do. Some commentators take 14:14–16 as Christ reaping the harvest of the redeemed and only 14:17–20 as portraying judgement.

45. The crystalline sea in front of God's throne, 4:6, is now shot-through with fire in token of the judgement about to be enacted. The hymn is called the hymn of Moses and the Lamb because it recalls the Israelites' victory song after their escape from Egypt, Ex 15, and now celebrates Christians' deliverance from an even greater foe.

   The vision of the sanctuary here, and of the Ark at 11:19, bear out Jeremiah's prophecy, 2M 2:4–8, that they would be seen again only at the time of the great re-gathering of God's people.

46. The battle is described at 19:11–21. Although Armageddon could mean 'hill of Megiddo' in Hebrew, there is no hill near Megiddo, which is in the plain of Jezreel. It is probably best taken as the name not of a place but an occasion, the final battle between good and evil that issues in the establishment of God's kingdom. Many battles have, however, been fought near Megiddo. Sisera was slain there by Jael, Jg 4,5, and Josiah by the Egyptians, 2K 23:29.

47. There are parallels between the trumpets and bowls and the plagues with which Moses tormented Pharaoh. For example the first trumpet recalls the seventh plague, the second trumpet and the third bowl the first, the fourth trumpet and the fifth bowl the ninth, and the first bowl the sixth plague.

48. This is the same beast as we have already encountered at 11:7 and 13:1.

49. It is assumed that Christians will be aware of this, and similar, prophecies.

50. Through its master, the devil, the beast was alive from creation, Gn 3. It was defeated by Christ on Calvary and its activities severely circumscribed, Rv 12, so in that sense it is no longer alive. It is yet to come in that it will be unfettered for a short time at the end of the age, Rv 20:3; see 1:8.

   If the exegesis hereabouts seems forced it is because the symbolism is particularly obscure and seems more than elsewhere to reflect contemporary Rome. Therefore, although our main aim is to interpret Rv in a universal sense and relegate allusions to Rome to a separate discussion in appendix 4, in this instance it might help to tackle appendix 4 first.

51. Evil's lack of moral fibre means that it cannot even be faithful to itself, see Mt 12:25–28.

52. The ten 'kings' are powers of evil since they are opposed to Christ. They are best taken as 'the principalities and the ruling forces who are masters of the darkness in this world, the spirits of evil in the heavens' identified by Paul at Ep 6:12 and may be equated with the hosts of evil mustered at 16:12–16. The battle against the Lamb is described at 19:11–21.

53. Where the woman astride the beast was brazenly dressed and foul, Christ's Bride, the Church, the community of believers, is attired in white and chaste. Where the whore's city is wiped-off the face of the earth and becomes a byword for decadence, the Lamb's city, the new Jerusalem, is destined for eternal glory.

54. This is not to be taken literally. The grisly details are given to underline the dread fate that awaits evil-doers.

55. The false prophet is the beast of 13:11 representing false religion.

56. This is the great tribulation again. Here it comes after the beast is destroyed. At 17:8–11 it was the beast who brought it about. But there is little gain in trying to reconcile details of events for which so much is expressed in poetic and symbolic terms. The reference to Ezekiel's gory account of Gog and Magog, Ezk 38–39, brings home the horror of this final war.

57. First resurrection implies a second, the resurrection of the dead at the end of time.

58. Many see a weakness in the Augustinian explanation in that it seems to do less than justice to verses 3, 4 where they refer to Satan being sealed in an Abyss and the martyrs coming back to life with its suggestion of physical resurrection.

   The millennium has an interesting parallel with Ezekiel 35–48 where: Israel's enemies, symbolised by her traditional foe Edom, are defeated; God breathes new life into her and she enjoys a long spell of peace; this is shattered by a massive attack by Gog; God intervenes to save her and we have a vision of a new Temple. This is matched in Rv with the binding of Satan, Christ's millennial reign, Satan's last attack, God's intervention and the new Jerusalem.

59. The first death, though it is never referred to as such, is physical death on earth.

60. Like the Holy of Holies in Solomon's Temple, 1K 6:20, and (probably) the Dwelling. The whole city is a Temple.

61. Note the unity of God and the Lamb. Together they are the Temple and they share the same glory and throne, 21:22 – 22:3.

   Some commentators feel that references to 'nations', 'kings' and 'treasures' in 21:24–26, to healing in 22:2, and to the embargo on the unclean in 21:27; 22:14–15 indicate an earthly rather than a heavenly condition and consequently see these verses relating not to eternity but to conditions on earth during the millennium. However this would violate the chronology, especially in respect of the last judgement, as well as ignoring the poetic symbolic nature of the whole text and John's frequent use of earthly figures to describe heavenly realities.

62. The title 'morning star' points to Jesus bringing the dawn of eternity.

63. While v 12 speaks of judgement according to deeds, v 14 promises blessings to those who have washed their robes clean in the blood of the Lamb (implied by 7:14). But there is no conflict.